FORMAL
PRINCIPLES
OF
LANGUAGE
ACQUISITION

T0204864

FORMAL PRINCIPLES OF LANGUAGE ACQUISITION

Kenneth Wexler and
Peter W. Culicover

The MIT Press
Cambridge, Massachusetts
and London, England

First MIT Press paperback edition, 1983
© 1980 by
The Massachusetts Institute of Technology

This book was set in VIP Times Roman by Grafacon, Inc. and printed and bound by Murray Printing Company in the United States of America.

Library of Congress Cataloging in Publication Data

Wexler, Kenneth.
    Formal principles of language acquisition.

    Bibliography: p.615
    Includes index.
    1.   Language acquisition.   2.   Learning ability.
3.   Generative grammar.   I.   Culicover, Peter W.,
joint author.   II.   Title.
P118.W47   401'.9   79-25652
ISBN 0-262-23099-2 (hard)
        0-262-73066-9 (paper)

CONTENTS

Contents

Contents

Contents

Contents

PREFACE

The attempt to discover the principles governing the growth of language in the young child has acquired a new life with the development of modern linguistic theory. This book is an exploratory study of those principles. The approach is that of learnability theory, which attempts to deduce properties of the language learner from what is known about the mature state and (to a lesser extent) other empirical properties, such as the linguistic environment of the child.

This book differs from most work in language acquisition in that it is not a study of the developing speech of the child. For reasons advanced in the text, we believe that much can be learned from the study of learnability theory. Our approach is not necessarily incompatible with the usual approach and we hope for a productive interaction between the two fields in the future. We believe there has already been at least a beginning (see chapter 2).

Learnability theory further differs from the more usual approach to language acquisition in degree of formalism. We attempt to construct a precise theory of language and language acquisition. Throughout the book we stress the conceptual, theoretical, and empirical implications of learnability studies. We do not survey the literature in related mathematical fields, which so far does not seem to have any implications for the theory of language learning. But we cannot do without mathematics completely. In chapter 4 we present somewhat detailed and complicated mathematical material because the details and method bear crucially on theoretical and conceptual issues. However, the reader can understand the spirit and many of the results of learnability theory without a detailed reading of how these results were attained.

To justify the attempt to construct a formal general theory of language learning, we can do no better than to quote Noam Chomsky:

The search for rigorous formulation in linguistics has a much more serious motivation than mere concern for logical niceties or the desire to purify well-established methods of linguistic analysis. Precisely constructed models for linguistic structure can play an important role, both negative and positive, in the process of discovery itself. By pushing a precise but inadequate formulation to an unacceptable conclusion, we can often expose the exact source of this inadequacy and, consequently, gain a deeper understanding of the linguistic data. More positively, a formalized theory may automatically provide solutions for many problems other than those for which it was explicitly designed. Obscure and intuition-bound notions can neither lead to absurd conclusions nor provide new and correct ones, and hence they fail to be useful in two important respects. (1957, 5)

We may add that in learnability theory formalization has led to mathematical analysis from which theoretical conclusions can be drawn that would otherwise be extremely difficult, perhaps impossible, to reach.

We would like to thank Greg Carlson for reading the manuscript of chapters 5 and 7 and for a number of useful comments. Noam Chomsky provided stimulating discussion and constant encouragement. The members of the Winter 1979 Proseminar in Cognitive Science at Irvine pointed out a number of problems in the manuscript of chapter 4. Kathy Alberti, with some help from Lillian White, deserves much credit for her excellent job in typing a difficult manuscript. Gerry Delahunty made up the bibliography.

For a number of years we have received support from the Linguistics Program of the National Science Foundation (Grant BNS74-23469 A01). We wish to thank Paul Chapin for his encouragement of a new field of research. At an earlier stage Alan Bell was also helpful in this regard.

We feel fortunate to have been working in the Program in Cognitive Science in the School of Social Sciences at the University of California, Irvine. In an atmosphere in which significant new theoretical ideas were actively encouraged, no matter what the disciplinary origin, we were able to pursue the logical conclusions of our ideas. We would like to thank our colleagues in the school for their efforts in maintaining such an atmosphere. Dean Christian Werner has been particularly supportive and appreciative of our efforts.

Henry Hamburger was an integral part of our earlier mathematical research, and he has made many highly useful comments on our later endeavors. We regret only that the demands of other research made it impossible for him to collaborate with us in the later work represented in this book. We have no doubt that the book suffers for it.

In many other ways, Sherry, Paul, and Stephanie Wexler and Pam Coker were helpful and supportive throughout the writing of this book. We would like to give them a special thanks.

Wexler wrote chapters 1, 2, 3, 4, and 6; Culicover wrote chapter 5; and chapter 7 was jointly written. Much of the research of chapters 5 and 7 was jointly carried out.

The formal study of language learnability is a new field with only a tiny number of researchers. It is clear that the results presented in this book should be looked upon as tentative. A number of the directions taken could have been otherwise. For example, much of the syntactic framework is a simplified version of the standard linguistic theory based on Chomsky's *Aspects of the Theory of Syntax* (1965). Only a lack of time and energy has prevented us from attempting to study in detail the learnability properties of the intriguing linguistic theories developed more recently.

We believe that learnability theory provides a perspective rich with implications for the study of language and mind. If this book stimulates others to attempt the study of the difficult and important questions raised in learnability theory, then, even if the answers proposed differ from ours, we will have succeeded beyond our expectations. Looking forward to the future of learnability theory is an exciting prospect.

FORMAL
PRINCIPLES
OF
LANGUAGE
ACQUISITION

CHAPTER 1

METHODOLOGICAL
CONSIDERATIONS

1.1 Learnability Theory as a Theory of Language Acquisition

This book presents a study of various aspects of the problem of first-language acquisition, especially the acquisition of syntax, though we do give some consideration to semantic matters. The field is complex and difficult; nevertheless, it is one in which we can make some progress. In the end we will propose a number of rather precise conclusions, which should be looked upon as tentative. It should be obvious that such a stance is the proper one to take regarding a problem that has remained unsolved for centuries.

The general view that informs our study is that language is learned by a child who brings a great deal of knowledge about language to his task. In many ways this view can be considered a conclusion, for we will offer many pieces of evidence along the way in support of the view. We will even argue that the evidence leads to the conclusion that there are innate principles of mind which the child uses in learning his language. The specification of some of these principles will be a primary task of this study.

The empirical bedrock of our investigations is one solid and overwhelming fact: given the appropriate conditions, any normal human child can learn any natural language.[1] It is this fact that has remained unexplained, and we take it that the central problem of learning theory (with respect to language) is to explain this fact.

There have of course been many attempts to explain the fact of language acquisition. In general these attempts have been vitiated by a conception of human language so inadequate that no progress at all could be made. Attempts made to explain language learning by processes such as association or stimulus-and-response have almost always conceived of language as a list of connections—for example, connections between words and things. Occasional attempts have been made to transcend this limitation in psychological and philosophical accounts, but rarely has an even roughly adequate account of a subpart of human competence been considered. In particular, no theory of acquisition can explain the acquisition of the rich and intricate system of syntax. (We are ignoring here the contributions of linguistic theory to this question.)

Any theory of language acquisition must contain, explicitly or implicitly, a theory of the linguistic ability that is ultimately attained by a child. If no explicit theory is given but, rather, only a statement of learning procedures, then these learning procedures, by their very nature, will be able to produce only certain kinds of learned abilities. These abilities must include what is biologically possible for humans if the theory is to be adequate. The belief that humans are capable of learning anything, and thus that a theory of learning must account for this fact, has no empirical support.[2] The concomitant belief, that any logically possible system is a possible human language, is also completely unfounded. The problem is to find out exactly what are possible human languages and how these are learned.

We must begin, therefore, with a theory of what constitutes a possible natural language, where "possible" of course means biologically possible rather than logically possible.[3] The question of what constitutes a possible natural language has been under intense investigation by linguists. We will begin by assuming a theory of natural language that represents a formalization of part of what some linguists consider to be the appropriate representation of natural language. In particular we will assume the framework for syntax known as *transformational grammar*. We will give reasons for this choice and will discuss alternatives in chapter 6.

What makes the problem of language acquisition so intriguing is not only the central role of language as a characteristic human ability. The very complexity of language adds a difficulty that lends interest to the problem. It is well known, for example, that many (most) sentences that a person hears or says have not been encountered by that person previously. Thus a language cannot be learned as a finite list of sentences. Rather, as work in generative grammar has amply demonstrated, we must conceive a language to be given (at least in part) as a set of rules called a grammar. In the theory of generative grammar the rules generate an infinite set of structures, which may be identified with sentences. The set of rules is finite, of course. We may look upon the problem of language acquisition as the problem of mastering this set of rules.

The set of rules is taken to represent the adult's linguistic *competence*. The reader unfamiliar with linguistic theory should realize that these rules are taken to be *descriptive*, not *prescriptive*. In other words, the rules are part of a scientific theory that describes a person's (usually implicit, unconscious) knowledge of his language. The linguist's task is to discover what these rules are. As an idealization, we assume that every speaker of a dialect has internalized the same set of rules, though there are interesting ways in which this requirement can be relaxed (see Wexler, Culicover, and Hamburger 1975). This idealization has proved to be a very fruitful way of conducting linguistic research.

Of course, there are many possible natural languages, and the child must have a way of selecting which is his. The selection is based upon his experience with language. We will have to discuss what this experience consists of. For now, let us simply call the information about language that a child uses to construct his language the *primary data* from his language.[4] We will also sometimes refer to the primary data as the *input* or *information*.

To have a fully explicit theory of language acquisition, we need more than a restriction on the class of possible languages and the information on which the selection or construction is based. We must specify a procedure for constructing a grammar based on the class of possible grammars and the input data.

To summarize, we have the following situation: the child is born with a schema of some sort as to what constitutes a possible natural language. Based on experience of a certain sort, the child then constructs a language (grammar) by using a certain procedure. This construction takes place over time. At any given time the child may have a grammar that is not the ultimate adult grammar. Ultimately (again in a sense that has to be specified) the learner constructs the "correct" grammar of his language. We then say that he has learned the language.

When we have specified such a theory, how will we know it is correct? The usual empirical descriptive linguistic tests can be made for the class of languages assumed to be possible. In particular, we can check whether all known languages fall into this class. But how are we to check whether the theory of language acquisition is correct? Obviously, a fundamental criterion that must be imposed is that it must be possible for the procedure to learn any possible language, given appropriate data from that language. To be even more restrictive, the learning must take place under those conditions of time and human abilities (memory restrictions, for example) that in fact hold for human language learning.

Although such considerations seem elementary, the investigation of language acquisition has not proceeded in this way. It seems reasonable to conclude that a primary requisite of a theory of language acquisition would be the demonstration that the proposed procedure can learn any of the assumed possible languages. No theories of language acquisition of which we are aware are concerned with this demonstration.[5] In this book we will be concerned with the formal specification of the class of possible languages, primary data, and language learning procedures, and with demonstrating that the learning procedure can learn any language in the class. Only at that point can we begin to discuss such notions as the efficiency of the procedure. When we have completed this task, we can be in a position to assess directly the kind of innate structure that is necessary to allow language learning to proceed. These innate structures will then become hypothesized linguistic universals.

The important fact that makes these investigations possible is that for any interesting or conceivably adequate definition of what it means to "learn" a language, there are classes of languages that can be shown to be *not* learnable.[6] Thus, proceeding from the empirical generalization that the class of natural languages is learnable, we can exclude a class of languages that is *not* learnable from consideration as the class of "possible human languages." The discovery of those principles that make a class of languages learnable is an intricate and difficult matter, which we will discuss in some detail. It is important to stress that these principles are not intuitively given; they can be discovered only by theoretical and empirical research.[7]

1.2 Learning Procedures and Principles of Mind

1.2.1 Principles and Procedures

It is useful as a starting point to distinguish two classical positions on the question of learning. These have been delineated differently in many different kinds of theories, so we will not here attempt to do justice to any particular formulation. However, for heuristic reasons it will be useful to counterpoise the theories.

Empiricist theory allows for a class of sensory or peripheral processing mechanisms by means of which the organism receives data. In addition, the organism possesses some set of inductive principles or learning mechanisms. The accounts of these differ somewhat from theory to theory, but two properties seem fairly consistent. First, the mechanisms are relatively weak in terms of the abilities that they can learn.[8] Second, the mechanisms are quite general; that is, they are not related to the learning of any particular subject matter or cognitive ability, nor are they limited to any particular species.[9]

Rationalist theory also assumes that a learner has sensory mechanisms and inductive principles. But rationalist theory assumes that in addition the learner possesses a rich set of principles concerning the general nature of the ability that is to be learned. For example, when learning how to construct visual space and to see objects, the learner makes use of a set of visual principles or abilities and not simply sensory mechanisms and inductive principles. The same is true for logical and other abilities. Note that both the rationalist and empiricist theories must assume that the learner has some kind of inductive or learning ability. Thus the question of the existence of these cannot distinguish the theories.

Suppose that humans have various abilities (or faculties) that allow them to learn various domains: language (possibly divided into subdomains), vision, thinking, and so on. Call these domains $D_1, D_2, \ldots$ For each domain there is a set of principles about that domain that we can take to be innate, or given, to the learner. For domain D_i, call these innate principles P_i. In addition, for each domain there is a learning mechanism that tells the organism how to create and change its hypothesis about the domain on the basis of data from the environment and in accordance with the principles of the domain. Let LP_i be the learning mechanism for domain D_i.[10]

Now there are various possibilities for the relations between these constructs. A strong empiricist theory might make the claim in (1).

(1)
i. For all i, $P_i = \emptyset$ (the empty set), and
ii. For all i, j, $LP_i = LP_j$.

Assumption (i) states that there are no special innate principles, for any domain. Assumption (ii) states that there is exactly one set of learning mechanisms, which applies to all domains.[11]

A rationalist theory, on the other hand, would assume that in general $P_i \neq \emptyset$; that is, there *are* innate domain principles. It is not clear exactly what assumptions about LP_i would satisfy a rationalist theory. A pure innateness theory would naturally assume that for all i, $LP_i = \emptyset$. However, for language at least, nobody has ever made such a suggestion, because it is clear that humans can learn different languages.

One possibility is that assumption (ii) might be correct even though assumption (i) fails. That is, it is conceivable that humans do have one general learning mechanism, which applies to the data from different domains and uses innate principles particular to those domains. There are many reasons why it is difficult to evaluate this issue. First, to our knowledge, there exists little study of inductive methods used naturally by humans in various domains. Second, it is exceedingly difficult to think of significantly varying learning mechanisms. In general, two kinds of learning mechanisms have been proposed. The first is some kind of simple associationist or stimulus-response connection. The second is some kind of hypothesis-formation ability. Although these mechanisms may be formulated in many different ways, their general properties seem to remain the same. Where there is significant variation in concepts of learning, the differences are in the structure of various domains as, for example, in the different theories of language or of perception.

1.2.2 Linguistic Constraints and Cognitive Constraints

It is sometimes suggested that the attempt to solve the problem of language learning by the discovery of formal constraints on grammars is misguided. The argument can take two forms. In one, a distinction is first made between the form of language, on one hand, and the hypothesis-formation (or learning) procedure, on the other. In our terminology here, this amounts to a distinction between P_i and LP_i. It is suggested that constraints on the learning procedure (LP_i) and not on the form of language (P_i) can be responsible for the ultimate form of language and for making language learnable. The reason given is that constraints on the learning procedure make the problem of learning language more easily solvable.

But it is here that we believe the confusion lies. (See Wexler 1978a for further discussion of this point.) The argument depends on the kinds of constraints that are postulated. The usual kinds of constraints on learning mechanisms discussed in psychology put limitations on the mechanism. For example, there are various kinds of short- and long-term memory limitations, or limitations on the computational complexity of a learning mechanism, or limitations on the complexity of input that a learning mechanism can handle.[12]

But if the learning procedure constraints are constraints such as these, constraints that limit the power of the learning mechanism, then for a fixed attained adult linguistic system, the stronger these constraints on learning, the stronger will the formal constraints on possible grammars have to be. The situation can be seen in figure 1.1 (taken from Wexler 1978a). The diagram is not a flow chart, detailing processes that operate in time. Rather it is simply a representation of the logical structure of the problem. Based on input data, the mechanism of learning (the system for constructing and changing hypotheses, abstracted from the formal constraints on grammars) creates a complex

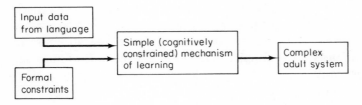

Figure 1.1
Outline of the learnability problem

adult linguistic system, under a set of formal constraints. Since in general the creation of the adult system is a nontrivial task, it is clear that the less powerful the learning mechanism (the more cognitive constraints placed on the mechanism) and the less complex the input data, then, in order to achieve a given complex adult system, the greater will the formal constraints on grammatical possibilities have to be.

To take one further example of cognitive constraints, first recall Chomsky's (1965) idealized "instantaneous" model of language learning: all the data is available to a language learner at one time and the learner selects a grammar at one fell swoop. (It is important to realize that this model was proposed as an idealization for the purposes of linguistic theory, with the clear recognition that it contains false assumptions about the actual time-course of language learning by the child.)

As a description of the child constructing his grammar, this model clearly (and deliberately) ignores the fact that at any one time only a little data is available to the child, who constructs his grammar over the course of time, using a little bit of data at a time. It might then be suggested that this cognitive constraint on the amount of data available might make the learning problem easier, thus vitiating the need for some formal constraints on grammars. But this conclusion is logically wrong; exactly the opposite holds. With all the data before the learner at one time, with no problems of loss of data because of memory limitations, with no restrictions on the complexity of a computation based on large amounts of data, the learner has a relatively easy time. Allowing the learner only a bit of data at a time, and not allowing him to remember past data, puts a severe cognitive restriction on the learner which will make his job more difficult. Thus, in general, stronger formal constraints will be needed.

This first form of an attempted argument against the need for formal constraints on grammars for the purposes of learnability stresses the existence of constraints on the learning mechanism (hypothesis-formation system). A second form of the argument is somewhat more subtle. This approach agrees with the need for constraints on the notion of "possible human language" but suggests that the only kinds of constraints necessary are general cognitive constraints and not specifically linguistic constraints.

The important point to realize about this kind of argument is that the question is an empirical one, which must be settled by the usual theoretical and empirical arguments available to science. There can be no a priori decision that only one kind of constraint is permissible in a theoretical system.

The question is empirical on two levels. First, with regard to linguistic description, suppose that on the basis of linguistic analysis a constraint is formulated as a universal of language. Now it is perfectly possible logically that the purported linguistic constraint is a special case of, or follows from, a more general cognitive constraint, that is, a constraint that applies to all cognitive systems, not just the linguistic system. But by no means is it necessarily the case that the constraint is this general. The hypothesis may be put forth that the constraint *is* a general cognitive constraint, but in order to find evidence for the hypothesis, other cognitive systems would have to be analyzed and theories about them developed. In general, of course, a scientist prefers generalizations, but the cognitive domains that are referred to outside of language (such as thinking and problem-solving) are not for the most part the subject of any kind of reasonably well specified theory, so it doesn't even make sense to assert the existence of a constraint that applies to these domains. One might almost as well suggest that the linguistic constraint applies to black holes, which would make the constraint even more general.

The second level on which the question of linguistic versus cognitive constraints is empirical regards the explanation of language learning. Can language be learned if its form is constrained only by general cognitive constraints or are specifically linguistic constraints neces-sary? The main thrust of this book is that the learning of a large portion of syntax is possible if specifically linguistic constraints are invoked. Without these constraints we cannot prove that language is learnable. Once again, these linguistic constraints may be special cases of, or follow from, more general cognitive constraints. But until we have more understanding of these other cognitive systems, we have no way of telling whether there is anything at all to these more general pos-sibilities. At present the constraints that we need are quite specifically linguistic. More general theories would be intriguing, as insightful generalization always is, but until we have reason to believe the generalizations (or to even formulate them coherently), we must re-main skeptical.

1.3 Performance and Acquisition

1.3.1 The Learning of Competence
Linguistic theory is a theory of the knowledge that a speaker has about language. The theory idealizes away from factors involved in the use of this knowledge, factors such as memory and other aspects of produc-tion and comprehension. Syntactic theory even idealizes away from other areas of a speaker's knowledge, such as his knowledge about how to use utterances in various situations. This idealization is called a theory of linguistic *competence*, as opposed to *performance*. To review these concepts, well known in linguistic theory, we may take perfor-mance theory to be the study of real-time processing of language, in-cluding models of the speaker and hearer and related phenomena. Competence theory, on the other hand, is intended to represent a na-tive speaker's knowledge of a language in a way that is neutral between speaker and hearer and is abstracted from such considerations as memory. Performance theory cannot develop without a competence theory, and studies of linguistic performance usually proceed from some competence theory, adequate or not.

The learning theory developed in this book studies the learning of some aspects of syntactic knowledge. In other words we study the learning of linguistic competence, idealizing away from the learning of performance. We have not studied, for example, how a child learns to actually produce a sentence or the perceptual strategies that he might use for decoding a sentence that he hears. In a way analogous to the argument for linguistic theory, we would argue that the study of the learning of performance strategies depends on the study of the learning of linguistic competence.

Some confusions are possible, because learning itself may be viewed as a performance. It is not obvious, however, that this is the only correct way to view learning. Just as the notion of language or of the linguistic competence of an idealized native speaker is an abstraction we create so that serious inquiry may proceed, we also create the notion of learning by an idealized learner. For example, we do not include the concept of *attention* in our theories. Yet a number of aspects of performance are represented in our theory of learning. For example, we will be concerned with the complexity of the input that the learner must use in order to create his language. To the extent that the complexity demanded by our theory is not greater than the complexity actually used by a learner, we will consider that we have support for our theory. We will see that progress can be made in the creation of a plausible learning theory.

That our theory of learning describes some aspects of performance is not surprising. The same is true of linguistic theory. For example, the linguistic theory for a language describes possible orders of words in sentences. Clearly this fact will also be relevant to performance. Exactly which facts are to be accounted for by competence theory is not determined a priori. In linguistic theory it is taken as a working hypothesis that a competence theory can be developed independently of a performance theory. The value of such an approach is determined by the insight achieved. Similarly, we adopt as a working hypothesis the claim that a theory of language learning can be created independently of performance considerations in language learning (such as lack of attention). Ultimately a complete theory would have to include all such (empirically true) conditions. The fact that our theory does not explain the real-time course of events means simply that it is incomplete as a description of the world, as is linguistic theory. But again, as in the case of linguistic theory, the fact that a real-time course of events is not described or explained does not mean that the theory cannot be successful. Rather it means that the theory is a theory of only part of the world and that it can potentially be successful in explaining that part of the world.

1.3.2 Developmental Psycholinguistics

A large literature has grown up in developmental psycholinguistics. This literature is for the most part concerned with the speech of young children. Much data has been collected concerning children's production and, less often, comprehension of speech. On the whole, however, the field ignores what we take to be the central problem in the theory of language acquisition, namely, the construction of a system that will learn natural language.

Although we find various attempts at theory construction, we find no concern with demonstrating whether the constructs of the theory are sufficient for language learning. Of course, only with the development of the mathematics of symbolic logic in the twentieth century and, in particular, the development of formal theories of natural language in the past twenty-five years, could this question be asked in a precise and potentially answerable way.

To repeat, for us the central problem of the theory of language acquisition is to show that the assumed structures and devices that the child brings to bear in learning language actually have the capacity to learn any natural language, under the appropriate circumstances, given limitations such as those on memory and access to data. To the extent that investigations don't deal with this question, the topic of the investigations is something other than what we take to be the central problem of the theory of language acquisition. There are a number of empirical studies in developmental psycholinguistics that are relevant to the problem. For example, such studies might be concerned with the nature of input to the language learner.

Other studies, of course, might be directed toward some other end. An investigator might simply be interested, for example, in what it is that children tend to say. The investigator might discover that young children tend to speak about things and events that they are familiar with. Abstractly, one might say that the goal of such a study would be the specification of a theory of children's utterances. Such studies, of course, might incidentally contribute data relevant to the construction of a language acquisition theory. [13]

1.4 Learnability and Linguistic Theory

1.4.1 Explanatory Adequacy

Studies of learnability are intrinsically related to studies in linguistic theory. Chomsky (1965) distinguishes various criteria for linguistic theory. He writes:

A grammar can be regarded as a theory of language; it is *descriptively adequate* to the extent that it correctly describes the intrinsic competence of the idealized native speaker . . . a linguistic theory must contain a definition of 'grammar,' that is, a specification of the class of potential grammars. We may, correspondingly, say that *a linguistic theory is descriptively adequate* if it makes a descriptively adequate grammar available for each natural language. (p. 24)

But descriptive adequacy is not a sufficient criterion for linguistic theory. Chomsky continues:

Although even descriptive adequacy on a large scale is by no means easy to approach, it is crucial for the productive development of linguistic theory that much higher goals than this be pursued. To facilitate the clear formulation of deeper questions, it is useful to consider the abstract problem of constructing an 'acquisition model' for language, that is, a theory of language learning or grammar construction . . . we can say that the child has developed and internally represented a generative grammar . . . He has done this on the basis of observation of what we may call *primary linguistic data* . . . on the basis of such data, the child constructs a grammar—that is, a theory of the language of which the well-formed sentences of the primary linguistic data constitute a small sample . . . As a precondition for language learning, he must possess, first, a linguistic theory that specifies the form of the grammar of a possible human language, and, second, a strategy for selecting a grammar of the appropriate form that is compatible with the primary linguistic data. As a long-range task for general linguistics, we might set the problem of developing an account of this innate linguistic theory that provides the basis for language learning . . . To the extent that a linguistic theory succeeds in selecting a descriptively adequate grammar on the basis of primary linguistic data, we can say that it meets the condition of *explanatory adequacy*. That is, to this extent, it offers an explanation for the intuition of the native speaker on the basis of an empirical hypothesis concerning the innate predisposition of the child to develop a certain kind of theory to deal with the evidence presented to him. (pp. 24–26)

He summarizes the problem in a slightly different way:

Certain problems of linguistic theory have been formulated as questions about the construction of a hypothetical language-acquisition device. This seems a useful and suggestive framework within which to pose and consider these problems. We may think of the theorist as given an empirical pairing of collections of primary linguistic data associated with grammars that are constructed by the device on the basis of such data. Much information can be obtained about both the primary data that constitute the input and the grammar that is the 'output' of such a device, and the theorist has the problem of determining the intrinsic properties of a device capable of mediating this input-output relation. (p. 47)

For a class of grammars to be *learnable*, at the very least we mean that there exists a procedure that can take data from a language in the class and select the grammar that generates that data.[14] Ultimately, of course, we want this selection to be done in a manner that replicates the empirically true situation in language learning, so further conditions will have to be added to the definition of *learnability*. Ignoring these conditions for the moment, we can see that if a class of grammars $\mathscr{K}$ is learnable, and if $\mathscr{K}$ is also descriptively adequate, then the theory of language that specifies $\mathscr{K}$ as the set of possible grammars has attained the criterion of *explanatory adequacy*. That is, the linguistic theory specifies not only a descriptively adequate grammar for each natural language but allows the grammar to be selected from primary data.[15] In this sense, studying learnability is very much like studying explanatory adequacy, except for one difference in methodology; namely, in learnability studies we are more interested than has generally been the case in linguistic theory in demonstrating that the selection of the descriptively adequate grammar can actually proceed from the primary data. In this sense, then, we provide a more explicit working out of part of the problem of explanatory adequacy. (The particular hypotheses that we explore may be different from those studied to date in the framework of explanatory adequacy. See note 15.)

From the statement of the problem of learnability so far, it might appear that the major problem is to discover a strong learning procedure or mechanism (the *LP* devices of section 1.2.1). This appearance is misleading, however. Actual work in learnability theory proceeds most readily by constraining the class of possible grammars. The reason is that the strength of learning mechanisms, even in principle, is limited. If the hypothesis space through which they have to search is large enough, the mechanisms, no matter how powerful, will fail. And it turns out that in linguistic theory the hypothesis space is too large to allow, even in principle, construction of a descriptively adequate grammar from the primary data. Thus learnability theory must be concerned with constraining the form of possible grammars.

The situation in learnability theory exactly parallels that in linguistic theory. Chomsky (1965, 34–35) writes:

This account is misleading in one important respect. It suggests that to raise a descriptively adequate theory to the level of explanatory adequacy one needs only to define an appropriate evaluation measure. This is incorrect, however. A theory may be descriptively adequate, in the sense just defined, and yet provide such a wide range of potential grammars that there is no possibility of discovering a formal property distinguishing the descriptively adequate grammars, in general, from among the mass of grammars compatible with whatever data are available. In fact, the real problem is almost always to restrict the range of possible hypotheses by adding additional structure to the notion 'generative grammar.'

Despite the fact that in general strong learning mechanisms will not solve the problems of linguistic theory, there are reasons for trying to state these mechanisms precisely. Linguists working toward the criterion of explanatory adequacy attempt to do so by "adding additional structure to the notion 'generative grammar.'" Often it turns out, however, that it is unclear exactly how to do this. For example, two competing linguistic theories might be offered, each of which can account for the same set of data. Each theory allows for grammars that are descriptively adequate for the range of known data.[16] In other words, restricting the possible forms of grammars by adding universal conditions can often be done in more than one way while preserving accountability to the data. The problem for linguistic theory is to determine which of these sets of universal conditions is correct. If a theory of learning mechanisms is stated, we can look for those sets of universal conditions that allow the class of grammars to be learnable, those that allow the condition of explanatory adequacy to be met. This can be done only if there is a way to calculate whether or not a class of languages is learnable, according to some definition of *learnable*.

In linguistic theory the problem of alternative attempts to restrict the form of grammars can be met in some cases. The solution is to note that if one class of grammars is a subset of another, the smaller class cannot be harder to learn or to select on the basis of primary data than the larger class. In these cases linguists naturally choose the theory that allows for the smaller class of grammars, since this decision cannot hurt, and may actually help, in attaining the goal of explanatory adequacy. In other words, choosing a hypothesis space that is a subdomain of another hypothesis space is without question the appropriate strategy.

There is a problem of generality with this solution, however. It works only when two alternative linguistic theories restrict classes of grammars in such a way that one class is a subset of the other class. In general this condition is not met; we often have noncomparable (by the subset criterion) classes of grammars allowed by competing theories.

It is logically possible, however, that one of the alternative theories might provide a class of grammars that is learnable in the appropriate sense and the other theory might provide an unlearnable class of grammars. If we can show this, the choice of theories is clear: the theory that provides the learnable class of grammars is preferred.[17] Thus the specification of learning procedures and the computation of whether learnability holds of a class of grammars can make a real difference in the choice of a theory that comes closer to meeting the criterion of explanatory adequacy.

This is one way that the learnability criterion can play a role in the development of linguistic theory. There is a somewhat stronger, though related, way for learnability theory to be linguistically useful. In fact, most applications of learnability theory to linguistic theory to date have been of this second kind. The difference between the two uses of learnability theory is not so much a logical difference as a methodological difference.

Suppose that we are studying the question of whether a particular linguistic theory provides a learnable class of grammars, in an appropriate sense of *learnable*. Suppose, furthermore, that we discover that the answer to this question is negative. The class of grammars is not learnable. Then we can ask whether further restriction of the class of grammars will make the class learnable, and we can try particular hypotheses as to the forms that such restriction should take. We might discover that a particular restriction was such that we could then prove that given this restriction the class of grammars is learnable. At this point, since the restriction can be shown to aid in reaching the criterion of explanatory adequacy, we can adopt the hypothesis that the restriction is a universal condition on the form of language, specified by linguistic theory. It then becomes natural to test the hypothesized restriction in terms of its descriptive adequacy. Given linguistic data, does the restriction actually hold?

In this second use of the learnability criterion in linguistic theory, the criterion itself becomes a source for the discovery of (hypotheses of) linguistic universals, rather than simply a test of the adequacy, on learnability grounds, of linguistic theories. Suppose that the hypothesized restriction in fact found empirical descriptive support. That is, not only is the restriction useful for proving learnability, but it allows the linguist to account for linguistic data (judgments of grammaticality, and so on) that could not be accounted for without the restriction. In this case we have evidence of two very different kinds (learnability and descriptive evidence) for the hypothesized restriction. When two kinds of evidence of such different sorts support a hypothesis, we have good reason for taking the hypothesis seriously.

1.4.2 Feasibility

Chomsky (1965) discusses a criterion for linguistic theory that is even stronger than explanatory adequacy. This criterion, *feasibility*, is rarely mentioned in the linguistic literature but is nevertheless important. Essentially, to meet the criterion of feasibility, a linguistic theory not only provides a procedure that can select a descriptively adequate

grammar from primary data but also has the property that the procedure selects a grammar under empirically accurate restrictions on such
parameters as access to data and time to success. Chomsky writes:

We may therefore ask whether the grammars that these [learning] principles can provide, in principle, are at all close to those which we in
fact discover when we investigate real languages . . . If the answer to
this question of adequacy-in-principle is positive . . . we can then turn
to the question of feasibility: can the [learning mechanisms] succeed in
producing grammars within the given constraints of time and access,
and with the range of observed uniformity of output? (pp. 53–54)

He adds:

As observed earlier, the critical factor in the development of a fully
adequate theory is the limitation of the class of possible grammars.
Clearly, this limitation must be such as to meet empirical conditions on
strong (and, a fortiori, weak) generative capacity, and, furthermore,
such as to permit the condition of explanatory adequacy to be met
when an appropriate evaluation measure is developed. But beyond
this, the problem is to impose sufficient structure on the schema that
defines 'generative grammar' so that relatively few hypotheses will
have to be tested by the evaluation measure, given primary linguistic
data. We want the hypotheses compatible with fixed data to be 'scat-
tered' in value, so that choice among them can be made relatively
easily. This requirement of 'feasibility' is the major empirical constraint on a theory, once the conditions of descriptive and explanatory
adequacy are met. (pp. 61–62)[18]

In our terms, feasibility may be called "easy learnability," that is,
learnability from fairly restricted primary data, in a sufficiently quick
time, with limited use of memory. Although the conceptual distinction
between feasibility and explanatory adequacy is real enough, to a certain extent the exact border between the two is arbitrary and terminological. The criterion of explanatory adequacy demands that a
procedure exist for selecting a descriptively adequate grammar from
the primary data. The criterion of feasibility demands, among other
requirements, that the primary data be restricted to what the child
actually has access to. But the nature of the primary data isn't specified
a priori. If the original definition of primary data specifies only what the
child actually has access to, this part of the criterion of feasibility will

be part of the criterion of explanatory adequacy.[19] Other aspects of the criterion of feasibility do not seem to be included under the notion of explanatory adequacy. For example, a theory that meets the criterion of explanatory adequacy must select a descriptively adequate grammar based on the primary data, but there is no requirement that the selection be done quickly. The selection process might take inordinately long, compared with how quickly a language learner would make the selection. The criterion of feasibility imposes this further requirement of speed.

We might view explanatory adequacy and feasibility as two ends of a continuum, defined by imposing stronger and stronger conditions on linguistic theory. The criterion of explanatory adequacy would be defined by the minimal conditions that we could place on a function that selects a descriptively adequate grammar from primary data. As we add more realistic conditions of learning to this criterion we proceed until we finally reach a theory that includes all the empirically true restrictions on the human learner of a first language. This final criterion is feasibility.

Actually this is the way that work in learnability theory has proceeded: by adding more and more restrictive conditions to the criterion of adequacy for a theory. Viewing the criteria of explanatory adequacy and feasibility as a continuum does not change the logical structure of the problem, however. It simply helps us isolate various aspects of the problem for separate attack, in the interests of attaining insight into these difficult and significant issues.

Interesting parallels hold between the study of feasibility and the study of explanatory adequacy. We earlier pointed out (following Chomsky) that, perhaps surprisingly, it is not the specification of stronger learning procedures that is important in working toward the goal of explanatory adequacy but, rather, restrictions on the form of grammar. Similarly, one might think that specification of efficient learning mechanisms (the *LP* of section 1.2.1) was the most important problem in working toward the criterion of feasibility. However, it turns out that although specification of more efficient learning mechanisms can play a role, and someday may play a more significant role in reaching the criterion of feasibility, up to now restriction of the form of grammar has been the most important problem in working toward that goal. (See section 4.5 for some promising directions in reduction of computational complexity.) Perhaps part of the reason is that we do not yet know how to make aspects of mechanisms (order of hypothesis construction, for example) play a significant role in attaining these criteria. In actual work in learnability theory, the form of grammar is still sufficiently unrestricted that parts of the criterion of feasibility can be attained only by further restricting the form of grammar.

Chomsky writes:

In short, the most serious problem that arises in the attempt to achieve explanatory adequacy is that of characterizing the notion 'generative grammar' in a sufficiently rich, detailed, and highly structured way. A theory of grammar may be descriptively adequate and yet leave unexpressed major features that are defining properties of natural language and that distinguish natural languages from arbitrary symbolic systems. (p. 36)

This last sentence is true because a descriptively adequate theory of language may allow grammars that cannot be grammars of natural language; the only requirement is that if a grammar is a possible grammar for a natural language, it must be allowed by the descriptively adequate theory. Let us say that a major feature of natural language is that no natural language has the feature P. It is quite conceivable that the feature P is true of infinitely many arbitrary symbolic systems. A descriptively adequate theory might in fact contain all these systems of which P is true. Thus the theory, although descriptively adequate, does not express the fact that no natural language may have the feature P. An explanatorily adequate theory might demand that all grammars with the feature P be excluded from the class of allowable grammars or else no appropriate selection procedure for grammars might exist.

Interestingly, the sentence in question is also true if we replace "descriptively adequate" by "explanatorily adequate." A theory of grammar may be explanatorily adequate and yet leave unexpressed major features that are defining properties of natural language and that distinguish natural languages from arbitrary symbolic systems. Suppose no grammar for a natural language can have the feature P'. Yet an explanatorily adequate theory might allow grammars with the feature

P'. That is, a selection procedure could exist that, from primary data, would learn any natural language, even if grammars with feature P' were allowed by the theory. But the criterion of feasibility might rule out grammars with property P' because otherwise learning might take too long or might not satisfy some other property of feasibility.

This brings us to another parallel between feasibility and explanatory adequacy. The study of feasibility does not have to wait on the attainment of an explanatorily adequate theory any more than the study of explanatory adequacy must wait on the attainment of descriptive adequacy.

It is not necessary to achieve descriptive adequacy before raising questions of explanatory adequacy. On the contrary, the crucial questions, the questions that have the greatest bearing on our concept of language and on descriptive practice as well, are almost always those involving explanatory adequacy with respect to particular aspects of language structure. (Chomsky 1965, 36)

If [the linguist] wishes to achieve descriptive adequacy in his account of language structure, he must concern himself with the problem of developing an explanatory theory of the form of grammar, since this provides one of the main tools for arriving at a descriptively adequate grammar in any particular case. In other words, choice of a grammar for a particular language L will always be much underdetermined by the data drawn from L alone. Moreover, other relevant data (namely, successful grammars for other languages or successful fragments for other subparts of L) will be available to the linguist only if he possesses an explanatory theory. Such a theory limits the choice of grammar by the dual method of imposing formal conditions on grammar and providing an evaluation procedure to be applied for the language L with which he is now concerned. Both the formal conditions and the evaluation procedure can be empirically justified by their success in other cases. Hence, any far-reaching concern for descriptive adequacy must lead to an attempt to develop an explanatory theory that fulfills these dual functions, and concern with explanatory adequacy surely requires an investigation of evaluation procedures. (pp. 41–42)

In the work to follow we will demonstrate once again that considerations of explanatory adequacy provide "one of the main tools for arriving at a descriptively adequate grammar." We will do so by showing that the criterion of learnability leads us to hypothesize that natural language has certain properties, properties we can then test descriptively. To the extent that these tests support the hypothesized properties, the criterion of learnability will have been a tool in attaining descriptively adequate grammars. We will further demonstrate that feasibility too can be a major tool for arriving at a descriptively adequate grammar. The requirement that natural languages be easily learnable, in particular that they be learnable from fairly simple data, will lead us to hypothesize that natural language has certain properties, which we can then test descriptively.

All of these considerations are consistent with the notion that feasibility is a natural extension of explanatory adequacy and that in many ways the two concepts represent more or less stringent requirements on the same continuum of conditions to be imposed on linguistic theory. The criterion of *learnability* is imposed in an attempt to work toward the goal of explanatory adequacy and feasibility. In doing so, we hope also to shed light on the description of particular natural languages.

1.5 An Example

An example will help to demonstrate our methodology and to show how learnability theory can bring to light principles of linguistic theory.[20] We want to show that a given learnability property K holds for the class of possible grammars we are considering. (For example, K might be that every grammar in the class is "easily" learnable.) Given the assumptions of the theory, we cannot show that K holds. Often, in fact, we can find an example G of a grammar that is possible according to the theory such that the learnability property K does *not* hold for G. There are then two options. First, we can discover that a small modification of the learnability property K (call the new property K') would disallow the counterexample; that is G meets property K'. If K' is tolerable, we might be satisfied with this result. Second, and more commonly, we might find that no such modification K' is possible but that the addition of a new assumption H to the theory would disallow the counterexample, according to property K. This can happen in two ways. First, H might disallow G as a possible grammar. Second, H

might still allow G but constrain its operation in such a way that K is satisfied by G.

The following examples are developed more fully in chapter 4. There the goal will be to show that transformational grammars are learnable from very simple data. In order to attain this goal it is crucial to show that if a system that the learner has attained is not "perfect," that is, if the learner's system makes an error on some structure (behaves differently from the way the adult system does on that structure), then there is a "simple" structure on which the learner's system makes an error. This last statement (that the existence of an error implies the existence of an error on a simple structure) will be the "learnability property" K.

To be more precise, recall that a sentence is the terminal string of a surface phrase-marker (one to which transformations have applied). For a given deep structure P we say that the learner makes a *detectable error* on P if the terminal string of the surface structure that the learner's system maps P into is different from the terminal string of the surface structure that the adult's system maps P into. The *degree* of a phrase-marker is its depth of embedding of S (sentence). We now make K more precise by defining the learnability property K as follows: If a grammar makes a detectable error on some p-m, then there is a p-m P of degree 1 such that the grammar makes a detectable error on P.

We now proceed to construct a formal example (allowed by our definition of *grammar*) such that K does not hold of the example. Consider the phrase-marker P in (2). P is dominated by the sentence node S_1. There is one embedded sentence, dominated by the sentence node S_0. Thus P is of degree 1. The words (lexical items) of P are represented by lower-case letters. Now, suppose there is one transformation that applies to P in the adult system. This transformation T is a *raising* transformation. That is, it *raises* a node from one embedded sentence to a higher sentence. In particular, T raises node H from S_0 and attaches it as a right daughter of A (right sister of E). The learner, however, has hypothesized a different transformation. This is the transformation T′, which also raises H, but attaches it as a left daughter of B (left sister of F). The surface structures may be seen in (3). What is important about (3) is that it shows that the learner has *not* made a detectable error on P, because the terminal strings of the sur-

(2) $P = S_1$

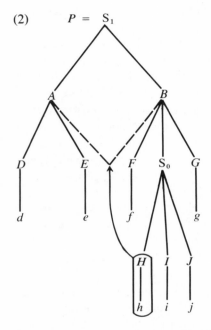

face structures are the same for both the adult and the learner, namely, *dehfijg*. This is true despite the difference in the surface structures.

Suppose now that the grammars are constructed so that there are no detectable errors on any degree-1 phrase-marker. The learnability property K then implies that there are no detectable errors on *any* phrase-marker, of whatever degree. But suppose that one other raising transformation, T'', is in both the adult's and the learner's systems; T'' raises A from S_1 and places A on the right of the next higher sentence (dominated by node S_2), as shown in (4). In the adult's system, A dominates the terminal string *deh*. Thus when A is raised, the terminal string of the surface structure of the degree-2 p-m dominated by S_2 will end in *deh* for the adult system. In the learner's system, however, A dominates *de*. Thus when A is raised, the terminal string of the surface structure of the degree-2 p-m dominated by S_2 will end in *de* for the learner's system. By definition, the learner will make a detectable error on the degree-2 phrase-marker. But we have already shown that there

(3)

a. Surface structure of P for adult: b. Surface structure of P for learner:

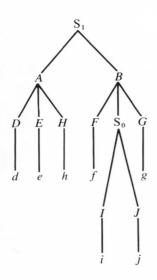
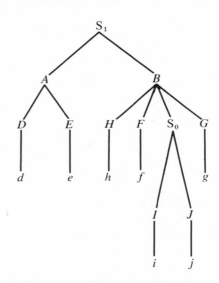

will be no detectable error on any degree-1 phrase-marker. Consequently, the learnability property K does not hold.

The move that we will then make in chapter 4 is to incorporate the first of the possibilities mentioned in the outline of the method given above. That is, we will modify K. The new learnability property K' will be: If a grammar makes a detectable error on some p-m, then there is a p-m P of degree 2 such that the grammar makes a detectable error on P. In other words, we retreat to the goal of showing learnability from data of degree 2 rather than degree 1.

Since in the artificial example just considered the phrase-marker on which there was a detectable error was of degree 2, the example does not contradict K'. Ultimately, of course, it must be proved that K' holds of all possible examples (as we do in chapter 4).

Now we want to consider an example in which our response to the failure of the learnability property is not to change the learnability property but to constrain the operation of our grammars. The example is shown as a degree-3 phrase-marker P in (5).

(4)

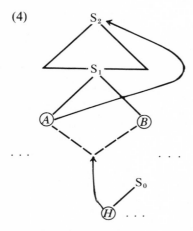

We assume, as before, that transformations obey the cyclic principle, applying to S_0, S_1, S_2, and S_3 in that order. At S_1, Q is raised. As in the previous example, the child's system attaches the raised node to a "wrong" position (that is, different from the adult's). Specifically, for the adult, Q becomes a daughter of D, and for the child, a daughter of E (see (5)). The difference for the adult and child attachments is indicated by the dotted lines under D and E. But the child does not make a *detectable* error on the phrase-marker dominated by S_1, because the terminal strings of the surface structures are the same (*fgqhilb*) for child and adult. Then A is raised from S_1 to S_2. Both child and adult do this identically. The attachment is indicated by the dotted line between S_2 and A in (5). This raising (of A) is different from the second raising in the previous example (4) because when we raise A in (5), no detectable error occurs. This is because A dominates the same terminal string for both the child and adult (*fgqhi*). However, at S_3, E is raised to the left of the phrase-marker, once again, identically for the adult and child (see (5)). Thus the terminals that start the terminal string of the fully transformed phrase-marker are the terminals dominated by E: for the adult the terminal string of the fully transformed phrase-marker starts with *hi*, whereas for the child the terminal string starts with *qhi*. Thus the child makes a detectable error on the degree-3 phrase-marker P. But there is no detectable error on any phrase-marker of degree 2 or

(5)

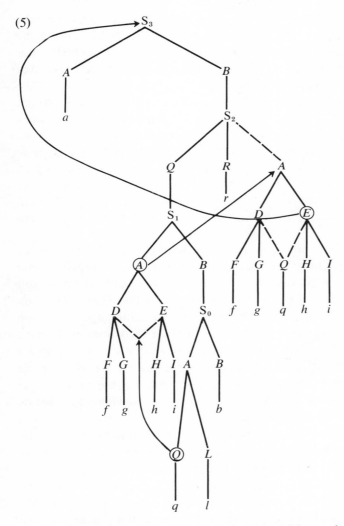

less. (The grammar has to be chosen so that this result can be formally demonstrated. This is done in chapter 4.)

What has happened in this example is that an error made at S_1 was not detectable and remained undetectable even when the error was raised to S_2. But a transformation applying at S_3 uncovered the error and made it detectable. In our previous example we tried to solve the problem by changing the learnability property K to K', that is, by assuming that the learnability property said that if a detectable error existed, then one existed on a phrase-marker of degree 2 (K') instead of degree 1 (K). We decided that the move from 1 to 2 was tolerable. We might be tempted to emulate that move here, by changing K' to K'', where "degree 2" is changed to "degree 3." But this move won't work here because the problem is not one of simply adding another level. The error of the mistakenly attached Q can continue to be moved up to higher and higher levels and might be uncovered only after a quite high level is reached. For example, A itself might be raised to S_3 or, in other examples, a node dominating A might be raised to S_3. The error might be discovered only when E is raised to S_4. And the process could continue.

This result would not be satisfactory, because the goal is to prove that if a detectable error is made, it is made on a phrase-marker of quite low degree. If we continued in the manner just outlined, the result would be failure to achieve our goal. (There would be a finite bound on the process, but in general the bound would be quite large.) Thus the move to a different learnability property will not work here. Instead we adopt the second method outlined earlier: we search for an assumption that will disallow the counterexample. We find such a hypothesis to be what we will call the *Raising principle*: If a node has been raised, it is frozen; that is, further transformations may not analyze nodes below the raised node.[21] The Raising principle has been assumed just to rule out (5) and similar examples. When A is raised from S_1 to S_2, A becomes frozen by the Raising principle. None of the nodes that A dominates may be analyzed (thus may not be affected) by a further transformation. In particular, since A dominates E, E may not be affected by a transformation. Thus E may not be raised from S_2 to S_3; therefore no detectable error will be created, and the derivation of P does not contradict learnability property K'.

In order to preserve a learnability property, we have been led to hypothesize a constraint on the operation of transformations. This constraint can be taken to be a universal principle in the language learning mechanism and, concomitantly, a universal principle of natural languages. The theory thus leads us to a hypothesis, namely, that the Raising principle is universal. Linguistic methods can then be used to test the hypothesis for its descriptive adequacy (as we do in chapter 5). If linguistic evidence is found for the hypothesis (Raising principle, in this case), we have two very different kinds of evidence for the Raising principle. On the one hand, an abstract analysis of conditions under which human learning can take place leads us to the Raising principle. On the other hand, direct linguistic evidence might support the principle. Whenever evidence of such radically different kinds is found for a hypothesis in science, it is considered that the argument for the hypothesis is relatively strong.

CHAPTER 2

FOUNDATIONS OF A THEORY OF LEARNABILITY

2.1 A Framework for the Theory of Language Acquisition

In the framework that we have adopted in chapter 1, a theory of (first) language acquisition may be looked on as a triple $\langle \mathcal{G}, \mathcal{I}, LP \rangle$ where

(1)
i. $\mathcal{G}$ is a class of grammars (the possible grammars),
ii. $\mathcal{I}$ is a class of possible sets of input or data $I(G)$ from grammar G in $\mathcal{G}$, and
iii. LP is a language learning procedure that maps inputs into grammars.

For the theory to be adequate, it must be the case that

(2)
i. Descriptively adequate grammars for every natural language are in $\mathcal{G}$,
ii. $\mathcal{I}$ includes the sets of information about language available to a normal language learner, that is, if G can be learned from a particular kind of experience $I(G)$, then $I(G)$ is in $\mathcal{I}$, and
iii. Every grammar G in $\mathcal{G}$ can be learned by procedure LP from every information set $I(G)$ in $\mathcal{I}$.

The goal of learnability theory, then, is to find a specification of a class of grammars $\mathcal{G}$ which includes grammars for all natural languages and to find a language learning procedure *LP* so that *LP* can learn any of the grammars from the appropriate kind of data. What it means to *learn* a grammar must be specified precisely. We will define *learn* to mean "learn according to a criterion *C*," where *C* will also have to be specified by our theory.

As specified in (1) and (2), these notions still do not have nearly enough substance to be called a theory. Rather, (1) constitutes a framework for a theory and (2) defines what it means for a theory to be adequate. When we have filled in actual, clearly specified instances of $\mathcal{G}$, $\mathcal{I}$, *LP*, and *C*, then we may say that we have a theory. We will investigate a number of such theories.

Proposition (1.i) states that the specification of a class of possible grammars is part of a theory of language acquisition. We have to specify $\mathcal{G}$ because of a fundamental element of our methodology; namely, we set as the goal of learnability theory to show that every possible grammar is learnable (2.iii) (but see section 2.1.1 for an alternative). Also, we want to ensure that every grammar that is a grammar for a natural language is learnable. We do this by requiring that every grammar for a natural language is in $\mathcal{G}$ (2.i), and thus, since every grammar in $\mathcal{G}$ is learnable, it follows that every grammar for a natural language is learnable.

Proposition (1.ii) specifies that the kind of information about his language that is available to the learner is part of a theory of acquisition. Every set of experiences from which language can be learned is in $\mathcal{I}$ (2.ii). Although this information may sometimes be enriched in one way or another, the important point is that the theory must allow language to be learned from unenriched information, if it is true that a child can naturally learn language in this way (2.iii). In general it will turn out that if language can be learned from a particular set of experiences, it can also be learned from a richer set of experiences.[1] Thus it will be most important for the theory to specify in $\mathcal{I}$ the *minimal* sets of data from which language can be learned. In the theories that we analyze, the *kind* of information that is allowed to the learner is the same, whatever language he is learning. The framework, however, doesn't require this. It is conceivable that different kinds of natural languages require different kinds of data in order to be learned. We see no reason to assume that this is true for the core of grammar, but we would not be surprised if linguistic constructions of somewhat special kind did require certain special kinds of experiences (for example, special teaching methods). Since we will not be concerned with those constructions in this book, we will assume that the kind of data available to the learner is the same no matter what language he is learning.

Proposition (1.iii) specifies the language learning procedure, *LP*. *LP* is the only part of the theory that is one element and not a class ($\mathscr{G}$ and $\mathscr{I}$ are both classes, or specifications of classes). Since the learner starts off without any knowledge of exactly which of the possible languages is his, he has to start with something fixed. This is the procedure, which includes notions of such things as grammatical form (and perhaps $\mathscr{G}$). The procedure specifies how input is mapped into hypotheses about grammar. *LP* explicitly involves the class of grammars. It is not clear how to interpret the notion of more than one possible procedure. One interpretation would be that different individuals are born with different means for learning their language. There is much reason to believe, however, that except in pathological cases the possibility of learning central notions of grammar does not differ from individual to individual. The idealization under which we work assumes that there is an idealized language learner; it does not allow the possibility of varying skills. Certainly the mysteries of how language learning can proceed are difficult enough at this stage of our investigations without considering the question of varying skills.[2]

These three requirements provide a framework for the study of language acquisition, a framework in which both empiricist and rationalist points of view (and many intermediate ones) might find expression. For example, if (1.iii) specifies a set of stimulus-response learning mechanisms, we will have taken a step toward formulating an empiricist theory of language acquisition. Of course, for the theory to be adequate, $\mathscr{G}$ and $\mathscr{I}$ would have to be specified in empirically adequate ways, and the stimulus-response mechanisms would have to be capable of mapping experience into the appropriate grammars. It is well known that when stimulus-response theory is formalized explicitly enough for study, such mechanisms cannot carry out the learning of the kinds of grammars that linguistics has shown to be necessary to adequately describe natural language.[3]

The interaction between the procedure *LP* and the class of grammars is very important. In fact, since the procedure has to select a grammar, there is no way of defining the procedure without mentioning at least some aspects of the class of grammars. Thus our separation of the problem of learning into the two parts of specification of mechanism and specification of domain principles (Section 1.2.1) is to some extent a heuristic device. The interaction between form and procedure is inescapable.

Consider an "evaluation procedures" theory (Chomsky 1965, chapter 1), in which it is assumed that the theory specifies a class of grammars together with an evaluation procedure that linearly orders the grammars in the class. The procedure then selects the most highly valued grammar compatible with the primary data. In this evaluation procedures theory the procedure must interact somewhat with the notion of grammar, because somehow the class of grammars that are compatible with the data has to be selected. Although stated in the framework (Chomsky 1965, 31 (14v)) abstractly as an integer assigned to each possible grammar, in the actual construction of a linguistic theory the evaluation measure will be defined by a procedure that depends heavily on notions of linguistic form. In fact, the point of the evaluation measure is to select grammars with particular forms over grammars with other forms when both grammars are compatible with the primary data. One approach to part of this problem is to define "notational transformations" (Chomsky 1975c), which determine equivalent (in a very special sense) grammars to which the evaluation procedure will apply.

In this evaluation measure theory, then, the class of grammars plays a direct part in the procedure for learning language. In other theories the representation of the class of grammars may not play such a direct role in the procedure. Nevertheless, the procedure will be intimately involved with aspects of grammatical form. This will be true even of theories that construct grammars piece by piece. The pieces (for instance, syntactic transformations, in theories we will consider) will be heavily constrained by assumptions on grammatical form. These assumptions will be built directly into the procedure. In general, as less direct reliance on the class of grammars is explicitly built into the theory, more reliance on grammatical form will have to be explicitly built into the procedure.

2.1.1 A Variant of the Framework: Attainability

Although what we have specified up to now is only a framework, hardly a theory, still there are possible variants, which could in principle have empirical consequences. In (2.iii) we required that every grammar in the set of possible grammars be learnable. A reason for this assumption is that we naturally want to be able to show that every grammar of a natural language is learnable; we do this by requiring that all grammars of natural languages be included in the class of possible grammars and that all possible grammars be learnable.

There is an alternative, however. As before, let $\mathscr{G}$ be a class of (possible) grammars. We do not require, however, that every grammar G in $\mathscr{G}$ be learnable from data $I(G)$ of the appropriate form. Instead, we define the class of *attainable grammars* as those grammars in $\mathscr{G}$ that can be learned by *LP* from data of the appropriate kind from $\mathscr{I}$. In order for this kind of theory to be adequate, the class of attainable grammars must include descriptively adequate grammars for all languages that can in fact be learned. (In particular, the grammars for all natural languages must be attainable.)

The attainable grammars are a subset of $\mathscr{G}$. Quite possibly they are a nontrivial subset; that is, conceivably there are possible grammars that are not attainable. These might include, for example, grammars whose form is perfectly appropriate and that in fact are learnable by procedure *LP*, but for which *LP* demands very complicated data or information, data not available to the language learner.

At first glance it might seem that the two kinds of frameworks are interchangeable, really notational variants. But this is not necessarily so. Whether our first framework can be translated in some cases into the second framework remains an open problem. In all work in learnability theory to date the first framework has been assumed; we have made it the goal of the current analysis to produce adequate classes of grammars that are completely learnable. In terms of the second framework, we prove that the class of attainable grammars equals $\mathcal{G}$, the class of possible grammars. That is, all possible grammars are attainable. In order to reach this result (for part of the problem of language learning) we have to both restrict the scope of the problem (essentially to the learning of syntactic transformations) and restrict the system.[4] If this latter restriction turns out to be too severe in that the restricted system will not allow all the grammars for natural language, one way to proceed might be to relax the restrictions and give up the goal of proving that all possible grammars are learnable (attainable). Perhaps some of the learnability problems that cause us to put restrictions on the class of possible grammars in chapter 4 do not actually arise, because grammars containing these problems are not attainable. Thus no adult has attained such a grammar, and no child has to learn such a grammar.

We have not pursued the implications of this position. Doubtless there will be intricacies. To be adequate, the attainable class of grammars must include the class of grammars that are grammars of natural languages (grammars actually attained by learners and hence unquestionably attainable). If some possible grammars are not attainable, it is conceivable that we could formulate formal conditions that pick out just these possible but nonattainable grammars. We might be able to put these conditions back into the class of possible grammars, deleting the nonattainable grammars from $\mathcal{G}$ and allowing the class of possible grammars to be totally learnable. It is an empirical question whether an entirely adequate theory can be stated in this way.

The question is confounded because the restrictions that have been placed on the class of grammars because of learnability problems are often double-edged. For example, many restrictions are constraints on the functioning of rules, placed there so as to solve learnability problems. In this sense the restrictions become part of the language learning procedure LP, which has to carry out grammatical derivations as part of its functioning and thus is constrained by the restrictions. On the other hand, even when the restrictions have been invoked in order for the language learning procedure to work better, the restrictions become part of the definition of the class of grammars $\mathcal{G}$. Thus placing a restriction on the procedure LP means that a new question will arise regarding the descriptive adequacy of the class of grammars $\mathscr{G}$. If this restriction is part of descriptive adequacy, then even for a theory in the alternative (attainability) framework to be adequate, the restriction will have to be built into the class of grammars $\mathscr{G}$, or at least will have to be a characteristic of the class of attainable grammars.

From the point of view of this second (attainability) framework, some universals of language are built into the organism directly, part of his language learning procedure. Other universals result because grammars of a certain form, though not ruled out directly by the initial constraints and procedure that the organism uses to learn language, will not be attainable. Let us call universals of the first kind *innateness* universals, and those of the second kind *attainability* universals. It is important to stress that the decision whether a particular universal will be of the innateness or attainability kind cannot be made a priori. It is an empirical question what goes into the procedure and initial constraints, on the one hand, and what the theorist will calculate from these (together with the input) as not attainable. The usual kinds of theorizing and empirical research will be necessary in order to answer this kind of question.

It might seem at first glance as if essentially *all* universals could be of the attainability type, that is, as if all universals could result from the procedure's not being able to learn certain kinds of grammars. The argument would be that we could weaken the initial constraints on grammars considerably, letting the initial class of grammars $\mathscr{G}$ be very large. The procedure *LP* would also be very general, with not much in the way of particular linguistic constraints. The procedure would only be able to learn (attain) certain grammars, of course. These would be the attainable grammars, and universals would be the properties of those attainable grammars.

The problem with this argument is that there might turn out to be no procedure of this general kind, which, unconstrained by linguistic restrictions, will be able to select (attain) descriptively adequate grammars for natural languages. There is no reason to think that the set of grammars attainable by a procedure not subject to linguistic constraints will include the set of grammars that are descriptively adequate for natural languages. In fact, everything we know about linguistic theory and learnability theory indicates that this is the case.

Consider a particular example, often used to argue for the innateness of formal universals of grammar (see, for example, Chomsky 1975a, 30–33). Syntactic transformations are particular kinds of mappings, namely, structure-dependent mappings of a certain kind. They are not arbitrary mappings. The strong attainability view would hold that this property would not be built directly into the organism that is learning language. Rather, the property would emerge because only grammars possessing this property could be attained.

On this (strong attainability) view the language learning procedure is uninformed about the nature of syntactic transformations. Let us say that the procedure assumes that they are mappings and nothing more. (Even this is an assumption about what the learner starts off with, but perhaps it would be allowed by the strong attainability point of view.) From the strong attainability point of view one would then argue that if data from a language with structure-dependent transformations were presented, the general procedure could learn (attain) that language, whereas if data from a language with arbitrary, non-structure-dependent transformations were presented, the procedure could not learn that language.

However, there is no reason to think that a procedure capable of performing in this way can exist. Sentences don't come with the information attached that they are generated by structure-dependent transformations, and the data are limited. There is no reason to think that the procedure will be able, from the primary data, to determine a grammar for the language which includes structure-dependent transformations and not arbitrary transformations; for any such procedure there might be many natural languages for which the procedure would determine grammars that contain arbitrary and not structure-dependent transformations. In short, the attained grammar will not be descriptively adequate. It is important to realize that this result would not be the lack of a mere nicety. The point is that the attained grammar would be severely different, in important respects, from the grammar that a child would learn from the same set of data. Quite possibly the grammar might fail even in weak equivalence; that is, the grammar attained by the theory might not even allow the same set of sentences as the grammar attained by the child. The complexity and difficulty of the problem of learning transformations (see chapter 4) even when the learner is informed as to the nature of transformations, leads us quite clearly to the belief that it will not be possible for an uninformed procedure to select appropriate grammars from the primary data.

Though it is clear that some constraints will have to be built into the learner, this does not mean that all universals will have to be built in. In general it appears to us that restrictions on the *kinds* of rules there are and on the functioning of these rules will be built into the class of grammars and procedure (for instance, the notion of transformational rule). The kinds of possible but nonattainable grammars there are might be those that use the means allowed by the formal assumptions, but use them in too complex a way. A grammar with an exceedingly large number of transformations, for example, might be possible but not attainable, because the procedure couldn't learn the grammar in an appropriate amount of time. It is important once again to stress that whether to account for a particular universal on grounds of innateness or of attainability is an empirical question. Our suggestions as to this very preliminary, very rough characterization arise simply from an inspection of what appear to be the kinds of universals that are useful in linguistic and learnability theory. For example, it does not appear to us that the statement that a grammar has less than, say, 500 transformations will be central in the pursuit of the goal of feasibility, the learning of grammar under natural conditions.

Such grammars (with large numbers of transformations) might not be attainable, however. Saying that grammars contain only structure-dependent transformations, however, helps exceedingly in the learning of transformations. A more precise and general characterization of what kinds of universals follow from attainability considerations would be an interesting study, one we have not pursued further.

We adopt as a working hypothesis the assumption that all (biologically) possible grammars are learnable. It could be empirically wrong. In this book we pursue the implications of this assumption. Even if the assumption turns out to be false, we expect that many of the results attained will carry through, possibly in a somewhat different form or with a different interpretation. On the other hand, recent work in linguistic theory is making it more plausible that this assumption is correct, though possibly with qualifications. Chomsky (1977) conceives of very restricted possibilities for "core grammar," with grammars for natural languages differing by a choice of parameters. Beyond core grammar, languages could differ in a wider variety of ways. One possibility is that all grammars realized by fixing the parameters for core grammar are learnable, but that the wider variation allowed by processes outside of core grammar is such that some possible realizations of those processes are not learnable. In fact, one would expect that core grammar would be learnable quickly and from simple data. Thus it might turn out that the working hypothesis of this book is in fact empirically correct, although it might have to be limited to core grammar. The results on degree-2 learnability in chapter 4 are supportive of the claim that linguistic theory has identified constructs of core grammar that are quickly and easily learnable because the organism starts with rich notions of linguistic structure.

2.2 An Elementary Theory of Learnability

To construct a theory of learnability we have to provide explicit definitions of the class of possible grammars ($\mathscr{G}$), the kind of information available to the learner ($\mathscr{I}$), the procedure for selecting a grammar (LP), and the criterion or definition (C) of what it means to learn a language. Since there are so many concepts in the theory, each of which has to be precisely articulated, we will proceed in this section by holding some of the concepts fixed at a fairly general level, while considering other of the concepts in more detail and deriving some of their properties. We will not be concerned for the moment with justifying the particular definitions of the concepts we introduce. In fact, a theme throughout much of this book will be that certain assumptions are wrong, that they won't work for the solution of the learnability problem. In particular, in this section we will not be concerned with most of the known properties of possible grammars. We will simply assume that a grammar G is an explicit device (set of rules, say) that generates a language $L(G)$. $L(G)$ is a set of *sentences*, that is, a set of finite strings on a (terminal) vocabulary. Of course, a language is more than a set of strings, but we will not consider other properties in this section.[5]

It is obvious that language learners are presented with examples of sentences from their language.[6] Therefore we will assume that the input to the language learner consists of a set of sentences. Since no language learner has access to an infinite set of sentences, we will assume that the set of sentences from which the language learner selects his grammar is finite. So we have as input to the language learner a finite set of sentences, sufficient for language learning to occur, which we will call the *set of primary data*. For language $L(G)$, the primary data are a finite subset of $L(G)$.

The procedure LP is another construct, the exact nature of which we will not discuss in this elementary theory. We simply want LP to be consistent with our other definitions. Thus LP will select grammars based on a set of primary data. In other words LP will be a function f, taking a set of primary data into a grammar. And f will have to satisfy the criterion of learnability; that is, it will have to select the correct grammars according to our definition of the criterion.

A problem with specifying the learnability criterion C more explicitly is that the definition of the criterion interacts with the definition of the input, or primary data. We have said that the input is a finite set of sentences, but we haven't said which finite set. Certainly we can't assume that *any* finite set will do; language is not necessarily learnable from a set consisting of one sentence, for example. In some sense we want to say that the set of primary data is big enough, but we have to explicate what "big enough" means.

We adopt the following solution. We assume that the criterion specifies that there exists *some* finite set of data D (sentences) that is "big enough"; that is, the learning function f will map D into the correct grammar, the grammar that generates the language from which D was taken. Clearly, by itself this definition of the criterion is not strong enough. Suppose that f maps another set of data from the same language $L(G)$ into another grammar G'. Surely we should allow this; we cannot require that the procedure select the correct grammar from every set of data. Rather, we want the procedure to select the correct grammar from a set of data that is "big enough," which means that if a set of data D' is bigger than D, the correct grammar is selected from D' also. D' is bigger than D, for these purposes, if D' contains D (if every sentence of D is a sentence of D').

To summarize, the language learning procedure LP is a function f that assigns to each finite set of sentences a grammar from the class of grammars $\mathcal{G}$. The criterion of learnability requires that for each grammar G in the class $\mathcal{G}$ there be a finite set of sentences $D \subseteq L(G)$ such that $f(D) = G$ and if D' is a bigger finite set of sentences contained in the language (that is, if $D \subseteq D' \subseteq L(G)$), then $f(D') = G$. D can then be called a set of *primary data* for G.[7] The point is that for a sufficiently large set of data, the correct language is chosen and further data do not change the choice.

One interesting property of this definition is that we have not put a bound on the size of a set of primary data for a grammar G. Although a finite set of data (of size $C(G)$, say) exists for each G in a learnable class $\mathcal{G}$, still there may be no finite bound over $C(G)$. There are infinite classes of grammars such that a bounded set of primary data exists for each grammar. For example, the class $\mathcal{G}$ introduced later in this section is such that a set of primary data of size 1 exists for each grammar in $\mathcal{G}$. One can also construct examples of classes of grammars that are learnable but do not meet this *bounding* requirement. Bounding of the size of a minimal set of primary data over a class of grammars (see note 7) would seem to be a natural requirement to add to the criterion of learnability, although we have not done so here.[8] The consideration of these issues is perhaps relevant to the discussion of the alternative framework of *attainability* in section 2.1. Perhaps grammars for which the set of primary data is very large are not attainable, although possible. In this book we ignore this possibility, in favor of the requirement that all possible grammars be learnable.

Actually, the requirements are still a bit too strong for our purposes. If $\mathcal{G}$ allows two grammars that generate exactly the same languages, the primary linguistic data cannot distinguish between them. We will therefore allow in this elementary theory any weakly equivalent grammar (any grammar that generates exactly the same set of sentences as the correct grammar) to be selected.

We can bring these requirements together in the *set model* of language acquisition.

(3) Let $\mathcal{G}$ be a class of grammars on some fixed terminal vocabulary. The class of grammars is *set-learnable* if there exists a function f from finite subsets of the class of all strings on the vocabulary into $\mathcal{G}$ such that for each $G \in \mathcal{G}$ there exists a finite set $D \subseteq L(G)$ such that

i. $f(D) = G'$, where $L(G') = L(G)$,

and for each finite set D' such that $D \subseteq D' \subseteq L(G)$,

ii. $f(D) = f(D')$.

We call f the *learning function* (for $\mathcal{G}$). Note that (3) actually requires one property in addition to those discussed so far. To satisfy the requirement that some grammar that generates the correct language is selected for each set of data bigger than the set of primary data, we could have allowed a different grammar to be selected for each set of data that contains D, as long as the grammar generates the correct language. Instead we have required that the same grammar be selected by f for all the supersets of D. Thus the definition satisfies the notion that at some time a grammar for a language is selected and does not change when further data are added.[9]

In this elementary theory, we ignore the role of time, concentrating on the relation between the primary data and the selection of a grammar. In later sections we will explicitly consider the role of time, including such matters as the gradual formation of hypotheses. It will be seen that much of the structure of the problem of learnability is not dependent on considerations of time but is inherent in the relations between available data and the class of possible grammars. On the other hand, a number of the complexities in the learnability problem arise from limitations on the available primary data which are due to time-bound aspects of the actual unfolding of learning.

We will now construct an artificial example to illustrate the definitions. There is not supposed to be anything languagelike about the example. It is formulated in a simple manner so as to be as clear as possible. Let $\mathcal{G} = \{G_1,G_2, \ldots\}$ be an infinite class of grammars generating languages defined in the following way.

$L(G_1) = \{a,aa,aaa, \ldots\}$
$L(G_2) = \{aa,aaa, \ldots\}$
$\ldots$
$L(G_i) = \{a^i,a^{i+1}, \ldots\}$
$\ldots$

In short, $L(G_i)$ contains all strings of length i or greater defined on the single word a. (a^i means a string $a\ldots a$ of length i.) Grammars for these languages can be constructed in many ways.[10] Intuitively, this class of grammars is learnable according to our definition because the shortest string in each language provides enough information to allow a guess as to which language is the source of the data. More formally, we can define a learning function f in the following way. Let D be a finite set of data from a language generated by one of the grammars in $\mathcal{G}$. That is, D is a finite set of finite strings on a. Let j be the length of the shortest string in D. Then we define $f(D) = G_j$.

This definition of the learning function f has the property that, for a set of data containing only one string a^j, the grammar that generates the language for which a^j is the shortest string is selected by f. That is, $f(\{a^j\}) = G_j$. If D is a finite set of data such that $\{a^i\} \subseteq D \subseteq L(G_i)$, then $f(D) = G_i$ (because any string in $L(G_i)$ is of length at least i). Thus $\mathcal{G}$ is learnable by the learning function f, according to our definition. It turns out that for this example the minimal set of primary data for any grammar contains just one string (see note 7). Namely, for G_i the minimal set of primary data is $\{a^i\}$. In general the minimal set of primary data will be larger (and there could be more than one minimal set of primary data).

What makes even this elementary theory of learnability interesting is that there are many classes of grammars that are not learnable. We will now construct an example of such an unlearnable class. Let $\mathcal{H} = \{H_0,H_1,H_2, \ldots\}$ be an infinite class of grammars generating the following languages:

$L(H_0) = \{a,aa,aaa,aaaa, \ldots\}$

$$L(H_1) = \{a\}$$
$$L(H_2) = \{a,aa\}$$
$$L(H_3) = \{a,aa,aaa\}$$
. . .
$$L(H_i) = \{a,aa,aaa, \ldots ,a^i\}$$
. . .

In other words, $L(H_0)$ consists of *all* strings on a, and for $i \neq 0$, $L(H_i)$ is finite, consisting of all strings of length $\leq i$. We will not bother to define the grammars H, which can easily be done in many ways.

The class $\mathcal{H} = \{H_0,H_1, \ldots \}$ is unlearnable. The intuition behind the proof is that for any finite set of data D (a set of strings on a), the learning function could choose either one of infinitely many finite languages that contain D, or it could choose H, which generates the infinite language. If the function always chooses finite languages (for example, a conservative strategy would choose the smallest language that contains D), then when data from $L(H_0)$ is presented, the function will still never choose H_0, as it must if H were learnable. If, on the other hand, the function f consistently chooses the grammar for the infinite language H_0, it will never choose a finite language and thus will never be correct when data from one of the finite languages is presented. No combination of strategies will allow $\mathcal{H}$ to be learnable.[11]

Suppose it were argued that, although no such learning function exists, the notion of learning that we have proposed is too strong. If a learner adopted the radical strategy of guessing the grammar that produced the largest language containing a given set of data, his only problem would be that he might accept too many sentences; that is, he would overgeneralize. But in fact we claim, as does linguistic theory, that speakers have the ability to distinguish grammatical from ungrammatical strings. It is clearly necessary for the rules of the language that humans learn to rule out many strings as ungrammatical. The problem of fixing just the correct set of sentences, neither too small nor too large, is precisely the task. Also, and even more important, the ultimate task is to be able to show that the learner (as we theoretically characterize him) will learn descriptively adequate grammars of a language. Allowing the learner to radically overgeneralize the adult language changes the problem in a very noninsightful way, by allowing solutions of the learnability problem that are not constrained by the necessity of achieving descriptive adequacy.

First ideas about what characterizes learnability in the elementary sense of set-learnability are not necessarily correct. For example, infinity is not related in a straightforward manner to the notion of learnability. In the examples presented, $\mathscr{G}$ is learnable despite the fact that it generates an infinite number of infinite languages, whereas $\mathscr{H}$, which contains only one infinite language, is not learnable. In fact, we can prove the following theorem characterizing set-learnable classes of grammars:[12]

Characterization Theorem for Learnable Classes of Grammars: Let $\mathscr{H}$ be a denumerable class of grammars which generates the class of languages K. Then $\mathscr{H}$ is set-learnable if and only if K does not contain an infinite subset of languages $K' = \{L_0, L_1, L_2, \ldots\}$ such that

i. $L_0 = \bigcup_{i=1}^{\infty} L_i$, and

ii. for every finite subset F of L_0, there are an infinite number of $L_i \in K'$ such that $F \subseteq L_i$.

2.3 Text-Learnability

Even though we want to concentrate on the learning of grammar from example sentences, a number of features of the learning situation that were omitted from the elementary theory of set learnability presented in the last section need to be considered. These omissions revolve around the notion of time, which is not mentioned at all in the definition of set-learnability. In this section we will present a theory that does make assumptions about the role of time.

It is clear that information about his language is presented to the learner in pieces, over time, rather than all at once. As an idealization, suppose that time is discrete. Thus we can count time as $t_0, t_1, t_2, \ldots$ Learning begins at time t_0. We can assume that one piece of information about his language is presented to the learner at each time t_i. Since we are considering only information that consists of example sentences, we can assume that one sentence from his language is presented to the learner at each time t_i.

Hypotheses also change over time. Thus we can suppose that at each time t_i, the learner has a hypothesis that a particular language in the class of possible grammars is the actual grammar from whose language he has been receiving data. The learning procedure LP guesses a grammar at each time. Also, since we are considering that LP acts in time, we will require that LP be effective (computable), rather than simply a function. [13]

In set-learnability we require that a finite set of primary data exists such that for every set containing the primary data, the correct grammar is selected. In integrating this notion with the role of time, we require that a finite time exists such that the correct grammar is selected at that time and at all later times. The set of data presented up to the time the correct grammar is selected can be looked on as the primary data. As further data come in at later times, the set of data becomes a superset of this primary data. Since the selected grammar doesn't change, the set-learnability condition will be met.

In set-learnability we require that a large enough set of primary data exists that the correct grammar can be selected from that set. We indirectly capture that notion in a time model by requiring that an appropriate time exists at which the selection can be made. But how do we know that enough data will be presented by some finite time? Suppose, for example, that a language included all the strings on the word a. But suppose that the same string, say aaa, is presented at every time. Surely we do not want to require that at some time in this particular sequence the correct grammar can be selected. In set-learnability the set of primary data can be taken to be as complete as necessary (though only finite). We want to insure that the data in a time model can also be as complete as possible. We can capture this property by demanding learnability only when the sequence of presented data contains all the strings in the language. Then, by taking a sufficiently large time, the set of primary data can be taken to be as big as necessary. Note that the requirement that the sequence of data contains all the strings in the language means that for any string in the language there is a finite time at which it is presented; the requirement does *not* imply that there is a finite time such that every string in the language will have been presented by that time. The requirement essentially says that learnability has to take place only under conditions where there is no systematic withholding of information. As an illustration, consider the class of grammars $\mathscr{G}$, from section 2.2. Suppose that sentences of length less than 10 were not presented. Then there would be no way for a procedure to distinguish between $G_1, G_2, \ldots, G_{10}$.

These requirements concerning the role of time can be brought together in the theory of *text-learnability*.[14] First, an *information sequence* $I(L)$ of language L is a sequence of sentences of L such that every sentence of the language appears in the sequence. Let $I(L) = a_1$, $a_2, \ldots$ be an information sequence. Then a *sample* (to time t) of I is $S_t(I) = \{a_1, \ldots, a_t\}$. Thus a sample is an unordered set.

A *learning procedure LP* is an effective function from the set of samples into the set of grammars in some class. We conceive of $LP(S_t(I))$ as being the guess that LP makes at time t when presented with the information sequence I.

(4) We say that the class of languages G is *text-learnable* if there is a learning procedure LP such that for any $G_i \in \mathscr{G}$ and any information sequence $I(L(G_i))$ there exists a τ such that $t > \tau$ implies both

i. $LP(S_t(I)) = LP(S_\tau(I))$ and
ii. $L(LP(S_\tau(I))) = L(G_i)$.

Condition (i) requires that the guessed grammar does not change after some finite time τ. Condition (ii) requires that this unchanging guessed grammar has a language equal to the language of the grammar from which the data is being presented. Gold (1967) showed that none of the usual classes of grammars studied in mathematical linguistics are text-learnable. This includes the finite-state and context-free grammars, for example. In fact, Gold showed that any *superfinite* class, that is, any class of grammars that generates all the finite languages on a vocabulary and at least one infinite language is not text-learnable.[15] We will call this result the Superfinite theorem. Also useful in deciding whether certain classes of grammars are not learnable is the following proposition, which follows immediately from the definition of learnability. The proposition holds for both set-learnability and text-learnability.

(5) If a class of grammars $\mathcal{G}$ is not learnable, and if a class of grammars $\mathcal{H}$ generates a class of languages $L(\mathcal{H})$ that is a superset of the class of languages $L(\mathcal{G})$ generated by $\mathcal{G}$, then $\mathcal{H}$ is not learnable.

Once a stock of examples of unlearnable classes of grammars is built up, other classes of grammars can be shown to be unlearnable by showing that the class of languages generated by a class of grammars contains all the languages generated by one of the unlearnable classes of grammars. We will refer to this result as the Superset theorem.

Most of the usefulness of our models of learnability from sentences stems from the fact that we can show that interesting classes of grammars are not set-learnable. Set-learnability leaves out the role of time in learning, which text-learnability includes. But an obvious result is that if a class of grammars is not set-learnable, then the class is not text-learnable.[16] Therefore, if we prove that a class of grammars is not set-learnable, we will know that it is not text-learnable. Thus in order to achieve results concerning nonlearnability from sentences, we will have to consider only set-learnability.

2.4 Restricting the Class of Grammars

The criterion that set-learnability imposes on grammars is really quite weak and insufficient. Only the correct set of strings has to be discovered and nothing more abstract with respect to descriptive adequacy. Nevertheless, it is difficult for classes of grammars to meet the requirement of being set-learnable. We have provided a simple example of a class of unlearnable grammars, and many more classes of grammar can easily be proved unlearnable by the application of either the Superset theorem or the Characterization theorem.

Suppose that we are willing to simplify the problem at first by considering only some of the formal constructs of grammar for which linguistic theory provides evidence. A long-studied type of linguistic rule is the phrase structure rule. Many properties of this kind of rule are well known. In particular, much of the content of the theory of phrase structure rules can be formalized within the theory of context-free grammars. Because of the simple formulation of these grammars, mathematical analysis of their properties has proceeded much further than for other kinds of linguistic rules, for example, transformations.[17]

It is easy to show that the class of context-free grammars is not set-learnable, since even greatly restricted subsets of the class of context-free grammars are not set-learnable. The unlearnable class of grammars $\mathscr{H}$ in section 2.2 can easily be formulated so that each of the grammars H_i is context-free, for example. Set- (and text-) learnability depends on reasonably simple convolutions of sets, and the individual grammars that generate these sets do not have to be very complex, at least in any obvious sense of complexity, in order for nonlearnability to be provable. Grammars are easily constructed that are not learnable because the languages that the grammars generate meet the condition of the Characterization theorem.

It may be that simple constructs of grammar are too simple for the learnability problem. That is, allowing more complicated constructs and formalisms might allow us to restrict the class of languages so that the unlearnability condition of the Characterization theorem is not met. It may be that the class of context-free grammars is too large to represent the class of natural languages. Only certain context-free grammars will be possible as parts of grammars of natural language. Allowing other kinds of grammatical rules might allow the class of context-free grammars to be sufficiently small so that set-learnability might be achieved. The general notion underlying our search here is that a class of grammars each consisting of two simple parts might be more easily learnable than a class of grammars each containing one relatively complicated part. Remember that we are working under the assumption that all (biologically possible) grammars are learnable, although this might not be the case. See section 2.1.1.

Suppose that we allow syntactic transformations in our grammars.[18] It is fairly well established that such operations are needed for descriptive adequacy of a theory of grammar. Transformations also yield additional power in construction of a grammar for a particular language, so it is conceivable that the context-free part of the grammar can be simplified while maintaining descriptive adequacy.

Since transformations are particular kinds of operations that map phrase-markers into phrase-markers, an initial set of phrase-markers has to be provided for transformations to apply to. This is done by including a context-free grammar as part of every transformational grammar. Thus a transformational grammar, for our purposes here, consists of a context-free grammar (often called the *base grammar*) and a set of transformations.

Suppose that a transformational grammar, in a degenerate case, contains no transformations at all (or only an *identity* transformation). Then the transformational grammar will be identical to the context-free part of it. The class of transformational grammars will include all these degenerate grammars. Allowing the context-free part of the transformational grammar to be *any* context-free grammar, we see that the class of transformational grammars includes all context-free grammars. Since the class of context-free grammars is not learnable, it follows from proposition (5) of section 2.3 that the class of transformational grammars is not learnable.

However, we have not made effective use of the strategy we are pursuing. The strategy is to simplify the inherent complexities of one part of the grammar by using power from another part. Suppose that it is *not* the case that *any* context-free grammar can be part of a transformational grammar. To take this notion to an extreme, suppose that there exists only one context-free grammar as part of a transformational grammar. That is, suppose there is one fixed context-free grammar B such that every grammar in the class of transformational grammars $\mathscr{T}$ that we are considering is defined by a set of transformations on B.

The assumption that only one base exists for all natural languages is often called the Universal Base hypothesis (UBH). There is ample linguistic evidence that the Universal Base hypothesis in its strongest form, outlined here, is wrong.[19] But we will consider the assumption for the light it throws on the learnability problem.

The point of invoking the Universal Base hypothesis is in line with our general strategy: by adding a component (transformations) to our grammars, we hope to restrict another component (the base) in such a way that the resulting grammars are learnable. In particular, if there is only one base, common to all grammars, the base will not have to be learned but can be assumed by the learning procedure. Although each grammar will differ because it will have a different set of transformations associated with it, these transformations would seem to be somewhat limited in that they operate on the structures produced by the same base grammar. In addition, the assumption that all the languages generated by this class of grammars are defined by transforming a common base leads to the speculation that the languages will be similar in certain ways and perhaps the complexities that lead to unlearnability will not result.

In short, our hypothesis is that if we fix any context-free base grammar and consider the class of transformational grammars defined on that base, the class of transformational grammars will turn out to be set-learnable. This hypothesis is false, as can be demonstrated by constructing a counterexample, a class of transformational grammars defined on a universal base such that the class of grammars is not learnable.[20] Consider the class of languages $K = \{L_0, L_1, \ldots \}$, where

$$L_0 = \{a^j c b^j \mid j = 1, 2, \ldots \} \cup \{b^j a^{j+1} c b \mid j = 1, 2, \ldots \},$$

and for $i > 0$,

$$L_i = \{a^j c b^j \mid j = 1, 2, \ldots \} \cup \{b^j a^{j+1} c b \mid j = 1, 2, \ldots, i \}.$$

Clearly conditions (i) and (ii) of the Characterization theorem apply to K and therefore any class of grammars that generates K (or a superset of K) is not set-learnable. To demonstrate the falsity of our hypothesis that every class of transformational grammars on a universal base is learnable, we have to show only that K can be generated by a class of transformational grammars on a universal base. We omit this demonstration here. It is accomplished by Wexler and Hamburger (1973, section 4). The universal base grammar B is taken to comprise the three rules:

S→a Sb
S→acb
S→abc.

The grammar for language L_i contains $i + 2$ transformations.

Therefore, even making an empirically too-strong assumption (that a universal base grammar exists) we can show that it is not the case that all classes of transformational grammars are learnable. It is possible that our hypothesis was, in a sense, not strong enough. If the Universal Base hypothesis were correct, there would only be one base, and it would have a particular form. If we could discover what that base is (which rules it consists of), it is conceivable that we could show that the class of transformational grammars on that (actual) base are learnable, even though it is not true that the class of transformational grammars on an arbitrary universal base is learnable.

We do not hold out much hope for this possibility. Peters and Ritchie (1973a) have shown that there is a fixed (simple) base such that the set of transformational languages on this fixed base is equal to the set of recursively enumerable languages. This set includes, for example, all the context-free languages. Thus it immediately follows from the superset proposition of section 2.2 and the Peters and Ritchie result that the class of transformational languages on a fixed base is not learnable. (It is still useful to consider learnability here for reasons given in note 20). The power of Peters and Ritchie's transformations could be restricted to yield fewer languages.[21] But the classes of languages that guarantee nonlearnability are really small and simple compared with the class of recursively enumerable languages; we consider it highly unlikely that any restriction on transformational operations which still preserves the character of transformations, even when defined on a fixed context-free base, will yield a learnable class of grammars. If such cases do exist (and they very well might not), there is no reason to think that they will attain anything like descriptive adequacy. In short, transformations are powerful devices and set-learnability requires extremely limited classes of languages. At present there is reason to suspect that transformational grammars cannot be sufficiently limited to allow both descriptive adequacy and set-learnability.

It is important that we not be misunderstood. Restricting the power of possible grammars has been, and continues to be, the most important method in our attempt to move toward learnability. In particular, such restriction not only allows some fairly strong learnability results but leads to some very interesting linguistic principles (see chapter 4). Our previous remarks mean that such restriction will not be enough to solve the learnability problem. Rather, we have to find the appropriate framework of constructs in which to state the learnability problem so that it may be amenable to solution by the device of restriction of grammatical possibility. Set-learnability (or text-learnability), it seems, is not the appropriate framework; the data are not rich enough to allow learnability.

2.5 Procedure and Criterion Changes

We have to find changes in the theory of learnability that will allow the theory to provide learnable classes of grammars. An important way of doing this is to restrict the class of possible grammars. However, we have seen evidence that restriction on the form of grammar by itself may not be sufficient to allow the theory to be successful.

We can consider changing other aspects of the learnability theory. From the perspective of the study of learning as it has developed within psychology, it might seem that the learning procedure *LP* would be the most likely place to increase the power of the theory. However, the evidence we have already presented shows that this is not the case. Many of the classes of grammars that we consider are not set-learnable, which means that no procedure can learn the class (no procedure can learn every language in the class).

There are two ways of looking at this limitation on procedures. Certainly any adequate theory would demand that the procedure for grammar selection be effective (computable). In studies of text-learnability we have shown that no effective procedures exist for learning a grammar in the defined sense. Church's Thesis (see note 13) says that we will never be able to formalize a sense of *effective procedure* more powerful than the ones we have now. Thus if no procedure exists according to current definitions, no more powerful procedure can exist.

But there is another, perhaps even more powerful, sense in which we have demonstrated a limitation on procedures. Within the theory of set-learnability we have demonstrated that many classes of grammars are unlearnable. This means that no function exists that makes the proper selection of grammars from the data. This limitation is not dependent on the lack of *computable* functions. Rather, *no* functions exist that can make the selection.[22] There is a logical limitation on what can be inferred from finite data which has nothing to do with effectivity. Thus there is no hope that any kind of increase in the power of procedures will yield learnability according to our definitions.[23]

An analogy to another case of noneffectivity may help make clear how powerful a limitation it is to lack a function that can make the correct choice. It is well known that for many classes of grammars—for example, the class of context-free grammars—there is no effective procedure for deciding, for any two grammars A and B in the class, whether the language $L(A)$ generated by A is a subset of the language $L(B)$ generated by B, whether $L(B)$ is a subset of $L(A)$, or whether neither is the case. The subset problem is undecidable for the class of context-free grammars.[24] Yet it is, of course, the case that either $L(A)$ is a subset of $L(B)$ or $L(B)$ is a subset of $L(A)$, or that neither holds. Thus a function f exists which takes a pair of grammars A and B and maps the pair into one of three values, say, A when $L(A)$ is a subset of $L(B)$, B when $L(B)$ is a subset of $L(A)$, and 0 when neither is the case. That is, a function exists that makes the proper selection, even though this function can't be effectively computed. In contrast, for classes of grammars that are not set-learnable no such selection function exists.[25]

Another possibility is that the criterion C of set-learnability is too strong. But it is exceedingly difficult to think of how to appropriately weaken this criterion while holding the other constructs of learnability theory fixed. For reasons given in section 2.1.1, we continue to assume that all biologically possible languages are learnable. As explained there, it might be fruitful to explore the implications of changing the learnability criterion by relaxing this assumption. We do not pursue those implications in this book.

One logical possibility is to allow languages to be learnable from an infinite set of data; we could allow the set of primary data to be infinite. This choice, however, suffers from dual problems. First, the assumption is clearly and fundamentally false; learners do *not* have an infinite amount of data available. The false assumption changes the character of the problem. Second, if we allow infinite sets of primary data, then all classes of grammars become learnable (cf. note 22). Thus no discrimination is possible between theories of grammar, at least with respect to learning of sets of strings. Assuming in learnability theory that learners have infinite data available would be rather like assuming in linguistic theory that grammars can contain an infinite number of rules. In both cases the formal problem becomes much easier, but the character of the problem has changed to the point that significant results cannot be attained.

It is difficult to see how the criterion given in the theory of set-learnability can be relaxed in some other way. It might be more plausibly argued that the criterion should be strengthened, so that even fewer classes of grammar would be learnable. As discussed in section 2.2, we might want to put a bound on the size of the set of primary data needed, the bound being taken over all grammars in the class so that no grammar would need a set of primary data of a size greater than the bound. Or (in the theory of text-learnability) we might want to demand that the procedure "know" when it had learned the correct grammar; that is, we might demand that the procedure shut off at some point that the procedure computes (in a strong case, the same point for all grammars) and that at the point of shutoff the chosen grammar be correct. As it is now in the theory of text-learnability the procedure keeps going, learnability ensuring only that from some finite time on, the guessed grammar is correct.

A way of relaxing the criterion would be to assume only that a correct grammar (a grammar that generates the correct language) is chosen at some finite time, but with no guarantee that the procedure stay with a correct grammar. This criterion is surely wrong for empirical purposes, since we begin by assuming that at some time humans do achieve a correct grammar and stay there. Somewhat stronger would be a criterion that demanded that the learner achieve a correct grammar at some finite time and at infinitely many finite times after that; in other words, the learner has to keep cycling back to a correct grammar, though no guarantee is made about the grammar in between the times at which a correct grammar is chosen. This is wrong for the same kind of empirical reasons as the last suggestion.

A somewhat weaker criterion than that of text-learnability would be the assumption that the learner has to have a correct grammar from some finite time on, though the grammar could be different at different times, as long as the generated language was correct. This also seems too weak, although it does allow for the possibility of a learner's reorganizing his grammar even after the correct language has been achieved. (The original text-criterion also allows for reorganization, before *some* time after which the grammar doesn't change.) We can't expect much help from this weakening, since all the unlearnable classes of grammars we have exhibited remain unlearnable under this weakened definition. [26]

This leaves for consideration only changing the kind of information or data available to the learner. The nature of input data is a complex question that rests heavily not only on the kind of logical and empirical arguments we have been giving but also on detailed empirical considerations. We will discuss the nature of input data in section 2.7.

2.6 Learnability and Descriptive Adequacy

First, however, it is important to point out that even if we had succeeded in weakening the class of grammars or criterion, or strengthening the notion of procedure, sufficiently for appropriate classes of grammars to be set-learnable, still we would have been far from a solution to the problem of language learnability. Set-learnability requires only that a grammar be chosen that generates a correct language, looked on as a set of strings. There is no requirement that further structural properties of the chosen language or grammar be of any particular form. In short, we have not required that the procedure select descriptively adequate grammars for the language from which it is receiving data. A correct set of strings is selected if the learnability criterion is met, but no constraints are put on the structural descriptions of sentences or on the structures available for semantic interpretation.

Although the criterion of set-learnability does not require anything more of an attained grammar than that it generate the correct set of strings, it is conceivable that in some cases grammars are achieved that do have the correct properties, even given the kinds of procedures and information allowed by the theory of set-learnability. To formally study this question we would have to define a new criterion, which would mention some property of the selected grammars or, perhaps, of the structural descriptions generated by the grammars. Then we would have to prove, for the learnability criterion to be met, that the defined property holds of selected grammars even though no information about the property is given to the learning procedure.

It will be useful to distinguish between weak and strong learnability. Recall that two grammars A and B are *weakly equivalent* if A and B generate the same sets of strings: $L(A) = L(B)$. A and B are *strongly equivalent* if they generate the same sets of structural descriptions (for the same sentences), where we have to define exactly what is meant by *structural description*. Two theories of grammar are strongly (weakly) equivalent if for any grammar allowed by one theory there is a strongly (weakly) equivalent grammar allowed by the other theory.

For any theory of learnability, we say that a class of grammars is *weakly learnable* if the grammar that is selected is weakly equivalent to the grammar from which the data have been taken. A class of grammars is *strongly learnable* if the grammar that is selected is strongly equivalent to the grammar from which the data have been taken. Exactly what strong equivalence means depends, of course, on what we take structural description to mean. In general the characterization of structural description is an empirical question.

As an example of how set-learnability can guarantee that a correct set of strings is selected, even though the structural descriptions are wrong, consider the learnable class of grammars $\mathcal{G}$ introduced in section 2.2. Suppose that $\mathcal{G}$ is defined by the rules given in note 10. When a sufficiently large set of data from $L(G_3)$ is presented, the learning function f that we defined in section 2.2 will select G_3. Consider some sentence of $L(G_3)$, say, $a^5 = aaaaa$. This string will have the derivation given in (6). Suppose constituent (phrase) structure is part of the structural description of a sentence, that is, part of a speaker's knowledge of language.[27] In particular, suppose that an adult speaker has the knowledge that the constituent structure of a^5 in $L(G_3)$ is (ignoring irrelevant details) $[[aaa][aa]]$. Then the phrase-marker in (6) is wrong (not descriptively adequate), since the structure in (6) is $[aa[aaa]]$. If the phrase structure of a sentence (or part of it) is knowledge that an adult speaker has, the theory of learnability has to guarantee that this knowledge is part of the selected grammar.

(6)   S

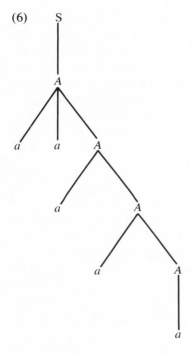

Note that in formal terms $\mathscr{G}$ is strongly learnable. That is, G_3 itself is selected, not a grammar that is weakly equivalent to G_3. Of course, G_3 is strongly equivalent to G_3, under any definition of structural description. That a correct grammar (given the class of grammars) is selected by f in all cases is due to the fact that only one grammar for a particular language exists in $\mathscr{G}$; thus if a grammar for the correct language is chosen, the grammar has to be correct. This fact leads to the hope that perhaps strong learnability could be attained by suitably restricting the class of grammars so that a correct one (strongly equivalent to the grammar that generates the language from which the data come) is selected. Although restricting the class of grammars in this way is important and necessary, it seems unlikely that the problem can be totally solved by this approach, without changing the criterion.[28]

Whatever the nature of the class of grammars, procedure, and input, we will have to define the notion of criterion so that it requires that descriptively adequate grammars are selected, if the learnability condition is met. In the next section we will consider the nature of the information available to the learner. Ultimately, this information will have to be sufficiently rich that descriptively adequate grammars are learned. It is possible, of course, that descriptively adequate properties of natural language are learned even in the absence of information relevant to the properties. In fact, the results are particularly impressive, for both linguistic and learnability theory, when we can show that descriptively adequate properties of grammars can be learned even when the input in no obvious way contains the property.[29]

2.7 The Nature and Function Of Input

We have so far been taking the primary data available to a learner to be example sentences and have demonstrated that the theories of set-learnability and text-learnability are unsatisfactory. They even fail on grounds of weak learnability. More important, nothing like descriptive adequacy can be attained under these theories. We have to look for richer systems of input data, with an eye to coming closer to solving, as a start, the problem of weak learnability, and ultimately the problem of strong learnability. Although a stronger form of input may be considered for reasons of weak learnability, sometimes the stronger form of input moves us in the direction of partial success with respect to strong learnability. To the extent that the stronger form of input is also empirically justified, success with respect to descriptive adequacy of learned grammars (under this form of input) will give us greater confidence in the correctness of the assumed form of input.

2.7.1 Preanalysis
Before turning to a consideration of possible enrichments of the input system, we must note that the concept of information, data, or input has to be taken in a special sense, because, in one sense, the only information is the physical data impinging on the learner's senses. In a broader sense, any conception of information will assume that the learner imposes order on the raw information. Thus, what the theory will consider information will be this preanalyzed information.[30] It may be that part of this preanalysis of information has to be itself learned. If

this is the case, then we simply assume that this kind of learning takes place first and in sufficient measure that the level of learning that we investigate can take place. This assumption does not solve the problem of how (if at all) the preanalysis system is learned. Rather, this problem is ignored so that progress can be made in understanding a different level of learning. Ultimately, all such levels must be investigated if we are to have an adequate theory. Of course, this is the usual situation in science, where certain assumptions and idealizations, incompletely understood in themselves, are made so that investigation can proceed. It is impossible to proceed without such limitation on scope of inquiry, and any language learning theory will have this limitation. In fact, essentially every discussion in the literature of the information available to a child learner has operated under this kind of idealization, although the particular form of the idealization varies. Even the simple artificial examples that we have considered so far operate under this kind of idealization. We have assumed that input data consist of sentences that are strings of words. But, of course, a learner is not presented with sentences segmented into words; the learner himself has to do the segmentation based on the environmental cues and his innate and learned linguistic abilities.

To take another example, a bit ahead of what we have discussed so far, suppose that we are trying to develop a theory of the learning of syntactic transformations. Much of this book will be devoted to a detailed analysis of this problem. We will have to assume that the learner is capable of preanalyzing the information. For example, we will assume that the learner can assign the correct syntactic category to words that he hears. Of course, since the assignment of categories to particular phonetic shapes is not universal across languages, this information (given in the lexicon of a linguistic theory for a language) will have to be learned. Nothing in the theory to be presented in this book investigates how the lexicon is created (learned). We simply assume that enough of it has been developed so that the processes we postulate for learning transformations can operate.

If we didn't make a particular idealization, some other idealization would be necessary. Suppose, for example, that a theory doesn't make the assumption that part of the lexicon is already developed, but tries to explain the learning of the lexicon. Perhaps the theory assumes that the child isolates particular phonetic shapes and attaches these (on the basis of some kind of evidence) to semantic readings and syntactic (such as category) information. This theory assumes that the learner can isolate particular phonetic shapes as words. Since words themselves are not universal (different shapes are words in different languages), the theory is being carried out under an idealization or limitation of scope. If an attempt is made to do away with this limitation, a theory will have to be created to explain how the child "learns" to create phonetic shapes from a physical signal; the theory that does it will have to make particular assumptions about physics and neurobiology. Although very powerful when it works, this reductionist approach has been successful in only a few domains of science. The major criticism of the approach is that if rigidly adhered to it doesn't allow work to proceed, work that in many cases can yield important scientific insight.

Thus when we later investigate the learning of transformations we will assume that for sentence (7), the learner (child) can at the very least assign the structural description (8).

(7) The juice spilled.
(8) $_{Det}$[The] $_N$[juice] $_V$[spilled].

Det, N, and V are standard symbols in generative grammar, standing for particular kinds of phrases: *the* is a determiner, *juice* is a noun, and *spilled* is a verb.[31]

At the very least, then, we assume that the child who is learning transformations is presented with exemplars of grammatical sentences from his language, together with the kind of structural information presented in (8). Now this last is really not an accurate way of speaking. The child is not "presented with" the structural information. Det, N, and V are in no way given in the linguistic signal. Rather, the child creates this structural information from the knowledge that he already has. (Once again, even the separation of the phonetic stream into words is not given but created.) Since in this work we are not analyzing how this creation takes place but rather are only assuming the results of the creation, we can speak of the child as being presented with the information, without loss of theoretical power. This way of speaking simplifies the discussion and will be especially useful in simplifying formal notation as illustrated in figure 2.1. Essentially this notation replaces schema (a) by schema (b). Since the middle box in (a), *creation of structural information*, is not analyzed in the theory, (b) is a picture that will do as much work as (a). This simplification is especially important since there will be a number of unanalyzed aspects of the presented data in the theory. Thus we gain much in notational convenience (especially in formalisms) if we adopt the kind of simplification represented in the figure. The simplification should not be misleading if it is remembered how to construct (a) from (b).

2.7.2 Negative Information

So far we have considered that the only kind of information available to the learner consists of grammatical sentences (strings) from the language he is learning. This kind of data presentation does not directly give information to the learner about which strings are ungrammatical. If the learner hears a sentence, he can assume that it is in his language.[32] But if he does not hear a sentence, it does not imply that the sentence is ungrammatical. Possibly he has simply not yet heard the sentence. The learner can make only inferences about strings he has not heard, and we have seen the limitations of such inferences.

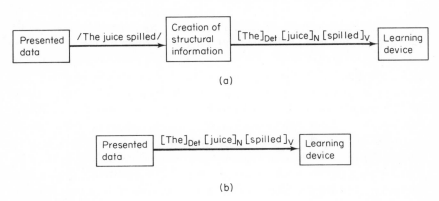

Figure 2.1
Convention about input representations

It is conceivable, however, that in some form the learner is given information about which strings are ungrammatical or *negative information*.[33] Examples of sentences, on the other hand, constitute *positive information*. Probably the existence of positive information is noncontroversial; at least we know of no challenge to its existence. But negative information is another matter. Therefore, we should consider, as an alternative to the earlier theories of strictly positive information, theories that allow both positive and negative information. (There is no need to consider theories in which the only information given is negative.)

One way to model a situation in which both positive and negative information are available to the learner is by assuming that at each time t, the learner is told whether a particular string is in the language. Gold (1967) studied various forms of this scheme, which he called "informant" presentation. Note that if a learner is told that a string is in the language this essentially constitutes an example of a sentence. (That is, the learner can take as an example a string that receives the answer "yes.") It is obvious immediately that informant presentation is at least as powerful as text presentation. Gold showed that in most cases informant presentation is in fact stronger than text presentation. In particular, the classes of context-free and context-sensitive grammars are learnable by informant presentation, whereas we have seen that these classes are not learnable by text-presentation.[34] Thus negative information is powerful. If we can assume the existence of negative information, we should have much help in the problem of learnability.[35]

It is therefore necessary to ask whether negative information is in fact available to a language learner. It is clear that parents do not simply present labeled nonsentences to children in a systematic manner; no parents (or other speakers) say "Here is a sentence, and it is ungrammatical, and here is another one, and this one is ungrammatical, and here is a third, which is grammatical." Even as a first step in looking for the existence of negative information we have to turn to the concept of correction, the concept that when the child produces an ungrammatical sentence, he is somehow informed that the sentence is ungrammatical.[36] The child will have to have some abilities of preanalysis in which some kind of event is translated into the information that the sentence he has spoken is ungrammatical. If some event can result in the learner's deciding that a sentence is ungrammatical, we can call this negative information. Of course, this interpretation is consistent with the general need for preanalysis.

The question therefore becomes: Is the child corrected when he produces an ungrammatical utterance?[37] In the opinion of those who have studied corpuses of children's speech, there seems to be very little of this kind of feedback. For anecdotal evidence, see Braine 1971, 159–161, but at least one study approaches the question directly. Brown and Hanlon (1970) analyzed a corpus of mother-child interactions and measured the proportion of nonapproval responses of the mother to "primitive" (ungrammatical) and to well-formed expressions of the child, and found no significant difference between the two proportions; mothers did not differentially disapprove grammatical and ungrammatical sentences. Brown and Hanlon also considered the possibility that a more subtle process of correction was going on than approval or disapproval, namely, that the child was understood more readily when he uttered a grammatical sentence than when he uttered a primitive sentence. In other words, the learner would have to translate noncomprehension by the listener into an assumption that his sentence was ungrammatical.[38] To examine this question Brown and Hanlon measured the proportion of times that mothers produced comprehending responses to grammatical and primitive sentences and again found no significant differences. Mothers seemed to understand ungrammatical sentences about as well as grammatical ones. The investigators pointed out that, in fact, what parents correct are semantic mistakes, not syntactic ones.

This evidence is only partial, of course. For example, it might be that mothers try especially hard to understand children's utterances, whereas other adults or children differentially understand grammatical and ungrammatical utterances. There is much room for empirical research on these questions, but Slobin (1972) claims that in the many societies the Berkeley group has studied there is no evidence that children are corrected for ungrammatical utterances.[39] At the moment, it seems that our theories of language acquisition should not assume that any nonsentences, labeled as such, are presented to the child.[40]

2.7.3 Special Arrangement of Examples

It is sometimes suggested that the argument that special restrictions on grammar have to be assumed for the purposes of learnability is misguided, because the argument ignores the possibility of what has been called by Levelt "intelligent text presentation." Presumably the claim is that, somehow or other, presenting sentences in some special way will provide information that will help learnability. A frequent suggestion is that presenting simple examples of language to children will aid them in learning language, thus making less necessary a component of innate linguistic structure. A version of this idea is presented by Brown (1977, 20), who writes, "But it has turned out that parental speech is well formed and finely tuned to the child's psycholinguistic capacity. The corollary would seem to be that there is less need for an elaborate innate component than there at first seemed to be."

Two questions are relevant to such claims. The first is theoretical: Why should we expect particular kinds of orders of presentation to help with the problem of language acquisition? What properties of input can help, and in what ways? In particular, is it possible that certain properties of input will allow us to do away with the necessity for hypothesizing special, innate structural abilities? The second question is empirical: What are the properties of input to the child? Do these have the characteristics claimed for them by those who assert that properties of intelligent text presentation are central to language acquisition? Interestingly, the answers to both questions, so far as we can tell at present, argue against the central importance of "intelligent text presentation." First, there is no theoretical justification for the claim that simplified input aids language learning. Second, the best empirical evidence is that input to children in general does not have the special characteristics anyway.

Turning to the first question, unfortunately we rarely see an explanation of why simplicity or fine-tuning should be useful to a child learning language.[41] The idea simply exists—unexplained (or unproved). If we do see some kind of justification for simplicity of input in language learning, it will not be of such a nature that a less elaborate innate component will be called for. We must distinguish between at least two major possible functions of simple and fine-tuned speech to children, with respect to language acquisition. On the one hand, simplified speech might be necessary because of a general limitation in children's cognitive capacities (like inability to deal with a long sentence because of memory limitations) or because special kinds of speech might attract a child's attention. This kind of explanation is sometimes given, and seems plausible. But this function of simplified speech to children will not decrease to any large extent the need for an innate structural component, because that need is demonstrable on the basis of a grammar's not being inferrable from data even when we assume an ideal learner, one with no problems of memory, attention, time. A second possible use of simplified speech with respect to language acquisition would be to help somehow with the logical problem of creating a grammar based on the primary data, again given no limitations of attention, and so on. Such arguments are rarely given, but it is this kind of argument that would be necessary to diminish the force of the argument for innate linguistic structure.

Levelt (1975b) attempts to provide one argument; he criticizes the lack of attention in LAD theories to the possibility of "intelligent text presentation" (p. 15).[42] Horning is quoted by Levelt:

Does language acquisition by children suggest means for improving our grammatical inference procedures? We believe that it does, and we conjecture that an important distinction between the child's experience and that we have assumed for our procedures is this: The child is not initially presented the full adult language he is ultimately expected to learn. Rather, he is confronted with a very limited subset, both in syntax and vocabulary, which is gradually expanded as his competence grows . . . We should not expect our inference procedures to perform well when confronted directly with complex languages. (Horning 1969, 15–16)

Levelt adds that "it is suggested [by Horning] that the procedure should first be exposed to small sublanguages, which are later combined and expanded," and continues:

These perceptive remarks have not been followed up in computer science . . . The result is that at present no formal models of the LAD variety are available to psycholinguists for the analysis of their new empirical findings on adults' speech to children. It should, however, be obvious that from the purely syntactic point of view the urge for strongly nativist assumptions has been diminished by these findings. (Levelt 1975b, 16)

But limiting the input in the way suggested by Horning will not help us to solve the language learning problem. Simply, less information is being given to the learner than before. In reference to figure 1.1 (section 1.2.2) input is being restricted. Thus more formal constraints than before will be needed. Limiting input will make a stronger nativist case, rather than a weaker one. Levelt does not indicate how this limitation on input will help to solve the language learning problem. He is careful to point out that no results exist in this direction.

Brown's claim is that special properties of fine tuning do away with the necessity of innate structural principles. In his Introduction to Snow and Ferguson 1977 he asks: What does Baby Talk (BT) accomplish?

A number of authors in this volume have driven home the principal point. The by-now overwhelming evidence of BT . . . refutes overwhelmingly the rather off-hand assertions of Chomsky and his followers that the preschool child could not learn language from the complex but syntactically degenerate sample his parents provide without the aid of an elaborate innate component. But it has turned out that parental speech is well formed and finely tuned to the child's psycholinguistic capacity. The corollary would seem to be that there is less need for an elaborate innate component than there at first seemed to be. (Brown 1977, 20)

The usual logical gap exists in this quotation. In what way does the "evidence of BT" refute "overwhelmingly" the claim that an "elaborate innate component" is needed? The evidence under review (Snow and Ferguson 1977) does *not* show that parental speech is uniformly well formed, nor that the speech is "finely tuned to the child's psycholinguistic capacity." (We will shortly turn to these matters.) But even more important than Brown's incorrect summary of the results in the papers he is reviewing is the logical gap. On what grounds can one say that an innate component is not needed if speech to children *is* well

formed and *is* "finely tuned to the child's psycholinguistic capacity"?
On none at all, except assertion.

In another passage Brown seems to deny what we have just quoted
him as saying. He writes:

The discovery that speech to very young children is not a complex
degenerate sample, but a sample fine-tuned to the child's psycholinguistic capacity, is certainly an advance over past views in the
sense that it is true as they were not, but whether it is an advance in the
sense of making the total acquisition problem simpler is not clear. Look
at it this way. The older view posed the problem as: AS→CS (adult
speech to child speech); the new view poses it as: AS→BT→CS (adult
speech to baby talk to child speech). It may be easier to develop a
theory deriving CS from BT than deriving it from AS, but notice that
the new view includes a new problem: AS→BT. (p. 22)

Once again, Brown does not show how it is "easier to develop a
theory deriving CS from BT." As we have argued, if it were true that
BT is simpler in the sense, say, of containing fewer structures than
adult speech, there might be less information in BT on which a learner
could construct his grammar. At any rate, Brown gives no argument
(an argument would depend, of course, on a theory of language learning). But in this passage Brown does see a further problem with the
theory that no innate components are needed for language acquisition—how is BT derived from adult speech? No theory exists of
how an adult knows how to train a child in language acquisition, which
is what the notions of Brown (and others) demand. Can such a theory
be created sufficient to do the job without the assumption of a strong
innate component for the adult? Brown does not entertain this question
in any form in which an answer might be realizable.

We do not mean to claim that sequential characteristics of the input
can play no role in learning. We are claiming that such aspects of the
input cannot play such a major role that there is no need for special
linguistic constraints. It is possible, in a formal sense, to code aspects
of the grammar to be selected into the input sequence. Consider the
unlearnable class of grammars $\mathscr{H}$ from section 2.2. Suppose we
adopted a special convention regarding input order of sentences in the
theory of text-learnability: Sentences have to be spoken in order of

increasing length (shortest first), and, in the case of a finite language, when the longest sentence is reached, the process starts all over again, from the shortest sentence. Thus the input order for language $L(H_0) =$ $a, aa, aaa, \ldots$. The input order for language $L(H_i) = a, aa, aaa, \ldots,$ $a^i, a, aa, \ldots, a^i, a, \ldots$. There is now a strategy that will learn $\mathscr{H}$: Guess H_0 until the first sentence (a) is repeated; then, if the sentence preceding a is a^i, guess H_i. This strategy will select the correct grammar in every case, for these input sequences.

It is highly unlikely that much information about linguistic structure is coded into the input sequence in natural language in the same way as in this artificial example, though it is conceivable that there is some useful sequential coding.[43] First, notice that to put much learning weight on this kind of scheme would mean that both the adult and child would need to know a special coding of grammars into input. There is no evidence for the existence of such knowledge (compared with, say, the linguistic evidence of adults' knowledge of structure). Thus assuming such a special coding does not allow us to do away with the need to assume innateness; rather it replaces an explicitly defined scheme of innate universals for which evidence exists by a completely undefined scheme for which no evidence exists. Second, despite the great utility of actually using certain sentences at certain times (in certain situations), according to the sequential coding hypothesis adults must present special training sequences, which may not be related to the contingencies of use. Besides there being no evidence for such a training sequence (of course, we are not sure what to look for, since the codings are not defined), it is quite implausible that such training sequences will override the necessities of language use.[44] Third, though different children have different linguistic environments, they learn essentially the same grammar. Fourth, putting the learning burden on a coding into sequence does not help, so far as we can see, with strong learnability, with the necessity of the child's learning descriptively adequate grammars (cf. section 2.6).

Turning to the second (empirical) question, some knowledge does exist concerning the nature of speech to children, and there is evidence that this speech (called baby talk or BT) does have special characteristics. These special characteristics do not, in general, code the grammar being learned in any way that can be seen to help in the problem of learnability. In fact, a real question exists as to whether BT is crucial in language acquisition.

In considering empirical studies concerning BT and its usefulness in language acquisition, it is important to distinguish between those studies that simply assert that BT plays a major role in acquisition and those studies in which the nature and role of BT is actually investigated. Levelt writes:

From these studies it appears that adults in addressing children use short, simple sentences with little embedding and inflection (Sachs et al., Snow) . . . Sentence boundaries are well marked in speech to young children (Broen). More generally, intonation is high and 'exaggerated,' clearly marking for the child what he should attend to. Overheard speech is therefore not to be considered as important input. (Labov (1970) moreover showed that such adult-to-adult speech is not as ungrammatical as had been generally supposed.) The syntactic complexity of adult's speech grows with the child's syntactic competence. More specifically, it seems that new semantic features are introduced by the child, to which the adult reacts with the more advanced syntactic construction by which they can be expressed (Van der Geest et al.). (1975b, 15)

Levelt then adds:

From the point of view of the syntactic structure of the child's 'observation space,' all this amounts to what I called earlier 'intelligent text presentation': the child is presented with grammatical strings from a miniature language, which is systematically expanded as the child's competence grows.

These conclusions do not follow from the actual results presented in the relevant papers. There really is no evidence that presentation from a "miniature language" takes place, or that such presentation has any role in language acquisition. Compare the quotations from Levelt with the following, from students of BT.

Ferguson, one of the early students of BT in the modern linguistic literature writes, "Given the wide variation in the details of the structure and use of BT from one community to another and from one family to another, it seems highly unlikely that it is a crucial element in the acquisition process"[45] (1977, 233).

Snow (1977) reviews much of the literature on mothers' speech to children. She writes:

Many of the characteristics of mothers' speech have been seen as ways of making grammatical structure transparent, and others have been seen as attention-getters and probes as to the effectiveness of the communication. But experiments in which language acquisition is the dependent variable and quality of input the independent variable have unfortunately been rare, and those few that have been performed have not all led to the conclusion that the input greatly affects language acquisition.[46] (p. 38)

Slobin, while arguing that the characterization of the primary linguistic data available to a child as "meager and degenerate" is a "bit too severe," states the problem in reasonable terms:[47]

The preliminary findings presented below suggest that the primary linguistic data represent a subcode which may be tuned to the language processing strategies of LAD or LAS. It should be noted at the outset that this suggestion in no way solves the problem of language acquisition posed by Chomsky, but at least it begins to clarify some of the parameters which must govern the work of LAD and LAS. (1975b, 284)

We earlier indicated that not only has Brown not given any idea how the properties of BT allow language acquisition to proceed without the assumption of a structural innate component, but even his description of parental speech as "finely tuned to the child's psycholinguistic capacity" is in doubt. The literature on such questions is difficult to review. And not only because of its size. A general problem is that the drawing of conclusions from data is often done in an unsound manner. Often the proper statistical procedures are not used. Even more important, a proper grasp does not exist of the relation between particular empirical results and particular theoretical statements. In general there are three kinds of possible empirical results that scholars claim demonstrate the crucial role of BT in language acquisition, doing away with the need for special structural principles.

1. Speech to children is simple, compared with speech to adults.

2. Speech to children becomes more complex as a child's (psycho)linguistic abilities increase (in a causal sense).
3. The more that a mother uses the special (simple) properties of BT, the more will her child develop language.

We will consider the evidence for all three of these propositions. Unequivocal answers are hard to obtain since notions such as "simple" can be defined in many ways. Nevertheless, consideration of the empirical literature leads to the conclusion that, as far as we can tell today, if definitions are made in the sense most relevant to the issues at hand, all three propositions are false.

Fortunately, a study by Newport, Gleitman, and Gleitman (1977)—henceforth NGG—is considerably more sound than most of the literature, on both counts mentioned: appropriate statistical techniques and appropriate theoretical conclusions from empirical data. In addition, in contrast to much of the literature the study approaches the problem in an open manner, asking: What can be learned empirically about the nature of BT and its role in language acquisition?[48]

A major question that must be asked is how Motherese (special talk of mothers to children) influences language learning. This relates to proposition 3 about BT. As NGG point out:

Notice that the finding that Motherese exists cannot by itself show that it influences language growth, or even that this special style is necessary to acquisition—despite frequent interpretations to this effect that have appeared in the literature. After all, Motherese is as likely an effect on the mother by the child as an effect on the child by the mother. (p. 112)

NGG attempted to study the question by interviewing children twice, with six months between the two interviews. Suppose that the extent to which mothers use certain features of Motherese is correlated with the language growth of the child. As NGG point out, this correlation is not sufficient to support the interpretation that Motherese is responsible for language growth. To take one example from NGG, suppose language growth is more rapid when a child is least sophisticated linguistically. Suppose also that Motherese is used more when the child is least sophisticated linguistically. There is no reason to suppose that

Motherese causes the child to learn faster. NGG perform a partial correlational analysis, measuring correlations between the use of features of Motherese and language growth when other factors are held constant. Such techniques are standard in the analysis of multivariate problems in psychology but have not been characteristic of language acquisition studies.

We cannot discuss NGG's conclusions in any detail. In summary,

[They] show that certain highly limited aspects of the mother's speech do have an effect on correspondingly limited aspects of the child's learning. Many other identifiable special properties of Motherese have no discernible effect on the child's language growth. The maternal environment seems to exert its influence on the child only with respect to language-specific structures (surface morphology and syntactic elements that vary over the languages of the world), and even then only through the filter of the child's selective attention to portions of the speech stream. (p. 131)

An instance of the effect of mother speech is the finding that the growth in mean number of elements in the child's verbal auxiliary yields a large partial correlation with the mother's tendency to ask yes-no questions and to expand the child's utterances. The growth rate for noun inflections also correlates with aspects of Motherese. "In contrast, the measures of child language growth that we take to be indices of universal aspects of language structure and content are, so far as we can see in this limited study, insensitive to individual differences in maternal speech styles" (p. 133). For example, "The child's growth in the use of complex sentences . . . is unaffected by the aspects of Motherese examined here . . . These phenomena of language use seem to be dependent on cognitive and linguistic maturity. While they are functions of the child's age, they are not related to specifiable features of the maternal environment" (p. 133).

NGG argue from their data that "the child is biased to listen selectively to utterance-initial items and to items presented in referentially obvious situations: the child acts as a filter through which the linguistic environment exerts its influence." (p. 137). We will return in the next section to NGG's second hypothesis. The first hypothesis (that the child listens especially to utterance-initial items) is used to explain why the growth in the number of elements in the auxiliary correlates with the number of yes-no questions that a mother asks (questions of the form "Did NP . . .," "Have NP . . .," "Can NP . . ."). These questions start with an auxiliary. If children listen to beginnings of utterances, the more such questions are used, the more input children will have concerning auxiliaries.

Such results, if they can be substantiated by further research, are in no way inconsistent with the hypothesis of innate structure (as NGG realize). There is no reason to expect that the child's language learning structures (including linguistic and attentional mechanisms) will be such that parameters like time to learn will be completely unaffected by the characteristics of input. But note that making available to the child learner more instances of auxiliaries (in positions to which he is paying attention) does not inform the learner how to create a grammar that will cover such instances. His grammar formation process may have more chances to work, and thus speed up somewhat. But the structure is still not given in the input to the learner. Yet all learners wind up with the same structure. To make clear our position again, we do not mean to say that special characteristics of mother's speech have *no* effect on *any* aspect of the growth of language in the child. In fact, such a result would surprise us. We simply are saying that what is known about BT in no way can eliminate the need for an innate structural component for language learning. Nor can the constructs of BT be responsible for the child's development of language. In our view the evidence points to the conclusion that the *child* is primarily responsible for language acquisition, not his mother or other adults or children in the environment.[49]

Another characteristic of BT that many authors have seen as important for language acquisition is its simplicity (proposition 1). But the data of NGG show that there is no reason to consider BT simple, in a syntactic sense. Of course BT is short, but shortness is not to be confused with simplicity. The notion of "simple" is often used in the literature without being well defined.[50] NGG try various definitions, proceeding from the notion of language lessons. For example, presenting subject-verb-object declarative sentences to the listener sounds simple compared with presenting other kinds of sentences. But the data show that Motherese is less simple in this way than adult speech. That is, children hear a smaller proportion of subject-verb-object sentences. Again compared with adult speech, a higher percentage of the utterances in Motherese involve optional movement or deletion transformations. And "there is a wider range of sentence types and more inconsistency to children than [when mothers talk] to the experimenter" (NGG, 122). In one sense, however, speech to children is simpler than speech to adults: "The sentences to children are shorter because they go one proposition at a time. Embeddings and conjunctions are rare in the Motherese corpora." Newport, Gleitman, and Gleitman summarize, "Overall then, 'syntactic simplicity' is a pretty messy way to characterize Motherese" (p. 122).

About the role of syntactic simplicity in language acquisition, NGG conclude on the basis of their data:

We can hardly agree with such writers as Levelt (1975) who asserts that Motherese has been shown to present the child with a syntactically limited subset of sentences in the language; and that 'from the purely syntactic view the urge for strongly nativist assumptions has been diminished by these findings'. On the contrary, nativist assumptions are left intact by a close look at Motherese—they neither gain nor lose plausibility. The point is that demonstrating that speech to children is different from other speech does not show that it is better for the language learner. Most investigators have jumped from the finding of a difference, here replicated, to the conclusion that Motherese is somehow simple for inducing the grammar. But the finding that Motherese has properties of its own does not show that these give acquisitional support. Notice, at any rate, that the view of Motherese as a syntactically simple corpus merely transfers a very strong claim about the child (that, owing to restrictive and rich hypotheses, he can deduce the grammar from haphazard primary data) to a very strong claim about his mother (that she has some effective notion of what constitutes syntactic simplicity so that in principle she can choose utterances on this basis). (p. 123)

Brown's claim that parental speech is "fine-tuned to the child's psycholinguistic capacity" is challenged by the lack of evidence in the literature for this proposition (see note 50) and, more directly, by the data of NGG. They find that maternal speech does *not* "grow syntactically more complex in a fine-tuned correspondence with the child's growing linguistic sophistication"; the proportion of simple declaratives increases with MLU (mean length of utterance) of the children, and the sentence range narrows.[51] They add, "Our findings suggest . . . that many features of the mother's speech change in accordance with the child's age, not his competence with constructional features of the language" (p. 145). Thus proposition 2 seems to be false.

We have presented a good deal of evidence against the assumption that, in any way that has been explicated so far, BT is crucial for syntax acquisition. But BT does have special properties. In dealing with biological phenomena it is always reasonable to ask about their function. What is the function of BT? NGG present arguments and evidence, which we will not summarize, that the function of BT is communication with a young child. In their words, "Along with some other investigators (see Shatz & Gelman, this volume), we believe this language style arises primarily in response to the pressures of communicating with a cognitively and linguistically naive child in the here-and-now, not from the exigencies of the language classroom" (p. 124).[52]

Another aspect of Brown's argument about the lack of a need for an "elaborate innate component" is the claim that parental speech is "well formed." This is generally, though not universally, true. NGG found that only one utterance out of 1,500 spoken to children was a "disfluency." Four percent of the utterances were unintelligible. Cross (1977) found in mothers' speech that 3.3 percent of the utterances were "disfluent," 2 percent were unintelligible, and 9.8 percent were run-on sentences. This is hardly a picture of uniformly well-formed utterances. It is true that adult-to-adult speech has been found to be somewhat less grammatical. Nevertheless, even a small percentage of ungrammatical sentences could conceivably cause trouble for a language learner uninformed as to the nature of language (see note 47).

In summary, evidence from studies of children's speech does not challenge the need for special structural principles to be invoked in the explanation of language acquisition, especially syntax acquisition. As for semantic acquisition, we know too little about how to describe the ultimate abilities to make firm conclusions about what is needed for their learning. The situation with respect to pragmatic and cognitive considerations is even less clear (see note 46). As we have said before, we do not claim that conditions of input have nothing to do with language acquisition, only that such conditions cannot play a role in the acquisition of language so central that special structural principles are not needed. In our view, the only way to discover the exact role that such input conditions play is to create a theory of language learning that can account for the fact that language is learned, and to incorporate in this theory empirically acceptable assumptions about the role of input. Short of such a theory, precise arguments simply cannot be made about how particular environmental conditions function in language acquisition.

2.7.4 Structural Information as Input
In section 2.7 we have been left with the problem of trying to modify learnability theory's conception of the input to the learner in order to help solve the problems of weak and strong learnability. We have seen, however, that many proposals along these lines cannot be right. Apparently, almost no negative information about syntax is presented to the child. In general the input to the child is not syntactically simple, and even if it were, we have argued that this might cause the learnability problem to be more rather than less difficult. Especially from the standpoint of learning syntax, the input to the child cannot be looked on as a series of graded lessons (fine-tuning).[53]

In this section we will suggest an enrichment of the input that does help in the problem of language acquisition. One property seems to emerge from a number of studies. There are devices in a child's environment which help to ensure that in a good number of cases the child has a reasonable chance to interpret an utterance correctly even if he is not able to understand the entire syntactic structure of the utterance. Of course, no external force can directly feed a correct interpretation into the child. The interpretation has to be accomplished by the child, based on his abilities and the environmental situation. But it might be possible that in a number of cases the child has an understanding of the situation which matches the correct interpretation of the utterance, even if he doesn't understand (or only partially understands) the syntactic structure of the sentence.

We do not intend anything like the suggestion that syntax is unnecessary because people can understand from situations. It is obvious that adults understand the structure of sentences, so they can correctly interpret utterances even when the referents are distant in time and space and there is nothing in the nonlinguistic environment to hint at the interpretation to be given to the utterance. It is the learning of this ability that has to be explained. We are merely suggesting that there are cases when the child will receive external information that helps in the interpretation of the utterance (which happens with adults also). It is conceivable that the kind of information thus available is useful as data to the child in language acquisition.

Before proposing a method of incorporating this kind of information into our theory of the input, we can consider what kind of evidence actually exists that such information is available. First, one can look at utterances to children as they occur. Slobin writes:

Most studies of child language comprehension put the child into a situation where there are no contextual cues to the meanings of utterances, but in real life, there is little reason for a preschool child to rely heavily on syntactic factors to determine the basic propositional and referential meaning of sentences which he hears. Judith Johnston and I have gone through transcripts of adult speech to children between the ages of two and five, in Turkish and English, looking for sentences which could be open to misinterpretation if the child lacked basic syntactic knowledge, such as the roles of word order and inflections. We found almost no instances of an adult utterance which could possibly be misinterpreted. That is, the overwhelming majority of utterances were clearly interpretable in context, requiring only knowledge of word meanings and the normal relations between actors, actions, and objects in the world. (1975b, 30)

We must be careful not to overinterpret such a result. For example, "knowledge of word meanings" is not necessarily a well-understood concept and might even include some knowledge that is normally called syntactic. Nor are we sure exactly what Slobin means by "interpretation." For example, in English, without the knowledge of inflections one cannot know whether past or present tense is indicated. Is determining tense part of "interpretation"? Perhaps Slobin means that, if knowledge of the situational context is added, the utterance becomes interpretable. At any rate, even if the claim is not accepted at its fullest strength, there seems to be reason to believe that in many instances a child could interpret an utterance correctly without knowledge of its entire syntactic structure.

Newport, Gleitman, and Gleitman (1977) provide some suggestive evidence that the extent to which mothers match their utterances to concepts that are at the same time in the child's consciousness correlates with linguistic development. One of a number of examples involves affirmative imperatives:

Affirmative imperatives are poor constructions from which to learn the language from the point of view of reference-making. They rarely map clearly onto the non-linguistic context: one says 'Throw me the ball' just when it is not being thrown and often when it isn't even in hand. Appropriately, then, the more frequently the mother produces imperatives, the more slowly the child grows not only in auxiliary structure but also in noun-phrase inflection. (pp. 140–141)

Other interpretations of these data are possible, but NGG argue why their interpretation is best. Note also that although NGG find evidence that producing "a construction when the child's attention is fixed on the notion that construction refers to in the language" increases language growth somewhat, still these results do not show that such techniques are necessary for language acquisition to proceed.

This view (NGG's) is consistent with Brown's conclusion that "what I think adults are chiefly trying to do, when they use BT with children, is to communicate, to understand and to be understood, to keep two minds focused on the same topic" (1977, 12). Brown further offers evidence (p. 19) for his conclusion:

How should they do so if not by talking about things the child is prepared to understand? If you do not speak to a very young child about what he knows and what interests him, he will, as Gleason points out, tune you out. The lead, it now appears, is not in the parents' hands as far as early content is concerned. It appears to lie in an interaction between the nature of young children and the nature of the physical world. Only now, perhaps, can we properly understand the amazing uniformities in what is named and what kinds of relations are talked about in Stage 1 speech. These uniformities, which are universal as far as they have been tested, appear to arise not from the predilections of parents, but from the nature of human children and the world they live in.[54]

A tendency to talk to children about things they understand does not necessarily imply that children can interpret the utterance without understanding the syntax of the utterance. But it does make this possibility more plausible. For example, much of the evidence on which Brown bases his conclusions about the motivation for BT is that of Cross (1977).

Some of Cross's measures relate to "referential characteristics," which involve "utterances that referred to the immediate context (i.e., to the child's or the mother's activities or to persons and objects in the recording situation), as well as those that referred to non-immediate events (i.e., events, people or objects that were removed from the child's perceptions)" (p. 159). In Cross's data, 73 percent of mothers' utterances made "immediate reference." (Cross's subjects were specially selected as those who "showed signs of rapid language acquisition.") The greater the child's linguistic understanding the more the mother refers to nonimmediate events (correlation = +0.72).[55] Certainly referring to an immediate event makes it more possible to interpret an utterance from the situational context than if reference is to a nonimmediate event.

Once again, we are not arguing for the necessary existence of certain training procedures. Rather, we are suggesting that the child has a certain ability, the ability in some instances to extract interpretations from situations (often the situations will be supplemented by some linguistic knowledge, such as meanings of words, or partial syntactic knowledge). Some evidence suggests that mothers, desiring to communicate with the child, tend to produce utterances in situations where this possibility exists.

How can we use this ability of the child in our conception of the input to the language learner, as we attempt to move in the direction of weak and strong learnability? We imagine that the child is presented not only with sentences (strings of words) but also with the interpretations of the sentences. That is, we conceive of one datum for the language learner as a pair consisting of a sentence together with its interpretation.

We have shown that the class of transformational grammars on a universal base is not even weakly learnable (section 2.2). Is it possible for input that contains interpretations to help in the solution of that problem (and the problem of strong learnability also)? How we formulate the problem depends on our theory of interpretation, in particular on which syntactic level the theory relates to interpretation. We have adopted a theory (based on Chomsky 1965 and Katz and Postal 1964) that semantic interpretation is defined on the syntactic deep structure of a sentence. Syntactic transformations apply to the deep structure without changing the meaning of the sentence, yielding a surface structure. (These assumptions constitute a form of what is often called the Katz-Postal hypothesis.) There is good reason in linguistic theory to assume that at least some of the interpretation of a sentence is to be carried out on the surface structure. One proposal that has received some attention is that the basic grammatical relations are defined in the deep structure but notions such as "focus" and "scope of quantification" are defined on the surface structure (see, for example, Jackendoff 1972). If grammatical relations are defined on deep structure, much information about interpretation that children have will be relevant to deep structure.[56] As a start on the problem we will assume, for purposes of current theory, that the semantic interpretation is defined on deep structure. It would be important to question this assumption in future work. This is especially true to the extent that semantic information not defined on deep structure is crucial to the learning of grammar.[57]

Transformations are mappings from phrase-markers into phrase-markers. The kind of information that might help a learner of transformations would be information about the phrase-markers that the transformations map from and to. Although children hear surface sentences (strings of words), there is not much reason to believe that they are presented with information about what the surface phrase-marker is.[58] The deep structure is the level of structure of a sentence before transformations apply. If much semantic interpretation is related to the deep structure of a sentence, and if a child sometimes has available the semantic interpretation of a sentence even when he doesn't understand its syntax, perhaps it is plausible that in some cases the child might be able to compute what the deep structure of a sentence is even when he doesn't understand the syntax of a surface sentence.

We are proposing that the possibilities of semantic interpretation might sometimes allow the learner to reconstruct the deep structure of a sentence. Exactly how he does this we cannot explicate here.[59] We assume that the child has cognitive abilities that allow him to do it. A more adequate theory would explicate these abilities. In part some of the abilities must be learned, because we know, for example, that there is no universal base grammar: different languages have different base grammars. However, it is conceivable (and there have been proposals to this effect) that the possibilities for base grammars are very limited. Therefore, it may be that the central rules of base grammars are learned easily and early. At the point when transformations are being learned, the syntactic rules of the base grammar may be available to the child. Suppose that the rules of translating between the base grammar and semantic interpretation are available to the child (as they will be if they are innate or if they are learned first). Then if the child has semantic interpretation of some sentences available, he will be able to reconstruct the base phrase-marker. In contrast to fine tuning, the property of input that we are suggesting here does give the language learner more information.

To put the assumption in formal terms, we can assume that one input to a learner is a pair (b,s), where b is a base phrase-marker and s is the surface sentence (string, not phrase-marker) that is derived from b by the operation of the set of transformations of the grammar. Of course, in no way is b actually presented to the learner—our justification for this form of input is that the learner constructs the deep structure by a form of preanalysis. The notation is simpler if we assume that the child is presented with a (b,s) pair, but the actual interpretation that is to be given to this assumption can be reconstructed on analogy with figure 2.1. The formal demonstration that (b,s) pairs work will be given in chapters 3 and 4.

Of course, it is more plausible that only some (not all) utterances in situations are such that the child will be able to reconstruct the deep structure. Again for formal and notational purposes, we will make an assumption that appears to be at variance with this state of affairs. We

will assume that the sequence of inputs to children is a sequence of
(b,s) pairs. It is not necessary to justify this formal assumption by
assuming that the child can invariably reconstruct the deep structure of
a sentence that he hears. Brown (1977) quotes Gleason (1977) to the
effect that children will tune out utterances that they don't understand,
so a child may simply not pay attention to some utterances. Or, even if
he doesn't ignore an utterance, he may not use it as part of his input for
language learning. (That is, if the child cannot reconstruct the deep
structure, he may simply not use the utterance to form hypotheses
about transformations).[60] All we really need to assume is that
"enough" (b,s) pairs are presented to the child.

CHAPTER 3

A LEARNABILITY
RESULT FOR
TRANSFORMATIONAL
GRAMMAR

Following the suggestion and rationalizations of the last section, we will consider a theory of learnability in which the input consists of a sequence of (b,s) pairs, where b is a base phrase-marker (generated by the context-free base grammar) and s is the surface string (sentence) of the surface structure which is derived from b by the operation of the transformational component. This decision implies that once again we are considering as the class of grammars the class of transformational grammars on a universal base.[1] The input is a sequence of pairs (b_1,s_1), (b_2,s_2), . . . generated by the adult transformational grammar A, where s_i is the terminal string of $A(b_i)$. In order to achieve success, the learning mechanism must ultimately select a set of transformations that performs the correct mapping of base phrase-markers into surface sentences.[2]

3.1 The Class of Transformational Grammars

Formal details of the class of transformational grammars whose learning we investigate in this first (b,s) theory may be found in Hamburger and Wexler 1975. For reasons of space we will not repeat those details here, especially those that are standard. (We assume some general knowledge of transformational grammar.)[3]

For our purposes, a transformational grammar consists of a context-free base grammar, which generates base phrase-markers, and a set of transformations, which apply to phrase-markers. Transformations apply to a base phrase-marker to ultimately yield a surface structure. The terminal string of words associated with the surface structure is the surface string or (surface) sentence.

We make a special assumption about the base context-free grammar B, namely, that S (the distinguished sentence symbol) is essential to all recursion in B. This means that if a node of any category D dominates another node of category D, a node of category S must occur between the two D nodes.[4] We assume the *principle of the transformational cycle:* the transformational component is applied at a level only after it has been applied at all dominated levels.[5]

Each transformation consists of a *structural description* (S.D.) and a *structural change* (S.C.).[6] The structural description is a finite sequence of (nonterminal) symbols from the base grammar and of variables $(X, Y, Z, \ldots)$ that stand for arbitrary (possibly empty) strings.

If the structural description *fits* the current phrase-marker, then the structural change is carried out; that is, if the transformation is applicable, then it must be applied. The transformations are thus said to be "obligatory." We have not studied learnability properties of components with optional transformations. Clearly, this would be an important area of future study. We have begun by using obligatory transformations for two reasons: First, determinism makes the learner's task more manageable and thus simplifies our own task; second, linguistic developments have led linguists to alter some descriptions to use obligatory instead of optional transformations (e.g., in early accounts of transformational grammar, the passive was optional, but since Chomsky (1965) it has usually been treated as obligatory). (Hamburger and Wexler 1975, 145)

Ultimately the problem of the learning of optional transformations must be solved. (For further discussion see Wexler 1978a). More recent treatments of linguistic theory (for example, Chomsky and Lasnik 1977) return to optionality.

Even if the assumption that all transformations are obligatory turns out to be wrong, the results obtained under such an assumption are still worth pursuing. Even with the assumption a very large number of learnability problems exist, as is apparent from this chapter and, especially, chapter 4. For reasons discussed in Wexler 1978a, the need to study the learnability of optional transformations will create further problems. Thus in restricting ourselves to obligatory transformations we are dealing with only part, though a significant part, of the problem of the learning of transformations. We can certainly expect many of the results obtained to carry over to a theory that includes optional transformations. This is especially true of some of the most interesting results in learnability theory—the demonstrable need to assume, on learnability grounds, particular formal universals of grammar.

A number of assumptions concerning the operation of transformations are made in Hamburger and Wexler 1975. Three of them concern the use of variables: variables may not be copied, they may not be shifted, and two variables may not appear consecutively as elements of structural descriptions. The motivation for these three assumptions is well-formedness of transformational applications (and to a large extent they are standard); we make these assumptions here also. The other assumptions are more substantive and are motivated on learnability grounds; we could not see how to prove convergence unless the assumptions (six of them) were made. However, most of these assumptions have been replaced in the new theory developed in chapter 4 by other, more effective assumptions. Therefore, we will not discuss the original assumptions here.[7]

A set of transformations is the transformational component of a grammar. A transformational component is *deterministic* if at every stage in a derivation there is at most one transformation that can apply (that fits the partially derived structure) and if this transformation applies in only one way (there is only one way the transformation fits the structure). We assume that the adult transformational component is deterministic. The learner's component may be nondeterministic, but it will become deterministic in the limit.

Determinism has been assumed because we are studying the learning of only obligatory transformations. If two such transformations can apply simultaneously, it is not clear how the derivation should be carried out. We will discuss determinism further in a number of places in chapter 4.[8]

A base grammar B has a distinguished subset of terminal symbols. These appear at the bottom of fully derived phrase-markers. We will call these terminal symbols words or *lexical items*. They will usually be denoted by small letters, whereas nonterminal categories will be denoted by capital letters. By definition, these terminal symbols cannot be rewritten. Although Hamburger and Wexler made no assumptions about the introduction of lexical items, it will be useful to assume that a lexical item w may be introduced only by a rule of the form $D \to w$. That is, w has no sisters when it is introduced. In a phrase-marker the node labeled D which dominates w is called a *lexical category* node. In chapter 4 we will assume that transformations may analyze lexical category nodes, but not lexical items. If P is a phrase-marker, then $*P$ is the *terminal string* of P, that is, the left-to-right sequence of lexical items at the bottom of P.

3.2 Properties of Learning Procedures

The appropriate definitions of learnability for the (b,s) case can be constructed on analogy with the definitions for set- and text-learnability. We obtain different definitions depending on which of the two definitions we build the analogy on. Either definition is straightforward. We will consider only text-learnability by way of example. The relevant concept is *function-learnability*. We will want to define the concept of learnability for a class of functions F with domain A and range R. If $f \in F$, an *information sequence* of f will be a sequence of pairs $(a, f(a))$, $a \in A$, such that for every $a \in A$ there will be at least one instance of $(a, f(a))$ in the sequence. F is function-learnable if an algorithm LP exists such that for every $f \in F$ and for every information sequence of f, LP eventually guesses f (at some finite time) and doesn't change its guess after that time.

An important property of function-learnability is the following result.[9] *Proposition:* Every enumerable class of functions is function-learnable. The proof is straightforward. Suppose f is the presented function. Enumerate the functions $f_1, f_2, \ldots$. The procedure guesses f_1 first. If f_1 is not correct, there is an element $a \in A$ such that $f_1(a) \neq f(a)$. By the definition of *information sequence*, eventually $(a, f(a))$ is presented. When the guessed function turns out to be wrong on a datum, the next function in the enumeration is chosen, in this case f_2. The procedure continues, choosing the first function in the enumeration compatible with all the data so far. Since f is in the enumeration, eventually f is selected as the function and will remain as the selected function, since there will be no data that are not compatible with f.

It follows from the preceding proposition that the class of transformational grammars on a universal base is function-learnable in the sense that the mapping of base grammars into surface strings is function-learnable.[10] Thus we have our first positive result, a case of learnability.[11]

Although learnability from (b,s) data is possible by the method of enumeration, a different theory is developed in Hamburger and Wexler 1975. There are reasons that enumeration procedures are not appropriate as theories of learning. A major reason is that the enumeration procedure requires that at each time t, a grammar is selected that is compatible with all the data presented to date; therefore memory for the entire set of data is required. A better theory would be one in which learnability is possible without requiring that the learner have available at any time the entire sequence of data presented up to that time.[12]

Clearly a child does not have the entire set of sentences he has heard all available at one time for constructing his language. A child, of course, may recognize a large number of sentences, many of which he has heard. But the most reasonable hypothesis is that he has constructed a set of rules that will generate some of the sentences he has heard and some he has not heard. There is no reason to suppose there is a special memory store for just the sentences with which he has happened to come into contact.

Despite the fact that the assumption of perfect memory for past data is false for a child, requiring that our learnability theory not have this property is a decision that requires some discussion. Of the very large number of properties that we can take to be true for language learners, we have to decide which should be part of a theory of learnability. A useful distinction seems to be that learnability theory (at least as a theory of competence) should be concerned with the logical and computational problems of the relation between available data and attained grammar (or competence). Other factors will of course play a role in actual language acquisition, factors such as motivation and attention and matters of developing motor skill. It may be that a learner doesn't pay attention to an input because he is hungry, say. Such factors are legitimate objects of study, but since they do not seem to be concerned with the logical and computational problems of the relation between data and grammar, the problem of how it is possible to attain knowledge of language, they will not be considered factors that must be taken account of by learnability theory.

This division of properties of the learner into those that are and are not relevant to learnability theory is somewhat rough, of course. In all likelihood it will be difficult to make many decisions concerning which set a particular property belongs in. We can make working hypotheses, however. For example, the decision about whether a learner is corrected for ungrammatical utterances (given negative information) might affect the logical structure of some aspects of the learnability problem, whereas certain kinds of problems of attention and motivation may not.[13] If a learner does not pay attention to a particular datum, it is conceivable that the datum (or an equally useful one) will appear later, and he will pay attention to it then. Hence it is not necessarily the case that problems of attention are intrinsically related to the logical and computational problem.

In the foregoing sense, properties of memory for past data seem to involve logical and computational problems concerning the relation of data to attained grammar. Enumeration procedures, as we have defined them, require the selection of grammars compatible with all past data. If the data available to the learner is more sharply restricted because of lack of memory, it is not at all clear that procedures equivalent to the enumeration procedure can be found. We will therefore consider the lack of memory for past data to be part of the learnability problem. The learning procedure that we define will have the property that the grammar selected at time $t + 1$ will depend only on the grammar selected at time t plus the new data presented at time $t + 1$.

The decision to disallow unbounded memory will have interesting consequences for our theory. In particular, in order to achieve learnability, more restrictions on grammars will be necessary. This is consistent with the general point made in section 1.2.2 that as the computational capacities of the learner are restricted, a larger set of specifically structural (linguistic) assumptions will have to be invoked. In terms of the distinctions made in section 1.4.2, properties involving memory for data, since they are concerned with restricting the availability of potential data instead of characterizing the nature of the data themselves, should be considered to play a role in the criterion of feasibility instead of explanatory adequacy. But note that the decision to invoke bounds on memory for past data in learnability theory has two related implications. First, the class of grammars will have to be further restricted. Second, the restrictions on the grammar (and possibly on other aspects of the theory) might lead to constraining the learning theory in such a way that the theory constructs more descriptively adequate grammars for languages. This possibility is in line with the general point, made in section 1.4.2, that the study of feasibility is an important element in the study of explanatory adequacy, just as the study of explanatory adequacy is an important element in the study of descriptive adequacy.[14]

Hamburger and Wexler invoke an additional property that might disallow enumeration procedures:

The most striking characteristic of the learning procedures posited is that only minor changes in the learner's model are made in response to each input datum. Specifically, the learner can hypothesize at most one new transformation in response to a datum or can reject at most one of those already hypothesized. Since it alters only one rule at a time, the learning procedure used here is much more plausible as a psychological model than the procedures considered in the literature of automata theory (e.g., Solomonoff, 1974) which allow repeated wholesale rejection of entire grammars (sets of rules). Whatever may be the merits of all-or-none models of learning for simpler tasks, it is clear that no child learns an entire language at a stroke. (1975, 138)

The issue is somewhat subtle, especially the question of whether the gradual-change property would rule out enumeration procedures. First, it is clear that hypotheses are formed and changed by the child somewhat gradually, with knowledge of language building up over a period of a few years. But we do not have any precise knowledge about how gradual the process is, or in what ways. The Hamburger and

Wexler theory adds or rejects one transformation when a disconfirming datum is presented, but there is no reason to think that this is the appropriate level of gradualness. There have been arguments for reorganization of grammar by a child that might go beyond this amount of gradualness. It is difficult to understand these issues precisely, because we have little understanding of how grammatical knowledge changes with presentation of a datum, and proposals for reorganization and such are in general not stated precisely enough for their properties to be understood.

Second, it is not clear that no enumeration procedures obey a version (perhaps even the correct version, whatever that may turn out to be) of the gradualness property. We showed that transformational grammars were learnable from (b,s) data by an enumeration procedure as long as there existed an arbitrary effective enumeration for the grammars. But proposals involving enumeration procedures (like the *evaluation procedures* of Chomsky (1965, 1975a)) do not posit arbitrary enumerations. Rather, the enumerations are given as a measure of simplicity. In fact, as we pointed out in section 1.1, in concrete proposals (say, Chomsky 1975c) the enumeration is given by a procedure for measuring simplicity, which is defined on the grammar.[15] Thus, in moving from grammar to grammar in the enumeration, we are moving between grammars that are maximally close to each other in terms of simplicity. We might expect that often these grammars will share many characteristics, inasmuch as the simplicity measure puts them close together. For example, the two grammars might differ only on the status of a particular low-level rule. Sometimes there might be larger differences, large enough perhaps to justify the name of *reorganization*. All we are arguing here is that it is not a priori clear that enumeration procedures will not have the appropriate gradualness property.

A third question is whether ignoring the property of gradualness would affect the validity of learnability theory. Considering the lack of gradualness as a simplifying assumption, will we get essentially the same results as we would if we did not make the assumption? The question again is subtle. One argument in favor of not making the assumption is that, if significant results can be attained without the idealization, everything else being equal, we should not make the idealization. That is, the reason for making an idealization that is known to be false is to allow work to proceed. If it can proceed at least as well without the idealization, then we should not make the idealization.[16] At least on these grounds, it seems reasonable to assume gradualness, as we have done. The lack of knowledge about exactly which concept of gradualness is correct, however, should lead us to be very tentative in asserting that this property is an important characteristic of the theory.

Chomsky (1975a, 119–122) raises further questions about the degree to which idealizations concerning learning should be accepted at current stages of inquiry. He defines an *extensional* approach to the question of input to the learning procedure. In this case the input at a given time consists, not of the last attained grammar plus the new data, but rather of the language generated by the last attained grammar (where *language* is sentences with formal and semantic properties) plus the new data. The *intensional* approach is of the form that we have been considering, where the input to the learning procedure consists of the last attained grammar plus the new data. Now, if the learning procedure is to be effective, and if infinite languages are allowed, a grammar—or "name" in Gold's (1967) sense—must be assigned to each language. What Chomsky's extensional proposal amounts to, we believe, is the following condition on intensional procedures: If the language generated by grammar G is the same as the language generated by grammar G', then the grammar selected by the learning procedure when a new datum d is presented and the last grammar was G will be the same grammar as the one selected when d is presented and the last grammar was G'. In short, fixing the last language plus the new datum will fix the next grammar.

Let LT_i be the learning theory at stage S_i. Chomsky writes (using S_5 as an example), "We may now ask whether we falsify the account of learning by assuming that the input to LT_5 is the language generated by the grammar available at stage S_5 rather than the grammar itself" (p. 120). More generally, he writes:

If there were answers to such questions as these about various properties of the learning process, we might develop a more realistic theory of language learning. It might reveal that our simplifying assumption, namely, that the mechanism for language learning is extensional and instantaneous, was far off the mark. It would follow, then, that the conclusions suggested with regard to universal grammar would also have to be modified.

Frankly, I doubt that the simplifying assumption, though obviously false, significantly affects the validity of the analysis based on it. If our initial assumption does indeed seriously falsify the situation, if there are substantially different stages with fundamentally different LT_i's, if these are in an important way intensional, and if furthermore the character of LT_i depends significantly on grammars (or other cognitive structures) already attained, then we would expect to find substantial differences in the result of language learning depending on such factors as order of presentation of data, time of presentation, and so on. But we do not find this, at least at the level of precision of currently available analytic tools. Nor does ordinary experience suggest that this is so. Despite considerable variety in learning experience, people can communicate readily (at the level of communication relevant to this discussion), with no indication that they are speaking fundamentally different languages . . .

There are, it appears, striking uniformities in steady state attained, through wide variation in conditions of learning. These facts suggest that the initial idealization, with its falsifying assumption about instantaneous extensional learning, was nevertheless a legitimate one and provides a proper basis for pursuing a serious inquiry into human cognitive capacity. At some stage in the progress of inquiry it will no doubt have to be qualified, but one may seriously question whether this stage has been reached in the study of linguistic competence and universal grammar. (pp. 121–122)

We agree that humans learn essentially the same grammar and that, under many conditions, the existence of the kinds of learning theory properties that Chomsky mentions would seem to lead to the conclusion that different learners should acquire different grammars.[17] Thus, if Chomsky's statement is taken as an argument against the notion that these kinds of learning properties (intensionality, and so on) are crucial factors in the character of the attained grammar, we would agree. However, from our point of view, there is reason to invoke these properties in learnability theory.

We can start from Chomsky's assumption that adult speakers have internalized the same grammar. If we then assume that these realistic learning properties exist, we have a problem: How can these properties, which seem to lead to different attained grammars, be compatible with the assumed fact that different learners achieve the same grammar? From our point of view, the answer will be that it is not necessarily the case that these properties will lead to different grammars for different learners. In some cases, particularly if the class of possible grammars is heavily enough constrained, these learning properties, which seem to lead to wide variation, will in fact not be able to lead to such variation. In other words, constraining the class of possible grammars will help to solve a problem created by the assumption of (possibly) realistic learning properties.[18]

Consider an analogy. We know that children learn language, but learning from different inputs will lead to different grammars for different learners, which we know is false. So we can idealize and assume that there is only one language in the world. Clearly the assumption is false, but it might be a useful idealization. Of course, at current stages of inquiry we do not have to make such a radical idealization. Rather, linguistic theory treats the existence of what appear to be two incompatible facts as a problem and solves the problem by assuming heavy constraints on the form of grammars, which makes the assumption of the existence of only one language unnecessary.

The question of whether a particular idealization has to be abandoned at a particular stage of inquiry does not have to be absolute. Different problems might allow for different idealizations.[19] Of the idealization of learning as an instantaneous process, Chomsky writes that "at the present stage of our understanding, I think we can still continue profitably to accept it as a basis for investigation" (1975a, 245 n.4). We agree that for many problems yet unsolved this idealization is appropriate. For example, the conception of learning as instantaneous, though false, will nevertheless imply the correct principle (the same principle that a more complete and true theory would imply) that a theory aiming for explanatory adequacy (explaining learning) must prefer a class of grammars $\mathcal{G}$ over a superset of $\mathcal{G}$, assuming both satisfy descriptive adequacy. There are many cases of actual linguistic work where this principle is important, and there is no reason to assume that its range of potential applications has been reached. Thus the instantaneous theory allows for a methodology that can continue to solve important problems.

Notice, however, that for some actual linguistic examples this principle cannot decide which theory to prefer; these are situations in which neither proposed theory provides a set of grammars that is a superset of the set provided by the other theory. Chomsky provides an example of each kind of situation:

There is, indeed, a serious objection to global rules. This device enormously increases the class of admissible grammars and thus moves us a long step away from our goal of attaining explanatory adequacy in linguistic theory and accounting for the possibility of language learning. Thus one would accept global rules only under the pressure of powerful evidence, which, I believe, has so far not been forthcoming. But the trace theory does not extend the class of admissible grammars. Nor does it restrict this class. Rather, it changes the class and is thus immune to the methodological objections that are rightly raised against the introduction of global rules. (1975a, 117)

As we pointed out in Culicover and Wexler 1977, the learnability theory in principle might be able to distinguish between some classes of grammars for which the subset principle fails: one class of grammars may be learnable and the other not learnable, in which case we would certainly prefer the learnable class. (See section 2.1.1 for a possible modification of this claim. Certainly, the natural languages must be learnable.) Furthermore, it is possible in principle that both classes of grammars are learnable in an "instantaneous" theory, but not in a theory that assumes other learning properties (since, as we have argued, many of these properties make the learning problem more difficult). In such a case, the assumption of a theory with these learning properties would be useful—it would help to solve a problem. In short, to argue that in some cases we should consider relaxing an idealization is not to say that a current idealization has to be abandoned in all cases. Linguistic theory can proceed and make advances under an idealization with false learning properties; we are simply suggesting that rejecting the idealization in some cases can lead to further insight.

The only way to show the value of rejecting an idealization is to illustrate with work in which rejecting it leads to results and insight. For example, we might not accept enumeration procedures with unbounded memory for past data as models. Rejecting these procedures and assuming more "realistic" (and less powerful) procedures might allow us to obtain insight not possible otherwise. In fact, as we have shown, an unconstrained class of transformational grammars is learnable from (b,s) data via enumeration procedures. In the hypothesization theory, with no access to past data, however, we cannot prove learnability for an unconstrained system. Rather, we have to assume certain constraints on the forms of transformational grammars. If these assumptions are empirically confirmed, we have a case in which we have attained insight by relaxing an idealization. An even more striking case involves the idealization that all data are potentially available to a learner. In chapter 4 we investigate constraints with which it is possible for language to be learned from quite simple data. Relaxing the idealization of unlimited access to data leads to a considerable number of results and (we believe) insight—in particular, to further constraints on grammars, postulated as innate mechanisms of mind, together with an illustration of how these structures play an important functional role (in allowing grammars to be learned).

3.3 A Learning Theory for Transformational Grammars

For the kinds of reasons that we have given, we will pursue a theory that has the properties of gradualness and no memory for past data. It will turn out that the pursuit of these (and other) properties will have the interesting effect of bringing to light new structural linguistic properties and of providing further evidence and justification (of a different kind) for known properties. The ultimate goal will be a unified theory in which linguistic and other properties can be understood both in themselves and in their relations to one another.

In this section we will sketch a first theory (Hamburger and Wexler 1975). In chapters 4 and 5 we will pursue a different theory, in fact, a major improvement over the one that we will sketch now. The improvement will be twofold. First, the results concerning the central problems of learnability (explanatory adequacy and feasibility) will be greatly strengthened. Second, the descriptive linguistic principles brought to light by the theory will be more adequate than those that emerge from the first theory.

The reasons for sketching the preliminary theory now are more than historical. The mathematical and conceptual aspects of the theory can be divided into two kinds, those concerning the linguistic systems and those concerning the learning mechanisms or procedures. The linguistic systems will have quite different properties in the two theories, and the mathematical analyses based on these systems will be correspondingly different. However, the learning mechanisms and analyses introduced in the original theory will, for the most part, carry over to the new theory, with some modification. Thus, introducing the original theory will help to motivate and explain the learning mechanisms. In addition, comparison of the more limited kinds of results obtainable with the first theory will show directly the kinds of roles that various properties of the new theory play in attaining the stronger results.

3.3.1 Input
For a fixed context-free base grammar B, a set of transformations defines a set I of (b,s) pairs. For each b generated by B, I contains the pair (b,s) such that s is the surface string of the phrase-marker b derived by the transformational component applying to b. Thus all potential information is in I.

In this theory we change the requirements on the sequential presentation of information. Instead of requiring that every (b,s) pair appear at least once in any information sequence, we invoke a probabilistic requirement, the assumption that every (b,s) pair in I has a fixed probability greater than 0 of appearing at time t, and that this probability of appearing at time t is independent of the past history of the system.[20] In other words, we assume that the probability of a datum's appearing does not depend on what the learner knows or on how old the learner is. These conditions can be greatly relaxed, as suggested in note 20. They can be replaced with a condition that simply asserts that every datum of sufficiently low complexity has a probability of occurring that is bounded from below. This condition is much more plausible than the original conditions, but either will allow our proofs to work.

One reason that we have moved to a probabilistic presentation scheme is that we want a theory in which the learning procedure does not have unlimited memory for past data. Allowing all data to appear at the next moment of presentation with non-zero probability means that there is always a chance that a useful datum will appear, even though the learner does not have it in memory.

3.3.2 Criterion

The criterion of learnability is the following: With probability approaching 1, the learner must eventually (at some finite time) select a correct grammar and that grammar must remain unchanged for later times. "Correct" here means that the grammar performs the correct (b,s) mapping, the same mapping as in the adult grammar.[21] A somewhat more formal definition will be given later in our statement of the mathematical results. We use the probabilistic definition because we use probabilistic presentation of data and will allow a probabilistic procedure. The reasons for using a probabilistic format, again, trace back at least in part to the requirement of no memory for past data.[22]

3.3.3 Learning Procedure

The learning procedure (LP) is a hypothesis-formation-and-changing procedure. At any time, the state of the learner's knowledge is represented by a finite set of transformations. (The base grammar is held fixed so it doesn't have to be part of the formal representation of the state of a learner's knowledge.) At each time, the learner is presented with one datum ((b,s) pair) d. In response to d, LP may or may not change its state of knowledge (its guessed grammar, or set of transformations). The first decision LP must make is whether it is correct for $d = (b,s)$. If the set of transformations at time t (which we represent as C_t, for child's component at time t, A being the adult component) is such that the base phrase-marker b is mapped into the surface string s, then LP considers that it is correct on d and makes no change in the hypothesized set of transformations. In other words, if (b,s) is presented at time t, and if $*C_t(b) = s$, then $C_{t+1} = C_t$. (Recall that for any phrase-marker P, $*P$ is its terminal string.) This is what has traditionally been called in psychology "learning on errors." Logically, if the learner is correct on a datum, he receives nothing indicating that he should change his hypothesis if he observes that datum. This require-ment of no change on corrects will also insure that once the learner has hypothesized a correct set of transformations, he will never change it. Thus, if we can insure that a learner will eventually select a correct grammar, the entire statement of the criterion will be satisfied, as the learner will never deviate from that choice.

The situation when the learner is incorrect on a datum is more com-plicated. The learner is incorrect on $d = (b, s)$ at time t if $*C_t(b) \neq s$. In this case we want LP to change C_t. The decision as to how to change C_t is not at all obvious. We want the learning procedure to have the property of gradualness. Thus we have created a procedure that changes only one transformation at a time (in general, a moment of (discrete) time is associated with the presentation of one datum). It is not at all obvious that the decision to change only one transformation at a time is the correct version of gradualness, but we adopt it as a begin-ning.

If we could guarantee that LP never made a mistake, we would have to add (hypothesize) transformations only until a correct component (set of transformations) was arrived at. But we cannot guarantee that there will be no errors; that is, it will happen that some selected trans-formations will be wrong. Therefore, in order for LP to ultimately arrive at a correct component, it will have to eliminate (reject) trans-formations as well as add them. Therefore we must have two pro-cesses, *hypothesization* and *rejection*.

The learning procedure LP will do only one of these at a time (that is, for a given datum): on each datum either (i) no change occurs or (ii) a transformation is hypothesized or a transformation is rejected, but not both. This property of LP has been assumed for conceptual clarity and mathematical and conceptual simplicity, not because it is necessarily correct. In fact, it is probably wrong, because it means that there is no direct concept in LP of correction or modification of a transformation. If a transformation T is to be modified to T', it must be by rejection of T on datum d and hypothesization of T' on some later datum d'. Certainly the assumption of the possibility of direct modification is consistent with our intuitions about intelligent learning procedures.[23] Many of the learning assumptions are motivated because of their simplicity or because of technical reasons involving proofs of learnability. Modification of *LP* in the direction of more intelligent procedures should be pursued, although our estimate is that the essential characteristics of the problem will not change.[24]

Suppose in fact that a datum (b,s) is presented for which the current selected set of transformations C_t is wrong. *LP* will either reject a transformation in C_t or hypothesize a new transformation. The set of transformations that *LP* considers available for rejection are those that applied in the derivation of b. That is, suppose $*C_t(b) = s' \neq s$. Those transformations in C_t that applied in yielding s' as the surface string of the transformed b are available for rejection. The rationale for this decision is that the idea of rejection is to eliminate a transformation that causes an error. One way to obtain a wrong derivation is for a wrong transformation to apply. Thus, allowing rejection of a transformation that has applied allows for the possibility of rejecting an incorrect transformation.[25]

The question of what transformations are available for hypothesization is a bit more complicated. The idea is that *LP* should hypothesize a transformation that will transform a phrase-marker that has not been correctly derived into a correctly derived p-m (with respect to the terminal string). We assume that only those transformations are available for hypothesization which, applied to the top level of b (that is, last in the cycle), create a correct p-m, one whose terminal string is s.[26] In other words, if the terminal string $*C_t(b) \neq s$, but T is a transformation such that the terminal string $*T(C_t(b)) = s$, with T applying at the top (last cycle), then T is available for hypothesization.

Why do we have to add only transformations that apply at the top level of the current phrase-marker? The rationale is twofold. First, suppose we wanted to add a transformation that applied at a lower level of the phrase-marker. In keeping with the idea of adding transformations that change the derivation so that the final terminal string is correct, we would have to add a transformation that applied at some lower level and, taken together with the transformations that applied earlier and later in the cycle, yielded a correct surface string. The computational burdens for this procedure seem very large, even compared with what we have already assumed. First, a transformation has to be selected to apply at some lower level and then tried out with all the later transformations; this involves quite a bit of computation. Second, in the procedure that we have adopted, *LP* has to calculate only the terminal string of phrase-markers yielded by the application of transformations that it wants to test for possibility of hypothesization. But if transformations at a lower level could be hypothesized, their effects on the phrase-marker would have to be evaluated, since further transformations will apply. This is a much larger computational burden, one we would prefer to do without.[27]

There is a second rationale for not hypothesizing transformations that apply at a lower level. Suppose that what is wrong with a transformational component is that a transformation T is missing and that T should apply at some lower (non-top) level i. But then consider the base phrase-marker b' which is formed from b by removing all levels above i. Since T is not in the transformational component C_t, T will not apply to b' at *its* top (level i), so an error will be caused by T not applying at the top of the base phrase-marker b'. That is, the terminal string $*C_t(b')$ will not be equal to the terminal string $*A(b')$. When b' is presented, an error will occur and hypothesization of T will be possible because the error occurs at the *top* of b'. Thus there will be no need to hypothesize T at level i of b, since the hypothesization can take place at the top level of another phrase-marker b'.[28] For these reasons we have assumed that hypothesization takes place only at the top level.[29]

The definitions of the sets of transformations available for hypothesization and rejection are crucial aspects of *LP*. It remains only to specify how *LP* works. At the beginning the learner's component C_0 has no transformations. When a datum d is presented, if C is correct on d (performs the correct mapping), C doesn't change. (We sometimes suppress the subscript t on C.) If C is incorrect on d, *LP* hypothesizes one transformation from the set available for hypothesization or rejects one transformation from the set available for rejection. Which of the transformations will be selected, and whether it will be one of those available for hypothesization or rejection, is determined with uniform probability.[30]

There is one complexity that we have so far ignored. Recall our assumption that adult transformational components are *deterministic* in the sense that at any stage in a derivation, at most one transformation fits the structure and this transformation fits in only one way. We want to insure that in the limit, the learner's component is also deterministic. At any rate, if the component is not deterministic, some derivations will not be well-defined, given our preliminary assumption that there are only obligatory transformations. It will sometimes turn out that the learner's component C is nondeterministic on some datum $d = (b,s)$. In this case we say that $*C(b)$ cannot be computed and treat the datum as if C makes an error. That is, hypothesization or rejection will take place on d. We want the transformations that caused the nondeterminism to be available for rejection in such a case. Therefore we take the set of transformations available for rejection to be not the set of transformations that *applied* to b, as we earlier indicated, but the set of all transformations *applicable* at any stage in the derivation. (This will include all transformations that are applicable up to and including the lowest level of nondeterminancy, as applicability is not defined past that point.) Thus transformations that cause nondeterminancy, if they ever apply, will be available for rejection. *LP* will insure that the learner has no such transformations in the limit.[31]

A flow chart of the learning procedure *LP* appears in figure 3.1, taken from Hamburger and Wexler 1975, fig. 12. In the chart, $hyp(d,$ C) is the set of transformations available for hypothesization given that the current component is C and the presented datum is d. The transformational component starts out empty. A new datum $d = (b,s)$ is presented. *LP* calculates the surface string $s' = *C(b)$. Then there is a decision. If C is nondeterministic on b (if $C(b)$ "can't be computed"), *LP* moves to the pick-*hyp*-or-*rej* box. If s' can be computed (if C is deterministic on b), then a decision is made. If $s' = s$, there is no error and no change is made in the component, *LP* cycling back to the next datum. If $s' \neq s$, there is an error and *LP* moves to the pick-*hyp*-or-*rej* box. If *hyp* is picked, a transformation is selected from those available for hypothesization and added to C. If *rej* is picked, a transformation is selected from those available for rejection and eliminated from C. Then *LP* moves on to the next datum.

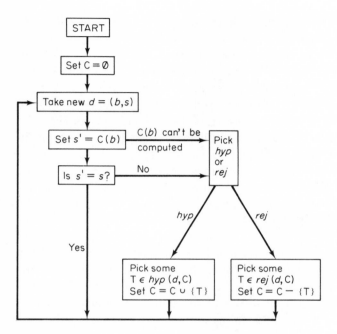

Figure 3.1
Flow chart of the learning procedure

3.4 Proof of Convergence: An Informal Sketch

In this section we will provide a rough sketch of the proof that the system converges, that is, that learnability occurs. Mathematical formalisms and details of the proof appear in Hamburger and Wexler 1975. There is no need to replicate that proof here. What we are attempting to do is to show how particular properties of the grammatical and learning systems are important for the learnability results.

The proof is divided into two major parts. Part 1 derives properties of the grammatical system, and depends only on that system and not on the learning procedure or mechanism. Part 2 is a study of the properties of the learning procedure, but depends heavily not only on the definition of that procedure but also on the properties of the grammatical system derived in part 1. In this book we will be concerned with obtaining a far more powerful result than the one obtained in Hamburger and Wexler, namely, learnability from simple data. The key result that will make this possible is the construction of a transformational system from which more powerful results may be obtained. This is carried out in chapter 4, in which a new system with new properties is discussed. The results in chapter 4 will replace the part 1 results in Hamburger and Wexler. These results are not only based on different linguistic properties, but also involve a very different method of proof. Furthermore, the linguistic properties assumed in chapter 4 are assumed for specific reasons of learnability and can be seen to play specific roles in allowing learnability from simple data. We will present the assumptions, the specific reasons for the assumptions, and the proof in detail in chapter 4. For these reasons we will not discuss the original proof of the part 1 (grammatical system) results in Hamburger and Wexler but will simply state the results. [32] The part 2 results, which involve the learning procedure, will go through for the chapter 4 system with essential details unchanged from the original proof, except for some simplification resulting from a stronger part 1 result (see section 4.5). We will therefore discuss the properties of the part 2 proof here. [33]

First, however, let us consider a crucial property that the linguistic system will have to possess. The learning procedure *LP* hypothesizes transformations based on evidence that some transformation is needed and rejects transformations based on evidence that some transformation may be wrong. It makes sense to think that, barring difficulties, such a system should ultimately be able to select a correct transformational component. Transformations are hypothesized or rejected only when a detectable error occurs, that is, when the learner's transformational component maps the presented phrase-marker b into a surface string s' that is different from the presented surface string s. Any datum d has a finite probability of appearing at any time, so it would appear as if an error, if it existed in the learner's system, could occur in the input sequence. This is an important property, because the learner must be presented with an error if his system is to change, and change is necessary if he is ever to attain a correct component. But suppose the probability that an error-datum will occur is very small. The probability could be so small that the errors are ineffective in allowing learning to occur.

For example, suppose that errors occur only on very complicated data (as measured, say, by depth of the phrase-marker b). Very complicated data must have probabilities of presentation that, though assumed to be greater than 0, are vanishingly small. (This will follow from the fact that the probabilities of presenting data constitute a probability distribution—that is, the sum of the probabilities is 1—and the fact that there are an infinite number of possible data.) Suppose that errors occur only on very complicated data. In principle, the following might occur. At some time the learner has selected an incorrect transformational component. However, this component makes errors only on very complicated data, which have a very small probability of occurring. If one of them does occur, a new transformational component is selected (a transformation is hypothesized or rejected). This new component, we assume, also is not correct. However, the smallest datum on which the new component makes an error, we assume, is even larger (more complicated) than the last datum (on which the previous component made an error) and its probability of presentation is even smaller. In principle, the probabilities of presentation of error-data may go down so fast that the learner is not likely to be presented with errors, the learning system will not have enough of a chance to change its hypotheses, and convergence (learning) will not necessarily take place. In very rough terms, we would like the system to display the following property:

Property 1 (P1): Errors occur sufficiently often.

Or consider the following behavior. Suppose that $d = (b,s)$ is a datum on which an error occurs. Thus hypothesization and rejection will be possible on d. It should be clear that in general the larger d is (the greater the depth of b and the length of s), the more possibilities there will be for hypothesization and rejection (this can be proved). That is, the larger d, the more transformations will have applied, in general, and thus the more transformations available for rejection. But even more crucially, the larger d, the more ways there will exist for adding a transformation that will transform b appropriately, thus the more transformations there will be available for hypothesization. Now, determining the transformations that are available to be hypothesized is done by probabilistic selection (equiprobable selection under one scheme, but this is not necessary—see note 30). There is no way to tell which of the available transformations *should* be selected (at least under the procedures we have postulated). Of the set of available transformations only a small number will be correct transformations. In principle, the set of available transformations will grow as the size of d grows; so as d grows, the chance (probability) of selecting a correct transformation in principle might severely decline. Suppose then that the size of data on which errors occur is very large; it even seems to be possible that the size could grow with time, as the learner learns more transformations. It is possible in principle that the size of data on which errors occur is so large that the number of transformations available for hypothesization or rejection is very large and that consequently the chance of selecting a correct transformation is very small. Given these conditions the system again might not converge, that is, learning might not occur. The conclusion is that we need two properties. First, we need the following general property:

Property 2 (P2): Error-data exist for which not too many alterations (hypothesizations and rejections) are possible, so that there is a reasonable chance of selecting a correct transformation.

We have seen why we want P2 to be true and also what kind of behavior will lead to P2's being false. Thus we want a third property:

Property 3 (P3): If errors occur at all, then there are sufficiently small data on which errors occur.

The rationale for P3 is that if errors occur on small data, hypothesization and rejection can take place on these small data. There will in general be fewer transformations available for hypothesization and rejection on small data, and thus a better chance of selecting a correct transformation. Thus P2 will follow from P3.

But now consider P1 again. P1 says that errors must occur sufficiently often. According to P3, errors will occur on sufficiently small data. But as we have pointed out, the probabilities of very large data appearing become very small. The probabilities of small data appearing can be large enough (the idea being that there are only a finite number of small data, so that the probability of any of them appearing is greater than a lower bound greater than 0, whereas there are an infinite number of data larger than the small data, and thus the probability of one of these appearing *cannot* be bounded away from 0). Thus P3, although motivated here by P2, can also insure that P1 holds. In fact, the same considerations that led us to P1 and P2 point to the conclusion that P1 and P2 should hold together, that is, of the same data, so that we can conclude that P4 must hold.

Property 4 (P4): Errors exist for which not too many alterations (hypothesizations and rejections) are possible, so there is a reasonable chance of selecting a correct alteration, and these errors occur sufficiently often.

We thus see that P3 is a crucial property, which will lead to P4 (and both of its parts, P1 and P2) being true. In fact, the demonstration that P3 holds is the point of part 1 of the proof of learnability. Part 2 uses P3, together with properties of the learning procedure, to yield learnability. Although it may not seem obvious that it should be so, P3 is proved in a manner dependent entirely on the grammatical system and independently of the learning procedure *LP* (except for the definition of "error").[34]

Recall that the degree of a phrase-marker is its depth of S-embedding. Two transformational components A and C *disagree* on a phrase-marker b if they map b into different surface strings. That is, $*A(b) \neq *C(b)$. We now restate P3 as BDE:[35]

Boundedness of Minimal Degree of Error (BDE): For any base grammar B there exists a finite integer U, such that for any possible adult transformational component A and learner (child) component C, if A and C disagree on any phrase-marker b generated by B, then they disagree on some phrase-marker b' generated by B, with b' of degree at most U.

BDE (property P3) is the property of the linguistic system that plays the major role in the proof of convergence. That BDE holds is by no means obvious, and a number of linguistic assumptions must be made in order for it to hold (see note 7). Here we will give only the initial plausibility argument, ignoring the complications that make necessary the assumptions and mathematical analysis to be found in section 2 of Hamburger and Wexler 1975. As we have already pointed out, chapter 4 presents in some detail a different system and proof which allow a far stronger form of BDE to emerge.

As we pointed out in section 3.1, there is a restriction on the context-free base grammar B which is very useful in the proofs. B is assumed to be S-*essential,* which means that all recursion takes place through a distinguished category S, which is also the starting (top) category of the grammar. Thus, if a node of category D dominates another node of category D, there must be a node of category S between the two occurrences of D, as in (1). Thus we can break a phrase-marker up into levels, each dominated by a sentence S. Each level can contain no node that dominates another node of the same category within the level. Thus the levels are finitely bounded in their depth and width.

We add another assumption, the Binary principle.[36] This principle says that a transformation may apply to the level at which it is operating, plus the next lower level, but no further down. The Binary princi-

(1)

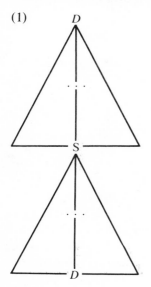

ple seems to imply that if an error occurs at the top of phrase-marker b, then an error will also occur on phrase-markers formed by dropping lower levels of b, to which the error-causing transformation doesn't apply. Given the bound on depth and width of levels, it seems to follow that an error will occur on a bounded phrase-marker, BDE following.

It turns out that this analysis is only right as a first approximation, that transformational systems have many possibilities that go beyond this analysis (in particular, that the application of earlier transformations can influence the possibilities for later ones). Thus the analysis will not work in this form, and a number of other restrictions must be added, together with a tortuous proof. We will ignore these here, but see Hamburger and Wexler 1975 for details of the original restrictions and proof (and note 7 for a quick sketch of the restrictions).

Before going on to a discussion of the learnability proof, we will state a more precise version of the convergence result. First, we need a definition of "moderate equivalence."[37] Recall that, for a p-m b, *b is the terminal string of b.

(2) *Moderate Equivalence:* For two transformational components C and A, C is *moderately equivalent* to A, with respect to a base grammar B, if and only if, for all phrase-makers b generated by B, *$C(b)$ = *$A(b)$. We denote moderate equivalence of A and C as C $\cong_M$ A.

The learnability theorem, or convergence result, is then the following (recall that C_t is the learner's component at time t):

Learnability: For all $\epsilon > 0$, $\exists t'$, Prob($C_{t'} \cong_M$ A) $> 1 - \epsilon$

In short, by selecting a large enough time, the probability can be made arbitrarily close to 1 that the learner will have selected a correct (moderately equivalent to adult) transformational component. By the property of *LP* that changes in components are made only when errors are discovered, once a component moderately equivalent to the adult component is selected by the child, there will be no errors and thus no changes at all in the selected component. As defined, learnability will imply the requirement that ultimately (with probability 1) a correct component is selected and after that the component remains unchanged (see chapter 2).

The method of proof of the convergence result is the following. The adult component A has n transformations in it, say, A $= \{T_1, T_2, \ldots, T_n\}$. At any time, the learner's current component has a finite number of transformations in it; say, at time t the selected component has m transformations, which we denote $C_t = \{T_1', T_2', \ldots, T_m'\}$. In the worst case, none of the m transformations in C_t is correct. Thus, in order to move from C_t to A, each of the m wrong transformations must be rejected, and each of the n correct transformations must be hypothesized. The minimum number of steps (pieces of time, presentations of data) for this to occur is $m + n$ because at most one alteration (hypothesization or rejection) can be made on a datum. In general, the change will take many more than $m + n$ steps because (1) some data won't contain errors and thus no change will take place in the guessed component, and (2) on some data (errors) on which changes *are* made, incorrect changes will be made, namely, (a) wrong transformations will be hypothesized, or (b) good ones (hypothesized after time t, when we have assumed only bad ones are in the learner's component) will be rejected. Nevertheless, it is possible that C_t can change to A in $m + n$ steps, and the method of proof will involve showing that the probability that this will happen is greater than a bound greater than 0. More generally, the probability of *any* possible component C_t changing to A by making correct changes on all the next pieces of data is bounded away from 0, and this change will take place in a number of steps less than a bound k. Once correct, the component will not change. That is, the probability that an incorrect component will change to a correct component in k or fewer steps is bounded away from 0. This statement is true for all times and no matter what the state of learning. It follows that convergence will take place as required by the definition of *learnability*.

This is the desired method of proof. The properties we have discussed (and others) will make this possible. The situation is schematized in (3). ($\mathcal{T}_i$ means that T_i is deleted from the transformational component.)

(3) $\{\mathcal{T}_1', \mathcal{T}_2', \ldots, \mathcal{T}_m'\} \rightarrow \{T_1, T_2, \ldots, T_n\}$

Note that there is no claim here that learning *will* take place like this.

In general, we would expect incorrect transformations to be added, some data not to be error-data, and so on. We are simply using this situation as a method of proof, showing that the probabilities that these kinds of sequences will occur are high enough that convergence takes place.

In light of this method of proof consider the properties that we have discussed so far. A datum d on which a learner's component makes an error will be called an error-datum. Changes will be made in the guessed component only when error-data occur. Thus we need to insure, for the proof, that there is a good probability that error-data will occur on each of the next $m + n$ steps. This is property P1, essentially; it follows from BDE, as we have pointed out. We can insure that there is a bound under the probability that an error-datum occurs on each of the next $m + n$ steps and that these error-data are of degree less than U. This too follows from BDE; it is part of the statement of P4. We will need P4 to hold because we need a sufficient chance of a good alteration occurring on each of the $m + n$ steps. A "good" alteration is defined as one that rejects an incorrect transformation or hypothesizes a correct transformation.

Showing that there is a sufficient chance for a good alteration to occur on any step involves two parts, stated in P5 and P6.

Property 5 (P5): There are data of low degree for which the set of transformations available for alteration include at least one good alteration.

Property 6 (P6): For these data there is a finite bound on the number of alterations available, so the probability of the good alteration occurring is bounded away from 0.

To see why P5 is true, suppose there is an error on some datum $d = (b,s)$ (guaranteed by BDE that such exists of degree less than U, given any errors at all). Suppose the learner's component C_t applies a wrong transformation T to b. Since there is an error on d, T (along with all other transformations in C_t which applied to b) is available for rejection. Since T is wrong, this is a good alteration. Suppose, on the other hand, that C_t does not apply any wrong transformations to b. Then all the transformations that C_t applied to b must be correct (must be in A).

Since we have assumed that learning has not yet occurred, there must be some transformation T in A that is missing from C. Consider the lowest level of b on which a correct transformation (from A) which applies at that level is missing from C. The sub-phrase-marker b' dominated by this level is correct up to its top. By the definition of *hypothesization* in *LP,* T can be hypothesized at the top level of phrase-marker b'. This is a good alteration. Since b is of degree less than U, b' is of degree less than U. Thus b' is a sufficiently simple datum on which a good alteration can be made. This yields property P5. At each of the $m + n$ steps a good alteration (hypothesization or rejection) is available.

Note that the concept of transformational cycle plays an important role in this last discussion which shows that P5 holds. The transformational cycle says that transformations apply to the lowest level of a p-m first, then the next higher level, and so on up the tree. If, instead, transformations were allowed to apply in different orders to a p-m, then it might happen that there is an error at the top of b' only because a higher transformation applied, the output of this higher transformation requiring the application (in the adult component A) of a transformation T at the lower level (top of b'). T might not apply if b' is taken out of b. There would then be no error on b' and no basis for the hypothesization of T on b'. Thus the assumption of the transformational cycle is used to derive P5.[38]

Property P6 says that for these error-data there are only a bounded number of alterations available. Let $d = (b, s)$ be an error-datum. Only transformations that the learner's component C_t applies to b are available for rejection. Property P7 (still to be discussed) says that for a given base grammar there is a bound on the size of the learner's component. Since only transformations in the learner's component at a given time can be rejected, there is a bound on the number of transformations that can be rejected. The only transformations available for hypothesization are those that apply to the top of a phrase-marker and map it into the correct string. It can be shown that the number of such transformations is bounded by a number that depends on the depth of b and the length of s.[39] Since the length of s is bounded (given A, which is fixed) for any phrase-marker of less than a fixed degree, it follows that there is a bound on the number of transformations available for hypothesization from any datum of degree less than U. From this result, together with the above mentioned bound on the number of rejections possible, P6 follows.

Properties P5 and P6 together state that there are data of low degree such that the set of transformations available for alteration includes at least one good alteration, yet there is a finite bound on the number of alterations available from these data. Thus the probability of a good alteration's occurring is greater than a bound greater than 0, since we have assumed that there is an equal probability that each alteration in the set of available alterations will occur. These alterations are of low degree and so occur sufficiently often. Thus P4 is established.

We need one other property. Our method of proof demands that the probability of getting from a bad to a good component in the next k steps is bounded away from 0, where k is fixed over all times and learning states. Suppose that a learner's component could get arbitrarily bad, so that it could have an arbitrarily large number of (wrong) transformations in it. That is, m (the number of transformations in C_t) is unbounded; thus $m + n$ is unbounded, and the number of steps that it would take to get from C_t to A is unbounded. Therefore we want a bound on how bad C_t can get. We impose such a bound by simply showing P7.

Property 7 (P7): For a base grammar there is a finite bound on the number of transformations there can be in a learner's component C_t, the bound holding over all times.

First, note that P7 was also involved in the demonstration of P6 and so is used twice in the proof. To see that P7 holds, we simply note that each transformation T in a learner's component is hypothesized on a phrase-marker such that T applies to the eligible structure of the phrase-marker (the part of the phrase-marker to which transformations can apply). Determinism implies that a component may have only one transformation for each eligible structure. Given the restrictions of the transformational system, one can show that there are only a finite number of eligible structures for a base grammar. There may be no more transformations in the learner's component than this number of eligible structures. This implies P7.

One of the restrictions insuring that there are only a finite number of eligible structures is the Binary principle. This is another example of the role of the Binary principle in the convergence proof.

We have sketched the major components of the proof. To summarize, we need to put a bound under the probability that m bad transformations will be rejected and n good ones selected in the next $m + n$ steps, the bound holding over all times, given that the transformational component contains exactly m bad transformations. Property P4 shows that there is a sufficiently large chance that error-data will occur on which there is a sufficiently good chance that good alterations will be made. Property P7 shows that there is a fixed (over time) bound as to how many of these alterations will have to be made for a correct component to be selected. Taken together these results yield a proof of the learnability (convergence) theorem.

We have passed over a very large number of difficulties and details. The reader who is interested in pursuing the argument with mathematical precision should consult Hamburger and Wexler 1975 and, for more powerful developments, chapter 4 of this book.

CHAPTER 4

DEGREE-2
LEARNABILITY

We are now ready to attack the following crucial problem in the theory of the learnability of transformational grammar. Although we have been able to show that transformational grammar is learnable, the complexity of the data that the learner has to use in order to converge to the correct grammar is far too large. Thus the problem arises: Can transformational grammar be learned from an input of reasonably small complexity? In this chapter, a proof is given that transformational grammar, given certain constraints, can be learned from data of degree less than or equal to 2.

To see the complexity of the data needed for learning according to the original theory, recall the method of proof sketched in chapter 3. First, if the learner has not yet learned the language, there is a reasonable chance for him to learn on the next input. Since in this system, learning takes place only when errors are made by the learner, this means that there must be a reasonable chance of an error occurring on the next input. This is guaranteed in the proof by showing that there must be an error on some phrase-marker of small degree. That is, there is a bound U such that the system will make an error on at least one phrase-marker of degree less than U. (In general, it will make an error on many such phrase-markers.) Thus the learner only has to have as input phrase-markers of degree less than U. Only small degree phrase-markers have to be input to the learner.

But what is U? Theorem 3 of Hamburger and Wexler 1975 gives the bound as $U = 10(E^2F)^2$, where F is the size of the largest set of siblings of any node in a base phrase-marker (that is, the largest "branching size") and E is the number of different sub-phrase-markers that may determine the fit of a transformation, given the various assumptions and restrictions made. To take a too simple artificial example to show how big U gets, suppose that all branching is binary. Thus $F = 2$. We also take a far too small estimate of the number of different structures generated by the grammar which may in principle determine the fit of a transformation. Suppose $E = 10$. Putting these numbers into the formula for U, we find that $U = 400,000$. In other words, the learner can concentrate attention on phrase-markers of degree smaller than 400,000.

Important as the convergence result is, the size of this bound is obviously absurd. We want to reduce it to a reasonable figure. We can reduce U from 400,000 (or bigger) to 2, although this requires new assumptions about constraints on grammars. In other words, we can show that even though a language learner will eventually learn a grammar that can deal with complex sentences, *in the process of learning* he need only deal with sentences containing embedded sentences that contain sentences, and no sentence more complex than these. It is reasonable to believe that information from highly complex sentences is not needed as input to the learning procedure. Thus this theoretical result is desirable.

After completing the original proof of convergence (Hamburger and Wexler 1975) we searched for empirical evidence for the assumed constraints. In particular, we hoped to find evidence for the various restrictions on raising. We can make a distinction between, on the one hand, conventions on rules which constrain their operation so that predicted distributions of acceptability judgments provide evidence for the rules and, on the other hand, conventions that the hypothesized rules fit (do not break) but that are not used to predict distributions of grammaticality. An example of the latter kind of constraint would be the statement that all rules of the base are context-free.

At first, we looked to show that the constraints were only of the latter kind. But we were surprised to discover that a modification of the constraints would help to predict subtle distributions of grammaticality judgments. (See chapter 5 for details.) This new constraint is called the Freezing principle. Not only is the Freezing principle descriptively useful, but it appears that it might play a crucial role in allowing transformational components to be learned from relatively simple data. The goal of this chapter is to prove degree-2 learnability.

4.1 Assumptions

4.1.1 Freezing Principle and Binary Principle

The *Freezing principle* (sometimes FP) says that if a transformation changes the structure of a node so that it is no longer a base structure, nothing under that node may be analyzed (and thus changed) by a further transformation. To state the principle more precisely: if A and B are nodes in a phrase-marker such that A dominates B, and there is no node C such that A dominates C and C dominates B, then A *immediately* dominates B. The *immediate structure* of A is the sub-phrase-marker consisting of A, the nodes $A_1, A_2, \ldots, A_n$ that A immediately dominates, in order, and the connecting branches. The immediate structure of A is a *base immediate structure* if $A \rightarrow A_1 \ldots A_n$ is a base rule. Otherwise, it is nonbase.

Definition: If the immediate structure of a node in a phrase-marker is nonbase, that node is *frozen*.

We can now state the Freezing principle.

Freezing Principle (FP): If a node A of a phrase-marker is frozen, no node dominated by A may be analyzed by a transformation.

Note that *no* node that A dominates may be analyzed, not just the nodes that A immediately dominates. Also note that by this definition, since A does not dominate A, if A is frozen, it may itself be analyzed by a transformation (unless some B that dominates A is also frozen).

Notation: A box around a node A in a phrase-marker indicates that A is frozen. In this example, C is frozen; that is, $C \rightarrow GH$ is not a base rule. Thus the nodes labeled G, H, M, and N may not be analyzed by a transformation.

Example:

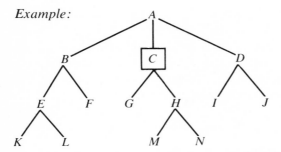

In line with the Freezing principle, we may think of the base grammar as providing *characteristic structures* of the language. Transformations sometimes distort these structures, but only these characteristic structures may be affected by transformations.

The essential characteristic that makes the Freezing principle different from the restrictions that we are attempting to replace by it (restrictions 2–5 of Hamburger and Wexler 1975, henceforth referred to as the original restrictions; see also note 7 of chapter 3) is that it gives a key role to this characteristic-structure conception of the base grammar. A second difference is that it applies to all transformations, not just raising transformations, as the most comparable parts of the original restrictions do (restrictions 4 and 5). In fact, FP is stated in a more simple manner than the original restrictions, because the definition of a frozen node refers only to the current (derived) phrase-marker. The original restrictions, on the other hand, have to use such notions as "nonexplicitly raised nodes," which depend on the history of the derivation. This is probably not a crucial distinction, from the standpoint of learnability, however, because these latter notions can be coded into the derived phrase-marker. (If we weren't referring to universal constraints, this latter kind of power would add problems of learnability.) It turns out, in fact, that in order to prove our final result, we will need one of the restrictions on raising, in addition to FP and other principles.

The Freezing principle leads to a very important property of the learning system, namely, the ability to learn grammar from exposure to relatively simple sentences. The crucial property of FP is that only base structures may be used to fit transformations.

The *Binary principle,* called the height-two restriction in Hamburger and Wexler 1975 and the Subjacency condition in an independent proposal by Chomsky (1973), allows transformations to apply to only those nodes lying at the level at which the transformations are cycling and the level immediately below that. Recall that we have assumed that S is essential to all recursion, that is, if a node labeled A dominates another node labeled A, then a node labeled S occurs between them. Thus a phrase-marker can be broken up into levels, each dominated by an S and including all the nodes and lines down to but not including the next S dominated by the original S. For simplicity, in the remainder of this chapter we assume that for any nodes S_i, S_j ($S_i \neq S_j$) in a base-phrase-marker such that S_i and S_j are labeled S, either S_i dominates S_j or S_j dominates S_i. This would rule out, for example, conjunction. The assumption is made for mathematical convenience only; it greatly simplifies formalisms and proofs. We believe that the proofs go through even without the assumption, but this has not been proved formally. In the example below, suppose that transformations are applying at cycle S_4. The Binary principle will allow transformations to apply to nodes A, B, C, S_3, D, E, F, K, and L, but not to S_2 or to any node dominated by S_2.

Example:

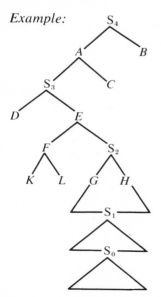

A Note on Notation: In syntactic work, usually the root S is labeled S_0 and lower S's are assigned higher indices. Thus, assuming linear embedding of S's, as we have, S_0 dominates S_1, which dominates S_2, and so on. This method has the advantage that when syntactic arguments are being constructed, phrase-markers can be written from the top down without calculating in advance the depth of the phrase-marker. We are departing from the usual practice because the opposite method is more convenient for the learnability analyses. For example, we perform such operations as dropping the lowest level of a base phrase-marker, which we can describe simply as dropping level 0, avoiding the cumbersome "level *i*, where *i* is the depth of the phrase-marker."

Very roughly, the proof of degree-2 learnability will proceed in the following way. The learning procedure *LP* can change its transformational component only when it has information that it is in error on some p-m *P* that, when correctly transformed, has surface string *s*. That is, the learner maps *P* into a surface string different from *s*. This is called a detectable error. In order to show degree-2 learnability, the crucial property of the system that must be shown is degree-2 error detectability: if a detectable error exists at all, then a detectable error exists on some phrase-marker of degree 2 or less. Degree-2 error detectability is a radical strengthening of BDE (section 3.4).

The proof will be by construction. Given that a detectable error exists on some phrase-marker *P,* we will create a degree-2 phrase-marker *P'* such that a detectable error occurs on *P'*. If the system is unconstrained, this property won't exist. (It is not true, for example, of the original, chapter 3, system). Section 4.1 will be concerned with developing the kinds of constraints that are necessary in order for this property of degree-2 error detectability to hold. Section 4.2 will consider the necessity of some of these constraints.

The proof of degree-2 error detectability is in section 4.3. Here we actually construct the degree-2 p-m *P'* on which an error occurs. The construction starts with a p-m *P* on which a detectable error occurs and forms *P'* by taking only the highest two levels of *P*. The kinds of examples offered in section 4.2 show that the construction is somewhat different from this, account having to be taken of the transformations that apply to the lowest level of *P'*. In section 4.4, various methods of showing learnability from data of degree less than or equal to 2 are discussed.

Note for Linguists: Throughout this chapter we will be doing proofs and analyses by construction. We will often construct phrase-markers by performing such operations as deletion on parts of other phrase-markers. It is important to realize that such language is part of the mathematical notation and does not, unless explicitly so stated, refer to transformational operations (part of linguistic theory), such as deletion transformations. The two notions must be kept strictly separated.

4.1.2 Cyclic Nodes and 0-Terminations

In recent work, including our own (Culicover and Wexler 1977), other phrase types, especially the noun phrase (NP) have been taken to be cyclic, to allow recursion without intervening S's, to define levels, and to count in the Binary principle.[1] Once again, for relative simplicity we will not consider this possibility but will take S as the only cyclic node. We think that the proof will go through even if we assume that there is a set of cyclic categories.

Recall that a p-m with no embedded S's is of degree 0. If a p-m has one embedded S, it is of degree 1. In general a p-m with i embedded S's is of degree i. It appears that we should be able to prove learnability of transformations from simple data if we can conclude that if a transformation applies to some base phrase-marker then it applies to a base phrase-marker of degree 0 or 1. But since the Freezing principle allows transformations to apply only to those parts of structures which are base, and the Binary principle allows transformations to analyze only adjacent levels, it appears that the two principles together should allow us to prove this result.

Consider a transformation T and any base phrase-marker P to which T applies at level i. We want to construct a degree-1 phrase-marker to which T applies. The obvious way to proceed is as follows: First, take the sub-phrase-marker P' dominated by the S at level i. T applies to P' at the top level. Now consider the nodes at which T fits P'. Delete all nodes under these nodes, forming the partially derived sub-phrase-marker P''. By the Binary principle the nodes at which T fits are either at the top level or one level down, so P'' is of degree 0 or 1. By the

Freezing principle the nodes at which T fits, and all the nodes dominating them, can be generated by the base, so P'' is generated by the base.

But we are not finished because P'' is not a terminal phrase-marker; it is only a partially derived structure, with respect to the base grammar. The natural way to complete the construction is to let each of the bottom nodes of P'' be rewritten by rules of the base until a terminal phrase-marker is reached, that is, until lexical items are inserted. Call this new phrase-marker P'''. It is a natural condition on a base grammar, of course, to require that this be possible. But we need more. Unless we ensure that the rewriting takes place without introducing another S, we will wind up with a P''' of degree greater than 1. We will show later by example that this condition can actually arise. Therefore, we will rule it out by assumption. First, we need a definition.

Definition: If A is a nonterminal symbol of a context-free grammar, a *termination* of A is a sub-phrase-marker dominated by A, generated by the rules of the grammar, and terminating in terminal symbols. A 0-termination of A is a termination of A containing no node labeled S (except for the possibility that $A = $ S).

Note on Notation: We will often ignore the distinction between a node and its label, that is, we will use A instead of the phrase "the node labeled A." In the previous definition we speak of A, which is a phrase-type, as dominating a phrase-marker. Of course, we mean that the node labeled A dominates the phrase-marker. This should cause no confusion, as the meaning will be clear in most cases, and when it is not, we will indicate the correct interpretation.

We can now make the following assumption:

Assumption (of 0-termination): Every nonterminal symbol in the base grammar has a 0-termination.

In other words, we require that every symbol can be rewritten until it terminates, without going through S. It now follows that the bottom symbols of P'' can be terminated without going through S, creating a P''' of degree 0 or 1. Thus P''' is a base phrase-marker of degree 0 or 1 to which T applies. This proves the following theorem:

Theorem 1. If a transformation T applies to a base phrase-marker, then there exists a base phrase-marker of degree 0 or 1 to which T applies.

Of course, if a transformation applies to a phrase-marker of degree 0, it applies to any phrase-marker of degree 1 formed by putting any level over the degree-0 phrase-marker to which it applies, and we have the corollary to theorem 1:

Corollary: If a transformation T applies to any base phrase-marker, then there exists a degree-1 base phrase-marker to which T applies.

Note: Of course, we mean that T applies to a p-m P if T applies to P or to any of its S-dominated sub–p-m's.

Example: To see that the assumption of 0-termination is necessary, consider the grammar G containing the rules: $S \rightarrow AB$, $S \rightarrow AD$, $B \rightarrow CS$, $D \rightarrow ES$, $A \rightarrow a$, $B \rightarrow b$, $C \rightarrow c$, $E \rightarrow e$. The assumption of 0-termination fails for G, since D has no 0-termination. Consider any transformation T with a structural analysis $ACAD$. T applies to the degree-2 phrase-marker (1). In fact, T applies to infinitely many phrase-markers. But T applies to no phrase-marker of degree 0 or 1.

(1)

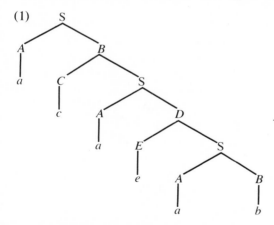

Notation: By the term *phrase-marker* we mean a terminal phrase-marker, a p-m in which lexical items are always inserted. If we do not want to put this requirement on a p-m, we will speak of a partially derived p-m.

If the reader objects that the experience of linguists makes categories that don't 0-terminate look very odd and therefore not worthy of formal study, we should point out that part of the goal of this analysis is to make such intuitions of the linguist explicit and to provide a theoretical explanation of them.

4.1.3 Detectable Errors and Learnability

It would appear at first sight as if we have almost reached our goal of showing that the system is learnable from data of degree 0 and 1. Recall that the original learnability proof essentially contained two parts (see section 3.4). First, we showed that if a learner's transformational component made an error, it made the error on a phrase-marker of degree less than a certain bound U (determined by the base grammar). Thus the probability of an error occurring on the next presentation of a sentence is greater than a certain lower bound p (p is the minimum of the probability of presentation of a certain set of base phrase-markers, the minimum being taken over all base phrase-markers of degree less than the bound U).

The second part of the proof was to show that if an error occurred, there was a probability greater than a certain lower bound that the learning procedure would alter its hypothesized transformational component in the right direction. Since there is a finite bound on the number of steps in the right direction that need be taken, the two parts of the proof combine to show that the probability of learning the grammar on a finite number (the number being given) of consecutive trials is bounded from below, no matter what the learner is currently hypothesizing.

This second part of the proof will clearly go through as before, even if the learner is presented only data of degree 0 and 1. The learning procedure is the same, and the original proof showed that if an error occurred on a phrase-marker of any degree then the probability of learning on consecutive trials was bounded from below. Thus a fortiori the result holds for p-m's of degree 0 and 1. (For more detail, see section 4.4 and note 55.)

In fact, one would be tempted to say that the first part of the proof must also hold for the degree-0,1 case, with the bound being 1. It might seem that theorem 1 shows that if an error is made on a component, an error is made on a base p-m of degree less than or equal to 1. The error in this argument is that theorem 1 asserts that if a transformation T applies to any p-m P, then it applies to a p-m P' of degree 0 or 1. But suppose T makes an error on P, that is, it does not map P onto the correct surface string. Does it follow that T makes this kind of error on P'? The answer is no, as we shall see by example.

The goal of our analysis is to find those assumptions about the form of grammar which will allow us to prove that if a transformational component maps a base phrase-marker onto an incorrect surface string, then it also does this for some base phrase-marker of quite low degree. If we can put a bound on this degree, we will have shown that the grammar can be learned from data of degree less than or equal to that bound.

First, we want to sharpen our notion of error. With an adult transformational component A as a standard, a child's component C makes an error if it differs from A in behavior.

Definition: If a transformational component C maps a base phrase-marker P onto a surface structure that is different from the surface structure obtained when A is applied to P, we say that C *makes an error* on P. If C makes an error on P, and if the surface *sentence* when C does the mapping is different from the surface sentence when A does, we say that C *makes a detectable error* on P.

Notation: In the notation of the original proof we say that $A(P)$ is the surface structure obtained when A is applied to P (that is, $A(P)$ is the final derived phrase-marker) and for any phrase-marker P, $*P$ is P's terminal string. Thus the definitions of *error* and *detectable error* become:

If $A(P) \neq C(P)$, then C makes an *error* on P.
If $*A(P) \neq *C(P)$, then C makes a *detectable error* on P.

The point is that only a detectable error will cause the learning procedure to make a change in the guessed component. We want to show that if a component makes a detectable error, it makes a detectable error on a phrase-marker of low degree.

Convention: We have assumed that adult components are deterministic; that is, at any given point in any derivation the structural description of at most one transformation will fit the phrase-marker, and it will fit in at most one way. The child's component becomes deterministic in the limit because any nondeterminism that arises is seen as a detectable error, thus causing a change in the transformational component. We can incorporate this into the current definition of *detectable error* by simply assuming that when a nondeterminism arises in any derivation, C simply maps the phrase-marker into a special filter symbol, say $\emptyset$: if C is nondeterministic on P, then $C(P) = \emptyset$. In this case, since A is deterministic, $*A(P) \neq *C(P)$ and, by definition, a detectable error has been made on P.

4.1.4 Nonuniqueness of Lexical Items
Consider a context-free base grammar having the following rules:

$S \to PQ$
$S \to DEB$
$P \to AS$
$Q \to A$
$Q \to BH$
$H \to FG$
$A \to a, B \to b, D \to d, \ldots, H \to h, P \to p.$

This grammar certainly meets the assumption of 0-termination. Suppose that the adult transformational component contains only one transformation, T_2; that is, $A = \{T_2\}$. What T_2 does is to raise H from an embedded sentence and place it after a final A in the matrix sentence. Formally,

$T_2: X - H - A \Rightarrow 1 - \emptyset - 3+2.$

Suppose the child's grammar contains T_2, but in addition it contains another transformation, T_1. That is, $C = \{T_1, T_2\}$. T_1 raises B from an embedded sentence and places it to the left of an F in the matrix sentence. It does this whenever there is another B between the moved

B and the *F*. Formally,

$$T_1: X - B - B - F - Y \Rightarrow 1 - \emptyset - 3 - 2{+}4 - 5.$$

C makes no detectable errors on a p-m of degree 0 or 1. The only way an error could be made is for T_1 to apply to a degree-1 p-m, but the only degree-1 p-m to which T_1 applies is P_1, as in (2) below.

Assumption: In chapter 4, for mathematical simplicity we assume that all transformational adjunction is sister-adjunction. The learnability problems that we uncover do not seem to be tied to this assumption, but the question should be investigated in more detail.

(2)

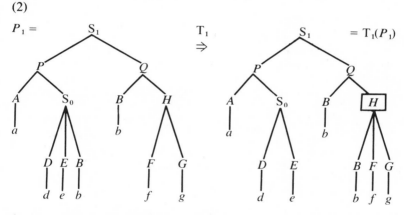

An error has been created here, because T_1 is not in A. Thus $A(P_1) = P_1$, while $C(P_1) = T_1(P_1) \neq P_1$. But no detectable error has been created because, although movement has occurred, the terminal strings remain the same, that is, $*A(P_1) = *C(P_1) = *P_1 = adebbfg$.

So we have shown that C does not make any detectable errors on a p-m of degree 0 or 1. But C does make a detectable error on a degree-2 p-m. Consider P_2, a p-m of degree 2 containing P_1 as an embedded sentence, as in (3). No transformation applies on the S_0 cycle to P_2. On S_1, in A, again no transformation applies, but in C, T_1 does apply, replacing the embedded P_1 by $T_1(P_1)$ as shown in (4). On S_2, T_2 will apply to both P_2 and P_3 (that is, in both A and C), but it will raise an *H*, which, because of the operation of T_1 in C, dominates different strings for the two components. That is, after the cycle on S_2, we have (5).

(3)

$P_2 =$

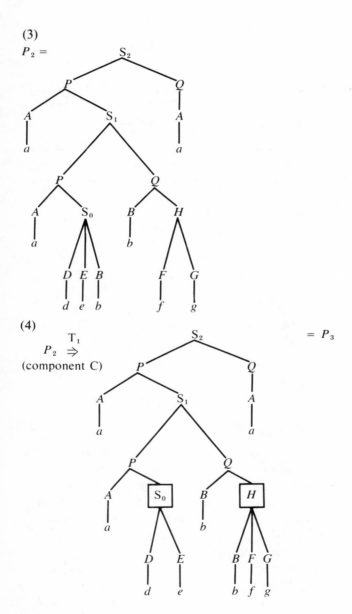

(4)

$$P_2 \underset{\text{(component C)}}{\overset{T_1}{\Rightarrow}} \qquad\qquad = P_3$$

(5)

A(P₂) =

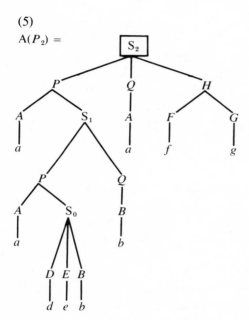

C(P₂) =

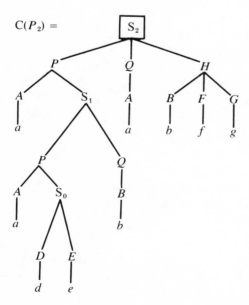

Not only is there an error at S_2, but it is a detectable error, because $*A(P_2) = aadebbafg$ and $*C(P_2) = aadebabfg$. Thus $*A(P_2) \neq *C(P_2)$ and P_2 is a degree-2 p-m on which a detectable error is made.

This example is pathological and not really very deep. The problem is that although T_1 moves a constituent and, in fact, reorders the original constituents, still no detectable error is made, because the lexical items (b) don't distinguish the original phrases. There are many solutions that one is tempted to try in order to rule out this example. One might assume that no string-preserving T can apply. But the string-preserving transformation could be broken down into the compounding of two transformations, neither of which is string-preserving. Or the example could be changed so that some other part of the string is changed and there are never two stages in the derivation with identical strings. A proposal might be made that T_1 in the previous example is a bit complicated as transformations go (but not very complicated; it has one moved target and a left and right context). Thus, if one assumed a constraint on the complexity of transformations, perhaps this example could be ruled out. But once again, this would not solve the problem, because the complexity could be put into the compounding of simple transformations.[2]

It turns out that there is a simple and elegant solution to this class of problems. Suppose the moved category (B) could be rewritten as another word. That is, simply add $B \rightarrow b'$ to the set of rules. Now let the first B be rewritten as b and the second as b'. That is, take P_1' as in (6). Now $*A(P_1') = adebb'fg$ and $*C(P_1') = adeb'bfg$. Thus $*A(P_1') \neq C(P_1')$ and P_1' is a degree-1 p-m on which a detectable error is made.

Recall that the lexical categories are a subset of the nonterminal symbols of the context-free grammar, such that the lexical categories rewrite only as terminal symbols (words or lexical items) and only the lexical categories rewrite as terminal symbols. The lexical categories are also sometimes called terminal categories. It turns out that we can rule out this entire class of pathological examples with the following simple assumption.

Assumption (Nonuniqueness of Lexical Items): Every lexical category rewrites as at least two lexical items.

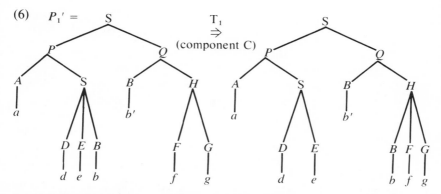

(6) $P_1' =$ ... $T_1 \Rightarrow$ (component C)

4.1.5 Order-Equivalence and Error Detectability

With the rather natural nonuniqueness assumption we will be able to show that if a transformational component incorrectly reorders a constituent, it makes a detectable error on some p-m. In the following definition we ignore inserted morphemes, although the obvious generalization is to consider an inserted morpheme as a category of its own.

Definition: Order the terminal category nodes of a p-m P from left to right, obtaining the sequence $1, 2, \ldots, n$. A transformation T reorders these nodes, possibly deleting some or adding copies of some. The *terminal category node order* $O_T(P)$ of P under T is the new left-to-right sequence $i_1, i_2, \ldots, i_m$ of these terminal category nodes in $T(P)$. If T doesn't apply, then $O_T(P) = 1, 2, \ldots, n$. These notions are extended in a natural way to transformational components. If A is a transformational component, then $O_A(P)$ is the sequence $j_1, j_2, \ldots, j_p$ of terminal category nodes in $A(P)$.

Note: If a deletion occurs, it is possible that $m < n$. If a copy occurs, then possibly $m > n$.

Example: Let T be the transformation $T: C - D - E - F - D - G \Rightarrow \emptyset - 2 - 1 - 4+1 - 5 - 6+2$. Then the p-m P is transformed as in (7). $O_T(P) = 3,1,2,5,1,2,6,7,3$. We have placed the numbers of the terminal category nodes under their corresponding lexical items. Note that the order $O_T(P)$ cannot be read off directly from the structural change of the

(7) P = $\Rightarrow$

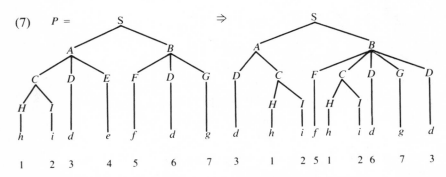

transformation T because C is not a terminal category node in P and thus even though C is referred to in the structural description of T, C may not be numbered in $O_T(P)$.

Note: It is important to note that we have assumed for the sake of the current proof that all lexical categories are realized in lexical items and thus we have ignored the possibility of dummy categories.

Definition: Two transformational components A and C are *order-equivalent* on a phrase-marker P if $O_A(P) = O_C(P)$.

Note on concepts of equivalence: Recall that two transformational components are moderately equivalent on a p-m P if they map P into the same surface string. Thus if two T components are order-equivalent, they are moderately equivalent, but it is easy to construct examples for which the converse does not hold. Also, if two T components are strongly equivalent on P (that is, at the least they map P into the same phrase-marker, called the surface structure), then they are order-equivalent. Unfortunately, again the converse doesn't hold. Thus the descending hierarchy of strength of these concepts is: strongly equivalent, order-equivalent, moderately equivalent.

These concepts may be extended in a natural way to become properties of T components on a fixed base grammar. For example, two T components are *strongly equivalent* on the grammar B if the components are strongly equivalent on all p-m's generated by B. Recall that two T components on B are *weakly equivalent* if their generated sets of surface strings are equivalent. Thus the descending hierarchy of strength is: strongly equivalent, order-equivalent, moderately equivalent, weakly equivalent.

Theorem 2: Let P be a base p-m of degree i. If two T components A and C are not order-equivalent on P, then there exists a base p-m P' of degree i such that there is a detectable error on P'.

Proof: We will construct an appropriate P' identical to P except possibly for a change in one lexical item. $O_A(P)$ and $O_C(P)$ are sequences of integers. Suppose the first element of the sequences where the two sequences differ (as they must, since by assumption, $O_A(P) \neq O_C(P)$) is the kth term in the sequence and suppose that this kth term (node number) is i for $O_A(P)$ and is j for $O_C(P)$. Thus the substring formed from the first $k - 1$ elements of $*A(P)$ equals the substring formed from the first $k - 1$ elements of $*C(P)$. Now if terminal category node i and terminal category node j in P dominate different lexical items, then there is a detectable error on P and the proof is completed by taking P' $= P$. Thus we can assume that i and j dominate the same lexical item w in P. We now take P' to be identical to P except that in P' terminal category node j dominates w', another lexical item, instead of w ($w \neq w'$). This is possible by the assumption of nonuniqueness of lexical items. Since, by definition, choice of lexical items doesn't influence application of transformations, the surface strings $*A(P')$ and $*C(P')$ will be identical through term $k - 1$, but for term k, $*A(P')$ will contain w while $*C(P')$ will have w'. Thus $*A(P') \neq *C(P')$ and a detectable error is made on the degree i p-m P'.

Note: Crucial use is made of the assumption of nonuniqueness of lexical items.

4.1.6 Higher-Degree Errors
We are tempted once again to say that our goal has been reached. That is, if a detectable error occurs on a degree-i p-m P, then A and C are not order-equivalent on P. We know by theorem 1 that a transformation that applies to a degree-i p-m will apply to a degree-1 p-m P'. Since A and C are not order-equivalent on P (they shift the categories differ-

ently), surely they are not order-equivalent on P'. Thus, by theorem 2, a detectable error is made on P', a p-m of degree 1.

The error in this argument is the assumption that if two transformational components are not order-equivalent on a p-m P, they are not order-equivalent on a lower degree p-m P' to which they apply. This assumption is not universally valid. Once again we resort to example.

(8)

a. The base rules:

$S \rightarrow AB$

$S \rightarrow HIJ$

$A \rightarrow DE$

$B \rightarrow FSG$

$A \rightarrow a,a'; B \rightarrow b,b'; D \rightarrow d,d'; \ldots ; J \rightarrow j,j'$

b. The transformational components:

$A = \{T_1^A, T_2\},$

$C = \{T_1^C, T_2\},$

where

$T_1^A: X - E - Y - H - Z \Rightarrow 1 - 2+4 - 3 - \emptyset - 5,$

$T_1^C: X - F - H - Y \Rightarrow 1 - 3+2 - \emptyset - 4,$

$T_2: A - F - X - B \Rightarrow 4+1 - 2 - 3 - \emptyset.$

Clearly the set of base rules meets the assumption of 0-termination and the assumption of nonuniqueness of lexical items. If we choose P_1, as in (9), it is clear that T_1^A and T_1^C are order-equivalent on P_1, but the phrase-markers into which the transformations map P_1 have different structures. It can be seen that no p-m of degree 1 generated by the base causes a detectable error. But when T_2 applies to a degree-2 p-m containing the transformed phrase-markers in (9), there will be a detectable error, because the effect of T_2 is to raise B, and B dominates a different string in the two cases. This may be seen in (10).[3] $*A(P_2) = fijgdefdehg$ and $*C(P_2) = hfijgdefdeg$; therefore $*A(P_2) \neq C(P_2)$. We have, therefore, shown that P_2 is a degree-2 p-m on which a detectable error occurs, but no detectable error occurs on a p-m of degree 0 or 1.

The child, in learning from a degree-1 datum, has hypothesized a transformation that correctly handles that datum and all other degree-1 data. The slight error he has made is to place the moved constituent (H)

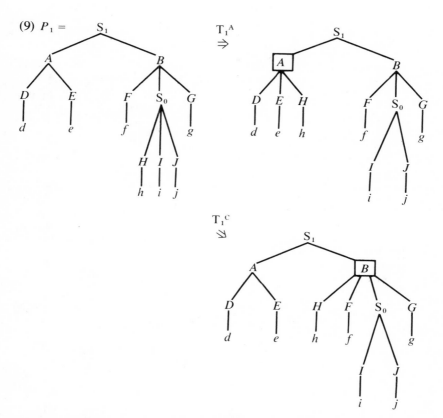

to the left of a certain constituent (F) rather than to the right of the
constituent immediately to that constituent's left (E), as the adult does.
Such errors seem natural, and there might be no reasonable assumption
that will rule out this kind of case.[4] However, a detectable error does
show up on a degree-2 datum, so perhaps our desired result can be
saved by increasing the necessary data to include degree-2 data. That
is, perhaps we can show that if a component makes a detectable error
then it makes a detectable error on some p-m of degree 0, 1, or 2.

4.1.7 Raising Principle
In order to make a proof based on this concept go through, it would be
necessary for all nondetectable errors to be of the kind illustrated in the
example given in (8)–(10). That is, a nondetectable error occurs on a

(10)

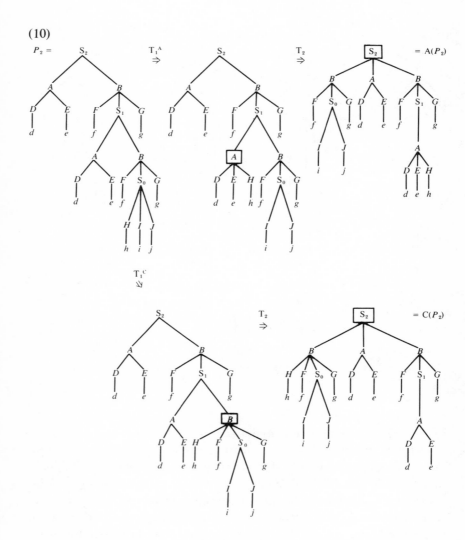

degree-1 p-m. By theorem 2, the two components must order the categories the same; otherwise there is a detectable error on a degree-1 p-m. One possibility is that, as in example (10), a transformation at the next level (the top of a degree-2 p-m) raises the constituent that creates the error and so causes a detectable error. The other possibility is that there is no such transformation. Thus there is no degree-2 detectable error. Then, at degree 3, by the Binary principle, the constituent that contains the error cannot be analyzed and thus no detectable error at all can be made.

Unfortunately, the last part of this "proof" is incorrect, namely, the assumption that the Binary principle doesn't allow a transformation at level 3 to be fit by the node at level 1 which contains the error. The possibility exists that this node was raised from level 1 to level 2 in such a way that no detectable error was created, but one *is* created at level 3. Again, an example.

First, note that we don't have to insert lexical items in our examples. We simply assume that all terminal category nodes can be rewritten as at least two lexical items. Thus, by theorem 2, whenever two components are not order-equivalent on a p-m of degree i, there is a p-m of degree i on which a detectable error is made. For the rest of this chapter we will write phrase-markers only down to the terminal category nodes. When we have shown that two components are not order-equivalent on P, we will know that there is a detectable error on a p-m P' of the same degree as P.

To begin to construct the example we will create, at level S_1, a nondetectable error of the sort already encountered. We will do this by letting A contain T_1^A and C contain T_1^C, which order the moved constituent in the same way but with different structures. The derivation is shown in (11). Note that symbols such as P_1 are not held constant from the last example to this example. We won't state the base rules, which obviously can be deduced from the base phrase-markers. Again, in all the examples to follow, the convention will be that, unless otherwise stated, the base rules in the example are exactly those realized in the base phrase-markers given.

To accomplish this derivation, let $T_1^A = F - G - X - K - Y \Rightarrow 1 - 2 + 4 - 3 - \emptyset - 5$ and $T_1^C = X - H - Y - K - Z \Rightarrow 1 - 4 + 2 - 3 - \emptyset - 5$. Now, at level 2, we

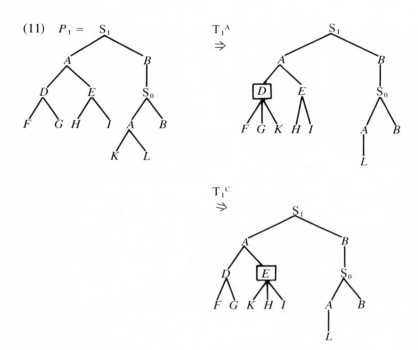

will raise A, which dominates, for both components, the terminal category string $FGKHI$. But we want to do this in a structure-preserving way, so that later the nodes under A may be analyzed. Therefore, we let the base grammar contain the following rules:

$S \rightarrow Q\ R\ (A)$
$Q \rightarrow S.$

Now take

(12) $P_2 =$

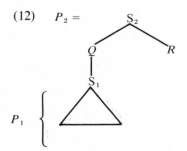

The phrase-marker dominated by S_1 is P_1, which was given in (11). After cycle S_1 we have two different embedded p-m's, $T_1^A(P_1)$ and $T_1^C(P_1)$, for the two components A and C. Now on S_2 we raise the A node that dominates the error, obtaining (13) and (14), for components A and C respectively. We can do this by letting $T_2 = A - B - R \Rightarrow \emptyset - 2 - 3 + 1$. T_2, of course, is in both A and C.

(13)   (14)

$\{T_1^A, T_2\}$ $\{T_1^C, T_2\}$

$P_2 \Rightarrow$ $P_2 \Rightarrow$

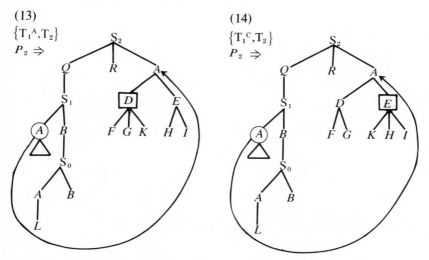

Once again, at cycle S_2, no detectable error has been created, because A has been raised as a whole, and the error that it dominates is not isolatable. Furthermore, A has been raised to a place where it can appear in the base, that is, $S \rightarrow QRA$ is a possible base derivation. Thus S_2 is not frozen. Hence A is analyzable.

On the last cycle, S_3, we raise E, which contains the error. Thus a detectable error will be created. We will also state the transformation T_3 in such a way that had it applied before cycle S_3, T_1 could not have applied, and thus no error could have been made at a level lower than S_3. T_3, of course, is in both A and C. We take $T_3 = A - Q - R - D - E \Rightarrow 5 + 1 - 2 - 3 - 4 - \emptyset$. P_3 is given in (15). After T_1^A and T_2 have applied to P_3 we have (16), and after T_1^C and T_2 have applied to P_3 we have (17). The only difference between the two p-m's is that K is in a different structural position, though not in a different order. Thus we have $A(P_3) =$

(15)

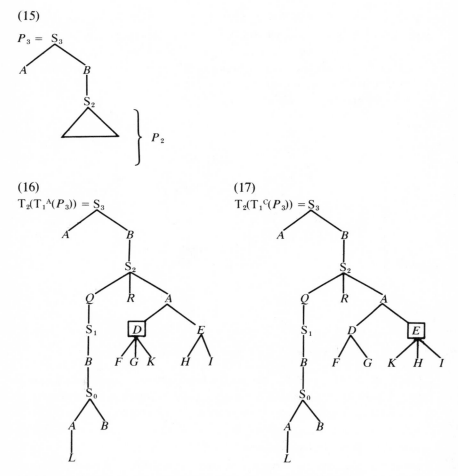

(16)
$T_2(T_1{}^A(P_3)) = S_3$

(17)
$T_2(T_1{}^C(P_3)) = S_3$

$T_3(T_2(T_1{}^A(P_3)))$, as in (18), and $C(P_3) = T_3(T_2(T_1{}^C(P_3)))$, as in (19). Thus $O_A(P_3) = HIALBRFGK$ and $O_C(P_3) = KHIALBRFG$, so $O_A(P_3) \neq O_C(P_3)$. Since P_3 is of degree 3, from theorem 2 we conclude that there is a p-m of degree 3 on which a detectable error is made. (Note that for convenience we have written the terminal category node orders as a sequence of the labels of categories of the node. When no confusion is caused by this procedure, we will follow it, as it makes the examples far clearer.)

(18)   (19)

$A(P_3) = \boxed{S_3}$ $C(P_3) = \boxed{S_3}$

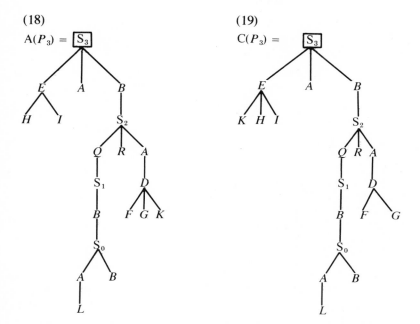

It remains to be shown that there is no detectable error on any p-m of degree less than 3. Note that for a detectable error to occur the sequence of transformations has to be: raise K (creating error), raise A, raise E. The structural descriptions of the three transformations in each component have been stated so that the transformations will apply only so as to *raise* a constituent. Therefore we will have to have a degree-3 p-m for all three transformations to apply and to cause a detectable error. The situation may be seen in (20). The dotted lines in (20) indicate a node attached by raising. The split dotted lines indicate that K is attached to D in one component and to E in the other. Thus there is a detectable error on a degree-3 phrase-marker, but no detectable error on a phrase-marker of smaller degree.

What allows this last example is that a node can be used to fit a transformation after being raised nonexplicitly, that is, as part of a subtree dominated by another node, which has been raised. We can rule out this possibility directly by assuming the following principle:

Raising Principle (RP): If a node A is raised, then no node that A dominates may be used to fit a transformation.[5]

(20)

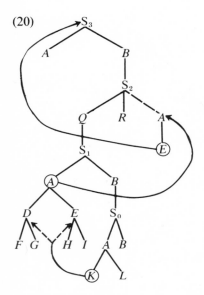

Since the effect of a raised node is the same as that of a frozen node, given the Freezing principle, we can use the same notation; that is, we can put a box around the raised node to indicate that no node that it dominates may be used to fit a transformation.[6] The Raising principle will rule out the example given in (11)–(19) because, since A is raised on cycle S_2, A is frozen by RP, and thus the E that A dominates cannot be raised at cycle S_3. The example given in (8)–(10) does not violate RP and will still be allowed. Therefore, we still can only hope to find a bound of 2, and not 1, on the minimal-degree detectable error for a system on which a detectable error exists.

4.1.8 S-Optionality
We would like the proof to proceed in the following manner. Suppose we have a degree-3 p-m P, as in (21). If a detectable error is created at S_3 and not on a lower cycle, we want to show that a detectable error exists on the degree-2 p-m P' created by dropping the sub-phrase-marker dominated by S_0 and substituting a 0-termination (sometimes known as a 0-extension) of the node D which dominates S_0 (the 0-extension exists by assumption). The idea is that a detectable error at

(21)

$P = S_3$

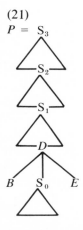

S_3 could not have been caused by nondetectable errors at S_0 because the Binary principle, the Freezing principle, and its extension, the Raising principle, will not allow what happens at S_0 to affect S_3 without causing a detectable error at S_1 or S_2.

The idea, in other words, is that the phrase-marker dominated by S_0 can be treated as a block and that if we substitute some nonsentential phrase (dominated by D) for it, the transformations that apply to S_2 and S_3 won't be affected. But suppose that a transformation T at S_1 depends on analyzing a sister of S_0, say, B (or any node dominated by that sister). If we replace (22a) by some other sub-phrase-marker (22b), it may be that T will not apply to the new p-m P'.

(22)
a.   b. D

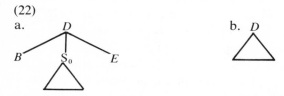

To see that this situation can actually lead to a transformational component in which a detectable error is made on a degree-3 p-m but none on a p-m of degree 0, 1, or 2, we construct an example in which no transformation operates at S_0 or at S_1, a nondetectable error-producing transformation affecting the subtle B operates at S_2, and the detectable

(23) $P =$

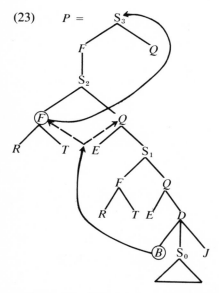

error-producing transformation operates at S_3. On S_2, B is raised by components A and C to different positions, but ones that produce no detectable errors: B is raised to become a right daughter of F by $T_2{}^A$ in A and to become a left daughter of Q by $T_2{}^C$ in C. On cycle S_3, a transformation T_3, which is in both components A and C, raises F and produces a detectable error on the degree-3 p-m P.

Assume that B is introduced on the right-hand side of no base rule except $D \rightarrow BSJ$. Following our plan of attack for the proof, we replace the phrase dominated by D in (23) by a 0-extension (say $[_D GH]$) to create the degree-2 p-m P'. In (24) we assume that $D \rightarrow GH$ is a base rule and that G and H are terminal categories. But $T_2{}^A$ and $T_2{}^C$ will not apply to P' since there is no node labeled B in P'. No error will be created under F on level S_2 and no detectable error will be created at S_3. Thus there is no detectable error on P'. In fact, with a simple formulation of the transformations (we have not bothered to actually define them here) it can be shown that there is no detectable error on any p-m of degree 0, 1, or 2, although there is a detectable error on the degree-3 p-m P.

(24) $P' =$

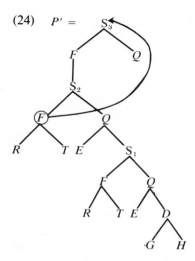

We want to ensure that if a transformation can analyze the sister or niece (or grand-niece, etc.) of an S, then it can continue to apply in the same way when there is no S there. In other words, we want to be able to remove the S and everything it dominates from the phrase-marker without affecting any of the structure outside of the S. The problem with this operation seems to be that it may be possible to drop an embedded S only by replacing it with an entirely different structure. We can simply rule out this possibility by assuming that an S can always be dropped, with the resulting phrase-marker still being a base structure. That is, we assume the following principle:

Principle of S-Optionality: S appears on the right-hand side of a rule in the base grammar only within parentheses denoting optionality, that is, as (S). And there is no rule of the form $A \rightarrow (S)$.

It immediately follows that if D is a node in a base phrase-marker and the immediate structure of D includes an S, then if we drop the sub-phrase-marker dominated by S, the remaining phrase-marker is still base.[7] Thus the principle of S-Optionality will rule out the example in (23)–(24), where $_D[BSJ]$ was a base structure but $_D[BJ]$ wasn't. In other words, whenever we have a structure with an S, we have a corresponding structure without the S. What we want is for a transformational component to behave identically with respect to detectable errors whether or not the S is there.

4.1.9 S-Invisibility

The principle of S-Optionality is not enough, however. It may be that the structural description of a transformation may fit a phrase-marker only when the S is absent. If we drop the lowest (S_0) sentence in a degree-3 p-m P to create a degree-2 p-m P', a transformation T may apply to P' at S_1 which didn't apply to P; this T may have the effect of not allowing a further transformation, which caused a detectable error on P, to apply to P'. There will then be no detectable error in P'.

To see that this can happen, we consider once again the example given in (23)–(24) but add to the base grammar the possibility that $D \rightarrow BJ$ (the rule introducing S now reads: $D \rightarrow B(S)J$), so that the principle of S-Optionality is now satisfied. Let P be as given in (23). P' is formed by dropping from P the sub-phrase-marker dominated by S_0, as shown in the following:

(25) $P' =$

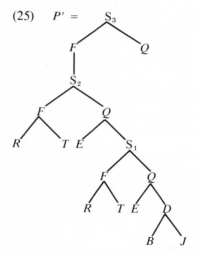

Add to both transformational components, A and C, the rule T: F - E - B - $J \Rightarrow 1$ - $3+2$ - $\emptyset$ - 4. In other words, move B to a position immediately before E. Now, at S_1, T will apply to P' but not to P, since there is no sequence B - J in P, but rather B - S - J. (There is no

(26)

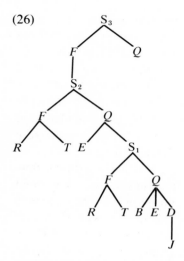

variable in the structural description of T between *B* and *J*.) After applying T at S_1 (the only transformation to apply at S_1) P' becomes (26).

When we showed the transformations T_2^A and T_2^C in example (23)–(24), we didn't have to bother to state their structural descriptions (which are the same for the two transformations). But now let us simply assume that the structural descriptions of T_2^A and T_2^C end with - *E* - *B* - *X* (we'll ignore the part of the S.D. that causes *B* to be raised to a particular position). In other words, *B* can be raised only when it immediately follows *E*. (Actually, even this assumption isn't necessary for our purposes, since the Freezing principle would block T_2^A and T_2^C from applying after T).

Hence T_2^A or T_2^C (depending on the component) will apply to S_1 in *P* and then T_3 will apply, causing a detectable error in *P*. But in *P'*, first T will apply, yielding (26). Then T_2^A and T_2^C will not be able to apply, since the p-m in (26) ends with - *B* - *E* - *J*, not - *E* - *B* - *J*. Thus no error will be created, and therefore no detectable error will occur on *P'*. In fact, for these components, although a detectable error occurs on a degree-3 phrase-marker, no detectable error occurs on a degree-2 p-m.

The problem is that a transformation can be prevented from applying simply by the presence of an S that does not take part in the transformation. To prevent this possibility, we will rule it out by assumption.

We want to formulate a principle of S-invisibility, which says (informally) that if a p-m P differs from a p-m P' only in that an optional S has been inserted into P' where there was no S in P, and if a transformation T applies to P, then T applies to P' with elements of the structural description of T fitting the same nodes in P' as in P and the transformational operations taking place in the same manner for P and P'. In other words, S is simply ignored. The intuition underlying the formulation of the principle seems quite clear, but it takes a little work to make sure there is a formal basis for the intuition.

The purpose of the principle of S-invisibility is to allow a transformation to apply to a p-m that contains an S if it applies to the p-m without the S. Not only this, but the transformation must apply in the same way as if the S were not there. Let T be a transformation with structural description (S.D.) $= B_1 - B_2 - \ldots - B_n$ and structural change (S.C.) $= B_1' - B_2' - \ldots - B_n'$. Each B_i' is a (possibly empty) sequence of integers between 1 and n and inserted morphemes. The point of our analysis: for each position i in the structural description of T, we want to construct a transformation T_i that will behave exactly like T but will ignore an S in the phrase-marker between B_i and B_{i+1}. Thus the first i terms in the S.D. of T_i will be the same as those for T, the next one will be S, and the last terms will be the terms of the S.D. of T from $i+1$ on. The structural change of T_i will also be like that of T but will have to leave S unchanged, shift the terms from $i+1$ on one place to the right, and take account of the fact that there has been a partial renumbering in the S.D. of T_i. Let M be the set of inserted morphemes. First, for any i, $0 \leqslant i \leqslant n$, define a function f_i from $M \cup \{1, \ldots, n\}$ into $M \cup \{1, \ldots, n, n+1\}$ in the following way:

$f_i(k) = k$ for $1 \leqslant k \leqslant i$ or $k \in M$, and
$f_i(k) = k+1$ for $i+1 \leqslant k \leqslant n$.

For $K = k_1 k_2 \ldots k_n$, a string of elements of $M \cup \{1, \ldots, n\}$, the string $f_i(K) = f_i(k_1) f_i(k_2) \ldots f_i(k_n)$.

Definition: Let T be a transformation with S.D. $B_1 - B_2 - \ldots - B_n$ and S.C. $B_1' - B_2' - \ldots - B_n'$. For any i, $0 \leqslant i \leqslant n$, T^i, the *position i S-invisible transformation* of T, has S.D. $C_1 - C_2 - \ldots - C_{n+1}$, where

(i) $C_j = B_j$ for $1 \leqslant j \leqslant i$,
(ii) $C_{i+1} = S$ and
(iii) $C_j = B_{j-1}$ for $i+2 \leqslant j \leqslant n+1$.
The S.C. of T^i is $C_1' - C_2' \ldots \ldots - C_{n+1}'$, where
(iv) $C_j' = f_i(B_j')$ for $1 \leqslant j \leqslant i$,
(v) $C_{i+1}' = i+1$, and
(vi) $C_j' = f_i(B_{j-1}')$ for $i+2 \leqslant j \leqslant n+1$.

Definition: For a transformation T with structural description $B_1 - B_2 - \ldots \ldots - B_n$, let $T^S = \{T^0, T^1, \ldots , T^n\}$ be the *set of S-invisible transformations* of T. For a transformational component $A = \{T_1, T_2, \ldots , T_m\}$, let $A^S = A \cup_1^m T_i^S$ be the *S-invisible amplified transformational component* formed from A. In other words, A^S includes the original transformations in A, plus all the S-invisible transformations that can be formed from these transformations. We can now assume the following principle:

Principle of S-Invisibility: For any transformational component A, in all transformational derivations replace A by the S-invisible amplified transformational component A^S.

For the remainder of this chapter we will assume this principle, always applying A^S; but for simplicity of notation we will identify A with A^S and thus always speak of applying component A.

Example: We can apply the principle of S-Invisibility to the example that gave rise to it. P is defined in (23) and P' is formed from P by dropping S_0, as in (25). The problem now arises that T: $F - E - B - J \Rightarrow 1 - 3+2 - \emptyset - 4$ applies to P' but not to P. Thus later error-producing transformations that apply to P do not apply to P'.

The reason that T doesn't apply is that there is an S in P between B and J, that is, between positions 3 and 4 of the structural description. But consider the position-3 S-invisible transformation T^3. If we apply the definition of S-invisible transformation, we find that T^3: $F - E - B - S - J \Rightarrow 1 - 3+2 - \emptyset - 4 - 5$. T^3 is part of A^S, and by the principle of S-Invisibility, A^S applies in place of A. T^3 applies to level S_1 in P, yielding (27).[8] But T_2^A and T_2^C, the error-producing transformations, won't apply to level S_1 in (27), because their S.D.'s end with $- E - B - X$.

(27) $T^3(P) =$

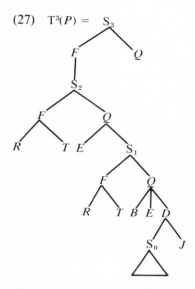

Therefore no detectable error will occur on P, and the principle of S-invisibility has invalidated the counterexample.

4.1.10 The Problem of Dropping S_0

Recall that we want to show that if P is a degree-3 p-m containing a detectable error at the top (S_3) level but none on a lower level, and if the hidden error is created at level S_2, then we still obtain a detectable error if we replace P by a p-m P' created by dropping S_0 from P. How—that is, at what point in the derivation—shall we drop S_0 from P? If certain choices are made, problems arise. There are examples in which the detectable error that occurs on the degree-3 p-m does not show up on the degree-2 p-m.

4.1.10.1 Before Transformations Apply The simplest choice is to drop S_0 before any transformations apply. Let P' be the p-m created by deleting the sub-phrase-marker dominated by S_0 from the base p-m P, as in (28). Clearly P' is still a base p-m, by S-Optionality. Also it is degree 2. Does it follow that a detectable error at level S_3 in P, caused by an error at S_2, implies a detectable error at level S_3 in P'? Unfortunately,

(28)

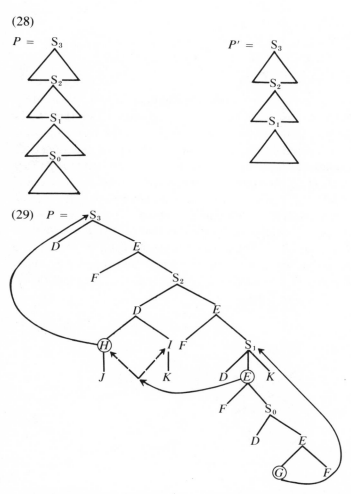

(29) $P =$

no. The problem is that dropping S_0 might not allow transformations to occur at S_1 which are essential for error-producing transformations at S_2, which are themselves essential for a transformation that produces a detectable error at S_3 to operate. For an example, see the phrase-marker P in (29). We take the transformational components to be $A = \{T_1, T_2{}^A, T_3\}$ and $C = \{T_1, T_2{}^C, T_3\}$ where the transformations are defined as

T_1: X - G - Y - K $\Rightarrow$ 1 - $\emptyset$ - 3 - 4+2,
$T_2{}^A$: J - X - E - Y - G $\Rightarrow$ 1+3 - 2 - $\emptyset$ - 4 - 5,
$T_2{}^C$: X - K - Y - E - Z - G $\Rightarrow$ 1 - 4+2 - 3 - $\emptyset$ - 5 - 6 and
T_3: D - X - H - Y $\Rightarrow$ 3+1 - 2 - $\emptyset$ - 4.

At level S_1, G is raised by T_1 (in both grammars A and C). We assume that $S \rightarrow DE(K)(G)$ is a rule of the base grammar, so that T_1 is structure-preserving at the point of attachment and the Freezing principle won't prevent transformations from applying to the raised G node. At S_2 a nondetectable error is created when component $A(T_2{}^A)$ raises E to attach H to the right of J and component $C(T_2{}^C)$ raises E to attach to the left of K. Since there is now an error under H, when H is raised at level S_3, a detectable error is created.

An important point of this construction is that G is in the structural description of $T_2{}^A$ and $T_2{}^C$. Thus G is necessary if an error is to be created. Suppose that we now create P' from P by dropping S_0, as in (30). T_1, which raises G, obviously cannot apply to P', since there is no

(30)

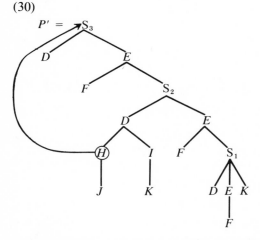

G in P'. But $T_2{}^A$ and $T_2{}^C$, which create the error, cannot apply either, because G is part of their S.D. The only transformation that can apply is T_3, which raises H; but since no error has been created under H, raising H will also not create an error. Therefore there is no detectable error (in fact, no error) on the degree-2 p-m P'.

The problem is that a structure-preserving transformation has created a (base) structure at S_1 which did not exist before the transformation and this structure is essential in order for the error-producing transformation to operate. Thus our hopes are dashed for taking any degree-3 p-m with a detectable error and forming a degree-2 p-m with a detectable error by dropping the most embedded sentence before transformations operate.

But note that in this example there is a degree-2 base p-m on which a detectable error is made, namely the phrase-marker P' given in (31). In

(31)

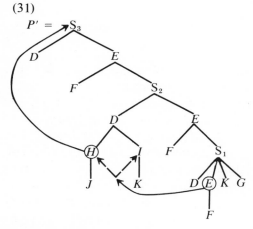

this P', $T_2{}^A$ and $T_2{}^C$ will apply, raising E and creating an error at level S_2. Then a detectable error will be created when T_3 raises H at S_3. This P' (31) was created by dropping S_0 *after* transformations (namely T_1) applied to S_1 in P. Thus we are led to consider the possibility that we can in general create the proper P' by dropping S_0 after all transformations at level S_1 operate.

4.1.10.2 After Transformations Apply With this method of constructing P', however, we run into an immediate problem when we consider non-structure-preserving raising transformations. Suppose P is as given in (32). If, at level S_1, G is raised to be a right sister of I, under D, then P', formed by dropping S_0 after transformations at S_1 apply, becomes (33). But if $D \rightarrow HIG$ is not a base rule, P' will not be a base

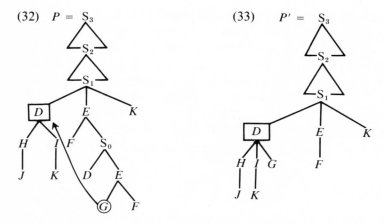

phrase-marker, contrary to what is demanded by our attempt to construct a degree-2 *base* p-m that contains a detectable error.

The obvious suggestion is to convert the nonbase p-m P' into a base p-m by dropping the nonbase structure dominated by the frozen node and substituting a 0-termination of it. Of course, not any 0-termination will do, because a structure might result that would allow a transformation to apply to P' that did not apply to P, and this transformation might prevent the error-producing transformations from applying, as in example (28)–(31). But we can take as the 0-termination the original structure under the frozen node, before the non-structure-preserving raising transformation applied. In (32), for instance, we would simply eliminate the G under D to obtain the P' shown in (34). (34), of course, is the same as the original P in (32) with S_0 deleted. The principle of S-Invisibility assures that any transformation that applies to P' (34) at level S_1 will also apply to P (32) at S_1. We are thus led to the conjecture that the appropriate degree-2 p-m P' can be constructed from the degree-3 p-m P by applying all transformations at S_0 and S_1 to P, then replacing the structures dominated by the highest frozen nodes in S_1 by the structures that these nodes dominated *before* transformations applied, and then dropping S_0.

In fact, if the only raising transformation that applies at level S_1 is a transformation T that raises one node to a non-structure-preserving position, then, given the Freezing principle, the set of possible analyses

(34) $P' = S_3$

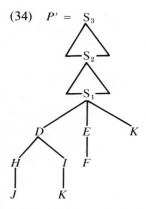

of the top level of S_1 after the transformation applies is a subset of the set of possible analyses *before* the transformation applies. If a transformation T' applies to the top level of S_1 after T applies, then T' must also apply before T applies. But then T and T' apply to the same structure, which is ruled out by the principle of Determinism (see the convention of section 4.1.3). Thus there can be no such T' which applies after T. But since the set of analyses of P' at S_1 equals the set of analyses of P at S_1 before T applies, no transformation can apply to P' at level S_1. Thus it is easy to see that in this case, if there is a detectable error on P, there will be one on P'.[9]

4.1.10.3 Problems of Context Recall that we are trying to find a method for constructing a degree-2 base p-m P' from a degree-3 p-m P so that whenever there is a detectable error on P there is a detectable error on P'. We are considering a method whereby the lowest sub-p-m, S_0, is dropped after transformations apply to S_0 and S_1 and the structure under frozen nodes in S_1 is replaced by the original base structures that these frozen nodes dominated. We want to find out whether this method of construction of P' will work. In the simple case just considered ($P' = (34)$), where the only transformation that applies at level S_1 raises one node in a non-structure-preserving manner, the proof based on the principle of Determinism and the principle of S-Invisibility goes through. That is, if there is a detectable error on P, there is a detectable error on P'. In some other cases the proof doesn't work. Basically they are cases where at S_1, both structure-preserving and non-structure-preserving operations take place, so that transformations may apply to P' that don't apply to P. This can occur in a number of ways. For example, one transformation might perform both a structure-preserving operation and a non-structure-preserving operation at S_1. This might be ruled out by a restriction on the definition of transformations or of raising transformations. However, there is still the possibility that two transformations could perform these operations. As a third possibility, only a structure-preserving raising transformation applies, but the Raising principle (that raised nodes are frozen) makes the structure behave as if there has been both a structure-preserving and non-structure-preserving operation. We will give, as an example, an instance of a fourth case, in which there is a structure-preserving raising, but the raised node has itself been frozen by an earlier transformation. When the frozen material is replaced by a base structure, to form P', a new transformation may apply to P' that does not allow the error-producing transformation to apply. The example will show the need for further assumptions if this method of constructing P' is to work.

In section 4.1.11 we will make these assumptions. Ultimately it will turn out that the method of constructing P' that we are considering is basically correct. It will be used in the final proof of degree-2 error detectability (theorem 8, section 4.4).

As far as possible, we will attempt to keep the same operations and structures as in our previous examples. We will want to raise G in a structure-preserving way, as in (29). However, to satisfy the requirements of the current example we want G to be frozen by a non-structure-preserving transformation applying at S_0. So we let G dominate LM in the base and define a transformation T_0 that moves L to the right of M, under G, thus freezing G, in accordance with the Freezing principle. The p-m P is given in (35). After the transformation (T_0) that moves L and the transformation that raises G apply, P becomes the p-m given in (36). According to our current conception, P' is to be formed by dropping S_0 from (36) and replacing the frozen structure under G with the original base structure that G dominated. This yields (37).

We now add to our transformational components a new transforma-

(35)

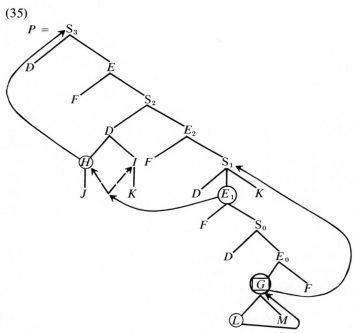

(36)

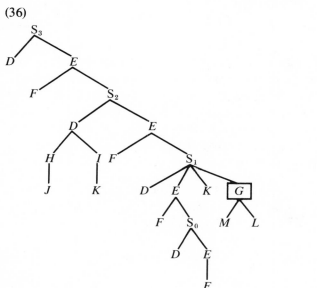

(37)

$P' = $

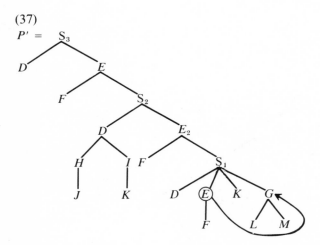

tion, T_1', which applies at level S_1 to P' but does not apply to the transformed P (36) at S_1. T_1' attaches E to the right of M. The resulting structure cannot be fit by the transformations T_2^A and T_2^C which produce the error. Thus there will be no error on P'.

The transformations needed for this example are the same as the four defined after (29), which we repeat below, and two new ones, T_0 and T_1'. That is, we define, $A = \{T_0, T_1, T_1', T_2^A, T_3\}$ and $C = \{T_0, T_1, T_1', T_2^C, T_3\}$ where

(37′)
$T_0: D - L - M - X \Rightarrow 1 - \emptyset - 3{+}2 - 4,$
$T_1: X - G - Y - K \Rightarrow 1 - \emptyset - 3 - 4{+}2,$
$T_1': X - E - Y - L - M \Rightarrow 1 - \emptyset - 3 - 4 - 5{+}2,$
$T_2^A: J - X - E - Y - G \Rightarrow 1{+}3 - 2 - \emptyset - 4 - 5,$
$T_2^C: X - K - Y - E - Z - G \Rightarrow 1 - 4{+}2 - 3 - \emptyset - 5 - 6,$ and
$T_3: D - X - H - Y \Rightarrow 3{+}1 - 2 - \emptyset - 4.$

After T_1' applies to P' (37), the resulting structure is (38). (It is irrelevant to the example whether G is frozen in (38).) The point in the derivation has been reached (cycle S_2) where the error-producing transformations T_2^A and T_2^C must apply. In order for their structural descriptions to be met, E_1 must be to the left of G. But this is not the case in

(38)

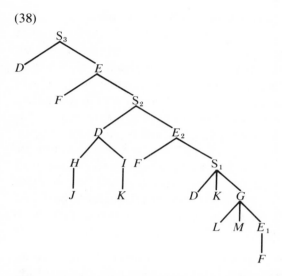

(38), owing to the operation of T_1'. Thus the error-producing trans-formations cannot apply, and there is no error on P'.

T_1' demands in its structural description that the nodes L and M be fit, in that order. Since at level S_1 in P (36) G is frozen, M and L cannot be analyzed, and T_1' cannot apply to P. The derivation of P goes through as before, and there remains a detectable error on P. Thus we still have a counterexample to our claim that we have the proper method of constructing P'. We could try the following interpretation of the Freezing principle: for obligatory transformations (which we have here), if a transformation fits a p-m except that one of the nodes fit by an element of the structural description is under a frozen node (so that the Freezing principle doesn't allow the obligatory transformation to apply), then the derivation is filtered out. If this filtered out (36), it would filter out P for both components A and C, and there would be no detectable error on P. However, the example has been constructed so that this filtering interpretation of the Freezing principle is not sufficient to rule it out as a counterexample. The reason is that T_0 has operated, so even if G were not frozen, T_1' couldn't apply to P (36) at S_1 because its S.D., which demands that L precede M, would not be met. Thus the problem remains.[10,11]

4.1.11 S-Essential Transformations and No Bottom Context

The essence of the example in (35)–(38) is that when P' is formed from P, a new transformation applies to the new 0-degree p-m dominated by S_1. This new transformation destroys the context under S_1 which is required for an error-producing raising transformation to apply at level S_2. But if we do not allow the context of the lower p-m in a degree-1 p-m to play any role in the determination of fit of a transformation that applies to the degree-1 p-m, these examples will be ruled out. In particular, T_2^A could not apply to level S_2 in P because an element of the S.D. of T_2^A, namely G, fits the node G in the lower p-m (S_1). If we ruled out the possibility of this kind of context effect, T_2^A could not apply to P at level S_1. Likewise, T_2^C requires that a context G under S_1 be fit and thus would be ruled out if we didn't allow such context effects. With T_2^A and T_2^C not applying, there is no error on P.

Notation: In this section *dominate* is taken to mean "weakly dominate," so that a node S dominates itself. No theoretical stance is indicated by this notation—if instead it meant "strongly dominate," we would simply change the definitions of other concepts so that their range of application would remain the same.

Definition: Let P be a p-m. Suppose that a transformation T with S.D. $= B_1 - \ldots - B_n$ applies to P at level S_i ($i \geq 1$, so that S_i dominates S_{i-1}). Suppose that for some i, $1 \leq i \leq n$, B_i fits a node in P that is dominated by S_{i-1} and B_i is not a variable. Then we say that T is *S-essential*.

In other words, an S-essential transformation is one for which the embedded S provides material essential to the fit of the transformation. Note that if the node that is fit is the embedded S itself, the transformation is S-essential. Strictly speaking a transformation is really not S-essential; rather, an application of a transformation is, since T may be S-essential in applying in one derivation and not in another. However, since it will cause no misunderstanding, we informally define a transformation to be S-essential. Before we can state the required principle, we will need some definitions. We want to state a principle that says that S-essential transformations can make no use of the context provided by the embedded S.

Definition: Let T be a transformation with S.D. $= B_1 - \ldots - B_n$ and S.C. $= B_1' - \ldots - B_n'$.

(a) Suppose there exists i, j, $1 \leq i, j \leq n$, such that

(i) $B_k' = k$ for all k, $1 \leq k \leq n$, such that $k \neq i, j$,

(ii) $B_i' = \emptyset$, and

(iii) $B_j' = i+j$, or $B_j' = j+i$.

Then we say that T *simply moves* B_i to B_j and T is a *simple movement* transformation. If T simply moves B_i to B_j, and if T applies to a p-m P at level S_h ($h \geq 1$), and if

(iv) S_{h-1} dominates B_i and

(v) S_{h-1} does not dominate B_j,

then T is a *raising* transformation.

(b) Suppose that there exists i, $1 \leq i \leq n$, such that

(i) $B_k' = k$ for all k, $1 \leq k \leq n$ and $k \neq i$ and

(ii) $B_i = \emptyset$.

Then T *simply deletes* B_i and T is a *simple deletion.* If T simply deletes B_i, and if T applies to a p-m P at level S_h ($h \geq 1$), and if

(iii) S_{h-1} dominates B_i,

then T is an *embedded deletion* (sometimes S-*essential deletion*).

(c) If T applies to a p-m P at level S_h ($h \geq 1$), then T is a *no-bottom-context* (NBC) raising (embedded deletion) transformation if T is a raising (embedded deletion) transformation such that the node B_i that T raises (deletes) is the only node dominated by S_{h-1} to which a nonvariable element of the S.D. of T applies.

In other words, a raising transformation moves a phrase from an embedded S to the next higher S, and an embedded deletion transformation deletes a phrase from an embedded S.[12] If these are no-bottom-context transformations, the raised or deleted node is the only node in the embedded sentence that can play a role in fitting the transformation. We can assume:

Principle of No Bottom Context (NBC): If T is an S-essential transformation, then it may apply only if T is a no-bottom-context raising or deletion transformation. In other words, if $T \in A$ or $T \in C$ can apply only in a way such that a node in the embedded S besides the raised or deleted node is fit by a nonvariable element in the S.D. of T, then T does not apply. We do not assume that the derivation is filtered out.

Our principle of No Bottom Context really assumes more than that the context of the embedded structure plays no role in an S-essential T. It also limits S-essential T's to two kinds, those that raise a constituent or those that delete a constituent, with no other effect. Note, though, that we still allow the context of the matrix sentence to play a role in fitting a transformation, though this context can't be changed by the transformation.

The criteria we have put on S-essential transformations are related to much work in syntax. For example, NBC will not allow a transformation to insert from a higher cycle into a lower one (compare Chomsky, 1965).[13] The strong constraints on S-essential transformations (in addition to no bottom context) have been made in order to simplify the proof. Whether they are necessary for the proof remains to be investigated.[14]

Example: Suppose that we define a transformation T: X - B - F - G - Y $\Rightarrow$ 1 - 4+2 - 3 - $\emptyset$ - 5 and apply T to the three phrase-markers in (39). T

(39)

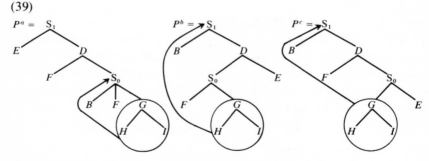

applies to all three phrase-markers in (39), moving G to the left of B. In fact, by definition, T simply moves G to B. The definition of ''simple movement'' depends only on the S.D. and S.C. of the transformation, and not on the p-m to which the transformation is applied. When T applies to P^a at S_0 (or at S_1 if this is not ruled out by some other assumption), T is not a raising transformation, since S_0 dominates B (that is, G is not raised). T applied to P^b, however, *is* a raising transformation, since S_0 does not dominate B (G is raised). T applied to P^b is not a no-bottom-context raising transformation, since F is a nonvariable element of the S.D. of T, which applies to a node (F) dominated by S_0. When T applies to P^c, however, T is a no-bottom-context raising transformation, since F is in the matrix structure and G, the raised element, is the only node in S_0 fit by a nonvariable element of the S.D. of T.

Turning back now to the example that motivated the principle of No Bottom Context, recall that the error-producing transformations were $T_2{}^A$ and $T_2{}^C$, which applied to P (35), raising E from S_1 to the same left-to-right position in S_2 but with different structures. But both $T_2{}^A$ and $T_2{}^C$ demand that an element G of their S.D.s fit P, which is accomplished by fitting G under S_1, even though E and not G is the constituent moved. That is, when $T_2{}^A$ and $T_2{}^C$ apply to P (35) at level S_2, they are not no-bottom-context raising transformations. (Nor are they deletion transformations, of course.) Yet they are S-essential transformations. Therefore, they violate NBC and cannot apply. But then no error is produced on P and the counterexample is avoided.

The general type of counterexample of which this last is an instance is as follows. A transformation applies at S_2 and causes a nondetectable error, which is discovered at S_3. If we attempt to form a degree-2 p-m P' by transforming up to S_1 and then taking 0-extensions of the lowest base structures in S_1 while dropping S_0, it happens that transformations apply to this new P' at S_1 which change the structure of S_1, blocking the error-producing transformations. Thus no error is made on P'. NBC would seem to rule out most of these kinds of examples because an error-producing transformation that operates at S_2 cannot use any context under S_1 to determine its fit. Therefore, even if the context structure has been changed at S_1 in P', still the error-producing transformation will apply.

4.1.12 Transparency of Untransformable Base Structures
Unfortunately, there are still some cases where this argument doesn't apply, cases where the error-producing transformations are blocked from applying at level S_2 in P' for reasons other than the structural context, as context is specified by the NBC principle. So far as we can

see, there are two ways that this can happen. Suppose that an error-producing transformation raises the node D from level S_1 to level S_2. When P' is formed, transformations apply to level S_1 of P' that don't apply to level S_1 of P. If these transformations either delete D or freeze (by FP) a node dominating D, the error-producing transformation at S_2 that raises D can't apply. Thus deletion and freezing are two methods of constructing counterexamples to our attempted proof.

As an example of how the Freezing principle will prevent an NBC error-producing transformation from applying, consider the transformational components A and C, which make use of the transformations defined in (37'). Replace the transformations T_2^A and T_2^C, which raise E when G appears to the right of E, with the transformations U_2^A and U_2^C respectively, which raise E regardless of the right context of E. That is, we define $A = \{T_0, T_1, T_1', U_2^A, T_3\}$ and $C = \{T_0, T_1, T_1', U_2^C, T_3\}$, where the new transformations are defined in (40):

(40)
$U_2^A: J - X - E - Y \Rightarrow 1+3 - 2 - \emptyset - 4$ and
$U_2^C: X - K - Y - E - Z \Rightarrow 1 - 4+2 - 3 - \emptyset - 5.$

When these new transformational components A and C apply to P (35) up to level S_1, they will produce (36), as before. P' (37) is then created, as with the earlier components, by replacing the frozen structures with base structures and dropping S_0. Once again, the transformation T_1' applies to P' at level S_1, although not to P, attaching E to the right of M, under G, yielding (38), repeated here as (41). (T_1', although context-dependent, is not ruled out by NBC, since it is not a raising transformation.) The one difference between (41) and (38) is that we have put a box around G in (41), indicating that it is frozen, that is, that $G \rightarrow LME$ is not a base rule. In (38) we left this unspecified, since whether or not G is frozen was not relevant to the earlier example. But now notice what has happened. When the new components A and C apply to P (35), they produce exactly the same p-m's as the earlier components did, because the new transformations (U_2^A and U_2^C) raise E exactly as did the transformations they replace (T_2^A and T_2^C). Thus a detectable error is created on P. On P' (37), however, first (41) is produced. Since U_2^A and U_2^C raise E independently of the context under S_1, they would

(41)

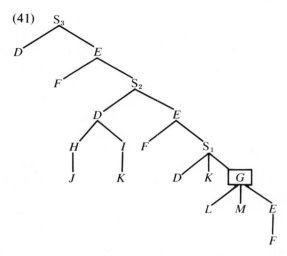

apply to (41) at level S_2. But they can't apply, because E is under a frozen node (G) in (41). Thus the error-producing transformations don't apply to P' and this detectable error on the degree-2 p-m P' does not occur even though there is a detectable error on the degree-3 p-m P and NBC is satisfied.[15]

Suppose that we tried to get around this problem by assuming the interpretation of the Freezing principle discussed at the end of section 4.1.10.3: if obligatory transformations (the kind that we have been assuming) would apply except for FP, the derivation is filtered out. In the current example this interpretation would mean that P' would be filtered out, for both components A and C, so there would be no detectable error on P'. But there would be no filtering on P. Thus a detectable error would remain on P but not on P', and we still have the counterexample.

The other operation that can apply to P' at S_2 and prevent an error-producing transformation from applying at level S_3, even if NBC is satisfied, is deletion of the phrase that would be raised by the error-producing transformation. Suppose that instead of moving E at level S_1 in P' (37), we delete E. This can be done by replacing transformation T_1' (see (37)) by a transformation U_1 which deletes E at level S_1 in P' but not in P (36). For example, we could define $U_1: X$ - E - Y - L - M $\Rightarrow$

1 - $\emptyset$ - 3 - 4 - 5. Then E will be deleted at level S_1 in P' (37), and the error-producing transformations U_2^A and U_2^C cannot apply to P'. Thus there will be no detectable error on P'. But U_1 cannot apply to P at level S_1 (compare (36)) because its structural description is not met (L and M being in the wrong order, even ignoring the freezing of G in (36)). Consequently, E will not be deleted at level S_1 of P, and the error-producing transformations will apply at level S_2, causing a detectable error at level S_3. Once again there is a detectable error on the degree-3 p-m P but none on the constructed degree-2 p-m P'.[16]

The general problem is that when we drop S_0 from P and replace the frozen structures with base structures to form P', it may happen that P' is transformable at S_2 whereas P is not, since no further transformations apply to it. We can rule out this possibility directly by assuming that whenever such an untransformable structure exists, we can find a new base structure that contains the base part of the original structure, the new base structure also being untransformable. In other words, untransformable base structures are transparent, in the sense that they will show up on the surface. First, recall that a partially derived base p-m is a p-m that does not necessarily contain lexical items (terminals) at the bottom nodes.

Definition: If P is a partially derived 0-degree base p-m, a *0-extension* (sometimes simply an *extension*) of P is a p-m created from P by replacing each nonlexical bottom node A of P by a 0-termination of A.

In other words, an extension of P is simply a fully derived 0-degree base p-m of which P is the upper part.

Example: The phrase-marker in (42a) is a partially derived base p-m and (42b) is an extension of (42a).

Principle of the Transparency of Untransformable Base Structures (TUBS): Let P be a partially derived 0-degree base p-m. If no transformations in an adult transformational component A apply to P (that is, none of the S.D.s fits P), then there exists a 0-extension of P to a fully derived base p-m P', such that P' is untransformable by A.

To see how TUBS will rule out our last counterexamples (the one concerning FP, given in (40)–(41) and the one concerning deletion

(42)

a.   b.

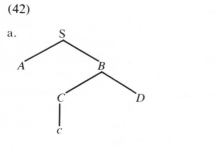
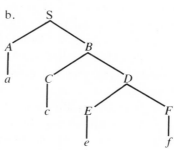

which followed, given by defining U_1), we first observe that P, fully transformed (by component A and also by component C) up to level S_1, is given in (36). No further transformations apply to P at level S_1. By the principle of S-Invisibility, no further transformation will apply to S_1 when we drop S_0. Thus when we drop S_0 we obtain (43) as the sub-p-m dominated by S_1 after all transformations have applied to it. Since no transformations apply to (43), by the definition of transformation it will follow that no transformation will apply to the base structure formed by dropping the sub-p-m dominated by G (except for G). This partially derived base p-m is given in (44). Thus (44) is an untransformable, partially derived 0-degree base p-m. TUBS guarantees that there exists a 0-extension of (44) which itself is untransformable; TUBS doesn't specify exactly which p-m this 0-extension is, but assume for illustrative purposes that it is (45). We now create P' from P by substituting

(43)   (44)

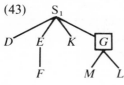
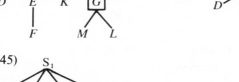

(45)

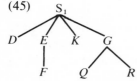

(45) for the p-m dominated by S_1 in P (35). No transformations can operate at level S_1 in P'. In particular, the node E under S_1 in P' can neither be deleted nor placed under a frozen node when transformations operate at level S_1. When the error-producing transformation raises E at level S_2 in P, it raises E in P' also. Therefore, there will be an error—and at S_3 a detectable error—on the degree-2 p-m P'. In general, TUBS works because it insures that the base structure of the transformed S_1 in P is recapitulated in the base structure of the transformed S_1 in P'.[17] By recapitulating this base structure, TUBS insures that the Freezing principle does not siphon off the error-producing configuration on a degree-2 p-m while not siphoning off the error on a degree-3 p-m.

Note that TUBS is not an absolute transparency principle (the opposite of "absolute neutralization," where some base structure never shows up as a surface structure). Such an absolute transparency principle would say that for any partially derived 0-degree phrase-marker P, there exists a 0-extension P' of P such that P' is untransformable. In other words, all base structures show up as surface structures. The absolute principle implies that the appropriate 0-extension exists for *any* structure, whereas the weaker TUBS principle that we have adopted requires only that the appropriate 0-extension exists for those structures that are themselves not transformable.[18]

4.1.13 Uniqueness and Ordering of S-Essential Transformations

An earlier problem arose when we raised a constituent containing an error in such a way that the error was hidden on that cycle but appeared on the next cycle, when a constituent under the previously raised node was itself raised again. Our solution to this problem was to block the raising of this latter node (that is, to adopt the Raising principle).

But there are other ways in which errors on one cycle may be raised and yet remain hidden.[19] These involve raising two (or more) nodes, where each of the nodes contains an error, preserving the sequence. Consider the p-m P in (46).

The operations that we want to construct are similar to ones we have created in earlier examples and can be defined transformationally. To

(46)

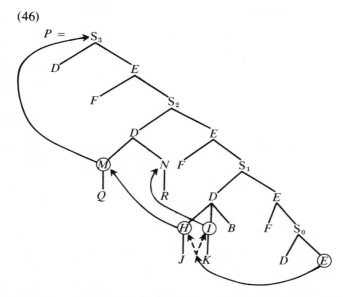

save space we won't define the transformations formally. Their operations are straightforward and should be clear from the diagram in (46)
and the following description (but see note 20).

No transformations apply at level S_0. At level S_1, E is raised to a
position between J and K. An error is made here: component A right-
adjoins E to J, whereas component C left-adjoins E to K (in component
A, E becomes a daughter of H; in component C, E becomes a daughter
of I). But the error is hidden, since E is in the same left-right position in
both components. Thus there is no detectable error at level S_1.

At level S_1, H and I both contain errors, that is, the strings they
dominate in C are different from the strings they dominate in A. At
level S_2, H and I are both raised (in the same manner for both components A and C). H is raised to become a right sister of Q under M, and I
is raised to become a left sister of R under N. Thus the error remains
hidden, because the same left-right positioning of terminal categories
has been preserved. This can be seen in (47). $A^2(P)$, which is P transformed up to level S_2 by component A, appears in (47a); $C^2(P)$, which
is P transformed up to level S_2 by component C, appears in (47b). The
terminal string of S_2 after transformations is $QJEKRFBFD$ for both

(47)

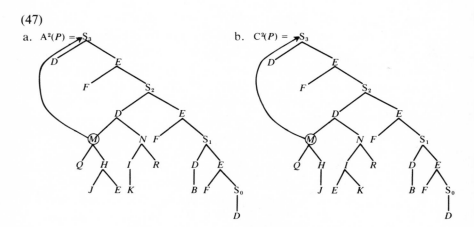

a. $A^2(P) = S_3$ b. $C^2(P) = S_3$

phrase-markers. Therefore, there is no detectable error at level S_2.[20] At level S_3, M is raised to the front of the p-m. Since M dominates different terminal strings in A and C (QJE for A and QJ for C), a detectable error is created at level S_3, although there is no detectable error on a p-m of degree 2 or less.

What makes this case different from earlier cases, and what makes the Raising principle inapplicable here, is that the detectable-error-producing transformation does not here have to raise a node dominated by a node that has been previously raised. Rather, a node (M) that dominates the raised node (H) is raised. (It is not even the raised node (H) itself that is further raised, so we can't take care of the situation by assuming that the node that dominates a raised node is frozen—that is, that M itself can move, but nothing that M dominates.) A case analogous to the earlier Raising principle case would have arisen if we had assumed (in (46)) that the D in cycle S_1 (which immediately dominates HIB) had been raised to S_2. Then a detectable error could be caused by raising H or I from under D to S_3, but RP will prevent this last operation.

The crux of the problem with examples like (46) seems to be that a pair of adjacent nodes are raised to a higher S where they remain adjacent (and in the same order, of course). It would seem natural, at least for these examples, to attempt to rule this possibility out directly. But it is not at all clear how to do this. One natural possibility would be to assume that a phrase, once broken up, cannot reconstitute itself; for instance, if HI is a phrase and H is moved, then I cannot be moved to the right of H to re-form the phrase. But this assumption isn't even sufficient for our current example (46), because that phrase-marker has been deliberately constructed so that HI does not constitute a phrase in S_1, before movement. Rather, HIB is a phrase.

A stronger formulation could be tried: if H and I are adjacent nodes, in that order (I is right-adjacent to H), and if H and I are both raised, the transformations that raise H and I cannot raise them so that I is right-adjacent to H.[21] But even this principle is not strong enough; though the raising transformations might not raise I so that it is right-adjacent to H, further non-S-essential transformations might apply which would have the same effect. Therefore, we could try an even stronger principle.

Principle of Adjacency: If H and I are both nodes in a p-m P, and I is right-adjacent to H, and if H and I are *explicitly* raised by distinct raising transformations (that is, not as part of a larger phrase), then if it ever happens again (after the raising transformations have applied) in the derivation of P that I is right-adjacent to H, the derivation is filtered out. (All statements about right-adjacency must be generalized, of course, to include left-adjacency.)

The principle of Adjacency will rule out (46) because H and I are adjacent and are both explicitly raised and are adjacent again. We think that the principle of Adjacency is strong enough to take care of all these kinds of counterexamples. If it runs into trouble in ways that we don't now foresee, another (possibly stronger) Adjacency principle could be tried; namely, if H and I are two *terminal category* nodes in a p-m P, I right-adjacent to H, and if H and I are both raised, but by separate transformations, then if it ever happens again in the derivation of P (after the raising) that I is right-adjacent to H, the derivation is filtered out. Given all our other assumptions, these two principles may turn out to be equivalent. The way that this modified principle will rule out our last example (46) is that for component A, say, K is right-adjacent to E, E and K were raised by separate transformations (E when H is raised, K when I is raised), and after the raising K is again right-adjacent to E. Thus the modified principle of Adjacency would filter out the derivation under component A. A similar kind of statement would filter out the derivation under component C.

In general, the principle of Adjacency says that if an adjacency bond is broken up by a raising, it can never be put back together. If this turned out to be descriptively adequate, it might even be extended to apply not only to raising but to all aspects of a derivation. That is, it might turn out that if an adjacency bond is ever broken up, it can never be put back together.

Although we have no reason to believe that the principle of Adjacency will not be sufficient for the purposes of the proof in this chapter, we would like to replace it with another assumption that seems to make the proof more manageable. Looking again at (46), it is clear that to produce counterexamples of this type, it is necessary that two raising transformations apply at one cycle (in this case the transformations that raise H and I at cycle S_2). If we rule out this possibility, none of these counterexamples can exist. (Recall that the Raising principle takes care of problems of this kind when there is only one raising transformation.) Therefore, we assume another principle:

Principle of Uniqueness of S-Essential Transformations (USET): At most one S-essential transformation may apply on each cycle.

As with a number of our other principles, USET can be interpreted in a number of ways. First, we could make it a condition on the transformational components. Second, we could require that if an S-essential transformation T_1 applies at a cycle, and if another S-essential transformation T_2 then fits the phrase-marker, T_2 does not apply. Or third, we could filter out any derivation in which two S-essential transformations applied on a cycle. Any of these interpretations will allow the proof to go through.

It is an interesting question whether two S-essential transformations ever apply on the same cycle. Or, more specifically, whether two raising transformations ever apply on the same cycle. See chapter 7 for some discussion. We have assumed this principle (USET) here because it makes the proof less cumbersome, while clearing up the particular kinds of counterexamples that we have just encountered. We think that the principle of Adjacency in place of USET will also allow the proof to go through, though more clumsily in the notation.

While we are making assumptions about S-essential transformations, we might as well make it easier on ourselves again, in attempts at a proof, by assuming still another principle:

Principle of Ordering of S-Essential Transformations (OSET): At a cycle, the S-essential transformations (at most one, given USET) apply before the non-S-essential transformations.

The OSET principle can be interpreted in any of the three ways that USET can. Moreover, OSET implies that no S-essential transformation can apply after a non-S-essential transformation, even if the non-S-essential transformation creates a context that would allow the S-essential transformation to apply.[22]

The Principle of Ordering of S-Essential Transformations can be looked upon as an extension of the strict transformational cycle, since it implies that if S_i dominates S_{i-1}, transformations that apply to elements in S_{i-1} must precede transformations that apply only to elements in S_i. Once again, it would be important to test the descriptive adequacy of OSET. At the moment, we are not sure OSET is necessary in the proof, though it is certainly convenient.

4.2 Necessity of Assumptions

For systems as complicated as the ones that we are considering, it is difficult to obtain absolute necessity results for properties of learnable classes of grammars. That is, it is difficult to prove that a constraint K (not tautologous to the definition of learnability, of course) must hold for every grammar in every learnable class of grammars. The reason is that if K does not hold, we can strengthen other properties, to the point of making the class of grammars learnable. In the absurd extreme, we can strengthen the definition of allowable grammars, so that there is only one grammar in the class (obeying no external constraints, say). This class, then, is of course trivially learnable. The point is to find empirically adequate properties that make the class of grammars learnable.

Despite this situation, an important class of necessity results can often be obtained. These are relative necessity results, results showing that for a given set of properties of grammars that can be proved to determine a learnable system, if we remove one property K, the class of grammars is no longer learnable. Thus K is a *necessary property* of the system.

These relative necessity results become quite important in the system we are analyzing. We have made a large number of assumptions, many of them in order to handle particular kinds of counterexamples to the hypothesis that if a transformational grammar makes a detectable error on a phrase-marker, the grammar makes a detectable error on a phrase-marker of degree less than or equal to 2. It is important to ask whether each of our assumptions is necessary (in this relative sense). The assumptions have been made in the belief, of course, that they are necessary, and they have been made sequentially to handle particular counterexamples. If it had been clear how to explain a counterexample on the basis of other assumptions in the system, a new assumption would not have been made. Without proof, however, it is quite conceivable that a convoluted combination of a subset of assumptions in a particular case would render another assumption unnecessary.

We have made five major structural assumptions about transformational grammars, distinct from the usual definitions and assumptions about these grammars existent in the linguistic literature (such as the definition of transformation, the cycle, and so on). We will now consider the relative necessity of each of these principles. They are as follows:

Binary Principle (BP)
Freezing Principle (FP)
Raising Principle (RP)
Principle of No Bottom Context (NBC)
Principle of the Transparency of Untransformable Base Structures (TUBS)

4.2.1 Binary Principle

At first sight, it seems clear that the Binary principle would be necessary for learnability; that is, without BP we could not prove that the existence of a detectable error implies the existence of a degree-2 detectable error. For if a transformation can apply more deeply than one S down from the current cycle, the transformation can be defined so as to require for its operation a p-m of large degree.

Example: The base grammar contains the following as its only nonterminal rules:

$$S \rightarrow \left\{ \begin{matrix} B \\ D \\ E \\ F \\ G \end{matrix} \right\} H$$

$$H \rightarrow I(S)$$

We define a transformation T, with structural description B - X - D - Y - E - Z - F - U - G - V, where X, Y, Z, U, V are variables; T will apply to the degree-4 p-m P given in (48). Suppose that T makes a detectable error on P. It is clear from the definition of T and the base grammar that T does not apply to any p-m of degree less than 4 (owing to the deliberate construction of the base grammar, with B, D, E, F, G in complementary distribution) and so cannot make a detectable error on any p-m of degree less than 4. Therefore, learnability from degree-2 data cannot be proved.[23]

But the possibility exists that BP itself is not necessary, that a modification of it might suffice. Perhaps transformations can apply indefinitely deep (for example, over variables), *but* there is always a small-degree phrase-marker on which the transformation could be learned. This wasn't the case with (48), but something is unsatisfactory about that example. In particular, the structural description of the transformation T is quite complicated. Perhaps if we made an assumption that limited the complexity of transformations, we could do without BP; that is, we could show that if a detectable error exists on some p-m,

(48)

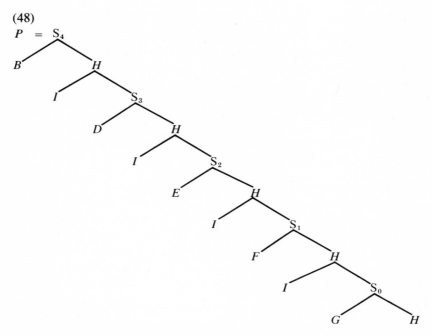

there is a small-degree p-m on which a detectable error exists. The example in (48) wouldn't be possible because T has too large an S.D. It is conceivable that this approach might work (but see note 11).

It might not even be necessary to go to an additional assumption in order to replace the Binary principle. One of our existing assumptions may do just this job, that is, ensure that transformations apply to some small-degree phrase-markers, even without BP. In particular, the principle of No Bottom Context might do the job. Actually, NBC is formulated so as to be compatible with BP: given that the depth that transformations can penetrate is one level down, only certain kinds of transformations can penetrate down that far (namely, those in which one phrase is raised or deleted and which don't depend on the context of the embedded S).

But we can extend NBC in a natural way to apply to transformations that apply deeper than one embedded S. If the Binary principle doesn't hold, we first say that an (extended) S-essential transformation T is one in which a nonvariable element of the S.D. of T fits a node dominated by an embedded S. This is the same definition of S-essential transformation as previously, but with BP not holding, it applies to a wider class of transformations. Now the extended NBC is simply as follows:

Extended Principle of No Bottom Context (NBC):
i. The only S-essential transformations are ones that raise one phrase or delete one phrase in an embedded S, and
ii. Only the context of the *matrix* (top) S can play a role in fitting the S.D. of the transformation (none of the context of any of the embedded S's can play a role).[24]

With this extended NBC it would appear that only two levels are necessary for fitting a transformation T: the matrix level, at which T applies, and the level from which a phrase is raised or deleted. Therefore we could create a degree-1 phrase-marker P' from a p-m P by eliminating all levels between the level at which T applies and the level from which a phrase is raised and by eliminating the embedded p-m's under the level from which a phrase is raised. T would apply to P' as well as to P.

Example: The phrase-marker from (48) is repeated here as (49a). Suppose that T raises F to become the left sister of B, that is, we define T: $B - X - F - Y \Rightarrow 3+1 - 2 - \emptyset - 4$. T is consistent with the extended NBC since the only context for the application of T is B, which is at the level at which T applies. Although P is a degree-4 phrase-marker, we can construct a degree-2 p-m P' by deleting all S's between the matrix level (S_4) and the level from which F is raised (S_1) and by deleting all S's dominated by the level from which F is raised (in this case only S_0). P' is shown in (49b). In general, S-Optionality will allow the appropriate S's to be dropped. P' is a degree-1 p-m to which T applies, raising F to the left of B.

If this procedure for constructing P' can always be applied (as appears at first sight to be the case), the Binary principle will not be necessary. Rather, the extended principle of No Bottom Context will always allow a transformation that applies to a complex phrase-marker to apply to a small one.

This argument is not quite right, however. There is at least one clear case where the procedure will not result in a degree-1 p-m to which the

(49)

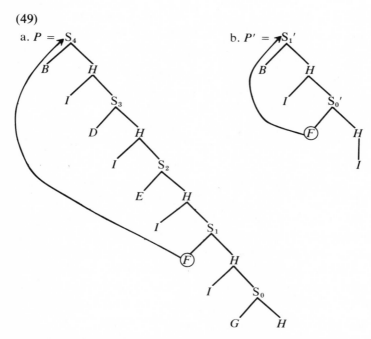

a. $P = S_4$

b. $P' = S_1'$

transformation applies. In addition, depending on other assumptions that must be made about S-essential transformations operating without the Binary principle, other counterexamples turn up.

The clear case involves the one way in which the context of an embedded S may affect the fit of an S-essential transformation, by specifying a boundary (between S's) category. This possibility was discussed in note 14. The example is rather tortuous and perhaps other, simpler, cases exist. But it is important to show that given current assumptions the Binary principle is necessary.

A degree-2 phrase-marker P to which a transformation that violates the Binary principle applies is presented in (50a); (50b) shows the degree-1 p-m P' that was constructed from P according to the method outlined. An error-producing transformation (T_2^A in component A and T_2^C in component C) raises M from S_0 to S_2 in P, violating BP. An error is made because T_2^A attaches M as a right sister of J, whereas T_2^C attaches M as a left sister of K. We can assume that the error is

(50)

a. $P =$

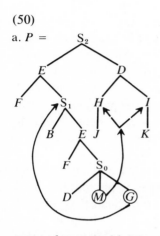

b. $P' =$

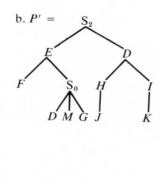

exposed at some higher cycle (not shown) by, say, raising H. Therefore there is a detectable error on a degree-3 p-m containing P. However, we want a condition on the raising of M; namely, we want M raised only when it is at the right boundary of S_0. In order for M to become a right boundary, we will raise G at cycle S_1. These operations can be affected by the following definitions of transformations.[25]

T_1: B - X - G - Y $\Rightarrow$ 3+1 - 2 - $\emptyset$ - 4
$T_2{}^A$: X - M - J - Y $\Rightarrow$ 1 - $\emptyset$ - 3+2 - 4
$T_2{}^C$: X - M - J - K - Y $\Rightarrow$ 1 - $\emptyset$ - 3 - 2+4 - 5

At cycle S_1, T_1 raises G. Then at cycle S_2, $T_2{}^A$ or $T_2{}^C$ (in components A and C, respectively) raises M, producing an error, which is uncovered at the next cycle (S_3, not shown). (Although it appears that the Freezing principle will interfere with this argument, we will shortly show why it doesn't have to.)

None of these transformations applies to P'. Since level S_1 has been eliminated, there is no B in P', so G cannot be raised by T_1; and $T_2{}^A$ and $T_2{}^C$ cannot apply, because the G between M and J prevent their structural descriptions from being met. The consequence is no error on P' and, of course, no detectable error on a higher cycle caused by the nonoccurring detectable error.

There is a possible objection to our analysis. Although the error-producing transformations don't apply to P' as we have constructed it, they will apply to a modification of the construction. First, note that since a later transformation applies to M, it must be that the raising of G is structure-preserving at the point of deletion (otherwise the Freezing principle would prevent a transformation from applying to M); that is, $S \rightarrow DM$ is a rule of the base grammar. Therefore we can modify P' to obtain a degree-1 base phrase-marker P'' by replacing the string DMG under S_0 by the string DM. With G no longer there, the error-producing transformations T_2^A and T_2^C can apply to P'', a degree-1 phrase-marker.

To this move we have the following response. We add a transformation T_0 to both components, the point of T_0 being to prevent the error-producing transformations. Since the structure of S_0 in P is different from the structure of S_0 in P'', we can define T_0 so that it applies to P'' but not to P. For example, we can take T_0 to simply delete M; that is, $T_0: D - M \Rightarrow 1 - \emptyset$. Since M no longer exists, it can't be raised. Alternatively, we could take $T_0: D - M \Rightarrow 2+1 - \emptyset$; that is, T_0 could permute D and M. The structure of S_0 in P', after being transformed (by T_0) would consist of a frozen (boxed) S_0 node dominating M and D ($_{S_0}[MD]$). Since S_0 is frozen, M may not be raised at S_1. Thus there is no error on P'. T_0 cannot apply to P because with G in S_0, the structural description doesn't fit. Therefore, for P, S_0 is not frozen, M can be raised at S_1, and the error remains. (Of course, the example depends on there being no automatic, unspecified end variables that would allow T_0 to fit P. But we haven't assumed these, and if we did, perhaps other examples exist.) Now, it may seem that, after all, T_0 will apply to P at cycle S_1 after G is raised. But, applying at S_1, T_0 is an S-essential transformation, and it doesn't fit the requirements on S-essential transformations laid down by NBC. On the other hand, T_0 can't apply to cycle S_0 after G is raised at cycle S_1, by the cyclic principle. Therefore, in fact, T_0 cannot apply to P, and there is nothing to prevent the error-producing transformations from applying to P.

We have shown that even if we adopt the extended NBC, relaxing the Binary principle allows the existence of a detectable error on a degree-3 p-m, whereas no detectable error exists on any degree-2 p-m. Therefore we have proved that the Binary principle is (relatively) necessary for the proof of learnability.

Can the Binary principle be shown to be necessary in a way that does not depend on the subtle use of the boundary context? Do examples that prove its necessity exist? In attempting to answer these questions we have to consider the kinds of assumptions that will have to be made when the Binary principle is relaxed. In particular, we have to consider what kinds of S-essential transformations can apply and what the principles of ordering these transformations are. In dealing with the example shown in (50), we suggested that NBC could be extended in a natural way to S-essential transformations that do not conform to the Binary principle. Other questions remain, however.

Recall that for the sake of making our current proof easier, we have assumed that only one S-essential transformation can apply at any cycle (USET). However, it seems likely that the principle of Adjacency can replace this assumption. At least, invoking the principle of Adjacency can solve the only counterexamples to our hypothesis that we have found for which we must invoke the assumption of one S-essential transformation per cycle. Therefore we should eventually look to see whether the same situation holds of our transformational system without the Binary principle. That is, if we allow more than one S-essential transformation per cycle, are the only counterexamples also counterexamples to the principle of Adjacency?

It is not at all clear what kinds of assumptions to make about how relaxing the Binary principle can allow restrictions on S-essential transformations to be violated. As a perhaps natural beginning, which differs minimally from the BP case (that is, which generalizes from USET in one simple direction), we can assume that at any cycle S_i, for any cycle S_j lower than S_i (that is, $j < i$), there is at most one S-essential transformation involving S_j. According to NBC these S-essential transformations can only raise or delete one phrase. So we have assumed that at a cycle, one transformation can operate into each of the embedded S-dominated phrase-markers, raising or deleting one phrase and not using any of the other context of the embedded phrase-markers.

These assumptions still don't answer the question of how these S-essential transformations are ordered with respect to each other. In the case of the Binary principle we assumed that S-essential transformations operate before non-S-essential transformations (OSET). It is a natural extension of this principle to assume that, at a cycle, transformations involving a lower embedded S will apply before transformations involving higher embedded S. That is, at cycle S_i, for all embedded sentences S_j, S_k (j, $k < i$), a transformation fitting a node dominated by S_j applies before a transformation fitting a node dominated by S_k if and only if $j < k$ (that is, S_k dominates S_j).

What we are trying to do is to see, when the Binary principle is dropped and these other constraints on the application and ordering of transformations are invoked, whether the existence of an error implies the existence of an error on a degree-1 phrase-marker (an error that is then uncovered one cycle later). Consider the p-m P sketched in (51).

(51) $P = $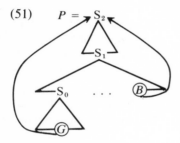

In P, two transformations apply. First, according to the ordering principle, G is raised from S_0 to S_2 (violating the Binary principle). Then B is raised from S_1 to S_2. Suppose that one of these transformations causes an error that is discovered at cycle S_3. Thus there is a detectable error on a degree-3 phrase-marker. Is there a detectable error on a degree-2 p-m? We can try a construction similar to that tried in example (50). Say that G causes the error. Then we can drop the top of S_1 (leaving S_2, and directly embedding S_0 in S_2). This gives us a degree-1 p-m P' that should allow G to be raised, again causing the error. Or, if raising B causes the error, we can drop S_0 to form P' and obtain the error caused by raising B in a degree-1 p-m. If both B and G cause errors, we select the construction of P' according to which of the errors is uncovered at cycle S_3.

Although this construction will work for many cases, it does not take into consideration the possibility of an interaction between the transformations that apply at cycle S_2 to S_0 and S_1. Suppose, for example, that the transformation that raises B from S_1 to S_2 can apply only if there is in the matrix sentence (S_2) a node labeled G, which has been put there by the transformation that raises G from S_0 to S_2. Then dropping S_1 or S_0 will not allow the interaction that produces the error-producing transformation.

Once again, however, note that if the raised G helps to determine the fit of the transformation that raises B, it follows from the Freezing principle that the grammar allows G to be generated directly in the base in the position in S_2 that it is raised into. Therefore we can construct P' by putting G into the matrix (S_2) level via the base rules, dropping S_0 and raising B from S_1 to S_2, and thus causing an error (this latter transformation allowed by the node labeled G in S_2).

This possibility can sometimes be vitiated by the following operations: If G is introduced into the top level of S_2 by a base rule, the nodes that G dominates may affect the phrase-marker via a transformation in ways different from the effect of the nodes G dominates if it is raised from S_0. There are at least three ways this can happen: via different structures under G, owing to transformations applying at S_0; via the Freezing principle; and via the Raising principle. In the case of P', where G is introduced by a base rule, transformations can operate which don't operate in P. These transformations can undo the error caused by raising B, or can cover it over in such a way that it can't be discovered at level S_3.

Again, to make these complicated possibilities clear, we resort to example. Consider the p-m P introduced in (52a). P', in (52b), has been constructed as just described, that is, by putting G into the S_2 level by means of the base rules, and dropping S_0. P is a degree-2 phrase-marker. At cycle S_0, transformation T_0 deletes Q, which is dominated by G. No transformations apply at cycle S_1. At cycle S_2, two transformations apply, both of them raising nodes. First, according to the ordering principle (the generalized OSET), the transformation that raises G from level S_0 to level S_2 applies. We call this transformation $T_{2,0}$ (adopting the notation that $T_{i,j}$ is an S-essential transformation that applies at level S_i and raises or deletes a phrase from level S_j, $j < i$). Then a transformation raising B from level S_1 to level S_2 applies. This

(52)

a. $P =$ b. $P' =$

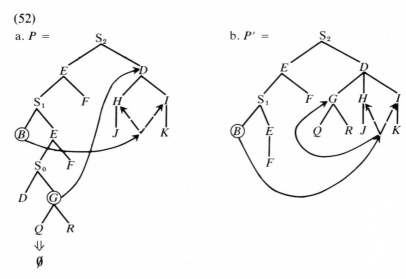

transformation makes an error; in component A, B is attached to the right of J, in component C, B is attached to the left of K. These transformations are called $T_{2,1}^A$ and $T_{2,1}^C$ respectively. The transformation that raises B is to be made dependent on there being a G in the matrix (top) sentence; thus the transformation will apply to P because $T_{2,0}$ has raised G.

P' has been constructed by putting G into the (structure-preserving) position to which it has been raised by $T_{2,0}$ and by dropping S_0. In addition, we assume that the deletion of Q (under G) in P is not structure-preserving, so in order to obtain a base structure for P' we have to expand G into a base structure. The only expansion that we know will be a base structure is $G \rightarrow QR$. (We assume that there are no others.)

B will be raised from S_1 to S_2 by $T_{2,1}^A$ and $T_{2,1}^C$, creating an error. But then the error is undone, because in the context of Q, B is moved to the left of Q. This movement does not depend on the structural position of B, only on the fact that B is to the right of Q. Therefore, it will apply to B in both components A and C, and both components will move B to the same place, even though B started out before the movement in different places. We call this transformation, which moves B in the presence of

Q, transformation T_2. T_2 cannot apply to P because Q has been deleted.[26] In (53) we show $A(P)$, which is P after all transformations in A apply to it, and $A(P')$, which is P' after all transformations in A have applied. $C(P)$ is the same as $A(P)$ except that B is attached as a left daughter of I (a left sister of K) and thus there is an error, but not a detectable

(53)

a. $A(P) =$ b. $A(P') =$

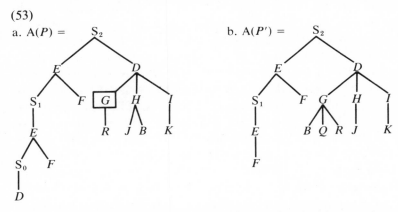

error on P. We can assume that at cycle S_3 a detectable error is created by raising H, which will dominate JB in $A(P)$ and J in $C(P)$. But in P', B has been moved to the left of Q, and $A(P') = C(P')$. Therefore, there is no error on P'. When H is raised at cycle S_3, it will dominate J in both components and no error (much less detectable error) will be created. Therefore, although there is a detectable error on a degree-3 p-m, there is no detectable error on the degree-2 p-m that we have constructed. In fact, there is no error in this example on any degree-2 p-m. Thus, if we can show that these transformations can exist, we have demonstrated the necessity of the Binary principle via a different kind of example.

The desired operations can be attained if we define the transformations in the following way.

T_0: $D - Q - X \Rightarrow 1 - \emptyset - 3$
$T_{2,0}$: $X - G - Y - H - Z \Rightarrow 1 - \emptyset - 3 - 2+4 - 5$
$T_{2,1}{}^A$: $X - B - Y - G - Z - H - W \Rightarrow 1 - \emptyset - 3 - 4 - 5 - 6+2 - 7$
$T_{2,1}{}^C$: $X - B - Y - G - Z - K - W \Rightarrow 1 - \emptyset - 3 - 4 - 5 - 2+6 - 7$
T_2: $X - Q - Y - B - Z \Rightarrow 1 - 4+2 - 3 - \emptyset - 5$

In particular, it should be noted in these examples that G is necessary in order to raise B (S.D.'s of $T_{2,1}{}^A$ and $T_{2,1}{}^C$). Also, T_2 will undo the error by moving B and attaching it to Q.

We have demonstrated in this example the (relative) necessity of the Binary principle. It is conceivable that new assumptions could be made that would rule out this example without invoking BP. But how to do this is not clear. The kind of example we are dealing with here is one in which the result of replacing a nonbase structure (in this case R under G) with a base structure (in this case QR under G) is that a transformation (T_2) applies which destroys the error. We have seen cases like this before. In fact, cases like this forced us to create the principle of Transparency of Untransformable Base Structure (TUBS). Recall that untransformable 0-extensions are required to exist only for untransformable structures. But suppose that we made an equivalent assumption here; that is, we assumed that an extension of G, after it had been raised into the top of S_2, existed such that S_2 was no longer transformable. In that case, since B can be raised, transforming S_2, we would be requiring that *any* partially derived phrase-marker could be extended to a 0-termination so that the 0-termination was untransformable. (Earlier we called this an absolute transparency principle.) But such a requirement would rule out the possibility of any transformations ever being able to apply, since the definition of transformation implies that a transformation applies to the entire set of extensions of a structure fit by the transformation's structural description. Therefore, this absolute transparency principle cannot be accepted. Whether there are more reasonable assumptions that will allow the Binary principle to be replaced is at present unknown. Nor do we know whether we have exhausted the class of types of examples that show that the Binary principle is (relatively) necessary. Conceivably, there are others.[27]

4.2.2 Freezing Principle

The Freezing principle eliminates the possibility of many types of derivations. But in order for the principle to be shown to be (relatively) necessary to the learnability proof, it has to rule out particular kinds of S-essential (probably raising) operations not ruled out by the other constraints. This is because the only constraint the current learnability criterion imposes on efficiency of learning is that it be done on data of degree less than or equal to 2.[28] Although we started this analysis with FP as a basic assumption, we have since adopted a number of other constraints. The Raising principle eliminates a number of possibilities. The principle of No Bottom Context, especially, appears as if it might make FP unnecessary. The reason is the great strength of NBC, which puts severe constraints on what an S-essential transformation might do.

There nevertheless remain at least two kinds of examples that show the necessity of the Freezing principle. The first are cases in which an operation that violates FP prevents the deletion of a phrase that is then raised to cause an error. NBC won't allow the context of the bottom phrase to play a role in fitting the error-causing transformation, but the transformation can still tell whether or not a phrase of the appropriate category is in the bottom phrase, ready to be raised. The second kind of cases involve the ability of a raising transformation to tell whether the phrase to be raised is a boundary phrase.

An example of the first (deletion) kind of example is the p-m P in (54a). In P, B is raised by transformation T_1 to a position to the right of

(54)

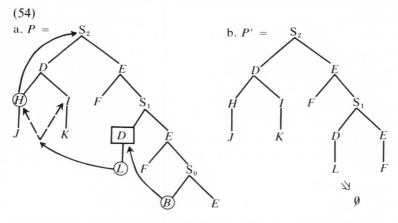

L, under D. We assume that this operation is non-structure-preserving at the point of attachment, that is, $D \rightarrow LB$ is not a base rule. We have put a box around D to indicate that it would be frozen if FP held, although we are assuming that it does not hold, in this example. We can define T_1: L - X - B - $Y \Rightarrow 1 + 3$ - 2 - $\emptyset$ - 4. Now, at the next level, cycle S_2, L is raised under H by component A and under I by component C. This causes an error, but not a detectable error. These transformations can be defined in a straightforward manner, as the error-producing transformations in previous examples were. (That is, write a right attachment of L to J in component A, and a left attachment to K in component C.) If FP held, this transformation could not apply, because L is under the frozen node D. But since we are not assuming FP, the transformation can apply. If H is now raised on the next (S_3) cycle, a detectable error is created on a phrase-marker of degree 3.

Can we find a p-m of degree 2 on which a detectable error is created? In an attempt to do this, we create P' (54b) as in our previous examples: we delete S_0 and extend the base part of S_1 (that is, up to D) to a 0-termination. This yields P'. By NBC, the transformation that raises L cannot pay attention to the context in S_1; therefore L is raised to S_2 in P', causing an error (unless the transformation is written so as to make L a boundary; we will show how that can happen after this example). Then when H is raised on cycle S_3, a detectable error is created on the degree-2 phrase-marker P'.

However, suppose we add a transformation T that deletes L at S_1 in P'. Then of course L can't be raised to S_2 causing an error. Therefore there will be no error on P'. We can write T so that it doesn't apply to P. That is, L is *not* deleted in P and is therefore raised, causing an error, and the detectable error remains on the degree-3 p-m P. To do this, we take T: X - L - F - $Y \Rightarrow 1$ - $\emptyset$ - 3 - 4. This means that L is deleted when it occurs immediately to the left of an F. In P, B has been raised to between L and F, so L is *not* immediately to the left of F; therefore L is not deleted. (Of course, L is immediately to the left of F before B is raised, but the principle of Ordering of S-Essential Transformations (OSET) prevents the deletion from taking place before B is raised.)[29] It follows that L is raised at cycle S_2 in P, and the detectable error is created at cycle S_3. Therefore, the Freezing principle is (relatively) necessary to the proof of learnability.

The Freezing principle would have prevented this counterexample because if L had been raised from cycle S_1 to cycle S_2, L could not have been under a frozen node. That is, LB would have to be possible under D in the base structure. Then P' could have been created by putting B into P' (54b) as a right sister of L. The existence of B between L and F would have prevented L from being deleted. Then L would be raised, causing an error, and a detectable error on the degree-2 p-m P' would be created when H was raised at S_3.

For the proof of necessity of the Freezing principle that we have just given, we have to make sure that none of the other assumptions have been violated. Obviously most of them have not been, but perhaps we should more carefully check the principle of Transparency of Untransformable Base Structures (TUBS), which says that any partially derived 0-degree base p-m that is untransformable has an extension to a full 0-degree base p-m that is itself untransformable. Actually, without FP, TUBS can't play a natural role in a proof of learnability, since the partially derived base p-m necessary to the construction of P' is the top base part of S_1, after it has been fully transformed. Nevertheless TUBS formally applies, even without FP, and we can check to make sure that it is not violated.

The partially derived base p-m in question would be the top base part of S_1 in P after P has been fully transformed up to S_1. This p-m is given in (55a). TUBS requires that (55a) be extendable to an untransformable

(55)

a. 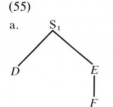   b.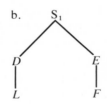

base p-m, but TUBS does not require that L be a label in this expansion. Thus, perhaps $D \rightarrow d$ is a sufficient expansion, or $D \rightarrow K \rightarrow k$. Without L in the expansion, the error-producing transformation, which raises L, cannot apply. Just to clear up any possibilities of confusion, in (55b) we show another partially derived base p-m (in fact, as we know, a fully derived p-m), with L inserted under D. But TUBS does not apply to (55b) because (55b) is not untransformable. In particular, the transformation that deletes L can apply to (55b). Thus TUBS is satisfied by our example, as are all the other assumptions, and the necessity of the Freezing principle has been demonstrated.

The second kind of example that could be used to show the necessity of the Freezing principle uses the boundary-category selecting capability of S-essential transformations (see note 14). In this case, we will not even need a deletion transformation. The example is shown in (56).

(56)

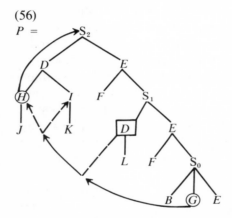

At level S_1, G is raised to the left of L, under D. We can assume that this operation is not structure-preserving, that is $D \rightarrow GL$ is not a base rule. Thus, D would be frozen if FP were assumed to apply. Since we don't assume that principle here, however, we can carry out the next operation, at level S_2. We define a transformation (different ones for component A and for component C, since we want an error) that raises G, but only when G is a left boundary of S_1. That is, in component A, the transformation is J - X - F - G - $Y \Rightarrow 1+4$ - 2 - 3 - $\emptyset$ - 5. Then, in P, G will be raised, causing an error, and the detectable error will come from raising H at cycle S_3. No error will be caused on a smaller degree P' because G cannot be at the left boundary of any degree-0 phrase-marker. Therefore, without FP there is a detectable error on a degree-3 p-m, but not on a smaller p-m. Thus we have demonstrated in another way the necessity of the Freezing principle.

Although we have found only these two kinds of examples, there may be more. Furthermore, it should be clear that without the very strong NBC principle, many other types of examples would be possible, in particular, any example in which the error-causing raising transformation that applies at S_2 demands that the matrix (top) structure of S_1 be of a form realizable only if a transformation that involved S_0 has occurred. Without NBC such examples are myriad. If NBC turns out to be (descriptively) too strong and we replace it by a weaker assumption, this will provide even further evidence for the necessity of the Freezing principle.

4.2.3 Raising Principle

The Raising principle freezes a node which has been raised: no transformations may apply to nodes under the raised node (compare note 6). In the example diagrammed in (11)–(19), we showed why we have to assume RP. However, at the time of that discussion, we had not yet postulated the principle of No Bottom Context. It turns out that the example violates NBC. In particular, the transformation T_3 (which applies to a degree-4 p-m and produces the detectable error) has structural description A - Q - R - D - E. When T_3 applies, it raises E, but the nodes fit by Q and R are in the bottom (embedded) p-m, as can easily be seen by inspecting (16) and (17), to which T_3 applies at level S_3. Thus T_3, and the example, violate NBC.

In order to demonstrate the need for the Raising principle in that example, T_3 must violate NBC. Suppose T_3 is taken as a raising transformation that satisfies NBC. Say, we replace T_3 by T_3', where $T_3' = A$ - X - E - $Y \Rightarrow 3+1$ - 2 - $\emptyset$ - 4. The derivation in (11)–(19) will still go through. However, the creation of the detectable error will no longer depend on A's being moved to the right (and raised). That is, there will be a detectable error on the degree-2 p-m P given in (57). An error is made at level S_1. The error is then uncovered when T_3' applies at cycle S_2. The derivation in (57) couldn't be carried out by T_3, since its structural description would not be met by P. In order to have a genuine counterexample of this kind we have to postulate a bottom-context-dependent transformation that will exclude the possibility of the derivation in (57). Otherwise, there is a detectable error on a degree-2 p-m, contrary to the result we desire.

The principle of No Bottom Context therefore rules out this coun-

(57)

$P =$

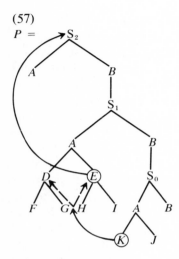

terexample. In fact, it appears at first sight as if NBC will make the Raising principle unnecessary. Suppose a detectable error is caused by raising a node at S_3 from under a previously raised node (thus violating RP). Then it appears that if we adopt NBC, thus not allowing the bottom context to play a role in the final detectable-error-producing transformation, we can cause a detectable error on a degree-2 p-m; namely, we don't raise a node from S_1 to S_2, but simply put the *top* of S_3 on top of S_1, and the error will be uncovered. This is how (57) was created.

This argument is correct for these kinds of examples but misses the possibility that the detectable error is uncovered by a non-S-essential transformation applying at S_3 (and the error cannot be uncovered on a smaller degree p-m). NBC allows the non-S-essential transformation to use the entire context in fitting its S.D., not just the moved node. An example appears in (58).

In (58), a nondetectable error is made by raising G at level S_1. This transformation can be defined in the same way as our earlier error-producing transformations. Then at level S_2, D is raised; D dominates the error so that the error is undetectable at cycle S_2. At cycle S_3, we raise M, which dominates D (thus M also dominates the error, making it nondetectable).

So far there is no detectable error. But then H is moved to the left of

(58)

$P =$

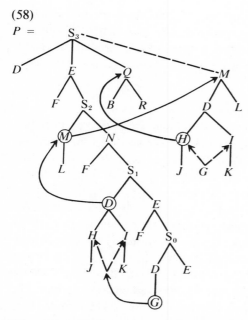

B, and the error is uncovered. In order to make this example work, we have to ensure that H can't be raised on an earlier (smaller degree) phrase-marker. The trick is to make the movement of H dependent on the raising of M. We do this simply by requiring that H be to the right of B in order for H to be moved. These operations can be carried out by three transformations (besides the error-producing transformation that raises G at cycle S_1):

T_2: L - X - D - Y $\Rightarrow$ 3+1 - 2 - $\emptyset$ - 4
T_3: X - M - Y - Q $\Rightarrow$ 1 - $\emptyset$ - 3 - 4+2
T_3': X - B - Y - H - Z $\Rightarrow$ 1 - 4+2 - 3 - $\emptyset$ - 5

T_2 raises D at cycle S_2. T_3 raises M at cycle S_3, moving M (and therefore H) to the right of B. T_3' (whose structural description includes B as a left context element) then attaches H to the left of B, causing a detectable error. The reader can check that there is no detectable error on any smaller degree p-m.

The Raising principle, of course, would exclude this example: it would not allow T_3' to apply to H, which is under the raised M (and also under the raised D, for that matter). Therefore, since a detectable error exists on a degree-3 p-m, but on no smaller p-m, when RP doesn't hold, we conclude that the Raising principle is necessary to the proof that transformational grammars are learnable from data of degree less than or equal to 2.

4.2.4 Principle of No Bottom Context

When example (35)–(38) was used to show why we had to assume the principle of No Bottom Context, we had not yet assumed the principle of Transparency of Untransformable Base Structures. It turns out that the example violates TUBS. In the example (see (35)), first the structure under G is transformed, then G is raised from S_0 to S_1. P' is formed by dropping S_0 and replacing the structure under G by a base structure. When this replacement takes place, another transformation, T_1' (defined in (37')) applies. T_1' prevents the error-producing transformation from applying. Note that after G is raised from S_0 to S_1, P is no longer transformable at S_1 (see (35)). Then by dropping S_0 and taking only the top base part of S_1, we obtain (44), a partially derived base p-m which, by the Freezing principle, is untransformable. Then TUBS guarantees that there is an extension of (44) which is itself untransformable, as in (45). But the example depends on (45)'s not existing; otherwise, the degree-2 p-m P' formed by replacing S_1 in (35) by S_1 in (45) would contain a detectable error and we would no longer have a counterexample.

Since the example used to motivate NBC also violates TUBS, it is conceivable that NBC is not necessary to the proof of the learnability of transformational grammar from degree-2 data. It is even plausible that this is the case. Suppose that a detectable error is made on a degree-3 p-m P. A nondetectable error is created by a raising transformation from cycle S_1 to cycle S_2. This error is then uncovered (made detectable) at cycle S_3. To create a degree-2 p-m P' on which a detectable error occurs, simply let all transformations apply to P up to level S_1, so that S_1 is no longer transformable. Then take the base part of S_1 and drop S_0 from it. This yields a partially derived 0-degree base p-m (dominated by S_1) which, by FP, is untransformable. TUBS therefore guarantees that the partially derived p-m can be extended to a fully derived 0-degree p-m that is untransformable. Substitute this 0-degree p-m for S_1 in P to construct a degree-2 p-m P'. Any transformation which applies to P must apply to P', in particular the error-producing transformations. Therefore there will be a detectable error on the degree-2 p-m P'.

Once again the prima facie argument is wrong. The possibility is missed that an error can occur at level S_1. Then there will not be a single partially derived p-m representing the base part of the effect of the transformational components on the top of S_1; there will be *two* top parts of S_1 after transformation, one for each transformational component. Yet this error at S_1 will not be the error that is ultimately detected. Rather, lacking NBC, this error will provide context that will allow another error to be created by a raising transformation (from S_1 to S_2). This latter error is the one uncovered at level S_3. In general, there can be a chain of errors, the first producing the context for the next to occur. However, the first is not directly detected. For example:

(59)

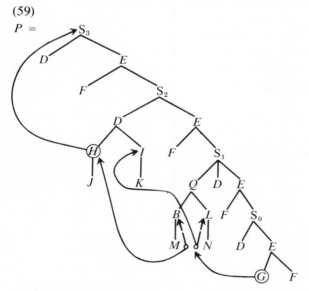

We define the two transformational components as $A = \{T_1^A, T_2, T_2', T_3\}$ and $C = \{T_1^C, T_2, T_2', T_3\}$ (that is, A and C agree except on one transformation), where the transformations are defined in (60).

(60)

$T_1{}^A$: X - M - Y - G - Z $\Rightarrow$ 1 - 2+4 - 3 - $\emptyset$ - 5

$T_1{}^C$: X - N - Y - G - Z $\Rightarrow$ 1 - 4+2 - 3 - $\emptyset$ - 5

T_2: X - J - Y - G - L - Z $\Rightarrow$ 1 - 2+4 - 3 - $\emptyset$ - 5 - 6

$T_2{}'$: X - K - Y - B - G - Z $\Rightarrow$ 1 - 5+2 - 3 - 4 - $\emptyset$ - 6

T_3: D - X - H $\Rightarrow$ 3+1 - 2 - $\emptyset$

First, an error is created on a raising transformation at cycle S_1, where component $A(T_1{}^A)$ attaches G to the right of M, under B, whereas component $C(T_1{}^C)$ attaches G to the left of N, under L. Thus, although there is no detectable error at level S_1, different structures are produced by the components. Given that we have not assumed NBC for this example, a raising transformation applying at cycle S_2 can exploit this difference in structures by referring to the context of S_1. In particular, after G is raised by component A, G is under B and is to the left of L. Therefore a transformation with structural description including . . . - G - L - . . . can apply after component A has applied to P through cycle S_1. In particular, transformation T_2 can raise G from S_1 to attach to the right of J (under H) in S_2. After component C has applied to S_1, on the other hand, G is under L and to the right of M. Therefore T_2 cannot apply after component C has applied to S_1. However transformation $T_2{}'$ demands an analysis that includes . . . - B - G - . . . and, therefore, $T_2{}'$ can apply after component C has applied to S_1. $T_2{}'$ raises G to attach to the left of K, under I.

Note that no detectable error has occurred through cycle S_2, because G has been raised to the same left-right position by both components, although to a different structural position. Then, when H is raised by T_3 at cycle S_3, a detectable error is created.

What is interesting about this example is that components A and C do not contain different transformations applicable to exactly the same structure at cycle S_2 to produce an error. Rather, the components contain the same transformations which could apply at cycle S_2. The difference in the structures of the input to the transformational components at cycle S_2 results in the selection of different transformations, which in turn results in different derived structures. A chain of non-detectable errors has occurred.

When S_0 is dropped and one of the derived structures of S_1 is taken as a replacement for S_1 to produce P' (say, the structure after A has applied is taken), then, since components A and C contain exactly the same transformations which can apply at cycle S_2, no error is caused. Therefore, of course, there is no detectable error. Since there is a detectable error on a degree-3 p-m, but none on a p-m of smaller degree, we conclude that the principle of No Bottom Context is necessary to the proof that transformational grammars are learnable from data of degree less than or equal to 2.[30]

4.2.5 Principle of Transparency of Untransformable Base Structures

The TUBS principle was the last assumption to be made. Therefore, that TUBS is (relatively) necessary to our proof follows from the fact that the examples motivating it satisfied all our other assumptions.

4.3 Proofs of Preliminary Theorems

4.3.1 Sketch of Proof

Our object now is to prove results that will eventually lead to a proof (section 4.4) of the major theorem, theorem 8, which states that if a detectable error exists, then a detectable error exists on a p-m of degree less than or equal to 2. In chapter 3 we sketched how learnability follows from this result. In section 4.5, we will show how learnability from degree-2 data follows. We will call theorem 8 Degree-2 Error Detectability. In proving degree-2 error detectability we will need not only the assumptions made to date, but other assumptions as well. These assumptions will not always be motivated by counterexamples for which the assumptions don't hold, as were the five major assumptions just discussed. Some of them will be assumed because they will be used to prove results along the way to the degree-2 theorem, and, at the moment at any rate, we cannot see how to prove the results without them. It remains for future research to show whether the assumptions are (relatively) necessary. (Note that the proof of necessity in section 4.2 does not take into consideration these new assumptions.)

The proof of degree-2 error detectability will be the result of a series of developments, but the basic idea of the proof is quite simple;

the intricacy comes in showing that the conditions of the simple idea are satisfied by our system. Suppose we have two transformational components, A and C, and there is a detectable error on a degree-i phrase-marker P, shown in (61a). Assume that i is the smallest degree phrase-marker on which an error occurs. If $i \leq 2$, the degree-2 theorem holds. Therefore we can assume that $i \geq 3$. The idea of the proof of the degree-2 theorem is to construct a degree-2 p-m P' (61b) on which a detectable error also will occur. (The detectable error occurs at level 2, the top level of P'.) P' will be constructed by transforming P up to level S_{i-2} by component A, deleting S_{i-3} and the entire sub-p-m dominated by S_{i-3}, deleting all parts of the tree under the frozen nodes (frozen by either the Freezing principle or the Raising principle) in S_{i-2}, and taking a 0-extension of these nodes. These operations can be seen in (61). The boxes under S_{i-2} in P (61a) indicate the lowest nodes in

(61)

a. $P = $

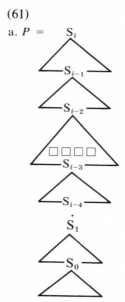

b. $P' = $

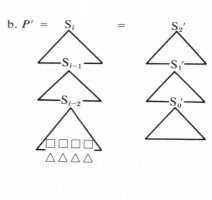

S_{i-2} (and not in S_{i-3} or below) that, after transformations in A apply up through S_{i-2}, are not strictly dominated by a frozen node (that is, the nodes with a box around them are either frozen themselves or are terminal category nodes; in either case the nodes dominating the nodes with boxes around them are not frozen). In other words, the p-m down to and including the boxed nodes represents a base structure, but as soon as we go under the boxed nodes, the structure is non-base. To form P' (61b) we drop all nodes under the boxed nodes and take a 0-extension of the boxed nodes (that is, a termination of the nodes, according to rules of the base grammar, which does not introduce an S). The 0-terminations are indicated by the triangles under the boxes in (61b). We can then relabel S_i as S_2', S_{i-1} as S_1' and the modified transformed S_{i-2} as S_0'. This then is the degree-2 p-m P'.

The proof centers around the existence of a certain kind of isomorphism. In the Substitution theorem (theorem 4) we show that if the isomorphism exists between two phrase-markers, the lack of a detectable error on one of the phrase-markers implies the lack of a detectable error on the other. To prove the degree-2 theorem (theorem 8) we show that the isomorphism exists between P and P' as we have constructed them above, so the lack of a detectable error on P' implies the lack of a detectable error on P, the result following. A major result along the way to proving that the isomorphism exists is theorem 7, which says that a property of "category raising equivalence" holds; that is, if two transformational components raise the same packet of terminal nodes, the nodes dominating the packets must be of the same category or there will be a detectable error. The reader probably suspects already that there is a certain similarity between P and P', although specifying the exact nature of the relevant preservation of structure (the definition of the isomorphism) is not as straightforward as it might seem.

4.3.2 Notation
We will need much notation in the course of the development of the proof. We list some of it here, along with some definitions. Let P be a base phrase-marker of degree i. The root of P is labeled S_i. This root dominates a sub-p-m with root labeled S_{i-1}, which in turn dominates a sub-p-m with root labeled S_{i-2}, and so on, until the lowest sub-p-m,

with root labeled S_0 is reached. Let P be a (perhaps nonbase) p-m, with root labeled S_i. Then Top(P) is the 0-degree p-m formed by dropping all sub-p-m's dominated by S_j, for $i \neq j$, from P. (Each node labeled S_j is dropped too.) If P is base, then of course Top(P) is formed by dropping the sub-p-m dominated by S_{i-1} from P. Top$^+$(P) is the 0-degree p-m formed by dropping all of the p-m P that is strictly dominated by S_{i-1}, but not S_{i-1} itself. Suppose that P is a p-m of degree i after transformations have applied. Then the eligible structure of P, denoted E(P), is the subtree dominated by S_i which includes all nodes to which further transformations are permitted to apply and the lines connecting these nodes (that is, E(P) does not include nodes ruled out by the Binary principle, Freezing principle, or Raising principle). Note that, in general, E(P) is a degree-1 (perhaps 0) *partially* derived base p-m, the Freezing principle or Raising principle possibly not allowing nodes that would complete the base p-m.

If we want to talk only about the top part of the eligible structure, we can calculate Top(E(P)). Note that Top(E(P)) = E(Top(P)).[31] Recall that *P is the string of terminal categories of the p-m P.

For a p-m P of degree i, $A^j(P)$, for $j \leq i$, is the p-m P transformed by transformational component A, up through level j. Thus $A(P) = A^i(P)$. $A^{j,e}(P)$ is the p-m derived by letting transformations apply to P up through level j, for $j \leq i$, then letting the S-essential transformation, if any, apply at level j. (The e stands for S-essential.)

For $j \leq i$, P_j is the p-m dominated by the node labeled S_j. In other words, the upper levels $j + 1$ through i have been deleted. Illustrations of many of these notations may be found in note 31.

Definition: For any strings t, v, we say that v is a *right (left) segment* of t if there exists a string x such that $t = xv$ ($t = vx$): We call x the *complement* of v (in t). A string x is a *substring* of a string y if there exist strings t, v such that $y = txv$.

Definition: A *packet* is a string of terminal nodes in a p-m, such that the string is exhaustively dominated by a single node. (By terminal nodes we mean terminal category nodes, not the nodes labeled by lexical items.)

A packet is the same as a phrase, except that it is a string of category nodes instead of lexical labels.

4.3.3 Raising of Equivalent Packets

Our goal is to prove theorem 4, the Substitution theorem. On the way, it will be useful to first prove theorem 3, which says if two components raise different packets, a detectable error exists.

4.3.3.1 Repulsion and No Copying
Notice two kinds of counterexamples to theorem 3:

(62)

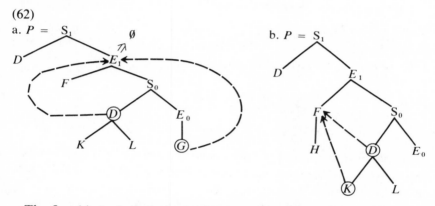

The first kind of counterexample is illustrated by (62a). At cycle S_1, component A raises D whereas component C raises G. (The dotted arrows indicate that the movements take place under different transformational components.) Then a singulary transformation deletes E_1. Even though different packets were raised by components A and C (KL and G, respectively), there is still no detectable error made on P. Therefore we will not be able to prove theorem 3 unless we rule out this kind of example. We will do so by making the unsubtle assumption that if the S from which a node has been raised is deleted, the derivation is filtered out.[32] This assumption will be part (i) of the principle of Repulsion.

The second kind of counterexample to theorem 3 is illustrated in (62b). Transformational component A raises the packet K, whereas component C raises the node D, thus raising the packet KL. Even though different packets are raised, there is no detectable error because the raised packets started out at the left boundary of the embedded sentence S_0 and finished at the right boundary of the matrix sentence S_1. (As usual, we are assuming there are no other transformations.) Once again we will simply rule out this kind of counterexample directly.[33] The assumption will be part (ii) of the principle of Repulsion, so called because a packet raised from a boundary of an embedded S is "repulsed" by that boundary; that is, material must appear between the boundary and the raised packet.

First we need the following definition.

Definition: A transformational component A *S-essentially applies to a packet K* at level S_i in a p-m P if there is a node B in S_{i-1} of P such that
i. $K = *B$ (B exhaustively dominates K), and
ii. either
(a) B is S-essentially deleted at S_i, or
(b) B is raised from S_{i-1} to S_i.
We also say in such a case that A *S-essentially applies to the node B.*

Principle of Repulsion: Let P be a base phrase-marker and let A be a transformational component. Suppose that at level i, A S-essentially applies to the node B. Suppose either
i. At level i, a node dominating S_{i-1} is deleted, or
ii. B is raised from S_{i-1} to S_i and either
(a) $*B$ is a right segment of $*A(P_{i-1})$, and $*[A(P)]_{i-1}*B$ is a substring of $*A(P_i)$, or
(b) $*B$ is a left segment of $*A(P_{i-1})$ and $*B*[A(P)]_{i-1}$ is a substring of $*A(P_i)$.
Then P is filtered.

Remark: It follows from the principle of Repulsion that all the sub-p-m's of P, from P_i on up to P, are filtered. In particular, we will usually be concerned with the filtering of P_i. Also, note that *dominating* in (i) means "weakly dominating," so S_{i-1} itself could be deleted. However, since this would be another S-essential transformation, USET would prevent the case from ever arising.

Example: The phrase-marker in (62a) violates (i) of Repulsion because D (or G) was raised and then E, a node dominating S_0, was deleted;[34] (62b) violates (ii.b) of Repulsion because, for component C, say, D is raised, D is a left segment of $A(P_0)$, and $*D*A(P_0) = (KL)(E) = KLE$ is a substring of $*A(P_1) = DHKLE$.

Before we go on to the proof of theorem 3, we rule out one possibility by making another assumption.

Assumption: There is no copying. That is, an integer appears at most once in the structural change part (the S.C.) of a transformational rule.

We make this assumption not because we believe there are no copying transformations in natural language but because the assumption makes the proofs go through more simply. In particular, the assumption that there is no copying implies that if a terminal category node N is in position i in $*A(P)$ and the same node N is in position j in $*C(P)$ and $i \neq j$, then $*A(P) \neq *C(P)$. This follows from the fact that if there is no copying, a node in the base p-m may appear at most once in the derived p-m. This conclusion will prove useful in the proofs. On the other hand, if copying is allowed, the conclusion doesn't follow, because N may appear at both positions i and j. (It is important to remember that N refers to a *node* in the base p-m, which may be repeated in the derived p-m if copying is allowed. N does *not* refer to a category.)

On the other hand, we do not have any counterexamples to show that the proof fails to go through without the prohibition against copying. Perhaps the proof will work with only slight modification, without the assumption. But at the moment, for simplicity, we will make the assumption. To the extent that copying is necessary, it will be important to relax the assumption. Recall that there is only a finite number of eligible structures for a given base grammar, and thus a finite number of structural descriptions. Given our constraints, no copying implies that there is only a finite number of definable transformations (for a fixed base grammar).

4.3.3.2 Further Assumptions and Proofs

Theorem 3: For any two transformational components A and C and for a p-m P of degree i, if component A S-essentially applies to a packet K at level S_i, $K \neq *A(P_{i-1})$, then either

i. Component C S-essentially applies to K at S_i, or

ii. Both $A(P)$ and $C(P)$ are filtered, or

iii. There is a detectable error on P or on a sub-p-m of P, or

iv. K is a right or left segment of $*A(P_{i-1})$, and component C S-essentially applies at S_i to a packet equal to the complement of K in $*A(P_{i-1})$.

Proof: Since P_{i-1} is a sub-p-m of P, if there is a detectable error on P_{i-1}, part (iii) of the theorem holds. Therefore, we can assume that there is no detectable error on P_{i-1}. That is, $*A(P_{i-1}) = *C(P_{i-1})$. By the principle of No Bottom Context, there are only two kinds of S-essential transformations, those that delete a single packet and those that raise a single packet.

Suppose, first, that component A S-essentially deletes the packet K at level S_i, as in (63). If S_{i-1} is then deleted at level i, the principle of

(63) S_i

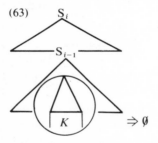

$\Rightarrow \emptyset$

Repulsion (part (i)) implies that P is filtered by A. Then either P is filtered by C in which case part (ii) of theorem 3 holds, or P is not filtered by C in which case there is a detectable error and part (iii) of theorem 3 holds. Thus we can assume that S_{i-1} is *not* deleted by A at level i.

By the principle of the Uniqueness of S-Essential Transformations (USET), no further S-essential transformation can apply to S_{i-1} or to a node dominated by S_{i-1}. Therefore, since S_{i-1} is not deleted at level i, the string left after deletion of K is a substring of $*A(P)$. This is the string $*[A(P)]_{i-1} = (*A(P_{i-1}) - K)$.[35] If there is a detectable error on P, then part (iii) of theorem 3 holds. Suppose that there is no detectable error on P. Therefore $*A(P) = *C(P)$. Then $*A(P_{i-1}) - K$ is a substring of $*C(P)$. But $*A(P_{i-1}) - K = *C(P_{i-1}) - K$. Therefore, $*C(P_{i-1}) - K$ is a substring of $*C(P_{i-1})$. The assumption of the theorem that $*A(P_{i-1}) \neq$

K implies that $*C(P_{i-1}) - K \neq \emptyset$. Since K is a substring of $*C(P_{i-1})$, the only way to delete K is for an S-essential transformation in C to apply to K. (USET implies that this must be accomplished by a single transformation.) Otherwise the entire $*C(P_{i-1})$ would have to be deleted and $*C(P_{i-1})$ could not be a substring of $*C(P)$ (since $*C(P_{i-1}) - K \neq \emptyset$). Therefore C S-essentially applies to K at level i. This completes the proof in the case where K is deleted by A.

Now suppose that A raises K. Suppose that K is not a right or left segment of $*A(P_{i-1})$. There are terminal category nodes t_1, t_2, and a terminal category node string x, such that $*A(P_{i-1}) - K = t_1xt_2$. That is, after K is raised by A, S_{i-1} exhaustively dominates t_1xt_2. By part (i) of the principle of Repulsion, S_{i-1} cannot be deleted at level i, so S_{i-1} dominates t_1xt_2 after P has been fully derived. That is, $*[A(P)]_{i-1} = t_1xt_2$. Thus t_1xt_2 must be a substring of $*C(P)$ (or else there is a detectable error on P).

Suppose that both t_1 and t_2 are raised by C to S_i. Then, by the Raising principle, K can never be deleted from between them, and t_1xt_2 cannot be formed, because x contains none of the nodes in K. If neither t_1 nor t_2 is raised, and if K is not raised (or S-essentially deleted), then t_1xt_2 cannot be formed.

Therefore, suppose one of them is raised. Without loss of generality, say t_1 is raised to S_i by C. Let D be the node that is explicitly raised. Then t_1 is the first (leftmost) node in $*D$. Now, either a node in K is raised with t_1, or it is not. Suppose a node in K is raised. Let N be such a node. That is, N is in K and N is in $*D$. But then there is a substring of terminal nodes z such that t_1zN is a substring of $*D$. By the Raising principle, D is frozen after it is raised. Since we have assumed that t_2 wasn't raised, zN doesn't include t_2. Therefore there is a string w such that, in $*C(P)$, the substring between t_1 and t_2 is t_1zNwt_2.

But we have already shown that t_1xt_2 is a substring of $*C(P)$, where x includes no nodes of K. Thus N cannot be in x, and we have a contradiction. (We have ignored the possibility of t_1 being deleted at level S_i, but this would create a detectable error, and thus satisfy part (iii) of theorem 3.)

The one remaining case (given that K is not a left or right segment of $*A(P_{i-1})$) is where no node of K is raised with t_1; that is, $*D$ contains no node of K. Since, by USET, no further transformations can apply within the embedded $C(P_{i-1})$, we know that there is a string z such that Kzt_2 will be a substring of $*C(P_i)$. Then there will be a string w such that $t_1 wKzt_2$ will be a substring of $*C(P)$. But, as before, we have already shown that $t_1 xt_2$ is a substring of $*C(P_i)$, with x containing no nodes in K. This contradiction proves that C S-essentially applies to packet K at level i, which is part (i) of the theorem.

The remaining case is when K is a right segment of $*A(P_{i-1})$. (If K is a left segment, the proof is analogous, but uses (ii.b) of Repulsion instead of (ii.a). We omit the proof in the left segment case.) By part (i) of the principle of Repulsion, S_{i-1} remains in $A(P)$. The situation is shown in diagram (64):

(64)

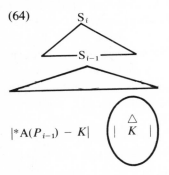

$|*A(P_{i-1}) - K|$

Let $\bar{K}$ = the complement of K; that is, $\bar{K} = *A(P_{i-1}) - K$. We know that $\bar{K}$ is a substring of $*A(P)$ (by part (i) of Repulsion). Thus, if there is to be no detectable error, $\bar{K}$ is a substring of $*C(P)$. By the Raising principle, either the entire K is a substring of $*A(P)$ or K is deleted at level S_i. First, suppose that K is deleted (by A) at S_i. Then K doesn't appear in $*A(P)$ and thus doesn't appear in $*C(P)$. If any node in K is not raised by C at S_i, then by part (i) of Repulsion, that node may not be deleted later. Thus every node in K must be raised. If a node in $\bar{K}$ is raised, along with K, then when K is deleted, by the Raising principle that node (in $\bar{K}$) must also be deleted. But then $\bar{K}$ cannot be a substring of $*C(P)$, as we know it is. So in the case where K is deleted in $*A(P)$, K must be raised by C (or S-essentially deleted by C). This is part (i) of theorem 3.

Therefore, we can suppose that K is not deleted by A at level S_i. That is, K is a substring of $*A(P)$ and thus of $*C(P)$. As before, we also know that $\bar{K}$ is a substring of $*C(P)$. Suppose that K is to the left of $\bar{K}$ in $*C(P)$. That is, for some strings w,x,y, we have that $*C(P) = wKx\bar{K}y$. Given the Raising principle (RP) and USET, this can happen only if K or $\bar{K}$ is raised by C (an explicit argument on strings can be given, but the conclusion is quite clear). This is conclusion (ii) or (iv) of theorem 3.

Suppose, therefore, that K is to the right of $\bar{K}$ in $*C(P)$. Thus there are w,x,y such that we have $*C(P) = w\bar{K}xKy$. Since we are dealing with the case where A raises a right segment of $*A(P_{i-1})$, we know by (ii) of Repulsion that $x \neq \emptyset$ (otherwise $\bar{K}K$ is a substring of $*A(P_i)$). First, suppose that neither a right nor left segment of $*C(P_{i-1})$ is raised by C. Then either K or $\bar{K}$ (or both) cannot be a substring of $*C(P)$, contradicting what we have shown. Now, suppose that C raises a *left* segment. And suppose that this segment includes a node of K. Since K is a packet (dominated exhaustively by a single node), and since only one node may be explicitly raised, all of K must be raised. This means that $*C(P_{i-1})$ is raised, which we have ruled out by assumption in the statement of theorem 3. If what is raised is a left segment that is less than K, then $\bar{K}xK$ cannot be a substring of $*C(P)$, with $x \neq \emptyset$. Thus $\bar{K}$ must be raised, which is part (iv) of theorem 3. The remaining case is when C raises a right segment. If this is not equal to K, then $\bar{K}xK$ cannot be a substring of $*C(P)$ with $x \neq \emptyset$. Therefore, K is raised—which completes the proof of theorem 3.

The assumption in theorem 3 that $K \neq *A(P_{i-1})$ is necessary because if the raised string is the entire phrase dominated by S_{i-1}, component C might produce the same (weak) effect by moving a node that exhaustively dominates S_{i-1}. An example is shown in (65). Component A raises the packet B to the left of D. Component C doesn't raise any packet, but at level S_1, a non-S-essential transformation in C moves E, which exhaustively dominates B, to the left of D. Therefore, the terminal string in both cases is $*A(P) = *C(P) = BD$.

This conclusion demands that a node that doesn't terminate after transformations have applied simply be ignored when we determine what the terminal string is. That is, S_0 in $A(P)$ doesn't terminate and is ignored. Other assumptions are possible, however. In fact, we will see

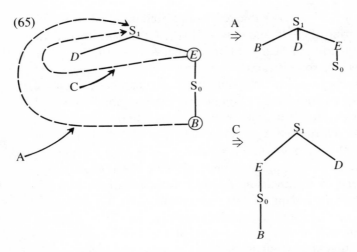

later that in order to obtain the results we desire we will have to make a different assumption. Interestingly, this assumption will also allow us to remove from theorem 3 the restriction that $K \neq {}^{*}A(P_{i-1})$. The assumption follows.

Principle of Designated Representatives (DR):
i. Suppose that K immediately and exhaustively dominates L in a p-m (that is, L has no sisters). Suppose also that L is raised or S-essentially deleted. Then L leaves behind (immediately and exhaustively dominated by K) a *designated representative* d_L, which depends on L. The designated representative d_L is considered to be part of the terminal string of lexical categories. For different categories $H \neq L$, $d_H \neq d_L$. For any lexical category H, $d_L \neq H$.
ii. If a designated representative is deleted, the p-m is filtered.

The idea of the principle of Designated Representatives is that when a packet that is exhaustively dominated by an S is raised, an element is left behind which is uniquely associated with a node that has been raised (or S-essentially deleted).[36] Therefore, if another component doesn't raise (or S-essentially delete) that packet, the designated representative won't appear in the terminal category node string, and there will be a detectable error. For example, in (65), when component C raises the node B, which is immediately and exhaustively dominated by S_0, an element d_B will be left under S_0. Therefore, $*A(P) = BDd_B$. In $C(P)$ no raising took place, and there is no designated representative, so, as before, $*C(P) = BD$. Therefore, $*A(P) \neq *C(P)$, and we have a detectable error.[37]

We are now in a position to eliminate the assumption in theorem 3 that $K \neq *A(P_{i-1})$. We do this in theorem 3'.

Theorem 3': Same as theorem 3, except the assumption that $K \neq$ $*A(P_{i-1})$ is eliminated.

Proof: Theorem 3' follows from theorem 3 except for the case where $K = *A(P_{i-1})$. In this case, suppose that the node that A S-essentially applies to is of category B. Then the principle of Designated Representatives implies that d_B is left behind as part of the terminal category node string. If d_B is deleted at level S_i, part (ii) of the DR principle implies that $A(P)$ is filtered. But then either $C(P)$ is filtered, which is part (ii) of theorem 3, or $C(P)$ is not filtered, which creates a detectable error, resulting in part (iii) of theorem 3. Therefore, we can assume that d_B is not deleted at level S_i. Now, we can assume that there is no detectable error at level S_{i-1} (otherwise (iii) of theorem 3 would be satisfied). That is, $*A(P_{i-1}) = *C(P_{i-1})$. Thus the number of occurrences of d_B in $*A(P_{i-1})$ must equal the number of occurrences of d_B in $*C(P_{i-1})$. Say this number is h. Now, since part (ii) of the DR principle says that none of these occurrences of d_B can be deleted (or else filtering occurs and the theorem is proved), and since when component A S-essentially applies to K, one more copy of d_B is formed (and this copy cannot be deleted or else theorem 3' is proved), we know that $*A(P)$ contains $h + 1$ occurrences of d_B. But if there is no detectable error on P (which is necessary or else the theorem is proved), the number of occurrences of d_B in $*C(P)$ must also be $h + 1$. But this extra copy of d_B can only be introduced into $*C(P)$ by an S-essential transformation in C applying to a node of category B at level S_i, and the packet that B dominates must be $K = *C(P_{i-1})$ (or else no d_B would be introduced). But either $*A(P_{i-1}) \neq *C(P_{i-1})$, in which case there is a detectable error on P_{i-1} and conclusion (iii) of theorem 3 holds, or $*A(P_{i-1}) = *C(P_{i-1})$, in which case component C S-essentially applies to the packet K at level i, and conclusion (i) of theorem 3 holds. This proves theorem 3'.

In proving the Substitution theorem (theorem 4), we will make use of theorem 3'; thus we will be assuming that the principle of Designated Representatives (DR) holds. Actually, we think that theorem 4 could be proved using theorem 3 rather than theorem 3', thus avoiding DR. But we have to assume DR anyway (in order to prove theorem 7, *category raising equivalence*), and our goal is to complete the proof under one set of assumptions (that is, the proof with DR does not seem to follow a fortiori from the proof without DR). The advantage of proving theorem 4 using only theorem 3 would have been to isolate more precisely where DR becomes necessary.

4.3.4 Substitution Theorem

4.3.4.1 The Proof The Substitution theorem (theorem 4) says that if certain relations exist between two phrase-markers P and P' and if there is no detectable error on P, then there is no detectable error on P'. The relations involve the substitution of certain phrases in one p-m for certain phrases in the other p-m, the structures otherwise being identical. This theorem will be useful for our final result because we will be able to show that for any p-m P there exists a degree-2 p-m P' that satisfies the relation between P and P'. Thus if there is a detectable error on any p-m P, there will be one on a degree-2 p-m P'.

Definition: For two partially derived p-m's $P = P'$, for any nodes D in P and D' in P' we say that D *corresponds to* D' (and write $D \equiv D'$) if D is in exactly the same position in P as D' is in P'.

Example:

In the example, the category of A' is A, and similarly for the other nodes in P'. S in P corresponds to S' in P', A to A', B to B', C to C', and D to D'. We are now ready to define the crucial isomorphism, *preservation*.

Definition: Let A and C be transformational components and let P and P' be base phrase-markers. We say that P *preserves* P' (and write $P \cong P'$) if

i. $E(\text{Top}(A(P))) = E(\text{Top}(A(P')))$,

ii. $E(\text{Top}(C(P))) = E(\text{Top}(C(P')))$, and

iii. Suppose D_A and D_C are nodes in $E(\text{Top}(A(P)))$ and $E(\text{Top}(C(P)))$ respectively, and suppose that the node D_A' in $E(\text{Top}(A(P')))$ corresponds to D_A and the node D_C' in $E(\text{Top}(C(P')))$ corresponds to D_C. That is, $D_A \equiv D_A'$ and $D_C \equiv D_C'$. Then $^*D_A = {}^*D_C$ if and only if $^*D_A' = {}^*D_C'$.

Remark: The relation $\cong$ is an equivalence relation. That is, it is reflexive, symmetric, and transitive. Assumptions (i) and (ii) should be self-explanatory. They simply require that for P to preserve P' the nodes eligible for transforming by a given component must be the same after transformations apply to P and P'. Assumption (iii) says that if one of these nodes in P transformed by A dominates a terminal string different from the string the node dominates when P is transformed by C, then the corresponding nodes in P' also dominate different terminal strings. After we prove the theorem we will show by example why we have to assume (iii) when it might seem at first glance as if (i) and (ii) are enough.

Theorem 4 *(Substitution Theorem):* Let A and C be transformational components, $P = P_i$ be a degree-i base phrase-marker, and $P' = P_j'$ be a degree-j base phrase-marker such that

i. There is no detectable error on P' or any of its sub-p-m's,

ii. There is no detectable error on P_{i-1} or any of its sub-p-m's,

iii. $\text{Top}^+(P) = \text{Top}^+(P')$, and

iv. $P_{i-1} \cong P_{j-1}'$ (with respect to A and C).

Then there is no detectable error on P.

Remark: Some of the properties of the assumptions of the theorem may be seen in (66). That is, (iii) requires that, before transforming, the matrix p-m's and the place of insertion of the embedded p-m be the same for P and P'. This is shown by the long equals sign between the matrix (top) p-m's. In addition, (iv) requires that after transforming, the

(66)

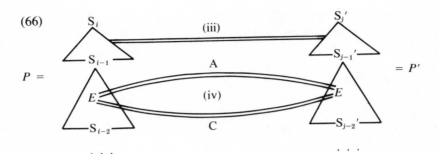

eligible structure of the top of P_{i-1} equals the eligible structure of the top of P_{j-1}'. This is true for both components A and C, and is shown by the two long equals signs labeled A and C which connect E (for eligible structure) in the two p-m's. The correspondence property of preservation—(iii) in the definition of *preserve*—is not shown.

Another way to look at the structure of the theorem is

(66′)

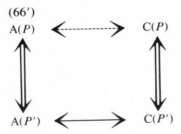

In this diagram, $A(P') \leftrightarrow C(P')$ is to be interpreted as $*A(P') = *C(P')$ (assumption (i)). The double arrow, as in $A(P) \Leftrightarrow A(P')$ is to be interpreted as $\text{Top}^+(P) = \text{Top}^+(P')$ and $E(\text{Top}(A(P_{i-1}))) = E(\text{Top}(A(P_{j-1}')))$, as follow from (iii) and (iv) respectively. Similarly for C. Under the further assumptions (not shown in the diagram) listed in (ii) of the theorem and also part (iii) of the definition of *preserve* (relevant to (iv) of the theorem), the conclusion is that we can complete the diagram. That is, $*A(P) = *C(P)$, as indicated in the diagram by the dotted single arrow connecting $A(P)$ and $C(P)$.

Proof: First we will clear away a special case. Suppose that P' is filtered by A or C, but not both. Then there would be a detectable error on P', contrary to assumption (i). Therefore, if one of the transformational components filters P', the other does. So assume that both A and C filter P'. Now, suppose that A filters P' *before* level j, that is, for some k, $k < j$, $A(P_k') = \emptyset$. But then $A(P_{j-1}') = \emptyset$, and therefore $E(\text{Top}(A(P_{j-1}'))) = \emptyset$. Therefore, by (iv) and the definition of $\cong$, we have $E(\text{Top}(A(P_{i-1}))) = \emptyset$. From this we can conclude that A filters P. Now, if A filters P' before level j, C must filter P' before level j, and so we can show that C filters P. Therefore there will be no detectable error on P, which is what we want. Suppose, therefore, that A filters P' at level j, but not before. But then, it follows from (iii) and (iv), since application of transformations depends strictly on eligible structures and since filtering depends strictly on application of transformations (determinism, and so on), that A will filter P. If A filters P' at level j, and not before, it follows from (i) that C filters P' at level j but not before. Therefore we can follow the same reasoning as for A, to show that C filters P. But then both A and C filter P, and there is no detectable error on P. Therefore, we have proved the theorem in the case where P' is filtered, and we can assume for the rest of the proof that P' is filtered by neither A nor C.

The goal of the proof is to show that there is no detectable error on P. To do this we will calculate the terminal strings $*A(P)$ and $*C(P)$ in terms of packets of nodes that are related to packets of nodes in P'. First, suppose that an S-essential transformation T in A applies to a packet at level j in P' (that is, that packet is dominated by a node in level $j - 1$). Suppose T applies to the node D_A' (of category D) which dominates the packet $*D_A'$. Since by (i) there is no detectable error on $P' = P_j'$ or on any of its sub-p-m's, and since we are assuming (see conclusion of last paragraph) that neither A nor C filters P', it follows that either conclusion (i) or (iv) of theorem 3' holds. Conclusion (iv) is a special case dealing with the raising of left or right segments and their complements. We will consider it briefly at the end of the proof, noting that its treatment will follow that of the conclusion (i) case. For now we assume that conclusion (i) of theorem 3' holds. Namely, C S-essentially applies to the same packet in P' as A does. More precisely, C applies at level j to a node D_C' dominating packet $*D_C'$ (D_C' is in level $j - 1$) and

(67) $*D_A' = *D_C'$.

Now, since there are no detectable errors on any sub-p-m's of P', we know that the embedded sentences from which D_A' and D_C' were raised (or deleted) have equal terminal strings. That is,

(68) $*A(P_{j-1}') = *C(P_{j-1}')$.

But we have assumed (USET) that at most one S-essential transformation may apply at a level. Thus the only effect on the embedded strings by S-essential transformations is the deletion of $*D_A'$ or $*D_C'$ (we have not allowed copying). But in subtracting the equal strings in (67) from the equal strings in (68) we are left with equals. That is,

(69) $*[A^{j,e}(P')]_{j-1} = *[C^{j,e}(P')]_{j-1}$.

After S-essential transformations at level j apply, the embedded sentence (level $j-1$) for component A has a terminal string identical to that for component C.

Now, since $P_{i-1} \cong P_{j-1}'$ (iv), it follows from (67) that there are nodes D_A, D_C in P which correspond to D_A', D_C' respectively, and

(70) $*D_A = *D_C$.

Since there are no detectable errors on sub-p-m's of P (ii) we also have the analogue of (68) for P, namely,

(71) $*A(P_{i-1}) = *C(P_{i-1})$.

By the definition of *correspond* we know that the category of D_A is the same as the category of its corresponding node D_A'. Therefore, since $\text{Top}^+(P) = \text{Top}^+(P')$, the principle of No Bottom Context implies that when an S-essential transformation in A applies to P' at level j, the transformation also S-essentially applies to P at level i. Exactly the same argument implies that when an S-essential transformation in C applies to P at level j, the transformation also S-essentially applies to P at level i. Therefore, the only (by USET) S-essential transformation applying to P at level i will apply to equal packets, $*D_A$ and $*D_C$, in components A and C respectively (see (70)). Therefore, after S-essential transformations apply at level i in P, the terminal strings are equal for A and C. That is,

(72) $*[A^{i,e}(P)]_{i-1} = *[C^{i,e}(P)]_{i-1}$.

It remains only to show that the non-S-essential transformations applying at level i do not disturb this equality of terminal strings between A and C.

In order to compute the structure of A(P) we must first consider the structure of $A^{i,e}(P)$, that is, the structure of P after S-essential transformations have applied at the top level. At most one S-essential transformation can apply (USET) and it must raise or delete a packet dominated by a node D_A. Now a node dominating D_A (after it is raised) may be part of the eligible structure $E(\text{Top}(A^{i,e}(P)))$, or D_A may be dominated by a node in $E(\text{Top}(A^{i,e}(P)))$. But by the freezing of raised nodes (Raising principle), a node that D_A (strictly) dominates may not be in $E(\text{Top}(A^{i,e}(P)))$. Thus after a raising transformation takes place there are (possibly empty) strings, x,y of terminal nodes in P and a bottom node N_A of $E(\text{Top}(A^{i,e}(P)))$ such that $x*D_Ay$ is the terminal packet dominated by N_A. If D_A is a bottom node of $E(\text{Top}(A^{i,e}(P)))$ (that is, no node dominating D_A is frozen) then $D_A = N_A$ and $x = y = \emptyset$. An example is illustrated in (73). In (73) D_A is raised at level i, attaching to

(73)

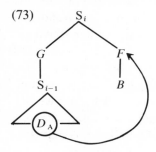

the right of B, under F. There are two cases. If $F \rightarrow BD$ is not a base rule, F is frozen by the Freezing principle and therefore the node labeled F is a minimal element of the eligible structure $E(\text{Top}(A^{i,e}(P)))$. That is, the node labeled F is N_A and $x = *B$ and $y = \emptyset$. On the other hand, if $F \rightarrow BD$ is a base rule, then F is not frozen and D_A itself is a minimal element of the eligible structure. That is, D_A is N_A, and $x = y = \emptyset$.

The embedded sentence P_{i-1} is also affected by an S-essential transformation T. After T has applied, if S_{i-1} is dominated by a bottom (minimal) node of $E(Top(A^{i,e}(P)))$ (that is, if a node dominating S_{i-1} is frozen, which can happen if the raising is not structure-preserving, and attaches in the appropriate place) then there are (possibly empty) strings u, v of elements in $Top(P)$ or in $*D_A$ such that $u*[A^{i,e}(P)]_{i-1}v$ is the packet dominated by a bottom node of $E(Top(A^{i,e}(P)))$. If no node dominating S_{i-1} is frozen, we still write that $*[A^{i,e}(P)]_{i-1}$ is part of the packet $u*[A^{i,e}(P)]_{i-1}v$, but $u = v = \emptyset$.

Aside from these two cases, $Top(P)$ is unaffected by an S-essential transformation. Let $E_1, E_2, \ldots, E_r$ be the sequence of bottom nodes of $E(Top(A^{i,e}(P)))$ excluding the nodes in $E(Top(A^{i,e}(P)))$ that dominate S_{i-1} and the raised D_A (if any). For all k, $E_k \in Top(P)$ and E_k is a terminal category. Then there exist positive integers m,n such that we can write

(74) $*A^{i,e}(P) = E_1E_2 \ldots E_{m-1}u*[A^{i,e}(P)]_{i-1}vE_mE_{m+1} \ldots$
$$E_{n-1}(x*D_Ay)E_nE_{n+1} \ldots E_r.$$

Without loss of generality we have taken $m \leq n$; that is, the raised node is raised to the right. The term $x*D_Ay$ has been put in parentheses because if no node is raised by the S-essential transformation (that is, if an S-essential deletion transformation applies) or if no S-essential transformation at all applies, the term $x*D_Ay$ does not appear. In that case we simply take $x = y = \emptyset$. That is, the parentheses are the optionality parentheses of linguistic theory.[38] At the end of the proof we will give an example that should help to make these calculations clearer. Note also that, given the restrictions on the definition of *raising transformation*, the only way a node dominating S_{i-1} can be frozen is for the raised node D to attach directly under a node N that also dominates S_{i-1} (although not necessarily immediately), such that N is frozen (its immediate structure is nonbase). In this case, of course, there are nodes in $E(Top(A^{i,e}(P)))$ between S_{i-1} and D_A. That is, $m = n$. (We assume that each E_k appears exactly once, $1 \leq k \leq r$.) In this case also, we take $x*D_Ay$ as part of v. (We can assume this is a case of the use of the optionality parentheses.)

We have already shown that when component A raises a node D_A'

from P_{j-1}' to $\text{Top}(P_j')$, A also raises a node D_A in P_{i-1} to $\text{Top}(P)$. Since all the relevant assumptions on which the demonstration is based (i)–(iv) are symmetric between P_i and P_j', the converse of this statement also holds. Now a raising transformation is the only transformation that affects the top p-m after S-essential transformations have applied but before non-S-essential transformations have applied, and NBC insures that the nodes D_A and D_A' are raised to the same place in the equal top p-m's (see (iii)). The Raising principle allows only the nodes D_A and D_A' to be part of the eligible structure of the top p-m after S-essential transformations apply, and not the nodes that D_A and D_A' dominate. The only other difference between the top of P and P' after the S-essential transformations apply is a difference in what P_{i-1} and P_{j-1}' dominate, but these also are not part of the eligible structure after S-essential transformations apply. Therefore we have

(75) $E(\text{Top}(A^{i,e}(P))) = E(\text{Top}(A^{j,e}(P')))$.

Therefore we can write

(76) $*A^{j,e}(P') = E_1 E_2 \ldots E_{m-1} u^* [A^{j,e}(P')]_{j-1} v E_m E_{m+1} \ldots$
$\quad\quad E_{n-1}(x^* D_A' y) E_n E_{n+1} \ldots E_r,$

where D_A' appears in (76) if and only if D_A appears in (74).[39]

Now, since the application of transformations is determined strictly by the eligible structure, the final derived string is a permutation (with possible deletions) of the terminal packets in the eligible structure. That is, there is an integer $q \le r$ and integers f, $g \le r$ and a one-to-one (that is, no copying) function p from $\{1,2, \ldots, q\}$ into $\{1,2, \ldots, r\}$ such that

(77) $*A(P) = E_{p_1} E_{p_2} \ldots E_{p_{f-1}} (u^* [A^{i,e}(P)]_{i-1} v) E_{p_f} E_{p_{f+1}} \ldots$
$\quad\quad E_{p_{g-1}}(x^* D_A y) E_{p_g} E_{p_{g+1}} \ldots E_{p_q},$

and

(78) $*A(P') = E_{p_1} E_{p_2} \ldots E_{p_{f-1}} (u^* [A^{j,e}(P')]_{j-1} v) E_{p_f} E_{p_{f+1}} \ldots$
$\quad\quad E_{p_{g-1}}(x^* D_A' y) E_{p_g} E_{p_{g+1}} \ldots E_{p_q}.$

Again, without loss of generality we have assumed $f < g$; that is, the raised node remains on the right of the embedded sentence. Also, a node dominating S_{i-1} in P might be deleted (if no S-essential transformation applies—otherwise Repulsion prevents this), so that $(u*[A^{i,e}(P)]_{i-1}v)$ has been placed in optional parentheses. (See note 38.) If in fact S_{i-1} has been deleted, then by convention take (in (77)) $x = y = *[A^{i,e}(P)]_{i-1} = \emptyset$. The same situation holds for $(u*[A^{j,e}(P')]_{j-1}v)$ in (78). In fact, $(u*[A^{i,e}(P)]_{i-1}v)$ appears in (77) if and only if $(u*[A^{j,e}(P')]_{j-1}v)$ appears in (78). Also, even if D_A has been raised, with $x*D_Ay$ appearing in (74), $x*D_Ay$ might be deleted by a singulary transformation at level i, and thus might not appear in (77). But we know that $x*D_Ay$ appears in (77) if and only if $x*D_A'y$ appears in (78).

From (77) and (78) we conclude that there are strings t_1, t_2, t_3 of terminals of Top(P) such that

(79) $*A(P) = t_1*[A^{i,e}(P)]_{i-1}t_2*D_At_3$, and

(80) $*A(P') = t_1*[A^{j,e}(P')]_{j-1}t_2*D_A't_3$.

Here, as by our earlier convention, if no raising took place, $*D_A = D_A' = \emptyset$.

We can repeat this entire construction for component C and conclude that there are strings u_1, u_2, u_3 of terminals of Top(P) such that

(81) $*C(P) = u_1*[C^{i,e}(P)]_{i-1}u_2*D_Cu_3$, and

(82) $*C(P') = u_1*[C^{j,e}(P')]_{j-1}u_2*D_C'u_3$.

But since we have assumed that there is no detectable error on $P'(i)$, $*A(P') = *C(P')$. Thus, substituting (80) and (82) we have

(83) $t_1*[A^{j,e}(P')]_{j-1}t_2*D_A't_3 = u_1*[C^{j,e}(P')]_{j-1}u_2*D_C'u_3$.

But from (69), we can take $w = *[A^{j,e}(P')]_{j-1} = *[C^{j,e}(P')]_{j-1}$ and from (67) we can take $z = *D_A' = *D_C'$. Therefore,

(84) $t_1wt_2zt_3 = u_1wu_2zu_3$.

We have assumed that there is no copying, so the elements in the sequence w are distinct from the elements in t_1. Likewise, the elements in w are distinct from u_1. From this fact and (84) we have $t_1 = u_1$. Likewise, z is distinct from t_2 and u_2. Taken together the conclusion is

(85) $t_i = u_i$, for $1 \leq i \leq 3$.

Then, using (85), (70), and (72) to substitute into (81) we have

(86) $*C(P) = t_1*[A^{i,e}(P)]_{i-1}t_2*D_At_3.$

Comparing (86) with (79) we conclude

(87) $*A(P) = *C(P).$

Therefore there is no detectable error on P.

  This proves theorem 4 except that we have not yet considered the case where conclusion (iv) of theorem 3′ holds. In this case, for P', A raises a left or right segment of $A(P_{j-1}')$, which we call $*D_A'$ where D_A is the node that dominates the raised packet. Component C raises a packet $*D_C'$, which is the complement of $*D_A'$ (in $A(P_{j-1}')$). Thus, equation (67) becomes $*D_A' = *D_C'$. A similar change takes place in (70). (To prove that this revised equation holds, one has to assume that nodes always terminate in lexical items.) The situation appears similar to the case we have already proved, in which A and C raise identical packets. That proof depended on the arrangement of the raised packet and the packet left behind. The same packets show up in this case. It appears that the proof will proceed along similar lines, although we have not written it out explicitly. The primary reason we have not attempted to write out the proof in this case is that in section 4.3.5.1, for reasons given there, we will have to make some new assumptions (about heads), which make conclusion (iv) of theorem 3′ impossible. This is proved in lemma 1 of section 4.3.5.2. Thus theorem 4 is proved without having to consider the case where conclusion (iv) of theorem 3′ holds.

4.3.4.2 An Example To clarify the proof, we give here an example of the calculations of equation (74). Suppose that P is as given in (88a). A raising transformation T raises D from S_1 to attach to the right of C, under F. On the assumption that no other transformations apply, the derived structure after this S-essential transformation applies is shown in (88b). The calculation of (74) depends on whether F is frozen or not in (88b). (F is frozen if $F \rightarrow BCD$ is not a base rule.) First, suppose that F is frozen. We want to calculate, in terms of (74), the terminal string of P after the S-essential transformation T has applied at level 2. First, $E(\text{Top}(A^{2,e}(P)))$ is given in (89). Each of the bottom nodes of $E(\text{Top}(A^{2,e}(P)))$ dominates a frozen packet in $A^{2,e}(P)$, and these pack-

(88)

a. $P =$

b. $A^{2,e}(P) = S_2$

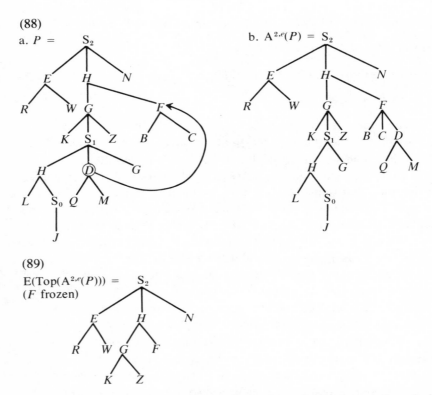

(89)

$E(Top(A^{2,e}(P))) = S_2$
(F frozen)

ets (plus the embedded sentence), taken in order, make up the whole terminal string $*A^{2,e}(P)$. That is, we can write the terminal string, according to (74), as in (90). Above each terminal packet (R, W, and so on)

(90) E_1 E_2 E_3 u $*[A^{2,e}(P)]_1$ v E_4 x $*D$ y E_5

$*A^{2,e}(P) =$ R W K $[\emptyset$ L J G $\emptyset]$ Z $[B$ C Q M $\emptyset]$ N

we have written the symbol from (74) that corresponds to the packet (E_1 above R, for example). Between each nonadjacent E_k and E_{k+1} occurs a frozen packet, set off by brackets. The parameters of (74) are $m = 4, n = 5, r = 5$.

Now, consider the same transformation T applying to P, but in this case assume that the transformation is structure-preserving at the place of attachment. In other words, F in (88b) is not frozen. Then $E(Top(A^{2,e}(P)))$ is given in (91). Since F isn't frozen, its immediate

(91)

$E(Top(A^{2,e}(P))) = S_2$
(F not frozen)

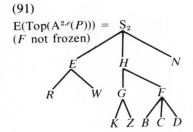

structure is eligible. But the Raising principle implies that the nodes that the raised D dominates are not eligible. Then we calculate the terminal string according to (74) as in (92). In this case, $m = 4$, $n = 7$, $r = 7$.

(92) E_1 E_2 E_3 u $*[A^{2,e}(P)]_1$ v E_4 E_5 E_6 x $*D$ y E_7

$*A^{2,e}(P) = R$ W K $[\emptyset$ $\overbrace{L\ J\ G}$ $\emptyset]$ Z B C $[\emptyset$ $\overbrace{Q\ M}$ $\emptyset]$ N

To take the remaining cases, in which the raised node is attached under a node that dominates S_1, suppose that a different raising transformation, T', applies to P. Call the revised component A'. T' raises D and attaches it to the right of F, under H. The derived structure is given in (93). If $H \rightarrow GFD$ is a base rule, then H is not frozen. In this case, since there are no frozen packets (except what S_1 and D dominate), the calculation of (74) is exactly the same as (92). (However, $E(Top(A'^{2,e}(P)))$ will be slightly different from (91), in that D will appear directly under H, not under F.)

If, on the other hand, H is frozen, we first calculate $E(Top(A'^{2,e}(P)))$, which is given in (94). The calculation according to (74) is then given in (95). Here, $m = n = r = 3$. As mentioned earlier, in this kind of case, $x*Dy$ is part of v. The frozen node H dominates the entire frozen packet $KLJGZBCQM$.

(93)

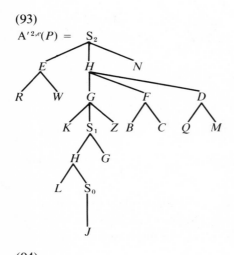

$$A'^{2,e}(P) = S_2$$

(94)

$$E(\text{Top}(A'^{2,e}(P))) = S_2$$
(H frozen)

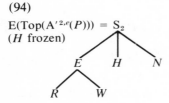

(95) E_1 E_2 u $*[A'^{2,e}(P)]_1$ v E_3

$$*A'^{2,e}(P) = R \quad W \quad [K \quad \overbrace{L \ J \ G} \quad \overbrace{Z \ B \ C \ Q \ M}] \quad N$$

4.3.4.3 Necessity of Assumptions about Corresponding Nodes At first sight it might appear that part (iii) of the definition of *preservation* ($\cong$)—section 4.3.4.1—is not needed in order to prove the Substitution theorem. The essential characteristic of the relation between P and P' that insures that their error behavior is the same seems to be that the eligible structures of P and P' are the same at the point when transformations are about to apply (parts (i) and (ii) of the definition of preservation). However, this is not enough for the proof of the Substitution theorem, as can be seen by the following counterexample. The common matrix of P and P' is given in (96). The partially derived phrase-marker in (96) is a schema for a degree-1 p-m, with different choices

(96)

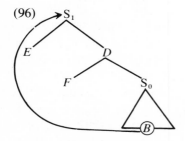

possible for the embedded 0-degree p-m dominated by S_0. At S_1 an S-essential transformation raises B. S_0 is to be filled in with one of four 0-degree phrase-markers, defined in (97a)–(97d).

(97)

a. $A(P_0') = S_0$

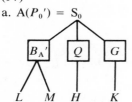

b. $C(P_0') = S_0$

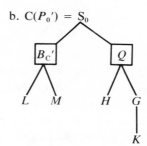

c. $A(P_0) = S_0$

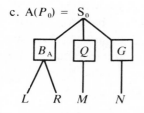

d. $C(P_0) = S_0$

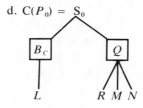

The nodes B_A', B_C', B_A and B_C are all of category B. They have been labeled distinctively here to show which p-m's they occur in. These four phrase-markers are the result of applying component A or C to P_0 or P_0', the 0-degree p-m's embedded in P and P', respectively. (For purposes of this example it is not necessary to define P_0 and P_0'—the transformed p-m's are all that are relevant.)

First, note that all the assumptions of the Substitution theorem except (iii) of the definition of preservation are met. (i) There is no detectable error on P' or on any of its sub-p-m's. B is raised by A and C at level 1, and the terminal string is $*A(P) = *C(P) = LMEFHK$. (ii) There is no detectable error on P_0 since $*A(P_0) = *C(P_0) = LRMN$. (iii) $Top^+(P) = Top^+(P')$, as given in (96). (iv) $P_0 \cong P_0'$, with assumption (iii) of $\cong$ relaxed. That is, $E(Top(A(P_0))) = (E(A(P_0))$ since P_0 is degree 0, and it can be seen in (98a) that $E(Top(A(P_0))) = E(Top(A(P_0')))$. Likewise, in (98b) it can be seen that $E(Top(C(P_0))) = E(Top(C(P_0')))$.

(98)

a.
$E(Top(A(P_0)))$
$= E(Top(A(P_0'))) =$

b.
$E(Top(C(P_0)))$
$= E(Top(C(P_0'))) =$

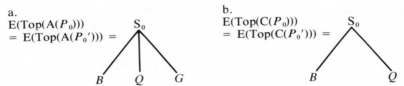

To see why (iii) of preservation doesn't hold, first note that B_A' corresponds to B_A, and B_C, corresponds to B_C'. But $*B_A' = LM = *B_C'$ and thus $*B_A' = *B_C'$, whereas $*B_A = LR$ and $*B_C = L$, implying that $*B_A \neq *B_C$. This contradicts (iii) of the definition of preservation.

Of course, it is the failure of just this property that leads to the failure of the Substitution theorem. $*A(P) = LREFMN$ and $*C(P) = LEFRMN$. Therefore, $*A(P) \neq *C(P)$ and there is a detectable error on P, contrary to the Substitution theorem. This detectable error doesn't occur on P' because although B is raised in P', B dominates the same packet under both components A and C. This example demonstrates the necessity of assumption (iii) of preservation for the proof of the Substitution theorem.

4.3.4.4 Existence of Untransformable 0-Extensions

Our next goal is to prove that if two transformational components raise identical packets of terminal nodes, then if the category of the dominating (raised) node is different for the two components, a detectable error occurs on a degree-1 p-m. This is Category Raising Equivalence. This result is important for the proof of our main result. If it did not hold, the two components could raise different categories without producing a detectable error. These categories could be attached to nodes still eligible for transformation (nodes not ruled out by the Raising principle). In theorem 3′ we proved that identical packets had to be raised, but said nothing about the categories of the nodes dominating these packets.

The proof of Category Raising Equivalence will proceed in the following manner. Given a case of two transformational components raising different categories, we will construct a degree-1 phrase-marker on which a detectable error occurs. We will do this in the usual way, by forming P' from P_i. P' drops all nodes under the frozen nodes in P_{i-1} and then takes a 0-extension of those nodes. If the bottom part of P' can be transformed, it may happen that a raising transformation that applied to P doesn't apply to P', contrary to the point of the construction. In theorem 5 we prove that an untransformable 0-extension exists. TUBS plays a major role here, for the kinds of reasons discussed when we introduced TUBS.

In order to prove Category Raising Equivalence (which we will do in theorem 7), it will be useful to prove also that the 0-extension in P' is such that the 0-degree bottom p-m is untransformable not only by component A but also by component C. This is the second part of theorem 5. On the assumption that there are no detectable errors on 0-degree p-m's, this result is almost obvious since A is not transformed; thus transformation of C should cause a detectable error. But C could be transformed without changing the terminal string. We might try to rule this out by prohibiting such string-preserving transformations. However this is not sufficient, because two non-string-preserving transformations could apply and their joint application could preserve the original string. That is, there might be transformations T_1 and T_2 such that $*T_1(P) \neq *P$, but $*T_2(T_1(P)) = *P$. What we want is to insure that a p-m never has the same terminal string at two different points in the derivation. Recall, as always, that the terminal string is a string of *nodes*, not categories or lexical items. Two nodes with the same terminal category, even the same lexical item, might interchange and the result would not be string-preserving. The principle of Nonuniqueness of Lexical Items (NULI) will assure that there will be another p-m on which a detectable error occurs (see theorem 2).

Assumption against String Preservation (ASP): If, in a transformational derivation applied to a base p-m P, the terminal string at any one stage of the derivation is ever repeated at a later stage, P is filtered out.[40]

Theorem 5: Let A and C be transformational components such that no detectable error occurs on any 0-degree p-m. Let P be a p-m (of arbitrary degree) that is not filtered by A.[41] Then there exists a 0-degree base p-m P' such that
i. $A(P')$ is an extension of $E(\text{Top}(A(P)))$, and
ii. $A(P') = C(P')$.

Proof: Let all transformations in A apply to P, so that P is no longer transformable under A. This yields $A(P)$. It follows from the Freezing principle that $E(\text{Top}(A(P)))$ is a partially derived 0-degree base p-m that is not transformable. Thus the TUBS principle (see section 4.1.12) implies that there exists a 0-extension of $E(\text{Top}(A(P)))$ to a fully derived base p-m P' such that P' is untransformable by A. That is, $A(P') = P'$, which is itself an extension of $E(\text{Top}(A(P)))$. This proves (i) of theorem 5.

Since there are no detectable errors on any 0-degree p-m, there is no detectable error on P. That is, $*A(P') = *C(P')$. But since, as shown, $A(P') = P'$, we have $*A(P') = *P'$. Thus $*C(P') = *P'$. However, if any transformations in C applied to P, it would then happen that at two different stages of the derivation (before and after C applied), P' would have the same terminal string. Therefore, by the assumption against repeating terminal strings (ASP), P' is filtered by C. It follows from (i) that P' is not filtered by A, so there is a detectable error on the 0-degree p-m P', contrary to assumption. Therefore our assumption that a transformation in C applies to P' is wrong, and $C(P') = P' = A(P')$, which proves (ii) of theorem 5.

4.3.5 Category Raising Equivalence
4.3.5.1 A Model (Heads)

Property of Category Raising Equivalence (CRE): Let P be a base p-m and A and C be transformational components such that there are no detectable errors on phrase-markers of degree 0 or 1. For any level i, if A applied to P raises a node of category F or S-essentially deletes the node at level i, then either both components filter P or component C raises or S-essentially deletes a node of category F at level i.

We will use the property of CRE in the proof of the main theorem, theorem 8. Therefore, it is important to prove the validity of this property. Since the possibilities of structural changes which the property rules out seem to involve complicated and perhaps pathological interaction, there might be many kinds of assumptions that would allow the property to be derived. Perhaps we could simply assume that the property holds and proceed from there. However, it is of interest to see how we might insure that the property holds. In this section we will provide one path toward that end, one having the advantage that it not only allows the property to be derived but makes use of some traditional (though partially implicit) properties of grammatical analyses (both transformational and phrase-structural).

We want to restrict the possibilities for transformations to operate in such a way that two different components allow the same sequence of terminal nodes (packets) to be dominated by different nodes. This is in essential respects equivalent to allowing transformations to permute nodes in a phrase-marker in such a way that a packet that was originally dominated by a particular node comes to be dominated by a different node. (We mean exhaustively dominated, of course.) It has long been considered a desirable goal to bar relabeling of phrases. Of course, direct relabeling is already ruled out in our framework, since we do not allow a transformational rule to simply change a category (rewrite a PP as an adverb, for instance). However, we have to do more: we have to restrict indirect relabeling, in which phrases take on new category membership by virtue of movement and deletion rules.

The path we will pursue makes crucial use of the notion of *head* of a phrase, a traditional grammatical notion that has received recent attention in grammatical theory, especially with respect to $\overline{X}$ theory.[42] By restricting opportunities for movement and deletion of heads, it will turn out that we can restrict in an interesting way the opportunities for relabeling and will therefore be able to prove that the property of category raising equivalence holds.

Assumption: In any base rule $F \rightarrow F_1F_2 \ldots F_n$ (F not a lexical category) exactly one of the F_i is designated as the *head* of F.

In this statement we have not explicitly allowed for notational conventions such as optional parentheses and disjunctive braces. That is, *base rule* is to be taken as *rewrite rule* of the usual definitions of context-free grammars. If we allowed notational conventions, the modified assumption would state that the head must be an *obligatory* category of the expansion (or conceivably an element of a set of possibilities, one of which is obligatory). For the present it seems simpler to define things the way we have. The move to notational conventions and $\bar{X}$ theory should be straightforward.

Assumption: If F_i is a lexical category and F_i is introduced in a rule $F \rightarrow F_1 \ldots F_i \ldots F_n$, then
i. F_j is not a lexical category for $i \neq j$, and
ii. F_i is the head of F.

In other words, at most one lexical category is introduced in a rule, and if a lexical category is introduced this category is the head of the phrase. It seems to us that these assumptions follow the principles both of head theory and of the usual practice in the writing of phrase-structure rules.

Thus we have the situation diagrammed in (99). In (99),

i. $F = F^i$ is the dominating node of any phrase,
ii. F^j is the head of F^{j+1} ($0 \leq j \leq i-1$),
iii. F^1 is a lexical category node,
iv. $F^0 = f$ is a lexical item node, and
v. we can call F^j the j-head of F.

One of the points that $\bar{X}$ theory is concerned with is how big i can get (this is related to the question of how many bars there are). These questions need not concern us here. Nevertheless we can be confident that the kinds of restrictions that $\bar{X}$ theory can put on phrase-structure grammars should be of central importance to the theory of learnability.

(99)

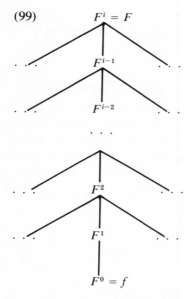

$$F^i = F$$
$$F^{i-1}$$
$$F^{i-2}$$
$$\cdots$$
$$F^2$$
$$F^1$$
$$F^0 = f$$

The following assumption will play a central role in the model for deriving category raising equivalence.

Principle of Heads (PH):[43] If F^{i-1} is the head of F^i, then no transformation may have the effect of removing F^{i-1} from under F^i; in particular,

i. F^{i-1} may be deleted by a transformation only if F^i is deleted by the same transformation application, and

ii. F^{i-1} may not be moved to a position such that it is not dominated by F^i.

Remark: In other words, throughout the course of a derivation a node immediately dominates its head. The assumption can, as usual, be realized in a number of ways, for example, by hypothesizing particular transformations or by filtering when the assumption is violated. We will not discuss the various possibilities, but for convenience in proofs will simply assume that if the principle of Heads is violated, the phrase-marker is filtered.[44]

It will also prove useful to make another assumption.

Assumption: S is never the head of any category.

This assumption, too, fits well with head theory ($\overline{X}$ theory) and, in fact, is probably derivable from the theory. We will not enter into a discussion of the formal properties of head theory here (but see note 44).

Theorem 6: Let A,C be transformational components and P be a base phrase-marker. Suppose, after transformations apply to level i of P, P has been filtered by neither A nor C and there is a node F (of category F) in $\mathrm{Top}(A(P_i))$ and a node G (of category G) in $\mathrm{Top}(C(P_i))$, category $F \neq$ category G, such that F and G dominate the same terminal packet, that is, $*F_A = *G_C$. Then there is a node F (of category F) in $\mathrm{Top}(C(P_i))$ such that either
i. G dominates F, or
ii. F dominates G and G is a j-head of F for some j.

Remark: Since the assumptions are symmetric in A and C, the corresponding conclusion holds for component C, that is, with A substituting for C, G for F, and F for G.

Proof: Although it appears complicated, the situation is really quite simple. By the definition of *head* we know that in the base phrase-marker P, $F = F^j$ immediately dominates its head F^{j-1}, and so on, to yield (100). By the principle of Heads, heads may not be removed by

(100)

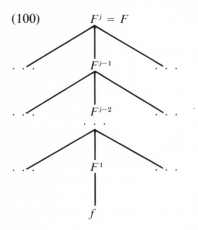

transformations. Thus (100) still holds after transforming, that is, in $A(P_i)$. Likewise $G = G^k$ has heads and in P and $C(P_i)$ we have the same situation, namely (101). But F and G dominate the same terminal

(101)

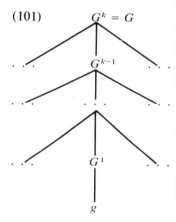

string. In particular, G dominates the lexical node f (the lexical head of F). (Note that g and f are the names of *nodes*, not lexical items.) But f is immediately dominated by F^1. In general F^h is immediately dominated by F^{h+1}. By inspecting (100) one can see that there are only two ways in which G can dominate f in $C(P_i)$. First, F could dominate G and G dominate F. That is, $G = F^h$ for some h, $1 \leq h \leq j$, which means that G is an h-head of F. And since G is in $\text{Top}(C(P_i))$ and F dominates G in $C(P_i)$, we know that F is in $\text{Top}(C(P_i))$. Therefore conclusion (ii) of theorem 6 follows. This situation is seen in (102). The second way that G can dominate f in $C(P_i)$ (again from an inspection of (100)) is for G to dominate F. In this case, F can either be an h-head of G (as in (103a)) or not (as in (103b)). In either case, (103a) or (103b), G dominates F, and in order to prove that (ii) of theorem 6 holds, we have to show only that F is in $\text{Top}(C(P_i))$. Suppose first that in the base p-m P, before transforming, F is in a higher cycle (level) than G. Say, F is in cycle k and G is in cycle h, where $k > h$. This can be seen in (104). We have already shown that after transformations apply, in $C(P_i)$, G dominates F. But since we don't allow any lowering transformations (transformations

(102)

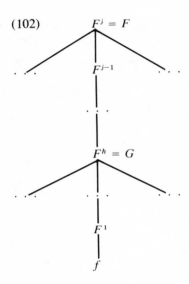

(103)
a.

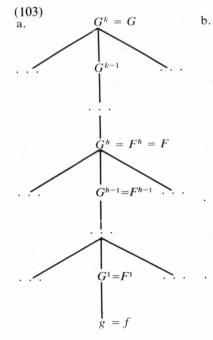

b.

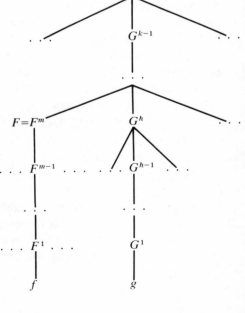

(104)

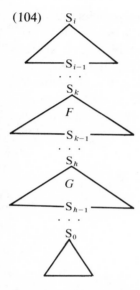

that move a node to a lower cycle), the only way that G could come to dominate F would be for G to be raised. According to restrictions on S-essential transformations (and the Binary principle), nodes can be raised only one cycle at a time. So the first raising of G must be from level S_h to level S_{h+1}. But the Raising principle will freeze G after it is raised. An effect of the freezing is that no node can be inserted under G;[45] so, F can never be inserted under G, contrary to what we have proved. Therefore we conclude that F cannot be in a higher cycle than G in P.

Now suppose that G is in a higher cycle than F in P. Say, G is in cycle k and F is in cycle h, where $k > h$. The situation is the same as (104), except that F and G are interchanged. Now we have to consider the effect of component A on P. As pointed out in the remark after the statement of theorem 6, the symmetric conclusion applies to component A. And we have already proved the conclusion except for showing that the relevant node in case (ii) is in the top 0-degree p-m. That is, we have already shown that in $A(P_i)$, either F dominates G, or G dominates F and F is a j-head of G for some j. Suppose the first case, that is, F dominates G in $A(P_i)$. But we have supposed that G is in a higher cycle than F in P, so the same argument (from the Raising principle) that we used earlier in the proof leads to a contradiction: G's being in a higher cycle than F in P is inconsistent with F's later dominating G. Therefore, suppose the second case, that F is a j-head of G in $A(P_i)$. By the principle of Heads, F must then be a j-head of G in P. But then G must dominate F in P. Furthermore, since G is in a higher cycle than F in P, a node labeled S must intercede between G and F. That is, G dominates S_{k-1}, which in turn dominates F. The situation can be seen in (105):

(105)

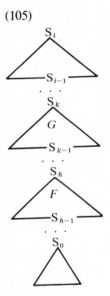

Since F is a j-head of G, and since G dominates S_{k-1} and S_{k-1} dominates F, the definition of *head* implies that S_{k-1} is an m-head of G, for some $m > j$. But we have assumed that S is not the head of *any* category. Therefore this case also contradicts our assumptions, and we can conclude that G is not in a higher cycle than F in P.

The one remaining case is where F and G are in the same cycle in the transformed phrase-marker P. Say F and G are both in cycle k in P. This situation is indicated in (106). Now, let transformations in component C apply up through level S_k. We know that G is in $Top(C(P_i))$. Therefore G (or a node dominating G) must be raised by an S-essential

(106)

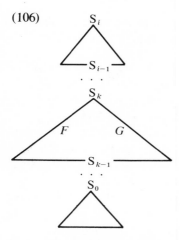

transformation from level S_k to level S_{k+1}. But, again by the Raising principle, if F is not under G when G is raised to cycle S_{k+1}, then F can never be inserted under G.[46] Therefore, F must be placed under G by the non-S-essential transformations applying at S_k. That is, G dominates F in $C(P_k)$. But since transformations don't lower nodes (put them in lower cycles), there may be no S node between G and F. That is, G and F are in Top($C(P_k)$). Once G is raised to S_{k+1}, the Raising principle prevents F from being moved from under G. It also prevents F from being deleted, since G is not deleted in P_i. Thus F continues to be raised with G to Top($C(P_i)$). That is, since G is in Top($C(P_i)$) and since G dominates F with no S in between, we conclude that F is in Top($C(P_i)$). This proves theorem 6.

Remark: It is interesting to note the role that the principle of Heads plays in the proof of theorem 6. Without the principle, there would be, for example, no requirement that G dominate f, the lexical head of F in P. Hence there would be no constraint on the relation between G and F, and the theorem could not be proved. As we indicated earlier, here we are just providing one model for the derivation of category raising equivalence; it is highly likely that others are possible. In particular, we think that head theory may play a crucial role in this constraint, but there are doubtless other properties of head theory that should be explored. Much remains to be done in this intriguing area of the relation between head theory and learnability theory.[47]

4.3.5.2 Idea of Proof and Further Assumptions We are now almost ready to prove that the principle of Category Raising Equivalence (CRE) holds (theorem 7). The idea of the proof is straightforward. If two components raise different categories F and G, we will construct a degree-1 p-m based on the two relevant levels; namely, the levels raised from and to. We will then show that the component that raises G in the original p-m has to be able to raise F in the constructed degree-1 p-m, or else there will be a detectable error on the degree-1 p-m, contrary to assumption. Then, using theorem 6, we will show that both categories F and G have to be in the top level of the original p-m which has been transformed by the component that raises G. The principle of No Bottom Context will then imply that since F is raised in the constructed degree-1 p-m, it is raised in the original p-m, along with G. But the principle of Determinism interpreted strongly (as we shall explain) or the principle that says that at most one S-essential transformation may apply at any level (interpreted strongly) will imply that a detectable error exists, contrary to assumption.

Actually, NBC is not quite enough to allow us to infer that if a node is raised in one p-m, then if the same category exists in the bottom of another degree-1 p-m and the top levels of the p-m's are identical, the node of the same category in the second p-m is also raised. This is because, as we earlier indicated, there can be a boundary effect (see note 14). Therefore, for the purposes of the proof of theorem 7, we will have to assume a slight strengthening of NBC.

Assumption: We strengthen NBC to assume that an S-essential transformation is independent of all bottom context. That is, any transformation can be assumed to have implicit variables around the node to which the transformation S-essentially applies, these variables applying only to elements in the lower p-m. This assumption will not allow the special effects discussed in note 14, but perhaps it can be eliminated on further study. At any rate, since it is stronger than NBC, it does not affect proofs of earlier theorems.

In the course of the proof we will have to show that both components A and C raise the same node in the constructed p-m. To do this we will have to eliminate the possibility that a nonbranching node K dominates another node L, and that one component raises K while the other component raises L. In order to make the proof work here we will use the principle of Designated Representatives, first discussed and defined in section 4.3.3.2. However, it is interesting to note that the principle of Heads would be sufficient. The principle of Heads will not allow L to be moved from under K (in particular, to be raised) because every node must have a head and thus L must be $K's$ head. Instead of doing the proof in this one-step, immediate way, however, we have chosen to use the principle of Designated Representatives. One reason is that the definition of *head* and of the principle of Heads may be too strong (possibly just in the case of nonbranching nodes). Therefore, it is instructive to see what other principle could be substituted. In addition, since we need DR, as shown in (65) and the ensuing discussion, we can use it here without making an additional assumption.[48]

We will have to make yet one other modification in the assumptions of the system. A key element of the proof will be the demonstration that two categories will exist in a p-m, both of them raisable, this not being allowed by determinism. But all that we will actually be able to show is that the two raisable categories exist in the p-m, and in fact that they are not frozen by RP. However, it will still be possible that one of the categories is frozen by FP, thus not allowing Determinism to rule out the p-m. In order to overcome this possibility we will make the following assumption:

Assumption of Freezing-Principle Strict Determinism (FPSD): The adult transformational component A is such that no two transformations (or applications of one transformation) simultaneously fit, even if one of them is ruled out by the Freezing principle.

The interpretation that we will make of this principle is the same as the interpretation given to the original principle of Determinism, namely, that component A simply has the property. Component C, on the other hand, may not satisfy the property. However, at any stage in the derivation of a p-m in component C, if two transformations simultaneously fit, even if one of them is ruled out by FP, the learning procedure considers that there is a detectable error. Thus FPSD implies that if two transformations simultaneously fit a p-m, there is a detectable error. So if we can show that two transformations simultaneously fit a p-m of degree 0 or 1, there is a detectable error on a p-m of degree 0 or 1. This implication will be used in the proof of theorem 7, to handle just the case that we have been considering.[49]

Recall that we are trying to provide a model that allows us to derive Category Raising Equivalence, which probably can be done in many ways. A fault with FPSD is that it seems to take away a good deal of the power of the Freezing principle, reducing many of its effects (though not all—consider the case where no other transformations apply) to that of Determinism. It would be important to find another assumption to allow the proof to work, or even better, to use some of the assumptions we have already discussed. Once again, we think that head theory and transformational assumptions relating to head theory would be quite helpful here. For example, the assumption that nonheads are cyclic nodes, discussed in note 47, would mean that nonheads would count in the Binary principle. This assumption, together with the principle of Heads, which says that a head may not be moved (or deleted) from under the node of which it is a head, might limit certain kinds of compounding of transformational operations to such an extent that the complicated convolutions of transformational applications necessary to attain equivalent terminal nodes of different categories might be impossible. Also, as mentioned earlier, these kinds of assumptions might simplify our whole problem, allowing us to eliminate other assumptions.

There is one other possibility that we have to deal with. In the proof of CRE (and of theorem 8 also), we will use the fact (proved in theorem 3′) that both components raise identical packets, if there is no detectable error. But a further possibility in theorem 3′, namely (iv), allows the complement of a packet raised by one component to be raised by another component, with no detectable error or filtering resulting. Examples can be constructed which show that this possibility can exist. It turns out that the assumptions that we have made about heads rule out this possibility, as can be seen in lemma 1.

Lemma 1: For any two transformational components A and C, and for a p-m P of degree i, if component A S-essentially applies to a packet K at level S_i, and if there is no detectable error on P and P is not filtered by C, then at level S_i component C cannot S-essentially apply to $\bar{K}$, the complement of K in $*A(P_{i-1}) = *C(P_{i-1})$.

Note: Here we have generalized the notion complement to be defined as the string of nodes formed by deleting K from the string $*A(P_i)$. That is, K does not have to be a left or right segment. Nevertheless, the latter case is all that we need.

Proof: By definition, every category has a lexical head in a p-m. Let s be the lexical head of S_{i-1} in $*A(P_{i-1})$. By the principle of Heads, s remains under S_{i-1}, no matter what transformations apply. Thus s is not in K, the packet to which an S-essential deletion or raising has applied. Since s is the lexical head of S_{i-1}, it also (by the principle of Heads) remains dominated by S_{i-1} in $C(P)$, and s can neither be deleted nor raised at level S_i. But we have already shown that s is not in K. Thus s, a node in $\bar{K}$, is not deleted or raised at level S_i. And thus $\bar{K}$ is not deleted or raised at S_i. This proves lemma 1.

4.3.5.3 An Example Before proving Theorem 7, it will be useful to look at an example that demonstrates a number of points. First, the example shows the kinds of compounding of transformational applications that result in equivalent terminal packets being dominated by different nodes in the two components without causing a detectable error. Second, the example will illustrate theorem 6. Third, the example will show why we have to assume FPSD. Fourth, the example will be suggestive regarding how the Binary principle together with the kind of strong relation between head theory and cycle theory that we have just discussed might play a fundamental role in ruling out many learnability problems.

The base phrase-marker P is shown in (107a), and the two stages of its transformational derivation under component A are shown in (107b)

(107) Component A:

a.

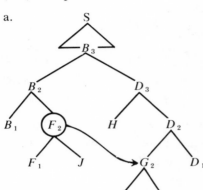

b.

⇒

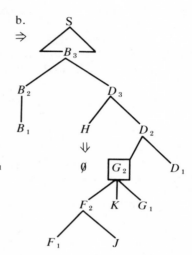

c.

⇒

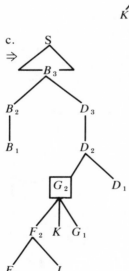

and (107c). P is repeated in (108a), and the two stages of its transformational derivation under component C are shown in (108b) and (108c). First notice that we have used subscripts on some of the categories in (107) and (108). This is because we want to show that we haven't violated the principle of Heads. A category with a subscript i is the head of an immediately dominating category with the same label and subscript $i+1$. For example, in (107a) D_2 is the head of D_3. We haven't assumed that each category is of the same height. For example, in (107a), D is of height 3, and F and G are of height 2. In head theory one might want to assume that each category is of the same height.

The transformations work as follows. In component A (107), first F_2 is moved and adjoined to the left of K, freezing G_2, which dominates K (the transformation is non-structure-preserving at the point of attachment). Then H is deleted.[50] On the other hand, in component C (108), G_2 is moved to the left, to become a right-adjunct of J, thus freezing F_2, which dominates J. Then H is deleted. The point of deleting H is that we do not want a detectable error, which would otherwise result. The terminal string in both cases is now $B_1F_1JKG_1D_1$. H is used as a device to avoid violating the principle that no two derivational stages of a p-m may have the same terminal string (section 4.3.4.4). Also note that the principle of Heads is not violated; in fact, none of the transformations move or delete a head.

Nevertheless, it turns out that $*G_{2_A} = *F_{2_C}$. That is, in the surface p-m's G_2 in A(P) dominates the same terminal packet, namely F_1JKG_1, as does F_2 in C(P). Suppose now that P were part of a larger p-m. Then, in component A, G_2 could be raised to a higher level, and in component C, F_2 could be raised, and there would be no detectable error. It is true that F_2 also exists in A(P) = Top(A(P)) (assuming P is degree 0), and in fact, G_2 exists in C(P) = Top(C(P)). But these nodes are frozen; therefore, even though we can show that a transformation will raise them (that is, F_2 in A(P) and G_2 in C(P)), the original principle of Determinism won't rule out the example. But Freezing-Principle Strict Determinism will create a detectable error. Note, in addition, how theorem 6 still holds. In A(P), G_2 dominates F_2, and in C(P), F_2 dominates G_2.

If all nonheads were cyclic nodes, counting in the Binary principle,

(108) Component C:

a.

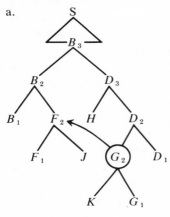

b.

⇒

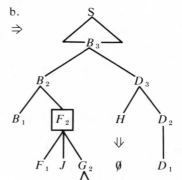

c.

⇒

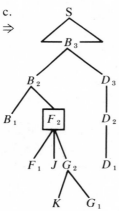

then S_3, D_3, and G_2 would be cyclic nodes. Therefore, the first transformation in component A could not apply. This is because the transformation has to attach F_2 to the left of K, which is dominated by too many cyclic nodes according to the Binary Principle. Once again, the development of head theory might tell us whether this situation is general, that is, whether these assumptions will simply not allow two different nodes in different components to dominate the same terminal packets.

4.3.5.4 The Proof

Theorem 7: The property of Category Raising Equivalence (CRE) holds. That is, suppose there is no detectable error on any p-m of degree 0 or 1. Suppose A and C are transformational components and that a transformation in A S-essentially applies to a node of category F at level i of a base p-m P which is not filtered by A. Then either
i. There is a detectable error on P, or
ii. Component C S-essentially applies to a node of category F at level i of P. Furthermore, if A raises F, then so does C; and if A deletes F, then so does C.

Proof: Consider first the packets (not the dominating nodes) that are involved. Suppose that at level i, component A raises terminal packet K. Then, according to theorem 3′, if component C does not raise an identical packet, either P is filtered by both components, or there is a detectable error on P. But P cannot be filtered by both components, because we have assumed that P is not filtered by A. That there is a detectable error on P is conclusion (i) of the theorem that we are proving. Therefore we can assume that component C raises an identical terminal packet, K. An identical proof exists to show that if A S-essentially deletes packet K at level i, so does component C. In fact, the remainder of the proof will be identical whether we are considering raising or S-essential deletion, so we will discuss only the raising case.

We have assumed that there is no detectable error on any 0-degree p-m. Also, C does not filter P_{i-1} or else there would be a detectable error on P_{i-1}. Therefore theorem 5 applies, and implies that there exists a 0-degree base p-m P_0' such that

(109) $A(P_0')$ is an extension of $E(\text{Top}(A(P_{i-1})))$, and

(110) $A(P_0') = C(P_0')$.

We now construct a degree-1 p-m $P' = P_1'$ by substituting P_0' for P_{i-1} in P. Thus $\text{Top}(P') = \text{Top}(P)$. Since F is raised from level $i - 1$ to i in P, we know by the Freezing principle that F is part of the eligible structure of $A(P_{i-1})$. Therefore (109) implies that F is part of the eligible structure of $A(P_0')$. That is, $F \in E(A(P_0'))$. Thus by the principle of No Bottom Context, F is raised in P' (from level 0 to level 1) by the same transformation that raises F from level $i-1$ to i in P. The situation is shown in (111). We have assumed that P is not filtered by A. But once F has been

(111)

raised, the Raising principle implies that the transformations that apply to level i of P apply to level 1 of P', and only these transformations apply. Therefore P' is not filtered by A either. Also there is no detectable error on P', since we have assumed that there are no detectable errors on degree-1 phrase-markers. Therefore theorem 3' and lemma 1 imply that component C must raise an identical packet from level 0 to level 1 of P', as component A does. Since A raises node F (of category F), we say that both components raise terminal packet *F.

Component C could have a transformation raising F, but there are two other possibilities, which we will show actually cannot hold. A nonbranching node K might dominate F and be raised or F might be nonbranching and dominate a node L, which might be raised. These two possibilities are illustrated in (112). The nonbranching property of

(112)

a. K b. F

course must hold of all the nodes between K and F (in (112a)) or between F and L (in (112b)). If $K = F$ (the nodes, not the categories) or $L = F$, then the category F is raised. So we suppose $F \neq K \neq L$. At this point the principle of Heads would rule out these two possibilities, because if a node is nonbranching, it must dominate only its head, which therefore could not be raised. But, instead we will use other principles to derive the result.

Suppose first that (112a) holds and component C raises K in P'. But (110) implies that (112a) is also the structure of a part of the tree dominating F in $A(P_0')$. (There could not be another F in $A(P_0')$ by the principle of Determinism.) Therefore, the principle of Designated Representatives implies that a designated representative d_F is left behind by component A when F is raised, since F has no sisters. But component C leaves no representative behind, or (if K has no sisters) leaves d_K behind. Since $K \neq F$, $d_K \neq d_F$, by DR. Also, part (ii) of DR says that if a designated representative is deleted, the p-m is filtered. But we have already shown that A doesn't filter P', and if C filtered P', there would be a detectable error on a degree-1 p-m, contrary to assumption. Therefore P' also is not filtered. And the designated representatives d_K and d_F, which are unequal, show up as part of the terminal strings in *$C(P')$ and *$A(P')$ respectively. Since designated representatives can only be introduced by S-essential transformations, and USET implies that there is at most one S-essential transformation per level, no further designated representatives can be introduced. So $*A(P') \neq *C(P')$, contrary to the assumption that there are no detectable errors on any degree-1 p-m's. Therefore K cannot be raised by component C. The same kind of argument works for case (112b). If L is raised by component C, then d_L is left behind, causing a detectable error, contrary to assumption. Thus we have shown that

(113) Component C raises F in $P_1{}'$.

By construction, $\text{Top}(P) = \text{Top}(P')$. Therefore, from (113) and the principle of No Bottom Context we derive (114):

(114) If $F \in \text{Top}(C(P_{i-1}))$, there is a transformation $T \in C$ that fits P at level S_i (the top) and raises F.

Now, as the first step in the proof we showed that at level i component C raised a packet $*F$. Suppose that the dominating node of this packet is G, where $G \neq F$. (That is, $G \in C(P_{i-1})$.) Now, we have assumed that A does not filter P. So if C does filter P, there is a detectable error, which is conclusion (i) of this theorem 7. Therefore, neither component filters P and from this we can conclude that neither component filters P_{i-1}. Thus we can apply theorem 6 and conclude that

(115) There is a node F (of category F) in $\text{Top}(C(P_{i-1}))$.

Now we can assume that level i is the smallest level in P such that nodes of different categories are raised. (For if it isn't so, then we can repeat the construction on the smallest p-m for which this assumption holds.) The proof of theorem 6 shows that G and F had to start out in the same cycle k of P. Then they are raised together. But, of course, G must be the category raised by component C. The same argument shows that F and G also have to start out in the same cycle k of P and that F has to be the raised category. But if $k \leq i-1$, the assumption that level i is the smallest level in P such that nodes of different categories are raised is violated. Therefore we can assume that F and G start out in level $i-1$ of P. But then the Raising principle can't prevent a transformation from applying to G.

Therefore (114) and (115), together with this last conclusion, imply (116):

(116) There is a transformation T ϵ C which fits P at level S_i (except possibly for restrictions imposed by the Freezing principle) and which raises F.

But since we have already assumed that component C raises node G, (116) implies that component C violates the assumption of Freezing-Principle Strict Determinism. Therefore, we conclude that our assumption that the equivalent raised packets can have different dominating nodes, F and G, is wrong, and we have proved theorem 7.

4.4 Degree-2 Error Detectability: The Proof

Theorem 8 (Degree-2 Error Detectability): Let A and C be transformational components. If there is a detectable error with respect to A and C on some base phrase-marker P, then there exists a base phrase-marker P' of degree ≤ 2 such that there is a detectable error on P'.

Proof: We will construct a phrase marker P' of degree ≤ 2 such that there is a detectable error on P'. To do this we will show that the constructed P' satisfies the assumptions of the Substitution theorem (with respect to the original p-m on which there is a detectable error).

Suppose that there is a detectable error on some base p-m $\bar{P}$. We construct P from $\bar{P}$ by defining P as the smallest degree sub-phrase-marker of $\bar{P}$ on which there is a detectable error. That is, given that $\bar{P} = \bar{P}_q$ we let $P = \bar{P}_i$ for that i, $0 \leq i \leq q$, such that there is a detectable error on $\bar{P}_i$, but no detectable error on $\bar{P}_r$ for any $r \leq i$. Thus the degree of P is i. If $i < 3$, then the theorem follows. Therefore we take $i \geq 3$. We note again that although there is a detectable error on P, there is none on any of its sub-phrase-markers. Therefore assumption (ii) of the Substitution theorem (theorem 4) holds.

Assumption (ii) of theorem 4 is defined only on P. To show that the other assumptions hold, we have to first define P'. By construction we will take $\text{Top}^+(P) = \text{Top}^+(P')$ so that assumption (iii) of the Substitution theorem holds. Since the constructed P' will be of degree $j \leq 2$, the theorem would follow if there were a detectable error on P'; so we assume that there is no detectable error on P' or on any of its sub-p-m's (assumption (i) of the Substitution theorem). It remains only to construct this P' of degree $j \leq 2$ and to show that $P_{i-1} \cong P_{j-1}'$, which is the final assumption (iv) of the Substitution theorem. There are two cases, depending on whether an S-essential transformation in A applies at level $i-1$ of P.

Case (i): Suppose that at level $i-1$ of P, no S-essential transformation in A applies. Then we take $P' = P - P_{i-2}$. That is, we simply take P' as the degree-1 base phrase-marker formed from the top two levels of P. By the principle of S-optionality, we can delete P_{i-2} and still obtain a base p-m. In P' we will relabel S_i as S_1' and S_{i-1} as S_0'. These p-m's appear in (117):

(117)

a. $P =$ b. $P' =$

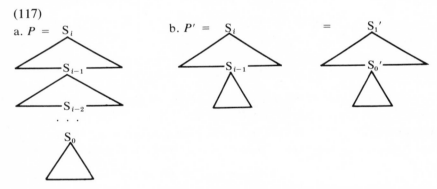

Now it only remains to show that $P_{i-1} \cong P_{j-1}'$, that is, that $P_{i-1} \cong P_0'$. First we must show that

(118) $E(\text{Top}(A(P_{i-1}))) = E(\text{Top}(A(P_0')))$.

But since P_0' is of degree 0, so is $A(P_0')$ and thus $\text{Top}(A(P_0')) = A(P_0')$. Therefore, $E(\text{Top}(A(P_0')) = E(A(P_0'))$. But since $P_0' = \text{Top}(P_{i-1})$ we have

(119) $E(\text{Top}(A(P_0'))) = E(A(\text{Top}(P_{i-1})))$.

But we have assumed that no S-essential transformation in A applies at level $i-1$ of P. Therefore, only non-S-essential transformations apply at level $i-1$ and by the principle of S-Invisibility, the presence of an S can have no effect on which transformations apply and how they apply.

Therefore, $\text{Top}(A(P_{i-1})) = A(\text{Top}(P_{i-1}))$, and thus

(120) $E(\text{Top}(A(P_{i-1}))) = E(A(\text{Top}(P_{i-1})))$.

Equation (118) then folows from (119) and (120). Now we have constructed P so that there is no detectable error on any sub-p-m of P. Thus there is no detectable error on P_{i-1} or any of its sub-p-m's. Suppose that $A(P_{i-1})$ were filtered. Then $A(P)$ would be filtered. But since there is a detectable error on P, this implies that $C(P)$ is not filtered and therefore $C(P_{i-1})$ is not filtered. The argument with A and C interchanged also works, so we have shown that $A(P_{i-1})$ and $C(P_{i-1})$ are not both filtered. Therefore, we have eliminated conclusions (ii) and (iii) of theorem 3'. Lemma 1 eliminates conclusion (iv) of theorem 3', which then implies that, since no S-essential transformation in A applies at level S_{i-1}, no S-essential transformation in C applies at S_{i-1}. Thus we can repeat the proof to obtain, for C,

(121) $E(\text{Top}(C(P_{i-1}))) = E(\text{Top}(C(P_0')))$.

In order to complete the proof that $P_{i-1} = P_0'$, we need only show that the correspondence property ((iii) of the definition of preservation) holds. Thus let D_A, D_C be nodes in $E(\text{Top}(A(P_{i-1}))) = E(A(\text{Top}(P_{i-1})))$ and $E(\text{Top}(C(P_{i-1}))) = E(C(\text{Top}(P_{i-1})))$ respectively, and let D_A', D_C' be the corresponding nodes in P_0', that is D_A' is in $E(A(\text{Top}(P_0')))$ and D_C' is in $E(C(\text{Top}(P_0')))$.

Case (i.a): Suppose that D_A does not dominate S_{i-2} and D_C does not dominate S_{i-2}. Then, since $\text{Top}(A(P_{i-1})) = \text{Top}(A(P_0'))$ and $\text{Top}(C(P_{i-1})) = \text{Top}(C(P_0'))$, we have

(122) $^*D_A = {}^*D_A'$ and $^*D_C = {}^*D_C'$.

Thus $^*D_A = {}^*D_C$ if and only if $^*D_A' = {}^*D_C'$, which is the correspondence property that we wished to prove.

Case (i.b): Now suppose that D_A dominates S_{i-2} and D_C dominates S_{i-2}. Since no S-essential transformations apply at S_{i-1}, by the principle of S-Invisibility there are strings t_1, t_2 of terminals such that

(123) $^*D_A = t_1{}^*A(P_{i-2})t_2$, and

(124) $*D_A' = t_1 t_2.$

Likewise, there are strings of terminals u_1, u_2 such that

(125) $*D_C = u_1 *C(P_{i-2})u_2$, and

(126) $*D_C' = u_1 u_2.$

For example, the structure of D_A and of D_A' may be seen in (127).

(127)

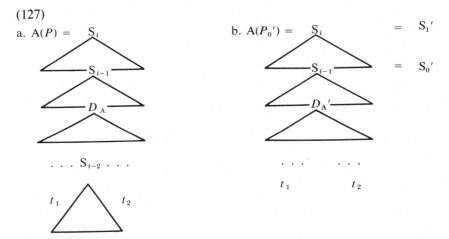

a. $A(P) =$ S_i

b. $A(P_0') =$ S_i $= S_1'$

S_{i-1} $= S_0'$

D_A

D_A'

$\ldots S_{i-2} \ldots$

t_1 t_2

Suppose $*D_A = *D_C$. Then (123) and (125) imply

(128) $t_1 *A(P_{i-2})t_2 = u_1 *C(P_{i-2})u_2.$

By construction, there is no detectable error on P_{i-2}. Thus,

(129) $*A(P_{i-2}) = *C(P_{i-2}).$

Since $*A(P_{i-2})$ is disjoint[51] from t_1, t_2 and $*C(P_{i-2})$ is disjoint from u_1, u_2 (which follows from the assumption of no copying), (128)–(129) imply that $t_1 = u_1$ and $t_2 = u_2$. Thus $t_1 t_2 = u_1 u_2$, and $*D_A' = *D_C'$. Thus $*D_A = *D_C$ implies that $*D_A' = *D_C'$.

We now pursue the converse part of the correspondence property. Suppose that $*D_A' = *D_C'$. Thus,

(130) $t_1 t_2 = u_1 u_2.$

By construction, there is no detectable error on P_{i-1}, that is,

(131) $*A(P_{i-1}) = *C(P_{i-1})$.

Suppose that $t_1 \neq u_1$. From (130) and the fact that all the elements in $t_1 t_2$ are distinct, it then follows that the last element of t_1 is unequal to the last element of u_1. Therefore we can conclude from (123) and (125) that the element preceding $*A(P_{i-2})$ in $*D_A$ is unequal to the element preceding $*C(P_{i-2})$ in $*D_C$. But $*D_A$ is a substring of $*A(P_{i-1})$ and $*D_C$ is a substring of $*C(P_{i-1})$. Together with (129) and the distinctness of the elements in $*A(P_{i-1})$ and also in $*C(P_{i-1})$, these facts imply that $*A(P_{i-1}) \neq *C(P_{i-1})$, which contradicts (131). Thus our assumption is wrong, and we conclude that $t_1 = u_1$. It follows also that $t_2 = u_2$. Thus, using (123), (125), and (129) we conclude that $*D_A = *D_C$. We have thus shown that $*D_A = *D_C$ if and only if $*D_A' = *D_C'$, which means that the correspondence property is proved for case (1.b).

Case (1.c): The remaining case is where only one of D_A and D_C dominates S_{i-2}. Without loss of generality, suppose that D_A dominates S_{i-2} in $A(P_{i-1})$ and D_C does not dominate S_{i-2} in $C(P_{i-1})$. Thus D_A and its corresponding node in P_0', D_A', can be written as in (123)–(124). Suppose that $*[A(P_{i-1})]_{i-2} = \emptyset$ (that is, the entire embedded sentence dominated by S_{i-2} has somehow been deleted, though, given the assumptions of case (i), not by an S-essential transformation). But then $*D_A = *D_A'$. Since D_C does not dominate S_{i-2}, $*D_C = *D_C'$, as in case (i.a). Therefore, the correspondence property follows; that is, $*D_A = *D_C$ if and only if $*D_A' = *D_C'$. Lastly, suppose that $*[A(P_{i-1})]_{i-2} \neq \emptyset$. But then since D_C does not dominate any elements from P_{i-2}, it follows that

(132) $*D_A \neq *D_C$.

Now suppose that $*D_A' = *D_C'$. Using (124) we have $D_C' = t_1 t_2$; since $D_C = D_C'$—as in case (1.a)—we have

(133) $D_C = t_1 t_2$.

But then $t_1 t_2$ is a substring of $*C(P_{i-1})$. Since $*[A(P_{i-1})]_{i-2} \neq \emptyset$, it follows from (123) that $t_1 t_2$ is not a substring of $*A(P_{i-1})$. Therefore there is a detectable error at level $i-1$, contrary to assumption.[52] Thus we can conclude that $^*D_A{}' \neq {}^*D_C{}'$. Given this last result, together with (132), it follows that $^*D_A = {}^*D_C$ if and only if $^*D_A{}' = {}^*D_C{}'$.

Therefore, we have proved for case (i) that $P_{i-1} \cong P_0{}'$. Thus the Substitution theorem implies that there is a detectable error on the degree-1 p-m P', and the proof is finished in this case.

Case (ii): Suppose that an S-essential transformation T $\in$ A applies at level S_{i-1} of P. We construct a degree-2 p-m $P' = P_2{}'$. We take the top two levels of P' to be the same as the top two levels of P. That is, we take

(134) $\text{Top}^+(P') = \text{Top}^+(P)$ and $\text{Top}^+(P_1{}') = \text{Top}^+(P_{i-1})$.

It only remains to define $P_0{}'$. There are no detectable errors on any 0-degree p-m (otherwise the theorem is proved). Now suppose that $A(P_{i-2})$ were filtered. Then $A(P)$ is filtered. Also, since there is no detectable error on any sub-p-m of P, it must be that $C(P_{i-2})$ is filtered. Therefore $C(P)$ is filtered. But then there is no detectable error on P, contrary to assumption. Therefore we assume that P_{i-2} is not filtered (by either A or C). It then follows from theorem 5 that there exists a degree-0 p-m $P_0{}'$ such that

(135) $A(P_0{}')$ is an extension of $E(\text{Top}(A(P_{i-2})))$, and
(136) $A(P_0{}') = C(P_0{}')$.

We pick any such $P_0{}'$. What we have done is to replace the degree-$i-2$ sub-p-m P_{i-2} in P by the degree-0 sub-p-m $P_0{}'$ in P'. All the assumptions of the Substitution theorem follow immediately, as before, except that we still have to show that $P_{i-1} \cong P_1{}'$. The construction may be seen in (137). (Also see (61).) Following the procedure used in case (i), we relabel S_i as $S_2{}'$ and S_{i-1} as $S_1{}'$.

Now, we have assumed that an S-essential transformation T $\in$ A applies at level S_{i-1}. If D is the node to which T applies, $D \in E(\text{Top}(A(P_{i-2})))$. But since $A(P_0{}')$ is an extension of $E(\text{Top}(A(P_{i-2})))$ (135), and since $\text{Top}(P_{i-1}) = \text{Top}(P_1{}')$ (by construction), NBC implies that T must apply at level S_1 to P'. Thus D will be raised or deleted in P', just as it was in P. Since only one S-essential transformation may apply (USET), and since nodes dominated by a raised node are not part

(137)

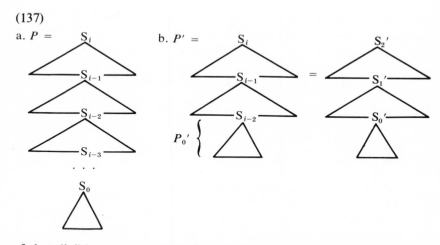

of the eligible structure (Raising principle), we have that the eligible structures of P and P' are the same after the S-essential transformation applies at level $i-1$. That is,

(138) $E(\text{Top}(A^{i-1,e}(P_{i-1}))) = E(\text{Top}(A^{1,e}(P_1')))$.

But since only eligible structures determine how the following singulary transformations apply, we conclude that (139) holds.

(139) $E(\text{Top}(A(P_{i-1}))) = E(\text{Top}(A(P_1')))$.

In other words, the eligible structures at the top levels are the same after *all* transformations (not just S-essential ones) apply.

Equation (139) is the first part of the definition of preservation. We must now show that the same equation holds, with C replacing A.[53] We have assumed that a transformation in A S-essentially applies to P at level $i-1$. Suppose the transformation applies to a node D_A (of category D). Since there is no detectable error on P_{i-1}, CRE (the property of Category Raising Equivalence, theorem 7) implies that component C also S-essentially applies to P at level $i-1$, applying to a node D_C (also of category D). Since $\text{Top}^+(P_1') = \text{Top}^+(P_{i-1})$ (134) and $A(P_0')$ is an extension of $E(\text{Top}(A(P_{i-2})))$ (135), NBC implies that component A must S-essentially apply to node D_A' at level 1 of P', where D_A' is of category D. But since there is no detectable error on P', CRE implies that component C S-essentially applies to a node D_C' (of category D) at level 1 of P. By NBC and Determinism there is only one transformation in C that can S-essentially apply to a given category, given the matrix p-m's are the same. Therefore, if D is raised by component C in P_{i-1} and P_1', it must be raised to exactly the same position. Therefore,

(140) $E(\text{Top}(C^{i-1,e}(P_{i-1}))) = E(\text{Top}(C^{1,e}(P_1')))$.

As (139) follows from (138) we have

(141) $E(\text{Top}(C(P_{i-1}))) = E(\text{Top}(C(P_1')))$.

This is the second part of the definition of preservation. It remains only to show that the correspondence property holds.

Now let D_A be in $E(\text{Top}(A(P_{i-1})))$, D_C be in $E(\text{Top}(C(P_{i-1})))$ and D_A', D_C' be the respective corresponding nodes in $E(\text{Top}(A(P_1')))$ and $E(\text{Top}(C(P_1')))$. We have to show that $*D_A = *D_C$ if and only if $*D_A' = *D_C'$. For simplicity we will prove the result only for the case where the S-essential transformation that applies at level P_{i-1} in A is a raising transformation. If it is an S-essential deletion the proof can be looked upon as a special case of the raising proof. Now, D_A may or may not dominate S_{i-2} and D_A may or may not dominate the raised node (call the raised node B_A). Aside from these two possibilities, the Raising principle and USET imply that D_A may otherwise dominate only terminals from $\text{Top}(P_{i-1})$. We have already seen (from CRE) that component C must raise a node B_C, of the same category as B_A. Without loss of generality, suppose that the raised node B_A is on the right of S_{i-2} after all transformations apply in P_{i-1}. Then we can write

(142) $*D_A = t_1(*[A(P_{i-1})]_{i-2})t_2(*B_A)t_3$, and
(143) $*D_C = u_1(*[C(P_{i-1})]_{i-2})u_2(*B_C)u_3$

where t_1, t_2, t_3, u_1, u_2, and u_3 are strings of terminals in $\text{Top}(P_{i-1})$. The parentheses of (142)–(143) are the optionality parentheses, as in the proof of theorem 4 and note 38. In proving (139) and (141) we proved that the node raised at level 1 of P' by A, B_A', is raised to the same position as B_A is, and the node raised in P' by C, B_C', is raised to the same position as B_C. Once again, the eligible structures determine all transformations and we can write

(144) $^*D_A{}' = t_1(^*[A(P_1{}')]_0)t_2(^*B_A{}')t_3$, and
(145) $^*D_C{}' = u_1(^*[C(P_1{}')]_0)u_2(^*B_C{}')u_3$,

where the corresponding optionality parentheses appear in (144) if and only if they appear in (142), and likewise for (143) and (145).

But theorem 3' and lemma 1 imply that $^*B_A = {}^*B_C$ and thus by USET, $^*[A(P_{i-1})]_{i-2} = {}^*[C(P_{i-1})]_{i-2}$. Also, t_1, t_2, and t_3 are disjoint from the other elements of $^*D_A$ (equation (142)) and u_1, u_2, and u_3 are disjoint from the other elements of $^*D_C$ (equation (143)). Therefore,

(146) $^*D_A = {}^*D_C$ if and only if $t_k = u_k$, $k = 1, 2, 3$, and if the corresponding optional elements appear (or do not appear) in both $^*D_A$ and $^*D_C$.

But exactly the same argument can be given for P', so that

(147) $^*D_A{}' = {}^*D_C{}'$ if and only if $t_k = u_k$, $k = 1, 2, 3$, and if the corresponding optional elements appear (or do not appear) in both $^*D_A{}'$ and $^*D_C{}'$.

But since the corresponding optional elements appear in $^*D_A$ if and only if they appear in $^*D_A{}'$ and likewise appear in $^*D_C$ if and only if they appear in $^*D_C{}'$, the conditions given in (146) and (147) are equivalent, so

(148) $^*D_A = {}^*D_C$ if and only if $^*D_A{}' = {}^*D_C{}'$.

This is the correspondence property that we wished to prove.[54]

Therefore, we have proved that $P_{i-1} \cong P_1{}'$. Thus the Substitution theorem applies, and it follows that there is a detectable error on the degree-2 phrase-marker P'. This proves theorem 8.

Note on the proof: It would be tempting to try to reduce the two cases to one, by constructing P' in case (i), in which no S-essential transformations apply at S_{i-1}, in the same way as for case (ii), in which an S-essential transformation applies at S_{i-1}. The case (i) construction would look like (137) of the proof. We would construct P' by substituting the appropriate $P_0{}'$ (from theorem 5) for P_{i-2}. However, since no S-essential transformation applies at S_{i-1} in P, it is possible that an S-essential transformation will apply at $S_1{}'$ in P', since $E(A(P_0{}'))$ is an extension of $E(\text{Top}(A(P_{i-2})))$. This transformation might destroy the context for a later error-producing transformation, as in a number of our earlier examples. Thus there would be no detectable error on P'.

Degree-2 error detectability (theorem 8) has interesting consequences for linguistic theory, in addition to its role in proving learnability. Suppose that an argument is constructed to show that a proposed grammar G is empirically wrong. Grammar G predicts that, for some base phrase-marker P, the surface sentence s associated with P is grammatical, whereas s actually is ungrammatical. Or the opposite holds: G predicts that s is ungrammatical whereas it is in fact grammatical. Degree-2 error detectability then implies that there exists a phrase-marker P' of degree 2 or less such that the same argument can be constructed on P'. In short, to the extent that the assumptions we have made are correct, it will never necessarily be the case that a phrase-marker of degree 3 or greater will have to be used in constructing an empirical syntactic argument about grammaticality. If degree-2 error detectability is false, then an argument about grammaticality that necessarily demands a phrase-marker of degree 3 or greater must exist. We know of no such arguments, within the bounds of the kind of linguistic theory discussed in this book. If any arguments that demand phrase-markers of degree 3 or greater are found, it would be interesting to observe which assumptions of our theory are violated.

4.5 Learnability from Data of Degree $\leqslant 2$

We have pointed out that degree-2 error detectability is sufficient to allow proof that transformational grammars are learnable from data of degree $\leqslant 2$. Let the statement "input is of degree 2" mean that the input sequence contains only (b,s) pairs such that b is of degree 0, 1, or 2, but that otherwise the definition of an input sequence is the same as given for the original theory in chapter 3 (for example, the probability of presenting a datum is non-zero). Let C_t be the learner's transformational component at time t, and A the adult component. $C_t \cong_M A$ means that C_t is moderately equivalent to A (see (4) of section 3.4 and section 4.1.5). Then Degree-2 Error Detectability may be formally stated as the following theorem.

Theorem 9: Let input be of degree 2. Then

$$\forall\ \epsilon > 0,\ \exists t',\ \mathrm{Prob}(C_{t'} \cong_M A) \geqslant 1-\epsilon.$$

The proof of theorem 9 is just the same as the proof of the original learnability theorem (Hamburger and Wexler, theorem 6), except that it uses the degree-2 error detectability result (theorem 8 of section 4.4) instead of bounded error detectability (theorem 3 of Hamburger and Wexler). Therefore, we will not repeat the proof here.[55] The informal sketch of the proof, as given in chapter 3, works as before.

The constraints and assumptions introduced in this chapter, which we will call the *degree-2 theory,* have structural properties that lead, as we have seen, to a far stronger property than the original system—to degree-2 error detectability and thus degree-2 learnability. It is natural to ask whether the degree-2 theory will allow a further simplification of the *learning* theory or of the proof of learnability.

One immediate simplification can occur in the learnability proof (theorem 9). In the original proof (sketched in chapter 3) we had to carry along and perform operations on phrase-markers of arbitrary degree i. For the degree-2 theory we have to consider only phrase-markers of degree 0, 1, or 2. Therefore a degree parameter i can be eliminated in the proof.

Aside from this notational simplification, it is not immediately apparent whether the learnability proof can be further simplified. Basically the proof is already fairly simple and intuitively rather straightforward. The mathematical and conceptual complications appear in the proof of the detectability properties, for example, theorem 8.

However, an intriguing possibility is that the degree-2 theory may allow a major simplification in the learning mechanism. First, recall that the proof of learnability given in Hamburger and Wexler 1975 and sketched in chapter 3 is carried out under the simplifying assumption that only one transformation applies per cycle. A corresponding proof of learnability exists for the more general (and empirically more correct) case in which more than one transformation may apply per cycle, as mentioned in note 26 of chapter 3. The learning procedure for the more general case, however, bears a heavy computational burden, which we would like to reduce. It may be that the degree-2 theory would allow this reduction.

The intricacies lie in the hypothesization procedure. In the case of one transformation per cycle a transformation T may be hypothesized when a detectable error occurs on a phrase-marker b if the following conditions are met: when b is transformed by the learner's component C up through the next-to-highest level and then T is applied to the highest level of this phrase-marker producing the derived phrase-marker b', the terminal string of b' is the correct (adult) terminal string, that is, $*b' = *A(b)$. In the more general case of more than one transformation per cycle, we would like to preserve this hypothesization procedure as much as possible. Specifically, we would like to be able to state the procedure so that a transformation T may be hypothesized when a detectable error occurs on b if the following conditions are met: when b is transformed by the learner's component C up through the next to highest level, if T is then added to C to apply to the highest level, the correct surface string is produced.

As explained in note 26 of chapter 3, this is *not* the hypothesization procedure that is adopted. To see why a change is necessary, consider the following example. Suppose that the learner's transformational component at some time is exactly the same as the correct (adult) component except that two transformations T_1 and T_2 that are in the correct component A are missing from C. Suppose furthermore that on some base phrase-marker b, T_1 and T_2 both apply at the top level and no other transformations apply to the top level. Also suppose that T_1 applies before T_2.[56] In order for the proof of learnability to go through as before, it must be possible for T_1 and T_2 to be hypothesized on b.[57] But in order for the procedure to hypothesize T_1, the correct surface string must be produced when T_1, together with C, applies to the top of the phrase-marker that is derived by applying C up through the next-to-highest level of b. But this will not be the case, because it takes T_1 and T_2 to yield the correct surface string, and T_2 is not in C. Likewise, T_2 cannot be hypothesized on b, because T_1 is not yet in C. Thus T_1 and T_2 cannot be hypothesized, and convergence cannot take place, at least according to the proof that we have so far developed.

In order to overcome problems such as this, the learning procedure that is used, as we described in note 26 of chapter 3, works differently. The procedure allows a transformation T to be hypothesized on b if the correct surface string is derived when T and C, *together with other transformations* (*not in* C), apply to the top of the phrase-marker that is derived from b by applying C up through the next-to-highest level. In the preceding example, T_1 could be hypothesized on b because T_1 together with T_2 applies to the top of the p-m to yield the correct surface string. Likewise, T_2 could be hypothesized on b because T_2 together with T_1 applies to the top of the p-m to yield the correct surface string. (Only one transformation is hypothesized at a time; we are describing the set of hypothesizable transformations.)

This modified learning procedure places a larger computational burden on the learner, since he now has to consider sets of transformations which, added to the current component, will derive the correct surface string. The original learning procedure demanded only that the learner calculate *one* transformation that could be added to the current component to derive the correct string. Since for n transformations the number of subsets of transformations is 2^n, this is a large increase in computational burden. In order to work toward the goal of *feasibility* (which includes considerations of computational efficiency) we would like to reduce this computational burden.

What is intriguing is that the linguistic assumptions that we have been led to in order to prove degree-2 learnability might also be of direct value in reducing the computational complexity of the learning procedure. The Freezing principle, in particular, might play such a role. Consider again the example just described, in which the learner's component C is missing only T_1 and T_2, which apply in that order to the top of b. We are going to attempt to construct a base phrase-marker on which T_2 can be hypothesized. Let C apply to b up through the next-to-highest level, and then let T_1 apply to the top of this p-m, yielding a p-m b' which is not necessarily a base p-m. Now, from b' we drop all S's except the highest one, and we also drop all lines and nodes under the frozen nodes. The Freezing principle tells us that T_2 applies to this partial base structure b' (we know that T_2 doesn't apply to any nodes in any lower S's because of the assumptions that at most one S-essential transformation applies (USET) and that S-essential transformations apply before non-S-essential transformations (OSET), and the fact that T_1 applies before T_2). To make b' into a fully-derived 0-degree base p-m, we take a 0-termination of the lowest nodes in b', which we assumed in section 4.1.2 that we can always do. This produces the base p-m b'' to which T_2 applies. Since T_2 is in the adult component A, the principle of determinism prevents any other transformations from applying to b''. Also, if any transformation in A applies to $T_2(b'')$, then that transformation would apply to b after T_2 applies (by S-Invisibility and other principles). Thus only T_2 applies to b''. Therefore T_2 can be hypothesized on b'' by the original learning procedure, which hypothesizes a transformation without consideration of other possible transformations.

Once T_2 has been hypothesized, T_1 can be hypothesized on our original phrase-marker b, again by the original (simpler) learning procedure. This is because T_1 when added to the learner's current component (which now includes T_2) maps the partially derived b into the correct surface string. Thus both T_1 and T_2 can be hypothesized by the original learning procedure, and convergence can take place.

It appears that this argument will generalize to any number of transformations missing from a learner's component (the transformations being learned in reverse order from their order of application). To make a complete argument go through, we would have to formalize the argument presented here and prove that, given the new degree-2 assumptions, convergence can take place with the original learning procedure. If the proof can be made to go through (an effort we will not pursue here), we will have shown that the degree-2 assumptions allow a major reduction in computational complexity. We thus would have the intriguing result that assumptions made for the purpose of demonstrating one aspect of feasibility (simplicity of the data from which learning can take place) also play a clear role in demonstrating another aspect of feasibility (simplicity and efficiency of the computations made during learning). It might turn out that the relation between linguistic structure and computational complexity will be a significant area of research.

CHAPTER 5

LINGUISTIC EVIDENCE FOR THE LEARNABILITY CONSTRAINTS

We demonstrated in chapter 4 that it is possible to place constraints on a class of transformational grammars that are sufficiently restrictive to allow a plausible learner to learn any member of this class given simple input data. We turn now to the empirical evidence for or against the adoption of these constraints as components of the theory of grammar for natural language. It seems to us that the approach to linguistic theory represented by chapter 4 would be of interest if it merely provided a range of plausible hypotheses to test. But a still more exciting possibility is that this approach can be ultimately sharpened to the extent of providing hypotheses that are in essence correct.

5.1 The Status of Linguistic Data

5.1.1 Remarks on Empirical Content

The formal results of the learnability studies are illuminating in many respects, but not conclusive in every respect. The enterprise is in fact a complex one, and it is because of this complexity that formal studies along these lines must be balanced with appropriately oriented investigations into the syntax of natural language.

The learnability studies require empirical grounding for a number of reasons and should not be taken in themselves as final proofs that the theory of grammar must take a particular form. In fact, what we have shown is that, given a variety of assumptions, transformational grammar is learnable from simple input data. We have not shown, however, that our set of assumptions is the only set that will allow learnability. In fact, the proof of Hamburger and Wexler (1973; 1975) indicates that learnability is attainable with different constraints, although the conditions under which learning will be possible are different in the two cases. In particular, and most importantly, Hamburger and Wexler's bound on the degree of minimal error was huge, whereas the bound given under current assumptions is 2. This is the result of chapter 4.

Thus we do not have absolute necessity for the constraints adopted in chapter 4. We do have, however, a characterization of the types of obstacles to degree-two learnability within the bounds set by the capacities of the learner and the richness of the learning environment, and we have a set of constraints that will allow us to surmount these obstacles and prove learnability.

In view of the unlikelihood of arriving at absolute necessity conditions (see the discussion in section 4.2), we are faced with the potential choice between sets of conditions, each of which is sufficient to prove learnability under possibly different assumptions about the learner and the learning environment. In the current research we have adopted a variety of specific assumptions about the intellectual capacities of the learner, the form in which data are presented to the learner, and the manner in which data are presented. Although our assumptions here are not arbitrary ones, nevertheless they are by no means obviously correct. It is certainly possible that changes in these assumptions in light of empirical psychological research would have clear consequences for whether or not given classes of grammars could be shown to be learnable. For some detailed discussion along these lines, see chapter 2.

In view of the substantial gaps in our knowledge concerning what the precisely correct nonlinguistic assumptions must be, it is important that empirical considerations be brought to bear to determine the extent to which particular constraints can be incorporated into linguistic theory. Our concern in this chapter will be to investigate the syntactic aspects of the learnability studies while holding constant the psychological and psycholinguistic assumptions.

5.1.2 Methodological Notes

We will concentrate on those constraints that, together, can be shown to be necessary for learnability, within our general framework. In view of this particular approach, it is worth making a few methodological remarks that may forestall some potential confusions about the thrust of our syntactic arguments. We are concerned here with the question of the empirical validity of constraints whose motivation is external to descriptive linguistics. In this regard this work contrasts with much research on grammatical constraints, which, though concerned with the same data, attempts to arrive at constraints that will satisfy the observed phenomena.

One example should serve as an illustration of the contrast, although it must be recognized that many pieces of linguistic research concerned with constraints on grammars satisfy in some degree the description to be given.[1] A clear case is provided by Ross's *Constraints on Variables in Syntax* (1967).

Ross motivated his investigation by pointing out the failure of Chomsky's (1964; 1968; 1973) A-over-A principle to rule out certain ungrammatical sentences. As stated in Chomsky 1973, that principle is as follows:

If a transformation applies to a structure of the form

$$[_\alpha \ldots [_A \ldots] \ldots]$$

where α is a cyclic node, then it must be so interpreted as to apply to the maximal phrase of the type A. (p. 235)

The A-over-A principle as stated restricts transformations from applying to a node such as A_0 in (1) at the level of α unless the transformation is so stated as to ignore A_1. Hence it blocks the extraction of the

(1) α

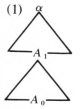

underlined noun phrase in (2a), consistent with the grammaticality judgment of (2b).

(2)
a. John met ₙₚ[the woman who knows ₙₚ[*which Senator*]].
b. **Which Senator* did John meet the woman who knows ∅?

Ross was concerned with replacing the A-over-A principle with a more general constraint or set of constraints. One failing of the A-over-A principle is that it does not block extraction of an adjective phrase (AP) in a structure parallel to (2), since in such a case the

(3)

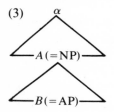

extraction rule is applying to a structure of the form (3). As the examples in (4) show, however, the category of what is extracted from the relative clause is irrelevant; the result is an ungrammatical sentence anyway.

(4)
a. John met ₙₚ[the woman who became ₐₚ[*how angry*]].
b. **How angry* did John meet the woman who became ∅?

Ross attributed the failure of extraction in these cases not to the category of the moved element and the dominating nodes, as the A-over-A principle requires, but to the particular configuration of the clause to which the extraction rule is applying. In this case the structure in question is that of a relative clause and Ross postulated a specific constraint that blocks extraction out of a relative clause (and certain related structures) called the Complex NP constraint.

Other similar inadequacies in the A-over-A principle led Ross to propose a number of other constraints, among them the Sentential Subject constraint and the Coordinate Structure constraint. (See Ross

1967 for discussion.)   While Ross's analysis encompassed a greater range of data than did Chomsky's original formulation, it did so at the expense of abstractness, generality, and elegance. However, there was no obvious way in which the various constraints proposed by Ross could be collapsed into a single constraint that would account for all of the data. Specifically, Ross, in abandoning the A-over-A principle, found it necessary to adopt, for every distinct configuration that blocks extraction, a distinct constraint.

We do not wish to imply here that there is any principled bound on the number of constraints. In fact, it appears quite likely that the Coordinate Structure constraint of Ross (1967) does not generalize to any other constraint. What we do wish to emphasize, in citing this example, is the considerable extent to which the form of the theory of grammar, as embodied in the constraints, conforms to the data. Thus, in Ross's framework, for examples involving complex NP's we have the Complex NP constraint, for examples involving sentential subjects we have the Sentential Subject constraint, for examples involving internal S's we have the Internal S constraint, for examples involving left branches we have the Left Branch condition, for examples involving bounding of rightward movement rules we have a Bounding convention, for pied piping examples we have the Pied Piping convention, and so on.

In essence, the contrast is between an approach that seeks abstract, formal explanations for the form that linguistic theory takes, and an approach that develops linguistic theory primarily in terms of the linguistic facts that have been recognized and subjected to analysis. These approaches are not in principle antagonistic, but we find that in the case of the latter, the constraints for the most part express generalizations about relatively accessible linguistic phenomena and do not follow from deeper principles. We will give some examples to illustrate.

What is particularly important to recognize here is the different status that a counterexample has in the two approaches. To the extent that a constraint expresses a generalization about the data, a counterexample can be readily identified when it occurs. But if a constraint is more abstract and has a deeper, nonlinguistic motivation, linguistic counterexamples will not necessarily be immediately apparent. Nor will apparent counterexamples necessarily falsify the theory. In fact, it seems to us that in cases where constraints have the external motivation of the sort shown in chapter 4, reanalysis of superficially contradicting data is in principle to be preferred over abandoning the constraints. It is not a priori obvious that a theory that is consistent with the linguistic data but does not account for learnability is to be preferred over a theory that accounts for learnability but appears to be inconsistent with some data.

An examination of the recent literature on the theory of grammar shows that the construction of theories that attempt to generalize the data has continued to be a major approach. We cite a few examples that have been proposed, indicating just the constraints themselves; the data are readily available from the literature and can often be reconstructed from the constraints themselves.

1. From Postal (1972b)[2]

Wh Constraint: Mark as ill-formed any derivation in which
(a) There are two nominal constituents, A and B, in the input structure of a Wh Movement rule, where:
i) A is a pronoun,
ii) B is a *wh* form,
iii) A is the left of B; and
(b) The corresponding constituents of A and B in the output structure of the Wh Movement rule, call them A' and B' respectively, are aligned such that B' is to the left of A'; and
(c) In the semantic representation, A and B (or, more precisely, their corresponding elements) are marked as stipulated coreferents. (p. 48–49)

2. From Ross (1972)

*Doubl-*ing *Constraint:*[3] All surface structures containing a subtree of the form (5), in which the node corresponding to V_a in remote structure was immediately dominated by S_i, and the node corresponding to V_b in remote structure was immediately dominated by S_j, and in which no S node intervened in remote structure between S_i and S_j, are ungrammatical. (p. 78)

(5)

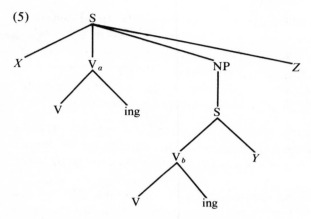

3. From Kuno and Robinson (1972)

Clause-Mate Constraint on Multiple Wh Words: Multiple *wh* words bound by the same Q must be clause-mates at the time of application of Wh-Q Movement. (p. 471)

Wh Crossing Constraint: A *wh* word cannot be preposed crossing over another *wh*. Time and place *wh* words . . . can cross over another *wh* . . . , but they cannot cross over the *wh* in the subject position. (p. 474)

Dislocation Constraint: Dislocation of more than one constituent from its original location is prohibited. (p. 477)

4. From Hankamer (1973)[4]

No Ambiguity Condition (NAC): Any application of Gapping which would yield an output structure identical to a structure derivable by Gapping from another source, but with the gap at the left extremity, is disallowed. (p. 29)

5. From Kuno (1973)

Internal NP *Clause Constraint:* Sentences containing an internal NP clause are ungrammatical. An NP clause is internal if it is neither the leftmost nor the rightmost constituent of its immediate parent node. (p. 375)

Self-Embedding and Conjunction-Juxtaposition Constraint: The immediate self-embedding of clauses and phrases of the same grammatical function and the juxtaposition of conjunctions, especially those of the same form, both add to the reduction in intelligibility of sentences. (p. 375)

Constraint on Surface Subject Clauses: Sentential subject NP clauses can appear only in sentence-initial position. (p. 375)

Predicate Deletion Constraint: Copulative sentences with sentential subjects cannot undergo deletion of postcopular elements. (p. 376)

What leads us to group these constraints together is not the relative specificity of their formulation but the relatively high degree of conformity between their content and the range of phenomena to which they apply.[5]

We do not wish to be misunderstood as condemning the research that lies behind these constraints. Nor do we wish to say that these constraints, because they have limited application, must be incorrect. All that we intend to do is to clarify the methodological difference between these constraints and the learnability constraints. It is this methodological difference that leads us to treat syntactic phenomena in this chapter somewhat differently here from the way they are generally treated in the literature.

In this chapter we are concerned with determining whether there is any empirical evidence for the central constraints that emerge from the learnability theory. In the course of this investigation, we encounter syntactic phenomena that are of interest from the point of view of linguistic description but are not directly relevant to this question. In general we can only give brief mention to such phenomena, whereas in more traditional approaches to syntax an in-depth analysis would no doubt be in order. On the other hand, there may be data that contradict a particular constraint. Here we must investigate the possibility that the most obvious account of the data (namely, that which contradicts the constraint) is not the right one. Sometimes this takes us relatively far afield, to the point that we are no longer discussing matters of direct relevance to the constraint. Again, this is a line of approach somewhat unfamiliar in the literature.

To give just one example, in section 5.2.5 we consider a possible counterexample to the Freezing principle, the applicability of conjunction reduction to putatively frozen structures. In the course of the discussion, we are led to investigate the hypothesis that there is no transformation of Conjunction Reduction, but a more limited lexical deletion transformation. From this we are led to consider Right Node Raising, a related phenomenon, where the Freezing principle is again violated. Again, we argue that there is no structural transformation here, but a limited lexical deletion rule. It is important to point out that we do not attempt to present a complete theory of conjoined structure. Consequently, many problems traditionally associated with conjunction phenomena in the literature are left unsolved; many are not even mentioned. Quite possibly the analysis that we propose raises even more problems, and many aspects of our proposals are left unjustified. Unfortunately, owing to the limitations of this study, we are unable to pursue each issue touched upon in the detail that it deserves. A completely adequate account would have to deal with these details.

To summarize, our approach to matters of syntactic description differs somewhat from that usually encountered in the literature. Most significantly, we are concerned with such matters primarily to the extent that they shed light on the empirical validity of the learnability constraints that have strong external motivation. It is to be expected, of course, that further consideration of those questions that we cannot pursue in detail here will take us that much further towards an understanding of the nature of grammatical constraints and the extent that their existence can be explicated in terms of learnability theory.

5.2 The Freezing Principle

5.2.1 Freezing in VP

5.2.1.1 The Dative Construction Recall that the Freezing principle prevents analysis by transformations of derived structures that are not also base-generable structures. An illustration of the interaction of FP with the rules of English grammar involves the dative construction. The analysis to follow appears elsewhere; we summarize the essential points here.[6]

The Dative transformation derives (6b) from (6a).

(6)

a. John gave a book about astronomy to Mary.

b. John gave Mary a book about astronomy.

There is some disagreement as to whether this relation is in fact a transformational one. For arguments that it may not be transformational in every case analogous to (6), see Oehrle 1976. Culicover (1976b, chapter 6) presents some of the standard arguments in favor of treating this relation as a transformational one. We take the position here that the Dative transformation is well motivated.

The output of Dative can be represented structurally in a number of ways. Depending on the actual output structure that we assign and the possible range of base structures that we permit, we will make different predictions as to the analyzability of this output structure. By observing the ways in which this structure is analyzable we can draw inferences, which may be testable on independent grounds, concerning the forms of both the possible base structures and the output structures of Dative. Of course, we can only hypothesize that the analyzability of the output structure is explicable by appeal to the Freezing principle and is not due to some independent mechanisms.

Suppose for the sake of discussion that the underlying structure of (6a) is (7).[7] In the absence of independent considerations the assumed

(7)

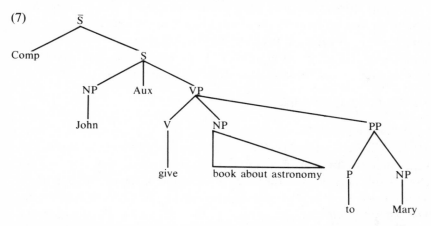

complexity of the branching in the VP can be varied with no effect on the essential characteristics of the analysis.

There are three plausible output structures for (6b). These are illus-

(8)

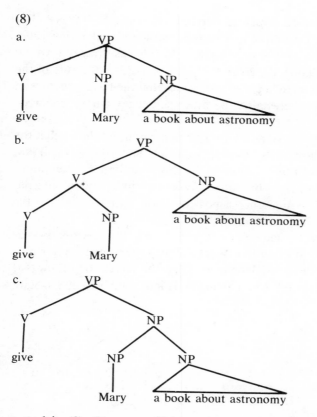

a.

b.

c.

trated in (8). Structure (8c) can be ruled out as a serious possibility because of the evidence against treating *Mary a book about astronomy* as an NP. We cannot passivize this putative NP, for example:

(9) *Mary a book about astronomy* was given by John.

No other transformation that applies explicitly to NP appears to treat this sequence of NP's as an NP.[8]

Let us introduce now the question of the underlying structure of the VP. If V NP NP is a possible base order, it may still be the case that the structure associated with this sequence in the base is not the same as the structure associated with the derived sequence V NP NP. For example, the derived structure may be (8b), while the underlying structure of V NP NP sequences may be (8a). In this case freezing would occur in (8b) at the node V_*, given that V $\rightarrow$ V NP is not a rule of the base. (We do not mean to suggest, of course, that the base structure of (6b) is (8a). Rather, there might be other sentences whose underlying structure is (8a).)

If we rule out V $\rightarrow$ V NP as a base rule in general, it follows that the logically possible alternative situation, in which (8a) is derived and (8b) is underlying, cannot arise. Let us make this simplifying assumption. The problem now becomes one of resolving two independent alternatives: (i) V NP NP is or is not a possible base structure; or (ii) the output of Dative is (8a) or it is (8b).

Consider next the consequences of introducing the Freezing principle (FP). Suppose first of all that V NP NP is not an underlying structure for any sentence of the language. Then the effects of FP on (8a) and (8b) are shown in (10). (A frozen node is indicated by a box around

(10)

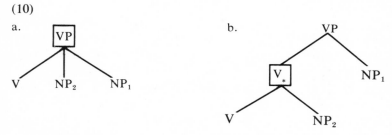

it.) Clearly, the two structures are differentiated by the fact that NP_1 is dominated by a frozen node in (10a) but not in (10b). Hence we would expect movement transformations to apply differentially to NP_1 and NP_2 if (10b) is correct, but not if (10a) is correct.

In fact NP_1 does not appear to be excluded from participating in a number of movement transformations while NP_2 is practically immobile. Consider the consequences of applying Wh Fronting, Topicalization, and Tough Movement to (11) and related structures.

(11) John gave Mary the books.

(12)

a. *Who did John give ∅ the books?
b. Which books did John give Mary ∅?
c. Who did John give the books to ∅?
d. Which books did John give ∅ to Mary?

(13)

a. *Mary, John gave ∅ the books.
b. These books, John gave Mary ∅.
c. Mary, John gave the books to ∅.
d. These books, John gave ∅ to Mary.

(14)

a. *Mary is tough for John to give ∅ books.
b. Good books are tough for John to give Mary ∅.
c. Mary is tough for John to give books to ∅.
d. Good books are tough for John to give ∅ to Mary.

These distributions follow if (10b) is the derived structure, since NP_2 cannot be moved, but NP_1 can. That is, in the (a) sentences, the movement of NP_2 yields ungrammaticality, but in the (c) sentences, where Dative has not applied, NP_2 can be moved. The (b) and (d) sentences, in contrast, show that the Dative transformation does not affect the movability of NP_1 at all.

Additional support for the proposal that the output structure of the Dative transformation is a frozen one has to do with Gapping.[9] In essence, Gapping deletes the verbal sequence in a conjunct when it is identical to that of the preceding conjunct, as (15) illustrates.

(15)

a. John sells cars, and Mary sells trucks.
b. John sells cars, and Mary, trucks.

The italicized verbal sequence, in this case the verb sells, is deleted under identity with sells in the first conjunct. (Gapping is in fact somewhat more complicated than this suggests, but for the present purposes this simple application will suffice.)

Returning to the output of the Dative transformation, we would not expect to be able to delete the verb in either (10a) or (10b). Although

Gapping is claimed[10] to apply only before variables consisting of single constituents, we still find it far more acceptable to apply Gapping in the untransformed Dative structures.

(16)

a. John gave Mary a book, and Bill $\begin{Bmatrix} \text{gave} \\ *\emptyset, \end{Bmatrix}$ Fred a magazine.

b. We sent the Democrats four hundred dollars, and the boss $\begin{Bmatrix} \text{sent} \\ ^{:*}\emptyset, \end{Bmatrix}$ the Republicans ten thousand dollars.

(17)

a. John gave a book to Mary, and Bill $\begin{Bmatrix} \text{gave} \\ \emptyset, \end{Bmatrix}$ a magazine to Fred.

b. We sent four hundred dollars to the Democrats, and the boss $\begin{Bmatrix} \text{sent} \\ \emptyset, \end{Bmatrix}$ ten thousand dollars to the Republicans.

Finally, consider the rule of Complex NP Shift.[11] The function of this transformation is to shift a heavy, immediately post-verbal NP to the end of the VP, as illustrated in (18)–(20).

(18)

a. We saw *the man you were telling us about* on television last night.

b. We saw $\emptyset$ on television last night *the man you were telling us about*.

(19)

a. I would consider *anyone who tries to climb that mountain in winter* stupid.

b. I would consider $\emptyset$ stupid *anyone who tries to climb that mountain in winter*.

(20)

a. Fred opened *the door to the attic* quickly.

b. Fred opened $\emptyset$ quickly *the door to the attic*.

Observe that Complex NP Shift cannot apply to the first NP in the sequence V NP NP, as predicted by FP. As the schemata in (10) show, the first NP is dominated by a frozen node after Dative has applied. The following examples show that Complex NP Shift is correctly blocked in this case.

(21)
a. John gave *the woman in the blue suit* the keys.
b. *John gave Ø the keys *the woman in the blue suit*. [12]

(22)
a. The teacher told *some of the students who were in the room* the answer to the question on the exam.
b. *The teacher told Ø the answer to the question on the exam *some of the students who were in the room*.

(23)
a. Every member of the club is obliged to send *national headquarters in Washington* a check for ten dollars.
b. *Every member of the club is obliged to send Ø a check for ten dollars *national headquarters in Washington*.

In sum, it appears that the Freezing principle correctly predicts some subtle grammaticality distributions in a number of unrelated constructions in which Dative plays a role. [13]

5.2.1.2 Complex NP Shift Returning to the transformation of Complex NP Shift, it is clear that this rule is non-structure-preserving and should cause freezing as a consequence. This can be seen in (24), which repre-

(24)

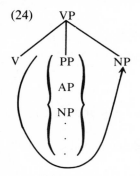

sents in schematic form the output of Complex NP Shift. [14] The structure of a sentence like (20b), for example, would be (25). [15]

(25)

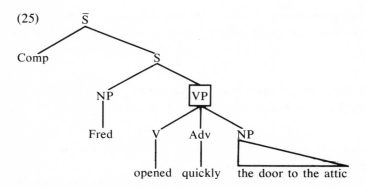

We would expect that no transformation ordered after Complex NP Shift could apply to this frozen structure. The following examples show that the extraposed NP cannot be analyzed by Wh Fronting, for example.

(26)
a. John sent to Horace *an expensive book about horned frogs.*
b. *What kind of frogs did John send to Horace *an expensive book about ∅?*

Similarly, the examples in (27) show that other movement transformations, like Topicalization and Tough Movement, cannot analyze the extraposed NP either. But, as the examples in (28) show, none of these transformations is blocked when the NP in question is VP-final in underlying structure.

(27)
a. *Horned frogs, John sent to Horace *an expensive book about ∅.*
b. *Horned frogs would be nice for John to send to Horace *an expensive book about ∅.*

(28)
a. What kind of frogs did John find an expensive book about ∅?
b. Horned frogs, John found an expensive book about ∅.
c. Horned frogs would be easy for me to find an expensive book about ∅.

Since the VP in (25) is frozen, we would expect that movement

transformations cannot apply to the constituent over which the complex NP has been moved, either. The examples in (29) show that this is
correct for Wh Fronting, Topicalization, and Tough Movement.[16]

(29)
a. John gave to Bill *the picture that was hanging on the wall.*
b. *Who did John give to Ø *the picture that was hanging on the
wall?*
c. *Bill, John gave to Ø *the picture that was hanging on the wall.*
d. *Bill would be easy for John to give to Ø *the picture that was
hanging on the wall.*

As can be seen in (30), however, these transformations can apply when
Complex NP Shift has not applied.[17]

(30)
a. John gave the picture that was hanging on the wall to Bill.
b. Who did John give the picture that was hanging on the wall to Ø?
c. Bill, John gave the picture that was hanging on the wall to Ø.
d. Bill would be easy for John to give the picture that was hanging
on the wall to Ø.

The examples in (31)–(32) show that just when the complex NP is
moved over an NP, the latter NP cannot be analyzed.[18]

(31)
a. They elected President of Mauritania the colonel who had engineered the recent coup.
b. *Which country did they elect President of Ø the colonel who had
engineered the recent coup?
c. *Mauritania, they elected President of Ø the colonel who had engineered the recent coup.

(32)
a. They elected the colonel who had engineered the recent coup
President of Mauritania.
b. Which country did they elect the colonel who had engineered the
recent coup President of Ø?
c. Mauritania, they elected the colonel who had engineered the recent coup President of Ø.

In (32) the length of the first NP renders the examples somewhat awkward; they are improved considerably by simplifying this NP, as in (33).

(33)
a. Which country did they elect the colonel President of $\emptyset$?
b. Mauritania, they elected the colonel President of $\emptyset$.

Finally, Gapping does not apply after Complex NP Shift, as predicted if the entire VP is frozen by the latter.

(34)
a. John sent to Horace an expensive book about horned pigs, and Fred $\begin{Bmatrix} \text{sent} \\ *\emptyset, \end{Bmatrix}$ to Susan a picture of himself.
b. John considers easy to please the directors who voted favorably on the bond issue, and Mary $\begin{Bmatrix} \text{considers} \\ *\emptyset, \end{Bmatrix}$ difficult to convince the other members of the board who failed to vote at all.
c. They elected President of Mauritania the colonel who engineered the recent coup, and we $\begin{Bmatrix} \text{elected} \\ *\emptyset, \end{Bmatrix}$ Vice President of Mauritania's Senate the woman who supplied him with arms.

The sentences in (35) show that Gapping is applicable when Complex NP Shift has not applied.

(35)
a. John sent an expensive book about horned pigs to Horace, and Fred (sent) a picture of himself to Susan.
b. John considers the directors who voted favorably on the recent bond issue easy to please, and Mary (considers) the other members of the board who failed to vote at all difficult to convince.
c. They elected the colonel who engineered the recent coup President of Mauritania, and we (elected) the woman who supplied him with arms Vice President of Mauritania's Senate.

Though the examples in (35) are not entirely acceptable, they are certainly more acceptable than the starred examples in (34).

5.2.1.3 Remarks on Rule Ordering In the preceding discussion of Dative and Complex NP Shift there has been the implicit assumption that the movement transformations such as Wh Fronting, Topicalization, and Tough Movement were ordered after them. Of course, the problem of language learning is simplified if the ordering of rules is a function of the general theory of grammar rather than something that has to be learned explicitly. The learnability theory developed in chapters 3 and 4 assumes only such intrinsic orderings. A typical instance of the theory-imposed ordering is that of Tough Movement, Dative, and Complex NP Shift. By the usual account, the structural description of Tough Movement involves material in a higher cycle than that which satisfies the other two rules; hence, by the cyclic principle,[19] it applies after them.

(36) $\bar{s}_1$[*it* be easy $\bar{s}_0$[for John to give *NP* to *NP*]]

By extending this notion of the cycle in certain natural ways and making some well-motivated assumptions about structure, we can induce a variety of other rule orderings from the theory alone. Following Williams (1974b) we assume that the transformational cycle applies at every node in a phrase marker. Thus it follows automatically that those rules that can apply entirely within the VP, such as Dative and Complex NP Shift, will apply before rules applying to material outside the VP, such as NP Preposing, Tough Movement, Wh Fronting. This eliminates the need for explicitly ordering Dative before NP Preposing.

To induce the other orderings, we follow a proposal that is by now generally accepted in the literature, namely, that the essential sentential structure is given by the two base rules:[20]

(B1) $\bar{S} \rightarrow$ Comp S
(B2) S $\rightarrow$ NP VP

It will follow from the structure generated by these rules that transformations that move constituents into Comp—Wh Fronting and Topicalization, for instance—will follow rules that apply completely on a lower domain of the phrase-marker, such as Passive, Complex NP Shift, and Dative.

We will assume, in fact, that there is no explicit rule ordering, and that all appearances of such rule ordering are consequences of the cyclic principle, the strict cycle, and the constraints on analyzability. When rules T_1 and T_2 apply to the same domain, if T_2 freezes something that must appear in order for T_1 to apply, then T_1 will always precede T_2 even though we are adopting the principle that rules within the same domain apply in all possible orders with respect to one another.

5.2.2 Other Applications
The foregoing should suffice for illustrative purposes. In the interest of brevity we will simply sketch out additional potential applications of the Freezing principle. First, Culicover (1977a) offers an account of the pseudo-cleft construction in English in which the focus constituent is moved into position by a non-structure-preserving transformation, freezing this constituent and rendering it unanalyzable by later transformations. (37) provides some typical data, and (38) illustrates the derivation of (37a). For the details of the argument, the reader is referred to the reference cited.

(37)
a. What Susan did was prove the theorem.
b. *Which theorem was what Susan did prove ∅?
c. *This is the very theorem that what Susan did was prove ∅.

(38)

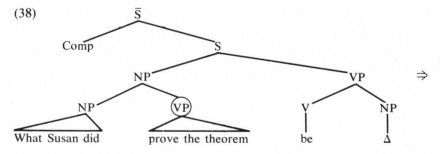

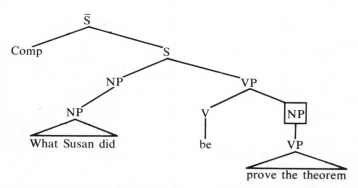

Another application involves the rule of *s*-contraction, which derives (39b) from (39a).

(39)

a. John $\begin{Bmatrix} \text{has left} \\ \text{is leaving} \end{Bmatrix}$.   b. John's $\begin{Bmatrix} \text{left} \\ \text{leaving} \end{Bmatrix}$.

Again, we can only sketch out the analysis.

Following Bresnan (1971), we view *s*-contraction as a rule that attaches the *'s* to the right. Evidence for this is provided by (40), which can be derived only if the contracted auxiliary does not attach to the subject NP. Wh Fronting derives (40) from *you do think who is leaving*. Note that we do not get (41).

(40) Who do you think's leaving?
(41) *Who's do you think ∅ leaving?

If attachment of *'s* to the VP freezes it, this explains why the following are ungrammatical.

(42)

a. *I wonder which one John's ∅.
b. *Mary asked how tall John's ∅.

In each case, since the VP is frozen we cannot look into it to find the [+wh] constituent.

It might be argued that the correct notion here is that contraction cannot occur to the left of a deletion site. This hypothesis is falsified, apparently, by data of the following sort.

(43) Mary believes that there $\begin{Bmatrix} \text{is} \\ \text{, } \text{'s} \end{Bmatrix}$ ∅ presently in the room a group of
at least one thousand Washington lobbyists.

Various problems emerge from such an analysis. These can be dealt with in a satisfactory way, but to pursue them here would take us too far afield.   ＼

5.2.3 Freezing at Node of Removal

Until this point the discussion of the Freezing principle has been concerned primarily with the syntactic consequences of non-structure-preserving attachment transformations. It is logically possible, also, that a transformation can be non-structure-preserving at a node from which a constituent has been moved or deleted. Suppose, for example, that prepositions in English obligatorily took NP complements. That is, suppose, that the rule of expansion of PP were PP → P NP. Any rule that moved the NP from beneath a PP, or deleted it, would freeze the PP, since PP → P would not be a rule of the base, by hypothesis. The frozenness of the PP in this case would be expected to block access of any later transformation to the isolated P.

(44)

One problem that arises in considerations of this sort is that of lexical subcategorization. For example, the verb phrase expands as either VP → V NP, or as VP → V. Hence removal of the NP would not freeze the VP. However, most verbs do not function both transitively and intransitively. This raises the possibility that lexical subcategorization might play a role in determining whether the particular application of a removal transformation is structure-preserving.

A complication of this issue is the possibility that some or all removal transformations may leave behind trace elements that have syntactic reality. If movement of an NP always left behind an NP trace, the question of subcategorization would not arise.

Chomsky (1973; 1975a; 1976; 1977) proposes an extreme formulation of trace theory in which all movement transformations leave behind an obligatory syntactic trace. For example, application of Wh Fronting to

(45) yields the surface structure of (46) in which a trace is present. The trace is indicated by *t*.

(45) $\begin{bmatrix} \text{Comp} \\ +\text{wh} \end{bmatrix}$ John tried to find *what*.

(46) $\begin{bmatrix} \text{Comp} \\ {\scriptstyle +\,wh} \end{bmatrix}$ [*what*] John tried to find t.

Assuming that every noun phrase (at least) is assigned an index in deep structure, *t* abbreviates an NP that contains no lexical items and has the same index as the NP that formerly occupied its position. This device allows Chomsky to represent a number of conditions on transformations as conditions on the surface structure distribution of coindexed constituents. For instance, in order to account for the ungrammaticality of (47)—

(47) *Who do you know $_{NP}$[the man $_{\bar{S}}$[that was hitting $\emptyset$]]?

—instead of adopting a constraint against moving *who* out of a relative clause, we could adopt a constraint that filters out surface structures in which an NP outside of the relative clause governs (is obligatorily coindexed to) a trace NP inside of the relative clause. See Chomsky 1973; 1975a; 1976; 1977 for the development of this theory of conditions on rules.

For our part, we will assume that traces of the sort discussed by Chomsky are at least not an automatic consequence of any movement transformation. In other words, though we do not rule out the notion of trace elements from our theory, we wish only to allow for the possibility that a transformation may specify that a trace is left behind. For some motivation for this position, see Culicover 1977a.

To pursue the question of the effects of subcategorization restrictions on freezing, we return to the rule of Gapping. Consider the underlying structure (48), noting in particular the presence of identical Aux, V, and interrogative NP.

(48) $_{\bar{S}}[\begin{bmatrix} \text{Comp} \\ +\text{wh} \end{bmatrix}$ $_{S}[$ $_{S}[$Bill *will find what* in Madison Square Garden]

and $_{S}[$Mary *will find what* in Shea Stadium]]]

Notice that the conjoined constituents are S and not $\bar{S}$. Thus there is a single Comp for the two conjuncts. While conceivably Gapping could apply at the conjoined S, it appears that one of the conditions for Gapping is not met: Gapping does not apply when the verb is followed by identical constituents in the two conjuncts. For example, Gapping applies in (50), but not in (49).

(49)

a. Bill will find a ring in Madison Square Garden and Mary will find a ring in Madison Square Garden.

b. *Bill will find a ring in Madison Square Garden, and Mary, a ring in Madison Square Garden.

(50)

a. Bill will find a ring in Madison Square Garden, and Mary will find a wallet in Shea Stadium.

b. Bill will find a ring in Madison Square Garden, and Mary, a wallet in Shea Stadium.

For a detailed discussion of this condition, see Stillings (1975).

For reasons having to do with parallel structure, it is possible to apply Wh Fronting in (48) to the two *wh* words simultaneously. For similar reasons, it is possible then to apply Inversion in the two conjuncts. Wh Fronting yields (51a), and then Inversion yields (51b).

(51)

a. $_{\bar{s}}$[what $_{s}$[$_{s}$[Bill *will find* $\emptyset$ in Madison Square Garden] and $_{s}$[Mary *will find* $\emptyset$ in Shea Stadium]]]

b. $_{\bar{s}}$[what will $_{s}$[$_{s}$[Bill *find* $\emptyset$ in Madison Square Garden] and $_{s}$[Mary *find* $\emptyset$ in Shea Stadium]]]

Interestingly, in (51b) the italicized portions satisfy the structural description of Gapping. The verbal sequence in the second conjunct is identical to that in the first conjunct, and the immediately preceding and following constituents are nonidentical.

Note now that *find* is a verb that obligatorily subcategorizes a direct object NP. If Wh Fronting yielded frozen VP's in (51) we would expect Gapping to be blocked, as in (16a), which we discussed earlier in section 5.2.1.1.

(16)

a. John gave Mary a book, and Bill $\begin{Bmatrix} \text{gave} \\ *\emptyset, \end{Bmatrix}$ Fred a magazine.

But, as (52) shows, Gapping can apply to (51b). Hence subcategorization does not play a role in the definition of structure-preserving, and the operation of the FP.

(52) What will Bill find in Madison Square Garden, and Mary, in Shea Stadium?

Additional examples of a similar type support this conclusion.

(53)

a. Where did Mary put the cat and Fred, the goldfish?
b. What did you trade to Susan, and Fred, to Mary?

In these cases the verbs *put* and *trade* subcategorize NP-PP sequences of a specific sort.

To summarize to this point, it appears that removal of a constituent from a structure in which it is subcategorized does not freeze that structure in case the constituent in question is an optional term in the base expansion of the category assigned to the structure. This still leaves open the question of whether it is ever possible to freeze a constituent by removing a subtree that it dominates. At present we know of no convincing case showing that this is more than a logical possibility.[21] It is quite possible that this restriction of FP to attachments would not affect the learnability proof in chapter 4.

5.2.4 Freezing and Conjoined Structures

5.2.4.1 Against Conjunction Reduction
Conjoined structures and the various ways of reducing them have always been a problem for linguistic theory. An example involving the dative construction will show why these structures are a problem for the current theory. Consider (54). Suppose that we apply Dative independently to VP_1 and VP_0.

The verb *gave* in both conjuncts is dominated by a frozen node. This means that a rule of Conjunction Reduction of the sort proposed by Ross (1967) would not be applicable to (55), and we would be unable to derive the grammatical (56).

(54)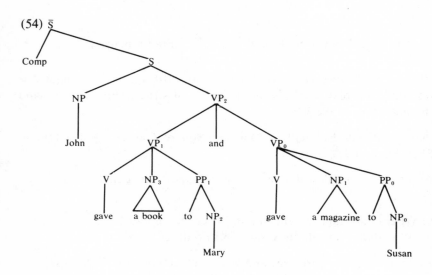

(55)

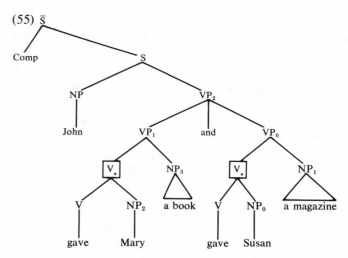

(56) John gave Mary a book and Susan a magazine.

The function of Conjunction Reduction in general is to remove identi-cal left or right branch constituents from conjoined structures and at-tach a copy of the identical constituents above the conjoined node that dominates both of them. If Conjunction Reduction were applied to (54), for example, it would give as output (57), which would be an intermediate

(57)

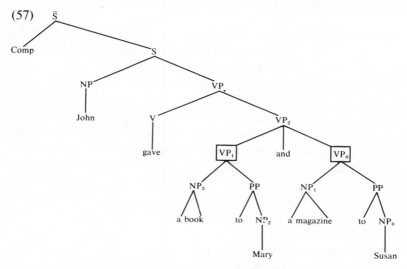

structure if we supposed that Conjunction Reduction preceded Dative in the derivation of (56), for example.

The structure in (57) poses a number of problems, however. It makes the claim that *a book to Mary* and *a magazine to Susan* are VP's in derived structure. More seriously, even, it does not provide a structure that will satisfy the structural description of Dative in both conjuncts. In particular, the right conjunct lacks the verb to which the indirect object would be adjoined.[22] Of course, we could adopt a convention for interpreting the structural description of a transformation when a conjoined structure is encountered, but unless we had a situation in which a common element in the two conjuncts was to be moved and simultaneously reduced to a single copy, it would be necessary in essence to reconstruct the original conjoined structure. For example, if NP_2 and NP_0 in (57) were both *Susan,* we could apply Dative simultaneously to both instances and attach one copy of *Susan* at the verb *gave,* getting *John gave Susan a book and a magazine*. But in order to apply Dative to (57) as it stands, it would be necessary to move *Susan* to a position where the second copy of the verb *gave* would have been if Conjunction Reduction had not applied. This does not appear to provide a particularly insightful solution to the problem.

5.2.4.2 Verb Deletion A possible means of avoiding this difficulty would be to posit a rule of (at least) verb deletion for conjoined structures, as contrasted with the general reduction rule of Ross (1967), introduced at the beginning of this discussion. Such a rule would delete only lexical material that is identical in the conjuncts, otherwise not affecting the structure. Because of the grammaticality of (55), this rule would have to apply even to the frozen derived structure in (55). A generalization that would permit this is that rules that apply to one constituent under identity with another, such as pronominalization and VP Ellipsis, are not restricted by any analyzability constraints, such as those proposed by Ross (1967).[23] We would have to formulate this rule of deletion in conjoined structures so that it fitted in naturally with this generalization, of course.

A solution along these lines again raises questions having to do with surface structure. Taking the most conservative input structure for (56), namely (55), we arrive by deletion at (58), in which *Susan a*

(58)

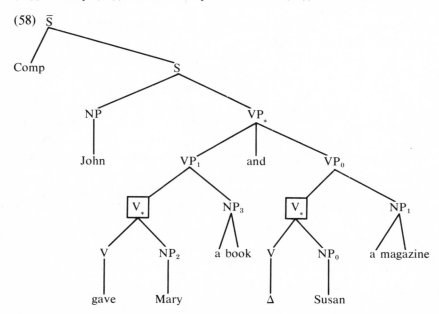

magazine is a VP. Unfortunately, we are unable to provide evidence to verify that this is the correct surface structure. The reason is not so much an empirical one as a theoretical one: because the reduction transformation applies to conjoined nodes, subsequent transformations cannot apply to just one of the conjuncts without violating the Conjoined Structure constraint (see Ross 1967). In cases such as these the Conjoined Structure constraint blocks the extraction of a constituent of one of the conjuncts. This prevents us from applying constituency tests to the conjuncts separately. The cyclic principle, on the other hand, prevents us from going down into the individual conjuncts and applying transformations within the conjuncts themselves. For at the time the reduction transformation is applied, we have moved out of the individual conjuncts to the conjoined node, and cannot move back down again without violating this principle.

Let us return now to the reduction transformation itself. There is some indication that a simple rule that deletes the verb will not work. When an adverb precedes the verb in the two conjuncts the result of deletion is, unexpectedly, unacceptable.[24]

$$
(59) \quad *\text{John} \left\{ \begin{array}{l} \text{completely} \\ \text{yesterday} \\ \text{just} \\ \text{obviously} \\ \text{happily} \end{array} \right\} \text{finished the coffee, and} \left\{ \begin{array}{l} \text{partially} \\ \text{almost} \\ \text{last week} \\ \text{certainly} \\ \text{angrily} \end{array} \right\} \emptyset
$$

the dessert that had been left over for him.

From this we can argue that the only thing that can be reduced is a left branch in a right conjunct, that is, a constituent that immediately follows *and*.

The argument goes as follows: When an adverb is moved into preverbal position, it freezes the V. This is shown by the fact that Gapping is blocked by the preverbal adverb (see (60)). The attachment of the adverb does not freeze the entire VP, because it is possible to question out of the VP: *Which coffee did John completely finish ∅?* The adverb is not attached at the S-node, as in (61), either. If this were the case, *finish the coffee* would be a VP, and would act like one with respect to transformations like VP Top and other rules that mention VP, such as VP Ellipsis.

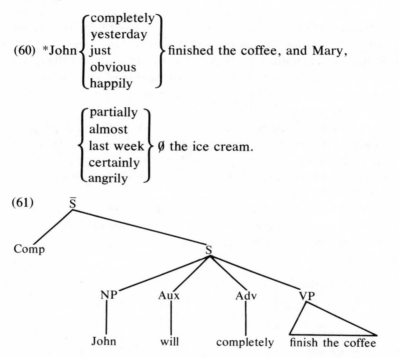

(60) *John $\left\{\begin{array}{l}\text{completely}\\\text{yesterday}\\\text{just}\\\text{obvious}\\\text{happily}\end{array}\right\}$ finished the coffee, and Mary,

$\left\{\begin{array}{l}\text{partially}\\\text{almost}\\\text{last week}\\\text{certainly}\\\text{angrily}\end{array}\right\}$ ∅ the ice cream.

(61)

However, this does not seem to be the case, as the examples in (62) show:

(62)
a. They said that John would completely finish the coffee, and

$\left\{\begin{array}{l}\text{completely finish the coffee he will}\\\text{*finish the coffee he will completely}\end{array}\right\}$.

b. They said that John would completely finish the coffee and he will (*completely).

The contrast in (62) shows that *completely* is a constituent of the VP.
    Now even if the verb is dominated by a frozen node after adverb

attachment, reduction of the verb won't be blocked, because the reduction transformation is not subject to the constraints on analyzability, as we have already argued. So, the argument goes, the ungrammaticality of (59) must be explained on other grounds: the structural description of the reduction transformation.

To summarize to this point, there exists a plausible rule for the derivation of reduced conjoined structures of a limited type which allows us to preserve the structure necessary for later application of transformations within conjuncts. This rule, if it is correct, must be included in the class of rules that are not sensitive to analyzability constraints. Furthermore, this rule can apply only to left branch constituents in a right conjunct that immediately follow *and*.

5.2.4.3 Parallel Extraction out of Reduced Structures This account of conjunction (at least for the special case considered thus far) provides us with structures that are not deformed in any way beyond the deletion of lexical material. This is particularly crucial if we maintain FP. Consider, for example, the structure (57) as a possible representation of (63). Note that VP_1 and VP_0 are frozen.

(63) John gave a book to Mary and a magazine to Susan.

It is a well-known fact that constituents of conjuncts may be moved out of them if conditions of parallel structure are satisfied. (We will assume these conditions here but will make no attempt to state them precisely. See Williams (1978) for a convincing proposal.) Even supposing that such conditions could be satisfied for the derivation of conjoined datives— . . . *gave Mary a book and Susan a magazine*— and even ignoring ordering problems, the frozenness of VP_1 and VP_0 would block Dative in (57).[25] This frozenness would also block all other extraction rules, such as Wh Fronting, which must apply to a structure like (57) after reduction has applied for the derivation of (64).

(64) Who did John give a book to ∅ and a magazine to ∅?

Though this sentence may not be judged completely acceptable by all speakers, it is certainly no worse than those in (65), where reduction has not applied.

(65)

a. Who did John give a book to and give a magazine to?

b. Who did John give a book to and take a magazine from?

Thus the marginal nature of (64) is not due to the reduction, it appears. The structure that results from the deletion rule does not appear to have the consequence of blocking the parallel application of larger transformations.

5.2.4.4 Left Branch Reduction Certain properties of this rule of verb deletion in conjoined structures suggest an extension along rather natural lines. First, the rule is not sensitive to frozen structures, which leads us to suspect that it is not in fact a transformation of the usual sort. Second, the rule applies to left branch verbs, which raises the possibility that it may apply to left branches in general. Third, if the rule is not a transformation of the usual sort but rather an operation by which conjoined structures may be reduced, it would be natural to seek an extension of it to right-branching structures as well.

We have already given a number of arguments to show that we are not dealing with an actual deletion of V. One more indirect argument may be mentioned here. Consider the structure in (66). The frozenness of VP_0 would block Wh Fronting from applying to its constituent *who*. Also, VP_1 and VP_0 do not satisfy the parallel structure conditions that would allow extraction of an NP from the two VP's. But, as we have already seen, (64) is a grammatical sentence.

To the extent that the reduction rule applies only to verbs, it is difficult to imagine what the proper formulation might be. Perhaps the rule replaces the verb by a $\emptyset$ pro-verb, or perhaps it simply deletes the lexical material beneath it, which is the way we have been viewing it up till now. The former possibility proves to be unattractive if reduction is extended to left-branching structures generally, as we will see.

It has long been recognized that an argument for reduction (as opposed to generating all conjuncts directly in the base) exists in those cases where the conjoined structure cannot be a conjunction of underlying constituents. This situation arises when (a) the constituents that appear in surface structure cannot be underlying constituents, and (b) the conjuncts in surface structure are not constituents at all. For exam-

(66)

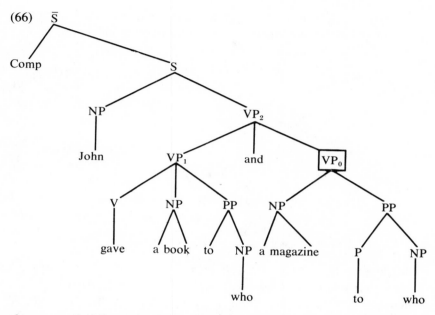

ple, we argued for reduction of V by noting that *a book to Susan* and *Susan a book* are not underlying constituents of VP; in fact they are probably not constituents at all, although we can see no way to get empirical evidence on this if they show up only in conjoined structures.

The same sort of case can be made for reduction of subjects. For an argument of type (a) we cite well-known examples of the sort given in (67):

(67)
a. John is eager to please and is easy to please.
b. John walked out the door and was hit by a snowball.
c. John is here and seems to be anxious to leave.

These are derived, respectively, from the structures illustrated in (68):

(68)
a. John is eager to please and it is easy to please John.
b. John walked out the door and a snowball hit John.
c. John is here and Δ seems $_S$[John to be anxious to leave].

An argument of type (b) relies on the assumption that the constituent $_{Aux}$[Tense Modal] is an immediate daughter of S, as illustrated in (69).

(69)

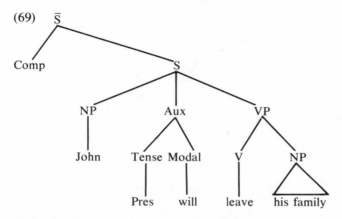

This position is defended by Culicover (1976a) and is based on arguments presented by Klima (in lectures), Jackendoff (1972), and Emonds (1970; 1976). Given this analysis, it follows that the italicized phrases in (70) cannot be underlying constituents, and (70) must have the underlying structure shown in (71).

(70) John *will leave* and *should be back soon*.

(71)

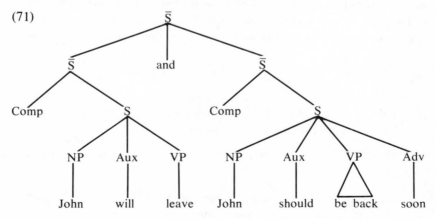

Another case of left branch reduction of this same sort applies to possessives. Note first that the italicized portion of (72) is not a constituent. On the contrary, *John's mother* is a constituent, as is well known.

(72) John's *mother's house*

These facts support an argument of type (b), in light of examples such as (73).

(73)
a. John's *mother's brother* and *father's sister* are married.
b. My *car's engine* and *boat's propeller* are rusted beyond repair.
c. We are confused by Fred's *publisher's refusal to respond* and *lawyer's refusal to negotiate.*

Another left-branch structure that undergoes reduction is illustrated by (74).

(74) Mary is much more interesting than Susan.

Bresnan (1973) argues that *much* is a determiner of the quantifier phrase, or QP, *much more*, as in (75). Once again we find that non-constituents appear to be conjoined in surface structures, as in (76).

(75)

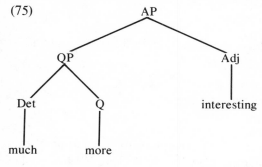

(76)
a. Mary is much *more interesting* and *more intelligent* than Susan.
b. I found a considerably *more useful* and *less expensive* device for fixing the faucet.

c. An obviously *more angry* and *more righteous* visitor entered the room.

By hypothesis these phrases are not constituents when the determiner is present, and hence the appearance of conjunction must be due to reduction.

Finally, we can find marginal evidence of left-branch reduction of the definite article in noun phrases.[26]

(77)

a. ?The man's questions and woman's answer were completely unrelated.

b. ?I was looking for the boy's bicycle and girl's scooter.

c.*?We were surprised by the man's refusal to discuss the problem and woman's reluctance to do so.

Let us introduce at this point a notational device to represent the deletion of lexical material only from beneath a node. In a structural change, we place double parentheses around the term that dominates the deleted material. So, for reduction of left branches we write

Left Branch Reduction Rule:
$A - X - and - A - Y$
$1 - 2 - 3 - 4 - 5 \Rightarrow 1 - 2 - 3 - ((4)) - 5$
Condition: $1 = 4$

It is easy to see how this reduction can be extended to right branches.

Right Branch Reduction Rule:
$X - A - and - Y - A$
$1 - 2 - 3 - 4 - 5 \Rightarrow 1 - ((2)) - 3 - 4 - 5$
Condition: $2 = 5$

This rule will derive sequences that correspond to the output of the putative transformation known as Right Node Raising, or RNR. We will show how the reduction approach is preferable to RNR in terms of descriptive adequacy. This demonstration involves an interesting and quite unexpected application of FP.

5.2.4.5 Right Node Raising The rule of Right Node Raising has been postulated for the derivation of sentences like the following.[27]

(78)
a. Mary buys, and Bill sells, pictures of Fred.
b. Mary buys, and Bill is believed to sell, pictures of Fred.
c. Mary buys, and Bill knows a man who sells, pictures of Fred.
d. Mary buys, and everyone claims that Bill sells, pictures of Fred.
e. Mary is believed to buy, and Bill sells, pictures of Fred.
f. Mary knows a man who buys, and Bill knows a man who sells, pictures of Fred.[28]
g. Everyone claims that Mary buys, and I think Bill sells, pictures of Fred.

This rule has the effect of producing a gap in the left conjunct. In many instances, such as those in (78), the conjuncts are clearly not base generable as such and must therefore arise during the course of derivation.

One hypothesis is that identical right branches in the underlying conjuncts are removed and a copy is attached at or above the level of the conjoined node. This is the derivation found in Postal 1974; 126 and Maling 1972. Such a rule, if it exists, is a perfect test case for FP, since it yields a multitude of different structures in its most general formulation. Some of these may be base structures, and others may not.

Consider the simplest case, that of (79). The derivation is given in (80)–(81).

(79) Mary buys, and Bill sells, pictures of Fred.

Because there is no base rule of the form $S \rightarrow S\ NP$, the node S_* is frozen. This predicts that it would be impossible to question out of the raised NP. The prediction is incorrect, as (82) shows.

Since we are attempting to demonstrate the correctness of FP, we cannot use it to rule out adoption of RNR as a transformation. However, finding independent reasons why RNR cannot be a transformation would lend plausibility to FP, since FP must rule out RNR.

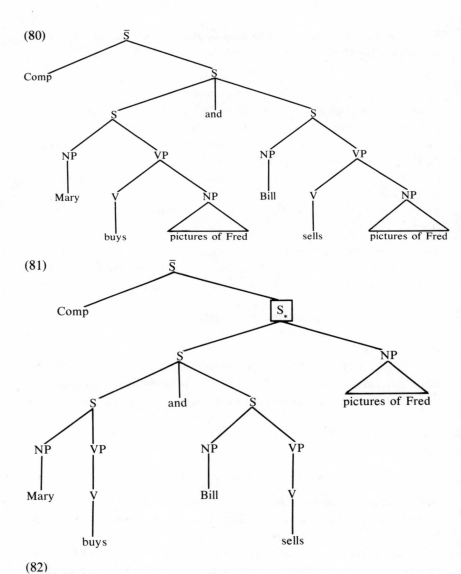

(80)

(81)

(82)
a. Who does Mary buy, and Bill sell, pictures of Ø?
b. I wonder who Mary buys, and Bill sells, pictures of Ø?

The argument against RNR is based on the fact that a raised node always behaves, vis-à-vis all constraints on analyzability, just as it would if it were in its original underlying position. Hence, whereas it is apparently possible to apply RNR to a constituent of a relative clause, if we then try to analyze this raised node, we find that it acts as though it were still within the relative clause. Consider (78c) again: *Mary buys, and Bill knows a man who sells, pictures of Fred.* If RNR in fact applies in the derivation of this sentence, it must violate the Complex NP constraint of Ross (1967) and more general constraints related to it, such as Chomsky's Subjacency condition (1973) and the Binary principle of Culicover and Wexler (1977). This last constraint will be discussed in detail in section 5.4. For the moment, note that Wh Fronting may not apply to a constituent of a relative clause when RNR has *not* applied.

(83) *Who does Bill know $_{NP}$[a man $_{\bar{S}}$[who sells pictures of $\emptyset$]]

If we consider the other conjunct in (78c) we observe that it permits Wh Fronting when it appears alone:

(84) Who does Mary buy pictures of $\emptyset$?

If RNR does not apply, and the right-branch NP's are left in their original positions, the presence of the one relative clause blocks parallel extraction by Wh Fronting from the two conjuncts.

(85) *Who does Mary buy pictures of $\emptyset$, and Bill know a man who sells pictures of $\emptyset$?

If RNR applies to give (78c), we would not expect the same result, because in this case the NP would no longer be in the relative clause in the second conjunct. But (86) is ungrammatical.[29]

(86) *Who does Mary buy, and Bill know a man who sells, pictures of $\emptyset$?

Similar results obtain if the left conjunct is the one with the relative clause, showing that the ungrammaticality of (86) is not due to the confusion of some superficial parsing strategy.

(87) *Who does Mary know a man who buys, and Bill sell, pictures of ∅?

Of course, if RNR applies to relative clauses in both conjuncts, Wh Fronting is again blocked.

(88) *Who does Mary know a man who buys, and Bill know a woman who sells, pictures of ∅?

To take another constraint, it appears marginally possible to apply RNR to conjoined structures just in case the structures are parallel. Thus (89) is ungrammatical, but (90) is marginally acceptable.

(89) *Mary buys, and Bill sells cars and, trucks.

(90)
a. Mary buys paintings of, and Bill buys paintings of and photographs of, sandy California beaches.
b. ?Mary buys paintings, and Bill buys paintings and photographs, of sandy California beaches.

In cases such as (90b), where the constituent that has been separated from the rest of the structure has internal structure, it is possible to apply further transformations. The conjoined structure in (90b) would not block Wh Fronting, for example, since the rule could apply in parallel fashion to the structure even if RNR has not applied, as in (91b).

(91)
a. ?Which beaches does Mary buy paintings, and Bill buy paintings and photographs, of ∅?
b. Which beaches does Mary buy paintings of ∅ and Bill buy paintings of ∅ and photographs of ∅?

Example (91a) can be made more complex by replacing *paintings and photographs* by *reproductions of paintings and photographs*. Normally such an increase in complexity would block Wh Fronting because of the Binary principle.

(92) *Who did you buy reproductions of paintings (and photographs) of ∅?

This is mirrored in the structures to which RNR has applied.

(93) *Which beaches does Mary buy paintings, and Bill buy reproductions of paintings and photographs, of Ø?

But (93) is not so much worse than (91a) that it constitutes a strong piece of evidence against RNR as a transformation.

We have established that RNR as a transformation does not succeed in predicting the grammaticality of certain structures, regardless of whether FP is correct. Rather, it appears that what is crucial are the constraints on analyzability defined on structures undeformed by an extraction transformation like RNR. This suggests that a deletion rule of some sort is more descriptively adequate, as embodied in the Right Branch Reduction rule, already given.

Let us sum up the argument. We discovered first of all that a Conjunction Reduction transformation of the sort proposed by Ross (1967) will not work if FP is correct, for two sorts of reasons. First, if a transformation causes freezing in the conjuncts, the reduction nevertheless seems to apply. Second, the reduction itself will cause freezing, but this does not seem to block other transformations from applying subsequently. We concluded that there was a rule that deleted lexical material in right conjuncts in constituents immediately after the conjunction. This rule is Left Branch Reduction, and does not obey the constraints on analyzability such as FP.

On the other hand, we found that a transformation of Right Node Raising constitutes another apparent counterexample to FP; RNR patently derives frozen structures (since it is non-structure-preserving most of the time). But, we found, this did not automatically lead to unanalyzability. What the data seem to show, in fact, is that RNR is a deletion transformation that applies to right branches in left conjuncts, that is, immediately before the conjunction. The fact that there is no true movement in these sentences explains why freezing does not occur. Furthermore, it explains why the acceptability of analyzing the raised right node correlates exactly with its analyzability in corresponding untransformed structures. Thus we have argued that two sorts of potential difficulties with the Freezing principle in conjoined structures are only apparent difficulties.

5.2.5 The Passive Problem

We noted in 5.2.1.1 that FP incorrectly predicts that (94) will be ungrammatical.

(94) John was given an encyclopedia for his birthday.

The reason for the prediction, as (95) shows, is that the node dominat-

(95)

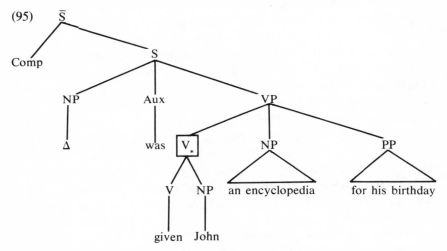

ing the indirect object after Dative has applied is frozen. Thus NP Preposing, which applies in the derivation of (94), should be blocked. In this section we will discuss two possible solutions to this problem.

5.2.5.1 Obligatory Δ-Filling One plausible solution relies on the formal statement of NP Preposing:

NP Preposing:
X - $_{NP}[\Delta]$ - Y - V - NP - Z
1 -   2 - 3 - 4 -   5 - 6 $\Rightarrow$ 1 - 5 - 3 - 4 - $\emptyset$ - 6

The crucial property of this rule that we are concerned with here is that it fills a dummy NP. As is clear from the following examples, this transformation is obligatory. If it fails to apply, we cannot still get a grammatical sentence by realizing the Δ as *there* or *it*, as happens automatically in the course of a derivation under some analyses.[30]

(96)

a. Bill saw Susan.

b. Susan was seen by Bill.

c. *$\left(\left\{\begin{matrix} \text{There} \\ \text{It} \end{matrix}\right\}\right)$ was seen Susan by Bill.

Thus we entertain the possibility of a convention that requires us to apply an obligatory Δ-filling transformation even in frozen structures. But we are unable to demonstrate that this is anything more than an ad hoc solution to the passive problem, because we can find no other clear cases in which a dummy must be filled by a constituent that potentially appears in a frozen structure.

There is one similar case, however, that carries with it some problems of its own, and a digression here would not be too much out of place. Consider the derivation of sentences like those in (97).[31]

(97)

a. It seems that Bill likes Susan.

b. Bill seems to like Susan.

A plausible source for these sentences is a structure with a dummy subject governed by the verb *seems*. Sentence (97b) may be derived by the familiar rule of NP Preposing, but this rule will not apply to the subject of the complement in (97a) because of the Binary principle, which we discuss in detail in section 5.4. A rule applying at the higher S cannot have access to the subject (or any other constituent) of the next $\bar{\text{S}}$ down. But the infinitive, we assume, is not an $\bar{\text{S}}$, but an S only.

(98)

a. $_S[\Delta$ seems $_{\bar{S}}[$that $_S[$*Bill* likes Susan$]]]$

b. $_S[\Delta$ seems $_S[$*Bill* to like Susan$]] \Rightarrow$ $_S[$*Bill* seems $_S[\emptyset$ to like Susan$]]$

In (98a) the dummy subject is not filled and is realized as *it* on this approach.

The problem, now, is the following: We have seen that Complex NP

Shift may apply to the subject of an infinitive, as in examples like the following.

(99)
a. I $\left\{\begin{array}{l}\text{consider}\\\text{believe}\\\text{thought}\end{array}\right\}$ the clowns wearing those funny hats to be very amusing.

b. I $\left\{\begin{array}{l}\text{consider}\\\text{believe}\\\text{thought}\end{array}\right\}$ ∅ to be very amusing the clowns wearing those funny hats.

Suppose that Complex NP Shift applies to the subject of an infinitive complement of *seems,* however.

(100)
a. Δ seems ₛ[the clowns wearing those funny hats to be very amusing]
b. Δ seems ₛ[∅ to be very amusing] the clowns wearing those funny hats

Even when the dummy subject is realized as *it* the resulting sentence is ungrammatical.

(101) *It seems ∅ to be very amusing the clowns wearing those funny hats.

This is in contrast with (102), which would have been derived had Complex NP Shift not applied.

(102) The clowns wearing those funny hats seem ∅ to be very amusing.

This situation is an interesting one, because it suggests a formally precise basis for discriminating between obligatory transformations whose failure to apply has no consequences, and those whose failure to apply leads to ungrammaticality. In a structure comparable to (100a), but where the complement of *seems* is S̄, NP Preposing will not apply, the dummy subject will be realized as *it,* and (103) will be derived.

(103) It seems that the clowns wearing those funny hats are very amusing.

The two cases are distinguished by the following convention: A derivation must be filtered out if an obligatory transformation is applicable but is blocked because there is no constituent that it can apply to.[32]

In the case of (101), Complex NP Shift moves the target constituent (in the sense of Bresnan (1976a)) to the right and freezes the node that it attaches to. All other aspects of the structural description of NP Preposing are present, but the target cannot be moved again because of FP. Hence the blocking of the transformation, which is obligatory, causes filtering. On the other hand, in (103), we must interpret the convention in such a way that the absence of a target does not filter the derivation. In this case, the Binary principle blocks access to the entire complement. Thus at no point in the derivation of (103) could it have been the case that there was an NP available for NP Preposing into the position occupied by the dummy subject. In (101) by comparison, the target is made inaccessible by FP.

The problem now is, what is the formal difference between the case where filtering occurs, and that where it does not (when the complement is *that*-S)? Perhaps in the history of the former sort of sentence there was a target that was rendered inaccessible to NP Preposing, whereas in the latter case, there never was an eligible target. If this in fact is the crucial difference, one must be suspicious of this explanation for how (101) is blocked, because it requires access to derivational history. Other things being equal, it is preferable not to resort to a filtering device of this sort, because of the considerable increase in descriptive power it affords beyond what appears to be absolutely necessary, assuming of course that this filter is not a universal principle. If it is universal, we can assume it is desirable, because (again everything being equal) it allows a reduction in descriptive power.

In short, though the proposed convention might work for this particular case, there is no good evidence that it is the best solution to the passive problem.

5.2.5.2 Underlying Passive A second possibility is that the passive construction is generated in the base, and not (necessarily) transformationally. Friedin (1975) and Bresnan (1978) have suggested that the active-passive relation is captured in the lexicon and that all passives are base-generated, while Wasow (1977) proposes that some passives are transformationally generated and others generated in the base. That Friedin's and Bresnan's proposal will solve the passive problem is clear, and we think their proposal has some merit on its own. For details see the works cited; we will not attempt to reconstruct the arguments here, nor is this the best place to discuss the problems inherent in such an approach.[33]

It is worth pointing out a piece of data that, though it could be accommodated under the first solution mentioned (obligatory Δ-filling), follows more naturally if the passive is an underived construction. We have already seen (section 5.2.1.1) that Gapping is blocked by Dative, as in (104).

(104)
a. John gave Mary a magazine for Christmas, and Sam gave Susan a set of electric trains for her birthday.
b. *John gave Mary a magazine for Christmas, and Sam, Susan a set of electric trains for her birthday.

In the passive construction, even with datives, Gapping is not blocked.

(105)
a. Mary was given a magazine for Christmas (by John), and Susan was given a set of electric trains for her birthday (by Sam).
b. Mary was given a magazine for Christmas (by John), and Susan, a set of electric trains for her birthday (by Sam).

The explanation of the ungrammaticality of (104b) is that the output of Dative is a structure with a frozen node dominating the verb. This is shown in (106a). In (106b), if NP Preposing has applied, the verb is still dominated by a frozen node, unless of course some pruning or other convention reduces the structure.

In order to generate (105b) when the passive is transformationally derived, we will have to introduce into the theory some way of allowing transformations access to the frozen V_* after NP Preposing has

(106)
a.

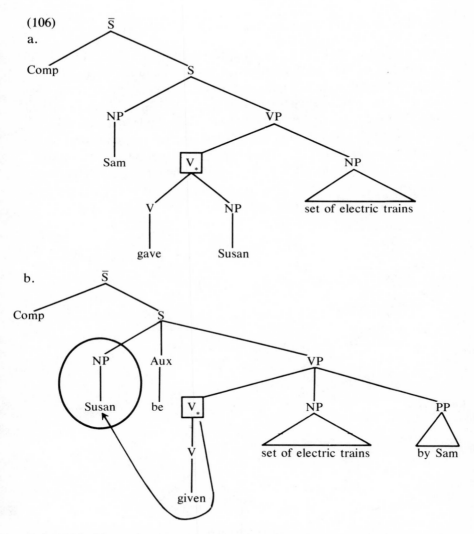

analyzed it. No such convention is required, however, if the passive is
not transformationally derived.[34]

5.3 The Binary Principle

The second crucial principle in the learnability proof of chapter 4 restricts the domain of application of transformations to specific and relatively local parts of a phrase-marker. The essential notion is that used in the proof of Hamburger and Wexler (1973; 1975) and involved in the Subjacency condition of Chomsky (1973). It is that a transformation can involve material only in the S on which it is cycling or the next S down, as illustrated in (107), where the current cycle is taken to be S_2. As a concrete illustration, we consider the structure in (108).

(107)

(108)

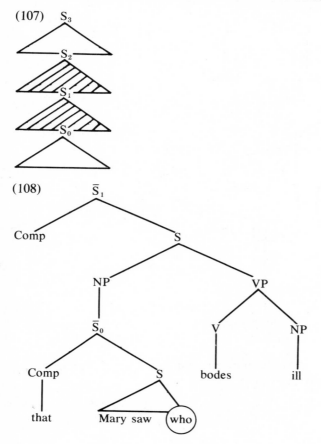

This basic notion may be elaborated in various ways. For example, it is possible to extend the set of relevant cyclic domains to NP, and to other nodes as well, and doing so has clear empirical consequences. For instance, if we take $\bar{S}$ and NP to be cyclic nodes in the sense of this constraint, when we are cycling on $\bar{S}_1$ in (108) it is impossible to analyze below the $\bar{S}_0$ node.

Consequently we would predict, correctly, that the circled *who* in $\bar{S}_0$ could not be moved into the Comp of $\bar{S}_1$, generating **who does that Mary saw bode ill?* To generate this sentence we would have to analyze below $\bar{S}_0$, which is the second cyclic node below $\bar{S}_1$, and not the next one below.[35]

It is also possible to interpret the phrase "cycling in a cyclic domain" in a variety of ways. A number of alternatives are explored in Culicover and Wexler 1977 in terms of their empirical consequences for the description of English.

This section states the two forms of the Binary principle (BP) given by Culicover and Wexler (1977) and summarizes the central cases to which they apply. After exploring the empirical differences between the two constraints, we find sufficient evidence to lead us to settle tentatively on one version rather than the other.

5.3.1 Binary Principle: Two Versions

We define the set $\{\bar{S}, NP\}$ to be the set of B-cyclic nodes. We suppose that the transformational cycle moves upwards through the phrase-marker, and that a rule must apply at the lowest node in the tree at which its structural description is met, if it is to apply at all to the elements crucially involved in the rule at that level of the transformational cycle. This is similar in certain respects to the proposal of E. Williams (1974a,b), the primary difference being that he proposes defining for each transformation the node at which it applies. Our assumption also incorporates a version of the strict cycle. We will find it useful to understand "apply a transformation" to mean that if the structural change is not carried out, either because the transformation is optional or because it is blocked by a constraint, the transformation cannot apply to the same configuration on a later cycle. This interpretation is not intended to rule out cases where a transformation is blocked and then the phrase-marker is restructured in such a way that formerly ineligible nodes become eligible. We will attempt to formalize this notion later in this chapter. We also assume, following Chomsky (1973; 1975a; 1976; 1977), that after a constituent has been moved into Comp, it can be moved thereafter only into a higher Comp node.

Suppose the transformational cycle is operating at a given node.[36] Starting from this node, we move down a path in the phrase-marker. Any transition to a B-cyclic node or from a B-cyclic node counts for the Binary principle. The principle is that we may move along a path just as long as the count is less than two. When the count becomes two, the node just reached is the lowest node in that path to which a transformation may apply. Consider an example. Suppose we are cycling on

(109)

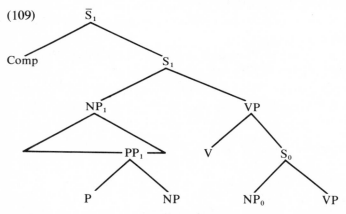

S_1. A transformation applying at this level may apply to PP_1 (for example, Extraposition of PP) since the path from S_1 to NP_1 counts as one transition, and from NP_1 to PP_1 counts as the second. A transformation applying at this level may apply also to NP_0 (Tough Movement or NP Preposing) or to an immediate constituent of NP_0.

At $\bar{S}_1$, we may apply transformations to NP_1, since counting down from $\bar{S}_1$ to S_1 counts as one transition, and counting down to NP_1 counts as the second. Note that we cannot apply a transformation to a constituent of NP_1 at this level. We may apply a transformation at this level to NP_0, however, since the path through S_1 to S_0 does not contain any transitions from or to a B-cyclic node.

(110)

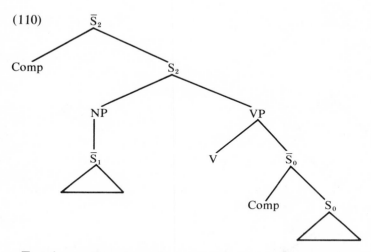

To take another example, consider (110). Again, at S_2 we may apply a transformation to a constituent of NP (say, Extraposition of $\bar{S}_1$). However, we may not apply a transformation at this level to a constituent of S_0, since the transitions to and from $\bar{S}_0$ will restrict transformations from going below this node. This will account for the failure of NP Preposing to apply to the subject of a tensed S or any other $\bar{S}$ with a complementizer.[37] We will refer to this version of the Binary principle as the *counting version,* or CV.

An alternative principle that has equivalent consequences in a large number of cases is the following: Consider a node A on which a transformation T is cycling. T may apply no further down in the phrase-marker than to the immediate constituents of the highest B-cyclic node dominated by A. Thus, if a transformation is applying to $\bar{S}_1$ in (111), its domain of application is that shown by the dotted lines. We will refer to this version of the Binary principle as the *domination version,* or DV.

Let us consider now what limitations these constraints impose on the accessibility of various structures to transformations. Consider (112), in which the subject is sentential. The domain of application of a rule applying at S_1 as constrained by CV is illustrated by the broken line, and the domain of application as constrained by DV is shown by a solid line. In (112) the two domains turn out to be the same.

(111)

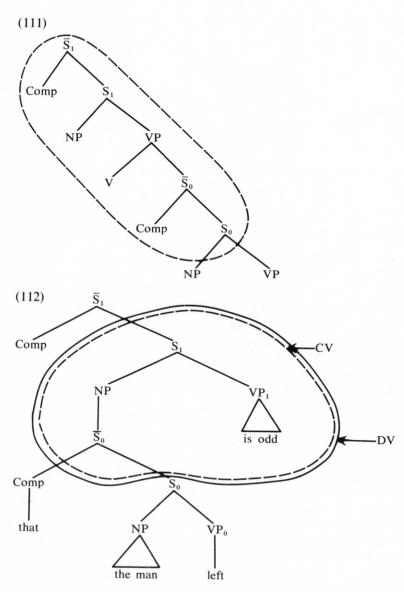

(112)

Observe that in either case a transformation applying at S_1 cannot involve constituents of $\bar{S}_0$ but can involve $\bar{S}_0$ itself. This permits ordinary Extraposition to apply, as in (113).[38]

(113) It is interesting $_{\overline{S}}$[that you should say that]

However, both constraints block Complex NP Shift of a constituent of VP_0 around VP_1.

(114)

a. $_{\overline{S}}$[That Mary gave *a bag full of time bombs* to Fred] impresses me.

b. $_{\overline{S}}$[That Mary gave $\emptyset$ to Fred *a bag full of time bombs*] impresses me.

c. $_{\overline{S}}$[*That Mary gave $\emptyset$ to Fred] impresses me *a bag full of time bombs*.

Similarly, both constraints will block the extraposition of a PP from the sentential subject to the right of the VP of the main clause.

(115)

a. $_{\overline{S}}$[That John gave a dollar *to Fred*] impresses me.

b. $_{\overline{S}}$[*That John gave a dollar $\emptyset$] impresses me *to Fred*.

Without the Binary principle (or some other constraint equivalent to it here) the rule that extraposes PP in (116) will derive (115).

(116)

a. A movie *about vampires* has been playing recently.

b. A movie $\emptyset$ has been playing recently *about vampires*.

In both (115) and (116) a PP has been moved out of a subject NP. Significantly, in the ungrammatical (115b) the NP dominates $\overline{S}$.[39]

As can be seen from the following structural description of Complex NP Shift, unless some sort of bounding is imposed on the rule, ungrammatical examples such as (114) will be derived. The crucial aspect of the rule is that there is no non-ad-hoc motivation for mentioning in the rule itself the VP around which the complex NP is extraposed.[40]

Complex NP Shift:

X - V - NP - Y

$1 - 2 - 3 - 4 \Rightarrow 1 - 2 - \emptyset - 4+3$

At the level of $\bar{\bar{S}}_1$ the domain of access of a transformation is as shown in (117). At $\bar{\bar{S}}_1$ it is possible to apply rules that move constituents

(117)

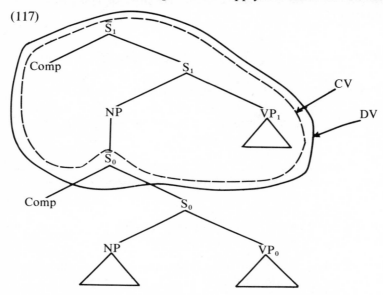

into Comp, such as Wh Fronting and Topicalization. These constituents may not be dominated by the sentential subject $\bar{S}_0$, however, as (117) shows. This captures in essence the Sentential Subject constraint of Ross (1967) and certain applications of the A-over-A principle of Chomsky (1964; 1968; 1973). Ungrammatical sentences like (118b,c) are blocked in this way.[41]

(118)
a. $_{\bar{S}}$[That Mary gave a bag full of cans to Fred] interests me.
b. *What does $_{\bar{S}}$[that Mary gave Ø to Fred] interest you?
c. *A bag full of cans, $_{\bar{S}}$[that Mary gave Ø to Fred] interests me.

An analogous situation exists for NP subjects. Consider the structure (119) in which the subject is an NP of the form *a story about NP$_*$*. With either version of the constraint it should be impossible to move NP$_*$ alone. This is correct, as sentences like (120) show.

(119)

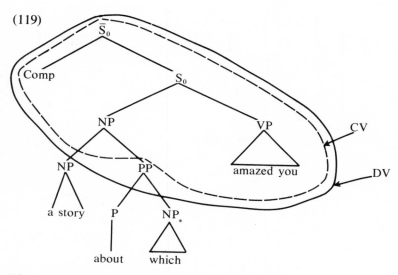

(120) *Who did NP[a story about ∅] amaze you?

If the structure is as shown in (119), DV permits movement of the PP but CV does not, regardless of where in the NP the PP is located. Judgments on such derivations vary; the best cases are like (121). We will make some further comment on these cases at a later point.

(121)
a. ?About whom did NP[a story ∅] amaze you?
b. ?Of which cities are NP[the mayors ∅] corrupt?

As Chomsky (1973) noted, extraction from right-branching sentential complements is possible and therefore constitutes a challenge for an approach of the sort being presented here.[42] Consider the examples in (122), which illustrate the apparent accessibility of such complements, and the structures (123) and (124), in which the domains of access are indicated.

(122)
a. Who is it $\begin{cases} \text{obvious} \\ \text{apparent} \\ \text{possible} \end{cases}$ s̄[that Bill hired ∅]?

b. Who does Fred $\left\{\begin{array}{l}\text{believe}\\\text{claim}\\\text{suspect}\\\text{know}\end{array}\right\}$ $_{\bar{S}}$[that Bill hired Ø]?

(123)

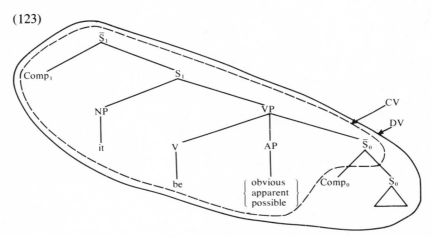

(124)

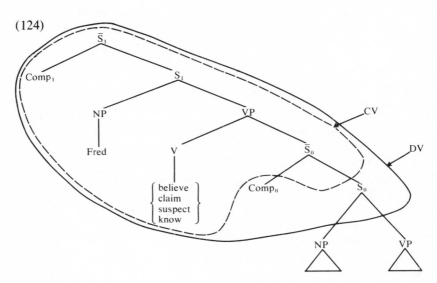

In neither structure is it possible for a transformation to move a constituent of S_0 directly from S_0 into $Comp_1$. Hence Chomsky (1973) proposes that the derivations of sentences such as those in (122) make use of successive cyclic movement of constituents. The constituents are moved into the Comp of the $\bar{S}$ in which they appear in deep structure, and hence into successively higher Comp's on successive cycles.

But even this route is blocked by CV and DV. If CV is correct, we must employ a convention that allows access to the contents of a Comp immediately dominated by an $\bar{S}$ within the domain of application of a rule. Hence at $\bar{S}_1$, CV will allow access to $\bar{S}_0$, and thus to the contents of $Comp_0$, by this Comp Accessibility convention.

If DV is adopted, an intriguing alternative suggests itself: At $\bar{S}_1$, transformations would have direct access to Comp but not to its daughters. The Comp Accessibility convention might then be understood as requiring the transparency of Comp, allowing access to its daughters. Or it may be possible to find evidence showing that Comp itself is moved in its entirety and is substituted for a higher Comp. This last possibility would completely eliminate the need for a special convention, if DV is the correct constraint.[43]

We will pursue this question further when we investigate the empirical differences between the two versions of BP. At this point it should simply be noted that either version entails successive cyclic movement into Comp.[44]

We omit discussion here of the application of the Binary principle to the analysis of Passive and Gapping; we will not demonstrate here how BP subsumes Ross's (1967) Complex NP constraint and his Left Branch condition; and we omit further discussion of how BP bounds rightward movement rules from extracting constituents of sentential complements. All these matters are taken up in some detail in Culicover and Wexler 1977, to which the reader is referred.

We conclude this discussion with one further illustration of the application of BP, to sentences involving Tough Movement. Consider a simple example, that of (125).

(125) It is tough for Jane to see Spot.

If, as has been argued in the literature,[45] the underlying structure of the infinitival complement in case there is no *for*-phrase is simply a VP, then in (126) Tough Movement will be able to apply with no problem.[46]

(126)

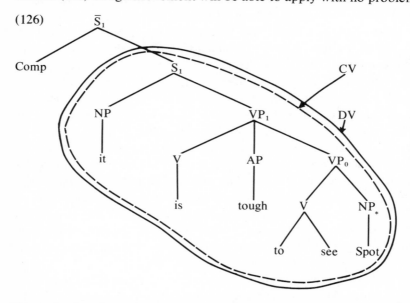

When the *for*-phrase is present, a complication arises: we have already claimed that the *for-to* infinitive contains an $\bar{S}$ node, which blocks access to its nonimmediate constituents. However, Chomsky (1973) notes sentences like (127) which show that the *for*-phrase may be part of the adjective phrase and not the infinitive in this construction.

(127) It is tough for Bill for Jane to see Spot.

In fact (127) cannot undergo Tough Movement, which follows from the fact that *for Jane to see Spot* must be a *for-to* infinitive if *for Bill* is part of the AP.

(128) *Spot is tough for Bill for Jane to see ∅.

Both versions of the Binary principle will, by the same token, block application of Tough Movement to NP's within *that*-complements. The

(129)

a.

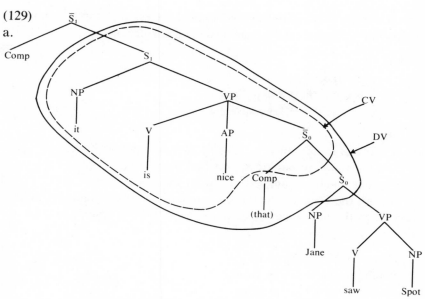

b.

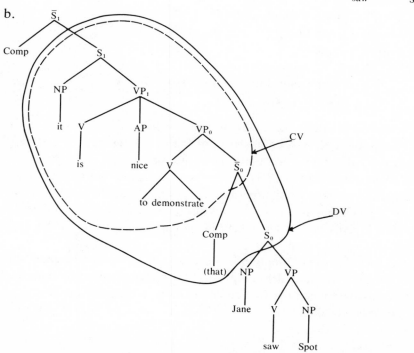

structures in (129) illustrate two typical cases, and the examples in (130)–(131) suggest that this analysis is a correct one.

(130)
a. It is nice (that) Jane saw Spot.
b. *Jane is nice (that) ∅ saw Spot.
c. *Spot is nice (that) Jane saw ∅.[47]

(131)
a. It is tough to demonstrate (that) Jane saw Spot.
b. *Jane is tough to demonstrate (that) ∅ saw Spot.
c. *Spot is tough to demonstrate (that) Jane saw ∅.

In sum, the Binary principle accounts for a substantial body of data related to the following phenomena, given certain attendant assumptions:

1. Complex NP Constraint
2. Sentential Subject Constraint
3. Bounding of Extraposition
4. Specified Subject Condition
5. Tensed S Condition
6. A-over-A Principle
7. Left Branch Condition
8. Limitations on Tough Movement
9. Limitations on Gapping

5.3.2 Empirical Differences between the Versions
5.3.2.1 Subject NP's
A comparison of the two versions of the Binary principle (BP) shows that they make different predictions only when the transformational cycle is operating at a B-cyclic node. At such a node, the counting version permits access as far as the next B-cyclic node(s) down that are dominated by this node, whereas the domination version permits access as well to immediate constituents of the next B-cyclic node(s) down.

Suppose that in (132) only $\bar{S}$ is a B-cyclic node. As can be seen, the two versions are equivalent here. As (133) shows, the two versions are also equivalent when the B-cyclic node on which we are cycling (say, $\bar{S}$) immediately dominates another B-cyclic node (say, NP). Finally,

(132)

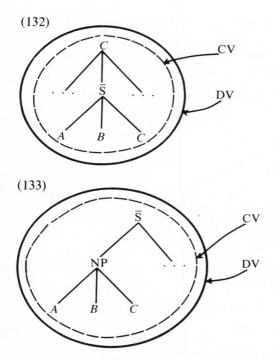

(133)

the two versions can be seen to be distinct just in case we are cycling at a B-cyclic node and there is some non-B-cyclic node between it and the next B-cyclic node down. In (134) the non-B-cyclic node is *C*.

(134)

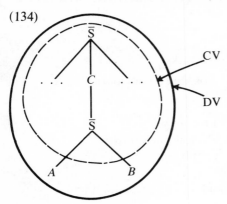

This difference allows us to seek empirical evidence that will distinguish the two versions. For example, only if we are employing the domination version will a transformation applying at $\overline{S}$ have access to a PP complement of a subject NP, as in (135).[48] We have already cited

(135)

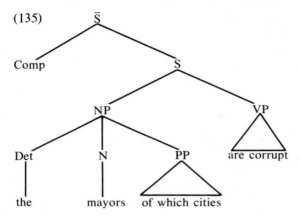

examples, such as the following, which suggest that this may be correct.

(136) ?Of which cities are the mayors corrupt?

A broader range of data shows that the marginal acceptability of (136) is a relatively isolated phenomenon. Wh Fronting, Topicalization, and Cleft Formation do not in general yield grammatical sentences when the PP is moved out of the subject NP.[49]

(137)
a. A pound *of potatoes* costs $1.90.
b. I think that a book $\begin{Bmatrix} about\ roses \\ by\ Fred \end{Bmatrix}$ would sell enough copies to break even.
c. Our hopes *for success* will be well rewarded.
d. A house *of redwood* on the next block burned down.
e. A friend *of Susan* introduced me to Bill.
f. A bowl *of cherries* is sitting on the table.
g. A man *from Philadelphia* was standing on the podium and waving his hands around.

(138)

a. *Of what does a pound ∅ cost $1.90?

b. * $\begin{Bmatrix} \text{About what kind of roses} \\ \text{By which famous physicist} \end{Bmatrix}$ do you think a book ∅ would sell

enough copies to break even?

c. *For what sort of success would our hopes ∅ be well rewarded?

d. *Of what kind of wood did a house ∅ on the next block burn down?

e. *Of whom did a friend ∅ introduce you to Bill?

f. *Of what fruit is a bowl ∅ sitting on the table?

g. *From which city was a man ∅ standing on the podium and waving his hands around?

(139)

a. *Of potatoes, a pound ∅ costs $1.90.

b. * $\begin{Bmatrix} \text{About roses} \\ \text{By Fred} \end{Bmatrix}$, I think that a book ∅ would sell enough copies to

break even.

c. *For success, our hopes ∅ will be well rewarded.

d. *Of redwood, a house on the next block ∅ burned down.

e. *Of Susan, a friend ∅ introduced me to Bill.

f. *Of cherries, a bowl ∅ is sitting on the table.

g. *From Philadelphia, a man ∅ was standing on the podium and waving his hands around.

(140)

a. *It's of potatoes that a pound ∅ costs $1.90.

b. *It's $\begin{Bmatrix} \text{about roses} \\ \text{by Fred} \end{Bmatrix}$ that a book ∅ would sell enough copies to

break even.

c. *It's of success that our hopes ∅ would be well rewarded.

d. *It was of redwood that a house ∅ on the next block burned down.

e. *It was of Susan that a friend ∅ introduced me to Bill.

f. *It is of cherries that a bowl ∅ is sitting on the table.

g. *It was from Philadelphia that a man ∅ was standing on the podium and waving his hands.

The weight of the evidence seems to lean against DV.[50]

5.3.2.2 Extraposition of PP A further piece of evidence in favor of CV relates to the rule that extraposes prepositional phrases from NP's. Some standard examples show that this rule applies to PP's in subject NP's:

(141)
a. A man just came in from MIT Press.
b. A review appeared last week of a new book about syntax.
c. Several pictures have just arrived of my entire family.

Akmajian (1975) gives a more elaborate discussion of this rule and some interesting implications that can be drawn from it.

The simplest statement of Extraposition of PP is the following:[51]

Extraposition of PP:

$$X - _{NP}[Y - PP] - Z$$
$$1 - \quad 2 - 3 \ - 4 \Rightarrow 1 - 2 - \emptyset - 4 + 3$$

Though very general, Extraposition of PP can apparently be constrained, by principles such as BP, from overgenerating wildly.

Consider now nominals in which the possessive contains a PP. We would like to investigate whether Extraposition of PP applies within these nominals, as it should if our statement of the rule is correct at least in essence. As it turns out, surprisingly, this rule cannot apply to a PP in a possessive NP. This is a consequence of the counting version of BP only.[52]

Some typical nominals are given in (142) and an illustrative phrase-marker in (143).

(142)
a. $_{NP}$[*The man from MIT Press*]'s *arrival* was delayed.
b. $_{NP}$[*The review of Mary's book*]'s *original publication* appeared in April.
c. $_{NP}$[*The story about George*]'s *conclusion* leaves him in Africa.

In each of these sentences the italicized NP contains a possessive NP which itself contains a PP. This PP may extrapose over a verb in other sentences where appropriate conditions are met (see 144).

(143)

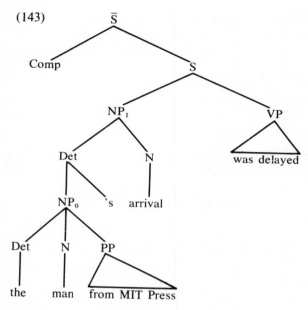

(144)

a. The man ∅ finally arrived *from MIT Press.*
b. The review ∅ appeared in April *of Mary's book.*
c. The true story ∅ has never appeared *about George.*

Some of the examples in (142) and many others like them are quite awkward, possibly because of the relative weight of the prenominal NP and the problems it creates for parsing strategies. One way of reducing the complexity is to paraphrase the possessive with a post-nominal *of*-phrase.

(145)

a. The arrival of the man from MIT Press was delayed.
b. The original publication of the review of Mary's book appeared in April.
c. The conclusion of the story about George leaves him in Africa.

We might expect to find that another way of reducing the complexity of such constructions would be to extrapose the PP from beneath the possessive to the right of the head N of the main NP. This yields extremely ungrammatical sequences, however.

(146)
a. *The man ∅ 's arrival *from MIT Press* was delayed.
b. *The review ∅ 's original publication *of Mary's book* appeared in April.
c. *The story ∅ 's conclusion *about George* leaves him in Africa.

The structure of these NP's is schematized in (147), with the domains of application at NP_1 given by CV and DV illustrated as usual. The

(147)

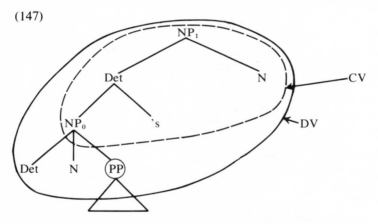

presence of Det is argued for in Culicover and Wexler 1977 in terms of the counting version of BP; it permits the principle to yield the Left Branch condition for the fullest possible range of cases, as noted in 5.3.1.[53]

As (147) shows, CV will prevent a transformation such as Extraposition of PP from applying to the circled PP, but DV will not. Counting from NP_1 takes us as far as NP_0; DV would allow a transformation access to the immediate constituents of NP_0, in this case PP.

It cannot be argued that PP is immediately dominated by a node between it and NP_0. This would, in our framework, exclude it from undergoing extraposition regardless of which version of BP we selected. But, as we noted earlier and in connection with the examples in (144), with either version of BP, the PP must be immediately dominated by NP if Extraposition of PP may apply at all, as schematized in (148).

(148)

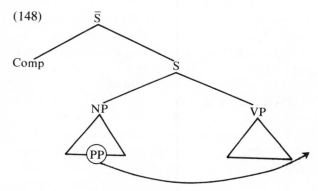

It may be that the extraposition rule must be stated more specifically in terms of the presence in the context of strictly sentential elements like V. But we gave an argument earlier against this, in connection with examples in which the PP had been extraposed out of object NP's. Thus it does not seem that we can block Extraposition of PP from applying strictly within the NP. On this basis it appears that CV does the better job of accounting for this rather surprising phenomenon.

5.3.2.3 A Right Branch Problem

Another difference between the two versions of BP is that CV does not require an additional Left Branch condition whereas DV does. There is more to the difference between the two versions than this, however. There is some evidence that the restriction extends to right branches as well, as shown by (149).

(149)

a. John knows $\left[_{NP}\left[\left\{\begin{matrix} two \\ several \end{matrix}\right\}\text{ women much nicer than Susan}\right]\right]$.

b. *How much nicer than Susan does John know $\left\{\begin{matrix} two \\ several \end{matrix}\right\}$ women ∅ ?

c. *Much nicer than Susan though John knows $\begin{Bmatrix} \text{two} \\ \text{several} \end{Bmatrix}$ women $\emptyset$, . . .

The need to restrict access to right branches of this sort depends, of course, on whether *how much nicer* is only an AP marked [+wh] or is a constituent of a reduced but still potent $\bar{S}$ (or any other category). In the latter case, either version of BP will block (149b). Otherwise a right branch condition would have to be adopted analogous to the Left Branch condition in case DV is the version of the constraint employed.

Suppose that we in fact required a right branch condition. What form would it take? A general constraint against movement of right branches is obviously too strong, as numerous cases of extraposition attest (compare 5.3.1, 5.3.2.2). A more specific constraint would appear to be ad hoc, however, since there are no other instances of restrictions against movement of right branches. In fact, CV gives just the right difference between, for example, Wh Fronting and Extraposition of PP, since at S it permits extraposition of the right branch and at $\bar{S}$ it blocks any access to it at all.

We can maintain DV, then, if we are willing to adopt a special Left Branch condition and an even more special Right Branch condition.

It is relevant to consider here an alternative explanation proposed by Bresnan (1975; 1976a). She suggests that there is no Left Branch condition at all, and that the phenomenon is an illusion caused by an interaction between the structural description of Wh Fronting and the Relativized A-over-A principle. Put simply, Bresnan is arguing that Wh Fronting must move the maximal phrase that satisfies the structural description of Wh Fronting given in (150).

(150) *Wh Fronting* (Bresnan):
$\bar{s}[Q - W_1 - \bar{x}[wh - W_2] - W_3]$
   1 - 2 -   3 - 4 - 5 $\Rightarrow$ 1 - 3 - 4 - 2 - $\emptyset$ - $\emptyset$ - 5

The way that Wh Fronting is stated, taken together with the Relativized A-over-A principle, will guarantee that if an NP dominates a left branch phrase in which *wh* is initial, the NP will be moved and not the lower phrase itself. If the *wh* phrase is a possessive, then the maximal NP, the one that is moved, dominates some NP of which this possessive is a determiner, as in (151). Thus the possessive itself will not be

(151)

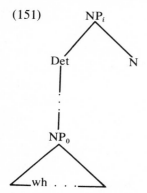

moved, and the Left Branch condition will be captured. Similar statements hold true for structures in which the left branch is an interrogative adjective phrase.

But this will not in itself rule out examples like (149b), because here the *wh* phrase is not initial in the NP. That is, *several women how much nicer than Susan* has roughly the structure shown in (152). The maxi-

(152)

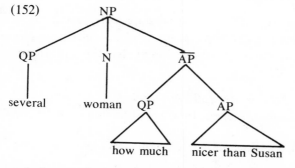

mal phrase of which the interrogative is the initial element is actually $\overline{\text{AP}}$ in (152) and not the NP. The Relativized A-over-A principle would require us to move this $\overline{\text{AP}}$, generating the ungrammatical (149b).

If the counting version of the Binary principle is correct, however, derivation of (149b) is ruled out. At the $\bar{S}$ node, Wh Fronting (and *though* Attraction) has access only to the NP and not to the $\overline{AP}$, as (153) shows.

(153)

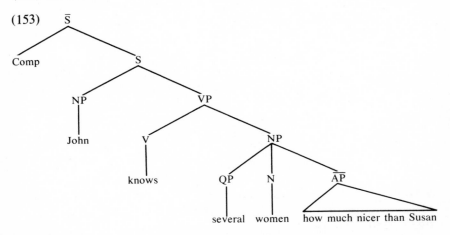

In section 5.5.3 in our discussion of Pied Piping we will argue that by assuming that this $\overline{AP}$ is a reduced relative clause dominated by $\bar{S}$ we can also block the entire NP from undergoing Wh Fronting, by invoking the Binary principle.

Another case that Relativized A-over-A will apparently not account for involves a transformation that topicalizes AP. This rule is *though* Attraction. In simple cases the rule derives examples like those in (154).

(154)

a. *Interesting* though John is ∅, he won't get a raise.

b. *Tall* though that mountain seems to be ∅, I'm going to try to climb it.

c. *Beautiful* though Mary has become ∅, she still is humble.

d. *Angry at Susan* though you are ∅, try to forgive her.

This transformation does not apply to NP's that contain Det, suggesting that the rule is stated in terms of AP alone and not in terms of NP and AP, or more generally, $\bar{X}$.

(155)

a. *An interesting man though John is ∅, he won't get a raise.
b. *Tall mountains though those peaks seem to be ∅, I'm going to try to climb one of them!
c. *A beautiful woman though Mary has become ∅, she still is humble.
d. *Angry people though you folks seem to be ∅, try to forgive Susan anyway.

In spite of the fact that the rule is stated in terms of AP, it is impossible to move the AP out of an NP.

(156)

a. *Interesting though John is a ∅ man, he won't get a raise.
b. *Tall though those peaks seem to be ∅ mountains, I'm going to climb one of them.
c. *Beautiful though Mary has become a ∅ woman, she still is humble.
d. *Angry though you folks seem to be ∅ people, try to forgive Susan anyway.

It seems that some condition to replace or supplement the Relativized A-over-A principle will be necessary for these examples. As is easy to see, CV will do the job.

A further difference between the two versions of the BP concerns the Comp Accessibility convention. It appears that CV requires the special convention that material in Comp can be moved into the Comp of the next higher $\overline{S}$, in spite of the BP. On the other hand, DV offers at least a possibility for accounting for this accessibility directly, since Comp is within the domain of the highest $\overline{S}$ in this case. We repeat as (157) the tree that illustrates the difference. If we were to adopt DV, we would be committed to movement of Comp, and not to movement of constituents under Comp. It is true, of course, that we could assume a Comp Accessibility convention for DV as easily as for CV, but this would eliminate just that feature of DV that makes it more attractive than CV.

To determine whether Comp itself is actually moved, it would be useful to have examples in which two fronted constituents are fronted

(157)

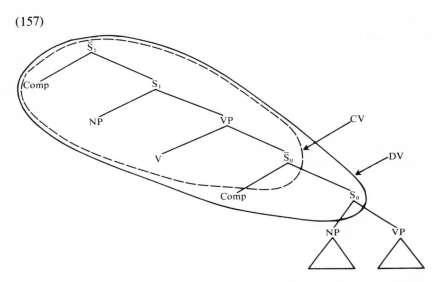

again on a later cycle. Furthermore, it would be important to show that both of these constituents *must* be moved on the later cycle, so that the inference would follow that it was Comp that was being moved and not the two constituents separately. In section 5.5.3 we discuss examples of just this type. However, we argue that it must also be possible to move constituents of Comp. If we are correct, we cannot capitalize on the property of DV that we have been considering.

To summarize, there are at least three possible empirical differences between the two versions of the Binary principle. In one case CV is superior in terms of the data itself, and in one case CV permits a simplification of the theory by permitting us to eliminate the Left Branch condition. The third case is unclear, although for reasons of elegance we would wish to choose DV instead of adopting a separate Comp Accessibility convention. The weight of empirical evidence, as far as we can determine, tentatively favors the counting version, and we will employ that version hereafter in this chapter. Nevertheless, we believe that the domination version is clearly the more natural constraint; any reinterpretation of the facts we have cited that would allow us to return to this version would certainly be welcomed.

5.4 The Raising Principle

5.4.1 Freezing of Extraposed Complements
5.4.1.1 Extraposed PP A variety of adjuncts to NP's may be extraposed from NP. As we saw in section 5.3.2.2, PP may be extraposed from NP, as in (158).

(158)
a. A review $\emptyset$ came out last week *of a new book by Fred.*
b. Some people $\emptyset$ greeted me *from Philadelphia.*
c. An analysis $\emptyset$ will be necessary *of all those samples.*

d. I $\left\{\begin{matrix}\text{sold}\\\text{gave}\end{matrix}\right\}$ a $\left\{\begin{matrix}\text{book}\\\text{picture}\end{matrix}\right\}$ $\emptyset$ to Bill $\left\{\begin{matrix}about\\of\end{matrix}\right\}$ *Fred.*

When extraposed from subject position, these PP's cannot be analyzed by transformations such as Wh Fronting.

(159)
a. *Which book did a review come out last week of $\emptyset$?
b. *What city did you expect some people to greet you from $\emptyset$?
c. *This is the only sample that an analysis is necessary of $\emptyset$.

d. *Sam met the man that I $\left\{\begin{matrix}\text{sold}\\\text{gave}\end{matrix}\right\}$ a $\left\{\begin{matrix}\text{book}\\\text{picture}\end{matrix}\right\}$ to Bill $\left\{\begin{matrix}\text{about}\\\text{of}\end{matrix}\right\}$ $\emptyset$.

In comparison, when the same NP's are in VP-final object position, Wh Fronting is applicable.

(160)
a. Which book did you volunteer to write a review of $\emptyset$?
b. Which city did you meet a lot of people from $\emptyset$?
c. This is the only sample that you have to provide an analysis of $\emptyset$.

d. Sam met the man that I $\left\{\begin{matrix}\text{sold}\\\text{gave}\end{matrix}\right\}$ Bill a $\left\{\begin{matrix}\text{book about}\\\text{picture of}\end{matrix}\right\}$ $\emptyset$.

In section 5.5 we propose to derive these examples by a restructuring rule. Otherwise, they would be blocked by BP.

Observing the formal operation performed by Extraposition of PP, we see that it raises the PP from the B-cyclic domain NP_0 to the

(161)

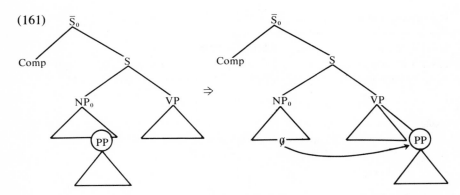

B-cyclic domain $\overline{S}_0$.[54] The ungrammaticality of the examples in (159) lends credence to the Raising principle as a constraint on grammars of natural languages, since what we appear to have is a case in which a raised constituent is frozen.

Notice that Extraposition of PP cannot yield a frozen structure through FP. There are both empirical and theoretical reasons for this. Given the theory of the base, the derived structure in examples like (158) is a possible base structure. Compare the examples in (158) with those in (162).

(162)
a. A review (of John's book) came out last week in the *New York Times*.
b. Some people greeted me with enthusiasm.
c. An analysis (of these samples) will be necessary for several reasons.
d. I gave a picture to Bill for Christmas.

Conceivably the structure derived by Extraposition of PP is different from the underlying structure of the examples in (162), but there is no evidence to suggest this possibility beyond the frozenness of the extraposed PP.

Empirically, if the freezing of the extraposed PP were due to FP, then the frozen node would be the one to which the PP was attached, not just the PP itself. Thus, the VP in the right-hand phrase-marker in

(161) would not be analyzable in our framework, and examples such as those in (163) would be blocked by the FP.

(163)

a. *Which newspaper* did a review ∅ appear in ∅ *of that new book by Fred?*

b. *Who* did that editor ∅ talk to ∅ *from the New York Times?*

c. *How necessary* will an analysis ∅ be ∅ *of these samples?*

d. Mary is the person *that* I gave a book ∅ to ∅ *about Fred.*

Since these examples are perfectly grammatical, they appear to be evidence against an account of the frozenness of the extraposed PP in terms of FP.

5.4.1.2 Extraposed Relatives Another extraposable constituent of NP is the relative clause. We will refer to the extraposition transformation in this case as Extraposition of Rel.

(164)

a. The reports ∅ are sitting on the table *which you ordered me to collect.*

b. There are several animals ∅ living in the zoo *that find our climate quite unpleasant.*

c. I gave an umbrella ∅ to Fred *that I found in the subway last week.*

It is well known that a nonextraposed relative clause cannot be analyzed. In our framework we explain this through the Binary principle: the $\bar{S}$ constituting the relative clause is not accessible from either the higher S or the higher $\bar{S}$ because of the intervening NP node. We illustrate this in (165); for discussion, see section 5.3.2.

When a relative clause has been extraposed, it no longer appears in a configuration such as (165). Then, whatever the constraint that blocks analysis of the relative clause in the unextraposed case, it will no longer apply. As we can see in (166), an extraposed relative clause does not appear in a complex NP like NP_0 in (165). As illustrated, the Binary principle will not apply correctly here, assuming accessibility of Comp in $\bar{S}_0$. Nor for that matter, will the Complex NP constraint of Ross (1967), since in (166) there is no complex NP after extraposition.

(165)

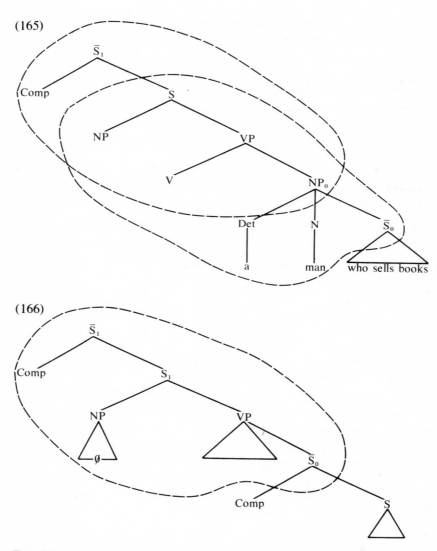

(166)

For this reason Ross was led to the conclusion that extraposition of the relative clause applied only on the last cycle and was ordered after all transformations that might otherwise analyze the relative clause, like

Wh Fronting, Tough Movement, and so on. Thus, these transformations would be blocked by the Complex NP constraint from applying to relative clauses that would later extrapose.

In Culicover and Wexler 1977 we observed a similar problem in our framework: Extraposition of Rel prevents BP from blocking access to the extraposed $\bar{S}$. However, because of the way BP is formulated, no transformations applying at $\bar{S}_1$ can access constituents of S_0. Thus BP almost eliminates the need for assuming that Extraposition of Rel is last cyclic.[55]

The problem is not quite eliminated, however. Recall the Comp Accessibility convention of section 5.3.1, which allows access to the Comp of the next $\bar{S}$ down from the cycle on which the transformations are applying, if $\bar{S}$ is within the domain defined on that cycle. Depending on the particular details of one's analysis of the relative clause, as many as three kinds of arguments can show that BP does not block extraction from extraposed relatives.

First, consider a relative clause with a *wh* word in initial position:

(167) The reports are sitting on the table *which* you ordered me to collect. (=(164a))

Suppose that *which* is [+wh], a reasonable position to take.[56] Then, as can be seen in (168), the relative pronoun in $\bar{S}_0$ will be within the scope

(168)

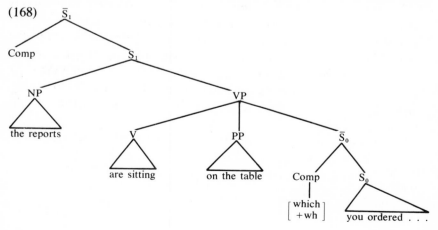

of Wh Fronting on $\overline{S}_1$, allowing the derivation of (169).

(169) *Which are the reports sitting on the table $\emptyset$ you ordered me to collect?

If the raised extraposed relative clause is frozen, this problem does not arise.

Second, there are some relative clauses that do not have a *wh* relative pronoun in surface structure but have *that* or no marker at all:

(170)
a. I gave the umbrella to Fred (that) I found in the subway last week.
b. There are several animals living in the zoo *(that) find our climate quite unpleasant.
c. The reports are sitting on the table *(that) you ordered me to collect.

We might wish to take the position that movement of a *wh* constituent into a Comp marked [+wh] seals off that Comp from further analysis.[57] If the examples in (170) were derived from *wh* relatives, this convention would block analysis of Comp. Even in extraposed position, the rest of the relative clause would be nonanalyzable because of BP.

But suppose that we lack this convention, or suppose alternatively that the sentences in (170) are not derived from *wh* relatives, but by deletion of a proform that is not fronted. On this latter view, *that* would be underlying.[58] Without a means of sealing off Comp, it will be possible to extract constituents of the extraposed relative by moving them into Comp of the relative clause and then into the higher Comp. Again, this will be blocked if the extraposed relative clause is frozen by the Raising principle.

Third, the italicized phrases in (171) are generally referred to as reduced relative clauses.

(171)
a. A book has just appeared *written by Fred*.

b. An astronomer came out *denying that the moon is approaching the Earth.*

c. A man phoned us *surprised at your remarks.*

As pointed out in Culicover and Wexler 1977, if reduced relatives are dominated by $\overline{S}$ in derived structure, the Binary principle will correctly block extraction from them, as illustrated in (172).

(172)

a. *Who has a book just appeared written by ∅?

b. *The Earth is the planet that an astronomer came out denying that the moon is approaching ∅.

c. *Which of my remarks did a man phone you surprised at ∅?

The possibility is still open, however, that reduced relatives are not dominated by $\overline{S}$ in surface structure, either because the higher nodes are pruned by the reduction transformation or because they are generated directly in the base as reduced structures. Without going into the question of which alternative is correct, we can still see that RP will block analysis of extraposed reduced relatives if BP does not. Thus RP and BP acting together will block analysis of any sort of relative clause in any position whatsoever, as required by the empirical evidence.

5.4.1.3 Extraposition of S Complement A last type of extraposition that yields support for the Raising principle is illustrated in (173).

(173)

a. I expressed my belief to Mary that the United States should give away a million tons of wheat a week.

b. A suspicion has arisen that you have been holding back on the IRS.

c. The implication follows directly from your remarks that deep structures are necessary for the survival of the human race.

We will speak of the rule that derives these sentences as Extraposition of S Complement, or ES. It is well known that the extraposed $\overline{S}$'s in (173) are not subject to analysis by later transformations. This is shown by the examples in (174).

(174)

a. *Exactly how many tons of wheat did you express your belief to Mary that the United States should give away?

b. *The IRS is the government agency that a suspicion has arisen that you are holding back on.

c. *How necessary for the survival of the human race does the implication follow from your remarks that deep structures are?

Once again, the impossibility of analyzing the $\overline{S}$'s moved by ES follows straightforwardly from RP.[59]

5.4.2 A Counterexample

An obvious counterexample to the Raising principle is provided by this last type of extraposition, ES. As (175) shows, the extraposition of a sentential subject seems to be a raising transformation, yet the examples in (176) illustrate the well-known fact that such extraposed constituents are in fact analyzable, contrary to the prediction of RP.

(175)

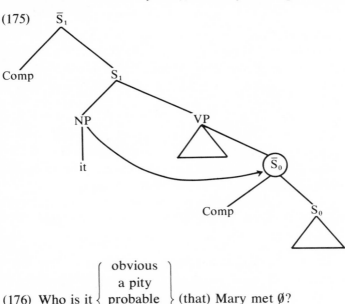

(176) Who is it ⎰ obvious / a pity / probable / likely / surprising ⎱ (that) Mary met ∅?

One way out of this difficulty would be to adopt the position argued for by Koster (1978), that the structure in (175) is in fact not transformationally derived but underlying. Another would be to allow the transformation of ES, but to explain the empirical evidence that supports RP in section 5.4.1 in terms of other principles. Because the matter is complicated and space is limited, we will leave the question open here. In section 7.1 we offer a suggestion about how an analysis of the second type might be developed.

Notice that if we were to abandon the Raising principle, and could explain the data of 5.4.1 in some other way, we would nevertheless have to deal with the counterexample in chapter 4 that motivated it in the learnability proof. In section 7.1.5 we sketch out one way in which the counterexample could be rendered nonconstructable by substantive linguistic assumptions about the base, about Comp, and about raising.

5.5 Restructuring

In this section we will discuss an apparent counterexample to the Binary principle, specifically, that it is possible to analyze a PP within an object NP, as in sentences like *Who did you lose a picture of?* An obvious solution to this problem is to extrapose the PP *of who* out of the object NP *a picture of who,* but this cannot be done in our framework for several reasons, which we will discuss in detail. What is needed, we suggest, is a special class of restructuring rules, which apply under certain restrictive conditions. A restructuring rule will in this case move the PP *of who* into a position where it can be analyzed without any violation of BP. Interestingly, restructuring may well provide the basis for an explanation of a set of phenomena usually referred to as "pied piping."

5.5.1 A Dilemma
Sentences like those in (177) appear to be perfectly grammatical. Yet, as (178) shows, their derivation would be blocked by BP as we have formulated it.[60]

(177)
a. Who did you lose a picture of?
b. Which house did you repair the roof of?
c. Which room was the sheriff sitting in the back of?
d. Who would it be impossible for John to have any advantage over?
e. Which book is Mary the author of?
f. Who did Susan propose mercy towards?
g. What did Horatio measure the length of?
h. Which problem did Sam propose a solution of?

(178)

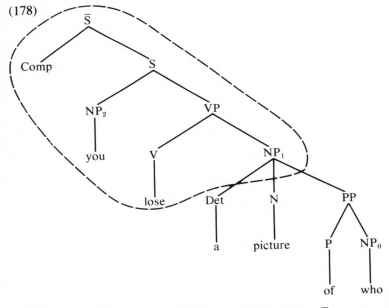

As (178) shows, a transformation applying at the $\bar{S}$ cycle (like Wh Fronting) may apply to NP_2 or NP_1, but may not apply to constituents of these NP's, such as NP_0. This restriction permits us to explain why constituents of subject NP's do not undergo Wh Fronting, as in (179).

(179) *Who did a picture of ∅ frighten you?

For this reason, revision of BP so that it will allow access to NP_0 on the $\bar{S}$ cycle will have the function of allowing derivation of (178) also.

We could repair this defect by adopting a special constraint against analysis of subjects, but given the general applicability of BP as formulated in section 5.3, this move lacks strong motivation. At the very least we will have replaced the very general Binary principle with a new Binary principle and a collection of special constraints.

Without ruling out the possibility that a consistent and compelling set of alternative constraints can be arrived at, let us pursue here the question of accounting for the grammaticality of the examples in (177) while maintaining the essential features of the current analysis. We note first that the examples in (177), illustrated in (178), can be derived without violating BP if the PP in NP_1 can in some way be located outside of NP_1 so that NP_1 no longer dominates it. One configuration in which this property holds is that in (180).

(180)

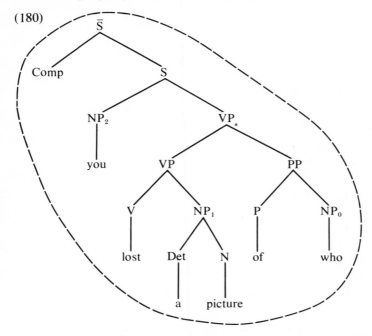

On the face of it, it appears that the sort of structure illustrated in (180) can be derived by an independently motivated transformation,

Extraposition of PP.[61] Yet for three reasons, at least, Extraposition of PP does not in fact provide an adequate solution to this problem.

First, we already have argued (in section 5.4.1.1) that a raised constituent cannot be analyzed by later transformations. Extraposition of PP is a raising transformation; the PP begins in the domain NP_1 and ends up in the domain $\overline{S}$, which contains NP_1.

Second, we have assumed for learnability reasons in the proof in chapter 4 that a string-preserving application of a transformation is impossible.[62] That is, if a transformation moves a constituent to the end of a variable, as in $X - B - Y \Rightarrow X - Y - B$ or $X - B - Y \Rightarrow B - X - Y$, this transformation is inapplicable whenever Y or X (respectively) is null. The derivation of (180) from (178) would be just this sort of string-preserving application.

These two reasons are theoretical ones and therefore derive much of their plausibility from the plausibility of the particular theory in which they play a role. A third reason relies neither on the Raising principle nor on the assumption of non-string-preserving application of transformations.

Let us suppose, perhaps counterfactually, that string-preserving application is permitted and that either there is no RP or that RP applies just when the raised constituent has not been raised by string-preserving application of some transformation. This last assumption will allow us to explain the frozenness of extraposed constituents while allowing constituents that have been extraposed by a string-preserving operation to be analyzed.

For the sake of precision, we will assume that Extraposition of PP adjoins the PP to the node on which the cycle is applying at the time the transformation applies. Application of Extraposition of PP to (178) will hence yield (180), whereas application of the transformation to a PP in a subject will give a derivation as in (181).

The following problem, first noted by Akmajian (1975), now arises: If PP can extrapose while preserving the terminal string, what is to prevent it from extraposing on successive NP cycles from a position deep within the NP to a position where it can extrapose out of the NP entirely? Illustrating first with a subject NP, we consider sentence (182), which has the structure shown in (183).

(181)

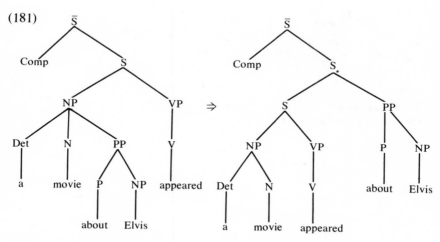

(182) A report about a review of a book by Chomsky has just appeared.

(183)

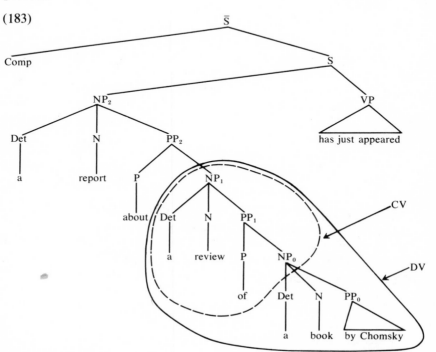

We have shown the domain of a transformation applying at NP_1 according to both the counting version (CV) and the domination version (DV) of the Binary principle. If CV is the correct version, Extraposition of PP cannot apply to PP_0, and no problem of the sort we are going to discuss will arise. However, if DV is correct, Extraposition of PP will apply to PP_0. Let us suppose that in this case adjunction takes the form illustrated in (184).

(184)

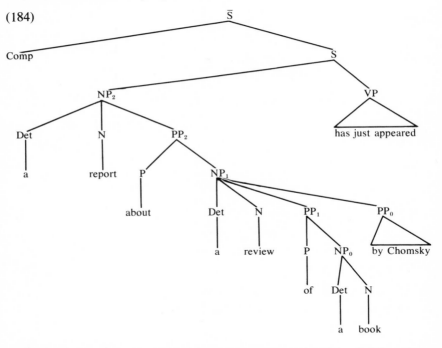

Similarly, on the NP_2 cycle PP_0 can extrapose (again), yielding the structure shown in (185). As Akmajian pointed out (1975, 120, n. 4), PP_0 can now extrapose out of NP_2. Though the resulting sentence is grammatical, it can have only the interpretation that the report is by Chomsky, not the book (or the review).

(185)

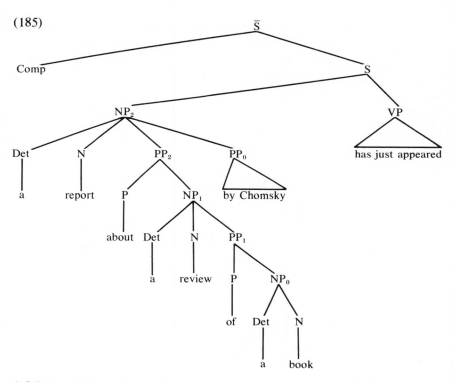

(186) A report about a review of a book has just appeared by Chomsky.

Similar examples show the general impossibility of extraposing any PP but that immediately dominated by the highest NP.

(187)

a. An attack appeared on the bulletin board against the proposal by Joan.

b. *An attack against the proposal appeared on the bulletin board by Joan.

(188)

a. A report appeared in the papers about the roof of the Senate Building.

b. *A report about the roof appeared in the papers of the Senate Building.

Extraposition of relative clauses is restricted in the same way. Thus, a relative clause cannot be extraposed out of an NP within an NP. If string-preserving extraposition were allowed, the relative clause could first extrapose from the lower NP to the higher one and then out of the higher one.

(189)

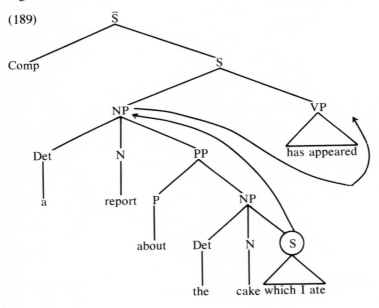

(190)

a. A report has appeared about the cake which I ate.

b. *A report about the cake has appeared which I ate.

The derivation of these ungrammatical examples by directly extraposing the lowest constituent out of the subject NP is blocked by BP.

   This argument against applying string-preserving extraposition depends on a number of specific assumptions: the domination version of BP, a weakened Raising principle, a particular convention for attaching extraposed constituents, among others. It may be that for independent reasons this argument cannot be carried through. For example, if the counting version of BP is correct (as we argue it is in section 5.3.2), then extraposition on a higher NP cannot apply to the PP dominated

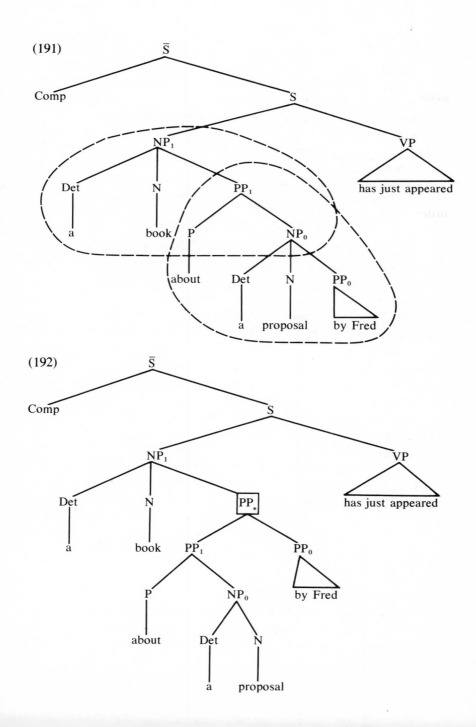

by a lower NP. Rather, extraposition on a higher PP can apply to the PP dominated by the NP the higher PP dominates. The difference is illustrated in (191). Here PP_0 is within the domain of transformations at PP_1, but not at NP_1. If extraposition applied at PP_1, however, the result would be a derived structure (192) that appears not to be a possible base structure.[63] Since this PP_* is frozen, we would not expect PP_0 to undergo extraposition out of NP_1 on the S cycle. Since PP_* is structurally different from the original PP_1 but displays the same order of terminal elements, extraposition of PP_* will not provide us with any evidence for or against string-preserving extraposition of PP.

(193) A book has just appeared about a proposal by Fred.

Consequently, if the counting version is correct, string-preserving extraposition may occur, but will not yield problems of multiple extraposition because of the particular attachment convention and the Freezing principle. In order for this to be the case, of course, we must still not apply RP in cases of string-preserving extraposition. But in order to account for the data discussed in section 5.4 by RP we will have to assume that RP applies when extraposition is not string-preserving.[64]

To sum up, we have one possible empirical argument against deriving the structure in (180) from (178) by Extraposition of PP and two theoretical ones: such a derivation would be raising and cause freezing, and it would involve string-preserving extraposition. The solution that we will propose for the problem originally raised in this section, namely, the analyzability of the object NP, will involve essentially a weakening of these theoretical arguments against extraposition in this case to allow a class of rules that we will call *restructuring rules*.[65] In short, a restructuring rule is precisely a *string-preserving movement rule that does not obey the Raising principle*. In the next section we will discuss further properties of restructuring rules and conditions that can or must be imposed on them.

5.5.2 Conditions on Restructuring
5.5.2.1 Formal Characterization
We hypothesize that all restructuring rules are of the form illustrated in (194), which correspond to the phrase-markers in (195).

(194)
a. $_\alpha[X \ _\beta[Y \ A \,]] \Rightarrow_R \ _\epsilon[_\alpha[X \ _\beta[Y]] \ A \,]$
b. $_\alpha[_\beta[A \ Y] \ X] \Rightarrow_R \ _\epsilon[A \ _\alpha[_\beta[Y] \ X]$

(195)
a.

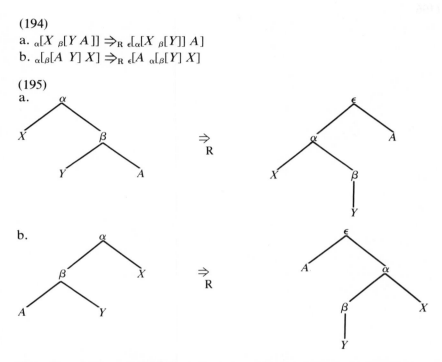

b.

Here X and Y are variables, and ϵ is a variable ranging over categories which will be made explicit momentarily. What is important to observe here is that the constituent A, which is restructured, is a boundary constituent of β before restructuring and a boundary constituent of ϵ after restructuring. We will call the output of a restructuring rule a *restructure*.

We will hypothesize that all restructuring rules are structure-preserving. That is, every restructure is a possible base configuration. We will understand restructuring rules to function in the following way: Suppose that $H \rightarrow Z\alpha(A)$ is a rule of the base. In a restructure derived from (196a), the value of ϵ is H. That is, the restructure is (196b). In other words, when A is restructured out of β into H, if it could have been a constituent of H in the base, it becomes a constituent of H in the restructure.

On the other hand, suppose that $H \rightarrow Z\alpha(A)$ is not a rule of the base, but suppose that $\alpha \rightarrow \alpha A$ is. Then the restructure will be derived by

Chomsky-adjoining *A* to the *α* that dominated it; thus the value of ε here is *α*. (197) illustrates. Conceivably we could formulate the theory of grammar so that the form of a restructure followed automatically from the structure-preserving requirement, but we will not attempt to do so here.

(196)

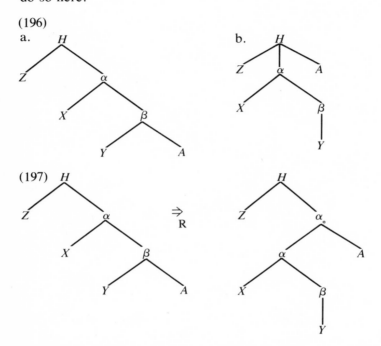

The characterization of restructuring rules that we have adopted here is in no way to be taken as a strong claim. Rather, we have made some assumptions that will allow at least the class of derivations that we believe to be necessary on empirical grounds. For example, we intend to restructure PP out of object NP's as in (198), where the PP is Chomsky-adjoined to the original VP. Sister-adjunction to VP would not be structure-preserving, since we do not assume that ₛ[NP VP PP] is a possible base structure. Of course, we could easily be wrong. In that case we might be led to a different view of the formal properties of restructuring.

Similarly, our formulation of restructuring will permit a derivation such as (199a). Given that ₙₚ[NP PP] is not a base structure, we rule out

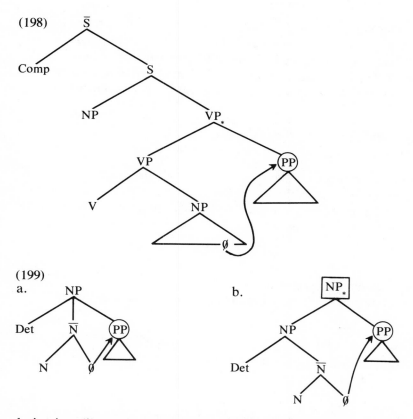

(198)

(199)
a.

b.

derivations like (199b). Only (199a) is a structure-preserving operation, and hence the only one allowed by the assumptions about the base and the function of restructuring rules. Again it should be noted that these assumptions are made purely on internal theoretical grounds and are neither supported nor invalidated by any empirical considerations that we are aware of.

We will assume that all restructuring rules apply at the end of the cycle. Thus, (196b) will be derived from (196a) after all transformations that can apply to H have applied. Whether this is correct or not is again an empirical question, but we have no evidence to bring to bear on it here.

Furthermore, it seems that certain restructuring rules are sensitive to lexical items. The classic case, cited by Akmajian, Steele, and Wasow (1979) and originally noted by Ross (1967), involves the idiom *make the claim*. Ross pointed out that the complement of *make the claim* can be analyzed, but generally the complement of *the claim* cannot be.

(200)
a. Who did Fred make the claim that Mary had seen?
b. *Who did Fred discuss the claim that Mary had seen?

On the other hand, it is an open question whether there really is restructuring going on in this case. The grammaticality of examples like (200b) does not completely decide the issue, because there are many sentences that should be grammatical if there were restructuring, but are not. For example:

(201)
a. With whom did John claim that Mary was living?
b. *With whom did John make the claim that Mary was living?

(202)
a. How quickly did John claim that Mary could run?
b. *How quickly did John make the claim that Mary could run?

(203)
a. Who did John claim likes oysters?
b. *Who did John make the claim likes oysters?

(204)
a. Where did Bill claim that Mary had put the beer?
b. *Where did Bill make the claim that Mary had put the beer?

Considerably more investigation would have to be undertaken to determine whether and in what ways lexical items should be permitted to govern the application of restructuring rules.[66]

5.5.2.2 Constraints on Transformations It appears that restructuring is subject to the constraints on analyzability that restrict the application of transformations, namely, the Binary principle and the Freezing principle. It is not possible, for example, to restructure a PP out of a relative clause, and the fact that it is not is explained by BP.

(205)

a. *Who did you meet the man that Mary $\begin{Bmatrix} \text{gave the money to} \\ \text{owns a picture of} \end{Bmatrix}$?

b.

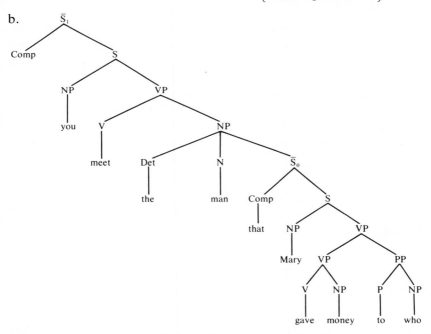

(205a) could be derived only if the PP *to who* was restructured out of $\bar{S}_0$ into the domain of Wh Fronting on $\bar{S}_1$. BP blocks direct access to constituents of $\bar{S}_0$ on the $\bar{S}_1$ cycle. And, apparently, BP blocks restructuring out of $\bar{S}_0$ as well.

Again, there are apparent counterexamples. If the PP in question is a constituent not of $\bar{S}$ in a relative clause, but of a PP, then it appears possible to question out of this PP.

(206)

a. Who did you meet the friend of a relative of?

b. Which books does the government specify the cost of the covers of?

Given that BP blocks direct access to the lowest PP's in (206), it would appear that restructuring does not obey the BP. We will return to these examples in section 5.5.3, where we will account for them as part of a more general discussion of pied piping. The derivations that account for the pied piping examples will permit the generation of (206), with no further machinery required.

Evidence that restructuring is restricted by the Freezing principle is forthcoming from a consideration of the Complex NP Shift. As we have noted in section 5.2.1.2, Complex NP Shift moves an NP to the end of a VP, freezing the VP. A typical derived structure appears in (207). Because the VP is frozen, it is not possible to analyze any of its

(207)

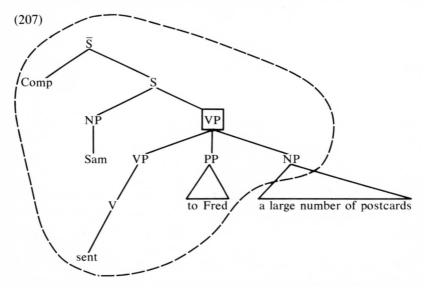

constituents, including the shifted complex NP. Because of BP, the only way to analyze the complement PP *of postcards* in the shifted NP would be to restructure it out of the NP. And because the FP blocks the restructuring, we are unable to derive the ungrammatical (208), which is considerably less acceptable, in our judgment, than a sentence like (209). (See discussion in Culicover and Wexler 1977.)

(208) *What sort of postcards did you send to Fred a large number of?

(209) What sort of postcards did you send Fred a large number of?

But in (209), the NP *a large number of what sort of postcards* is not dominated by a frozen node, because the sentence is derived not by Complex NP Shift but by Dative. See our discussion in section 5.2.1 for the differences between the two.

One further constraint that appears to apply to restructuring rules and transformations is concerned with the following sorts of examples. Suppose that we extrapose a PP out of a complex NP in object position, as in (210).

(210) Sam gave *a picture of Mary* ∅ to Susan *by Fred*.

As (211) shows, *a picture of Mary* is sufficiently complex to undergo Complex NP Shift.

(211)
a. Sam gave a picture of Mary to Susan.
b. Sam gave to Susan a picture of Mary.

However, Complex NP Shift cannot apply in (210).[67]

(212) *Sam gave to Susan by Fred a picture of Mary.

What might be crucial in (212) is that the constituent *by Fred* was a right daughter in deep structure of a constituent that has been moved to the right of it in surface structure. Let us suppose as a first hypothesis that there is a constraint against reordering constituents A and B where B was originally a right or left boundary constituent of A. This constraint (or any other theoretical device with the same effect) will block the derivation of (212) by preventing movement of the NP *a picture of Mary* to the right of *by Fred*.

Consider now the following examples, which we noted earlier as examples (137) and (138) in section 5.3.2.1.

(213)

a. A pound *of potatoes* cost $1.90.

b. I think that a book $\begin{Bmatrix} about\ roses \\ by\ Fred \end{Bmatrix}$ would sell enough copies to break even.

c. Our hopes *for success* will be well rewarded.

d. A house *of redwood* on the next block burned down.

e. A friend *of Susan* introduced me to Bill.

f. A bowl *of cherries* is sitting on the table.

g. A man *from Philadelphia* was standing on the podium and waving his hands around.

(214)

a. *Of what does a pound Ø cost $1.90?

b. * $\begin{Bmatrix} About\ what\ kind\ of\ roses \\ By\ which\ famous\ physicist \end{Bmatrix}$ do you think a book Ø would sell enough copies to break even?

c. *For what sort of success would our hopes Ø be well rewarded?

d. *Of what kind of wood did a house Ø on the next block burn down?

e. *Of whom did a friend Ø introduce you to Bill?

f. *Of what fruit is a bowl Ø sitting on the table?

g. *From which city was a man Ø standing on the podium and waving his hands around?

The original force of these examples was to show that a PP cannot be moved out of a subject NP by Wh Fronting. But as (215) illustrates, these PP's can extrapose to the right. Since they are [+wh],[68] we cannot rule out the logical possibility that these PP's could undergo Wh Fronting after extraposition. The fact that they cannot (cf. (214)) constitutes an interesting problem for our analysis.[69,70]

(215)

a. Our hopes will be well rewarded for success in the future.

b. Several houses are on the market of redwood.

c. Several friends arrived of the man I was telling you about.

d. A bowl is sitting on the table of the most beautiful cherries you have ever seen.

e. A man was standing on the podium from Philadelphia.

We can envision at least two ways of blocking Wh Fronting after Extraposition of PP. First, as we have mentioned a number of times, the extraposed PP is frozen by the Raising principle. This is what accounts for the fact that the PP cannot be analyzed and its NP removed:

(216) *Who did several friends arrive of $\emptyset$?

Conceivably, the mechanism by which a PP that dominates an NP that is [+wh] comes to be marked [+wh] itself is blocked because the PP is frozen. However, we will not be able to sustain this explanation because, as we will argue, the mechanism that performs this function is cyclic. Thus as soon as the transformational cycle moves up to a PP that dominates an NP marked [+wh], the PP will become so marked. By the time Wh Fronting applies, the frozenness of PP will have no effect, since it was marked [+wh] before extraposition froze it. For the substance of this argument, see the discussion in 5.5.3.

On the other hand, it may be that the definition of freezing is such that the only property of a frozen node that is accessible to transformations is its category. If so, a node marked [+wh] can still not undergo Wh Fronting if it is frozen. We are unable to find clear empirical evidence to resolve this question. Note, however, that the analysis of Pied Piping that we will propose below requires that it be possible to determine that a frozen node marked [+wh] is in fact so marked.

The second way of blocking Wh Fronting of the entire PP after Extraposition of PP is to invoke the constraint that blocks the reordering of a constituent and the constituent that dominated it in deep structure. By the same token, it will be impossible to move an extraposed PP to the left of the subject NP of which it was a part. This will account for the examples in (214) and for similar examples in which the extraposed PP is moved not by Wh Fronting but by Topicalization.

(217)

a. *Of potatoes, a pound ∅ costs $1.90.

b. * $\begin{Bmatrix} \text{About roses} \\ \text{By Fred} \end{Bmatrix}$, I think that a book ∅ would sell enough copies

to break even.

c. *For success, our hopes will be well rewarded ∅.

d. *Of redwood, a house on the next block burned down ∅.

e. *Of Susan, a friend introduced me to Bill ∅.

f. *Of cherries, a bowl is sitting on the table ∅.

g. *From Philadelphia, a man was standing on the podium and waving his hands around ∅.

Thus the constraint in question has not only initial plausibility but unsuspected independent support.

Recall that the intent of this discussion is to investigate whether it is reasonable to hypothesize that restructuring rules (and restructures) obey constraints on transformations. We have noted data that suggest that restructuring rules obey the Binary principle and the Freezing principle. It also appears to be the case that restructures obey this constraint on reordering. This is shown by the examples in (218)–(219). Those in (218) show the underlying structures; in (219) we have restructured the PP's and then applied Complex NP Shift.

(218)

a. I lost *an absolutely beautiful picture* of Bill.

b. Sam repaired *the part of the roof* on the north side.

c. Mary is *the author that I was telling you about* of that fantastic mystery novel.

(219)

a. *I lost ∅ of Bill *an absolutely beautiful picture*.

b. *Sam repaired ∅ on the north side *the part of the roof*.

c. *Mary is ∅ of that fantastic mystery novel *the author that I was telling you about*.

We have shown thus far that, to the extent to which empirical evidence can be brought to bear on the issue, there are virtually no differences between Extraposition of PP and restructuring PP out of objects except for the following: A raised restructured PP is not frozen, and restructuring cannot apply over a variable whereas an extraposition transformation must. This similarity raises the possibility that restructuring rules are simply a special class of transformations. On the other hand the fact that restructuring rules appear to violate two learnability constraints (the Raising principle and the prohibition against string-preserving operations) is a counterargument. Conceivably, though, there are conditions that would allow us to prove learnability without these assumptions.

A further argument lends support to this possibility. Note, first, that the reordering constraint as we have stated it is a constraint on derivations not on analyzability, as the Binary principle and the Freezing principle are. Whereas FP, for example, blocks analysis of a phrase-marker when it could not have been base generated, the reordering constraint blocks the derivation of certain structures as a function not of the configurations to which the rules apply, but of the underlying sources of these configurations. For example, there is nothing particularly objectionable about applying Complex NP Shift over a PP if that PP was never a constituent of the NP.

We have not attempted a precise formal statement of this reordering constraint. However, there appear to be certain clear counterexamples to the informal constraint that we have been entertaining.

Our tentative formulation of the constraint was that there could be no reordering of A and B when B was a boundary constituent of A. Schematically, if B has been moved out of A, A and B cannot then be reordered in (220). Suppose now that B has been moved out of A by a leftward movement rule, (221). If the constraint is simply that A and B cannot now be reordered with respect to one another, there are counterexamples.

(220)

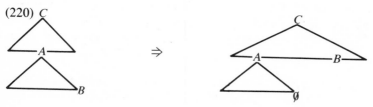

(221)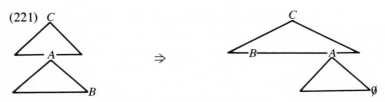

First, if NP Preposing is a transformation, there exists a rule that moves an NP to the left into subject position.

(222) *John* was arrested ∅ by the cops.

The constituent that dominated *John* in deep structure is the verb phrase, which after NP Preposing is *arrested by the cops*. As (223) shows, this VP can be moved to the left of *John* by VP Top.

(223) They said that John would be arrested by the cops, and *arrested by the cops* John was.

Either the constraint as we are understanding it here is wrong, or the passive construction is not transformationally derived. (See 5.2.5.2 for discussion of the latter possibility.)

Along similar lines, we find that the constraint will block derivation of sentences like (224), in which Tough Movement has preceded VP Top.

(224) They said that John would be easy to please, and *easy to please* he is.

Again either the constraint as stated is wrong, or there is no rule of Tough Movement. (Lasnik and Fiengo (1974) argue for the latter.)

But a possible revision of the constraint will allow examples like (223) and (224). We will not allow reordering just in case *B* was a right boundary constituent of *A* and was moved to the right of *A*, or if *B* was a left boundary constituent of *A* and moved to the left of *A*.[71] As can be seen, examples (223) and (224) involve a leftward movement of *B* out of *A*, where *B* was a right boundary constituent of *A*.[72]

5.5.2.3 Lexical Government We conclude this discussion of conditions on restructuring rules with some further remarks on the condition men-

tioned earlier to the effect that restructuring rules are lexically governed, and in fact are stated strictly in terms of lexical items.

It turns out that not every prepositional phrase in an object NP is
analyzable by Wh Fronting. On the face of it, this suggests that the
restructuring of PP's out of objects is due to a restructuring rule and not
to a special case of Extraposition of PP. Some examples are given in
(225)–(226).[73]

(225)
a. John stole a picture on that wall.
b. Bill tried to meet a friend from Chicago.
c. I found a box of pine.
d. We cooked the meat in the refrigerator.
e. John met a woman under serious investigation.
f. Sam proposed a solution of little interest.

(226)
a. *Which wall did John steal a picture on Ø?
b. *Which town did Bill try to meet a friend from Ø?
c. *What kind of wood did you find a box of Ø?
d. *How serious an investigation did John meet a woman under Ø?
e. *Whose refrigerator did you cook the meat in Ø?
f. *How much interest did Sam propose a solution of Ø?

The examples of (226) are to be contrasted with those of (177) in
which the PP complement of the object NP can be analyzed by Wh
Fronting.

(177)
a. Who did you lose a picture of?
b. Which house did you repair the roof of?
c. Which room was the sheriff sitting in the back of?
d. Who would it be impossible for John to have any advantage over?
e. Which book is Mary the author of?
f. Who did Susan propose mercy towards?
g. What did Horatio measure the length of?
h. Which problem did Sam propose a solution of?

Interestingly, where the PP can be analyzed, it cannot be paraphrased by a relative clause, and where it cannot be analyzed, it does admit a relative paraphrase. There are a few exceptions:

(227)
a. ?I lost a picture *that was* of Mary.
b. *Sam repaired the roof *that was* of the house.
c. *The sheriff was sitting in the back *that was* of the room.
d. *It would be impossible for John to have any advantage *that was* over Mary.
e. *Mary is the author *that is* of this book.
f. *Susan proposed mercy *that was* towards Fred.
g. *Horatio measured the length *that was* of the carpet.
h. *Sam proposed a solution *that was* of the problem.

(228)
a. John stole a picture *that was* on that wall.
b. Bill tried to meet a friend *who was* from Chicago.
c. I found a box *that was* of pine.
d. We cooked the meat *that was* in the refrigerator.
e. John met a woman *who was* under serious investigation.
f. Sam proposed a solution *that was* of little interest.

The examples in (228), which allow the relative paraphrase, are just those that in (226) do not allow Wh Fronting.

This suggests that the prepositional phrase complements in (225) are syntactically derived from relative clauses by a reduction transformation. If the reduced relative is an $\bar{S}$ in derived structure, the Binary principle will block analysis of the PP, as in (226), exactly as for unreduced relatives (see section 5.3.1). We would then lack any support for applying restructuring only to certain sequences of lexical items, since the difference between (226) and (177) would follow from a deeper syntactic difference.

Furthermore, a comparison of (226f) and (177h) indicates that in some cases a lexical characterization of the trigger for the restructuring will be difficult to state.[74] Thus, we argue, the superficial evidence that restructuring of PP is subject to lexical government masks a deeper structural difference with somewhat more explanatory force.

5.5.2.4 Blocking by Possessive Before concluding this discussion of restructuring it is important to take note of a fact pointed out by Chomsky (1973). He observed that object NP's cannot be analyzed when they contain a possessive, as in the following examples.

(229)
a. I lost Bill's picture of Susan.
b. Everyone disapproved of Sam's respect for Nixon.
c. We read about Markov's solution to the problem.
d. John applauded the government's mercy towards the victims.

(230)
a. *Who did you lose Bill's picture of?
b. *Who did everyone disapprove of Sam's respect for?
c. *Which problem did you read about Markov's solution to?
d. *Which victims did John applaud the government's mercy towards?

In general, the examples in (230) are worse than parallel examples lacking the possessive.

(231)
a. Who did you lose a picture of?
b. ?Who did everyone disapprove of indicating respect for?
c. Which problem did you read about a solution to?
d. Which victims did John propose mercy towards?

Chomsky proposes that the sentences in (230) be blocked by the Specified Subject condition extended to NP's:

Specified Subject Condition (SSC): No rule can involve X, Y (X superior to Y) in the structure
$$\ldots X \ldots [_\alpha \ldots Z \ldots -WYV \ldots] \ldots$$
where Z is the subject of WYV and is not controlled by a category containing X.

For $\alpha = \bar{S}$ we can account for the examples that motivate the SSC with the Binary principle; it is therefore worth considering whether we can account as well for the examples in (230) involving NP's in terms of the set of constraints that emerge from the learnability proof.

As elsewhere, we will avoid a lengthy digression by suggesting the outlines of a plausible analysis and not pursuing each point in detail. We note first that NP's with possessives inhibit Extraposition of PP from both subject and object position. (This was also noted by Akmajian and Lehrer (1977).)

(232)

a. $\left\{\begin{matrix} \text{Bill's} \\ \text{A} \end{matrix}\right\}$ picture of Susan is hanging on the wall.

b. $\left\{\begin{matrix} \text{*Bill's} \\ \text{A} \end{matrix}\right\}$ picture is hanging on the wall of Susan.

(233)

a. $\left\{\begin{matrix} \text{Sam's} \\ \text{Any} \end{matrix}\right\}$ respect for Nixon at this point $\left\{\begin{matrix} \text{is} \\ \text{would be} \end{matrix}\right\}$ surprising.

b. $\left\{\begin{matrix} \text{*Sam's} \\ \text{Any} \end{matrix}\right\}$ respect at this point $\left\{\begin{matrix} \text{is} \\ \text{would be} \end{matrix}\right\}$ surprising for Nixon.

(234)

a. $\left\{\begin{matrix} \text{Markov's} \\ \text{A} \end{matrix}\right\}$ solution to this problem has just appeared.

b. $\left\{\begin{matrix} \text{*Markov's} \\ \text{A} \end{matrix}\right\}$ solution has just appeared to this problem.

(235)

a. $\left\{\begin{matrix} \text{The government's} \\ \text{Public} \end{matrix}\right\}$ mercy towards the victims has been withheld.

b. $\left\{\begin{matrix} \text{*The government's} \\ \text{Public} \end{matrix}\right\}$ mercy has been withheld towards the victims.

(236)
a. We showed $\left\{\begin{matrix} \text{Bill's} \\ \text{a} \end{matrix}\right\}$ picture of Sam to Mary.

b. We showed $\left\{\begin{matrix} \text{*Bill's} \\ \text{a} \end{matrix}\right\}$ picture to Mary of Sam.

These facts would follow directly if it were the case that NP's with definite determiners such as *the* and possessives had the structure shown in (237a) while those with indefinite articles or quantifiers had the structure given in (237b). (Alternatively, we could assume that the structure in (237b) was exhaustively dominated by $\overline{\overline{N}}$, and that such a

(237)

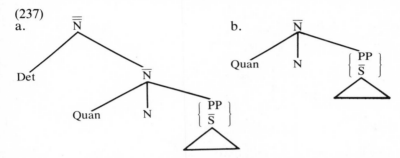

nonbranching B-cyclic node did not count for the Binary principle.) Given this difference, it would follow that in $\overline{\overline{N}}$ constructions the complement would not be accessible to extraposition transformations applying at a higher cycle, because of the Binary principle. The complement of an $\overline{N}$ would be accessible to such transformations, as illustrated by (238).

(238)

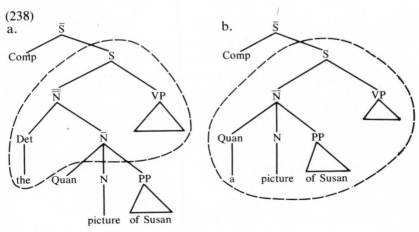

We need assume nothing more to prevent restructuring or Extraposition of PP out of objects. In the case of $\overline{\overline{N}}$, BP will block restructuring; in the case of $\overline{N}$ it will not.[75,76]

(239)

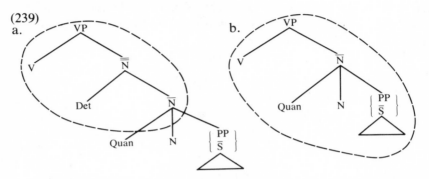

The problems that such an analysis raises are not inconsiderable. Significantly, it appears that extraposition is possible when the determiner is *that*, contrary to what we would predict.

(240)
a. That man called me up that I was telling you about.
b. That book has just been published about amoebas.
c. That new album has appeared by the Beatles.

In this case, we suggest, the extraposed constituent is in fact not a constituent of $\overline{N}$, but an immediate constituent of $\overline{\overline{N}}$. Jackendoff (1977a,b) argues that complements at this level are nonrestrictive, and in fact we do get only a nonrestrictive interpretation in cases where extraposition such as that illustrated in (240) is possible. Notice that where demonstratives are contrasted, we get only a restrictive interpretation. (This argument was suggested to us by Greg Carlson.)

(241)
a. That man that I was telling you about called me up, and this man that I was telling you about didn't.
b. That book about amoebas has just been published, and this book about amoebas is already a best-seller.
c. That new album by the Beatles has already appeared, and this new album by the Beatles is sold out.

(242)

a. *That man called me up that I was telling you about and this man didn't.

b. *That book has just been published about amoebas, and this one is already a best-seller (about amoebas).

c. *That new album has already appeared by the Beatles, and this one is sold out.

5.5.3 Application to Pied Piping

We have been arguing for the position that the apparent counterexample to the Binary principle can be eliminated by the introduction of a special class of restructuring rules. We leave open the question of the appropriate means of incorporating such rules into the theory of grammar, whether as transformations or as a special class of rules distinct from transformations.

Pursuing the consequences of a theory in which restructuring rules (whatever their ultimate interpretation) are allowed, we find, surprisingly, that such a theory allows us to account for aspects of a phenomenon known generally as *pied piping*. Many of the examples we will use in our discussion are based on those in Ross (1967), where the first discussion of the phenomenon appears.

5.5.3.1 The Basic Problem Two aspects of the problem of pied piping will concern us here. All cases of pied piping share the following characteristic: a node A undergoes Wh Fronting (or relativization), but A is not marked [+wh]; it only dominates a constituent B that is marked [+wh]. We distinguish two cases of pied piping.

The first case is the simple one, in which a PP undergoes Wh Fronting because it dominates an NP marked [+wh].

(243)

a. Who did you give the book $_{PP}$[to Ø]?

b. $_{PP}$[To whom] did you give the book Ø?

We will suggest a mechanism for generating both (243a) and (243b).

The second case is the classic Pied Piping convention of Ross (1967). Here, the node that is moved dominates but does not immediately dominate the constituent marked [+wh].

(244) These are the books NP[the height of the lettering on the covers
of which] the government prescribes ∅.

(245)

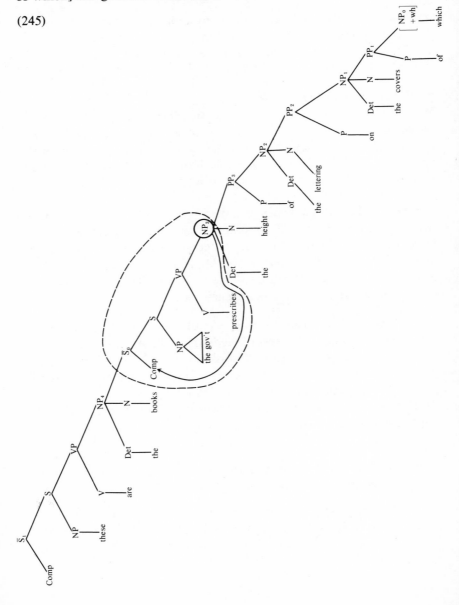

As seen in (244)–(245), it is NP_3 that undergoes Wh Fronting even though it is NP_0 that is $[+wh]$. The interesting property of such structures as (245) is that any NP that dominates NP_0 (except for NP_4) can undergo Wh Fronting. Thus, along with (244) we have the following:

(246)

a. These are the books $_{NP_2}$[the lettering on the covers of which] the government prescribes $_{NP_3}$[the height of $\emptyset$].

b. These are the books $_{NP_1}$[the covers of which] the government prescribes $_{NP_3}$[the height of the lettering on $\emptyset$].

c. These are the books $_{NP_0}$[which] the government prescribes $_{NP_3}$[the height of the lettering on the covers of $\emptyset$].

These examples are all problems for a theory that employs the Binary principle, since NP_2, NP_1 and NP_0 are all outside of the scope of Wh Fronting on $\bar{S}_0$, yet clearly they undergo the transformation. Sentence (244) is a problem as well if it is necessary to look at the $[+wh]$ NP_0 when applying Wh Fronting to NP_3 (or any other NP) on the $\bar{S}_3$ cycle. The solution that we will outline avoids these problems by application of restructuring.

5.5.3.2 Application of Restructuring We will leave discussion of the mechanism by which the feature $[+wh]$ is distributed through the complex NP to the next section. As the details of this discussion will show, on our analysis the distribution of $[+wh]$ must take place cyclically, and cannot be incorporated as a convention applying as part of Wh Fronting.

Assuming this, we note that PP_3 may undergo restructuring out of NP_3 on the VP cycle in (245). We illustrate the result in (247), where all $[+wh]$'s have been marked. By restructuring, PP_3 is now in the scope of Wh Fronting on the $\bar{S}_0$ cycle, as is NP_2. PP_3 cannot undergo Wh Fronting because of the Reordering constraint discussed in section 5.5.2, but NP_2 can. This accounts for the ungrammaticality of (248a) and the grammaticality of (246a), repeated below as (248b).

(247)

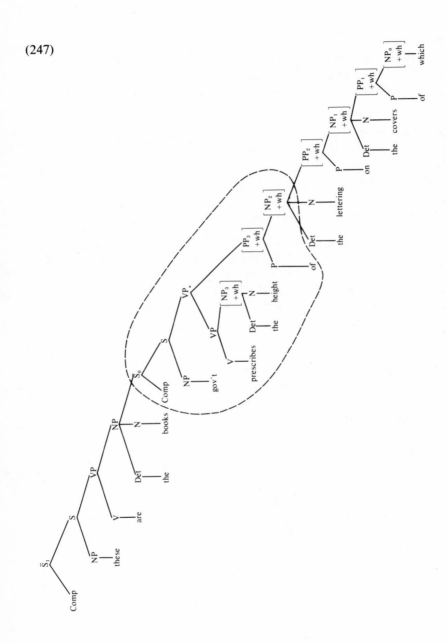

(248)

a. *These are the books of the lettering on the covers of which the government prescribes the height.

b. These are the books the lettering on the covers of which the government prescribes the height of.

Continuing with this line of analysis, we note that while PP_3 and NP_2 in (247) are within the scope of a transformation applying at $\bar{S}_0$, PP_2 and NP_1 are not. But (246b) shows that NP_1 must be. And (247) shows that NP_1 would be within the scope of such a transformation if restructuring could apply to PP_2 to raise it into the higher cyclic domain. Since the prior raising of PP_3 does not freeze it (the Raising principle does not apply to restructured constituents), there is no obvious reason why restructuring should not again apply (to PP_2 on cycle VP.), yielding (249) (p. 376). As before, note that $VP \rightarrow VP\ PP$ must be a base rule so that the Freezing principle will not rule out these derivations. Again, a constraint on reordering will block fronting of PP_2 but allow fronting of NP_1, accounting for the following.[77]

(250)

a. *These are the books on the covers of which the government prescribes the height of the lettering.

b. These are the books the covers of which the government prescribes the height of the lettering on. (= (246b))

Finally, restructuring of PP_1 at cycle VP.. will give the structure in (251) (p. 377) and will account for the examples in (252).

(252)

a. *These are the books of which the government prescribes the height of the lettering on the covers.

b. These are the books which the government prescribes the height of the lettering on the covers of. (= (246c))

Thus, as part of the pied piping analysis we derive the sorts of examples noted earlier as (206), in which an NP deeply embedded in an object NP can undergo Wh Fronting.[78]

(249)

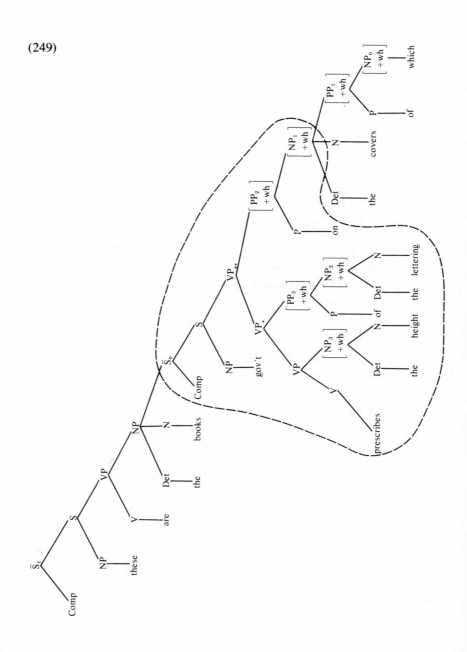

(251)

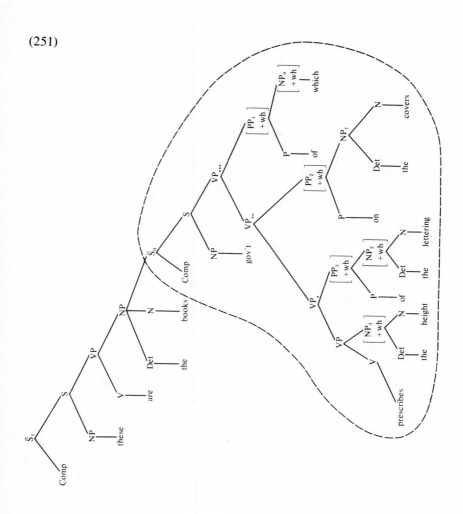

(206)

a. Who did you meet the friend of a relative of $\emptyset$?

b. Which books does the government specify the cost of the covers of $\emptyset$?

This is not an isolated exception to the Binary principle, but a particular fact among a whole range of pied piping phenomena.

There are three questions concerning our proposal to explain pied piping with restructuring. The first involves the mechanism of marking constituents as [+wh]. The other two have to do with a variety of other sentences that the structures (247), (249), and (251) appear to predict the grammaticality of. Some predictions are correct, and others present apparent difficulties for our analysis. We take up these problems in section 5.5.5.

5.5.4 Wh Copying

Let us first clarify the fact that in the analysis we are proposing it cannot be the case that constituents are specified as [+wh], by some sort of convention, at the point at which Wh Fronting applies. Looking back at (249), for example, we see that NP_1 is [+wh] because it dominates NP_0. But because of the Binary principle, at the time when NP_1 is accessible on the $\bar{S}_0$ cycle, NP_0 is not. Hence by strict interpretation of the Binary principle we cannot look at NP_0 to see that NP_1 dominates it.

There are two ways that we could relax this strict interpretation but neither is consistent with the facts. First, we could take the position that BP does not apply to this convention. If this were the case, we would expect to be able to apply Wh Fronting to any NP that dominated a [+wh] constituent. Yet (253) provides a clear counterexample to this prediction.

(253)

a. Mary knows $_{NP_2}$[the man $_{\bar{S}}$[that forgot $_{NP_1}$[what] to do]]].

b. *$_{NP_2}$[the man $_{\bar{S}}$[that forgot $_{NP_1}$[what] to do]] does Mary know?

In (253b) the NP containing the relative clause, NP_2, is fronted because it dominates an NP marked [+wh], namely NP_1. Similar examples were provided by Ross (1967) to show that the Pied Piping convention that he hypothesized must obey the constraints on transformations that he had argued for. Though our constraints take different forms from Ross's, the facts are the same and the conclusion is similar.

A second way of weakening the strict interpretation of BP is to formulate the convention (roughly) as follows:

When applying Wh Fronting at $\bar{S}_i$, an NP_j may undergo the transformation if there is an NP_k marked [+wh] such that (a) NP_j dominates NP_k and (b) NP_k is within the domain of rules applying at NP_j (*not* $\bar{S}_i$) as defined by the Binary principle. As an illustration we provide (254).

(254)

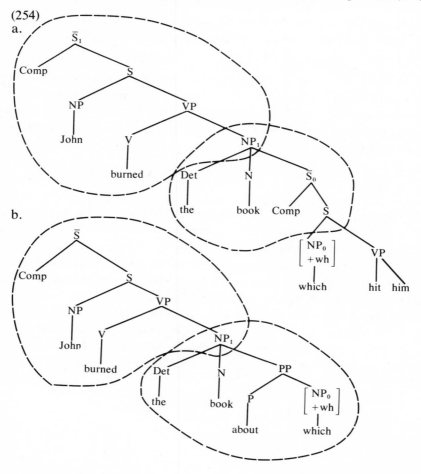

We find that in the case of (254a) the [+wh] NP, namely NP_0, is not within the scope of NP_1, according to BP. Hence NP_1 cannot undergo Wh Fronting, and we do not derive ungrammatical sentences like (253b) or (255).

(255) *The book which hit him did John burn?

On the other hand, in (254b) NP_0 is within the scope of NP_1, and NP_1 in fact can undergo Wh Fronting, most felicitously in a relative clause.

(256)
a. This is the painting the book about which John burned.
b. The book about which painting did John burn?

Though plausible, this approach overlooks the fact that pied piping occurs not only when [+wh] resides in a restructurable prepositional phrase, but when it appears in a possessive. Restructuring allows us to raise up deeply embedded interrogative noun phrases, but there appears to be no motivation whatsoever for restructuring possessives leftwards in the derivation of sentences like (257).

(257) John is the man *whose mother's brother's employer* I used to work for.

As the structure in (258) shows, without at least some (ad hoc) restructuring (the details of which are unclear to us), the view of pied piping that we are entertaining here will simply not work. The scope of a transformation at NP_3 extends only as far as NP_2. Hence under this analysis there does not appear to be any way to copy the feature up from NP_0 onto NP_3 without violating BP.

For the reasons just discussed we will adopt the following mechanism for transferring the feature [+wh] upwards in a phrase-marker: At any cycle, an NP or PP that dominates a node marked [+wh] may optionally be marked [+wh], subject to BP. We will call this Wh Copying.[79]

(258)

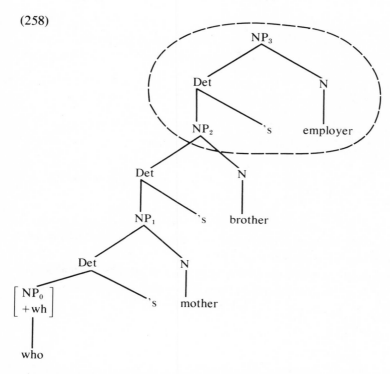

   To illustrate, consider the structure in (258). On the NP_1 cycle, NP_0 is in the domain and Wh Copying may apply. If it does, NP_1 is marked [+wh]. Then, on the NP_2 cycle, Wh Fronting may mark NP_2 [+wh] because NP_1 is [+wh] and accessible. Finally, on the NP_3 cycle, if NP_2 has been marked [+wh], NP_3 may be. If Wh Copying fails to apply at any point along the way, NP_3 will not be marked [+wh]. It will fail to undergo Wh Fronting, and this will lead to filtering of the sort discussed at various times in this chapter.
   A similar derivation applies to prepositional phrases. In a structure such as (259), Wh Copying may mark PP_1 [+wh] because NP_1 is [+wh]. If it does, PP_1 will undergo Wh Fronting; if it does not, NP_1 undergoes Wh Fronting. It is logically possible that NP_1 could undergo Wh Front-

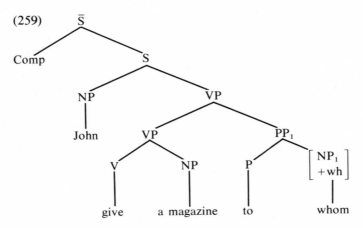

(259)

ing even if PP_1 were marked [+wh], but we will argue that this is ruled out for independent reasons.

For more complicated cases Wh Copying also applies successively at higher cycles. (260) illustrates one way in which [+wh] can be transmit-

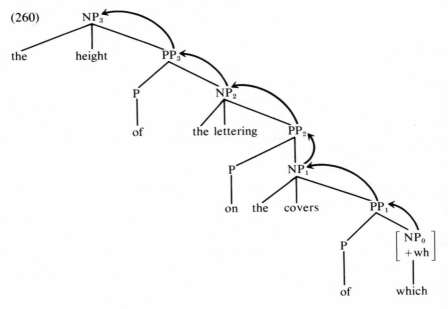

(260)

ted upwards. However, BP will block Wh Copying from marking an NP that dominates a relative clause containing [+wh], thus ruling out examples like (255). This is illustrated in (261). As can be seen, the

(261)

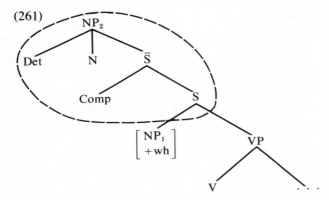

NP marked [+wh] in the relative clause is outside the domain of a transformation applying at NP_2, as defined by BP. If NP_1 is moved into Comp, on the other hand, the Comp Accessibility convention allows access to constituents of Comp on the higher cycle, but only for rules involving a higher Comp. Thus NP_2 will not be marked [+wh] in a structure like (262).

(262)

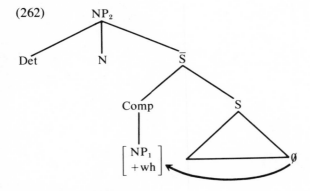

5.5.5 Further Issues
5.5.5.1 Other Examples Consideration of successive restructuring reveals that the sentences we have derived are not the only ones the

structures will generate. To see this, consider the tree in (251). Notice
that after three restructurings there are four noun phrases within the
domain of Wh Fronting on $\bar{S}_3$. Tree (251) itself presents a problem,
since all of these NP's are marked [+wh] as a result of Wh Copying,
yet only NP_0 can actually undergo Wh Fronting. Leaving this problem
aside until section 5.5.5.2, let us suppose that in the tree in (251) the
relative pronoun is not NP_0, but NP_1. That is, (251) is now a relative
clause on *covers* and not on *books*. The new underlying structure is
given in (263), with details omitted.

(263) These are the covers REL the government prescribes the
height of the lettering on which of the books.

Applying Wh Fronting to *which* yields the questionable (264).

(264) These are the covers which the government prescribes the
height of the lettering on ∅ of the books.

(265)

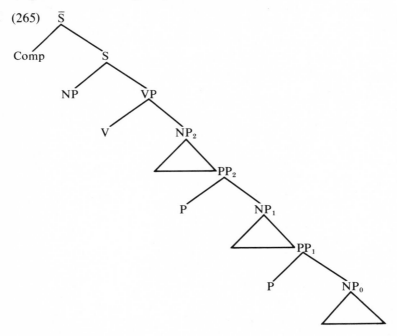

In fact our analysis predicts many more sentences of this sort. For ease of exposition, we first outline in schematic form the sorts of predictions that are made, and then proceed to list all of the relevant examples. Because of the difficulty of making firm judgments, and because of the real possibility that extragrammatical factors may be affecting these judgments, we will concern ourselves primarily with displaying the consequences of our analysis.

We begin with the simple structure (265). Suppose first that NP_2 dominates a $[+wh]$ that is not dominated by PP_2. If PP_2 is not restructured, Wh Fronting of NP_2 will take PP_2 along. If PP_2 is restructured, it will be left behind. Moving on, suppose that NP_1 dominates a $[+wh]$ that is not dominated by PP_1. In order for Wh Fronting to apply to NP_1, PP_2 must be restructured. If, furthermore, PP_1 is then restructured, NP_1 will undergo fronting alone. Otherwise, PP_1 will go along. But if NP_1 is fronted in this case, what is left of NP_2 cannot be fronted along with it. (266) shows why. After restructuring of PP_2, NP_2 and NP_1 are not attached.

(266)

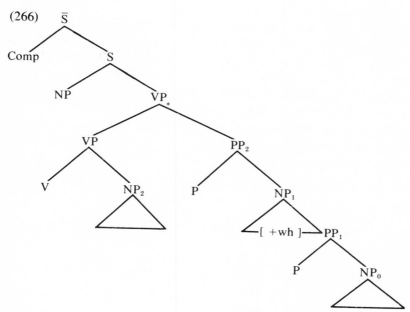

Returning to real examples, we begin with the NP *the height of the lettering on the covers of the books*. We relativize on each NP. The first examples show that it is impossible to move the sequence to the left of the NP marked [+wh] unless this NP happens to be the lowest in the structure.

(267)
a. These are the books the height of the lettering on the covers of which the government prescribes. (= (244))
b. *These are the covers the height of the lettering on which the government prescribes $\emptyset$ of the books.
c. ?*Fred made the lettering the height of which the government prescribes $\emptyset$ on the covers of the books.
d. This is the only dimension which the government prescribes $\emptyset$ of the lettering on the covers of the books.

In (267), (a) and (d) should be good, and (b) and (c) should be bad. To the extent that judgments can be made at all, the predictions are borne out moderately well.

Consider (266) once again. We can see that NP_1, because it is [+wh], should be able to undergo Wh Fronting regardless of whether PP_1 restructures. But in general, if NP_i is [+wh] in the base and no restructuring takes place, then NP_j, $j < i$, must move if NP_i moves. (This is nonclassical pied piping, where the highest NP is marked [+wh] in the base and not by Wh Copying.)

Once again we illustrate with real examples. Suppose first that all possible restructurings have occurred and that NP_0 is [+wh]. This gives us (268).

(268) Which books does the government prescribe the height of the lettering on the covers of?

Suppose next that all but one restructuring has occurred and that NP_1 is marked [+wh], as in (269).

(269) The government prescribes the height of the lettering on which part of the books?

Wh Fronting gives only (270).

(270) Which parts of the books does the government prescribe the height of the lettering on?

However, if NP$_1$ is marked [+wh] and the PP *of the books* restructures, we predict (271).

(271) Which parts does the government prescribe the height of the lettering on of the books?

For a more complicated example, consider (272), in which NP$_2$ is

(272)

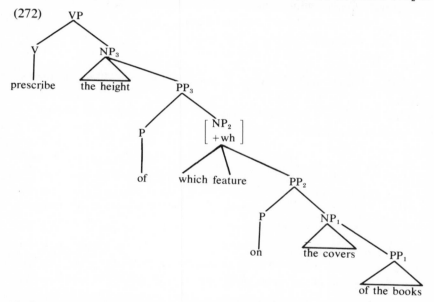

marked [+wh]. After restructuring PP$_3$, NP$_2$ can undergo Wh Fronting, giving (273).

(273) Which feature on the covers of the books does the government prescribe the height of?

But if PP$_2$ restructures also, then only *which feature* (that is, the remnant of NP$_2$ after PP$_2$ is removed) undergoes Wh Fronting.

(274) Which feature does the government prescribe the height of on the covers of the books?

Because of the Binary principle, it is impossible to restructure PP_1 without also restructuring PP_2. Thus it is impossible to apply Wh Fronting to only *which feature on the covers*.

(275) *Which feature on the covers does the government prescribe the height of of the books?

Similar examples hold when the NP marked [+wh] is NP_3. The examples in (276) should be grammatical and those in (277) should not be, by our analysis.

(276)
a. Which dimension does the government prescribe of the lettering on the covers of the books?
b. Which dimension of the lettering on the covers of the books does the government prescribe?

(277)
a. ?Which dimension of the lettering does the government prescribe on the covers of the books?
b. *Which dimension of the lettering on the covers does the government prescribe of the books?

The relative acceptability of (277a) may be due to there being an alternative structure for the NP in question, in which *on the covers of the books* is a sister of *of the lettering*. Then the former would restructure. In any event, the judgments here are extremely difficult to make, and there appears to be no clear-cut counterevidence to the predictions made by our analysis.[80]

5.5.5.2 Ghost *wh*'s We noted, in passing, an interesting technical problem with our version of Wh Copying which we will now look at in detail. Briefly, if every PP and NP in a structure is marked [+wh], restructuring may leave behind PP's and NP's that are marked [+wh] but do not dominate a true interrogative morpheme. For example, this is what has happened in (278). As (279) shows, fronting of *the height* does not satisfy the requirements of Wh Fronting.[81]

(278)

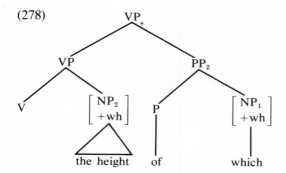

(279) *This is the monument *the height* the governor criticized Ø of which.

Our solution makes crucial use of the Freezing principle. We observe, first of all, that it is impossible to generate the feature [+wh] on an NP like *the height* in the base. That this is the case is shown by the fact that normal topicalized NP's do not trigger Inversion, as in *The height did John measure*. We would expect them to if they could be [+wh] in the base.[82]

Now, if we generate these NP's in the course of a derivation, the structure that we are generating is not a base structure. Hence the structure is frozen, by the Freezing principle.

Consider (280), in which the feature [+wh] has been copied onto

(280)

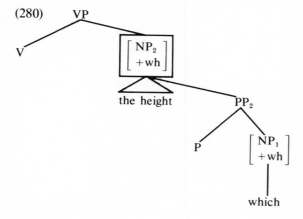

NP$_2$. Note that NP$_2$ is frozen. Since NP$_2$ is frozen, PP$_2$ cannot restructure into VP. Consequently it will be impossible for us to derive the "ghost *wh*" in (278).

It follows from the Freezing principle, then, that if a PP is restructured, it either is the highest [+wh] in the structure or dominates the highest. For if the highest [+wh] dominated the PP in question, that [+wh] would be frozen and restructuring would be blocked.

CHAPTER 6

FUNCTION, PERFORMANCE, AND EXPLANATION

In the preceding chapters we have discussed results that lead to some fairly specific conclusions. Considering the problem of the learning of syntactic transformations, we have demonstrated that, under certain assumptions, transformational grammars can be shown to be learnable from quite simple data. These results have led us to hypothesize certain principles derived from the learnability analysis as being empirically true of natural language. In chapter 5 we provided evidence that to some extent confirmed these principles. We have thus found support for some rather specific principles of mind. Naturally, there is no reason to think that these principles are perfectly correct or complete as they stand. We are just at the beginning of the study of language learnability. A large number of problems remain, some of which may demand reformulation of the results achieved to date. We discuss some problems and directions in chapter 7.

First, however, it may be useful to pause to reconsider the foundations of our subject, not from a technical point of view, but with respect to the question, Are we studying language acquisition correctly? In our view the methods we have used are justified by the results we have attained. The method, stated at its simplest, is to try to find a learning theory for the best generative grammatical description of human abilities that we can find.

One question that has been asked is, Why is it necessary to account for the learning of a generative grammar? The reasons are obvious to us. Generative grammar describes adult linguistic abilities. Therefore it should be the goal of the study of language acquisition to describe the basis for the learning of these abilities. If the study of language acquisition is not to account for the learnability of language, what is it to account for?[1]

It might be objected that we have chosen the wrong description of adult linguistic abilities. To some extent this remark is correct, though of limited relevance. We have simplified the problem by considering only partial aspects of an adult's linguistic competence, particularly syntax; and we have considered in detail only the learning of syntactic transformations. Even with respect to transformations we have simplified, not admitting certain kinds of constructs (such as rule features and domination as part of structural descriptions) in the definition of transformations. Our simplification has been principled; we have been working on only part of the problem of language acquisition, and there is no way to see how progress can be made unless we deal with one part at a time. But we have studied the learning of a major subsegment of linguistic theory (the theory of syntactic transformations) in some detail and with interesting results. We have also considered changes in linguistic theory as a result of learnability studies. So the fact that only part of linguistic theory has been studied is not fatal to the enterprise—rather, it is probably necessary if significant advances are to be made in the general problem.

Another objection concerning the description of adult linguistic abilities might be that transformational grammar itself is the wrong description of these abilities, so studying the learning of transformational grammar will not tell us anything about human learning. Our reason for selecting transformational grammar is that, in our view, it is by far the best and most coherent representation we have of adult human linguistic abilities, and the one with the most empirical support. Although much remains to be discovered about the nature of human language, in studying the learning of language we have to start with the best theory of language we have.

There are two possible objections to our view. One is that there are more adequate theories of generative grammar than the one we have chosen. Our answer is that we chose what appeared to us at the outset of our study to be the most convincing statement of a theory that was available, and we chose a subsystem of that theory as the object of learnability studies. To some extent other approaches have not been formalized enough to allow their learnability properties to be studied. If the lack of formalization simply reflected lack of an attempt to write a clear theory in a formal language, we could perform that formalization and proceed to study learnability. But often the lack of formalization implies that a theory is not clear enough to be formalized; in such a case the learnability properties of the theory cannot be studied without making a number of ad hoc assumptions. It also may happen that a theory is created in which no attempt is made to restrict the range of linguistic abilities, so that no formal restrictions are placed on language by the theory. This property, like vagueness, can lead to the impossibility of formalizing a theory. Certainly, if there are competing theories of grammar that are sufficiently precise to admit of formalization, the learnability properties of these theories should be studied. It may well be that learnability will help to choose between alternative theories, as in this book it has helped to choose between different versions of transformational grammar. Nothing about learnability theory per se rules out the possibility of studying the learnability of different linguistic theories. In chapter 7, we indicate possible directions for studying linguistic constructs that are not part of the chapter 4 theory.

A more radical objection might be that no system of generative grammar is an appropriate representation of human language. The reasons behind this objection are difficult to understand, since for us it is simply an empirical question concerning the description of linguistic abilities. On this question generative grammar has no serious competitors, in our opinion. Therefore, we will examine some particular versions of the objection that transformational grammar is the wrong object to study the learning of if one is interested in how children learn language.

6.1 The "Cognitivist" View

The first kind of objection has nothing directly to do with learning. Rather, it is an objection to grammar as a representation of linguistic abilities. Such a view is advanced by H. Clark and Haviland (1974), who claim that grammatical knowledge cannot be studied independently of linguistic performance, and, in fact, that grammatical theory itself cannot coherently exist. Clark and Haviland distinguish between the views of the "Grammarian" ("static theory") and the "Cognitivist" ("dynamic theory"). They argue for the superiority of the "Cognitivist" view on a number of grounds.

To begin with, Clark and Haviland take a position against the use of grammaticality judgments as linguistic data. They write,

For the Cognitivist, the Grammarian's enterprise has seemed odd indeed. First, the Cognitivist has been puzzled by the Grammarian's choice of primary data—especially judgments of grammaticality. Although it is important at some point to be able to account for grammaticality judgments, surely they are not the *raison d'etre* for the study of language. We do not speak in order to be grammatical; we speak in order to convey meaning. We do not attempt to comprehend speech in order to detect violations of grammaticality; we comprehend in order to detect meaning. In so far as comprehension and production go awry, we are willing to say that a sentence is somehow unacceptable or ungrammatical, and these processes can go awry in a variety of ways. But surely it is more important to account for the essential function of language, namely, how it is used to convey meaning. (p. 116)

This quotation demonstrates a number of confusions. First, note a fundamental confusion here about how a science chooses its data. The crucial data for the construction of and distinction between theories are not generally given a priori; rather, the development of theoretical and empirical work in a science brings changes in the kinds of data that are relevant at any time. Of course, somebody could choose to say that he is interested only in certain data and not in others, and could proceed to study only those data.[2] But on the assumption that the goal of science is to increase insight and knowledge about the world, this is not the way that a rational scientist would proceed. Nor is it the way that successful sciences have chosen their data. Surely biologists who are interested in solving the problem of genetic transmission do not have a particular a priori interest in X-ray photographs. Yet the development of theoretical and empirical work in molecular genetics led to the crucial importance of such photographs as data in the construction of theories of genetic transmission.

Correspondingly, in linguistic theory we do not have a priori evidence that grammaticality judgments (and other forms of data that linguists use) are the data on which theories should be based. What makes these data relevant is the insight obtained from using them. Grammaticality judgments and data like judgments of ambiguity, synonymy, and anomaly are important because rich and insightful theories have been created based on these data. Furthermore, the data allow theories to be discriminated, one from the other.

Clark and Haviland claim that grammaticality judgments should not be used as data by linguists because "we do not speak in order to be grammatical." But even if this notion were true, no logical relation can be established between the purpose of our speech and the kind of data on which to base linguistic theories. Function can also be established in biology. For example, the function of certain molecules is associated with genetic transmission. But this function once again does not dictate choice of data. We do not say that the biologist's enterprise is odd because he uses X-ray photographs although it is not the purpose or function of the relevant molecules to provide photographs.

The last sentence quoted from Clark and Haviland demonstrates another confusion, that between what is accounted for, and what is used as data. One of the questions that linguists attempt to account for is the relation between form and meaning. The kinds of judgments that linguists use as data turn out to be quite relevant to the investigation of this question. Certainly, such a relation would play a central role in a theory of how language is "used to convey meaning." Once again, a priori arguments cannot be given against the relevance of a particular kind of data.

Of course, one might argue the plausibility that certain kinds of data might be relevant to certain questions. This kind of argument is really pertinent only when we are in the pretheoretical stage of science. In the case of linguistic theory, there are already a large number of positive instances of how the data aid in the construction of theories. But even if one were to consider only the plausibility argument, setting aside the large body of linguistic theory and data that have been developed,

Clark and Haviland have no case. They speak of one of the advantages of the "Cognitivist" approach as being able to account for "how long people take in comprehending a sentence." Now, the time taken for comprehending a sentence gives no direct information about the structure of a linguistic system or how language is "used to convey meaning." On the other hand, judgments of grammaticality do give relevant evidence of certain linguistic structures, and judgments of synonymy or implication give relevant evidence about semantics. Thus the plausibility argument goes strongly in favor of linguistic kinds of data as being relevant to a theory of language.

However, we do not wish to make too much of the plausibility argument. The relevant test is whether a particular kind of data are useful for theory construction, and in this test, grammaticality judgments win out over reaction-time data.[3] It is logically conceivable that reaction-time data could aid in the construction of linguistic theories. But it is not particularly plausible. Surely the onus is on Clark and Haviland to find a kind of data that is more useful than grammaticality judgments for the construction of linguistic theory and to demonstrate the usefulness of that data. Until then the linguist (or psychologist, for that matter) should ignore a priori statements about what kinds of data are acceptable or most important and should continue, as any rational scientist would, to use the most useful data. In short, grammaticality judgments and other linguistic intuitions may provide the clearest route to discovering truths about language. At the present time they certainly provide the most important route to such discoveries.

Besides questioning whether grammaticality judgments should be part of the data of linguists, Clark and Haviland suggest that such judgments should have a different explanation. Namely, grammaticality judgments would be explained on the basis of comprehensibility of sentences. They write (p. 118) that the Cognitivist "would be able to predict acceptability judgments from certain failures in the process of comprehension, and this is as it should be. Note that such judgments, as normally elicited, are not a product of speech production and hence have nothing *per se* to do with the process of production." But as has been pointed out quite often, comprehensibility and grammaticality are *not* the same. Sentences can be comprehensible and not grammatical and vice versa. Examples are legion. To take an example whose theoretical basis we have studied in section 5.2.1, we may question the object of the preposition in (1a) to obtain (1b) and in like manner (2b) may be constructed from (2a).

(1)
a. John threatened the men who lived upstairs with a hammer last night.
b. Which hammer did John threaten the men who lived upstairs with ∅ last night?

(2)
a. John threatened with a hammer last night the men who lived upstairs.
b. *Which hammer did John threaten with ∅ last night the men who lived upstairs?

Note that, although (2b) is clearly odd, it is quite comprehensible, with the same meaning as the grammatical (1b). Or consider a sentence like

(3) *John wants win.

Sentence (3) is perfectly comprehensible but clearly ungrammatical. As has often been pointed out, we use grammatical knowledge in comprehension, but we use other abilities also. If the utterance is ungrammatical, a normal tendency is to find a way of understanding it anyway. Of course, an ultimate explanation of all cognitive abilities would have to explain this ability to make sense of ungrammatical utterances. This ability doubtless makes use of syntactic knowledge, but there is no reason to confuse the two.

    Clark and Haviland write,

Imagine that certain constructions, because they refer to less accessible aspects of knowledge, take longer to interpret than others. Concomitantly, these same constructions will tend to be less acceptable than others because acceptability is in most cases simply a reflection of how quickly one can construct a sensible interpretation of a sentence. (p. 140)

No examples or data are given to illustrate these clearly empirical statements. Yet they seem simply false. Consider a sentence like (4).

(4) The middle name of the fourth mayor of New York City had an even number of letters in it.

On the assumption that the reader (like the authors) has no knowledge about whether (4) is true or false, we may safely say that there are constructions in (4) that "refer to less accessible aspects of knowledge." Yet (4) is perfectly acceptable (as well as perfectly grammatical). Of course, there is no reason to think that it takes long to "construct a sensible interpretation" of (4), though it is difficult to say, without knowing what Clark and Haviland mean by "construct[ing] a sensible interpretation."

Clark and Haviland say that "Cognitivists" want to know by what "process" "people decide that certain sentences are unacceptable." They claim that, for example, linguistic constraints will have to be formulated in "process" terms. An example is the Coordinate Structure constraint (CSC, Ross 1967) which rules out sentences like (5) (Clark and Haviland's (43)) as ungrammatical.

(5) *Who did Bill see Mary and?

The constraint is specified by Clark and Haviland as "The Coordinate Structure Constraint: in a coordinate structure, no conjunct may be moved, nor may any element contained in a conjunct be moved out of that conjunct" (p. 171). They go on to say,

Here again, however, the constraint, as presently formulated, is independent of the process by which the grammaticality judgment has presumably been made. And again, there are several ways the listener could judge (43) [our (5)] to be ungrammatical. He could do so only upon failing to find two complete conjuncts adjoined to the *and* or only upon failing to find a missing case function for the *who* (where it is forbidden to look inside a coordinate structure), or both. Regardless of which it is, the listener will make the judgment only when there is a failure in one of the ordinary procedures he uses in the process of comprehension, and the Coordinate Structure Constraint should reflect this. Note that there are really quite low level rules the listener could use to exclude [(5)]. It is not simply the case that conjunctions cannot be *moved* out of coordinate structures, but rather coordinate structures must always have conjuncts adjoined to both sides of the *and*. Thus

(45) *Bill saw Mary and

can be judged as unacceptable only by inspection of the constituent *Mary and,* which is incomplete and therefore unacceptable. The listener does not need to know that the second conjunct had been moved elsewhere, as in [(5)], or even that there ever was a second conjunct. (pp. 121–122)

First, to consider the general point, it is true that grammatical theory does not specify a real-time process whereby the decision that (5) is ungrammatical is made. But the hypothetical processes Clark and Haviland allude to take account of the linguistically specified CSC (except for the last one, the "low level rules," to which we shall return). Many real-time models could be consistent with the Coordinate Structure constraint. It is the task of the performance theorist to discover how the constraint is realized in real time. Once again, the situation is familiar in other areas of psychology. For example, psychophysicists often assume that a signal produces a certain sensation strength, but for purposes of idealization no time course of events is specified.

What is most interesting about the last quotation from Clark and Haviland is the consideration of a process model without the Coordinate Structure constraint, the suggestion that "there are really quite low level rules the listener could use to exclude [(5)]," namely, that there must be "conjuncts adjoined to both sides of the *and.*" Thus (6) (Clark and Haviland's (45)) is also ungrammatical.

(6) *Bill saw Mary and

Their argument is interesting because it demonstrates clearly why linguists would want to adopt the Coordinate Structure constraint and not Clark and Haviland's suggestion. First notice that the ungrammaticality of (6) follows immediately from the statement of the grammar. Namely, the base rules will not generate (6) since *and* appears in the base only with conjoined phrases, and there is no transformation that deletes one of these conjoined phrases. Clark and Haviland's theory, on the other hand, will fail on a large number of other kinds of data quite well known to linguists. To take only some of the most immediate and obvious data, if more than two elements are conjoined, we will produce an ungrammatical sentence, as predicted by the CSC, if we question one of them.

(7) *Who did Bill see Mary, Ø and John?

Since there are conjuncts on both sides of *and* in (7), Clark and Haviland's theory would have to predict that (7) is grammatical. One might imagine reformulations of the theory to handle this datum.

Or consider what happens when other kinds of phrases are conjoined. If we question *caviar* in (8), in which verb phrases are conjoined, we obtain (9).

(8) John drank wine and ate caviar.
(9) *What (kind of caviar) did John drink wine and eat Ø?

Once again, though the CSC rules out (9), Clark and Haviland's theory must accept it because there are "conjuncts" on both sides of *and*.

Perhaps Clark and Haviland would want to formulate the explanation so that any incomplete constituent is unacceptable. Perhaps then (9) would be ruled out on the grounds that *eat* is an "incomplete" verb phrase (though it is not clear how exactly to do this). Sentence (7), on the other hand, would not be ruled out by this formulation. Still worse, incomplete phrases in English are perfectly grammatical if they arise from rules. Thus the ordinary operation of Wh Fronting leaves an incomplete constituent, as in (10) and (11).

(10) What did John eat Ø?
(11) Who did John give the book to Ø?

In (10) *eat* is incomplete in the same sense as in (9). In (11) *to* is an incomplete prepositional phrase. Yet these sentences are perfectly grammatical.

The general point is crucial to scientific methodology. Any single datum can in principle be explained or predicted by an infinity of principles or laws. Even in practice scholars might suggest a large finite number of explanations for the ungrammaticality of (5). However, linguists use a large number of empirical observations to narrow the class of possible explanations. It is simply not following the principles of scientific methodology (or of rational inquiry) to consider only one datum to the exclusion of all others.

Note that grammaticality judgments play a large role in the testing of the Coordinate Structure constraint. It of course may be that the CSC is wrong and should be reformulated, but empirical data are necessary in order to test this claim.[4] What is interesting about a constraint like the Coordinate Structure constraint is that *linguistic* structure must be used in the formulation of the constraint. It is perhaps ironical that Clark and Haviland use grammaticality judgments in an attempt to suggest alternative explanations. On the other hand, until some more useful data come along, that is what we have.

In summary, Clark and Haviland's criticism of the use of grammaticality judgments as data is based on a fundamental confusion and their proposal that the explanation of such judgments should lie in accessibility of knowledge is clearly wrong empirically. Their proposed explanation of a datum ignores (and fails on) the mass of data that were used to support the linguistic principle that they are trying to replace.

On rational scientific grounds the "Cognitivist" view (as defined by Clark and Haviland) offers no challenge at all to transformational grammar as a representation of linguistic abilities. The presentation of such a view makes it obvious why no concrete work along its lines has appeared. The easy grounds for dismissing it help to show why linguistic theory has proceeded as it has.

6.2 A "Performance Model"

An argument against the necessity of studying the learning of transformational grammar is provided by Schlesinger (1971).[5] He notes that arguments have been made that, because linguistic structure is so complex and removed from the possible linguistic experience of the child, the conclusion must follow that the child is endowed with innate structure which helps him to learn language. Thus a "learning theory" with no particular innate linguistic structures could not account for the learning of language. Schlesinger's response is to argue that the child does not have to acquire anything as complex or "abstract" as a generative grammar. He discusses a different kind of model, which is not supposed to be a generative grammar but a "performance model." This performance model contains, first of all, "input markers" or "I markers." The I marker is supposed to formally represent "the speaker's intentions which are expressed in the linguistic output" (p. 65). These intentions, of course, are not utterances. "The term *realization rule* will be used for the rules which turn I markers into utterances" (p. 68). Realization rules are supposed to be very much like transformational rules except that they apply to I markers, not phrase-markers. The important point is that there is no level of analysis in the model in which phrase-markers are the appropriate representation—realization rules map between I markers and utterances, with no intermediate level.

By doing away with phrase-markers Schlesinger claims that he has somehow made the problem of language learning easier. In fact, the problem of language learning was one of his reasons for doing away with phrase-markers. Thus Schlesinger writes,

The exclusion of P markers from the performance model is motivated by considerations of simplicity, and also, in part, by certain considerations about language acquisition. The crucial problem in current thinking on language learning seems to be how to account for the fact that a child acquires the underlying P markers which are posited by generative grammar. Some theories of language acquisition have been criticized for being unable to explain how the child learns these deep structures which, by definition, are not exhibited in the speech of the environment . . . The only way out of the difficulty is believed by these theorists to lie in the assumption of an innate propensity for arriving at these underlying structures. . . Now, if our above reasoning [i.e., that there are no P markers, but only I markers] is correct, this difficulty vanishes. No underlying P markers have to be learned. Utterances are produced directly from the I markers which represent the intentions of the child in a given situation, and which therefore do not have to be learned. Let us elaborate on this point. What the child has to learn are the correspondences between I markers and the utterances of persons in his environment. The I marker is inferred from situational cues. When the mother points to a ball and says: "Give me the ball," the task of the child consists in learning to associate the I marker representing the situation, with the utterance he hears. This is tantamount to learning a realization rule. Language learning still remains a fairly complicated task, of course, but it is one which does not pose insurmountable difficulties for an explanation in terms of learning theory. (p. 69)

Schlesinger gives only the sketchiest account of how his I markers and realization rules will account for the properties of, say, English. Numerous linguistic criticisms can be brought to bear. One major problem involves the "position rule" Agent + Action (p. 73). Rules of this kind are supposed to represent children's utterances better than rules that incorporate syntactic structures. One example given is *mail come*. Obviously, if "agent" is to be understood in the usual way, *mail* is not an agent.[6] What is interesting about the sentence, however, is that *mail* is a subject, thus providing evidence that grammatical relations might exist in children's language, and not just roles such as "agent." Realization rules of the type proposed by Schlesinger can therefore not allow *mail come* to be an "acceptable" utterance, at least under the usual interpretation. Thus Schlesinger's analysis fails as opposed to the "grammatical" analysis with respect to the very child data that he cites.

But even if we ignore all the linguistic criticisms that could be brought against Schlesinger's proposal, we cannot ignore one problem that underlies the entire proposal: Schlesinger's model in no way makes it easier to solve the problem of language acquisition. We would need a highly complex set of rules to map between intentions (I markers) and utterances. Schlesinger does not show how these could be learned. Instead, he takes a few simple examples of child speech and hints at how this small finite list could be learned. A basic error is the assumption that doing away with phrase-markers eliminates a problem. Rather, it can be argued that specification of levels actually makes the problem of language learning easier, because fewer possibilities are available for the mapping between semantic interpretation and utterance. In Schlesinger's model, so little attention is paid to the problem of capturing linguistic competence (or performance) that it is impossible to see what would have to be assumed about the relations between I markers and utterances.

What is important to notice about this "model" is that because we have no conception of what possibilities and constraints the model will have to assume, we can have no conception of the difficulties of constructing a learning theory for the model. Which makes it puzzling why Schlesinger writes that, aside from "information which one must ascribe to linguistically expressed intentions of the speaker and his way of looking at the world," the proposal "involves only processes that appear to be amenable to an explanation within a learning theory framework" (p. 95). Schlesinger does not specify what he means by "learning theory," but references in the paper suggest that he has some kind of stimulus-response framework in mind. Nowhere is a linguistic theory or a learning theory specified, and nowhere is a demonstration given that the learning theory can acquire adult abilities, given a specified form of input.

There can be no question, of course, that the organism comes to any learning task with some innate equipment; the question is only how much is innate. The soundest approach seems to be to make as few assumptions as possible, and to try to explain with these as much as possible. Currently, the nativists seem to be in favor of a much easier approach: they put down as much as possible to the organism's innate propensities . . . Explaining human behavior by invoking instincts has long ago become disreputable in psychology because it does not constitute an explanation at all. (Schlesinger, p. 100)

Schlesinger has explained nothing at all by his approach. He has not described either adult or child linguistic abilities, nor has he explained how language learning takes place. It is true that he has assumed little, aside from the ability to form I markers from situations (a strong assumption, by the way, similar to an assumption we make in chapter 3) and some generalities, such as that I markers are mapped into utterances. But he has explained nothing. In fact, there is not even a test given in Schlesinger's paper for whether his model is successful or relatively successful.

Once again, as has often been pointed out, note that it is simply wrong to say that invoking innate principles does not constitute an explanation. Suppose that, in fact, there are innate principles. Then invoking them would constitute an explanation. And, of course, biological explanations often invoke innate principles. What is true is that evidence must be brought to bear, whether one argues for or against innate principles.

Schlesinger has, in actuality, assumed a very strong innate capacity for the organism, namely, knowledge of what I markers are and how to construct them from situations. Now, of course, this ability may be innate, but why is it the only kind of ability that is innate (with respect to language learning)? So far as we can tell, Schlesinger gives two arguments for why I markers can reasonably be taken to be innate. First:

The relations represented in I markers may be taken to be linguistic universals. In [*John catches a red ball*] the relation between catching and a ball is given in the situation and not imposed by a language. No speaker of any language whatsoever will conceive of the action-object relation as holding, say, between catching and John. It is these relations which are incorporated in the I marker, and this justifies the statement that I markers are not learned, at least not in the way underlying P markers would have to be learned. (p. 70)

And second:

I markers are determined by the innate *cognitive* capacity of the child. There is nothing specifically linguistic about this capacity . . . It is just the way the child views the world, and will be the same whether he learns to speak, or fails to learn to speak due to some organic or environmental handicap. (p. 70)

Taking the second argument first, presumably Schlesinger's position is that somehow it is reasonable to postulate cognitive nonlinguistic capacities as innate, but not to postulate specifically linguistic capacities. No support is given for this position. In fact, from what we know of biology we would expect the opposite. It is well known, for example, that visual abilities are given by specifically visual innate capacities (Hubel and Wiesel 1959). Why is the cognitive way "the child views the world" more acceptable as an innate principle than the linguistic way the child views the world?

The second part of this second argument is difficult to understand. Suppose that the child has some "organic handicap." Why would anybody think that nevertheless his cognitive capacities, his way of "viewing the world," will be undisturbed? Cases of brain damage are well known in which it appears that the person's conceptual system has been damaged. Schlesinger's statement appears simply false, unless what he has in mind by "organic handicap" is a special kind of handicap that, by definition, does not affect cognitive capacity. What is interesting is Schlesinger's belief in "cognitive capacities," as opposed to linguistic capacities, so strong that the cognitive capacities cannot be damaged organically. (Alternatively, Schlesinger might mean only that cognitive and linguistic abilities are separate and linguistic abilities can be damaged without damaging cognitive abilities. But why shouldn't the opposite handicap also be possible?)

Schlesinger's first argument, that these conceptual abilities appear to be universal (and thus presumably innate), may have something to it. But note how strong the assumption and how unlikely it is to hold in the strongest form. The assumption is that all people, no matter what their culture, will interpret situations, independently of the linguistic input, in exactly the same way (Schlesinger does allow for some learning of the ability). Now, it is one thing to take this assumption as a working hypothesis, an example of what may be innate, but it is quite another thing to say that this "universality" implies that these interpretive abilities are universal in a way in which linguistic universals cannot be. We know very little of the calculus of concepts and of how they differ from language to language. There is no science of concepts that is even roughly comparable to linguistics, even at the descriptive level. In fact, a major thread in anthropological thinking has been that different cultures interpret the same objective situation in different ways. We cannot claim that it is definitively given that, for example, the concept "agent" applies in exactly the same way to the same objective situation in different languages. Yet "agent" is an element of Schlesinger's I markers.

Contrast this situation with that of what it is about linguistic structure that Schlesinger doesn't want to assume is innate: phrase structure. It is difficult to conceive of a descriptively adequate grammar for any natural language that did not make reference to phrase or constituent structure. Almost all linguistic theories, despite differences on other points, make use of notions of constituent structure.[7] What makes it clear that no principles of constituent structure are given to the organism?

Schlesinger's hints at what the concepts in an I marker might look like seem to be wrong on empirical grounds. Thus "a 'concept' may be looked upon as a set of words differing from each other only in their syntactic markers, e.g., good (adjective), well (adverb), goodness (noun)" (p. 71). He proposes that the sentence *The swim tired John* may be produced by the realization rules because "swim (verb, transitive), swim (verb, intransitive), swim (noun)" is part of the appropriate I marker, and thus *swim* may be a noun (p. 71). Since *eat* is not a noun, we don't have the sentence *The eat tired John*. Elsewhere Schlesinger suggests that these "concepts" may be universal, and this fits in with his general position that the ability to construct I markers from situations is universal. But there is no reason to believe that the category of a "concept" is universal across languages. In some languages, *swim* may be a verb and not a noun, and in some languages *eat* may be a noun. (In English, *window* is not a verb, which shows that English has nouns that are not verbs.) Furthermore, any one language, say English, may change in this respect over time. Thus the assumption that the category of a "concept" is universal is wrong.

By assuming that the category set of a concept is universal, Schlesinger is incorporating much syntactic, constituent structure information into his assumed universal innate cognitive capacity. Once again, one cannot give a methodological argument against assuming any particular kind of innate ability. We must simply use all the evidence at our command to discover what are the innate cognitive capacities that allow for language learning.

Consider another example. Schlesinger discusses why children produce utterances that are ungrammatical in the adult language, such as *more wet*. His model assumes that children know (from their I marker) that *more wet* is a "modifier + head" construction. "Gradually, the child comes to learn that in the *modifier + head* construction the head is a noun, and thus he avoids such mistakes. Eventually the more complicated rules of adult language are acquired" (p. 80). He goes on (pp. 80–81),

How are these category rules learned? A category rule is based on word classes: given a certain relation, only words of such and such a class may appear in the given position. Word classes are perhaps learned as acquired stimulus and response equivalences, in the manner described by Jenkins and Palermo (1964), Jenkins (1965), and Palermo in this volume. After word classes have been formed, a category rule may operate alongside the position rule, e.g.

modifier + *head*

adjective   noun

Notice the vague specification of how learning is to take place: "After word classes have been formed, a category rule may operate alongside the position rule." But we aren't told how these rules are formed by the child. There is no dynamic theory of change, no sketch of rule construction. In short, although this paper is an argument for "learning theory," there is no learning theory.

Not only does Schlesinger not explain how these "rules" can be learned, he produces no evidence that he has a correct account of the child's utterances. As he points out in another part of the paper, there are other modifier + head constructions in addition to adjective + noun (adverb + adjective, for example). Therefore, it cannot be (as presumably Schlesinger would have it) that the reason the child comes to know that *more wet* is a "mistake" is that in the modifier + head construction "the head is a noun." But there is an alternative. Rather than not knowing which grammatical classes may occur in which position, the child may not know which grammatical class a word belongs to. Perhaps *wet* is a noun for the child who said *more wet* (perhaps it is an adjective too; this does not matter). Perhaps Schlesinger cannot consider this possibility because he has assumed that *wet* is universally not a noun and that this information is given to the child innately.

Once again, it is important to have working hypotheses. However, we should try to keep two important aspects of methodology before us at all times. First, we must attempt to formulate precise and testable theories. Second, we must not assume that we have any special a priori insight into what kinds of principles underlie the workings of the human mind. Schlesinger's proposals do not explicate adult or child linguistic abilities in a way that fits with the empirical facts. No learning theory is given for the hypothesized abilities. And there is no reason to believe that even these (incorrectly specified) abilities are learnable by the kind of learning mechanism that Schlesinger hints at.

6.3 A Functional View

It is sometimes suggested that language acquisition should be explained in "functional" terms, though it can be difficult to understand what this means. Various proposals differ, to the extent that they are understandable. Most of these proposals offer little of explanatory value, especially with regard to the problem of language acquisition.

To consider one example of such explanation, E. Clark (1973) is concerned with the function of language. By *function* she means "the pragmatic and semantic reasons for a child's choice of one syntactic form over another in a particular situation." Grammatical theory, of course, does not attempt to predict what sentence will be uttered in a particular situation. If we are ever to have a satisfactory account of utterances, in this sense, much of the explanation will have to come from factors external to grammatical theory. Thus as part of performance theory it is reasonable to study extralinguistic reasons for "choice of utterance."

But Clark's claim is much broader. It is difficult to find an explicit statement of the general approach, but a number of statements in the paper make it clear that Clark is claiming that children acquire particular syntactic structures only when they have a "need" for them. It is important to realize that this statement is different from saying that children (or adults) "use" particular syntactic structures only when they have a need for them, a statement that is either false or tautologically true, depending on the interpretation of *need*. If *need* is defined, as it sometimes is, as some set of "motivators" such as food, then it is clear that in general no particular syntactic form is necessary to communicate these needs. On the other hand, if *need* is taken in its most general form, so that doing something is proof that there was a need for doing it, then the statement is trivially true and is without scientific interest.

Clark is concerned with sentences with coordinating conjunctions, sentences with subordinate clauses coming after the main clause, and sentences with subordinate clauses coming before the main clause. She writes,

In children, though, we have functional reasons for differentiating all three description types, for we must answer the question, Why does a particular form develop at all? In the child, as in the adult, *He ate and he left* is simplest . . . With this perfectly adequate way of describing two events, why should the child develop either of the other two forms? The first reason is that he comes to recognize what theme is and finds occasion to talk about the second event, rather than the first. He needs an alternative order of mention, one that is not chronological. So he acquires the use of *He left after he ate,* for that allows him to speak of the second event as theme. In using this form, however, he learns that it also implies a contingency relation. Later, when he wants to imply contingency while still speaking of events in their chronological order, he acquires the third description type, *After he ate, he left.* Thus, for functional reasons, the child develops *He ate and he left* first, *He left after he ate* second, and *After he ate, he left* last. This, in brief, is the argument for the hypotheses I have presented. (p. 593)

The underlying question, then, is Why does a particular form develop at all? It has been pointed out before that this is rather like asking, Why does a child learn to walk? Crawling is a "perfectly adequate" way of getting between two points in a room. With respect to walking, of course, the question that we ask is, How does a child learn to walk? What is the underlying biological basis of this achievement? The corresponding question for language might be, How does a particular form develop? What is the underlying biological basis of this achievement? To take another example, we could ask, Why does the heart develop? We could answer, Because blood has to be circulated in the body. But this still does not answer the embryological question, How does the heart develop? If Clark's method were extended to the development of the heart, we would have to ask, as each new part of the heart develops in the embryo, Why did this particular structure develop at all?

Clark does specify some aspects of "need," for example the need to express a theme. An underlying though unexpressed assumption seems to be that needs develop first, and then syntactic forms are developed to meet these needs. But the theory, as given, is wrong.

The question that now arises, is why, in that case, is there a sentence-type with the subordinate clause preposed? Isn't this a redundant structure given the presence of the coordinate clause construction where the theme is also the first event? Compare "He opened the door and came in" and "After he opened the door, he came in." The coordinate sentence is less specific in describing the relation between the two events, whereas the subordinate clause (*after*) is very specific and contrasts with *when, as, since, while,* and so on. The contingency relation of *when, since, after,* and so on cannot be expressed by a coordinate clause construction . . . The child does not need to develop the construction with a subordinate clause first until he wishes to describe more specific temporal relations than the one indicated by *and* or *and then*. (Clark 1973, 594)

Independently of the adequacy of Clark's account of the semantics and pragmatics of conjunctions, her explanation of why the preposed subordinate clause develops cannot be right. For there is another conjunction in English, *before,* just as specific as *after,* which will allow the contingency relation to be expressed, the first event to be theme, and the order of events to be the same as the order of mention. This is true of *He opened the door before he came in.* On Clark's account, it follows that there is no "reason" for preposed subordinate clauses, and therefore they will not exist, contrary to fact. Possibly Clark would argue that the *before* sentence could not develop because *before* cannot develop; she writes, "Conjunctions like *before* are uncommon in English" (p. 591). No evidence is given for this observation. Since adult speakers of English have developed the ability to use *before,* one wonders what the "need" would be that would cause the development of sentences with *before.*

The point is that insight into how language is acquired is not very likely to be gained by asking what the "need" is that causes development of each form. It is more reasonable, and more in keeping with the practice of developmental theorists in, say, biology, to ask how a form develops. Our point of view is that a child (at birth, or maturationally), is set to develop language, and he does this according to a biological program. One may ask, from an evolutionary point of view, why a particular form has developed in a language, and there may eventually be reasonable answers on this evolutionary level. But, biologically, we can assume that the child has capacities to acquire the adult language, and he does this, just as he learns to walk.

Functional considerations may play some role in explaining why certain forms develop at certain times, but as of yet we see no evidence that this occurs, or how it occurs. What is important is that if such considerations are to be studied, an articulated theory and description of data must be presented. Even if functional considerations play a role, they do not explain in any way *how* language is learned, how the child creates his grammar. Rather, they give only motivations for such creation. The central mystery of *how* remains untouched. Even Clark's (incorrect) "functional" account assumed a syntactic transformational analysis (preposing of subordinate clauses). Clark is careful not to claim that functional considerations can replace grammatical considerations.

6.4 Strategies

The notion of strategy has been suggested as crucial to the study of language acquisition. It is important to understand what is meant by *strategy*. In one proposal, Fodor, Bever, and Garrett (1974, 495) write, "It is obvious that a transformational grammar cannot be the *only* output of the child's language-acquisition mechanisms; computational procedures for effecting the production and comprehension of sentences must also be developed. In particular, the growth of child language appears to be, at least in part, explicable as a developing mastery of sentence processing heuristics." So much is unexceptionable and is tantamount to the statement that besides developing a competence theory, we must eventually state a performance theory and explain how the performance system is acquired. In this sense, *heuristics* presumably means something like "sentence processing procedure." But such a statement leaves us in the same position as before. A theory of adult performance must be stated, and a precise theory must be developed of how this adult performance is acquired by the child.

Fodor, Bever, and Garrett go on to suggest that "the child's linguistic maturity may be indexed in part by the extent of his mastery of heuristic procedures for relating specific surface features of sentences to properties of their deep organization" (p. 495). They offer evidence that children's heuristic procedures are different from adults' procedures. For example, they claim that 3½-year-old children tend to identify the first NP in a sentence with the "actor." Such a child will tend to incorrectly interpret a sentence like *The horse is kissed by the cow*.

First, there is a problem in interpreting the experimental results. It might be, not that these children have a certain (wrong) "sentence processing strategy," but rather that they cannot syntactically understand certain sentences at all. They might then have a "strategy" for responding in these experiments to sentences that they cannot syntactically understand. Whether these experimental results are relevant to linguistic competence at all is questionable. The interpretation of the results that we have given is supported by Fodor, Bever, and Garrett's data concerning nonsense V-N-N and N-N-V sequences. Even here, with nonsentences, children of about 3½ interpret the first N as the actor (according to the authors). Thus there is no reason to think that the experimental results reflect processing strategies for sentences. Rather, it seems most reasonable to conclude that when the child does not understand the sentence, he resorts to some "strategy." A glance at the data on page 500 of Fodor, Bever, and Garrett 1974 will show that this strategy is far from unanimous, even at the age where it occurs most frequently. (Individual data are not reported.)

Second, and more important, even if these procedures are adequate representations of children's performance procedures at this age, we still do not know how the adult procedures are learned. Adults understand passive sentences correctly. What allows a child to pass from incorrect to correct procedures? Talk of "heuristic procedures" as opposed to "rules" in no way helps to solve the problem of language acquisition.[8] We still need a precise and constructive theory of how the adult system is acquired. Since we have no adult performance theory that is reasonably general and precise, it is difficult to see how we can construct a theory of the acquisition of this performance.

Fodor, Bever, and Garrett (p. 502) write, "There exist no satisfactory models of a language-acquisition device capable of inducing a grammar from a corpus, and there is very little unequivocal evidence that such an induction does, in fact, take place. On the other hand, it seems clear that some of the child's developing linguistic capacity is organized into perceptual heuristics for projecting structural analyses, and that these heuristics have specifiable ontogenetic careers." In this book we present a model for inducing (the transformational component of) a grammar from a corpus. In some respects the model is satisfactory, in others not. It is satisfactory in that it can learn a particular version of transformational grammar. On the other hand, no model exists that can learn a performance system—which is not surprising, since no performance system is well-enough specified.

Fodor, Bever, and Garrett object to a theory of language acquisition that assumes that the ultimate output of the device is a transformational grammar. Their objection has three parts. First, they object that no devices capable of "inducing" a grammar exist. This objection has (in part) been vitiated by the results in this book, since we do produce devices capable of the induction, for a significant part of the problem. Of course, there might be empirical and theoretical objections to parts of the theory we present. But it is surely no objection to the possible correctness of a theory that solves some difficult problems that it is not unexceptionable in the form developed to date. In particular, the state of the development of the theory is clearly far superior to that of any theory based on heuristics, so any such objection would have to count far more heavily against a heuristics theory.

Fodor, Bever, and Garrett's second objection is that "there is very little unequivocal evidence that such an induction [of a transformational grammar] does, in fact, take place." The kind of evidence that they demand here is ontogenetic evidence. To us, the fact that transformational grammar is the best theory for an adult's linguistic competence is enough to insure that the output of a language acquisition device should include (among other concepts) a transformational grammar. But FBG deny the "psychological reality" of some aspects of transformational grammar (especially transformations). It would take too much space to discuss their objections to the psychological reality of transformations in detail here. In our opinion, these objections are based on an arbitrary notion of psychological reality—namely, a concept is "psychologically real" if it plays a particular kind of role in a particular kind of experimental procedure (or perhaps psychological process like remembering). There is no reason to choose this arbitrary notion of psychological reality.

Nevertheless, let us consider the ontogenetic evidence that FBG would hold against the notion that a transformational grammar is part of the output of a device that learns natural language. They list three predictions that such a transformational theory makes (p. 484). The first prediction is that "structures that are introduced in the adult grammar by a single rule, or by a number of interrelated rules, are mastered more or less simultaneously by the child." They point out that there are very little data concerning this claim. The one detailed longitudinal study that is relevant is by Bellugi (1967) and Klima and Bellugi (1966). Bellugi (1967) concludes that "much of the apparatus comes in a relatively short period of time and appears in a variety of structures" (quoted in FBG, 485). FBG merely add that the data are not "unequivocal." The general verdict then: not much data, but what exists is compatible with the theory that transformational grammar is developed.

The second ontogenetic prediction that FBG derive from transformational language acquisition theory is that "the productions of the child ought themselves to permit a natural representation by a transformational grammar." When FBG look at the data relevant to this claim, once again they cannot show that the claim is wrong. Rather they can only attempt to show that other interpretations are possible and that the data are not "decisive" (p. 490).[9] But independent of the data, we see no reason why the prediction should be made. If by "productions" they mean something like utterances, there is no reason that a transformational grammar should provide a "natural representation." A grammar, according to linguistic theory, is not a grammar for a corpus. There may be all sorts of reasons why children's utterances, even if related to a child's transformational grammar, are not naturally representable by such a grammar. There may be performance factors (such as memory), for example. Thus, we deny the validity of the second prediction.

The third prediction is based on the derivational theory of complexity. "If what the child is learning is a grammar, then the grammatical complexity of a structure, as measured by the number of rules required for its derivation, should be a predictor of the ontogenetic stage at which the structure is mastered, with grammatically simpler structures becoming available to the child earlier than grammatically complicated ones.'' On this question again FBG find that the data are compatible with other views. They also give some empirical evidence against the prediction. But predictions here are difficult to make because the measure of complexity depends on the particular model of grammar. Many of their data can be disputed on the grounds that the underlying grammatical analyses may not be correct. Again, independent of the data, we do not see that this third prediction follows from the theory that transformational grammar is one of the outputs of the language acquisition device. There may be all sorts of reasons why the derivational theory of complexity does not hold. For example, performance and pragmatic factors might have to be taken into account in the prediction of order of acquisition of structures.

Fodor, Bever, and Garrett's third objection to the theory that transformations develop is that ''perceptual heuristics'' develop. But this is in no way incompatible with the view that transformations develop; in fact, a performance component is part of the usual framework. In the beginning of this section we argued, on empirical grounds, against the particular sketch of one simple ''strategy'' (interpret first N as ''actor'') proposed by FBG. But there is no reason to believe that we will never be able to come up with a more adequate performance theory.[10] The basic point is that the very existence of these performance factors makes it difficult (but not necessarily impossible) to make predictions about ontogenesis (of the kind that FBG make). The situation is commonplace in science. When atoms were first proposed, a natural prediction would have been that if they exist, we should be able to see them; otherwise we shouldn't believe in their existence. Limitations in our eyes make it impossible for us to see atoms. Does this prove that they aren't real?

6.5 Other Considerations

There have been suggestions of other ways to state a basis for the theory of language acquisition. Many scholars claim that ''cognitive'' or ''semantic'' considerations are sufficient for language learning.[11] Some versions of these proposals allow no role at all for syntax. In other versions, syntactic phenomena are derived from cognitive or semantic considerations.

We do not have space to consider all these proposals. Basically, they all suffer from lack of explicitness. There is in general no way to even begin to see how to construct a theory of adult abilities along these lines. Nor is there more than the faintest hint of a precise specification of how a learning theory capable of learning adult systems could be created. In our opinion, when empirical considerations are taken into account and set ideas are not allowed to color evaluation of theories, there is no reason at all to accept any of these alternative accounts. Of course, the theory presented in this book does not account for many important topics, the "learning" of semantics, for instance. To the extent that progress is made in creating an adequate semantic theory, we can expect that it will be possible to study learnability properties of semantics.

CHAPTER 7

FURTHER
ISSUES

This chapter is concerned with a variety of topics. Section 1 contains a brief survey of several of the assumptions made for purposes of the proof in chapter 4 and considers possible interactions between the learnability constraints and empirically motivated conditions on the grammars of natural languages. Section 2 addresses itself to the question of the role of semantics in a theory of language learnability. The discussion is largely theoretical; pursuit of the empirical issues noted there would lead us far beyond the bounds of the current investigation. Finally, in section 3 we point out a number of open problems in language learnability and speculate about the directions in which solutions to these problems might lie.

7.1 Linguistic Interactions

7.1.1 Other Assumptions
In chapter 5 we examined in considerable detail the empirical evidence bearing on the Freezing principle, the Binary principle, and the Raising principle. Here we will take note of a number of further assumptions that play a role in the proof in chapter 4:[1]

Nonuniqueness of lexical items (section 4.1.4): Every lexical category rewrites as at least two lexical items.

Principle of S-*Optionality* (section 4.1.8): S appears on the right-hand side of a rule in the base grammar only within parentheses denoting optionality, that is, as (S).

Principle of S-*Invisibility* (section 4.1.9): For any transformational component A, in all transformational derivations replace A by the S-invisible amplified transformational component A^S. (That is, by convention, if the grammar contains a transformation in which S is not part of the structural description, the grammar will contain another transformation that is identical except that S has been added to the structural description between all constants.)

Principle of No Bottom Context (NBC) (section 4.1.11): If T is an S-essential transformation, then it may apply only if T is a no-bottom-context raising or deletion transformation. (That is, the raising or deletion of a constituent in a lower cyclic domain, when triggered by a constituent in a higher cyclic domain, may not depend on the context in the lower domain.)

Principle of the Transparency of Untransformable Base Structures (TUBS) (section 4.1.12): Let *P* be a partially derived 0-degree base phrase-marker. If no transformations in an adult transformational component A apply to *P* (that is, none of the S.D.'s fit *P*), then there exists a 0-extension of *P* to a fully derived base p-m *P'* such that *P'* is untransformable by A.

Principle of Adjacency (section 4.1.13): If *H* and *I* are both nodes in a p-m *P*, and if *I* is right-adjacent to *H*, and if *H* and *I* are each explicitly raised by a raising transformation, then if it ever happens again (after the raising transformations have applied) in the derivation of *P* that *I* is right-adjacent to *H*, the derivation is filtered out. (Similarly for left-adjacency.) (Replaced by USET.)

Principle of Uniqueness of S-*Essential Transformations* (USET) (section 4.1.13): At most one S-essential transformation may apply on each cycle. (Replaces Principle of Adjacency.)

Principle of Ordering of S-*Essential Transformations* (section 4.1.13):

At a cycle, the S-essential transformations apply before the non-S-essential transformations.

Principle of Repulsion (section 4.3.3.1): Let P be a base phrase-marker and let A be a transformational component. Suppose that at level i, A S-essentially applies to the node B. Suppose either
i. At level i, a node dominating S_{i-1} is deleted, or
ii. B is raised from S_{i-1} to S_i and either
(a) *B is a right segment of *$A(P_{i-1})$, and *$[A(P)]_{i-1}$*B is a substring of *$A(P_i)$, or
(b) *B is a left segment of *$A(P_{i-1})$, and *B*$[A(P)]_{i-1}$ is a substring of *$A(P_i)$.
Then P is filtered.

Principle of Designated Representatives (section 4.3.3.2):
i. Suppose that K immediately and exhaustively dominates L in a p-m. Suppose also that L is raised or S-essentially deleted. Then L leaves behind a *designated representative* d_L which depends on L. The designated representative d_L is considered to be part of the terminal string of lexical categories. For different categories $H \neq L$, $d_H \neq d_L$. For any lexical category H, $d_L \neq H$.
ii. If a designated representative is deleted, the p-m is filtered.

Assumption against String Preservation (ASP) (section 4.3.4.4): If, in a transformational derivation applied to a base p-m P, the terminal string at any one stage of the derivation is ever repeated at a later stage, P is filtered out.

Assumption of Heads (section 4.3.5.1): In any base rule $F \rightarrow F_1 F_2 \ldots$ F_n (F not a lexical category) exactly one of the F_i is designated as the *head* of F.

Assumption of Lexical Heads (section 4.3.5.1): If F_i is a lexical category and F_i is introduced in a rule $F \rightarrow F_1 \ldots F_i \ldots F_n$, then
i. F_j is not a lexical category for $i \neq j$, and
ii. F_i is the head of F.

Principle of Heads (PH) (section 4.3.5.1): If F^{i-1} is the head of F^i, then no transformation may have the effect of removing F^{i-1} from under F^i; in particular,

i. F^{i-1} may be deleted only if F^i is deleted by the same transformational application, and

ii. F^{i-1} may not be moved to a position such that it is not dominated by F^i.

Assumption that S is never the head of any category (section 4.3.5.1).

Let us now consider whether assumptions made on empirical grounds (in contrast to those made for the learnability proof) may be stronger than the formal assumptions, or may perhaps interact with them in more complex ways. We will restrict our discussion to the more clear-cut cases.

7.1.2 Nonuniqueness of Lexical Items

We consider first the assumption of Nonuniqueness of Lexical Items, or NULI. This assumption was adopted to permit proof of theorem 2, which we repeat:

Theorem 2: Let P be a base p-m of degree i. If two T components A and C are not order-equivalent on P, there exists a base p-m P' of degree i such that there is a detectable error on P'.

Intuitively, if the child's transformational component derives a surface structure different from the one the adult's component does, then the sentences corresponding to the two derivations will be different. The notion "surface structure" is understood here as the precise sequence of terminal categories, individually indexed. So, if lexical categories C and C' are the same and contain the same lexical items, the surface structure is different when we interchange them in a particular phrase-marker, even though the two structures would be identical otherwise. But the corresponding sentences, on which the notion "detectable error" is defined, would be identical in such a case.

It is of some interest to consider whether other constraints adopted in the proof will rule out the sorts of examples that motivate NULI, or whether we can find empirically motivated restrictions that will allow the proof of theorem 2 to go through. Consideration of the motivation for NULI (see the discussion in section 4.1.4) suggests that it might be possible to eliminate NULI in favor of the assumption against string preservation, or the assumptions concerning heads. However, we will see that NULI is independently necessary.

The assumption against string preservation is relevant here because the example that motivated NULI in chapter 4 involved simply permutation of a constituent A around another constituent A, violating ASP (which was motivated later in the chapter). However, it is possible to construct examples that do not violate ASP but which are counterexamples to theorem 2. What is crucial is that the two transformational components yield the same string but different surface order of underlying constituents. In constructing the examples in question, we could have stipulated that the permutation transformation simultaneously deleted some other constituent in the structure, thus avoiding this violation of ASP.

The examples constructed to motivate theorem 2 involved movement of lexical categories (but not lexical items). The assumption of Lexical Heads stipulates that any lexical category is the head of the phrase of which it is an immediate constituent. The principle of Heads rules out movement of lexical categories away from the phrases of which they are heads. It might be supposed, therefore, that these assumptions will allow us to do without NULI. However, other examples can be constructed which show the independence of NULI from the assumptions about heads.

The crucial aspect of the example that motivates NULI is that a given category can dominate a unique string of lexical items. In the simplest case, the category in question is a lexical category itself. But suppose that there were phrase structure rules $A \rightarrow BC$ and $C \rightarrow D$, and suppose B and D were distinct lexical categories, each containing only one lexical item. Then the constituent A would not be a lexical category itself, but it would dominate a unique string of lexical items.

Given the existence of lexical categories that contain unique elements, we can construct counterexamples to theorem 2 which do not involve explicit movement of lexical categories by transformations. It appears, therefore, that NULI cannot be eliminated. Of course, there is no reason to doubt the empirical validity of this assumption. If other assumptions could do the job of NULI, we would be admitting the possibility that a language could contain a lexical category that contained one lexical item.[2]

7.1.3 Principle of Adjacency and USET

The principle of Adjacency rules out explicit raising of adjacent constituents in such a way that they are adjacent in derived structure (and in their underlying order). USET, a stronger assumption, rules out the application of more than one S-essential transformation on any cycle. Raising transformations are, of course, S-essential.

We will suggest that certain assumptions about Comp will rule out violations of the principle of Adjacency when $\bar{S}$ alone is taken to be a binary cyclic node. However, recall that we are assuming that NP, as well as $\bar{S}$, is binary cyclic. On a strict interpretation of the notion of *degree*, any simple sentence containing an NP would be of degree zero, because it would contain only one $\bar{S}$. But if the notion of degree were to be modified to take into account the binary cyclicity of NP, such a sentence would be of degree 1. We have not explored the consequences for the learnability proof of such a change, but certainly at least some purely technical alternations would have to be made.

Suppose for the sake of discussion that NP is viewed as functioning as $\bar{S}$ does with respect to the learnability proof. To prove learnability from degree less than or equal to 2, we will then have to extend the principle of Adjacency or the NP counterpart of USET to NP's. Interestingly, there is clear counterevidence to both assumptions involving the extraposition of constituents from NP's.

Let us call the counterpart to USET for NP's UNPET, for Uniqueness of NP-essential Transformations. A counterexample to UNPET will arise if we can show that two constituents may be raised out of the same NP. The following examples suggest that this is the case:

(1)
a. $_{NP}$[a book $_{PP}$[by Fred] $_{PP}$[about amoebas]] has just appeared.
b. $_{NP}$[A report $_{PP}$[by Bill] $_{\bar{S}}$[that the world is flat]] has come to our attention.
c. $_{NP}$[A painting $_{PP}$[by Bill] $_{\bar{S}}$[that Mary owns]] is hanging on the wall.

(2)

a. A book has just appeared by Fred about amoebas.

b. A report has come to our attention by Bill that the world is flat.

c. A painting is hanging on the wall by Bill that Mary owns.

The examples in (2) show that both of the complements may be extraposed and are hence raised, violating the assumption of UNPET. These examples would also constitute violations of the principle of Adjacency if we could show that the order after extraposition was just the same as the order before extraposition. However, in the case of these particular examples, the underlying order of constituents is not fixed, so extraposition could yield the mirror image in the output structure of the underlying order. That is, (2a), for example, might not be derived from (1a), but from (3).

(3) A book about amoebas by Fred has just appeared.

Successive extraposition will yield just the right order in these cases.

   In order to test the principle of Adjacency we need a case in which the underlying order is fixed. If the surface order is the same, then we

(4)

have a violation of the principle, but if it is reversed, we do not. Unfortunately, we have not been able to find examples that are sufficiently clear to test the principle of Adjacency adequately.[3]

It is interesting to note, now, that substantive assumptions about the base component of English, along with the Binary principle and the Freezing principle, render it impossible to construct examples that will motivate the principle of Adjacency for NP's. In order to construct a counterexample, we would have to start with a structure like (4), which by assumption is degree 3. To construct the example, a constituent of NP_0 would have to be raised into NP_1, causing an error. Then adjacent

(5)

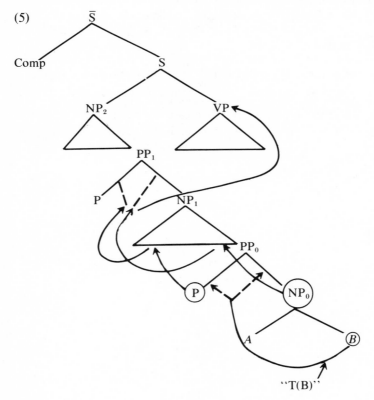

constituents of NP_1 would have to be raised into NP_2, concealing the error. The error would only show up on the raising of some constituent of NP_2 into the S, as (5) illustrates.[4] The error in (5) is caused by the adjunction of B to either P or NP. The sequence $P\,B\,NP_0$ is raised, first into NP_1 and then into PP_1. Finally, NP_0 is raised into VP.

Because of the structure of NP's in English, the construction of such an example appears to be impossible. To illustrate, suppose that the following are the rules that expand NP in the base.

(6)
a. NP $\rightarrow$ Det N PP
b. PP $\rightarrow$ P NP

To construct an example of the sort illustrated in (5) we must allow for the possibility of attaching some constituent B in structure-preserving fashion to the right of P or the left of NP. Otherwise the Freezing principle would block the derivation. Although there does not appear to be a rule of English that does this, suppose for the sake of illustration that there is one. Cycling on PP_0 in NP_1 gives us one of the following:

(7)

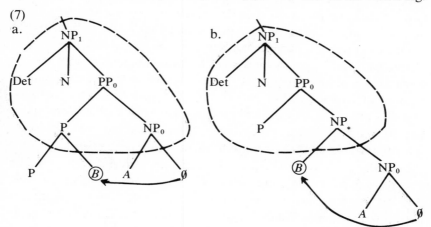

(Notice that the adjunction here is Chomsky-adjunction. For the reason, see note 4.)

To construct the example, we must now raise a constituent from PP_0 into NP_1. The scope of a transformation applying at NP_1 is shown by the dotted lines in (7). Only P_* and NP_0 may be raised in (7a), and only P and NP_* in (7b). But a look at (6) shows that neither P nor NP can be an immediate constituent of NP. Thus any such raising transformation will cause freezing at the level of NP_1. The structures in (8) give just one example, where P and NP are raised between Det and N.

(8)
a.   b.

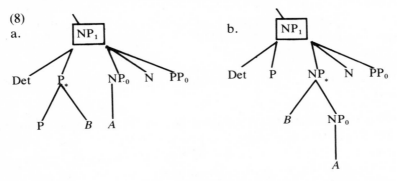

Although in principle derivations of the sort illustrated in (5) must be ruled out, we see that the structure of the base (for English, at least) may be sufficient in itself. And the Binary principle rules out derivations that skip over the intermediate stages that result in freezing. In order to show that we can do without the principle of Adjacency completely we would have to show that the base component rules out the construction of all examples of the sort shown in (5). In our opinion, such an approach would be very promising. More generally, combination of a precise theory of the base, together with such constraints as FP, BP, and RP should make many other constraints unnecessary, since the examples that give rise to them would not occur.

Consider the way in which we would go about trying to construct a counterexample to the principle of Adjacency, given sequences of $\bar{S}$'s. Assume that $\bar{S}$ dominates only S and Comp and that once a constituent has been moved into Comp, it can only be moved into a higher Comp.[5] Consider the structure in (9). The scope of transformations applying at VP_2 and S_2 is indicated by a broken line; that of transformations applying at $\bar{S}_2$ by a solid line. Suppose that the adjacent constituents that we wish to raise are NP_0 and PP. If the theory allows movement of two constituents into Comp, these two constituents could be moved into

(9)

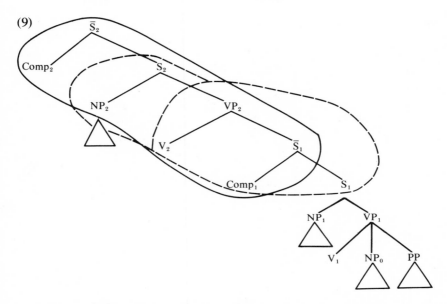

Comp$_1$ on the $\bar{S}_1$ cycle, yielding the structure in (10). Moving to the VP$_2$ cycle, we find that by assumption we cannot apply any transformations to the two constituents in Comp$_1$. The same is true at the S$_2$ cycle. At the $\bar{S}_2$ cycle we have access to Comp$_1$ by the Comp Accessibility convention of chapter 5. There are two possibilities, now. Either it is possible to move just one of the constituents of Comp$_1$ into Comp$_2$, or it is necessary to move all constituents of Comp$_1$ into Comp$_2$ if any are moved. (The latter might be accomplished by allowing only movement of Comp$_1$ itself.) If it is not possible to move just one constituent of Comp$_1$ into Comp$_2$, it will not be possible to violate the principle of Adjacency, given structures of the sort illustrated in (9).

If we wanted to do without the principle of Adjacency (or USET), we might assume either that at most one constituent may be moved into Comp on any cycle (assuming that movement into Comp is the only allowable raising from $\bar{S}$ to $\bar{S}$), or that Comp-to-Comp movement must apply to all constituents in Comp. Emonds (1976) independently argues for the position that what we have been speaking of as movements into Comp are in fact substitutions for Comp. From this it follows that only

(10)

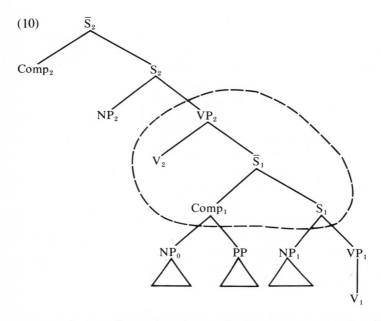

one such transformation is applicable on any cycle. However, Emonds's approach is ruled out for us by other constraints, such as the Binary principle and the Freezing principle. By the latter, movement into Comp would be non-structure-preserving, and hence would freeze $\bar{S}$. This would rule out, for example, successive cyclic Wh Fronting. The Binary principle would rule out nonsuccessive cyclic Wh Fronting, however.

Limited empirical evidence suggests that it is possible to move two constituents into Comp. Consider the following examples.

(11)
a. Yesterday what do you think John said?
b. What do you think (that) John said yesterday?
c. *What do you think (that) yesterday John said?
d. *Yesterday I wonder what John said.
e. *I wonder what yesterday John said.
f. *I wonder yesterday what John said.

Example (11a) shows that two constituents of the embedded $\bar{S}$ may be moved into the Comp of the higher $\bar{\bar{S}}$. In (11b) we see that just the *wh* phrase may be moved, and in (11c) we see that if the adverb is fronted in the lower $\bar{\bar{S}}$, it cannot be left behind when the *wh* phrase is moved into the higher $\bar{\bar{S}}$. These facts follow if what is raised in (11a) is a Comp that contains both *what* and *yesterday*.

This evidence is somewhat weakened, however, by the observation that a doubly filled Comp cannot appear in an embedded $\bar{\bar{S}}$, as illustrated by (11e,f). But it is possible that these last examples can be explained in a way that does not rule out the suggested analysis for (11a). For example, it could be that movement of a *wh* phrase into a Comp marked [+wh] freezes the structure so as to block later movement into that Comp, whereas movement of a *wh* phrase into a Comp marked [−wh] does not freeze the structure. This will allow us to explain the ungrammaticality of sentences like *What yesterday did John do?* For grammatical sentences like *Yesterday, what did John do?* we would require an analysis along the lines of Chomsky 1977, in which the adverb *yesterday* would be generated outside of Comp in a position designated Topic: $_{\bar{\bar{S}}}[\ _{\text{Top}}[yesterday] \ _{\bar{\bar{S}}}[\ _{\text{Comp}}[what] \ . . .]]$.

To the extent that empirical evidence can be found, it appears that all constituents in Comp must be raised into the higher Comp. This can be accomplished in a natural way in the current framework by adopting the convention that movement of a constituent into a Comp that is already filled is non-structure-preserving. The frozenness of the Comp will then allow raising of only the entire Comp, but none of its individual constituents; (12) illustrates.

It is suggested in section 5.5.2.4 that a nonbranching B-cyclic node might not count for the Binary principle. If this is the case, $\bar{\bar{S}}_0$ in the output structure in (12) will be analyzable with respect to transformations applying at $\bar{\bar{S}}_1$. This may explain why it is possible to extract the subject of an embedded $\bar{\bar{S}}$ if there is no complementizer; we can have *Who do you imagine ∅ will leave?* but not **Who do you imagine that ∅ will leave?* An analysis along these lines raises a number of complex problems that we cannot do justice to here. For some discussion of alternative analyses, see Bresnan 1977 and Chomsky and Lasnik 1977.

(12)

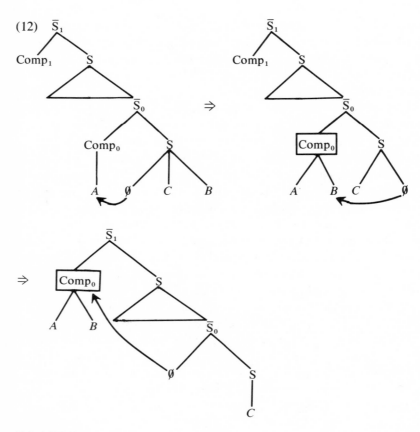

7.1.4 NBC

The principle of No Bottom Context makes an interesting distinction between subjects of complements and other constituents of complements (see note 9 of chapter 4). We will pursue in somewhat more detail a number of implications of this principle here.

Consider first the case in which we are dealing only with sequences of $\overline{S}$'s. The question is whether, given such a structure, an example can be constructed that motivates NBC.

On the face of it, it appears that such an example cannot be constructed. Suppose that we are cycling on $\overline{S}_1$. By the Comp Accessibility

(13)

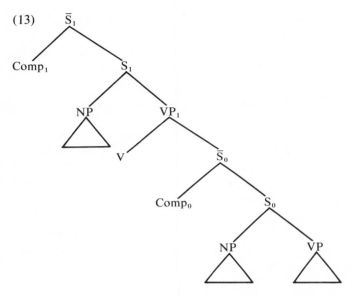

convention, we can have access to constituents of $Comp_0$. But if there are two (or more) constituents in $Comp_0$, it is frozen, so one constituent cannot serve as a context for movement of the other.

However, because movement from Comp can only be into another Comp, the Freezing principle is not necessary here. Even if a constituent of a lower Comp could serve as a context for a raising from $Comp_0$ into $Comp_1$, no detectable error of the desired sort could be constructed. In order to construct the example, we would have to raise a constituent from S_0 into S_1 in such a way that it blocked a transformation from applying to S_1, thus allowing an error-producing transformation to occur on some higher S_2, the error being detected on a still higher S_3. The discussion of NBC in chapter 4 gives details of how this counterexample would have to be formulated.

Because of the Binary principle, when we are applying transformations at $\bar{S}_1$ we cannot look into S_0; hence constituents in S_0 cannot serve as context for Comp-to-Comp movement.

Suppose that we are applying a transformation at VP_1 or S_1. By the Binary principle, we have access to $Comp_0$ or S_0. We cannot extract a constituent from $Comp_0$, however, for reasons just noted. Conceivably we could at this level apply to $Comp_0$ itself a transformation that had as its context S_0. Strictly speaking, this would constitute a violation of NBC. However, since Comp and S are always and only sisters in the base, mention of S in the structural description of such a transformation would be redundant. If any other constituent were to become a sister of Comp and S, freezing of $\overline{S}$ would result. Thus, NBC is not needed here.

Significantly, it is possible to construct examples of the sort that motivated NBC but that do not involve sequences of $\overline{S}$, only of S, that is, sequences of infinitive clauses. Strictly speaking, the definition of *degree* does not allow recursion through S or VP to contribute to the degree of a structure, but intuitively, at least, we would like to be able to show that detectable errors will show up on structures of limited complexity, regardless of the superficial marking assigned to the verb. The formal proof of chapter 4 does not deal with this problem, because there we simply assumed that all recursion involved S and did not assume the base rule $\overline{S} \rightarrow$ Comp S.

In extending the framework to take into account empirically motivated levels of structure, we might proceed in the following ways. On the one hand, we might assume that both $\overline{S}$ and S, as well as NP, were B-cyclic. This raises certain problems, which are discussed in Culicover and Wexler 1977. At the very least, it would entail a revision of the Binary principle.

On the other hand, we could assume that NBC applied not to just the B-cyclic nodes but to the recursive nodes. Although it is not clear how to provide a formal characterization of this notion, intuitively the recursive nodes for English are at least $\overline{S}$, NP, S, and perhaps VP, if the following rules are rules of the English base component.

(14)
a. VP $\rightarrow$ V S
b. VP $\rightarrow$ V VP

The S here is, of course, the infinitival S of sentences like *I want John to leave,* and the VP may correspond to the infinitive in sentences like *John managed to leave.*

The notion that NBC captures, in its extension to such nodes, is that when applying transformations at a recursive node, it is impossible to involve immediate constituents of that node *and* constituents of a more deeply embedded node of the same category if the contextual aspects of the latter govern the applicability of the transformation. An intriguing possibility is that this particular way of extending NBC to non-B-cyclic nodes is just what is needed to solve a problem raised by Culicover and Wexler (1977, note 54). There we observed that the non-B-cyclic recursive nodes allowed the construction of examples that in spirit prevented establishment of a bound on the degree of error for transformational components. Such examples could not be ruled out by the Binary principle. But quite possibly NBC will do the job, since it prevents transformations from being fit by constant terms on lower cycles, except for the target.

Interestingly, there is empirical evidence to suggest that NBC must in fact be extended to the non-B-cyclic recursive nodes, confirming our theoretical intuitions along these lines. Consider the structure in (15).

(15)

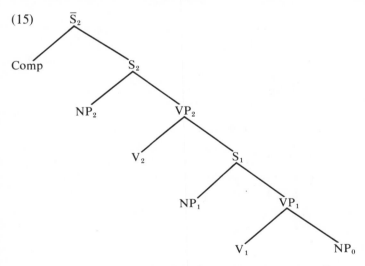

Notice that S_1 is not immediately dominated by an $\bar{S}$.

Consider next the following structural description:

(16) NP - X - V - NP - Y

    1 - 2 - 3 - 4 - 5

Without some constraint to the contrary, the structural description of (16) will be satisfied in two ways at the S_2 cycle. This is shown in (17). In both factorizations, NP_2 satisfies the first term of the structural

(17)
a.

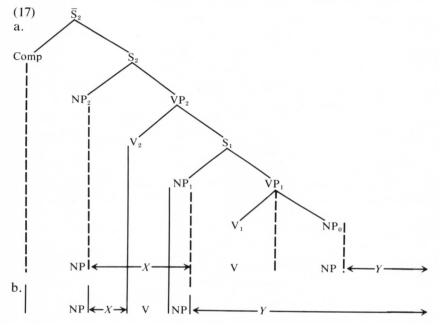

b.

description. In (a), V_1 satisfies the third term; in (b), V_2 does so. In (a), NP_0 satisfies the fourth term; in (b), NP_1 does. Informally, (17) embodies the claim that either the higher verb or the lower verb may govern the application of a transformation with a structural description of the form given in (16). To make the consequences more concrete, consider the following plausible formulation of the transformation NP Preposing, the transformation that moves the object into subject position in the derivation of passives:[6]

NP Preposing:
$\Delta - X - V - NP - Y$
$1 - 2 - 3 - 4 - 5 \Rightarrow 4 - 2 - be+en - 3 - \emptyset - 5$

Suppose that we have the deep (or possibly derived) structure (18).

(18) Δ believes $_S$[John to have seen Susan]

Applying NP Preposing as in factorization (b) of (17) gives the grammatical (19). (Here, *John* corresponds to NP$_1$.)

(19) John is believed to have seen Susan.

Applying factorization (a) gives the equally grammatical, but incorrect, (20).

(20) Susan believes John to have been seen.

In (20), *Susan* is no longer interpretable as the direct object of *see*, and *John* is no longer interpretable as the subject of *see*.

It is easy to see how NBC rules out factorizations such as (17a). V_1 is a bottom context and hence cannot be used to satisfy the structural description. On the other hand, V_2 is not a bottom context, so the transformation will apply only in terms of the latter. To the extent that the theory independently allows us to invoke NBC in cases such as (17)–(18), it appears to have correct empirical consequences.[7]

Along similar lines, consider Equi-NP Deletion applying between subjects. Suppose that the sentence in (21a) is derived from the sentence in (21b) by the following rule:

Equi-NP Deletion:
NP - X - V - NP - Y
1 - 2 - 3 - 4 - 5 $\Rightarrow$ 1 - 2 - 3 - $\emptyset$ - 5
Condition: 1 = 4.

(21)
a. Fred expects to leave.
b. Fred expects $_S$[Fred to leave].

Once again, NBC rules out ungrammatical (or otherwise incorrect) derivations by correctly discriminating between the NP immediately following the highest verb, and NP's immediately following verbs in the complement. For example, compare (21b) with (22).

(22) Mary believes Fred to like Mary.

If *like* satisfies the third term in the S.D. of Equi, we will derive *Mary believes Fred to like* ∅ by deleting the second instance of *Mary* under identity with the first. Since *like* allows Equi to apply normally, as in *Mary likes to play tennis,* we cannot rule out this derivation through the employment of a rule feature associated with the verb.

Another interesting case has to do with Tough Movement. In Culicover and Wexler 1977 we discussed the following version of this transformation.

Tough Movement (TM):
it - X - [+TM] - Y - V - Z - NP - W
1 - 2 -   3   - 4 - 5 - 6 - 7 - 8 ⇒ 7 - 2 - 3 - 4 - 5 - 6 - ∅ - 8

This formulation is extremely inelegant; there have been various proposals about how one or another term can be eliminated. Wilkins (1977) argues, for example, that only *it* and the NP term need be mentioned, since *it* can be subcategorized by the [+TM] element and other constraints on the analysis of variables will prevent application of the rule to the wrong NP. Crucially, TM cannot apply to the subject of the infinitive, nor to the object of the *for*-phrase in the higher clause.

(23)
a. It is nice for the rich to do the work.
b. The work is nice for the rich to do ∅.
c. *The rich is(are) nice for ∅ to do the work.

(24)
a. It is nice for the rich for the poor to do the work.
b. *The work is nice for the rich for the poor to do ∅.
c. *The rich is(are) nice for ∅ for the poor to do the work.

For a discussion of why (24b) is ungrammatical, see our discussion of the Binary principle in chapter 5.

The generalization about TM that has to be captured is that it moves only postverbal NP's of the infinitive clause. This is why term 5 is mentioned in our statement of the rule. But notice that this is a bottom context under the extended version of NBC (25), so this particular formulation of the rule would be ruled out by our assumptions. It seems, therefore, that if NBC is correct, it will be necessary to adopt some constraint (such as that proposed by Wilkins) to block access to the

(25)

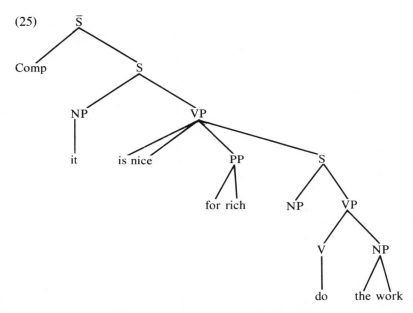

preverbal NP's. Of course, this is just what is desired anyway, in order to rule out on theoretical grounds such complex statements as the structural description of TM given here.[8]

Finally, given certain empirical assumptions of chapter 5, where $\bar{S}$ and NP are the B-cyclic nodes, the Binary principle will prevent access by transformations to lower B-cyclic domains, rendering NBC dispensable for these cases.[9] We have already seen this in the case of $\bar{S}$; for NP, if we adopt the counting version (CV) of the Binary principle, constituents of a lower NP cannot be seen from a higher NP.

(26)

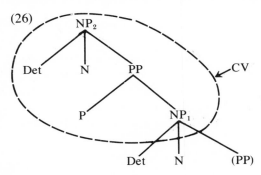

On the other hand, if the domination version (DV) is adopted, the lower context will be accessible, and it appears therefore that in such a circumstance NBC would be required. Surprisingly, CV was the ver-

(27)

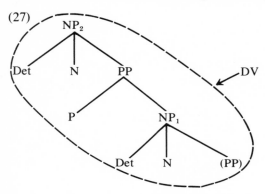

sion that we tentatively settled on in our discussion of the Binary principle in chapter 5. Notice that if we adopt CV, we can restrict NBC to just the non-B-cyclic recursive nodes. We can define this class of nodes easily enough as the class of nodes that yield recursion without going through any B-cyclic nodes. Because of the Binary principle, stating NBC in terms of just this class of nodes allows us to cover all the cases for which NBC was originally conceived. It is interesting to note that the Binary principle (or rather, the counting version) here allows us to state the domain of NBC in a general way; if we had to apply NBC to $\bar{S}$ and NP, we would be faced with a much more difficult task in terms of finding an appropriate general characterization of the scope of NBC.

7.1.5 Raising Principle

In section 7.1.3 we pointed out that possibly the base component of English, through interactions with the Binary principle and the Freezing principle, renders the principle of Adjacency and USET unnecessary. Similar observations can be made concerning the Raising principle. But, if we do not assume the Raising principle, we must seek other explanations for the phenomena noted in section 5.4 in support of this principle.

7.1.5.1 Function of the Base in Raising The Raising principle freezes a raised constituent, where raising is defined in terms of B-cyclic domains. To recapitulate briefly, the reason for adopting this principle is to block the following situation: an error is produced on the S_1 (not $\bar{S}_1$) cycle through a raising transformation operating on a constituent of S_0. The error is raised from S_1 into S_2 by a transformation that raises some constituent that dominates the constituent containing the error. Another transformation applies to reveal the error by raising it from S_2 to S_3. A derivation with these properties is illustrated in (28). Originally, K was a sister of L in S_0. It is incorrectly attached to E instead of

(28)

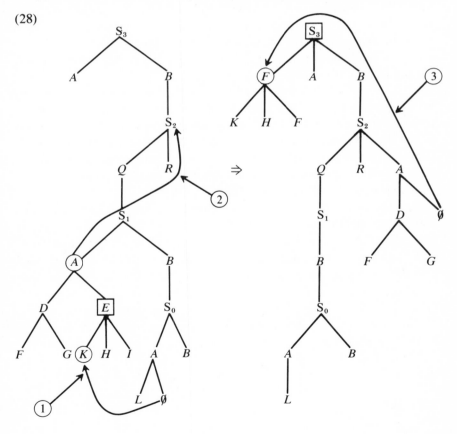

to D in S_1. Then A is raised to the right of R in S_2, and E is raised to the left of A in S_3.

To construct examples such as these, it is clearly necessary to raise constituents successively (although perhaps indirectly) over a phrase-marker of degree 3. It is important and intriguing to consider whether it is possible to construct derivations of this sort given the actual (theoretically specified) base component of English and the other constraints on grammars such as the Binary principle and the Freezing principle that we have adopted.

There are two cases: (i) raising from $\bar{S}$ to $\bar{S}$, and (ii) raising from NP to $\bar{S}$ or NP. As we saw in the case of the principle of Adjacency and USET, the base component of English tends to limit considerably the range of examples that can be constructed. However, since the two types of problems are quite different, we must consider the examples for the Raising principle independently.

First, consider the case in which the degree-3 phrase-marker on which we are trying to create a detectable error does not crucially involve NP cycles. Such a phrase-marker is shown in (29). Notice that it contains no structures of the form $_{NP}[X \, \bar{S} \, Y]$. Because of the Binary principle the $\bar{S}$'s in such structures would not be analyzable; hence they could not participate in the construction of raising examples of the sort that motivate the Raising principle.

Next, note that in (29), as in previous examples, the Binary principle blocks raising directly from $\bar{S}_0$ into VP or S_1. The only way that a constituent of $\bar{S}_0$ may become a constituent of $\bar{S}_1$ is by movement first into $Comp_0$ and then into $Comp_1$. To construct an example based on (29) that possesses the essential features of (28), the rule moving the constituent in question from $Comp_0$ to $Comp_1$ must create an error in $Comp_1$. But we can show there can be no detectable error formed in Comp, given certain assumptions. First, suppose that $Comp_1$ is empty before raising. When raising occurs, attachment is straightforward. Second, suppose that some other constituent has already been moved into (or generated in) $Comp_1$. Then the only kind of imaginable error is between attachment to Comp and attachment to this constituent.

To illustrate, suppose that $Comp_1$ contains a constituent Q, and suppose that both daughter- and Chomsky-adjunction are allowed by the

(29)

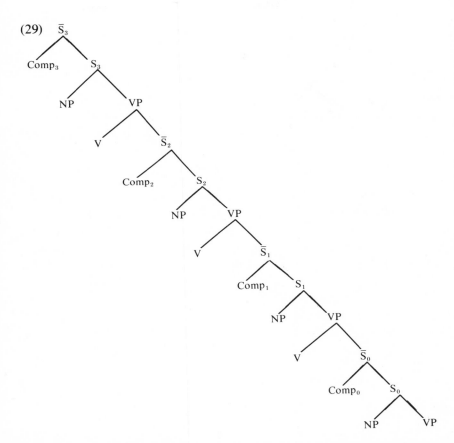

theory.[10] This will result in the following two possibilities, assuming that the constituent raised is NP. We have independently found it necessary to adopt the convention that Comp is frozen if it immediately dominates two constituents. Thus the structure in (30a) will be frozen and this error will be hidden, given that (30b) is the correct structure. If (30b) is correct, however, there is still no error, because Q_* can never be analyzed on a higher cycle. To see this, consider the structure in (31). If $Q \rightarrow NP\ Q$ is not a rule of the base then of course Q_* is frozen.

(30)

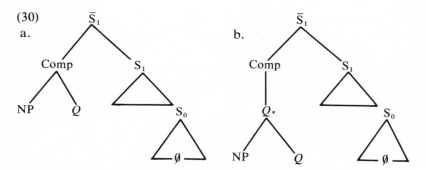

Suppose that Q_* is not frozen. Since no constituent of Comp can be moved anywhere but into a higher Comp, Q_* cannot be moved into S_2. By the Comp Accessibility convention, the node immediately dominated by $Comp_1$ can be moved into the higher $Comp_2$. But NP and Q cannot be moved separately into $Comp_2$. Other things being equal, both of the intermediate structures in (30) will give derivations in which it appears that the entire $Comp_1$ has been moved up into $Comp_2$.

(31)

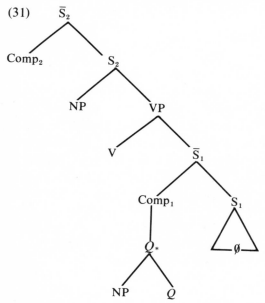

If this were all that the theory allowed, we could say that we had failed to create a detectable error. However, suppose for the moment that movement of Comp results in pruning of the $\bar{S}$ that dominated it. This opens up the possibility that transformations will apply if NP Q is raised by raising Comp in the structure (30a), but this is avoided in (30b) if only Q_* is raised.

Assuming that all transformations are obligatory, the raising of Q_* will block some transformation that would apply if $Comp_1$ were raised. This would create a detectable error, but on a degree-2 p-m.

To try to create a detectable error on degree 3, we must disallow the possibility that raising of only Q_* blocks a transformation and thus produces an error. Suppose, therefore, that raising of Comp does not cause pruning. If (30a) is correct, raising of NP Q into $Comp_2$ will give (32a) whereas raising of NP Q in the case of (30b) will give either (32b.i) or (32b.ii). Both of the structures in (32b) are the same, as far as higher cycles are concerned, because of the Binary principle. The structure in (32a) is frozen (since Comp dominates two constituents). Since it cannot be analyzed, it will not create an error in higher cycles.

Concentrating on (32b), then, we see that no matter how high either $Comp_1$ or Q_* is raised, as long as the raising of Q_* cannot be distinguished from the raising of Comp, there will be no detectable error on degree greater than 2. If the two raisings can be distinguished, there will be a detectable error, but it is detectable the first time that the raising occurs, on degree 2. If we cannot create a detectable error, there is no reason to adopt the Raising principle for this case.

Consider now the situation in which raising involves NP crucially. The difference between such a case and that just considered is that it is possible to raise constituents from NP to NP and from NP to S without involving Comp. Suppose, for example, that we have the structure in (33). To construct a suitable example we must raise a constituent from NP_0 into NP_1, causing an error to occur. Suppose for the sake of argument that PP_0 is raised into NP_1 by attachment between P and NP_0, as in (34). Assume that the adjunction is Chomsky-adjunction.[11] This raising does not have to be structure-preserving, and let us suppose that it is not. Note that raising cannot take place directly into NP_1 from NP_0 because of the Binary principle.

(32)
a.

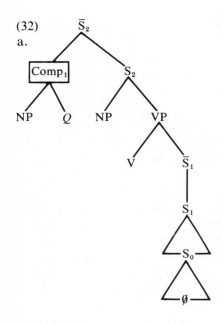

b. (i)

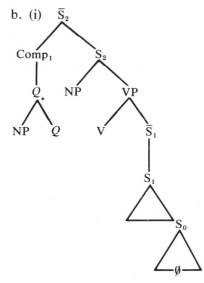

(ii)

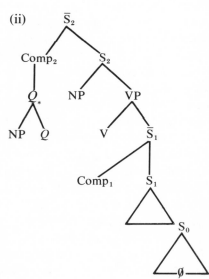

(33)

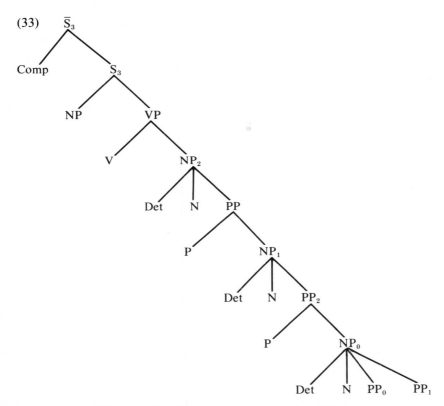

To continue constructing the example, on the next cycle the node dominating NP_* must be raised into NP_2. Suppose once again that there is an appropriate rule, this time one that moves PP_2 to the right of PP_3. This rule must apply at PP_3, however, because of the Binary principle. It cannot apply on NP_2. The resulting structure, as shown in (35), is frozen.

In order to get a detectable error on degree 3 we would have to raise NP_* into S_3. In principle this could be accomplished by extraposing PP_2 or PP_3 into S_3. As the structure in (35) shows, however, this will not make the error detectable, owing to the Freezing principle. It is important to recognize that the particular structures assumed are crucial: The Binary principle counts B-cyclic nodes to prevent the derivation

(34)

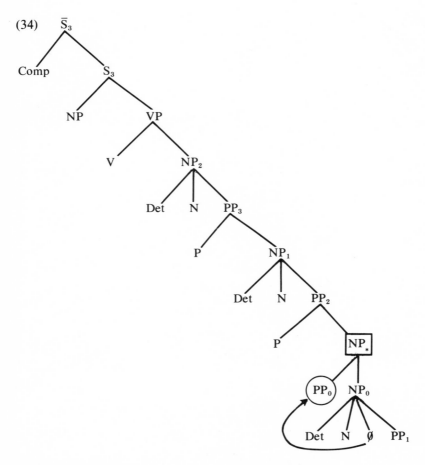

of intermediate structures that are analyzable on later cycles; the Freez-ing principle operates on derived structure, comparing it against possi-ble base structures to prevent detection of the error.

To summarize, it appears that given certain assumptions about Comp and the English base component we might not be able to con-struct examples that will lead us to assume the Raising principle. This is a topic that deserves further investigation.

7.1.5.2 A Parsing Strategy Suppose that we could find no learnability reasons to motivate the Raising principle. We would still be faced

(35)

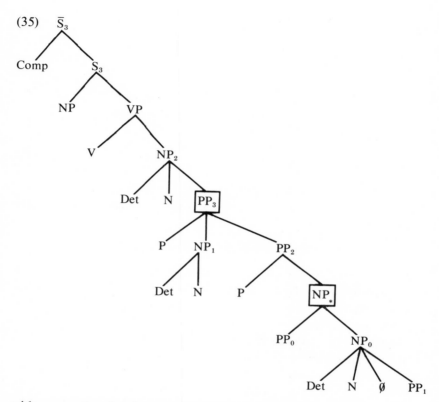

with accounting for the empirical motivation given for this principle in section 5.4. It might be that the Raising principle is correct, but for other considerations than learnability. In a sense this is what we will suggest here, but with sufficient qualifications that the ultimate proposal is likely to bear little resemblance to the original Raising principle.

Let us review briefly the empirical evidence for the Raising principle. Essentially it is of one type: a constituent extraposed from a noun phrase into S cannot be analyzed. We illustrate with (36), where A is a variable ranging over extraposable constituents, and X is a variable of the usual sort. For details of the evidence, see section 5.4.1. We will provide a few illustrative examples here in the course of the discussion.

In section 5.4.2 we took up the issue of Extraposition of Sentential

(36)

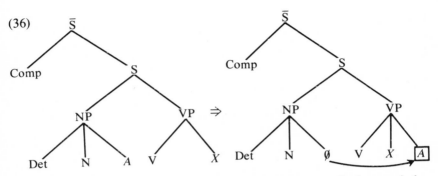

Subject, or Extrap. We noted that, contrary to the prediction made by the Raising principle, Extrap does not result in freezing of the extraposed sentential subject.

(37) Who is it obvious ₅[that Mary dislikes]?

It appears, therefore, that we can resolve a potentially serious problem if we dispense with the Raising principle. Of course, it may be that there is no rule of Extrap, as we discussed in 5.4.1. But if it should turn out that the preferred analysis did adopt this rule, it would not be reasonable to insist on the Raising principle if all motivation for it had been explained on grounds other than learnability.

Let us suppose, therefore, that the unanalyzability of an extraposed constituent is explicable in terms of performance considerations. To give a suggestion of how an account might go, consider a typical example: (38c) illustrates roughly the derived structure of (38b). We use * in the tree to indicate the position from which a constituent has been removed.[12]

The crucial characteristic of this structure that we would like to exploit is that it is not possible to determine that a constituent has been extraposed from the NP *an analysis* until the end of the sentence is reached. At this point it is necessary to backtrack in some way and reintegrate the extraposed constituent with its underlying source.

In this particular case, in order to return the PP *of which sample* to its original position it would be necessary first to fill the * of the PP with *which sample*. Without a fully worked out theory of performance we

(38)

a. An analysis will be necessary of all those samples.

b. *Which sample will an analysis be necessary of ∅?

c.

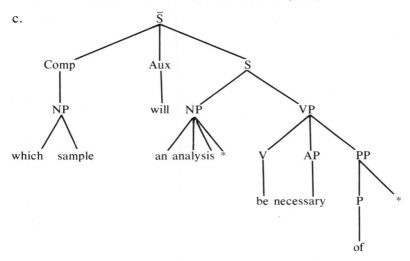

cannot explain why it is that this would put a greater strain on the performance mechanism than other derivations involving two operations. We may speculate, very tentatively, as follows:

Suppose that when the parser encounters *an analysis* it concludes that it is an NP, interprets it, and assigns it a role in the semantic representation. In this case, since no main verb has been encountered, *an analysis* must be the subject. Proceeding to *of* *, the parser would note the gap and the filler *which sample*. But the partial structure arrived at in the parse would demand that the PP *of* * be reintegrated with an earlier constituent, which has been interpreted already. In order to complete the parse, the parser would have to reconstruct the PP by reversing Wh Fronting, arrive at an interpretation for the reconstructed PP, and assign the object of this PP a semantic role in terms of the already interpreted NP *an analysis*. This reconstruction would be ruled out by the theory of derivational complexity that we would construct for examples of this general sort.

The foregoing is in no sense an explanation, because such a theory of derivational complexity does not exist. Assuming that it did exist, however, and assuming that it functioned as we are viewing it here, we would be in a position to formally distinguish the cases that motivated the Raising principle from those that motivate Extrap.

Unlike the structure in (38), the structure (39) of the extraposed sentential subject example (37) contains a dummy element (namely, *it*) in subject position. The principle of Designated Representatives (inspired in part by examples such as these) will in any event require the insertion of *it* under an NP that dominates no lexical items. Consider now the parsing of this structure, in this hypothetical performance explanation.

(39)

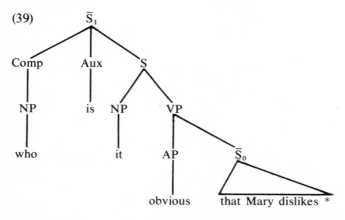

When the parser encounters the dummy subject, it would create "holder" in the semantic representation where the subject will go. When $\bar{S}_0$ is encountered, it is parsed, and the fronted *wh* phrase is reintegrated with $\bar{S}_0$. The resulting structure is interpreted, and this interpretation is assigned to the subject slot of the sentence. It would not be required in this case to reintegrate the extraposed constituent with an already constructed semantic structure, nor would it be necessary to determine the role of the extraposed constituent in terms of a constituent that had already been assigned a role itself. If we could construct a well-founded theory of derivational complexity to capture the formal difference between these two cases, we would have begun to develop an adequate account of at least this aspect of linguistic performance.

This approach to the problem is given suggestive support by the following facts. It is possible to construct sentences in English which have PP's in subject position. For example,

(40)
a. *From here to Boston* is five hundred miles.
b. *Inside the room* is very dark.
c. *To Chicago* looks like about thirty miles.

These PP's are, we presume, dominated by NP. Notice that they can undergo NP Preposing in sentences like

(41)
a. From here to Boston is believed to be five hundred miles.
b. Inside the room is generally thought to be very dark.
c. To Chicago was assumed to be about thirty miles.

The structure of (40c) is

(42)

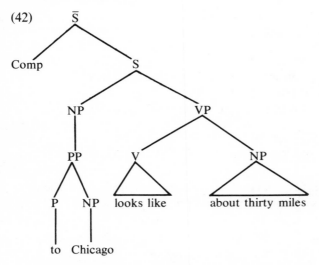

Although the NP exhaustively dominates PP, there is no principled reason why it should not be able to extrapose. In fact, as the examples in (43) show, such PP's can extrapose.

(43)

a. It is five hundred miles from here to Boston.

b. It is very dark inside the room.

c. It looks like about thirty miles to Chicago.

This is precisely what we would expect, given the principle of Designated Representatives.

In our discussion of the Raising principle one of the extraposition rules yielding a frozen structure is the rule that extraposes PP. There is no reason to believe that the rule that extraposes PP in (43) is formally any different from the rule that does so in, for example, (38). Yet in the case of (44) it is possible to analyze the extraposed PP.

(44)

a. Which town is it five hundred miles from ∅ to Boston?

b. Which room is it very dark inside ∅?

c. Which city does it look like about thirty miles to ∅?

Predictably, when these PP's are in subject position, they are not analyzable because of the Binary principle.

(45)

a. *Which town is [from ∅ to Boston] five hundred miles?

b. *Which room is [inside ∅] very dark?

c. *Which city does [to ∅] look like about thirty miles?

The force of these data is that we cannot invoke the Raising principle to rule out (38) without also ruling out (44). Without the Raising principle, an explanation of the sort proposed may well be correct; certainly some alternative is necessary. Interestingly, we find again that the analyzable extraposed constituent is just the one that leaves a dummy behind. We could stipulate that the Raising principle is not applicable just when this occurs, but without theoretical motivation such an account would fall far short of being a satisfactory explanation.[13]

7.1.6 Briefly Noted

The assumption of No Copying was adopted to simplify the proof. As noted in chapter 4, there is no reason to believe that it is necessary for the proof, but we have not investigated this question in detail. Similarly, the principle of Ordering of S-Essential Transformations (OSET) was adopted for simplicity; in this case, however, we know of no empirical evidence against the assumption; that is, we know of no case where a transformation must apply within an S before a transformation involving that S and the next S down. Such a case would be one, for example, in which a derived subject could govern deletion in a lower $\bar{S}$ or trigger extraction out of a lower $\bar{S}$.

So far as we know, there is no reason to doubt the empirical validity of the principle of S-Optionality, which requires that if S appears on the right-hand side of a phrase structure rule, it must appear within parentheses. Nor are we able to find any empirical disconfirmation of the principle of the Transparency of Untransformable Base Structures (TUBS). It is worth noting here that the examples used to motivate TUBS in chapter 4 make crucial use of successive raising transformations into S. As we observed in the preceding section, certain plausible assumptions about the base, together with the Freezing principle and the Binary principle, effectively rule out some such examples. Hence it may be that TUBS can be dispensed with under a more restricted theory of the base, although this is not absolutely certain without a thorough reanalysis of all of the relevant examples in chapter 4.

Turning to the principle of S-Invisibility, we again find no empirical evidence to disconfirm. This principle insures that if a transformation applies with A adjacent to B, the same transformation will apply even if an S intervenes. It is relevant just for those transformations that mention consecutive constant terms with no intervening variable in the structural description, as in X-A-B-Y. If a variable intervenes, as in X-A-Z-B-Y, the presence of an intervening S will not be sufficient to block the transformation.

S-Invisibility would follow from the assumption that there always is a variable between any two constant terms in a structural description. For arguments in favor of such a constraint, see Wilkins (1977). Much of S-Invisibility will follow from NBC, as pointed out by John Truscott.

7.2 Invariance Principle

An important result of learnability studies (see chapters 3 and 4) is that the class of transformational grammars is learnable if the learner is presented with data of the form (b,s) where s is a surface string and b the corresponding deep structure. A realistic interpretation of this requirement is that the learner must have semantic information presented along with the surface string and is capable of arriving at the correct deep structure on the basis of this information. In this section we speculate on how the relation between semantic structure and deep structure might be learned. We will point out that a particular assumption that constrains this relation has clear empirical consequences. Our discussion must unfortunately remain sketchy, though, because at present there is insufficient empirical evidence to allow a true evaluation of the adequacy of this (or alternative) constraints.

Briefly, the situation is roughly as follows. We have proved formally that if the learner has access to the deep structure, he can learn the grammar. Without this information we cannot prove that language is learnable.[14] (See chapter 2.) It is unreasonable to assume that the learner has direct access to deep structures, so we assume as a plausible alternative that semantic information (available from the context of the utterance) allows the learner to infer the deep structure. In order for this inference to take place, the learner must have available a learnable class of mappings from semantic structure to deep structure. Part of the learning task is to discover which member of the class holds in the language in question.

To explain how it is that this mapping is learnable, we must assume that it is constrained in some way. We suppose that it is constrained in the strongest way possible. This hypothesis leads to certain specific predictions about linguistic universals, *if* certain assumptions about semantic structure are made.

But here the empirical investigation is stymied. For one thing, we don't know what semantic structure looks like. For another, the cross-linguistic evidence about universals of syntactic structure is sketchy and, where available, is concerned with surface structure, not deep structure. It seems clear that our strong hypothesis is too strong, but it is not clear how to revise it suitably.

Nevertheless, the importance of semantic information for learning is obvious, and we intend to highlight by this discussion the fact that a correct explanation of precisely how the semantic information is utilized in the learning task will have important empirical consequences for syntactic analysis in general. Because of the very preliminary nature of this kind of investigation, and the inadequacy of the available data for our purposes, we are restricted to a discussion whose speculative nature must not be overlooked.[15]

7.2.1 Universal Base Hypothesis Replaced

The fact that, given certain constraints, reasonable procedures exist which can learn language, and the fact that these constraints appear to hold for natural language, together constitute remarkable evidence in support of the proposed theories of language and of language acquisition. However, one of the assumptions of the theory as so far developed is clearly wrong. This is the presumption that a single set of context-free rewrite rules is at the core of every language; in other words, the presumption that there is a universal base (see chapter 3). That this Universal Base hypothesis (UBH), in its strictest sense,[16] is wrong becomes obvious when attempts are made to write grammars for languages other than English and it is discovered that the order of constituents in deep structure is not the same as it is for English.[17]

Suppose that we drop UBH. That is, we still require that every language have a context-free base, but we allow the base to vary freely from language to language. Then the class of possible languages will include the class of context-free languages and thus, by known results,[18] will not be learnable if no base information is presented—that is, if the language learning data consist only of a sequence of grammatical sentences from the language.

But what of the scheme in which base information is presented? Suppose that (base phrase-marker, surface string) pairs—(b,s) pairs— are presented, and suppose that the base is not universal. From this presentation scheme, the base grammar is easily learnable, since information about the context-free rules is directly given in the phrase-markers, and since any context-free grammar contains only a finite number of rules.[19]

Thus, from this strictly formal point of view UBH is extra baggage: it is completely unnecessary to assume UBH in order to prove learnability. But without UBH the interpretation to be given to the results is absurd. Recall that the justification for proposing that the (base, surface string) pair presentation scheme constitutes a reasonable model of the situation faced by the child is that we might suppose that there is a one-to-one relation between the semantic representation of an utterance and the deep structure, so that the child might derive the latter from the former, with the semantic representation available from the context or situation of the utterance plus meanings of the words. (We will often omit reference to this knowledge.) But if there is no universal base, nor any constraint on the form of the base other than that it must be context-free, there is no reasonable explanation for how the child is able to derive the structure of each utterance. Different languages could have different deep structures associated with semantically equivalent utterances in identical situations, and thus we cannot assume that the child can derive the deep structure from the situation. That is to say, the only circumstance in which it is plausible to assume that the child has the (base, surface string) pair available is one in which the base can be determined by the child from the semantics of the situation. It would be implausible to suggest that the base phrasemarker is made available to the child totally through the linguistic input.

If we assume all of the current theory except for UBH, we cannot show that language is learnable. Yet UBH is wrong. What we need, therefore, is a replacement for UBH which will be plausible in itself and will allow the learnability theorem to be proved. A particularly elegant and effective replacement would not assume the universality of the base but, rather, would allow a proof that the base could be learned from the linguistic evidence and the universal semantic characterization of the context in which the linguistic evidence appears.[20]

Observe that UBH operates in the language acquisition theory in two ways. First, by assuming a single base it restricts the class of possible grammars. Second, with auxiliary assumptions it makes it possible for information about deep structures to be provided to the learner. We want to replace UBH by a set of assumptions that will fulfill both of these functions.

First, it will be useful to consider the various levels of semantic and syntactic representations and the mappings between these levels. In terms of syntax, there is a level of surface structure (SS) and a level of deep structure (DS), which are related by transformational mappings (T). In terms of semantics, there are also two levels. The first, which we might call the *mental world* (W) corresponds to objects, relations between objects, events, statements about these objects and events, and so on, which humans have mental access to. The second semantic level we might call the level of semantic representation (SR); it is meant to correspond to a linguistic encoding of the cognitive objects, events, and so on, of the first level. These two semantic levels are connected by a mapping (M), which has to some extent been studied by logicians.[21] The syntactic and semantic levels are connected by an interpretation mapping (I) between the level of semantic representation and the deep structure. These relations are depicted in figure 7.1.

The two upper levels in the figure are both surface levels in the sense that they are relatively open to direct observation. Surface structure represents sequences of words as they are observed in speech, and mental world represents objects and their properties in our perception. Both semantic representation and deep structure are deep levels in that they are not immediately observable but are, rather, constructed levels.[22]

A completely adequate theory of language acquisition would have to explain how the child learns the mappings T, M, and I. We have already dealt in some detail with T (chapters 3 and 4). The M mapping is a problem for psychology about which little is known: How do perceptual events come to attain a semantic representation? Now, let us deal with I.

A first question might be, Why postulate I at all? Why not eliminate the level of deep structure and simply have one mapping directly from the semantic representation (SR) to the surface structure (SS)?[23] The

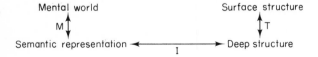

Figure 7.1
Semantic and syntactic levels

reason is that postulating a level of deep structure helps very much to explain how the mappings can be learned. In linguistic terms, by assuming a level of deep structure, a universal set of semantic representations, and constraints on the forms of I and T, we greatly reduce the possible derivations between SR and SS. Moreover, the reduction is accomplished in a natural way, which greatly facilitates the learning of these mappings or makes them learnable by a plausible restricted procedure.

A natural assumption to make is that there is a close correspondence between the semantic representation and the deep structure, an idea that has been partially represented as the assumption that grammatical relations are universal but the order of the constituents is not.[24] This assumption can be stated very simply and precisely: A grammar produces the constituents of the semantic representation as a set (unordered), and then ordering rules immediately apply which order the constituents. These ordering rules are of a specially limited form. In particular, they apply by ordering the immediate constituents introduced by each rewriting rule, and they may not reach down to order any other constituents.[25] Also, the semantic grammar (the set of rules introducing the unordered constituents) is universal; that is, every language has such a scheme for semantic representation. The ordering rules are not universal, but all ordering rules follow the constraints proposed. We call this universal constraint on ordering rules the Invariance principle. Note that we hypothesize this principle in order to initiate an investigation into the problem that we have noted here; certainly the Invariance principle is too strong, and too concrete as well. It seems to us very likely that the true relation between semantic structure and syntactic structure is of a more abstract nature.

To consider now a very simple artificial example, suppose the semantic grammar contains the following rules:

(46)
$$S \rightarrow \langle A, B \rangle$$
$$B \rightarrow \langle C, D \rangle$$
$$C \rightarrow \langle E, F \rangle$$

The notation $\langle A, B \rangle$ indicates that A and B are unordered sisters. The

(47)

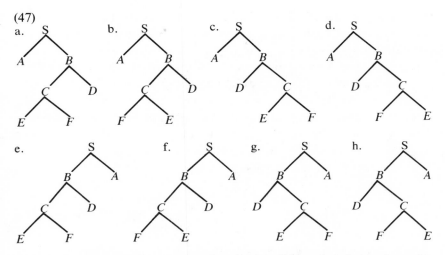

Invariance principle then constrains the possible ordered structures to those given in (47). No other ordered structures are possible, given the semantic grammar (46). Note that as a corollary of this prediction, the Invariance principle predicts that certain orders of constituents are not possible in deep structures. Of the 4! = 24 orders definable on the four terminal symbols (we are assuming here for simplicity that the rules are obligatory) A, D, E, F, the eight for which there is a structure in (47) are possible. The other sixteen are impossible. Examples of impossible orders include *AEDF* and *DAEF*.

Now notice how simple it becomes to "learn" the syntactic base of a grammar.[26] Assume for the moment that the child is presented with pairs of semantic representations and deep structures. The procedure for learning the order of constituents is quite simple and straightforward. Each time one of these (SR, DS) pairs is presented, the learner gets precise information about the order of various constituents. Thus each time a semantic representation (categorial component) rule is used in a derivation, the ordering rule also applies, and the learner adds a rule to his grammar (if he doesn't already have it) which specifies the order of these constituents.

Of course deep structures are not directly presented to the learner, but strings of formatives are. Consider for simplicity the case where no transformations apply. Then the string is the terminal string of a deep structure.

To take an example, now assume that the rules of (46) are optional and that each of the symbols except S terminates in lexical items; that is, add the rules $A \rightarrow a$, $B \rightarrow b$, . . . , $F \rightarrow f$ to the grammar (46). On the first data presentation, suppose the learner is presented with the (SR, SS) pair (48).[27] The learner (assuming that the lexical item tells him

(48)

$$\left(\begin{array}{c} S \\ A \qquad B \\ C \qquad D \end{array} \;,\; cda \right)$$

which category it is) knows that the order of categories is CDA, and, given the semantic grammar (46), this can happen only if the ordering rules include $\langle A,B \rangle \rightarrow BA$ and $\langle C,D \rangle \rightarrow CD$. These two rules are thus added to the learner's grammar and constitute part of the mapping I between SR and DS.

Now, suppose we assume that the semantic grammar is universal. Since any such grammar (set-system context-free grammar) contains only a finite number of rules, and for each of these rules only a finite number of ordering rules are possible (precisely $n!$ if n constituents are introduced by the rule), it turns out that there are only a finite number of possible ordering rules.

In fact, according to the procedure just outlined, as soon as one example of each rewriting rule has been introduced, the correct set of ordering rules will be learned. Thus, not only will convergence take place, but for a given semantic grammar there is a bound on the amount of time or data needed for convergence. Moreover, this learning should take place quickly. There is some empirical evidence, in fact, that the learning of the basic order of sentence constituents does take place quickly.[28]

Suppose now that the Invariance principle doesn't hold. The only assumption now is that the semantic (unordered) tree is mapped into an ordered tree by an effective function. If (SR, SS) pairs are presented as before, this mapping is still learnable, for we can show any such mapping is learnable in this sense.[29] The procedure is to enumerate the possible mappings and to guess them in turn, going on to the next one whenever a mistake is made (whenever a pair appears in the data which is not related by the currently hypothesized mapping). The new guess must generate all the pairs in the data to date.

As was pointed out in chapter 3, such a procedure is quite unlikely to be the human procedure. It requires all past data to be stored, and we do not believe that this is the case. It requires the rejection of an entire grammar each time a contradictory datum appears, which does not seem plausible. And we do not get degree-2 learnability; thus the procedure is implausible in terms of the time and data required for learning. See chapters 1 and 2 and section 3.2 for discussion of the relevance of these issues to learnability theory.

For example, suppose the set grammar is given by the following rules:

(49)
$$S \rightarrow \langle A,S \rangle$$
$$A \rightarrow a$$
$$S \rightarrow c$$

On this base it is easy to construct effective rules that will generate the class of languages $L = \{L_1, L_2, L_3, \ldots \}$ where

$$L_1 = \{c,ca,aac,aaac, \ldots\}$$
$$L_2 = \{c,ca,caa,aaac,aaaac, \ldots\}$$
$$L_3 = \{c,ca,caa,caaa,aaaac,aaaaac, \ldots\}$$
$$\ldots$$
$$L_i = \{c,ca,caa, \ldots ,ca^i,a^{i+1}c,a^{i+2}c, \ldots ,a^{i+j}c, \ldots\}$$

Language L_i is generated by an ordering rule that orders $\langle A,S \rangle$ as SA if there are i or fewer A's in the (unordered) tree and as AS if the number of A's is greater than i.

This class of languages (given the base forms) is identifiable by the general pair procedure, but there is no bound on the time or amount of data needed to converge. Suppose, for example, that the procedure enumerates grammars in the order $G_1, G_2, \ldots$, where G_i generates language L_i, and even suppose that strings are presented in order of increasing length. Then language L_i will take $i + 1$ units of time (or pieces of data) before it is (correctly) selected. For example, L_3 will be selected only after the sequence $c, ca, caa, caaa$ has been presented.[30]

7.2.2 Levels of Adequacy in Semantics

What kind of evidence indicates that the semantic base is universal? To consider a specific example, what are the reasons for believing that subject-predicate is the basic semantic division of a sentence in all languages? For that matter, why is it the basic division in English?

First, of course, the subject-predicate analysis works; we can define a semantic model on this analysis such that our intuitions about logical implication are captured in an appropriate manner.[31] We might say that a semantic theory that met this criterion had reached a level of *descriptive adequacy*. However, as in syntax, there are other descriptively adequate theories, and the problem remains of how to select among them. A linguistic theory that correctly selects among competing descriptively adequate accounts is said to have *explanatory adequacy*.

To consider a concrete example, suppose, instead of the subject-predicate analysis, we claimed that in English the subject and verb formed one of the two major constituents and the object was the other major constituent. Thus *the man stole the book* would have an analysis roughly like that in (50a), where we have titled the new subject-verb constituent the "subjicate." Is it anything more than convention that tells us that (50a) is not correct? Before we answer this question, consider the usual analysis (50b). Consider how the semantics for this sentence is given. For simplicity, we will consider only the simplest *extensional* semantics and ignore sense, but none of our conclusions

(50)

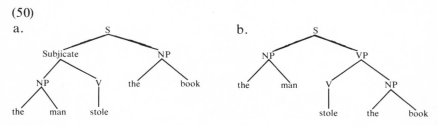

will be modified by this simplification. Also for the sake of exposition we will make other special simplifications that would not be possible in a more general treatment.

We can let the NP *the book* refer to an object. The verb *stole* is a function on objects, whose range is a set of objects (people, say) who stole the book. This set is the extension of VP. The extension of *the man* is an object (person). If this object is an element of the extension of VP, the sentence is true. Otherwise, it is false.

Suppose we have a sentence with an intransitive verb, say, *The man ran,* as in (51). In this case VP again represents a set of objects, and if

(51)

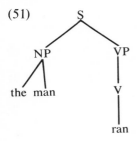

the object denoted by *the man* is one of them, the sentence is true, otherwise false. Thus under the subject-predicate analysis the major (highest up) semantic rule is the same for both SV and SVO sentences.

Turning now to the subjicate-NP analysis, note that we cannot apply the same semantic rules to (50a). Rather, we will have to let *steal* denote a function that takes the object denoted by *the man* into "the set of objects that the man stole," this being the extension of the subjicate. If the object denoted by *the book* is an element of this set, the sentence is true, otherwise false. So far we have had to define different rules for this analysis, but there is no reason to prefer one analysis over the other.

Consider now the sentence with an intransitive verb whose subject-predicate analysis is given in (51). Suppose we tried to give it a subjicate-NP analysis. We could try (52). Clearly the semantic rule needed is that used in (51) (true if extension of *the man* is an element of extension of *ran*) and not that used in (50a). That is, two separate rules are needed for two different structures under the subjicate analysis,

(52)

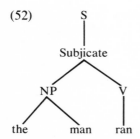

whereas for the subject-predicate analysis only one rule is needed. Thus the subject-predicate analysis is preferred.

In fact we should note that (52) would not be appropriate in any theory in which only one rule of interpretation could be associated with a given categorical structure, because here the rule for interpreting _{subj}[NP V] would have to be different from the one needed for (50a). Rather, we would have to try, say, (53). But if we introduce (53) in

(53)

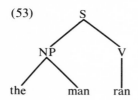

place of (52), we still are forced to the conclusion that two semantic rules are needed, one for (50a) and one for (53), whereas under the subject-predicate analysis only one rule was needed.

To summarize, the syntactic rules for the two analyses are given in the following:

(54)
a. The subject-predicate analysis:
S → NP VP
VP → V (NP)
b. The subjicate analysis:
$$S \rightarrow \begin{Bmatrix} \text{Subjicate NP} \\ \text{NP V} \end{Bmatrix}$$

Subjicate → NP V

One could argue on the basis of the syntactic rules that the subject-predicate analysis is simpler or captures a significant generalization. While we would argue this, we also want to point out that there is semantic evidence for the subject-predicate form, namely, the fact that we need only one rule to define truth given this analysis, whereas two rules on two different structures are needed for the subjicate analysis.[32]

7.2.3 Empirical Adequacy of the Invariance Principle

7.2.3.1 Background A test of the Invariance principle can be envisioned, given certain auxiliary assumptions. Suppose that no language had transformations. Given this, we would predict from the Invariance principle that all realizations of a particular semantic category in all languages would be members of a very small set, namely, the set of expansions that can be gotten by imposing an ordering on sisters of a node. For example, the structure (55) has only the realizations in (56a) and not those in (56b).

(55)
$_A[\text{B } _C[D\ E]]$

(56)
a.   *BDE*   b. **DBE*
    BED   **EBD*
    DEB
    EDB

If there were no transformations, a demonstration of the empirical adequacy of such a principle as the Invariance principle would be the discovery of universals of word order (or constituent order) consistent with predictions such as (56a,b).

Since there are transformations, however, certain nonbase orders can in principle occur. But the Freezing principle will restrict the occurrence of such orders in the following way: If a transformation is structure-preserving, no new order will be derived; if a transformation is non-structure-preserving, the resulting structure should be demonstrably frozen. Furthermore, by assuming a particular internal structure to a phrase marker, as in (54), the range of possible reorderings can be predicted in terms of the widest domain of freezing.

Suppose we had a transformation T whose function was to insert a constituent, say F, between B and D in the sequence BDE. Suppose also that F is not generated in the base in this example, so that attachment of F is non-structure-preserving. If DE is dominated by C (as in (55)), and if F is attached to C, then C will be frozen, but A will not be. This is illustrated in (57a). On the other hand, suppose that A has no internal structure. Then when T applies, F is attached as a daughter of A, and hence A is frozen, as shown in (57b).

(57)

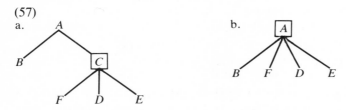

The empirical difference in the two cases is that in (57a) B can undergo transformation after T has applied, but in (57b) it cannot. Of course, there is no guarantee that in any particular case we will find just this sort of crucial transformation and data to decide questions having to do with the internal structure of a phrase, but because of the Freezing principle there is at least a prima facie possibility of drawing the appropriate distinctions.

However, since there may be transformations that apply only in roots as well as postcyclic transformations, it may not always be the case that even a non-structure-preserving reordering will have consequences in terms of the Freezing principle. In general we must allow for the possibility that a particular ordering will have to be transformationally derived even where we cannot independently motivate the transformation that derives it. (A case in point is the Kikuyu NP as noted in 7.2.3.2.) Such a lack of evidence, however, should not be interpreted as negative evidence. We believe that it is tolerable in case there is strong independent motivation for the order of constituents in deep structure.

7.2.3.2 Predictions There is a good case for not accepting the Invariance principle as formulated as correct in its strongest form. Nevertheless some predictions that follow from it appear to be substantially correct. The clearest case concerns the noun phrase.

Bartsch (1973) argues that the semantic properties of NP's can be captured by assigning to them a structure of the form given in (58). (We

(58)

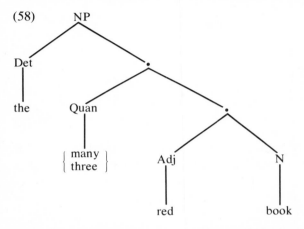

understand Det here to be a morphologically unbound determiner.) Taking (58) as correct, we should expect to find in natural language only the orders in (59a).

(59)

a. Det Quan Adj N   b. *Det N Quan Adj
   Det Quan N Adj   *Quan Det N Adj
   Det Adj N Quan   *Quan Det Adj N
   Det N Adj Quan   *Quan N Det Adj
   Quan Adj N Det   *N Det Quan Adj
   Quan N Adj Det   *N Det Adj Quan

With one exception, we find that none of the orders ruled out (shown in (59b)) occur. The empirical evidence is in Culicover and Wexler 1974. The exception is Kikuyu, which has the order N Det Quan Adj. Here we would want to say that this order is derived transformationally from Det Quan Adj N. As far as we know there is no reason not to adopt this analysis.[33]

7.2.3.3 Problems Predictions that are far more problematic arise when sentential word order is considered.[34] Suppose, for example, that in semantic structure the fundamental organization is subject-predicate. From the unordered structure in (60) we would predict only the orders in (61a), where $S = NP_{subj}$ and $O = NP_{obj}$.

(60) $_S[NP_{subj} \ _{VP}[V \ NP_{obj}]]$

(61)
a. S V O   b. *V S O
    S O V   *O S V
    V O S
    O V S

It is well known, however, that there are languages whose basic or only order is VSO. In the framework provided by (60), such languages will occur just in case the syntactic direct object (that is, the NP immediately dominated by VP) functions semantically as the subject, or there is a transformational derivation that results in V being placed in the front of every clause. Supposing for the moment that the language lacks such a derivation, a sentence whose meaning was "John kissed the horse" would have the underlying structure (62a). As we noted in Wexler and Culicover 1974, this raises an interesting possibility. Such a language, if it existed, would have (62b) as the structure of an intransi-

(62)

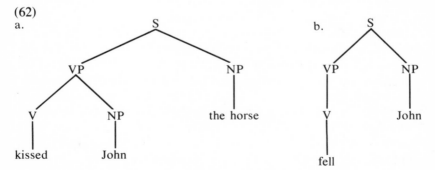

tive sentence. Notice that the subject of the intransitive bears precisely the same relation to VP and S in (62b) that the object NP *the horse* bears to VP and S in (62a). If structural configurations such as these

determined case marking, we would expect to find that in this language
the object of the transitive verb is marked in exactly the same way as
the subject of the intransitive. This case-marking pattern in fact does
exist and is one of the ways of characterizing *ergative* (as opposed to
accusative) languages. In such a language we will have sentences like
the following, where *abs* indicates the absolutive case that is shared by
the two sentence types, and *nom* indicates the nominative case.

(63)
a. Kissed John-*nom* the horse-*abs*. "John kissed the horse."
b. Fell John-*abs*. "John fell."

It turns out, however, that many languages display the ergative
case-marking system that do not have fixed VSO order in transitive
sentences. More important still, there are languages that appear to
have fixed VSO word order but do not display ergative case marking. It
does not appear that we can make a good case for SVO or SOV underlying order in such languages.[35] Further sorts of counterexamples can
be constructed by examining the predictions that the Invariance principle would make for structures related to but more complex than (60).

For example, it seems straightforward that VP can dominate PP as
well as NP and V. If VP contains PP, PP cannot be separated from the
V by NP_{subj}.

(64) $_s[NP_{subj}\ _{VP}[V\ NP_{obj}\ PP]]$
(65) *V $NP_{subj}\ NP_{obj}\ PP$

Note that (65) is impossible even in the ergative system as outlined. PP
still must be part of VP, and in (65) there is no unbroken sequence of
constituents containing V, NP_{subj}, and PP, and excluding NP_{obj} (where
NP_{subj} is the ergative syntactic object and NP_{obj} the ergative syntactic
subject). Rather, for the ergative system the order would have to be

(66) $_{VP}[V\ NP_{subj}\ PP^*]\ NP_{obj}$

where PP* represents the full sequence of PP's in the VP. As far as we
know, there is no language of the sort illustrated in (66).

Counterexamples of this sort should lead us to weaken somewhat
our strong version of the Invariance principle. Also, although it seems
that there are OSV languages of the ergative type that we have dis-

cussed, in which the semantic subject is the syntactic direct object, namely, Dyribal and West Greenlandic,[36] many if not most VSO languages are not of this type.[37] They provide a second class of counterexamples calling for a weakening of the Invariance principle.

7.2.4 Weak Invariance

7.2.4.1 Methodological Preliminaries A number of questions arise when we consider how to weaken the Invariance principle. Recall that our goal is to explain how the learner can determine which phrase is which when presented with examples of grammatical sentences and their meanings. To do this, we would like to show that there is a principled bound on the number of syntactic configurations that can express a particular semantic configuration. The assumption of any particular principle from which this bound follows implies particular syntactic universals, as we have seen. In part the problem is to find just those principles consistent with the range of syntactic variation among the world's languages.

Unfortunately, existing understanding of the actual range of syntactic variation is not sufficiently sophisticated to allow us to make use of the data that currently exist in the literature on syntactic universals.[38] The main problem, in our view, is that the available data for the most part provide generalizations about surface structure constituent order, whereas our theory makes direct predictions only about deep structure constituent order. An illustration of the complexity of the situation in English may be useful in clarifying what the problem is.

Suppose for the sake of discussion that the Invariance principle in its strongest form is correct. If in addition there is a semantic category corresponding to VP, then every language will have VP. We have already discussed the class of constituent orders that will not be consistent with this particular set of assumptions; one of these orders is OSV.

The order OSV is a possible surface order for English, as sentences like (67) illustrate.

(67)
a. John, I like.
b. The beans, I couldn't eat.
c. That Fred is a genius I can easily believe.

However, we would not wish to say that English is a counterexample to the Invariance principle, because the OSV order of English is transformationally derived and is not an underlying order, on the usual account.[39]

If we sought to maintain the Invariance principle in its strong form, it would be necessary to show that apparent counterexamples arise through the application of transformations to underlying structures that do not contradict the predictions made by the principle. Hence we are committed to detailed analyses of the syntax of those languages in which counterexamples appear, analyses whose intricacy is comparable with those set forth for English, Japanese, French, and a few other languages. It is fair to say that it is likely to be some time before there exists a substantial body of analysis of sufficient depth and breadth across the languages of the world to satisfactorily test the accuracy of universals of underlying structure.[40]

We should not overlook the tradition in linguistics, initiated to a considerable extent by Greenberg (1963), that is concerned with surface structure universals. It might be thought (and in fact at one time seemed to us) that such observations could be used to test the predictions of the Invariance principle to some extent. This is so because surface structure universals are usually couched in terms of the basic or unmarked constituent orders of a language. Possibly these might correspond to our underlying constituent orders.

There are two reasons these data cannot be used in the way suggested. First, the criteria for determining basic word orders are not formal, grammatical ones, but informal and heuristic. Steele (1978b), for example, suggests the following (p. 593):

1. "Marked variations are usually either not mentioned in descriptive studies or are identified as such."
2. Marked orders are in fact marked in some way, as with intonation or with a marker.[41]

Concerning the first criterion, there appears to us to be no particular reason to believe that the failure of descriptive grammarians to mention a particular construction is evidence that the construction does not reflect underlying constituent order. Nor can we rely, in general, on the judgments of such grammarians as to which constructions are basic, when they are actually mentioned, in the absence of close analysis of the language.

Similarly, though it may be the case that a particular marker or intonation is indicative of a derived syntactic structure, there is no reason to believe that interpretations of constituent order data based on Steele's second criterion will be especially useful in the absence of close analysis of the languages in question. To take an example from English, the passive construction displays OVS order (on one definition of S and O).

(68) John was-visited by-the-police.
        O   pass-V   S

Possibly we would want to say that this is clearly a nonbasic order because of the passive morphology: the verb *to be,* the passive participle, and the *by* phrase. But exactly the same morphology appears in an unmarked construction.

(69) John was unemployed by the time he was sixteen.[42]

Once again, superficial notions of marking cannot be diagnostic, in general, for the underlying/derived distinction. It might be objected that the unmarked/marked distinction is not intended to correlate with the underlying/derived distinction. In such a case, however, it is not clear what explanatory force universals couched in terms of the former might have.

The second reason the existing data on linguistic universals is difficult to use in the context of the present approach is one of terminology. Many of these universals are expressed in terms of the notions subject (S), and object (O). However, it is not at all clear what is meant by S and O. In the case of the English passive in (68), for example, the order is superficially S V Agent, since in fact *John* is the syntactic subject. On the other hand, it appears from the literature that S is usually understood to be the agent, that is, the NP that corresponds to *John* in the English sentence *John ate the pie*. But in that case the order of the passive is in fact OVS in English.

Although this does not appear to be a crucial problem for the analysis of English, it becomes serious when we consider languages that are as yet only superficially described. For then it is entirely unclear precisely what is meant in the description by "subject." This adds a further confusion, in light of the difficulties concerning the criteria for defining basic and nonbasic orders.

7.2.4.2 Grammatical Relations We will view the problem of constraining the mapping from semantic structure to syntactic structure in the following way: The semantic representation of a given sentence posseses a particular topology, in that there are various elements distributed in some relation to one another.[43] Assuming that the relevant aspects of semantic structure can be represented as a phrase-marker, we are able to define grammatical relations on the semantic structure of the same sort that have been defined on syntactic structure. So, for example, if (70) is the semantic representation of *John caught a fish,* we could define the relation subject-of so that the semantic representation of *John,* call it *John*,* is the subject.

(70)

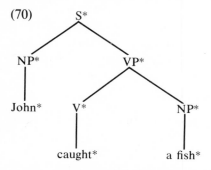

For a particular language it is necessary to specify, for each relation on semantic structure, the corresponding relation (or relations) that it is mapped into in syntactic structure. The set of such mappings must be learnable, and the goal of the theory is to explain how this is so.

The general form of such a theory is the following: There exist a set of possible relations on semantic structure, a set of possible relations on syntactic structure, and a set of possible mappings between them. The most restrictive view is that the first two sets are identical in membership and that the set of mappings between them consists of the identity mapping This is, in essence, a very strong version of the

Invariance principle, where what is the subject in the semantic representation is realized as the subject in the syntactic representation, and so on.

Notice a very important point. When we speak of a set of grammatical relations, we are speaking of a set of relations defined on the topology of a phrase-marker. We are not speaking of identity of *label*, where a particular noun phrase might be, for example, the direct object in two sentences but would bear a different syntactic relation to the subject in the two cases. For example, in a VSO language, O and S would be sisters; in an SVO language they might not be.

In weakening the Invariance principle we must relax somewhat the restrictions on how a grammatical relation may be defined. In the case of the strong Invariance principle we allowed for the definition of *direct object* as only the NP immediately dominated by VP. This committed us to the position that all languages had VP's, since all languages have direct objects and we allowed for only this one sort.

Seen this way, the Invariance principle is maintained in its original essential form; the class of grammatical relations is broadened, yielding a slightly less restrictive theory. We assume, as before, that semantic representation is universal. As before, we assume that the mapping between semantics and syntax preserves grammatical relations. The empirical question is, How are the relations defined?

7.2.4.3 Limiting the Cardinality of Mappings Defining the grammatical relations is of paramount importance for the problem of the learnability of the class of mappings between syntactic and semantic representation. Suppose, for illustration, that in principle there could be a grammatical relation $subject_{i,j}$, where this relation is defined as in (71) and diagrammed in (72).

(71) An NP_k is $subject_{i,j}$ of the jth clause in the phrase-marker if NP_k is immediately dominated by S_i.

Suppose, furthermore, that we have an SVO language. Letting (72) be a semantic representation, we can state part of the mapping between

(72)

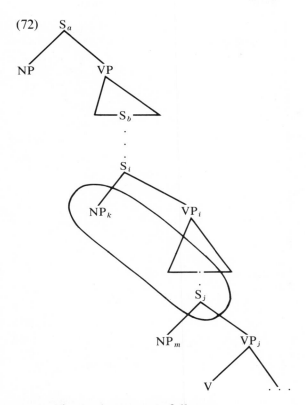

semantics and syntax as follows:

(73) If NP_m is the subject of S_j and NP_k is the *subject*$_{i,j}$ of S_j, then in the syntactic representation, NP_m is the subject of S_i and NP_k is the subject of S_j.

Intuitively, the two subjects are being interchanged. Applying (73) and (72) will give the deep structure (74).

It is clear that if we allow the definitions of grammatical relations like (73), there is no bound on the number of possible relations. This follows directly from the fact that there is recursion in natural language. An infinite number of relations of the form *subject*$_{i,j}$ exist. Moreover, we can also imagine relations of the form *object*$_{i,j}$, which switch two objects. Beyond this, we can see relations of the form *subject-object*$_{i,j}$,

(74)

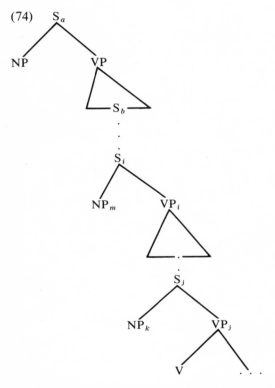

which switch subject and object in two clauses, those of the form $subject_{i,j,k}$, which involve three clauses, and so on.

This situation prevents learnability in the following way: If there is no bound on the number of relations statable on semantic structure, we cannot prove that there is a particular bound on the size of the phrase-marker (or structure) required to learn the mapping: for the relation $subject_{1,1000}$ we would require a phrase-marker of degree greater than or equal to 1000, for the relation $subject_{1,1001}$, a phrase-marker of degree greater than or equal to 1001, and so on. For every relation of the form $subject_{i,j}$ there exists a relation $subject_{i,k}$, where k is greater than j. Even for a universal base (with a fixed ordering of constituents) this is the case.

To show learnability of the set of mappings from semantic structure to syntactic structure we would therefore like to show that the set of relations is finite. To do this, we may restrict the set of nodes in a semantic representation over which a grammatical relation may be defined. A natural restriction that will do just this is the Binary principle.

The Binary principle restricts the scope of a transformation at a node to the set of nodes that can be reached in two or less transitions involving B-cyclic nodes; $\bar{S}$ and NP are the B-cyclic nodes. In (75), the *Binary domain* at $\bar{S}_2$ consists just of the nodes circled.

(75)

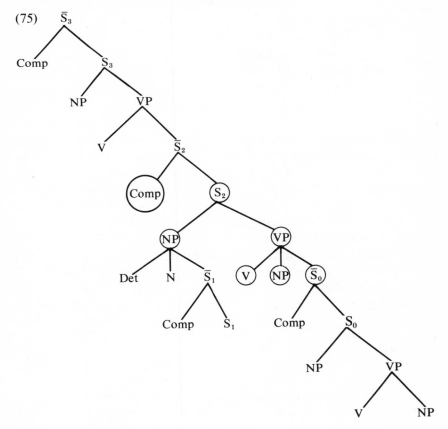

Such a restriction will allow us to define just the usual grammatical relations and any others involving constituents of a simple S only (up to $\bar{S}$). Because of the Binary principle, it is impossible to formulate a grammatical relation that makes reference to two distinct levels of a phrase-marker. Thus the set of possible grammatical relations is rendered finite, and the set of possible mappings is (perhaps) rendered learnable as a consequence. [44]

We must point out here an important problem with this analysis. Our formulation of the Binary principle (in Culicover and Wexler 1977, and in chapter 5) allows access from an $\bar{S}$ down into a chain of infinitives. This suggests that perhaps a hypothesis that we earlier entertained and rejected (Culicover and Wexler 1977) may in fact be correct: the S-node in the infinitive is Binary-cyclic (or every infinitive contains an $\bar{S}$). We will not pursue the question further here. [45]

An important prediction follows from this approach to grammatical relations. Suppose that we have a language in which the relative order of constituents is unconstrained. Every constituent will enter into some grammatical relation. This grammatical relation will not be realized in surface structures by relative constituent order, of course, but by some other form, such as case-marking. Regardless of the order of constituents, however, all of the constituents of the same clause will have to be *contiguous* in the syntactic deep structure—that is, two constituents of a clause may not be separated by a constituent of another clause—because the grammatical relations are defined, both in the syntax and in the semantics, over constituents of a single clause. Only contiguity can indicate, in the absence of rigid order, which bearer of a particular relational marker belongs to which clause. To our knowledge, languages that possess this property of totally free order are also constrained in the way predicted. [46]

7.3 Open Problems

The preceding chapters represent, in our view, progress in our understanding of language learning and its relation to linguistic theory. But we have simply scratched the surface of the problem that we have been studying. We will conclude by pointing out a few of the general questions that still remain open, and by speculating on lines of inquiry that might prove fruitful in some cases. Because of the vast range of still open questions, we will not attempt to provide a systematic catalogue but will simply mention a few that are most salient to us at the present time.

7.3.1 Input

We have assumed for the learnability proof (chapters 3 and 4) that the learner is presented with only grammatical utterances and is presented with all utterances in the limit. In this regard we note two sorts of open problems. On the empirical side, we wonder what the input to the child actually is, in terms of the grammaticality of the input, correction for errors, and the types and complexity of the structures over which the input ranges at various stages in the child's development. On the theoretical side, we wonder about the effect on the learning procedure of input that is not grammatical.

To speculate a bit, let us consider a (b,s) pair related in the usual way, where b is the underlying structure for the surface string s. It may be that in the adult grammar a single transformation T accounts for the relation between b and s. Or it could be that no transformations are involved in the derivation of s from b, or that many are. Suppose that in the context represented by b the adult, through a slip of the tongue, utters the ungrammatical s'. We can imagine many possible relations between the base structure b, the grammatical sentence s, and the error s'. Under at least some circumstances the relation between s' and b is such that it is logically possible for the learner to be led to hypothesize a transformation T′ that is not part of the actual adult transformational component. A question that is worth considering, therefore, is whether this logical possibility is allowed for by the theory, and if it is, what empirical consequences might be expected to follow from it.

One intriguing possibility is that the form of a grammar is so severely constrained by the learnability constraints that in the vast majority of cases errors are not taken by the learner to be serious evidence. That is, T′ cannot be a transformation applying in the derivation of s' from b because it would have to violate one (or more) of the constraints. Along related lines, the set of possible transformations might be so severely restricted by the theory that there simply do not exist transformations for most of the errors that can occur.

It is also conceivable that errors might be flagged as such by the adult in some way, for example, by immediate self-correction. However, it is important to point out the well-known fact that adults often provide the child with transformed and untransformed variants of the same construction, perhaps in the interest of clarification (see Snow 1972). Thus it is not at all obvious that self-correction by the adult would not serve the purpose of highlighting the error as evidence to be attended to (or at least to be taken seriously) rather than as an error that is to be discounted.

Suppose, in any event, that it is possible for an adult to make an error that could be a grammatical sentence in the language but happens not to be. To take one particular case, suppose that the adult's error involves moving some target constituent C to the wrong place. Schematically, the situation is as follows:

(76)
$b:$ . . . C . . .
$T: \Rightarrow C$ . . . $\emptyset$ . . .
$T': \Rightarrow$ . . . $\emptyset$ . . . C

Assuming that both T and T' are possible transformations, the learner will hypothesize T'. If the learner already has hypothesized T, T might be eliminated from the learner's grammar because, by Determinism, there cannot be in a grammar two transformations that can apply to a single structure at some stage of the derivation. However, since T is a transformation in the adult's grammar, sooner or later the learner will encounter positive evidence for it. This will help to correct the error. Because of Determinism again, T' cannot be retained.

Determinism is based on the assumption that all transformations are obligatory. Suppose that we hypothesized, alternatively, that all transformations were optional. Then we would have a problem. In the case schematized in (76) the learner, when presented with the datum . . . $\emptyset$ . . . C, could already have in his grammar transformation T. He might then hypothesize a transformation T' that derives . . . $\emptyset$ . . . C from C . . . $\emptyset$ . . . No later datum will rule out this transformation;

given the assumption that all transformations are optional, the learner will never again have to apply T' in order to derive a grammatical sentence. Of course, if all transformations are obligatory, then the next time the learner encounters b, application of T' will cause a detectable error and it will therefore be eliminated.

Consider another case in which we do not get automatic correction by subsequent grammatical examples. Suppose that the adult erroneously applies a transformation T to a constituent C' to which it cannot apply in the adult's grammar. (For example, suppose that the adult erroneously clefts an adverb and says *It is very early that I'm leaving.*) The learner adds C' to the set of constituents to which T may apply, or, if T has not yet been hypothesized, guesses T applying to C' and extends it to other constituents (the correct C) on the basis of later data.[47]

Given optional transformations, the failure of T to apply to C' in any of the resulting adult's utterances will not be sufficient to show the learner that an error has been made. In fact, unless the learner is explicitly corrected for ungrammatical utterances of his own, it is difficult to see how the error in the transformation can be detected through any later experience.

On this view of the situation, the child's exposure to ungrammaticality will in fact lead to change in the transformational component. In a more realistic characterization of the language learning process grammars may be somewhat more resistant to radical change stimulated by sporadic ungrammatical input. As we have suggested, the theory may be so restricted that very few errors will count as serious.

Nevertheless, even though the adult may in fact make very few serious errors in speaking to a child, the child will surely encounter utterances that have the status, for a learner, of serious errors. We have in mind cases where the learner is exposed to the influence of a number of dialects. Sentences of these dialects do not, of course, count as errors, but the learner has no way of knowing that these sentences are not in the dialect of his parents, just as there may be no way for the learner to know that a serious error is a datum that is not to be considered as evidence for grammar. We might expect that both errors and exposure to other dialects would lead to change in grammars over time.

The evidence from linguistically isolated communities suggests that the influence of errors in the absence of contact with other dialects or languages is not sufficient to cause radical change in short periods of time.

By the same token, we would expect greater change in communities with relatively denser population. From the point of view of the learner's grammar, every input datum not consistent with it is grounds for changing the grammar. Exposure to different dialects of the same language will lead the learner to attempt to incorporate all of the dialect differences into his own grammar, to the extent that they are mutually compatible. This may yield a grammar that is different in certain respects from any of the grammars producing the input data. It is reasonable to suppose that the greater the contact between different grammars, the greater the degree of difference in the grammars that are hypothesized as a consequence of the contact. It would certainly be of interest to make these notions precise. A common theme in modern linguistics is that first-language acquisition may well be the basis for language change (of the noncontact variety). But no explicit theory has been suggested.

7.3.2 Learnability

At various points in this book we have touched upon alternative assumptions, the choice between which might affect the learnability of the class of grammars under consideration. In section 7.1.1, we considered whether certain assumptions can be eliminated in favor of other assumptions more adequate from the point of view of linguistic description. In a number of instances it can be shown that learnability is not affected by the choice of assumption; sometimes, however, the formal proof is simplified, as in the cases of the principle of Adjacency and USET in section 4.1.13.

Given learnability, it is worth considering the contributions that various alternative assumptions might make to the complexity of the learning procedure. For example, it would be of some interest to show that a particular set of assumptions (all plausible on linguistic grounds) allow for learnability (convergence to a correct grammar), given time considerations roughly comparable to those actually observed in human language learning. More precisely, restriction of the input data to sentences of degree less than or equal to 2 might contribute significantly to the rate of learning, compared with the situation where there is no bound on complexity of input. Although it may not be correct to assume that the input data is actually restricted along these lines, it might be that at a certain stage in development, the learner ignores as evidence sentences above a certain level of complexity. On the other hand, while the learner does not require complex data for learning, not ignoring such data might speed learning by providing more evidence about errors.

Along related lines, it might turn out that the time to learning cannot be significantly reduced in the case of degree-2 learnability by adopting various alternative hypotheses. But, at the same time, a significant and empirically plausible reduction in the time to learning might be achieved by imposing the further restriction on the class of grammars that it be learnable from data of degree less than or equal to 1.

Clearly, degree-1 learnability would require severe restrictions on raising, perhaps even the elimination of all raising except raising through Comp. The proof in chapter 4 shows that the interaction of various raising transformations is primarily responsible for the majority of obstacles to degree-2 learnability. It seems reasonable to suppose that further restriction of raising will simplify the learnability problem. Nevertheless, the matter is still very complicated, as the discussion of section 7.1 indicates.

Another problem worth investigating is the extent to which the Binary principle can be eliminated, to allow unbounded rules. It is possible that other assumptions might rule out the counterexamples that motivate the Binary principle in chapter 4, but it is not at all clear what such assumptions should be. Consider the discussion in section 4.2.1 and our remarks about NBC in section 7.1.4. The problem is further complicated by the introduction into the linguistic theory of a class of B-cyclic nodes; it may be that the interaction between the Binary principle and the syntactic structure depends not only on the number of B-cyclic nodes in a path but on the categories of these nodes. Some discussion of this problem appears in Culicover and Wexler 1977, where we consider the possibility that both $\bar{S}$ and S are B-cyclic. Wilkins's (1977) Variable Interpretation constraint offers another possible

way to eliminate the Binary principle, but its consequences for learnability still have to be investigated.

7.3.3 Linguistic Theory

Finally, the form taken by linguistic theory has an enormous effect on
the question of learnability. Without a precise characterization of what
is to be learned, the question of whether it can be learned is virtually
meaningless. On the other hand, learnability theory, once underway,
can provide important insights into the proper formulation of linguistic
theory.

We have noted the latter relationship, for example, in our assumption of head theory to simplify the proof of chapter 4 (section 4.3.5.1).
It is important that the classically central linguistic notion *head* is central as well to learnability theory. Quite possibly further restrictions on
the base component of the sort investigated by Jackendoff (1977a,b)
will allow further simplification of the proof.

As a parallel development, a variety of proposals have been made to
restrict the expressive power of transformations. The most extreme is
Chomsky's proposal (1973; 1975; 1977) that *core grammar* is composed
of cyclic transformations that are structure-preserving, in the sense of
Emonds (1970; 1976), and context-free. Hence the cyclic movement of
a constituent of a given category C will be to a position in the structure
occupied by a dummy element of the same category. Thus the rule may
be expressed as "move C," since no further conditions are allowed in
the theory.

A related proposal is that of Wilkins (1977). She proposes, in essence, that transformations contain implicit variables. Thus A-B is always equivalent to A-X-B. Baker (1977) suggests that the structural
descriptions of transformations must in fact be of the form X-A-Y-B-Z,
which also would serve to restrict expressive power.

As we noted in chapter 4, note 11, transformations may interact in
such a way that simply restricting their expressive power does not in
itself guarantee that the relevant kinds of counterexamples to (degree-
2) learnability are ruled out. It is worth investigating precisely under
what circumstances what restrictions will suffice.

The movement away from the standard theory of transformational grammar represented by Chomsky's recent attempt to restrict the theory of transformations in the direction of core grammar entails the development of other, nontransformational aspects of the theory of grammar. For example, the trace theory of Chomsky (1973; 1975; 1977), Fiengo (1976), and others introduces an entirely new element into the question of learnability. It is not clear to us what effect on learnability will result from the assumption that every movement transformation leaves behind a trace constituent coindexed with the moved constituent. However, let us speculate.

The theory on which all our learnability proofs are based assumes that semantic interpretation is done on syntactic deep structures. We assume that from the situational context the learner can infer a semantic interpretation from which (after some initial relatively simple learning) he can infer a syntactic deep structure. Thus, for the learning of syntactic transformations, after the original base learning, we can assume that the input to the learner is a sequence of (b,s) pairs, where b is a base phrase-marker and s is the surface sentence (string, not phrase-marker) derived from it. (See chapters 2 and 3.)

This rationale for the assumption that syntactic deep structures are part of the input to the learner is weakened under any proposal in which some or all semantic interpretation is done on surface (or derived) structures. To take one proposal in some detail, let us consider a version of *trace theory* as presented in Chomsky's and Fiengo's work. On this account, when NP Preposing takes place as part of the derivation of the passive, we derive a structure like (77a) from a structure like (77b).

(77)
a. NP_i V t_i by NP_j
b. Δ V NP_i by NP_j

In this theory, interpretation is done on derived structure, so the interpretive component knows that NP_i is the direct object of V because a *trace* t_i has been left.

It appears, prima facie, that trace theory would cause quite a bit of trouble for learnability theory, because there is no semantic basis for assuming that deep structures are available as input to the learner. But this may not in fact be the case.

First, we can still assume that the learner can infer semantic interpretations from the context; there is now no rationale for the assumption that from the semantic interpretation the learner can create a deep structure. Second, interpretation is not done on exactly what has traditionally been called surface structure. Rather, surface structure has been amplified by traces. The trace t_i in (77) indicates that its coindexed noun phrase NP_i was moved from the position of t_i; thus NP_i is to be interpreted as an underlying direct object with respect to some aspects of semantic interpretation (and of course as a subject with respect to other aspects—these details have to be spelled out in a precise theory). But since the learner is given the semantic interpretation along with the surface string, it may be possible for him to conclude from this interpretation that there is a trace t_i in the correct position. Hence he may be able to build, from the semantic interpretation and the surface string, the trace-amplified structure. Given the assumptions of the theory, once this is done and the learner sees that there is an NP_i and a trace t_i, he knows that NP_i has been moved from position t_i by a transformation. Given that each of these steps can be accomplished under plausible conditions, there would be a basis for the learner to construct the deep structure and hence the transformation.

The problem here is to provide a formal account of how the learner infers the presence of traces, given the semantic interpretation and the surface string, and then determines what position the traces have in the surface structure. In the case of the passive or the *wh* question in English, for example, it is possible to hypothesize alternative analyses in which the surface constituent order is a deep constituent order as well and no movement transformation is actually involved. In English, of course, there are associated cues to suggest that the surface order is not simply one of many possible orders available in the language (in contrast with a language that is case-marked and allows relatively free constituent order). For instance, the passive construction is morphologically marked with the auxiliary *be* and the past participle, and the application of Wh Fronting in main clauses correlates with Inversion.

Still, it is a problem for any transformational account to explain how the learner distinguishes between a language that has rigid word order and movement transformations and a language that has free word order and no movement transformations. In a trace-theoretic account, the information that a transformation has been involved in the derivation of a particular sentence is put to a somewhat different use than in an account that does not make use of traces.

The second part of the problem appears at first to be peculiar to trace theory, though. Given the learner's recognition that a transformation has moved a constituent, on what basis does the learner infer the position from which the constituent has been moved? Consider the *wh* question in English. The learner is presented with (78) and must infer (79) as the trace-amplified surface structure.

(78) (Wh you did see *wh* + someone, who did you see)
(79) Who did you see t?

Here (78) represents the pair consisting of the semantic representation, on which no linear ordering is imposed, of course, and the surface string; (79) represents the trace-amplified surface structure. We have omitted labeled bracketing.

The learner must determine, in essence, that the trace appears to the right of *see*. The information that (78) provides is simply that there is a trace, and that it is associated syntactically with the verb *see*. Thus the learner is faced with two possibilities, *see t* (as in English) and *t see* (as in German, perhaps).

What is the basis for choosing between these two hypotheses? We might suppose that the subcategorization restrictions on *see* in the lexicon of English will provide sufficient information. If *see* is entered as [+__NP], the absence of an NP in the surface string will perhaps support the inference that there should be a trace in postverbal position—provided that elsewhere in the surface string there is a fronted NP that is not syntactically composable to form a constituent corresponding to a component of the semantic representation.

But what is the basis for deciding that *see* has the subcategorization restriction in question? Here we begin to touch on matters having to do with the lexicon, matters we have not investigated closely in our study of learnability thus far. It is useful to observe that in order to account for language learnability in a trace-theoretical context, it will be necessary to account as well for the learnability of lexical entries and perhaps of more general lexical structure.

Significantly, a non-trace-theoretic approach may not call for a theory of the lexicon in the same way. Suppose that the learner is presented with (78). In a standard theory, the learner must infer the deep structure underlying the surface structure, which in English would be roughly (80).

(80) Wh you did see wh+someone

Since constituent order is imposed on deep structures, the learner must be able to infer that wh+$someone$ is ordered to the right of see. On what basis is this inference made? Here, it seems reasonable to suppose that this inference is based on the learner's knowledge that English has a base rule of the form VP → V NP.

To speculate, then, the trace-theoretic approach may not be identical to the non-trace-theoretic approach in terms of the problems that each raises for learnability theory. Investigating this possibility would necessitate a detailed study of the precise role that the lexicon plays in the two approaches and of any formal differences in the organization of grammars that seemed required for descriptive adequacy in terms of the two approaches. Such investigations have not been carried out. However, a few points are worth noting in connection with the development of *filters*, which has taken place along with the (logically independent) development of trace theory (see Chomsky and Lasnik 1977). Filters are required when we attempt to simplify the structural descriptions of transformations radically, by eliminating all contextual information regarding their applicability.

Since eliminating context conditions from transformations often leads to the derivation of ungrammatical sentences, to maintain this approach it is necessary to adopt a system of output filters that will mark as ungrammatical those classes of sentences that the grammar should not generate. Chomsky and Lasnik (1977) report a preliminary investigation into the problem of how these filters are to be constrained. Without going deeply into details, we can see that the notion of a filter potentially presents a challenging problem for learnability theory.

Suppose that the following sequences are derived by the movement of A into initial position by a generally stated (optional) transformation:

(81)
a. AB . . . $\emptyset$ . . .
b. AC . . . $\emptyset$ . . .

Suppose, in addition, that a generally stated rule optionally deletes B or C. Suppose, however, that *AC . . . $\emptyset$ . . . is not a grammatical sequence. Thus, the grammatical sequences are just the following:

(82)
a. AB . . . $\emptyset$ . . .   c. B . . . A . . .   e. . . . A . . .
b. $A\emptyset$ . . . $\emptyset$ . . .   d. C . . . A . . .

To maintain generality, we adopt a filter of the following form:

(83) Any sequence of the form AC. . . is ungrammatical.

Consider now how a learner would learn (83).

The sequence AC . . . could be generated only from a deep structure of the form C . . . A . . . (a derivation that is non-structure-preserving). Call this deep structure D. Some of the (base, surface string) pairs that the learner will be presented with are then those in (84), in which the surface strings are (82b,d,e).

(84)
$(D, A\emptyset$ . . . $\emptyset$ . . .$)$
$(D, C$ . . . A . . .$)$
$(D,$ . . . A . . .$)$

Of course, the learner will never be presented with the pair $(D, AC$ . . .$)$, because the filter will rule out the ungrammatical sequence in the adult speech. Thus, the child will never have a detectable error on the basis of which the filter can be hypothesized. Given D, the rule of fronting A, and the rule for deleting B and C, the child will always be able to match the grammatical string uttered by the adult with a string that his own grammar generates.

It seems, therefore, that filters of this sort are not learnable via the hypothesization methods of chapter 3 unless the learner is explicitly corrected when he violates them. As Chomsky and Lasnik (1977,437) point out (and as has been an assumption of learnability theory—see section 2.7), it is unlikely that such correction takes place. Under the assumptions we have made here it does not appear that such filters are learnable unless they are in some sense universal or follow (for the learner) from universal principles. It would be important to investigate, therefore, whether there are plausible assumptions about the learning task that would allow for the learning of filters such as those proposed by Chomsky and Lasnik.[48]

Along another dimension are recent developments in Montague grammar. Here we must simply note that though the question of learnability of Montague grammars is a potentially interesting one, we have little idea as to the extent to which our current work can be easily adapted to this very different formalism in a natural way. It seems clear that the characterization of grammar presented by Montague himself (1973) is far too unrestricted to permit learnability to be proved, since he allows his grammars to contain rules that are in fact arbitrary effective functions. However, recent work by Partee (1975) and others may point toward plausible restrictions that may make the question of learnability more interesting in this context.

Finally, there are basic learnability problems in aspects of linguistic competence other than syntax. In phonology, for example, it is impossible to construct a learning context that is analogous to that for syntax. In the case of learning the transformational component we can hypothesize that the learner is provided with information about the rules indirectly in the pairs (b,s). The deep structure b is independently specified by the theory, since it is mapped not only into surface structures but into semantic structures. In the case of phonology, however, we do not have this dual interpretation of underlying phonological structures.

The learner is presented with only superficial phonetic information, on the basis of which he must infer both the underlying phonological representations and the rules relating them to the phonetic forms. Unless the class of phonological components is enormously restricted, and unless the set of possible underlying representations is equally severely constrained, this will present a learnability problem. Kean (1975) offers some suggestions about how to sufficiently constrain phonological theory.

7.3.4 Uncharted Territory

At various points in this book we have touched upon questions that we have not dealt with in any detail, if at all. Here we wish simply to recall a few that seem of greatest import for future study. A very important one is, What is the relation between semantic structure and deep structure? It is not at all clear to us what this relation actually is, nor do we believe that the appropriate form for expressing semantic content has been discovered. In many cases, the facts are unclear. There is not even clear agreement as to where the boundary between semantics and pragmatics (in the general, nonindexical, sense) might lie.

In chapter 5 we mentioned numerous problems of syntactic description. Many are unresolved. Those having to do with Comp are particularly important, and though we believe that some inroads have been made, most of the questions we raised are very much open. It goes almost without saying that we have not attempted to carry our research across to other languages. Certainly it is important to determine whether any of the learnability constraints are operative in languages other than English, and if they are not, to what extent the differences can be accommodated within a modified unified approach.

And last is the course of language acquisition. The theory that we have developed here is a theory of language learnability (and language learning), not a theory of the developing language of children. Nevertheless, it is not inconceivable that there could be some contact between the two theories. In particular, the theory of language learnability might constrain in significant ways the lines of development in principle available to the child on the basis of primary data. At the present time we see no aspects of our own work that are particularly applicable to this question, except that any constraints that are part of linguistic theory must operate in the emerging grammars as well as in the adult grammar. The main problem, as we see it, is how to demonstrate that any of the constraints operate in the grammars of children, who lack metalinguistic capacities. Errors found in child language are suggestive, but it seems extremely likely that they greatly underdetermine the theory. Possibly the crucial errors are the ones that children never make, but the data are far from clear; nor have extensive studies of the appropriate sort yet been done.[49]

We believe that the development of a framework of formal language learnability has been and will continue to be of considerable value in helping us to sharpen a variety of crucial theoretical issues in formal linguistics, language acquisition, and linguistic universals. The demand that a linguistic theory provide a class of grammars that is learnable, in the appropriate sense, yields a potentially fruitful set of particular hypotheses concerning the analysis and explanation of linguistic phenomena. Learnability considerations allow us to evaluate claims concerning the form and function of linguistic data available to the language learner. And the criterion of learnability may be applied to all aspects of a linguistic theory with interesting, although not always conclusive, results. In some cases we are led to reconsider traditional analyses; in others, the formal learnability theory itself may require refinement; in others still, it seems that both the primary data and the formal analyses within linguistic theory must be refined before results from learnability theory can be reasonably expected. In general, it is our belief that formal learnability theory offers an exciting perspective on a broad range of current issues and the possibility of real progress in our understanding of the nature of human language.

NOTES

Notes to Chapter 1

1
We cannot physically specify what "normal" means in this case, but that does not mean there is anything circular about the conclusion. The case is the same as in any kind of developmental theory. For example, general principles of embryology may be stated which do not hold for pathological cases. In fact, the use of "normal" in this way is a cornerstone of almost all work in biology. The argument could even be made that the situation is in essential respects the same in the physical sciences. Whatever the conclusion on the philosophical questions involved, the use of "normal" here is in no essential respect different from its use in biology in general.

2
We must distinguish between two kinds of learning. We have in mind learning in the sense in which a child can learn his first language: naturally, without explicit instruction and drill and with no particular struggle on his part. There is a second sense of "learning," in which explicit instruction and drill, specially arranged situations, and particular efforts at learning and discovery *are* allowed. There may be systems capable of being learned in this second sense that may not be capable of being learned in the first sense. We are concerned in this book with systems that may be learned in the first (natural) sense.

3
This distinction, along with a number of others in this chapter, has been repeatedly made by Chomsky. Cf., for example, Chomsky 1975a.

4
The term *primary data* is taken from Chomsky (e.g. 1965, chap. 1).

5
In speaking of theories of language acquisition in this section we are not considering linguistic theories as such. The work of Chomsky (1965 and many other places), in particular, is concerned with whether the theory of language has been stated so that any natural language can be learned. Formal questions of proof of learnability, however, have not in general been developed in linguistic theory. See sec. 1.4 (and chap. 3) for discussion of the relation between learnability and linguistic theory. See Peters 1972 for a discussion and formalization of the "projection problem."

6

The original proof that there are unlearnable classes of languages appears in Gold 1967. See Wexler and Hamburger 1973 and chap. 2 for further examples and for a characterization theorem.

7

In general the innate principles of mind that the evidence in this book leads to are *formal universals* (see Chomsky 1965, chap. 1). Not only are these principles not intuitively given, they are not part of our conscious experience, in general. Furthermore, it is probably true, to the extent that we can determine, that these principles are not even capable of being brought to consciousness. The principles are justified, not because we can come to some kind of intuitive understanding that they are correct, are operating within us, but rather because the postulation of the principles explains empirical data or integrates and makes coherent isolated bodies of theory that are themselves based on empirical data. In short, the kind of justification that exists for these principles is the kind of justification that exists for the postulation of principles in any science (the well-known, successful ones) that is willing to postulate abstract principles to explain empirical data.

8

Levelt (1975d, III, 160–161) claims that empiricist theory does allow strong learning mechanisms:

Confusion is frequently caused by the identification of the empiricist version of LAD [Language Acquisition Device] with behavioristic learning theory. An empiricist theory only states that the organism disposes of little or no foreknowledge of the grammar, but that it can deduce the grammar by means of strong heuristic procedures. These procedures are part of the a priori equipment of the child.

The question is partly terminological. But it is difficult to know what kind of "strong procedures" Levelt could have in mind. Possibly they don't exist. Levelt gives no examples and, in fact, writes that "just as in the rationalistic model the nature of the foreknowledge in question must still be defined more completely, empiricists still face the task of analyzing the structure of the inference mechanisms of which they speak." For the problem of language acquisition there is an extensive and delineated attempt at providing a rationalistic theory (transformational grammar), whereas there is no corresponding study of the "structure of the inference mechanisms of which [empiricists] speak." It is likely, given our results in this book, that no such successful mechanisms could be created. This may be one reason there is as yet, to our knowledge, no serious study of "strong" empiricist mechanisms.

Levelt, by the way, does mention one result in this context (p. 161).

At present, however, the only thing which is known with precision on this point is that all regular grammars, as well as all the more complex grammars which fall into Miller and Chomsky's (1963) *tote schema,* are learnable by means of a certain S-R mechanism in which correct responses are confirmed and incorrect responses are not confirmed (Suppes, 1969).

However, this argument is in error, as may be seen in the criticisms of Suppes' results presented by Arbib (1969), Nelson (1975), Kieras (1976), and Batchelder and Wexler (1979). Among other points, all these voice one fundamental criticism, in varying forms. Suppes' result holds only when the so-called S-R learning mechanism operates in the following manner: After each word in a sentence is spoken, the child is presented with information ("reinforcement") that is dependent on the child's internal state and not only on the word that was uttered. Of course, it is quite improbable that a child receives information after each word. But really incongruous (as all the cited references point out) is the assumption that the reinforcer knows the child's internal state. In Suppes' framework there is no way of getting around this limitation. Suppes' results (and others in the cited articles) have value in that they show the implausibility of S-R mechanisms as the foundation of complicated learning. If such mechanisms demand empirically impossible conditions for their realization, the mechanisms must be suspect.

9
This characterization is true not only of traditional approaches in psychology (e.g. Hull 1943) but of a number of more modern approaches. See chap. 6 for further discussion.

10
Chomsky (1975a) calls the entire apparatus (principles, constraints on form, etc.) responsible for mapping experience into competence the "learning theory." In a more traditional terminology (in psychology, especially, but also in linguistics and philosophy) only the mechanisms responsible for time-to-time change (the S-R connections, or the hypothesis construction mechanisms) are called part of the learning theory. Constraints on form, etc., receive no name in this traditional psychological terminology, because they are assumed not to exist.

11

A theory might not even break up human abilities into domains. In some ways this is equivalent to (i) and (ii).

12

The kinds of "cognitive constraints" on language learning that are most often discussed are really constraints on language use. That is, the constraints don't make reference to a procedure for inducing a grammar but, rather, constrain the grammar attained at a particular time in its use in the production or comprehension of sentences. An example is the hypothesized constraint against producing a sentence that contains more than one transformation (Bellugi-Klima 1968).

13

Even if one were primarily interested in the performance aspects of a young child's language, it is difficult to see how an adequate theory could be created without taking a theory of the child's linguistic competence into account. One would have to attempt to achieve an adequate description of the child's linguistic ability, which (as argued in section 1.4) is to a good degree dependent on the creation of an adequate learning theory for language, which itself depends on the learnability criterion we are discussing. (See Wexler, in press, for discussion.)

Recently a number of investigators have become actively concerned with the important goal of integrating studies in child language with studies in the nature of language (linguistic theory). These include Roeper (1978) and Mayer, Erreich and Valian (1978).

14

Languages in general are infinite objects, so a theory that specifies the possible languages actually specifies the possible grammars. Thus the "class of possible languages" is really taken to be the class of languages generated by the class of possible grammars. Note also that the criterion of learnability that we will be studying in this book does not guarantee that the exact grammar that generates the language from which primary data is presented to the learner is actually chosen by the learning or selection procedure. We guarantee only that a grammar equivalent to the grammar that generates the data is selected. The notion of equivalence will vary in different contexts, but generally two grammars will be defined to be equivalent in the relevant sense if the two entire (infinite) sets of data that could in principle be generated from the two grammars are equivalent. For example, if the set of data consists only of grammatical sentences, two grammars are equivalent in the relevant sense if they are weakly equivalent, that is, if the two grammars generate the same sets of sentences (strings). The criterion of learnability, as developed to date, does not guarantee, so far as is known, that a descriptively adequate grammar is chosen in all cases. However, the example just given is somewhat misleading: in general, more than just the correct set of sentences being chosen will be guaranteed by the criterion. And it may turn out that the assumptions are such that descriptively adequate grammars are chosen, although this outcome is not demanded by the criterion and thus is not proved. In general, it is important to specify all the kinds of judgments that go into the definition of descriptive adequacy, so that the learnability criterion can be strengthened.

15
As in note 14, an equivalent grammar may be selected. In informal discussion we will often ignore this possibility and speak of selecting "the grammar" from which data is presented. It is important to note that there might be possible grammars (ones that meet the biologically given constraints on form) that are not learnable. These grammars could not be grammars for natural languages (see sec. 2.1.1 for discussion). In this book we study the implications of the hypothesis that all possible grammars are learnable. We can expect the results to be relevant even if the hypothesis turns out to be false. The hypothesis is not necessary to a theory of learnability.

16
In actual linguistic practice it usually turns out that no theory can account for all the data that is known about a language. So the most that could be said is that the two theories account for the same subset of the known data. In fact, it often happens that competing theories account for different sets of data, each of the theories being successful on a set of data for which the other theory fails. These situations will make our subsequent point, about the usefulness of the learnability criterion when two theories account for the same data, even stronger. We can therefore ignore these complexities here.

17
Culicover and Wexler (1977) provide a formal artificial example for which exactly this situation can be proved to arise. See sec. 3.2 for further discussion of the relation between linguistic theory and learnability theory. If the hypothesis that all possible grammars are learnable (see note 15) turns out to be false, we could still use an explicit learnability requirement in comparing theories of grammar. For example, we

could check whether the grammars provided for natural languages by a particular theory were learnable.

18

Two grammars are *strongly equivalent* if they provide the same set of structural descriptions for sentences. They are *weakly equivalent* if they generate the same set of sentences. What Chomsky means by meeting "empirical conditions on strong (and, a fortiori, weak) generative capacity" is that for each natural language the class of possible grammars specified by the theory includes a grammar that is strongly equivalent to the grammar for that natural language (i.e., the requirement that descriptive adequacy is met).

19

The data that a child can use in selecting his language is more restricted than that available to the linguist for the purpose of theory construction and testing. For example (as discussed in chap. 2), it seems that in general information about what sentences are ungrammatical is not available to the child. Also, many sentences (very long or complex ones) are probably not available to the child. If we rule these out of the definition of primary data, the criterion of explanatory adequacy becomes more complex. Of course it is probable that a child won't hear only short sentences. Language can be learned under a variety of conditions, including quite different sets of sentences as exemplars. The requirement of feasibility will have to allow the appropriate grammar to be learned under these restricted possibilities of access to data.

20

This section assumes familiarity with a number of the concepts of linguistic theory, including the notions of phrase-marker and transformation. Readers unfamiliar with this theory might read any of a number of works, for example, Chomsky (1965). Introductory textbooks include Akmajian and Heny (1975) and Culicover (1976b).

21

A transformation T *analyzes* a node N in a phrase-marker if a nonvariable element A of the structural description of T applies to N.

Notes to Chapter 2

1

Performance considerations sometimes imply that richer sets of experiences might make for more difficult learnability problems. For example, too much information might overload an attentional system, causing the learner to pay attention to no information at all. We are ignoring such factors, which, at any rate, are little understood with regard to language acquisition.

2

Another interpretation of the possibility of more than one procedure would be that an individual learner tries more than one procedure, perhaps in serial order, perhaps in parallel, perhaps probabilistically. Whatever truth lies in these possibilities doesn't matter for the purposes of our framework, however, because even if such possibilities occur, the varying procedures are subprocedures of one larger procedure which includes the alternatives, together with a specification of how they come into play. For example, if the relevant notion is that a language learner matures and uses different procedures as he grows older, the larger procedure simply changes in time, defining subprocedures at each of the relevant time intervals. The important notion is that there is *one* procedure associated with the task of language learning, even if there are alternative subprocedures. In the theories in this book, we do not consider questions such as the possibility of different procedures being associated with maturing. Rather, we assume one fixed procedure. It is difficult to know what else to do at this stage of our investigation, given the paucity of knowledge about language learning procedures.

3

See the references in note 8, chap. 1.

4

We hope that the limitation of scope is temporary, simply part of a natural working procedure in which we can attack only part of a problem at any one time.

5

The conception of a language as a set of strings was introduced in Chomsky 1957, but even in that work it was made clear that a language is much more than a set of strings and that linguistic theory has to deal with other properties if it is to be descriptively adequate.

6

There may very well be other information available to the language learner. We will consider this information in later sections.

7

This definition is a generalization of Gold's (1967) "text learnability." By our definition, there may be more than one set of primary data for a language, even an infinite number. We can define a *minimal* set of primary data as a set of primary data that contains no subsets of primary data. There can be more than one minimal set of primary data for a grammar, even an infinite number. That is, D and D' are both minimal sets of primary data if both D and D' are sets of primary data and if no subsets of D or of D' are sets of primary data. It follows that if D and D' are both minimal sets of primary data, $D \neq D'$, then neither $D \subseteq D'$ nor $D' \subseteq D$.

8

In the theory of learnability that we are led to in this book the bounding requirement is essentially met (since degree-2 learnability holds—see chap. 4).

9

We ignore the possibility of changing a grammar indefinitely. Although an adult may change some small aspects of his grammar, these changes seem removed from the essential notions of grammar. The current idealization doesn't allow for such possibilities. It seems reasonable to demand that there be a point at which core notions of grammar have been learned.

10

For example, we could take G_1 to consist of the three rules $S \rightarrow A$, $A \rightarrow aA$, and $A \rightarrow a$; G_2 to have the rules $S \rightarrow aA$, $A \rightarrow aA$, and $A \rightarrow a$ and, in general, G_i to have the rules $S \rightarrow a^{i-1}A$, $A \rightarrow aA$, and $A \rightarrow a$. Note that for simplicity we have constructed the example so that no two grammars generate the same language. Nothing in the example hinges on the exact choice of grammars.

11

To prove that $\mathcal{H}$ is not learnable, suppose that f is a learning function for $\mathcal{H}$. By the definition of learnability, there must exist a finite set of primary data for each grammar in $\mathcal{H}$. In particular, let D_0 be a set of primary data for H_0. That is, D_0 is a finite set of strings on a such that for any set of data D such that $D_0 \subseteq D \subseteq L(H_0), f(D) = H_0$. Let $H_i (i \neq 0)$

be any grammar such that $L(H_i) \supseteq D_0$. (These clearly exist; in fact there are an infinite number of them.) $L(H_i)$ is itself a finite set of data. By the definition of learnability $L(H_i)$ must contain a subset that is the set of primary data for H_i. Thus $f(L(H_i)) = H_i$. But since $D_0 \subseteq L(H_i) \subseteq L(H_0)$, we know that $f(L(H_i)) = H_0$. Thus we have found a contradiction, which proves that no such learning function f can exist. A version of this example appears in Gold 1967.

12
The proof is omitted but may be found in Wexler and Hamburger 1973, sec. 1. There a slightly more restrictive definition of learnability is given, namely, that of *text* learnability (cf. sec. 2.3), a definition that demands effective procedures instead of simply the existence of a learning function. A complete Characterization theorem is not proved (necessary and sufficient conditions), but rather two separate theorems are proved. The first theorem (necessity) is essentially identical to the only-if part of the Characterization theorem given in this text. However, the second theorem (sufficiency) has to add conditions in order for us to achieve a proof, especially the condition that for any two grammars in the class, an effective procedure exists for telling whether the language of one grammar is a subset of the language of the other grammar. It is still an open question whether this assumption is necessary. That is, we have only proved the theorem using the assumption. However, we have not discovered any counterexamples without the assumption (that is, we have not discovered classes of grammars that meet all the conditions of the second theorem except for the existence of the subset procedure and that are not learnable). At any rate, the Characterization theorem in this text follows from the proofs of both of the "effective" theorems, since for our noneffective definition of learnability, the existence of an effective procedure for the subset question is not relevant. We simply need to know that a (not necessarily effective) function exists which selects minimal grammars. This clearly exists. The proofs in Wexler and Hamburger 1973 also involve the notion of time, and a slightly different notation. The time constructs can be omitted and the notation translated into the set notation in a straightforward manner. (Our original work demanded effective learnability. The idea to generalize to noneffective set-learnability arose in a conversation with Louis Narens.)

13
Intuitive notions of "effective" or "computable" can be formalized in a number of ways. Church's Thesis claims that none of these ways will be more powerful than the formalization provided by the theory of

Turing machines. The reader unfamiliar with these notions may consult
Davis 1958.

14
This definition is taken, with some notation and terminology changes,
from Wexler and Hamburger (1973). The definition is essentially that of
Gold (1967) but involves some technical modifications following
Feldman (1969) and Feldman et al. (1969). In original formulations,
learnability was called "identifiability in the limit."

15
The result follows from the Characterization theorem given in sec. 2.2.
To see this let the "universal" set L_0 of the Characterization theorem
be the infinite set in the superfinite class. If $L_0 = \{s_1, s_2, \ldots \}$, let the L_i
of the Characterization theorem be defined as $L_i = \{s_1, s_2, \ldots, s_i\}$.
These constructions meet the conditions of the Characterization theorem. Thus the class is unlearnable. This proves that a class of grammars
that generates a superfinite class of languages is not text-learnable
since the superfinite class is a superset of this unlearnable class.
See (5).

16
It is not known whether the converse is true. See note 12.

17
The mathematical theory of context-free grammars is studied in a
number of sources, including Chomsky 1963, Chomsky and Schutzenberger 1963, and Ginsburg 1966.

18
Syntactic transformations are a special (structure-dependent) kind of
mapping of phrase-markers (rooted, labeled trees, which represent the
structure of sentences) into phrase-markers. (See, for example,
Chomsky 1957; 1960; 1965.)

19
Since a context-free phrase structure grammar specifies the linear
order of constituents, the strongest version of the Universal Base
Hypothesis would claim that all languages have a single underlying
order. If we interpret this claim as equivalent to the claim that the
intuitively basic or canonical order of constituents in surface structure
is universal, then it is surely false: Japanese is verb-final and English is
verb-medial, for example. However, we could imagine a state of affairs
in which all languages shared this single base order, and the various

canonical orders were transformationally derived. The empirical evidence does not appear to support this view, in general, although McCawley (1970) has attempted to demonstrate that the underlying order of English is verb-initial (and thus is not directly reflected in surface structure). For critical discussion of McCawley's claim, see Berman 1974 and Wasow 1976.

20
Peters and Richie (1973a) have shown that every recursively enumerable set can be generated by the class of transformational grammars on a context-free base. Our desired result immediately follows. However, our examples will not use some very powerful devices used by Peters and Richie, including deletion.

21
In Peters and Richie 1973b, in which filtering is not allowed, it is shown that a more restricted class of languages is generated.

22
A function that can make the selection will always exist if we allow infinite sets of data to be used, that is, if the function is defined on infinite sets of strings. For example, if infinite data are allowed, $\mathcal{H}$ (sec. 2.2) would become learnable; f would be such that the set of primary data for $L(H_0)$ would be $L(H_0)$ itself, an infinite set. If we demanded that aspects of descriptive adequacy other than the set of grammatical strings be acquired, it would not be the case that all classes of grammars are learnable. (See sec. 2.6.)

23
We are keeping the notion of procedure separate from the notion of input and of linguistic possibilities. Procedure here (LP) is the learning mechanism of chap. 1.

24
Bar-Hillel, Perles, and Shamir 1961.

25
The analogy shouldn't be drawn too closely. For example, the subset problem has a more restrictive criterion; namely, an answer of A, B, or 0 has to be emitted, rather than simply a series of guesses, all of which except for the first finite number would have to be correct, as in text-learnability. The subset problem and learnability problem seem to differ as computational problems in that the first starts from a specification of rules (grammar) and tries to deduce a property of the grammars,

whereas the learnability problem starts from behavior or properties and tries to deduce the grammar. The latter problem appears to be more difficult, in general. It appears that the only way to solve it is to turn it into a variant of the former problem, with much of the structure given as starting information.

26
For example, $\mathcal{H}$ of sec. 2.2 is still unlearnable. The proof is clear, namely, there is only one grammar for any language in the class anyway. Without working out the details, it seems that the proof of the Characterization theorem can be maintained so that it will turn out that exactly the same classes of grammars are learnable under this weakened criterion as under the criterion of set-learnability as we have given it.

27
As we stress throughout this book, and as is stressed in linguistic theory, such knowledge does not have to be conscious. It is an empirical question what constitutes knowledge of a language, and consciousness is not criterial.

28
One way of achieving strong learnability solely by restricting the class of grammars would be for the theory of grammar to be such that the allowable grammars that generate a particular language (set of strings) all be strongly equivalent. There is no reason to think that the theory of grammar in general can be constrained to this extent, although it is an empirical question. The point is very much like the question in linguistic theory of whether, in general, there will be only one allowable grammar that is compatible with the primary data. Chomsky (1965, 36–37) writes,

It is logically possible that the data might be sufficiently rich and the class of potential grammars sufficiently limited so that no more than a single permitted grammar will be compatible with the available data at the moment of successful language acquisition, in our idealized "instantaneous" model . . . In this case, no evaluation procedure will be necessary as a part of linguistic theory—that is, as an innate property of an organism or a device capable of language acquisition. It is rather difficult to imagine how in detail this logical possibility might be realized, and all concrete attempts to formulate an empirically adequate linguistic theory certainly leave ample room for mutually inconsistent grammars, all compatible with primary data of any conceivable sort. All such theories therefore require supplementation by an evaluation measure if language acquisition is to be accounted for and selection of specific grammars is to be justified.

In the case of set-learnability theory, since a set of primary data is uniquely associated with a particular language (set of strings), if all the allowable grammars for that language are strongly equivalent, the grammars that a successful learning function could select from a set of primary data must all be strongly equivalent. Thus the problem is similar in strong-learnability and linguistic theory, except that we replace the notion of "one grammar compatible with the primary data" with the notion of "a class of strongly-equivalent grammars compatible with the primary data."

29
In some cases the property may be directly built into the language learning procedure. In other cases the property might emerge from the application of the procedure, although the property is not directly stated (as in the attainability framework discussed in sec. 2.1.1).

30
This conception, as we argue, is inescapable. For example, in Chomsky's (1965) framework for a theory of language acquisition it occurs directly. Not only does a child need "a technique for representing input signals"; he also needs "a way of representing structural information about these signals" (p. 30). In terms of linguistic theory this corresponds to "a definition of 'structural description'" (p. 31).

31
Recently, theories of the lexicon have begun to be more extensively developed. See, for example, Bresnan (1978), Roeper and Siegel (1978), and Wasow (1977). The goal of such theories should ultimately be the same as linguistic theory in general, namely, to explain how the child can learn language. Lexical theories might be such that certain structures can be most naturally learned if they are considered to be lexical. In addition, such theories of the lexicon might ultimately explain the kind of information that a child has early about the lexicon that helps in the problem of the learning of transformations, and how this information is learned. We do not consider theories of the lexicon in this book. Ultimately they should be a component of an adequate learnability theory.

32
We are ignoring, for now, the possibility that the string that the learner hears could be ungrammatical. For discussion see section 7.3.1.

33
Chomsky (1965, 25) leaves the question open and considers that the child might receive both positive and negative information, that is, instances of sentences (labeled as such) and nonsentences (labeled as such), the former arising naturally in the speech that the child hears and the latter coming from some kind of process of correction.

34
We have ignored certain technical modifications of this result, especially Gold's case of "anomalous" presentation and the role of primitive recursiveness. These considerations do not change the character of the discussion.

35
Note that there has been no demonstration that including negative information in the input will help with the problem of strong learnability. It is plausible, however, that negative information could help with this problem, that is, could help to ensure that descriptively adequate grammars are selected. This will be true, of course, to the extent that variations in structure will yield variations in output. In fact, many of the complexities of current work in linguistic theory involve puzzles as to why certain strings are ungrammatical, rather than why they are grammatical. That is, linguistic theory as it stands, uncomplicated by additional constraints, accepts certain strings that native speakers judge to be ungrammatical. A major puzzle is the question of, first, how to account for these ungrammaticalities descriptively (in a grammar) and, second, why the language learner chooses a grammar that rejects these sentences. If we could assume that the learner was somehow told that these particular sentences were ungrammatical, it would be clearer, at least in broad outline, why the attained grammars made the sentences ungrammatical. To the extent that we cannot assume that there is negative information (which is essentially what we will claim), then the existence of these ungrammatical sentences will have to be accounted for by other aspects of learnability theory, particularly by restrictions on the form of grammar that is possible, given primary data. Some examples appear in chap. 5. See Baker (in press) for related discussion.

36
This interpretation is analogous to Gold's (1967) "request informant."

37
Even if the child is corrected, there is no reason to believe that he takes

note of the correction in a way useful for language acquisition. Consider the mother-child interaction reported by McNeill (1966, 69):

Child: Nobody don't like me.
Mother: No, say "nobody like*s* me."
Child: Nobody don't like me.
(. . . Eight repetitions of this dialogue . . .)
Mother: No, now listen carefully; say "*nobody likes me.*"
Child: Oh! Nobody don't like*s* me.

38
Even if listeners do differentially comprehend grammatical and ungrammatical utterances of the child, the child might interpret the noncomprehension in a variety of ways. For example, the child might think that various pragmatic conditions (on conversation, say) were not being met, or that the listener was disagreeing. The Brown and Hanlon study is not a study of the effect of reinforcers, but a study of whether reinforcers exist that differentially reinforce the child's grammatical and ungrammatical utterances.

39
There really is a paucity of studies concerning the linguistic environment of the child, especially with regard to how this environment can aid in language learning. As far as we know, the Brown and Hanlon study has not been replicated. There are very few studies concerning whether children or other adults respond less appropriately to primitive utterances than do mothers. In a recent collection of conference papers (Campbell and Smith 1978) eight papers were published in a section entitled "Mother/Other–Child Interaction and Language Development." Of these, none reported any research relevant to the question of how the environment provided information on which the learning of syntax could be (even partially) based. One article was concerned with intonational contour. The other seven articles were concerned in one way or another with pragmatic considerations, for example, conversational rules.

40
A yet more subtle form of negative information may be available to the child. Brown, Cazden, and Bellugi (1968) discuss the occurrence of expansions in parent-child interactions. For example (see McNeill 1970, 108), if the child says "That mommy hairband," his mother might expand the utterance by replying, "That's mommy's hairband." Note that many other sentences could have been used for the expan-

sion. Which one is used depends on the situation. The child is receiving negative information, but not of the form "*That mommy hairband* is not a grammatical sentence." If he were, he would have no way of knowing that a semantic correction was not a correction of the form "That utterance is not a sentence." We might look on the expansion as informing the child that the utterance he has just made is not the correct utterance given the interpretation of the situation. Rather, the expansion is the proper surface sentence. The sentence the child uttered may be a sentence of the language, but it does not have the structure indicated by the correct interpretation of the situation. Thus, negative information is presented to the child, but a particular kind of negative information. This interpretation is consistent with the theory presented in chap. 3.

41
We will discuss the well-formed nature of speech to children later.

42
LAD refers to Language Acquisition Device. LAD theories are essentially any theory (for example, that of Chomsky, 1965) in which the language learner is thought of as forming hypotheses about grammar based on a starting configuration and the input data. Levelt is essentially criticizing the conclusion that a complex starting configuration (innate component) will be necessary.

43
For example, it has been suggested that sometimes adults utter a sentence to a child together with other sentences that are transformationally related to this sentence. Such data might make it easier for the child to learn the transformation. Although such presentation may be of some help, the child has the same general interpretive problem as for correction and other "training" routines. Note that often sentences are presented together which are *not* transformationally related. If the child assumes that (temporal) contiguity of sentences implies that they are transformationally related, he will often draw quite incorrect conclusions. Of course, this objection is not proof that such schemes won't work, but certainly any such training theory will have to explicitly come to grips with such problems. At present none do, and it seems reasonable to be skeptical about the possibilities.

44
Although there is evidence, which we will discuss shortly, that speech to children is in general different from speech to adults (for one thing,

speech to children tends to be shorter), this fact in no way implies a special sequence of utterances to a child which give him special information (coded into the sequence) that aids in language learning.

45
Ferguson adds,

If the effects of BT as a teaching device were decisive, this would certainly have been noticed long ago in many societies, and in particular by child development researchers. But in the absence of detailed experimental evidence one can still join Snow's (1972:561) observation that the speech addressed to young children 'in many ways seems quite well designed as a set of "language lessons." ' (1977, 233)

The conclusion that the speech addressed to young children seems 'well designed as a set of "language lessons",' does not mean that the speech actually functions as a set of language lessons. In fact, there is evidence, which we will discuss, that this speech does *not* function in this particular way (aside from its exemplar role, of course). All that similarity between speech addressed to children and language lessons might mean is that our commonsense understanding of what would constitute good language lessons agrees in some details with BT. The causative relations are completely unknown. It might turn out that our commonsense understanding of "language lessons" derives from an observation of BT. Or that BT derives from a commonsense understanding of "good language lesson." There are many other possibilities.

We have no particular reason to think that our commonsense understanding of "good language lesson" is in fact correct. Being immersed in a natural language situation is better in general, even for second language learning, than training according to any of our commonsense concepts of language lessons. Nor has learning theory in psychology or education been able to precisely state, and supply compelling evidence for, any particular notion of what a good language lesson is. In our opinion, the investigation of our folk notions of "good language lesson" would make an interesting study, along with such notions as our folk perception of how the physical world operates (which, of course, are quite different from the theories that have emerged from the study of physics). This folk perception of what constitutes a good language lesson should not be confused with what actually constitutes a good language lesson (if, in fact, there is such a thing).

46
Snow's admission that there is no empirical reason to believe that

particular details of mother's speech have an effect on what is learned is particularly interesting in view of her statement that:

The first descriptions of mothers' speech to young children were undertaken in the late sixties in order to refute the prevailing view that language acquisition was largely innate and occurred almost independently of the language environment. The results of those mothers' speech studies may have contributed to the widespread abandonment of this hypothesis about language acquisition, but a general shift of emphasis from syntactic to semantic–cognitive aspects of language acquisition would probably have caused it to lose its central place as a tenet of research in any case (p. 31).

It is not clear why the results of mothers' speech studies (which Snow admits do not show a language acquisition role for mothers' speech) should contribute to the "widespread abandonment of this [innateness] hypothesis." Incidentally, so far as we can tell from the literature, the innateness hypothesis was never widely held and so could hardly have been the subject of widespread abandonment. The hypothesis, as we discuss it in this book, is still accepted by very few psychologists (it is difficult to find examples). Perhaps a few more linguists than psychologists accept the view, but it does not seem to us to have been the "prevailing view" in the sixties, nor is it now the prevailing view.

It is also not clear why Snow seems to think that a shift to semantic and cognitive aspects of language acquisition would lead to an abandonment of the innateness hypothesis. Presumably she means that these aspects of language acquisition can be shown to be more clearly related to environmental influences than can the acquisition of syntactic structure. If so, the "abandonment" of the innateness hypothesis is not due to evidence that there are no innate principles of language. Rather, the crucial problem of the acquisition of syntactic structure has simply been ignored. If a scientist chooses to ignore a problem, the principles needed to solve the problem may be "abandoned."

It is not at all clear that semantic and cognitive aspects of language acquisition can be described and explained without the use of innate structural principles any more than can the acquisition of syntax. In our opinion the situation simply is that we have a good deal less formal structural knowledge about semantics (and even less about cognition) than we have about syntax. Thus there are fewer restrictions on imagining how semantic and cognitive principles can be "learned" in a way heavily dependent on the environment. Suppose that linguists had no knowledge of syntax. One might then imagine that sentences consisted of associations between words. It would be relatively straightforward to begin to construct a theory of how these associations could be learned (details would differ from theory to theory). We would not need too much in the way of innate principles, except for a few principles of association. Such theories have been tried in the past and are not totally nonexistent at present. Of course, the theories ignore the principles of syntax that have been discovered by linguists. If we ever determine precise and adequate structural theories for semantics and cognition (possible in principle but, especially for cognition, not realized as yet), it might turn out that these principles are not "learned" in a way heavily dependent on the environment. Until we have such principles, speculation may be of little value. As Chomsky has written,

I think it is fair to say that these empiricist views are most plausible where we are most ignorant. The more we learn about some aspect of human cognition, the less reasonable these views seem to be. No one would seriously argue today, for example, that our construction of perceptual space is guided by empiricist maxims. The same, I think, is true of the language faculty, which relates more closely to the essential nature of the human species. I suspect that the empiricist position with regard to higher mental functions will crumble as science advances towards an understanding of cognitive capacity and its relations to physical structures (1975a, 126).

47
LAS refers to Language Acquisition System, the same as LAD (see note 42). The "meager and degenerate" characterization is from Chomsky (1968, 68), as quoted by Slobin (1975b, 283–284):

I think that if we contemplate the classical problem of psychology, that of accounting for human knowledge, we cannot avoid being struck by the enormous disparity between knowledge and experience—in the case of language, between the generative grammar that expresses the linguistic competence of the native speaker and the meager and degenerate data on the basis of which he has constructed this grammar for himself.

Since "meager and degenerate" is not an exact term, it is difficult to know whether it is "a bit too severe." More important is to note that the characterization of the data is to be taken *in relation to* the ultimate knowledge of language that an adult speaker has. Certainly nothing like the rich structures that linguists have uncovered in language are part of the data available to a language learner. In fact, the very argument of those we have quoted that language input consists of simple aspects of language tends to make the input meager. As to "degenerate," suppose it is true that the great bulk of language addressed to a child is grammatical, lacks false starts, etc. Still, as Chomsky (personal communication) points out, even a very small number of ungrammatical sentences has to cause a problem for an uninformed learner.

In our view, the arguments here are qualitative arguments, which of course will be subject to controversy, since notions such as meager and degenerate can be interpreted differently by different authors. The essential point, as Slobin writes, is that the characterization of the input given by students of BT "in no way solves the problem of language acquisition posed by Chomsky." In our opinion, the ultimate resolution of these issues depends on a precise characterization of the relation between input and attained grammar, as we are attempting to (partially) accomplish in this book.

48

NGG appeared in Snow and Ferguson (1977), in which Brown's article appears as the Introduction; his discussion of the nature of BT and its role in language acquisition is based on the articles in the collection. NGG, as we have indicated, is a particularly sound study of these questions. It is interesting, therefore, that of the sixteen papers in the collection, the only one that Brown does not mention is NGG. (NGG, at 41 pages, is the longest article in the collection.)

49

Snow (1977) points to the interactional aspects of speech between a mother and child. Of course, interactional effects exist and are important if one is trying to explain why particular utterances occur. The child's response affects what the mother says and vice versa. How could it be otherwise in conversation? But, as always, we must not confuse the role of a concept in explaining, on the one hand, why certain utterances are made and, on the other hand, how language acquisition takes place. Even if it could be shown that interactional aspects of the language learning situation are crucial for language acquisition (for example, as motivation), this would still not vitiate the need for structural assumptions.

Consider the development of vision. Surely even here there is interaction. Mothers will point to objects, bring them into the child's line of sight, draw attention to special features. We know from animal studies that the crucial effects of experience on the development of vision involve the organism having experience at an early age (see Blakemore 1974 for a review). But nothing special in the way of tutoring is required for the development of vision. Of course, certain experiences might help the organism to learn particular things; for example, seeing a chair will help the organism to recognize chairs. There is no reason to believe that tutoring is more essential to the development of language than to the development of vision.

50

Snow (1977, 36) writes that "the broad outlines of mothers' speech to children—that it is simple and redundant . . . —are quite well established." She adds,

The central theme of mothers' speech research, of course, one which was present implicitly if not explicitly in all the studies mentioned above, is the relevance of mothers' speech to language acquisition. The generality of mothers' speech, including young children's ability to produce it, had to be established in order to show that all language-learning children, even those raised by fathers or older siblings, have access to a simplified speech register. No one has to learn to talk from a confused, error-ridden garble of opaque structure" (p. 38).

Since Snow offers no quotations, we don't know whether she means that someone has suggested that children learn to speak from a "confused error-ridden garble." This is not the view as put forth in the literature. Presumably Snow intends that an utterance is opaque if its structure is not immediately evident from surface aspects of the discourse. With regard to many of the properties that linguists have discovered are true of natural language, it is difficult to see how these are evident in the linguistic input, and Snow offers no evidence that they are. Her claim that all children have "access to a simplified speech register" is not substantiated by the NGG findings, at least with respect to most indices of syntactic simplicity.

What is the evidence for syntactic complexity of BT in the papers that Snow cites, in which she says "description of the characteristics of the speech was primarily accomplished"? Aside from mean length of utterance and a few other measures, she writes, "very few measures have really been intensively studied" (p. 32). However, she says that one paper (Pfuderer 1969) does concentrate on syntactic complexity. We don't have this paper available to us, but it is summarized in Andersen (1977, 363–364), the annotated bibliography to Snow and Ferguson (1977), in the following way:

This study indicates that a mother's speech to her child becomes increasingly complex during the child's second and third year. It is suggested that simplification in baby talk is directly correlated to the language production or comprehension of the child.

We do not know how Pfuderer measured syntactic complexity, but from the summary it does not appear as if the measures of complexity were compared with measures of the adult speaking to another adult (as in NGG). Also, the results summarized are the opposite of what NGG find. From what is summarized in Snow, there does not appear to be much evidence that BT is syntactically simple, in the sense of commonsensical notions of language lessons. Of course, that speech to children is short makes certain measures of complexity appear to be simpler for children. And NGG argue from their studies (p. 123) that "even the finding of low propositional complexity is probably better interpreted in terms of a gross bias toward brevity in maternal speech rather than in terms of a metric of syntactic simplicity."

McTear (1978), in a review of Snow and Ferguson (1977), writes that the notion that adults "reduce their syntax in order to teach their children syntax in a sort of language-teaching programme . . . is given very little support in the papers in this volume" (p. 524). Also, "Although many studies of BT suggest some relationship between BT and language acquisition, there has been little evidence of actual effects" (p. 528).

51

Another analysis performed by NGG concerns the effect of repetition on language growth. A common claim is that repetition by the mother aids language growth. A number of studies have found that the more advanced the child's age and linguistic abilities, the less the repetition by the mother. The usual interpretation is that as the child comes to know more about his language, he needs repetition less. But another interpretation is possible, as NGG point out. It may simply be that younger children are less likely to understand or attend to an utterance, and so it is repeated. In fact, "Newport (1976) showed that the child's tendency to respond to an utterance was unrelated to the serial position of that utterance in a repetition sequence" (NGG, 142). In NGG's data, the partial correlation between maternal repetitions and child growth scores is in fact negative, not positive (p. 142). Once again, the use of sounder methods of empirical analysis leads to a noneffect of what had been believed to be an effect of input.

52

Interestingly, Brown (1977) seems to share this conclusion, with respect to the intentions of parents, not their effects. He explicitly (p. 12) argues against the notion that parents' intentions are "to provide language lessons." But in a section entitled "What Does Baby Talk Accomplish?" Brown makes his remark about the evidence of BT refuting "overwhelmingly" the need for an "elaborate innate component." Therefore he must think that although intentions of parents are to communicate, the effects of the process are to strongly help somehow in language acquisition. The evidence from the BT literature is not consistent with this view.

53

The input to the child appears from the relevant studies to be mostly grammatical, but even a few ungrammatical sentences might cause trouble to an uninformed learner. At any rate, the theory of set-learnability assumes that the input is grammatical. Therefore the studies cannot help us here. For the purposes of analysis we will continue to assume that the input is grammatical. This simplifies our problem and lets work proceed. It still will turn out that we will need many structural assumptions. For a fully adequate theory we will ultimately have to study the effects of ungrammatical input. In chap. 7 we offer some speculations on how such a study might proceed. The theory must be robust enough to allow the correct grammars to be learned given the amount of ungrammatical input that can be expected for a child who learns language normally.

54

Brown is implying that children have innate cognitive capacities, having to do with perception and understanding of the world. If parents do not speak to children in categories that the children understand, the children will tune them out. According to this hypothesis there are uniformities in early speech because of these cognitive capacities. Even if this is uniformly true, the argument has no implications concerning the need for structural principles. It just provides evidence for the need for innate cognitive principles. There is no reason to think that both cognitive and syntactic principles won't be needed to explain language acquisition. See note 46.

55

Brown (1977, 13) points out the +0.72 correlation, but fails to note that the correlation in Cross's data of degree of nonimmediate reference with age of the child is +0.60. Thus almost all of the correlation of nonimmediate reference with linguistic development could possibly be attributed to effects of age. There is no way from Cross's presentation of data and analyses to surmise that age or comprehension ability (or some other variable) is causal. Cross argues in general that input is finely tuned to the child's abilities rather than age because the correlations with age were smaller than other correlations. For example, "Correlations with age exceeded those with language measures only twice in 26 discourse parameters" (p. 166). But there were six measures, including age. Even on a completely uniform assumption, a particular measure would be the highest of them all on the average 26/6 = 4.33 times. The figure of 2 is not so small. And most of the time the difference in correlations is not so large. The point, as NGG point out, is that without a partial correlational analysis, there is no way to draw the kinds of conclusions that Cross wants to draw. Many other statistical criticisms could be made. Brown (1977) must realize the weakness of the inference because he writes,

Very many of Cross's correlations are high, and I think she is right to conclude that mothers' speech is fine-tuned to the child's psycholinguistic development . . . I do realize that Cross's data do not prove these things and that I am responding quite selectively and with partiality because her major results, as she chooses to interpret them, accord well with my own experience (p. 13).

56
Much current research (e.g., Chomsky 1977) is carried out under the *trace theory,* which allows surface structure to play an even greater role in semantic interpretation. We will for the most part ignore trace theory in this book. However, one can imagine ways in which such a theory can help to provide (given the interpretation) syntactic information to the language learner. The learnability properties of such a proposal would have to be precisely investigated in order to determine how it interacts with the theory of learnability. See chap. 7 for some speculations on such a proposal.

57
Actually, the Katz-Postal hypothesis does not have to be assumed. Rather, we have to assume that the child has the ability to (sometimes) construct the deep structure of a sentence that he hears without totally understanding the syntax of the sentence. It would be an important area of future research to analyze how minimal this ability has to be.

58
It is likely that some information is provided by intonation, but we see no reason to believe that much structural information about the surface phrase-marker is available to the learner. But see note 56.

59
In chapter 7, we make some tentative and partial proposals concerning how a syntactic structure might be constructed from a semantic interpretation, but the problem is a difficult one. Even more difficult is the general problem for psychology of how one constructs an interpre-

tation from a situation. We have nothing to offer here, nor is much known about this problem.

60

There is a potential problem. If a child has in mind the wrong interpretation for an utterance, he may have no reason to think that he doesn't understand it. Given that he has an interpretation for the sentence, he might be able to create a deep structure that maps that interpretation, and might attempt to build a transformational account of the relation between that deep structure and the sentence string that he heard. In short, if b is the correct deep structure for the correct interpretation of the utterance, the child, instead of using the input (b,s), might use (b',s) and attempt to build a transformational system that maps b' into s. This problem then is a problem of wrong data, and is akin to the problem that would be caused by the presentation of ungrammatical sentences (unlabeled as such) as input. If the child actually does make this kind of mistake, the theory will have to take it into account. At present we do not. We assume that every (b,s) pair is correct.

Notes to Chapter 3

1
The assumption of a universal syntactic base is wrong, but there are suggestions on how to weaken the assumption to bring it more into line with what is known empirically, while preserving the essential characteristics and properties of the following analysis. (See chap. 2, note 19 and chap. 7.)

2
By choosing input to have this form we also move forward in the problem of learning descriptively adequate grammars (strong learnability), since knowledge of the transformational relation between base and surface is part of the linguistic knowledge (of structural descriptions) that a native speaker has. But we will not completely solve the problem, because we won't be able to guarantee that in the selected grammar all aspects of the structural descriptions are correct (match those of an adult native speaker).

3
For the formal theory of grammar, see Chomsky (1963). A general introduction to mathematical linguistics and automata theory is Hopcroft and Ulmann (1969). Ginsburg and Partee (1969) provide a mathematical model for transformational grammar.

4
It may very well be that in linguistic theory we would want to allow a set of essential symbols, such that recursion has to go through one of the symbols. For example an NP may dominate another NP without going through S. We see no reason why proofs similar to the ones we provide won't work with a larger set of essential symbols. But for simplicity we have made the assumption of a unique essential symbol.

5
The level of an S consists of itself and the non-S nodes that it dominates with no other S intervening (Hamburger and Wexler 1975, 144).

6
Hamburger and Wexler (1975, note 11) point out, "Although this terminology is in widespread use, Ginsburg and Partee (1969) speak of 'domain statement' and 'change statement.' Our structural descriptions are a special case of their domain statements with their D_0 required to be empty."

7

The six restrictions on the use of transformations that we had to adopt in order to prove convergence are listed on p. 147 of Hamburger and Wexler (1975). Restriction 1 is the Binary principle, which we will also adopt in the new theory (chap. 4). Restriction 2 forbids movement from an embedded S to an S at the same level. In chapter 4 this situation cannot arise because for reasons of notational simplicity we don't allow S's that aren't in a dominance relation. If such S's are allowed, we believe that restriction 2 may still be needed, but in another form. "Restrictions 3–6 are an interrelated set of conditions which involve the notion that certain new structures, once formed, cannot be analyzed by the structural description of subsequent transformations" (Hamburger and Wexler 1975, 148). In the chap. 4 theory these restrictions are replaced by another set of restrictions which have a double advantage. First, some of the new restrictions are much more natural from a linguistic point of view and, in fact, more adequate empirically. Second, the new restrictions allow a much more powerful result— degree-2 learnability. The major reasons for the assumption of the original conditions were a variety of cases whereby transformational behavior at a lower level of a phrase-marker was not in "error" and yet could alter later (higher) transformational behavior so that errors would occur at higher levels. The assumptions were made to explicitly bound these possibilities. Thus the assumptions were made, for the most part, to restrict raising possibilities, so that error structures couldn't be raised while the error remained hidden. The new conditions in chapter 4 (especially the freezing principle) are much more algebraic and structural in character, explicitly limiting the kinds of structures and behaviors that can occur, rather than merely the number of such structures. This algebraic flavor not only allows for a much stronger property of the system (degree-2 learnability), but seems more natural for actual linguistic structures.

8

The assumption of obligatory transformations together with Determinism implies Uniqueness: for a base phrase-marker there is at most one surface sentence. Interestingly, Chomsky and Lasnik (1977, sec. 2.2.1) find that Uniqueness generally holds for the quite different theory that they have developed.

9

In the definition of function-learnability, we have proceeded somewhat informally, taking advantage of analogy with preceding definitions. Any lack of explicitness can be easily filled in, and we will not be using the concept extensively in mathematical developments. Note in particular that two conditions have to be added for the proposition that every enumerable class of functions is function-learnable to be correct (cf. Gold 1967, 458). (1) For any function in the enumeration there must be an effective procedure for deciding whether it is compatible with the data received to date, and (2) there must be an effective method for finding a "name" for each function in the enumeration.

10

The proof that the class of functions defined by the class of transformational mappings is function-learnable, though not given in Hamburger and Wexler (1975), follows from properties proven there. Essentially what has to be shown is that the class of transformational grammars on a universal base may be enumerated. For an unconstrained transformational component this may not be true, but it is true for a system with the restrictions given in Hamburger and Wexler (1975). The property that makes one proof work is that there are only a finite number of "eligible structures" (cf. lemma 1 of Hamburger and Wexler). From this it follows that there are only a finite number n of possible structural descriptions of transformations, although with each structural description there are a countable number of transformations possible (for an example and discussion see p. 151 and figure 6 of Hamburger and Wexler). These transformations may be effectively enumerated. Thus possible transformations may be labeled T_{ij}, i being associated with the structural description and j with a particular transformation which has that structural description. Thus the transformations are as defined in the following array:

11	12	13	14	...
21	22	23	24	...
...	...	...	...	...
$n1$	$n2$	$n3$	$n4$	...

A transformational grammar may be identified with a finite number of transformations, that is, with a finite subset of the set of all transformations. Thus we can give an effective enumeration of the subsets of transformational components in the following way. First, enumerate all possible transformational components that contain transformations of the form T_{i1}. There are only a finite number of these, and it is clear that an effective enumeration of them exists. Next enumerate all possible transformational components with transformations of the form T_{i1} or T_{i2}. Once again there are a finite number of these and effective enumeration is possible. Proceeding, at step k enumerate all transformational components with transformations of the form T_{i1}, T_{i2}, . . ., or T_{ik}. Since any transformational component is finite, it will eventually be listed in this procedure. Thus the procedure provides an effective enumeration of transformational grammars on a universal base.

It is interesting to observe where the finiteness of the possible structural descriptions becomes important in the proof. If they were not finite, our array of transformations would not be bounded on the bottom by n; that is, in principle there could be a countable number of structural descriptions. Thus there would be an infinite number of possible transformations of the form T_{ik}, for fixed i, and the procedure we have defined would never get past transformations of the form T_{i1}. It follows that not all transformational components would be enumerated.

However, even this unconstrained class can be shown to be enumerable. Suppose our array continues indefinitely, past n. Then the transformations can be enumerated, according to a diagonalization argument. The grammars can then be enumerated by enumerating, for each k, the subsets of transformations that are enumerated before step k in this diagonalized enumeration. The proof essentially depends on the possibility of effectively enumerating the class of possible transformations.

Actually, two other properties have to be proved to show that the class of grammars is function-learnable, those listed in note 9. However, these properties follow in a straightforward manner from the definitions and properties of transformational grammars.

11

It is interesting to see why set-learnability by enumeration won't always work. Consider the class $\mathscr{H}$ from sec. 2.2. These grammars can be enumerated. H_0 will show up in this enumeration. Suppose data is presented from some grammar H_i, which appears after H_0 in the enumeration. Suppose, furthermore, that by time j each of the grammars that appear before H_0 in the enumeration has been discarded. Now H_0 is selected. But since all succeeding grammars will be compatible with H_0, the guess will always be H_0, and H_i will not be selected. This cannot happen with function-learnability because there is no analogous concept of superset. Every function is defined on the same domain; thus in the data particular knowledge will eventually be given about which element in the range an element of the domain is mapped into. In set-learnability, if an element is not in the presented language, the learner will never receive it and thus will not have definitive knowledge about it. In function-learnability, if the learner waits long enough, he will (eventually) have definitive knowledge about the value of a particular element.

In this regard it is interesting to consider a particular property of the (b,s) situation. Here we do formally have the function-learnability situation, since the domain is defined as the entire set of base phrase-markers. In the framework of Hamburger and Wexler, fairly unconstrained deletion is allowed, even deletion of an entire sentence. In order for the formal proof by enumeration to work, we must imagine that when a base p-m is entirely deleted, a datum of the form $(b,\emptyset)$ is presented to the learner. Otherwise, function-learnability would have to involve partial functions, and the same problems would arise as with set-learnability. Yet it is not particularly plausible to assume that $(b,\emptyset)$ is a possible part of the presented data (presumably this would mean that the learner understood a situation, and silence or a special mark indicated to him that the phrase-marker was deleted). Fewer possibilities of deletion will be allowed in the theory we will present in this book (chap. 4). However, we will allow filtering (see chap. 4), which provides the same problem. If an adult base p-m b is filtered (ruled out of the set of possible structures), and if the child receives no information about filtered sentences, then it is conceivable that the child will create a grammar in which b is mapped into a surface sentence instead of being filtered. The formal proof goes through in chapter 4 because we assume that the child does receive information about filtered phrase-markers. There may be other possible interpretations of filtering constraints, however, in which this problem will not exist.

12
This has also been pointed out by Braine (1971).

13
Taken to an extreme, of course, attentional and motivational factors will influence the logical problem. If the child pays attention to *no* data, the correct language cannot be selected. The division of properties is rough, in an attempt to allow work to proceed. To some extent the decisions depend on an answer to the question Which idealizations will, at the moment, produce the most fruitful results? If limitations on attention and motivation that might be proposed seem not to affect the logical character of the problem, they will be idealized away from.

Suppose that it could be shown that negative information is available to the child. Very many learnability problems would still be unsolved, especially those involving the learning of descriptively adequate grammars (strong learnability).

14
Chomsky writes,

We may ask, then, whether we would seriously falsify the account of learning (and if so, in what respects) by assuming that the input to [the learning procedure at a given stage] is the data so far utilized rather than the grammar that represents the child's theory at this point (along with other new data) (1975a, 120).

We are here suggesting that a way in which the assumption that all data so far utilized are input to the learning procedure "falsifies the account of learning" is that with this assumption the problem might be made easier in such a way that empirically correct conditions on grammars, conditions that play an important role in learning from restricted data, may not have to be invoked. The most pressing issue is not whether the assumption is false, but whether a particular idealization is most useful at a given stage of development of a field of study. See note 17 for further discussion.

15
Of course, as Chomsky points out, "an actual acquisition model must have a strategy for finding hypotheses" (1965, 203, n. 22).

16
An argument against enumeration procedures follows from the assumption that the data available to the learner at any stage is quite limited. We have argued that it is useful and important to make this assumption of bounded memory for data. But if we try to assume bounded memory for data together with an enumeration procedure for constructing a grammar, we may run into trouble. Suppose, as in the theory we will present, that only one new datum is available to a learner at a time. If the enumeration procedure picks the simplest grammar (first in the enumeration) that is compatible with only that datum, clearly learning will be impossible. The selected grammar will simply continuously shift, dictated by only one datum.

However, we might try an alternative procedure. As each datum is presented, the guessed grammar is not changed if the current grammar is compatible with that datum. If the currently guessed grammar is not compatible with the datum, select the next grammar in the enumeration that *is* compatible with it. If the assumptions about input are as given in the text, namely, each datum (b,s) appears at least once in each information sequence, then this next-grammar procedure will not always work. Suppose, for example, that a grammar G_2 is wrong on only one datum, (b,s). Let us say that (b,s) is presented at time 1, and grammar

G_1, first in the enumeration, is guessed. At time 2, datum (b',s') is presented, which is incompatible with G_1, but this datum is compatible with G_2, which is guessed. If (b,s) never appears again in the information sequence, G_2 will remain the guessed grammar, even though it is wrong (since it is not correct for (b,s)). However, we might assume alternative forms of input. Suppose we wanted to bar effects based on the fact that a datum appeared only once. Then we could require that all data appeared infinitely often in an information sequence. Under these conditions, if a guessed grammar is wrong, a datum will always appear to show that it is wrong, thus forcing a shift in the guessed grammar. Also, the correct grammar will have a place in the enumeration and will never be by-passed, because when its position is reached, it will be guessed, being compatible with any datum. (Of course, a grammar earlier in the enumeration which performs the same mapping would be selected if such existed.) Thus under many conditions unbounded memory for past data trades off with infinitely repeating data, inducing the same learnability possibilities. In general, giving much power to the possibilities of infinitely repeating data may not be too reasonable, given our general orientation that language is learned relatively quickly under a wide variety of input conditions. To require that the input be idealized as infinitely repeating may not only be false in at least some cases, but may prevent our obtaining otherwise attainable insights concerning necessary structural assumptions. This is especially true if we require that all the (b,s) pairs in the language be infinitely repeating in the input.

17
As Chomsky says, "these are imprecise and qualitative conclusions" (1975a, 122). To take one example, it is not altogether clear that intensional accounts will make it more difficult to show that the same grammar is selected, under varying orders of information presentation, than will extensional accounts. In the original instantaneous model there is one set of primary data, which has already been idealized away from order of presentation, so naturally order of presentation can have no effect. The theory of set-learnability has the same property, that is, order of presentation isn't even a concept in the theory. Even in the theory of text-learnability as we have defined it here (functions from samples (sets) of data) order of presentation cannot have an effect on the limiting choice of grammar. (See note 18 concerning another theory of text-learnability, in which order does have an effect.)

The idea of extensional theories is that at any time t the learner has a body of data, and he picks the simplest grammar compatible with that body of data. If the body of data is the finite set of data presented up to that time, as in the theory of set-learnability, then the ultimate grammar will be the same under different orders of presentation, since all calculations are based on the set of data. But consider an extensional theory, in which the input is not the data received at stage S_i but is the language generated by the grammar hypothesized at stage S_i (plus the new datum, of course). Suppose that at stage S_i, under information presentation I, the learner's selected grammar is G, and that, under information presentation I', the selected grammar is G'. In general, the language of G will not equal the language of G', that is, $L(G) \neq L(G')$. Suppose that the next datum is d, for both I and I'. Then, in the case of I, the input for the learning procedure at stage i is $L(G)$ together with d. For I', the input is $L(G')$ together with d. Since the sets of data input to the learning procedure are different for I and I', it could be that the grammar guessed at stage $i + 1$ is different for I and I'. Thus the *languages* guessed at stage $i + 1$ will be different for I and I'. The process can continue. The crucial question is: what happens in the limit? Will the grammars selected under I and I' be the same, as we demand on empirical grounds? There seems to be no reason to assume that the assumption of an extensional theory will guarantee such convergence, any more than an intensional theory will. The crucial property of a theory that assumes that the finite set of data encountered up to stage i is the input to the learning procedure at stage i (as in set-learnability) is that some finite set of data can be looked on as the set of primary data, for which the correct grammar will be selected, and such that for every superset of data the correct grammar will be selected. When any sequence of data presentation (say I or I') gets long enough, the set of data to date will include the primary data. But if the data is only the one new datum at stage i, plus the language of the stage i grammar, there is no reason to expect that any such set of primary data will exist. There is no reason to expect, for example, that the entire set of data presented up to stage i will be part of the selected language at stage i. This latter property would hold under the assumption that the grammar G selected for stage $i + 1$ was selected under the condition that $L(G)$ contain the language of the grammar selected for stage i, plus the new datum presented at stage i. There is no reason to believe that this property (of "strictly growing" languages) is correct, and even if it were correct, there is no reason to think that the grammars to which the procedure converges under information sequences I and I' will be equal. In short, although, at first, extensional theories seem to have the property of equivalent convergence under differing orders of presentation, they may very well have no significant advantage over intensional theories in this regard. The answer must lie in the properties of particular theories, with respect to descriptive and explanatory adequacy and feasibility.

18
For example, Gold's (1967) theory of text-learnability, unlike ours in chapter 2, is such that the order of presentation of data can have an effect on the resultant (steady-state) grammar; two different orders from the same language might result in two different grammars being selected, but these grammars must generate the same language (set of strings). With further enrichment of the input (e.g., function-learnability) further properties (e.g., equivalence of mappings) can be required. The point we make in the text is that it may be the case that by restricting the class of grammars in certain ways, further properties concerning equivalence of grammars selected under different orders of presentation might emerge, even if data is not directly presented concerning these properties.

19
The question of whether to relax an idealization is a standard scientific question, analogous to the question, for example, of whether higher-order terms in an expansion of a variable may be ignored. There are many cases in which the idealization works for a time and for certain problems (the terms are ignored with good results following) but, as precision and analysis deepen, it becomes useful to ignore the idealization, and to consider further terms.

20
The particular form of the probability distribution is not specified in the definition. A variety of well-known distributions have the non-zero feature. The requirement that the probability distribution be fixed, that is, that it not be dependent on the state of the learned system or on the time at which the datum is presented, is used in the proof of convergence (theorem 6 of Hamburger and Wexler 1975). It is invoked not because we believe that it is true but because it is needed, at least for the given proof. The proof depends on the probability that a datum from a particular finite set of data being presented at one time is greater than a bound p, and that this bound p holds over all times. If the probability distributions shifted from time to time (or depending on which of infinitely many states the system was in), the proof wouldn't work. We haven't investigated whether another proof would go through. However, we could allow the distributions to depend on the history and time if we added the requirement that over all distributions

(all times and histories) there was a lower bound to the probabilities of any of the data in a particular finite set appearing (namely, the data of complexity (depth of embedding) less than a certain bound $U(B)$ mentioned in the proof). Under these conditions the proof would go through. Given the results in chapter 4, $U(B)$ will be 2, so varying probability distributions depending on time and history are acceptable, so long as the probability of every (b,s) pair of depth 2 or less, for any time and history, is greater than a non-zero lower bound. This requirement seems reasonable to a first approximation, and frees us from any idealization concerning equivalent probabilities of presentation of a datum no matter what the time or history.

21
Thus it will not be the case that correct selection must be made on every information sequence (in the original sense—that is, every sequence of data that contains each datum at least once). Rather, correct selection must occur on a set of sequences of data of measure 1. (For discussion of the requirement that a finite time exists such that the selection is correct and unchanging after that time, see sec. 2.5.) The attained result is actually somewhat stronger than the defined criterion. Hamburger and Wexler (1975) proved that the mean time to converge to a correct grammar, which doesn't change thenceforth, is finite.

22
One might ask whether probabilistic presentation and a probabilistic criterion would allow set-learnability to be possible for a wider array of grammars. The answer depends on exactly how definitions are chosen. Horning (1969) has studied a probabilistic system in which probabilistic text presentation leads to convergence of the kind required here. Horning studies the class of stochastic context-free grammars. These grammars have probabilities associated with each of their rewriting rules. He also assumes that there is not only an enumeration of these stochastic grammars but that there is an a priori probability for each of the grammars. Learning is done by EB, an enumerative Bayesean procedure (Horning, p. 73) which maximizes the a posteriori probability of a grammar, given a sample. Following standard Bayesean arguments, this probability is maximized when the product of the a priori probability of a grammar and the probability of the sample, given the grammar, is maximized. At any time, the maximum is taken over a finite set of grammars in the enumeration, the set being chosen according to a particular computable function.

A procedure is said to *converge* for a presentation of data from a grammar G if for any $\epsilon > 0$, there is a time t such that for any time greater than t the probability of the procedure guessing G is greater than $1 - \epsilon$. The important result for our purposes is Horning's Corollary V.9: "The procedure EB converges to the best grammar under any stochastic presentation." Here, "best grammar" means that not only is the language guessed by the grammar the same as the language of the presented grammar, but the probabilities of sentences are the same; moreover, of grammars meeting these conditions the one with the highest a priori probability is selected. In this sense the class of grammars $\mathcal{H}$ of sec. 2.2, for example, will converge under stochastic text presentation.

These results raise a number of issues for us. Most important, to what extent are the learnability (convergence) results for (b,s) pairs dependent on the probabilistic presentation and criterion rather than on the form of the input or grammars? If learnability is possible from text, given probabilistic presentation and criterion, it seems that this, rather than structural form or input, might be the key factor. Note, however, that Horning's method (EB) uses probabilistic information in selecting the grammar. Our method (LP for learning procedure—cf. sec. 3.4) does not use such information at all. As we have pointed out, we use probabilistic presentation only to make sure that data is presented. LP does not at all take account of frequencies of presentation. In fact, the data do not come from a stochastic grammar and the probabilities of presentation are not necessarily related to the grammar in any structural way.

In addition, probabilistic presentation is not really necessary for the theory. Recall that probabilistic presentation was assumed so that we wouldn't have to assume that the learner had memory for past data. The assumption of probabilistic presentation could be replaced by any assumption that made sure that the relevant data was available to the learner at the appropriate times. The proof of the convergence theorem (cf. sec. 3.4) shows that there is a bound U so that only data of complexity (depth of embedding of b) less than this bound must be considered by the learner. There is a finite bound on how much data there can be. Call this finite set of (b,s) pairs D. Then, in place of the probabilistic presentation assumption, either of the following two assumptions would be sufficient for the convergence proof:

(i) Every datum in the finite set D is infinitely repeating (thus, in principle, if the learner needs this datum, he will always be able to have it available, in sufficient time).

(ii) The learner has memory for the elements of D that have been presented (and thus the data in D will be available to the learner when he needs it).

The same learning procedure *LP*, with only minor modifications, will allow convergence given either of these two assumptions, with only minor modifications in the proof.

In chapter 4 we show that U can be taken to be 2. Therefore, we would only require, under possibility (i), that every datum of degree less than or equal to 2 was infinitely repeating. Under possibility (ii), we would require that the learner have memory for data of degree 2 or less. One could imagine how conditions would exist under which even these requirements would be relaxed. Thus probabilistic presentation is not used as information for the learning procedure, nor is it the only assumption that will allow learnability. The crucial factors are the restrictions that allow the bound U to be derived. It would be an interesting exercise to try to calculate the minimum amount of data that would allow learning.

Horning's methods can be made to apply to grammars for which there are no natural a priori probabilities, as he points out (p. 80). Almost any probability distribution can be assigned. For example, if we have an enumeration of grammars $G_1, G_2, \ldots$, then the a priori probabilities can be taken to be $p(G_i) = 2^{-i}$. As Horning points out, the "probability" of a grammar can easily be interpreted as the inverse of "complexity" (thereby, of course, losing a relative-frequency interpretation).

Actually, the major element of Horning's stochastic systems that seems to allow so many classes of grammars (for example, the entire set of context-free grammars) to converge from text presentation is not the probabilistic presentation but, rather, the criterion of convergence. Horning notes that probabilistic presentation could be eliminated, with convergence still holding, "as long as the relative frequencies converge properly" (pp. 80–81). There might be a number of reasons why context-free grammars are learnable in Horning's sense but not in Gold's text presentation (cf. sec. 2.3). Essentially, for Horning, the measure of the class of information sequences for which the correct grammar is not selected at time t can be made arbitrarily close to 0, for sufficiently large t. In Gold's definition of text presentation, every information sequence must converge to the correct grammar and stay there. Also, the proof of nonlearnability for Gold's definition of text-presentation (cf. secs. 2.2 and 2.3) involves sequences that might have a 0 probability in Horning's formulation (or the relative frequencies would not converge in the alternative version). Incidentally, our requirement (of (b,s) learnability) is also stronger than Horning's criterion in that the (b,s) requirement has two parts. First, the probability that the learner will select a correct grammar at time t can be made arbitrarily close to 1. Second, if a correct grammar is chosen at any time, the selection will never change at later times.

23
It would appear to our intuitions that if we make the learning mechanism *LP* more intelligent, in terms of the definitions of the kinds of computations it performs, the problem of learning will not become more difficult. If we prove learnability with *LP*, we can prove learnability if we add further power to *LP*. For example, if we add the power to modify transformations to *LP*, then learnability will be preserved. Although this qualitative argument is appealing, we are not sure that it is true. It may be that lack of "intelligence" (as judged by our introspections and intuitions) actually helps in learning. Thus perhaps a procedure that modifies transformations instead of rejecting or adding a transformation might fall into a loop from which it can't exit, making convergence (learning) impossible. To some extent the simple aspects of *LP* were adopted because we couldn't see how to make more complicated procedures escape problems of loops, etc.

24
One question that might be asked is whether more intelligent learning procedures will do away with some of the necessity for assuming special syntactic principles. We feel that the answer is that it is unlikely, on a number of counts. First, it appears to us that convergence possibilities will not be strengthened by more intelligent procedures; in some cases they might even be weakened (see note 23). Second, the basic result concerning grammars we use to prove learnability (cf. BDE of sec. 3.4) is that if a transformational component behaves differently from the correct component, this different behavior will show up on a sufficiently simple phrase-marker (datum). It is the attempt to obtain this result that necessitates many of the syntactic assumptions (see note 7 and chap. 4). Yet even if it were not for the desire to prove learnability, we feel that the claim (of errors showing up on sufficiently simple data) is empirically correct. (We discuss the empirical status of the claim in relation to linguistic theory in the last paragraph of sec. 4.4.) Thus the syntactic constraints might be necessary just to be able to explain this empirical result.

More generally, we see no reason to assume that the learner is doing a lot of intelligent computation when he learns syntax. (By "intelligent" we mean the application of powerful general-purpose learning procedures. Certainly, in another sense, the application of specific linguistic constraints is a very strong form of intelligence. There seems to be nothing to the issue of whether special or general procedures are more intelligent except terminology.) A child develops his first language before he can do, say, complicated mathematics or science or other kinds of complicated problem solving. Perhaps the procedures that we have assumed are too strong, in which case the linguistic principles will have to be even more restrictive.

Little is known about the child's abilities to hypothesize at the (presumably) unconscious levels that we are discussing. Intuitions about such intelligent hypothesization derive from introspections concerning what we do when we solve problems (and in part, perhaps, from children's reports). But there is no necessary reason to think that unconscious procedures are identical or even similar to conscious ones. Whatever the state of our ignorance here, even if intelligent general procedures exist for the child, they do not appear to be sufficient for the problem of language learning. The contrary claim of Putnam (1967) is discussed in chap. 6, note 11.

25
Note that we do not require that a transformation be rejected such that without that transformation the correct derivation would have taken place (that is, at least the correct surface string s is derived). In many cases such a requirement would make it impossible to obtain any candidate for rejection, because no such transformations exist (even though the component contains a wrong transformation, which may even have applied on the current datum). We haven't investigated whether, with this alternative procedure, the proof would go through nevertheless.

26
We are discussing here only the case where one transformation applies per cycle. A transformation may be hypothesized only when no transformation in the current component C_t applies to the top level of b. The definitions and proof of convergence when we allow more than one transformation to apply per cycle (any finite number) are given in Hamburger (1971, chap. 6). The learning procedure LP has to be revised only with respect to which transformations are considered available for hypothesization and rejection. It is still the case that only one transformation is hypothesized or rejected at a time. The generalization for a transformation that may be rejected is fairly obvious; it is any transformation that applied in generating a wrong string. But now there are potentially more of these transformations, since more than one transformation may have applied per cycle.

The generalization of *LP* concerning what transformations may be hypothesized is somewhat more subtle; transformations are still hypothesized only at the top level of the p-m (but see the last paragraph of note 28). Now, however, a transformation T may be hypothesized if it, *together with other new transformations* added to the current transformational component, applied to the top of the p-m., yields a correct surface string. Intuitively, T has the potential (if other transformations are added) of allowing the learner's transformational component to behave correctly on the current datum. In the case of one transformation per cycle these generalizations reduce to the case discussed in the text.

Baker (1977, n. 4) produces an example of a simple transformational component that is not learnable via the procedure discussed in detail in Hamburger and Wexler 1975, a procedure based on the assumption that only one transformation applies per level. But Hamburger and Wexler (sec. 4.1) also point out results obtainable from the more general procedure discussed in this note. This procedure can learn the transformational component Baker presents. Thus his objections do not apply.

27

It is not even clear that effective procedures exist which will make the appropriate computations if hypothesization is allowed on lower levels. A key element in the proof of convergence is the proof that (given hypothesization takes place only at the top level) the number of transformations available for hypothesization is bounded by a number depending only on the depth of the base phrase-marker b and the length of the surface string s (lemma 7 and theorem 5 of Hamburger and Wexler 1975). It is not obvious that a corresponding bound exists if hypothesization can take place at lower levels. For example, it might happen that copying could take place at lower levels and deletions at higher levels, yet yield the same terminal string s as if these operations had not taken place. There might be an unbounded number of such compounding of copying and deletion transformations and thus an unbounded number of transformations available for hypothesization. It might be that the restrictions on the transformational system will not allow this, but we don't know at present. At any rate, the mathematics appears to be very much more complicated if we allow hypothesization at the lower levels. Allowing only transformations to be hypothesized which apply at the top greatly restricts the possibilities for hypothesization. If this method works, short of evidence to the contrary, there seems no reason to allow the more complicated possibilities.

28

There is one exception to this statement. If the transformation T that is missing from the learner's component and that applies at level *i* of *b* is *string-preserving* (does not change the terminal string), then if T doesn't apply, no error will be caused at the top level of *b'*. However, the string-preserving T could alter the *structure* of a phrase-marker. Thus the lack of the application of T to level *i* of *b* could result in different structure at level *i*, which causes the creation of an error at a higher level of *b*. For this reason Hamburger and Wexler (1975) do allow hypothesization of transformations at lower levels, but only hypothesization of string-preserving transformations, with no requirement that the hypothesized transformation have any other effect, such as the ultimate yielding of the correct surface string for *b*. It seems fair to say that the reasons for allowing such hypothesization are technical, and that we would prefer to do without such a possibility. In the transformational system that we develop in this book, we will discover important problems of learnability that will lead us to assume that string-preserving transformations don't exist (or that if such apply, the p-m is filtered) (sec. 4.3.4.4). Thus the necessity for hypothesizing string-preserving transformations will never arise. Without this possibility all the proofs involving convergence will go through a fortiori. We therefore ignore this possibility in our discussion of *LP* in the text.

In the more general situation—which we don't discuss in the text (see note 26)—where more than one transformation applies per cycle, non-string-preserving transformations may be hypothesized at lower cycles. However, any transformation T hypothesized on a lower cycle must be such that the application of T together with other transformations does not alter the terminal string. That is, all the transformations acting together are string-preserving. Interestingly, in the current theory we are led on learnability grounds to rule out such possibilities. In the last paragraph we mentioned a constraint against string-preserving transformations. The constraint, as defined in sec. 4.3.4.4, is actually more general, and we are led to the general form because of specific problems of learnability. The constraint filters out all derivations in which a terminal string is ever repeated at two stages of the derivation. Thus the situation in which transformations would be hypothesized at nontop (nonmatrix) levels of a p-m never arises for the new (chap. 4) theory, even when there is more than one transformation per level. Again, all the proofs involving convergence will go through a fortiori. For further discussion, see sec. 4.5.

29

One might think that the same argument would work for the class of transformations available for rejection: if an incorrect transformation T applied at a lower level i, there would exist a phrase-marker b' such that level i was the top of b'. T would then incorrectly apply to the top of b', causing an error. Thus T could be rejected at the top level of b'. Therefore we would have to reject only transformations that apply at the top level. The problem with this suggestion is that the incorrect transformation T may yield the correct surface string for b' but the wrong surface structure; in that case there is no detectable error on b' and no hypothesization will take place. Nevertheless, the wrong structure causes a detectable error to occur at the top level of the larger phrase-marker b. Thus we will have to have T available for rejection when it applies at the lower level i of b. Note that a wrong transformation T can yield the wrong structure but the right surface string, even though T is not string-preserving (cf. note 28). Both the adult and learner components may transform level i of b, with the same string but different structures emerging.

30

For example, if 10 transformations are available for rejection and 20 for hypothesization, the probability that one of the transformations available for hypothesization will be hypothesized is 1/30 and the probability that one of the transformations available for rejection will be rejected is 1/30. In the flow chart of the learning procedure LP (fig 3.1), we show the choice of hypothesization or rejection being made first. This is done for pictorial simplicity and is of no consequence.

In fact, the assumption of equal probability is for notational convenience only and is unnecessary. All that is needed for the proof is that every transformation available for hypothesization or rejection be selected with a probability greater than a nonzero bound, which depends on the total number of transformations available for hypothesization or rejection. Some heuristic power and perhaps efficiency of the procedure might be obtained from a more subtle selection of probabilities, including effects of past history, but so far nothing crucial hangs on the exact distribution.

31

Another alternative would be to attempt to insure that the learner never selects a nondeterministic transformational component. It may be impossible to insure this, however. There may not exist an effective procedure which, by inspecting a set of transformations, can tell whether that set is deterministic or not. Even if there is one, the computation would probably be quite difficult and long. The problem is not simply one of hypothesizing a transformation on a datum d and then checking to see whether the new transformational component is deterministic on d, for it may be deterministic on d but nondeterministic on other data.

32

A great deal of the complexity and difficulty of the proof in Hamburger and Wexler 1975 is due to the complexities of obtaining the part 1 results. We hope that the very different methods of chapter 4 are more perspicuous. One reason they may be is that we here present the material in a more didactic manner: before we actually present the proof itself, we try to obtain the needed results, show why the system fails, and then show how certain assumptions will overcome these failures. (Hamburger and Wexler started with the assumptions, then directly presented the proof.) A more substantive reason for what we hope is the relative perspicuousness of chapter 4 is that the method of proof is radically different. The original proof of the part 1 results in Hamburger and Wexler is essentially combinatoric, whereas the new proof in chapter 4 is essentially algebraic. Vast numbers of alternatives are possible for "strange" behaviors of transformational systems, hypothesized transformational components, and so on, but (in the original proof) we placed finite bounds on these alternatives, which allowed convergence to take place. The bounds were crude, depending on the sizes of various aspects of the grammatical system (such as the "widest" expansion allowed in a simple phrase-marker by the context-free base rules). The new proof is algebraic in the sense that it is not simply arithmetical possibilities that limit the strange behaviors. The assumptions are more structural, and similarities of structure are directly responsible for the limitations of behavior. Isomorphism of structure plays a direct and important role in the new proof. The new assumptions allow the new methods, and these assumptions are made necessary by the adopted goal of finding more feasible theories (see sec. 1.4.2). Limitation by combinatoric possibility is too weak to allow the powerful results needed to produce feasible theories. The historical development here, in our opinion, is an example of how conceptual development, or the changing of goals (here, the goal of providing feasible theories) can lead to mathematical and empirical methods and results that are simultaneously more adequate than the original methods and results.

33

In preparing the discussion to follow, we were aided by an unpublished manuscript by Henry Hamburger entitled "Framework, Obstacles, and Approaches." Details of the presentations differ.

34

The reason is that we prove that P3 holds of any possible transformational component, not simply of those that can be (or are likely to be) hypothesized by the learning procedure *LP*. In short, we prove that if *any* two transformational components differ in their behavior (mapping of base phrase-markers into surface strings), then they differ in their behavior on a small datum. The interpretation of this result used in the proof is that one of these components is the adult's, and the other is the learner's at a given stage. Thus if the learner differs in his mapping behavior from the adult, he differs on a small datum. It would have been sufficient to prove that if any attainable learner's component differs in its behavior from the adult's component (which provided the data from which learning took place), then the components differ on a small datum. (This result, of course, follows from the result that we *have* proved, and is thus weaker, but just as effective in the proof). However, trying to reach this latter result directly would appear to add great mathematical complexities, since analysis would have to be undertaken of what can be attained, whereas the more general result can ignore these complexities, since the proof is made for *any* transformational components. If we could provide an analysis of attainable (at any time, not convergence) components, and could find a proof directly from there, we might be able to provide more precise efficiency results, since time to learn, etc., will depend on what components are actually attainable at any time, and not on the set of all possible components. To date there have been no results along these lines.

35

This is proved in theorem 3 of Hamburger and Wexler 1975. The statement there has slightly different notation and a technicality that we have passed over, involving the fact that possible adult components are a subset of possible child components; namely, adult components must be deterministic, whereas child components do not have to be. (See sec. 3.3.3.)

36

The Binary principle is essentially equivalent to the Subjacency principle, independently proposed by Chomsky (1973), for reasons of linguistic description.

37

"Moderate" because (1) the requirement is stronger than weak equivalence, which means that the languages of A and C, conceived as sets of surface strings, are equivalent, and (2) the requirement is weaker than strong equivalence, which means (at least) that the surface structures (phrase-markers) of a structure transformed under A and C are equivalent. (Chap. 4 gives more formal definitions.)

38

The assumption of the transformational cycle plays a role throughout the proofs. It is used so often that its role is taken for granted. Without the assumption of the transformational cycle the entire theory would have to be reworked. We do not know whether a proof exists (rather, whether there are any reasonable conditions under which a proof exists) for learnability, if we do not assume the transformational cycle. In part, the question depends on exactly which assumptions about ordering of transformations, etc., are made to replace the transformational cycle.

39

This result follows from the nature of transformations as structure-dependent operations. It would not hold if transformations were arbitrary mappings of phrase-markers into phrase-markers. The structure-dependent nature of transformations is another property, like the transformational cycle discussed earlier, which plays a role in a number of aspects of the proof. It is very difficult to see how any kind of reasonable learnability result could be possible if transformations were taken to be arbitrary mappings of phrase-markers into phrase-markers. There would be huge numbers of possibilities. The property of structure-dependence gives a kind of finite grounding to the mapping possibilities. One might even speculate that problems of learnability provide a functional (evolutionary) motivation for the existence of the structure-dependence property. Of course, in principle other finite groundings are possible for mappings of phrase-markers into phrase-markers. For example, in a classic example (Chomsky 1965) we do not find transformations that perform permutations, yet these might be learnable finite groundings, in the sense of logical possibility. In general it would be interesting to study the learnability properties of various transformational systems to see to what extent the structure-dependent nature of transformations can be seen to be uniquely or specially associated with learnability, as compared with other possibilities for grounding transformations. Although the possibilities are intriguing, there is no reason to suppose that learnability is the only functional consideration relevant to the (evolutionary) selection of structural aspects of language. Thus, before precise results are obtained (linking structure and function) we can only speculate on the relation. In all this discussion it is important to note that functional reasons for selection relate to the evolutionary level of selection and not to the problem of language acquisition in the child, which relates to genetic mechanisms. (For discussion see chap. 6 and Chomsky and Lasnik 1977.)

Notes to Chapter 4

1
In chap. 5 and in Culicover and Wexler 1977, nodes that count in the Binary principle are called B-cyclic. Two kinds of sentence categories are defined in chap. 5, S and $\bar{S}$. No such distinction exists in chap. 4; S is the only sentence category.

2
Another possibility is that there might be a constraint against the same word appearing next to itself. Examples can be constructed which satisfy this constraint but share the problems of the given example. Suppose component A doesn't move B at all at S_0 or S_1. Component C moves one instance of B, then moves the second instance of B to where the first instance was, and then moves the first instance of B to the same left-right position as the second but in a different structural position. Then (say, by raising a node H which dominates this last moved B) a detectable error could be created at S_2, with none at S_1 or S_0.

3
FP prohibits analysis of any node under a frozen node. Therefore, if a frozen node dominates another frozen node, we will usually simplify notation by putting a box around only the higher (dominating) frozen node. In the second p-m in (10) the box around A indicates that A is frozen (i.e., A cannot immediately dominate DEH in the base). But in the third p-m we have not placed a box around A although it still immediately dominates DEH. This is because S_2, which dominates A, is frozen. In addition, in many of the examples to follow, if FP is not relevant to the example, we will not place a box around a frozen node. Unless it is explicitly mentioned or used in the development, it should not be assumed that a node without a box is not frozen.

4
In some cases there might be a "natural" principle that would tell the learner to attach a moved constituent to a particular phrase, but in other cases this doesn't seem to be so. For example, in the rule of Quantifier Movement a quantifier in the subject moves to the end of the subject, producing (ii) from (i):

(i) All the men have drunk wine.
(ii) The men all have drunk wine.

Whether the moved quantifier (*all*) remains in the subject NP or attaches to the auxiliary is not given a priori; it is not clear whether there is a natural principle that would allow only one of these possibilities. The issue may have to be settled for the child just as it is for the linguist, by hypothesization and testing.

5

The term "nonexplicit raising" is from Hamburger and Wexler (1975), as is the principle of the freezing of raised nodes (cf. note 6), which is one of the "restrictions on transformations." (Also see chap. 3, note 7.)

6

As often happens with scientific concepts, it is not always clear which should be definitions and which laws. We defined a frozen node as one with a nonbase immediate structure. The Freezing principle then asserted that no transformation could analyze any node dominated by a frozen node. We could, in light of this new principle, generalize the Freezing principle to say that a node may not be analyzed by a transformation if it is frozen or if it is dominated by a raised node. But perhaps it would be more elegant to define a frozen node as one for which no node it dominates may be analyzed by a transformation and then to state the Freezing principle as: A node is frozen if (a) its immediate structure is nonbase or (b) it has been raised. In either case the effect is exactly the same. We will often adopt the latter terminology when no confusion is possible. Thus when we speak of frozen node we will mean a node N such that the nodes that N dominates may not be analyzed by a transformation.

7

The second part of S-Optionality has been adopted because we want to preserve the principle that deleting S from a base phrase-marker leaves a base phrase-marker. If a node D dominates only S, deleting S doesn't leave a terminal (fully derived) base phrase-marker since D is a bottom node that is not lexical. The assumption of 0-termination implies that a degree-0 extension can be added to D. However, there will then be additional material under D which might affect the fit of transformations. Thus we adopt the second part of S-Optionality. One might imagine various ways of freeing ourselves from this assumption, but we will not pursue them here.

   Note also that, on the assumption that every category terminates (there is a derivation leading from the category so that all the bottom nodes of the derivation tree are lexical items), then the principle of S-Optionality implies the assumption of 0-termination. Simply delete subtrees dominated by S from the terminal derivation. The assumption that every category terminates is natural for context-free grammars, so assuming S-Optionality allows us to eliminate the need for explicit assumption of 0-termination.

8

Wilkins (1977) has proposed a much simpler, though quite a bit stronger, possibility: that only categories need to be listed in S.D.'s, and variables are automatically assumed to be present between each two adjacent elements of every S.D. If this proposal turns out to be descriptively adequate, we could adopt it. Then we wouldn't need the principle of S-Invisibility because, essentially, every category would be invisible in the relevant sense. Empirical differences between S-Invisibility and Wilkins's "elimination of variables" proposal exist in principle, namely, for cases in which S acts as if it is invisible (and perhaps NP also if the principle of S-Invisibility is to be extended to all cyclic nodes) but other categories do not.

The principle of S-Invisibility could be effected in other ways. We have interpreted the principle as a condition on the applicability of transformations; if a transformation applies to a p-m without the S, then it is made to apply to the same p-m with the S, and in the same way. In essence, S is treated as if fit by a variable even if the variable doesn't exist in the structural description of T. Alternatively, S-Invisibility may be interpreted as a requirement on the statement of transformations. That is, transformations are interpreted in the usual way, but the transformational component is such that the principle holds of it. In other words, no transformations apply to degree-0 p-m's without also applying in the same way to the same p-m with an embedded S. Under this second interpretation of the principle of S-Invisibility we must guarantee that there is an effective procedure for checking whether the principle holds for a given transformation. This is because we want the learning procedure to hypothesize only such transformations, so that the principle is true of the limiting set of transformations. (By the way, the principle could hold for a transformation in a given component but not hold for the same transformation in another component, so we must speak of the principle's holding for a component.) But there are only a finite number of 0-degree partially derived base p-m's and for each of these only a finite number of p-m's can insert S in accordance with the base rules. For any transformation T there is an effective procedure to check whether it applies to any partially derived p-m. Thus there is an effective procedure for checking whether the principle holds of any transformation. Of course, in general there is a much more efficient way of checking than to check every p-m, but right now we are concerned only that such a procedure exists.

There is a third alternative for realizing the principle of S-Invisibility that, together with other assumptions, would have the same effect. This is to modify the Binary principle so that when transformations apply at a cycle, they may only apply to nodes in the lower cycle that are not S's or sisters of S's. That is, nodes in the lower cycle that dominate S's are frozen with respect to transformations in the higher cycle. For example, when transformations are operating at level S_2 in phrase-marker P, given in (23), the node labeled D in S_1 is frozen. Thus no node under D in S_1 may be analyzed. In particular, B may not be analyzed and so cannot be raised by T_2^A or T_2^C. Therefore, no error will be caused and the problem will not arise. However, this version of S-Invisibility might not be strong enough for our purposes, because a singular transformation operating at level S_1 might analyze a sister of S_0, say B, and move it to a higher position in S_1. Then B could be raised to S_2, and the problem could repeat itself. Further analysis is necessary to determine whether this can actually occur. If it can, one might modify the proposal to suggest that it read: no sisters or nieces (or grand-nieces, etc.) of an embedded S may be analyzed by a transformation operating at a higher S. This proposal would also need further analysis.

For the moment, let us consider the first version of this third proposal, namely, that in the lower S the node dominating an embedded S is frozen. This version might be looked upon as a modification of the Binary principle (thus possibly allowing S-Invisibility to be merged with BP), and might have interesting empirical consequences. Suppose both S and NP are cyclic nodes to which we apply this modified BP. Consider the structure in (i): In Culicover and Wexler 1977 and in chap.

(i)

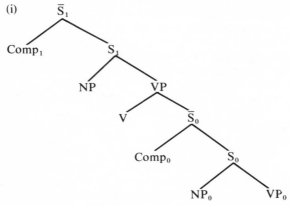

5 we formulate and offer evidence for a version of the Binary principle which, when T's apply at $\overline{S}_1$ in (i), allows nodes to be analyzed up to $Comp_0$ and S_0. But no nodes under these two nodes may be analyzed. But the modified Binary principle as we have just formulated it will freeze S_0 because S_0 is in the lower $(\overline{S}_0)$ cycle and dominates a cyclic node (NP_0). Thus in some cases this version of S-Invisibility will make correct empirical predictions. Problems immediately arise, and much empirical work would have to be undertaken to test the proposal. For these reasons we have chosen the less restrictive principle of S-Invisibility as given in the text. But these other possibilities might usefully be pursued.

9

Of course, this assumption of Determinism is an assumption of strict Determinism, where no two transformations may apply to a phrase-marker at a given time even if one of them applies only to the top of the p-m whereas the other makes essential reference to a constituent of an embedded S. We will later call these latter transformations *S-essential*. A natural principle, which can be looked upon as an interpretation (or extension) of the strict cycle, is that S-essential transformations precede non-S-essential transformations. Then the weak principle of Determinism says that no component has two transformations that could apply at the same time unless one of them is ordered first by the strict cycle, as just defined. If we adopt the weak principle of Determinism, the argument given in the text does not go through. But since the argument is not sufficient for all cases anyway, we might as well adopt the weak principle of Determinism.

10

Suppose that T_0 is not part of the transformational component, so the structure under G remains base. Since G is raised to S_1, the Raising principle will not allow L and M to be analyzed anyway. Thus the counterexample will hold. But in this case (where the Raising principle is doing the freezing), the filtering interpretation of the Freezing principle will rule out the counterexample.

11

Baker (1977) has suggested that certain learnability problems—which Culicover and Wexler (1977) discuss as the basis for the postulation of formal constraints on the operation of transformations—could possibly be handled by putting stricter limitations on the definition of *transformation*. Although attempts at restricting the notion of transformation are potentially valuable for the learnability problem and should be pursued, the problems we are dealing with here do not seem amenable to solution in this way. Consider the six transformations involved in the example (35)–(38). Each of these transformations moves exactly one constituent, deleting it in its original position and sister-adjoining it to another constituent. There are no other changes in the phrase-marker. As far as the complexity of the structural descriptions is concerned, besides mention of variables, the constituent to be moved, and the place of attachment, there is in each transformation at most one unchanged context element (exactly one for all transformations except T_1 and T_3, which have no context elements in their structural descriptions). Although this does not seem greatly out of line with what appears to be needed for descriptive adequacy, even this amount of complexity is somewhat illusory, because some of it has been built in to make the examples easier to understand, not for reasons intrinsic to the analysis. In particular, we have attempted to keep all base phrase-markers as similar as possible, thus minimizing the possibilities for expansion of a node. In the transformation T_0, L is attached to the right of M, but only when D is immediately to the left of L. If D were replaced by a variable in the S.D. of T_0, then T_0 could apply to level S_1 in P' (37). But T_1' also applies to level S_1 in P'. Therefore the principle of Determinism would be violated. The D was put into the S.D. of T_0 just so that T_0 would not apply to (37), violating Determinism. Suppose we had chosen instead to define T_0: $X - L - Y - F \Rightarrow 1 - \emptyset - 3 - 4+2$. That is, L is shifted to the right of F. This revised T_0 has no context elements in its structural description. Nevertheless, even when G is raised and P' (37) is formed, the new T_0 cannot apply at S_1 in P' because F is not to the right of L. Thus the problem of determinism will not arise. The reason we didn't choose this T_0 as an illustration in the text was simply that we would then have to assume a new base rule; namely, $E \rightarrow GF(L)$ would have to be possible so that T_0 doesn't freeze E_0 in P (35), preventing G from being raised at S_1. Thus some of the complexity of our transformations has been motivated by the desire to keep the number of base structures as small as possible, for ease of comprehension. Once again, it is important to pursue the possibility that limiting the complexity of transformations would be useful for learnability, but results so far do not suggest that limitations of complexity will be sufficient for learnability.

12

The definitions imply that, with transformations applying at cycle S_h, moving S_{h-1} is an S-essential transformation. By NBC, this movement must be a raising transformation. Thus it must be a simple movement. Since we have assumed dominate to mean weakly dominate, this movement of S_{h-1} does fit our definition of a raising transformation, and it is taken to be such in what follows. It is important to investigate whether this decision has the correct consequences. For example, does movement of S freeze S the way it would be required to by the Raising principle? If movement of S turns out to have properties different from raising nodes *strictly* dominated by S, then the definitions could be changed to reflect this fact. It would then be necessary to make sure that the proof works with the new definitions.

13

We could have defined an NBC principle in which bottom context had no effect and yet in which lowering was allowed. That is, a category from a higher sentence can move into a lower sentence and attach to a target in the lower sentence. We do not know whether this decision would have allowed the creation of counterexamples to the learnability theorem, or whether the current proof would still go through.

14

Besides the name of the raised or deleted node, there is one subtle way in which NBC will allow the structure of the embedded sentence to play a role in fitting transformations: NBC will allow the statement that the raised or deleted node is at the boundary of its clause. Consider the base phrase-markers (i) and (ii).

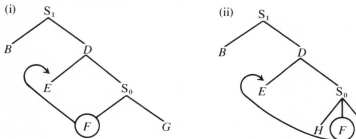

We can define a transformation T: X - E - F - $Y \Rightarrow 1$ - $3+2$ - $\emptyset$ - 4. This transformation will apply to (i) and raise F to become a left sister of E. Notice that the S.D. of T has no variable between E and F; therefore the S.D. doesn't fit (ii), where H exists between E and F, and T doesn't apply to (ii). NBC allows T to apply to (i) because no node under S_0 except F (the raised node) is fit by a nonvariable element of the S.D. of T. NBC could be modified to directly exclude this possibility—we will have to do this in sec. 4.3.5.2—but at the moment the formalism allows it. Right boundaries, of course, can be selected in the same way.

The result of the formalism allows interesting possibilities. In particular, in English, the subject of a clause (in deep structure) is always on the left boundary of the clause (excluding the complementizer node, which quite conceivably is passed over in fitting transformations, especially if it is empty). Therefore, if a transformation mentioned the last element of the matrix sentence, it could pick out the subject of the embedded sentence. No other NP in the embedded sentence can be picked out in the same way. The direct object, for example, is of course not uniquely associated with the right boundary of the clause; a number of different kinds of phrases may follow the direct object. This particular formulation of NBC thus leads to the prediction that transformations that raise or (S-essentially) delete NP's either apply to all NP's indiscriminately (with respect to syntax) or apply to subjects only. Although this prediction is made for English, it of course applies to all languages in which the subject is uniquely associated with the clause boundary and in which no other NP is uniquely associated with a clause boundary.

To avoid confusion, it should be clear that NBC won't allow a phrase at the boundary to be picked out simply by saying somehow in the definition of the S.D. that the phrase is at the boundary. Rather, the boundary phrase can be picked out in only two ways. First, the transformation can state a nonvariable element of the S.D. that fits a node in the matrix sentence adjacent to the boundary node in the embedded sentence. Second, the boundary node in the embedded sentence may be a boundary node of the entire sentence (the degree-1 p-m); therefore (in the case of a left boundary) if the transformation states *no* variable before stating the embedded node to be raised or deleted, the boundary phrase can be selected. The second case requires that we not assume there are, automatically, end variables in a structural description. The entire discussion, of course, assumes that Wilkins's proposal that variables appear automatically between adjacent elements in a structural description doesn't hold (see note 8).

15

There is, nevertheless, a detectable error on P. The E that S_2 immediately dominates in (41) will be attached to H or I by $U_2{}^A$ or $U_2{}^C$. Thus when H is raised by T_3 at level S_3, there will be a detectable error, although the E that S_1 dominates has not been raised to cause an error. But this problem can easily be fixed up by writing the S.D. of the U transformations so that they are raising transformations. In particular, we could require that there be an F between the node E and the node to which it is attached. For example, we would write $U_2{}^A$: J - X - F - Y - E - $Z \Rightarrow 1+5$ - 2 - 3 - 4 - $\emptyset$ - 6. Then the E that S_2 immediately dominates in (41) could not be attached to H or I by the U transformations. There might appear to be yet another problem, which arises even if we re-define the U transformations. Namely, if we drop S_0 from P (35), there is a detectable error on the resulting degree-2 p-m (E_1 is raised to S_2 causing an error, and the detectable error arises at S_3). But this is not really a problem, because our purpose here is only to show that the particular method of constructing P' that we have suggested (taking 0-extensions of the nonfrozen part of S_1) doesn't work. We have al-ready indicated why just dropping S_0 won't work in general. Neverthe-less, examples can be constructed like (35) in which there is *no* degree-2 p-m on which a detectable error occurs. That there is a de-tectable error on a degree-2 p-m in this case is simply an accident, resulting from our desire to keep the format of the examples similar to each other. Examples demonstrating the necessity of some of our as-sumptions may be found in sec. 4.2.

16
If it seems that U_1 is too complex, the considerations of note 11 should be kept in mind. For ease of understanding, we are attempting to keep the examples as similar as possible. But if we relaxed this requirement, and allowed, in this last example, the error-producing transformation at S_2 to raise L instead of E, we could prevent this transformation from applying to P' (37) by deleting L whenever there is an M to the right of L. This deletion transformation would be less complex than U_1 because it has only one context element in its S.D. The transformation wouldn't apply to P (36) because M is to the left of L in (36).

17
There is a weaker and, prima facie, more attractive TUBS principle (call it TUBS 2): If P is an untransformable partially derived 0-degree p-m, there exists a 0-extension of P to a fully derived base p-m P' such that $A(P')$ (the transformed P') is an extension of P. In other words, an untransformable structure P is still transparent, in the sense that it can show up on the surface, but it doesn't have to show up as the top part of a base structure (as in the original TUBS in the text). Rather, it can be the top part of a transformed structure. We do not know whether TUBS 2 is sufficient, together with all the other assumptions that we make, to prove learnability from data of degree 2. In particular, we will not be able to prove conclusion (ii) of theorem 5 (see sec. 4.3.4.4), which says that $A(P') = C(P')$, because TUBS 2 allows P' to be trans-

formed; although we can assume no detectable errors on P', it may be that A and C transform P' to different structures with the same terminal string. Theorem 5 is used to prove that the property of category-raising equivalence holds (theorem 7—cf. sec. 4.3.5.4); that is, under certain conditions if components A and C raise the same terminal phrase, the phrase must be dominated by the same node in both components. We do not know whether this theorem can be proved with the weaker TUBS 2. At the very least we would suspect that the principle (cf. sec. 4.3.3.2) that a movement or deletion from under a nonbranching node must leave behind a designated representative would have to apply to all transformations, not just to S-essential transformations. At the moment we have neither counterexamples nor proofs, and the question of replacing TUBS with the weaker TUBS 2 remains open.

18
It might be possible to find conditions on the definition of transformation and structural change that would imply TUBS. To take a (quite possibly unrepresentative) example, consider the base p-m P given in (i). First, suppose that E is moved to the right of the p-m P by a

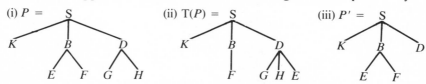

transformation depending in some way on the right context of E. The context might be H. If we interpret adjunction as sister-adjunction, we can write a transformation T: $X - E - Y - H \Rightarrow 1 - \emptyset - 3 - 4+2$. Applying T to P yields $T(P)$, given in (ii). Now suppose that D is expandable in the base grammar only as GH, and that no transformations other than T apply to P. Then the structure P' given in (iii) is a partially-derived, untransformable base structure, which has no untransformable 0-extension. Therefore TUBS is violated.

TUBS was violated in this example because the transformation that applied to P would not apply to P' because the required H doesn't exist in P'. Suppose, however, that we interpret adjunction $(+)$ as daughter-adjunction. Then we can write a transformation T' that has exactly the same structural effect as T but does not violate TUBS. Define T': $X - E - Y - D \Rightarrow 1 - \emptyset - 3 - 4+2$. Interpreting $+$ as indicating daughter-adjunction, $T'(P) = T(P)$, given in (ii). Moreover, T' applies to P' (iii), so P' is not untransformable. Therefore TUBS is not violated. In this case daughter-adjunction made it possible for a particular structural effect to be realized, without the violation of TUBS. This example, though, may be quite special, and the question could be investigated further.

If we are willing to obtain different derived phrase-markers, there is a way, in this example, of using sister-adjunction without violating TUBS. Simply take T' as is, but interpret + as sister-adjunction. Then T'(P) is given in (iv). As before, T' will apply to P' (iii) and TUBS is not violated.

(iv)

$$T'(P) = S$$

```
        S
    /  /|  \
   K  B  D   E
      |  /\
      F  G H
```

19
Counterexamples of this type were first pointed out to us by Doug Shaker.

20
The principle of No Bottom Context might appear to prevent the relevant transformations from applying at S_2. That is, a single transformation cannot raise both H and I. But we can allow H and I to be raised by separate transformations. Then it looks as if either H or I could be raised first, that is, either transformation could apply at one time in the derivation, since the context in which H and I occur is the same (and NBC further says that only the top context of S_2 is relevant to a raising transformation). Thus Determinism would be violated. This argument is almost right. It fails, however, to note that we can, say, make the raising of I dependent (in the S.D. of the transformation) on an H in the top p-m (under S_2). In that case the order in which the transformations apply must be: first, raise H; second, raise I. The principle of Determinism is not violated. The reader interested in pursuing this example to the extent necessary to formalize the transformations, should note that the transformation that raises H must be structure-preserving— that is, $M \rightarrow QH$ is a base rule, or else the Freezing principle will prevent H from being analyzed by the transformation that raises I. But then it is necessary to ensure that E cannot be raised from S_1 to become a daughter of H in S_2, via the transformation in A that applies at level S_1 to P (cf. (46)), because in that case S_0 can be dropped from P in (46) and a detectable error will occur on the resulting degree-2 p-m. That is, an error will occur when E is raised from the lowest level to the next

higher one. Then a detectable error will occur at the next level, when M is raised. These conditions can be satisfied in a variety of ways, within the bounds of our assumptions. To demonstrate this requires the precise statement of the transformations and base rules.

21
A more formal definition of adjacency: If H and I are nodes in a p-m P, I is *right-adjacent* to H if there is a structural description of P of the form X - H - I - Y. (The variables X and Y don't have to refer to phrases, of course.)

22
For example, in (i) a transformation T_1 moves D to the end of the p-m. A transformation T_2 raises H, but only when D is to the right of H, say, $T_2 = X$ - H - Y - $D \Rightarrow 1$ - $\emptyset$ - 3 - $4{+}2$. Therefore the only way in which these transformations can apply together is T_1 before T_2. But that would mean an S-essential transformation followed a non-S-essential transformation. The OSET principle will not allow this to happen. Therefore, only T_1 will apply to (i).

(i)
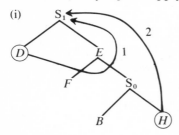

23
See Culicover and Wexler 1977 for examples in which no learnability at all is possible, even if the degree-2 requirement is relaxed.

24
If NBC and the Binary principle were shown to be wrong in some way and we wanted to slightly increase the power of S-essential transformations, a natural way might be to assume that besides the matrix context (that is, the context of the level at which the transformation applies), an S-essential transformation may use only the context of the level of the p-m from which the root of the phrase that was raised or deleted comes. For example, if an NP is raised from level S_i to level S_j, only the 0-degree p-m's at S_i and S_j could provide context for fitting the transformation.

25

If, in the interests of an assumption of simplicity of structural descriptions, we wanted to avoid the statement of an extra context element (J)
in $T_2{}^c$, we could modify the example by letting the structure of H in P
be $\lfloor_H\lfloor_J L\rfloor\rfloor$; that is, H directly and exhaustively dominates J, which in
turn directly and exhaustively dominates L. Then the error due to rais-
ing M could be made by having M attach in one component as a right
sister of L (under J) and, in the other component, as a right sister of J
(under H). Raising J at the next cycle (S_3) would then produce a detectable error; all transformations in the example state only two
nonvariables—the moved category and the category to which attachment takes place.

26

Although, for ease of understanding, in this example we have deleted Q
(transformation T_0), this deletion was not necessary. After G is raised,
RP prevents Q from being analyzed by a later transformation, so even
if Q is there, transformation T_2 cannot apply to P. Or we could have
permuted Q and R, assuming such permutation is not structure-
preserving, and FP would have prevented T_2 from applying to P.

27

Suppose we tried to create examples to show the necessity of BP, while
not allowing more than one S-essential transformation to apply at a
cycle. We could start by making use of the intermediate level. Consider
P, in (i) and P', formed from P, in (ii). No transformations apply to P at
S_0. At level S_1, D, which is in S_0, is deleted. Then at cycle S_2, B is
raised, causing an error, uncovered at the next cycle (S_3, not shown).
Now, without the intermediate (S_1) level, D cannot be deleted. So we

(i) $P =$

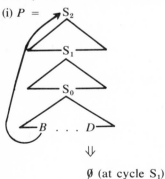

$\Downarrow$

$\emptyset$ (at cycle S_1)

(ii) $P' =$

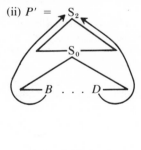

leave out S_1 in constructing P'. No transformations apply at level S_0 in P'. At the next higher level, S_2, it now turns out (that is, we construct it that way) that both B and D can be raised. This violates Determinism, and we would like to say that therefore no detectable error occurs on P', despite the fact that a detectable error occurs on P (or rather, P plus one higher level).

However, this is not right; we have misinterpreted Determinism, which says that component A is always deterministic; that is, it can't happen that B and D are simultaneously raisable. Therefore, component A will produce a terminal string on P'. If B and D are simultaneously raisable by component C, by convention there is a detectable error.

However, suppose that we reinterpret Determinism, and do not assume that component A has been defined so that two transformations can never simultaneously apply. Rather, we simply assume that whenever two transformations simultaneously fit a phrase-marker, that p-m is filtered out. In other words, we extend the definition for component C to apply also to component A. Under this reinterpretation of Determinism, component A will also map P' into $\emptyset$ and there will be no detectable error on P'. The crux of the example is that the occurrence of S_1 in P allowed D to be deleted and prevented Determinism from filtering P. Therefore we have an example that demonstrates the necessity of the Binary principle and applies only one S-essential transformation at each cycle.

It is not clear what to make of this reinterpretation of the Binary principle. In the proof, we use the original interpretation, but we think the reinterpretation might have the same effect. This question needs to be investigated more deeply.

28
Implicitly, other constraints are also postulated, such as "no memory for past data" and "rule-by-rule changes over the course of learning." These are constraints on the learning *procedure* (see chap. 3). It must be remembered that we are only at the beginning of the study of language learnability. More and more conditions must be required of a theory of language acquisition until we have reached a level of feasibility. Since the Freezing principle rules out so many derivations, by assigning the heavy role of the determination of characteristic structure to the base grammar, it is quite possible that FP will play an important part in helping to meet these future conditions to be imposed on a theory of language acquisition. See sec. 4.5 for some tentative results in this direction.

29
It must be recalled that we have adopted the weak principle of Determinism, which doesn't rule out transformational components if principles of ordering prevent two transformations that would otherwise fit the same p-m from being simultaneously applicable (see note 9).

30
In this example (59), since G is raised again, from S_1 to S_2, its attachment in S_1 to either M or N must be structure-preserving (otherwise, the Freezing principle would rule out the later movement of G). But then (i) is a possible base structure.

(i)

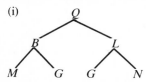

Suppose that (i) substitutes for the structure dominated by Q in (59) and that S_0 is dropped from (59). This forms P', a degree-2 p-m. But then both T_2 and T_2' apply to P' at cycle S_2, simultaneously. Therefore the transformational components are not deterministic, and our example has to be ruled out. But this will not be the case if we adopt the new interpretation of the principle of Determinism given in note 27, that when two transformations simultaneously apply, the derivation is filtered out but the transformational components are possible.

Even if we don't adopt this interpretation of Determinism, other examples show that NBC is necessary to the proof. The example we gave in the text has the advantage that only one context element is mentioned by T_2 (L), and by T_2' (B). However, let us allow ourselves somewhat greater complexity. Suppose, first, that we kept the error-producing transformations that raise G to under B or L at cycle S_1. Then, however, instead of further raising G to cycle S_2, we raise another node, say F, from level S_1 to level S_2. Transformation U_2 raises F to attach to the right of J when a string . . . -B-N- . . . is to the left of F (not immediately to the left, of course). Transformation U_2' raises F to attach to the left of K when a structure . . . -M-L- . . . is to the left of F. It is clear that U_2 will apply to P after component A has applied to S and U_2' will apply to P after component C has applied to S_1 (see (59)). In this case there is no problem with Determinism: if both G's appeared in a structure, as in (i), neither transformation would apply. Therefore we have produced another example to show the necessity of NBC, this example not needing the reinterpretation of Determinism.

31

For illustration of the notation, consider the p-m P in (i.a) to which a transformational component $A = \{T_1, T_2\}$ applies, yielding $A(P)$ in (i.b). T_1 raises D and T_2 raises H, as indicated by the arrows in (i.a). We

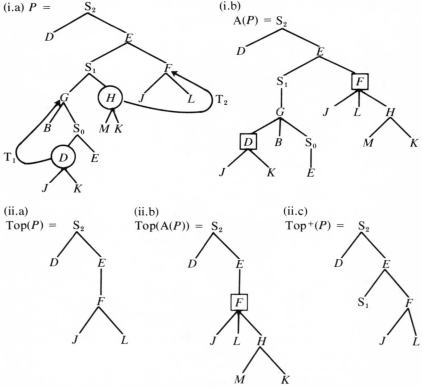

(i.a) $P = $

(i.b) $A(P) = S_2$

(ii.a) $\text{Top}(P) = S_2$

(ii.b) $\text{Top}(A(P)) = S_2$

(ii.c) $\text{Top}^+(P) = S_2$

assume that T_1 is structure preserving; that is, $G \rightarrow DBS$ is a possible one-step derivation. Therefore G is not frozen in $A(P)$, but D is frozen by the Raising principle, as indicated by the box around it. We assume that T_2 is not structure-preserving at the point of attachment; that is, $F \rightarrow JLH$ is not allowed by the base rules. Thus F is frozen by the Freezing principle, as indicated by the box around it. Although the Raising principle also freezes the H under F, we don't have to show this in the notation, since H is under a frozen node. We give below some other structures calculated from the definitions. Applying the Top operation to (iii.b) we calculate that $\text{Top}(E(A(P))) = $ (iii.a), which is $E(\text{Top}(A(P)))$, illustrating the commutativity of E and Top. The nodes

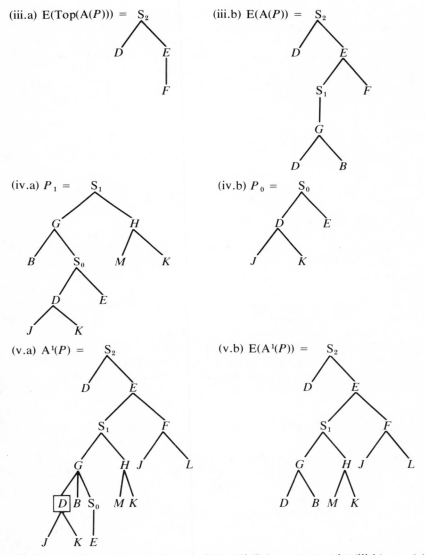

(iii.a) E(Top(A(P))) = S₂

(iii.b) E(A(P)) = S₂

(iv.a) P_1 = S₁

(iv.b) P_0 = S₀

(v.a) A¹(P) = S₂

(v.b) E(A¹(P)) = S₂

of (i.b) that have been left out of the eligible structure in (iii.b) are (a) nodes under F, ruled out by the Freezing principle, (b) nodes under D, ruled out by the Raising principle, and (c) S_0 and nodes under it, ruled out by the Binary principle. $A^1(P)$ means P transformed up through S_1, as in (v.a). We must be careful about placement of subscripts that indicate lower parts of phrase-markers. The effects of subscripts are different depending on whether placement occurs before or after transformation. For example, $A(P_0)$, which takes the lowest S of P and transforms it, is not the same as $[A(P)]_0$, which transforms P, yielding (i.b), and then takes the lowest S of this transformed phrase-marker. (No transformations apply to P_0, so $A(P_0) = P_0$, in this example.) This may be seen in (vi).

(vi.a) $A(P_0) = S_0$ (vi.b) $[A(P)]_0 = S_0$

32

We might be able to eliminate this assumption, still allowing examples like (62a), and yet prove theorem 4 (the Substitution theorem) and even theorem 8 (the Degree-2 Error Detectability theorem). We could not prove theorem 3, of course, but we might be able to prove a modified version of it; namely, if two transformational components raise different packets at a level, and the nodes dominating these packets are not deleted, there is a detectable error. This modified version of theorem 3 might be sufficient to allow the proof to go through, since if the different packets don't remain in the p-m, their effect might be restricted. At any rate, for relative simplicity we will keep the assumption mentioned in the text and prove theorem 3.

33

Although example (62b) shows that another special assumption is necessary to the proof of theorem 3, which theorem we use in the proof of theorem 4, the example does not show that the assumption is necessary to the proof of theorem 4, or of theorem 8. We have no counterexamples to show that the assumption is necessary to theorem 4 or 8, and the question is open.

It might seem that an assumption against rules that change structure but do not reorder terminal strings would rule out (62b), but there are examples similar to (62b) for which such an assumption does not hold. Consider the operations diagrammed in (62b) to show the beginning and final stages of a series of movements, each of which changed the terminal string. Later on we will give reasons for assuming that the same terminal string cannot appear at two different stages in a derivation, but even that assumption will not rule out examples like (62b), because we could raise D (and K in the other component) to the left of F in S_1 and then delete F. Then no two stages in the derivation would have the same terminal string, different packets would have been raised by the different components, and yet there is no detectable error. The only recourse appears to be to rule out the offending possibility directly, as in part (ii) of the principle of Repulsion.

34

Actually, (62a) can be ruled out by a weaker principle than part (i) of Repulsion. We could assume instead that if a node is raised at level i and then both the raised node and a node dominating S_{i-1} are deleted at level i, the derivation is filtered. Since in (62a) both the raised node (D in component A, G in component C) and a node dominating S_0 (E) are deleted, this weaker principle would imply that the derivation of (62a) would be filtered by both components A and C.

However, this weaker principle wouldn't apply to some other examples of this type. Consider the derivations sketched in (i). In (i.a) component A first S-essentially raises B to the right of F. Then a singular

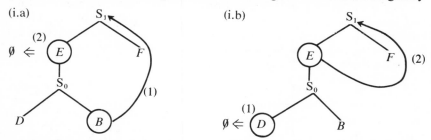

transformation applies, deleting E (and, of course, S_0 with it). The weaker principle is not violated because the raised node B is not deleted. The derived terminal string is $*A(P) = FB$. In (i.b), component C applies, first S-essentially deleting D. Then a singular transformation applies, moving E to the right of F. Again the weaker principle doesn't apply, and the derived terminal string is $*C(P) = FB$. Therefore, $*A(P) = *C(P)$, and there is no detectable error, even though the two transformational components S-essentially apply to different packets (B for component A and D for component C). Therefore we could not prove theorem 3.

However, part (i) of the principle of Repulsion will rule out this counterexample. In (i.a) a node is raised from S_0 and then a node dominating S_0 (namely, E) is deleted. Therefore Repulsion filters P. That is, $*A(P) = \emptyset$ (assuming, as previously discussed, that $\emptyset$ is the special filter symbol, besides denoting the empty string). On the other hand, since no node dominating S_0 is deleted by component C from (i.b), C does not filter P and we have $*C(P) = FB$. Therefore $*A(P) \neq *C(P)$. There is a detectable error, and this example does not constitute a counterexample to theorem 3, assuming the principle of Repulsion.

35

The subtraction operation is defined in the following way. For a string $x = x_1 x_2 \ldots x_n$ and a substring of x, $x' = x_i x_{i+1} \ldots x_j$ ($1 \leq i \leq j \leq n$), the string $x - y = x_1 x_2 \ldots x_{i-1} x_{j+1} x_{j+2} \ldots x_n$.

36

The principle of Designated Representatives obviously owes much to the long-standing idea in linguistic theory that deletion of a phrase can take place only under identity to another phrase or when a designated representative of the phrase is left behind (e.g., it for a NP). It might be the case on linguistic grounds that if K immediately and exhaustively dominates L and if L is raised, the designated representative that is left behind is d_K, not d_L (it depends on K, not L). Probably this assumption would work in the present case (proof of theorem 3'). However, when we introduce DR again (for proving category raising equivalence), it will be clear that the proof will work only if d_L is left behind (i.e., the designated representative depends on the moved or deleted category). Therefore we make this assumption here.

37

If a non-S-essential transformation in component A deletes E at level S_1, the designated representative d_B will be deleted, and the terminal string again will be BD. However, part (ii) of DR will then filter $A(P)$. Note that part (ii) of DR actually is not needed here, because E dominates S_0, a sentence to which an S-essential transformation has previously applied, thus allowing part (i) of Repulsion to filter $A(P)$. However, part (ii) of DR is needed for one special case, namely, one in which S_{i-1} is itself moved (or deleted) by an S-essential transformation applying at level S_i. Say a node F exhaustively and immediately dominated S_{i-1} before the S-essential transformation applied to S_{i-1}. After the transformation applies, a designated representative d_S is immediately and exhaustively dominated by F. However, Repulsion will not prevent F (or a node dominating F) from being deleted. Thus part (ii) of DR is needed in order to insure that d_S is not deleted.

38

We have used the optionality parentheses to make the situation more perspicuous linguistically. For a more traditional mathematical terminology we could delete the parentheses and replace $x*D_Ay$ by $f(P)$ where

$$f(P) = \begin{cases} x*D_Ay & \text{if } D_A \text{ is raised from } i - 1 \text{ to } i, \\ \emptyset & \text{otherwise.} \end{cases}$$

We will see in (76), which follows, that $f(P) = f(P')$. The terminology could be extended to other cases that we describe in terms of optional parentheses.

39
In terms of the notation of note 38, we replace $x*D_Ay$ by $f(P')$ where

$$f(P') = \begin{cases} x*D_A{'}y & \text{if } D_A{'} \text{ is raised from } i - 1 \text{ to } i, \\ \emptyset & \text{otherwise,} \end{cases}$$

and $f(P) = \emptyset$ if and only if $f(P') = \emptyset$.

40
Pullum (1976) discusses related phenomena under the name of the Duke of York Gambit.

41
The assumption that P is not filtered is made just to insure that $E(\text{Top}(A(P)))$ is well defined.

42
See Chomsky 1970 for the original formulation of $\bar{X}$ theory. Our formulations are very similar to those of Jackendoff (1977b).

43
The principle of Heads is different from a constraint proposed by Schwartz (1977), which says that a head may not be moved within the phrase of which it is the head.

44
The principle of Heads might be weakened in various ways; for example, deletion of a head might be possible and yet a way could be found to prove category raising equivalence. We will not discuss these possibilities. Also, a more stringent assumption might be considered, namely, some form of a requirement that transformations can't apply to (affect) heads at all (e.g., can't move or delete them). In this regard,

notice that in English the most characteristic transformations apply to the category NP, which is not a head in the usual systems (e.g., NP is not the head of the sentence when the NP is the subject, nor the head of the verb phrase when the NP is the direct object, nor the head of the prepositional phrase when the NP is the object of a preposition). A requirement like this might explain why VP, usually considered to be the head of S, is rarely affected by transformations (ellipsis being perhaps the chief counterexample, and perhaps also some forms of topicalization). At any rate, heads seem to be much more restricted than nonheads in their movement possibilities.

These notions of an abstract characterization of base structures together with an abstract characterization of the interactions between transformations and base structures seem to us pregnant with implications for learnability theory. In our opinion much insight will be found here. In particular, some of these assumptions might be quite useful in dealing with the problems raised throughout this paper, problems we have attempted to solve through restrictions on the application of transformations (though two of our assumptions crucially involve the base—namely, the Freezing principle and TUBS).

45
Recall that all adjunction is sister-adjunction, so if a node G is frozen (no nodes under it may be analyzed), nothing may be adjoined to a node under G and thus nothing may be inserted under G. The same result would follow if we allowed daughter-adjunction, on the assumption that no daughters may be inserted under a frozen node. We do not allow Chomsky-adjunction, in which new nodes are created. Presumably, if F is Chomsky-adjoined to G, a new node labeled G is created that would dominate the old G. This new G would also dominate F. On some assumptions this operation could take place even if the original G is frozen, since nothing takes place under the original G.

46
Also, USET would not allow two raising transformations to apply on the same cycle. But because ultimately we may wish to eliminate USET, we have used the Raising principle here instead.

47
There are so many rich structural possibilities that only some can be mentioned here, with no attempt at evaluation. It may be that if a node N is a head, the base rules are such that the category N never dominates N. This assumption would imply that certain categories are heads and others are nonheads. This might be consistent with certain ver-

sions of $\bar{X}$ theory. For example, perhaps NP is never a head, VP is always a head, and so on. The requirement might even follow from some version of $\bar{X}$ theory, in which categories are "projected" from certain "primitive" categories. This kind of requirement might put interesting restrictions on base theory. For example, in the expansion of the VP, the category V is always present and is taken as the head. Complements to the V are thus nonheads. It is well known (or at least is an assumption of a number of systems) that NP and S can be complements to the V. It is more questionable whether VP can be such a complement. On the assumption that VP is always a head, together with the assumption in the text that there is exactly one head of any phrase, VP could not be a complement to the V. This issue needs exploring, from the standpoint of both its theoretical and descriptive adequacy in syntax and its potential for learnability theory.

This assumption might be too strong, but there is a weaker assumption that might play an interesting role in learnability; namely, we could assume that if category K is a head, then K does not dominate another K which is a head of the top K. In other words, let K be a node of category j and height i (height i means that the head that K *immediately* dominates is an $i-1$ head of K). Then for any j, $j \leqslant i$, the j-head of K is *not* of category K. (This assumption, again. might almost come from $\bar{X}$ theory in that the projections X, $\bar{X}$, $\bar{\bar{X}}$, and $\bar{\bar{\bar{X}}}$ are by definition different categories.) This assumption might be related to a notion that the head sequence of a node (the sequence of j-heads) does not contain recursion. From this it is but a short step to proposing that the cyclic nodes are nonheads and perhaps the noncyclic nodes are heads. In some theories of English syntax, including our own (chap. 5), NP and S are cyclic nodes and they are not heads; VP is not a cyclic node and it is a head.

48

On the other hand, as we pointed out in note 36, we might want the designated representative not to depend on the category that was raised or S-essentially deleted but rather to depend on the category that exhaustively dominated the moved or deleted category. If so, the principle of Designated Representatives, as stated, would be the wrong one anyway. At any rate, we need *some* assumption about what happens when a transformation causes a nonterminating category to exist in a phrase-marker. This question has been raised before and obviously is worthy of further study. There might be a resemblance to some questions raisable in trace theory.

49

Freezing-Principle Strict Determinism is different from the filtering interpretation of the Freezing principle, which we earlier (sec. 4.1.10.3) considered and rejected in favor of other assumptions. Under that interpretation, the Freezing principle filters any p-m in which a transformation applies to a node made ineligible by freezing. However, this won't be sufficient for the proof here, because it is possible (and consistent with theorem 6 and with an example that we will shortly show) that the two raisable categories, one of them frozen, are present in both p-m's—those derived under A and under C. Then both p-m's will be filtered and there will be no detectable error, contrary to the result that we need to make the proof work.

Note that we don't need quite the full power of FPSD. The only cases that must be ruled out are where an S-essential transformation applies. Therefore, in place of this principle we could have assumed a principle of USET FPSD, which says the same as FPSD but only about S-essential transformations. For simplicity, we have stated the principle to apply to all transformations.

50

The deletion of H is not critical here. The same effect could be achieved by movement of H, say, to the right of the p-m.

51

For two strings x,y, we say that x is *disjoint* from y if and only if none of the elements in x appear in y and none of the elements in y appear in x.

52

Actually there is one pathological case that the proof does not seem to cover. Suppose $t_1t_2 = \emptyset$; that is, D_A dominates only S_{i-2}. Then it does not follow that there is a detectable error at level $i-1$, because we cannot claim that t_1t_2 is not a substring of $*C(P_{i-1})$. The one way that the correspondence property cannot hold then is for D_A to dominate only $*A(P_{i-2})$ and for D_C, D_A', and D_C' to dominate only the empty string. We can rule this possibility out by the simple assumption that nodes that come to dominate only the empty string are deleted. We make this assumption here because then this counterexample is eliminated (none of the nodes D_C, D_A', or D_C' could dominate only the terminal string, and the complete proof follows). If for some reason of linguistic theory we wanted to *not* delete these nodes, probably a different assumption would work, one saying that nodes that come to dominate only the empty string are not deleted but rather become ineligible for further transformation. This latter would have to be pursued in more detail to see how it enters into the proof. It would involve, it seems, a complication of the definition of eligible structure, which might then not be able to be defined as a subtree. On the other hand, such noneligible nodes might be able to be treated analogously to invisible S's (sec. 4.1.9).

53
It might appear that there is a simpler argument by which to prove that equation (138) holds with C replacing A, but this is fallacious. That is, since component C raises or deletes the same packet as A (by theorem 3), one might think that we could simply repeat the demonstration for A. But the problem is that one of the steps in the proof doesn't hold; namely, $C(P_0')$ is *not* necessarily an extension of $E(\text{Top}(C(P_{i-2})))$, which *is* true of A, and which was used in the proof.

54
The proof has been given in terms of "optional elements appearing" only because this method allows us to avoid the drawn-out specification of cases. It might make things clearer, though lengthier, to consider each individual case, for example, the case where both the embedded sentence and the raised node appear under D_A (equation (142)).

55
Briefly, the proof of theorem 9 can be seen to follow from the proof of theorem 6 of Hamburger and Wexler 1975 together with theorem 8 of sec. 4.4 in the following way. (We will use HW to identify propositions from Hamburger and Wexler; "HW-theorem 4" refers to theorem 4 of Hamburger and Wexler, whereas "theorem 4" refers to theorem 4 of this book.)

First, theorem 8 is the same proposition as HW-theorem 3 except that the finite bound U is shown to be $U = 2$. The proof of HW-theorem 4 is exactly the same for the system in this book, except that we don't allow string-preserving transformations, so that case HW-IIIa can't exist, which simplifies the proof. HW-lemma 6, HW-lemma 7, and HW-lemma 8 make no reference to specific grammatical properties; thus their proofs are exactly the same under the new system. HW-theorem 5 uses HW-lemma 1, which is that the set of eligible structures at any time in a derivation is a finite set. This can be immediately seen to hold for the new system. Otherwise HW-theorem 5 makes no reference to specific grammatical properties and therefore is proved in exactly the same way for the new system. HW-theorem 6 uses HW-theorem 3, HW-theorem 4, HW-theorem 5, HW-lemma 6, and no specific grammatical properties. These propositions hold for the new system, with HW-theorem 3 replaced by theorem 8, Degree-2 Error Detectability. Thus HW-theorem 6 goes through exactly as before except that a stronger result is obtained, learnability from data of degree ≤ 2. This is theorem 9.

56
The transformations are not explicitly (extrinsically) ordered. Recall that the only ordering of transformations that we have allowed is intrinsic ordering. Thus T_2 applies after T_1 because T_1 creates a structure to which T_2 can apply.

57
Or on some other phrase-marker. We assume in this example that no such others exist. Even if they must exist, the proof that one of them can always be hypothesized (HW-theorem 4) cannot go through.

Notes to Chapter 5

1
Many principles in linguistic theory are motivated by considerations of explanatory adequacy. We simply want to stress that learnability theory offers a clear kind of external motivation for a number of linguistic principles.

2
See Wasow 1972 for a discussion of this constraint and for a trace-theoretical solution with considerable theoretical implications.

3
See Milsark 1973, where it is argued that it is possible to find an explanation for the double *ing* phenomena within the grammar itself.

4
Stillings (1975) proposes an alternative account of Gapping, which does not have recourse to a constraint like NAC.

5
It is difficult to think of a formal measure of the notion "degree of conformity." Quite possibly our intuitions will not be shared by all readers in every case, but we think that the general relation we are concerned with is sufficiently clear.

6
See Culicover and Wexler 1977 for the most recent version. It should be noted that the Freezing principle makes use of a notion of "structure-preserving" that is related to but different from that of the important work of Emonds (1970; 1976). In our framework a transformational operation is or is not structure-preserving at a node, whereas in Emonds's framework the structure-preserving property holds of a transformation itself, and not of the various operations that it performs. It is conceivable that the two notions are extensionally equivalent in a theory in which transformations are severely constrained in other ways.

7
As can be seen from the phrase-marker in (7), we are viewing the basic sentential structure to be that originally proposed by Bresnan (1972), and, in a different version, by Emonds (1970). We are adopting the notation that appears to have become standard in generative grammar: $\bar{S}$ and S, rather than the S and S' notation we used in previous work.

8

Notice that sequences of NP's of this sort are conjoinable. In *John gave Mary a book and Sam a magazine,* conjunction must be transformationally derived if (8c) is not the correct structure. If, however, conjunction of this sort requires that the conjuncts be constituents at some stage of the derivation (as is suggested in Chomsky 1957), this example would constitute evidence for (8c). That is, on this view that only constituents are conjoined, in order to derive the example, *Mary a book* and *Sam a magazine* would have to be constituents at some stage of the derivation, as in (8c).

Recent proposals for a rule of Conjunction Reduction do not involve this condition; see Hudson 1976 for a summary. We will discuss the resolution of certain problems that conjunction raises for the approach adopted in this chapter. Our proposal does not require the conjuncts to be constituents.

9

For discussion of this rule and possible generalizations of it see Ross 1970; Jackendoff 1971; Maling 1972; Hudson 1976; Stillings 1975; and Hankamer 1973.

10

By Stillings (1975).

11

Cf. Ross 1967 for discussion of this rule.

12

It is interesting to note that in (21) a complex NP has been moved to the end of the VP, but this does not improve or preserve grammaticality; it leads to ungrammaticality, in fact.

13

The analysis sketched here is not completely without problems. In the first place, the following examples show that it must be possible to move the first NP in a V-NP-NP sequence if passive sentences are transformationally derived.

(i)

a. *John* was given ∅ a picture of Jefferson.
b. *Mary* was sent ∅ a box of chocolates for her birthday.
c. *Harold* was offered ∅ a chance to buy the Brooklyn Bridge but turned it down because the price was too high.

d. *Sam* was sold ∅ two tickets to the Beatles concert, only to discover that they were counterfeit.

In sec. 5.2.5 we will examine two more or less plausible solutions to this problem.

In the second place, Oehrle (1976) presents considerable evidence for the existence of V-NP-NP datives that have no V-NP-*to*-NP counterparts. For example, some idiomatic constructions of the form V NP_1 NP_2 lack an idiomatic interpretation in the order V NP_2 *to* NP_1.

(ii)
a. Bill gave Fred a dirty look.
b. ?Bill gave a dirty look to Fred.

A possible interpretation of this state of affairs is that (ii.a) is not transformationally derived. This presents a problem for the current analysis, because *give Fred* still acts as though it is a frozen structure: neither Gapping nor Wh Fronting may analyze it, for instance.

(iii)
*Bill gave Fred a dirty look, and Susan, Sam an even dirtier one.

(iv)
*Who did Bill give a dirty look?

And, as would be expected if (ii.a) were derived transformationally, it is possible to question the second NP in the sequence.

(v)
How dirty a look did Bill give Fred?

But if (iia) is not transformationally derived, we cannot use the Freezing Principle to account for (iii)–(v). If we proposed an alternative explanation for these data, we would raise the question of why such an explanation should not also be invoked for the nonidiomatic dative facts discussed in this section.

This issue appears to us to be an extremely complicated one, and we cannot do justice to it here; an entire monograph would be called for. We would have to determine, for each example, whether or not a transformational analysis is possible and justifiable, whether or not a plausible account can be given for the difference in interpretation between the two dative constructions, and so on. We do not see the problem as totally intractable, but in view of its complexity, we will say no more about it in this book.

Another, somewhat related problem is that in our account of Dative there are two V nodes. Consequently, we might expect that the higher V satisfies the structural description of NP Preposing, in part, thus allowing NP Preposing to apply to the direct object after Dative has applied. We would then have derivations of the following sort:

(vi)

$_{NP}[\Delta]$ $_V$[give Mary] $_{NP}$[a book] → *$_{NP}$[a book] was $_V$[given Mary].

We tentatively suggest that this derivation is blocked because the frozenness of the higher V blocks access to the feature on the verb that allows NP Preposing to apply. To develop this into a genuine explanation we would have to show independently (a) that NP Preposing is governed by features and (b) that freezing blocks access to features. As far as (b) is concerned, it appears that such an interpretation of freezing is needed for certain aspects of Pied Piping which we discuss in section 5.5. For (a) we offer the following argument.

There are numerous idioms in English of the form V NP P. A typical example is *take advantage of*. It is well known that for certain idioms of this form, NP Preposing may apply to either the NP that follows the preposition or to the NP that follows the verb:

(vii)

a. Mary was taken advantage of $\emptyset$.

b. Advantage was taken $\emptyset$ of Mary.

A natural explanation, proposed by Culicover (1967) and independently by Brame (1976) is that the structure of such idioms is the following: Either V_1 or V_2 can satisfy the third term of the structural description of NP Preposing, $_{NP}[\Delta]$ - X - V - NP - Y.

(viii)

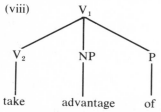

Culicover (1967) further notes that idioms of this general form fall into four categories. Category 1, the *take advantage of* category, allows two passives. Category 2 allows no passives; an example is *make eyes at*.

(ix)
a. *Mary was made eyes at (by all the boys).
b. *Eyes were made at Mary (by all the boys).

Dialects differ on the membership of particular idioms in particular categories and these examples represent our own judgments. Category 3 allows passives on the NP of the idiom only. An example is *take umbrage at*.

(x)
a. *Bill's remarks were taken umbrage at (by the audience).
b. Umbrage was taken at Bill's remarks (by the audience).

Finally, category 4 allows passives on the direct object of the idiom only. An example is *catch hold of*.

(xi)
a. Fred's arm was caught hold of by the officer.
b. *Hold was caught of Fred's arm by the officer.

We can get just this distribution of passive patterns by stating the rule of NP Preposing in terms of a verb marked [±passive]. The four patterns emerge from the marking of V_1 [±passive] and V_2 [±passive].

To the extent that this analysis can be maintained, we can block NP Preposing in the case of (vi) by not allowing NP Preposing to look at the feature [+passive] of the frozen verb. Of course, it is not at all obvious that the frozen verb has the feature [+passive] (since it is frozen), but it might turn out that all features of the lower node are copied upwards in the case of Chomsky-adjunction. If this is not the case, however, NP Preposing will still not apply because the higher verb will not have the feature [+passive] at all. Freezing will then play no role in the argument, but we will still need to assume that NP Preposing makes reference to this feature of the verb.

We should not overlook the possibility, discussed in sec. 5.2.5, that the passive is not transformationally derived at all. It is not clear, however, that in a nontransformational analysis there would be no counterpart of the problem to which this note is devoted.

14
An early discussion of this rule can be found in Ross (1967).

15
We are assuming here that Complex NP Shift moves the NP to the end

of the VP. This begs a number of questions that will be dealt with during the course of this chapter. First, it is logically possible that the NP is attached to S and not to VP, as in (i.a). However, it is easy to show that only the VP and not the entire S is frozen. In addition, we will argue that the transformational cycle applies on VP, and, by the strict cycle, (cf. Chomsky 1973) Complex NP Shift must apply on the VP cycle if its structural description is met there. Finally, the attachment could be either Chomsky-adjunction or daughter-adjunction in this case. If the former, there will be no empirical differences, since the highest VP is frozen in any case, as shown in (i.b).

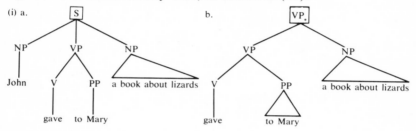

(i) a. ... b. ...

16

For the reader unfamiliar with the methodology traditionally employed in generative grammar, it should be noted that it is possible to block derivation of the ungrammatical examples in (29) by placing special conditions on the movement transformations themselves rather than by assuming a general constraint at the level of linguistic theory. The former solution is less highly valued because of the need to complicate linguistic theory to permit the statement of special conditions of the required sort on individual rules. Of course, this would be an unwelcome complication from the point of view of learnability theory also.

17

In Wexler and Culicover 1973, we entertained and provided an argument against accounting for phenomena of this sort by a perceptual strategy along the lines proposed by Bever (1970). We repeat the argument here: One might suppose that sentences like (29b) are unacceptable because the effect of Complex NP Shift is to derive a structure that could have had another derivation. Such an explanation of certain limitations on the transformation of Gapping is proposed by Hankamer (1973). In this particular case, movement of the object of the preposition *to* after Complex NP Shift has applied will give a derivation such as that schematized in (i).

(i)

$$\text{NP Aux V NP}_\text{C} \text{ to } \begin{bmatrix} \text{NP} \\ +\text{wh} \end{bmatrix} \rightarrow$$

$$\text{NP Aux V } \square \text{ to } \begin{bmatrix} \text{NP} \\ +\text{wh} \end{bmatrix} \text{NP}_\text{C} \rightarrow$$

$$\begin{bmatrix} \text{NP} \\ +\text{wh} \end{bmatrix} \text{NP Aux V to } \emptyset \text{ NP}_\text{C}$$

One might suppose, then, that the problem has to do with the juxtaposition of the preposition *to* and an NP that does not originate as the object of *to* in deep structure. To show that this is not the explanation, we observe that interposing an adverb between the preposition and the complex NP does not improve the sentence:

(ii)
a. *Who did John give to $\emptyset$ yesterday the picture that was hanging on the wall?
b. *Who did you send to $\emptyset$ reluctantly the money that you had been saving?
c. *Which drawer did Bill put into $\emptyset$ so abruptly the package that he received in the mail?

As (iii) shows, the ungrammaticality of these sentences is not due to the fact that there is an adverb following the preposition, since in general this does not yield ungrammaticality.

(iii)
a. Who did you talk to yesterday?
b. Which town would Mary go to most reluctantly?
c. This is the house that John moved into so abruptly.

It seems reasonable to conclude that there is no straightforward surface-structure-based perceptual strategy that will explain the phenomena discussed here.

18
Similar examples can be constructed when the complex NP has been moved over an AP. However, the untransformed sentences are not always completely acceptable. For example, we can derive (ii) from (i) by the rule of *to be* Deletion, and then derive from (ii) a sentence of the desired form.

(i) John considers the directors who voted favorably on the bond

issue to be $\left\{\begin{array}{l}\text{easy to please} \\ \text{angry at the American public}\end{array}\right\}$

(ii) John considers the directors who voted favorably on the bond

issue $\left\{\begin{array}{l}\text{easy to please} \\ \text{angry at the American public}\end{array}\right\}$

(iii) John considers $\left\{\begin{array}{l}\text{easy to please} \\ \text{angry at the American public}\end{array}\right\}$ the directors

who voted favorably on the recent bond issue.

As predicted, *easy* and *angry* cannot be fronted in structures like (iii).

(iv)
a. *How easy does John consider ∅ to please the directors who voted favorably on the recent bond issue?
b. *How angry does John consider ∅ at the American public the directors who voted favorably on the recent bond issue?
c. *Easy though John considers ∅ to please the directors who voted on the recent bond issue, . . .
d. *Angry though John considers ∅ at the American public the directors who voted on the recent bond issue, . . .

But as (v) shows, the untransformed structure (ii) cannot undergo these transformations either.

(v)
a. *How easy does John consider the directors ∅ to please?
b. *How angry does John consider the directors ∅ at the American public?
c. *Easy though John considers the directors ∅ to please, . . .
d. *Angry though John considers the directors ∅ at the American public, . . .

And (vi) demonstrates that in less complex examples both transformations can apply.

(vi)
a. How easy is John to please?
b. How angry is John at the American public?
c. Easy though John is to please, . . .
d. Angry though John is at the American public, . . .

Finally, the relevant examples are somewhat improved when *to be* is not deleted.

(vii)
a. How easy does John consider the directors to be to please?
b. How angry does John consider the directors to be at the American public?
c. Easy though John considers the directors to be to please, . . .
d. Angry though John considers the directors to be at the American public, . . .

Of course, when Complex NP Shift has applied, the adjective phrase becomes unanalyzable.

(viii)
a. *How easy does John consider to be to please the directors who voted favorably on the recent bond issue?
b. *Easy though John considers to be to please the directors who voted favorably on the recent bond issue, he does not intend to raise any embarrassing questions at this time.

It seems fairly clear that *to be* Deletion is responsible for the ungrammaticality of (v), but it is not clear to us why this should be so.

19
Cf. Chomsky 1965 for discussion of the general notion.

20
Variants of this proposal can be found in Bresnan 1972, as well as in Emonds 1970; Chomsky 1973; Wexler and Culicover 1973; Culicover and Wexler 1973a,b; 1977; and elsewhere.

21
We are ignoring for this part of the discussion our prior assumption that rules apply in an order determined by the domains on which they are defined, by the cyclic principle. Clearly Conjunction Reduction would have to follow any rule defined on the individual conjuncts, such as Dative. A way around this would be to assume that Conjunction Reduction is a precyclic (and possibly cyclic as well) transformation. As we will see, this does not help.

22
An additional point is that in order for Dative to move NP_2 onto V_1, it

would have to violate the Coordinate Structure constraint of Ross (1967).

23

Quite possibly the crucial characteristic of this deletion rule is that it deletes only lexical material under identity. If this were so it would be very interesting, because such deletion rules are just those that have no effect on syntactic structure and hence do not affect the applicability of later transformations. Consequently, no learnability problems of the sort that we are concerned with in chapter 4 will arise.

On the other hand, it is not at all clear how a rule that we have characterized as a lexical deletion transformation will generalize with pronominalization and VP Ellipsis. It is not out of the question that this rule should be characterized as a rule of interpretation of dummy elements, which would make the generalization somewhat more straightforward. (See Wasow 1972 and Williams 1977.) We have no explanation at this time of why rules of anaphora, like pronominalization and VP Ellipsis, are exempt from the learnability constraints.

24

We accounted for this in Wexler and Culicover 1973 with a non-structure-preserving transformation of adverb movement onto the verb. The deletion rule that would be blocked in (59) would then be Gapping, and not a rule of (verb) reduction that is insensitive to analyzability constraints. It seems to us now that Gapping applies only when the verbal sequence is bounded on the left by subject NP's in both conjuncts. Otherwise we would expect to derive (i), since no freezing is evident.

(i)

a. *Mary will visit Susan and might, Fred.

b. *Bill can't speak French and $\begin{Bmatrix} \text{used to} \\ \text{can} \end{Bmatrix}$, Polish

This follows from the formulation of Gapping proposed by Stillings (1975), which would also block derivation of (59) by Gapping.

25

The ordering problem is that the cycle will prevent us from applying Dative after Conjunction Reduction has given (57). The point here is that (57) must be ruled out for reasons that have nothing to do with the Dative transformation itself, if the Freezing principle is correct.

26
Given the range of constituents over which reduction applies, NP, V, Q, Adv, etc., it seems unlikely that they would all share the same null proform. In fact the determiners do not have a proform independently and it is not clear what such a form could be. It seems to us to be most straightforward simply to delete lexical material, especially since the role of various proforms, dummies, etc. (what Lightfoot (1977) refers to as "inaudibilia") is presently a matter of active theoretical dispute.

27
We give examples here where NP has undergone Right Node Raising (RNR). However, RNR is applicable to any right branch constituent, and the facts we discuss have their analogs in cases like the following:

(i)
a. Mary will, and John will not, buy the truck.
b. John gave a book, and Bill sent a money order, to Susan.
c. John walks, and Mary runs, slowly.
d. John believes, and it seems to be the case, that Mary buys trucks.

28
A pecularity of RNR is that it can go into islands, unlike other extraction transformations. This in itself is not sufficient to argue against the rule as an extraction transformation, but the case becomes quite strong when we discover that the "extracted" nodes behave as though they had never been extracted at all.

29
The ungrammaticality of this particular example could be accounted for by the Raising principle if there were truly a transformation of Right Node Raising. In this case the common node has been raised out of the relative clause, and would hence be frozen. But the Raising principle would also block grammatical sentences, on this account, in which the raised node is taken from parallel complements, as in (i), which is derived from (ii).

(i)
Who did Mary think that Bill saw, and Fred think that Susan tried to buy, a picture of?

(ii)
Mary thinks that Bill saw *who,* and Fred thinks that Susan tried to buy a picture of *who.*

Example (i) shows, incidentally, that the reduction of right branches in left conjuncts is also not subject to the analyzability constraints, in this case the Binary principle. This is exactly right if these cases are derived by a lexical deletion rule of the same sort that derives the conjunction reduction examples in the preceding section.

30
It is not obvious that there are any other rules that crucially involve Δ. If there are such rules, certain potential problems must be pointed out. For example, if Extraposition and *there*-Insertion both leave Δ behind, what determines that in the first case the Δ will be *it* and in the second case, *there?* An interesting by-product of the analysis of Extraposition by Koster (1978) is that this problem does not arise; on that analysis there is no rule of Extraposition at all. Of course, if there is a transformation of Extraposition this problem can be avoided by having the rule itself fill the dummy subject position with *it*.

There are also problems with *there*-Insertion if it leaves behind a dummy in the position occupied by the subject before the rule applies. If it did leave a dummy behind, NP Preposing could apply to the output, as illustrated in (i). The examples in (c) are derived from those in (a) by movement, by NP Preposing, of the italicized NP into the position occupied by Δ.

(i)

a. Δ $\begin{cases} \text{was } a\ man \text{ in the garden.} \\ \text{emerged } a\ woman\ in\ a\ white\ gown. \\ \text{appeared } a\ ghastly\ face \text{ at the door.} \end{cases}$

b. there $\begin{cases} \text{was a man in the garden.} \\ \text{emerged a woman in a white gown.} \\ \text{appeared a ghastly face at the door.} \end{cases}$

c. *A man was been ∅ in the garden.
   *A woman in a white gown was emerged ∅.
   *A ghastly face was appeared at the door ∅.

This is not necessarily a problem if there is some way of blocking NP Preposing in the case of intransitives like *be, emerge,* and *appear*. For example, if NP Preposing is triggered by the presence of the passive morphology, the rule will not be applicable with these verbs because they do not display such morphology.

31
An analysis along these lines was suggested originally by Bresnan (1972).

32

See Lasnik and Fiengo 1974 and Milner 1978 for some independent motivation.

33

It should be pointed out that, prima facie, Wasow's approach will not allow us to solve the passive problem. He argues for underlying passives just for those cases where the passive is ambiguous between an adjectival and a verbal interpretation. It does not appear to be the case, however, that the dative passive is ambiguous along these lines. See Wasow 1977, especially sec. 4.3, for discussion.

34

Another possibility is that the result of applying NP Preposing to a dative is, strictly speaking, ungrammatical but acceptable. This sort of possibility, of course, is always available in case there are counterexamples to a grammatical analysis, and we do not wish to make too much of it here. Briefly, to motivate such a solution in this particular case we would have to provide a theory of performance, specifically of comprehension, in which the rules assigning an analysis to a sentence like *John was given a magazine* operate flawlessly, even though this sentence is not generated by the rules of the grammar.

Such a solution is impossible if the rules that the performance mechanism employs are exactly the rules of the grammar, and if NP Preposing is in fact a rule. There is no reason to believe, however, that such a strict isomorphism holds. See Fodor, Bever, and Garrett 1974 for a critique of earlier attempts to construct performance models that closely parallel grammars. A similar attempt is found in some recent work of Bresnan (1978), where the grammar is formulated so as to further the parallelism.

On the other hand, it is possible that the task of the performance mechanism is not to reconstruct the deep structure of the sentence but to assign a reading to it with a minimum of computation. If this is the case, it is reasonable to suppose that in some cases the rules employed by the performance mechanism are not simply reversals of transformations. And from this we can conceive of a case in which the rules that are motivated in the performance mechanism for grammatical sentences will operate correctly for ungrammatical sentences.

This is not the place to speculate on what the performance mechanism might look like. It would be a great mistake, in our view, to try to argue for a solution along these lines without being very precise about the implicit claims that are made by any parsing strategy. It is all too easy to fall into the trap of proposing strategies on an ad hoc basis, when what is required, we believe, is a theory of performance that constrains severely the sorts of performance rules that can be hypothesized.

35
An intriguing possibility, but one that we cannot pursue in this book, is that languages differ according to which nodes are B-cyclic. To speculate somewhat, it might be that all languages have $\bar{S}$ and NP as B-cyclic nodes; some have in addition PP, and some have VP. In a language having PP as a B-cyclic node, it would be the case that the PP could be moved but never analyzed. This might explain, for example, why it is that in languages like French (and in fact most languages) it is necessary to "pied pipe" the preposition in questions and relative clauses. In French (i) is not grammatical.

(i)
*Qui pense-t-il de Ø?
Who thinks he about?
(ii)
De qui pense-t-il Ø?
About whom thinks he?
"Who is he thinking about?"

In a language having VP as a B-cyclic node, it would be impossible to analyze the VP. Hence, the only NP that could be questioned or relativized would be the subject. Notions like these might explain aspects of the Keenan-Comrie Accessibility Hierarchy (1977).

36
The counting version of the Binary principle described here is taken essentially verbatim from Culicover and Wexler 1977.

37
Alternatively, failure of NP Preposing to apply to the subject of a tensed S may be due to the presence of the Comp, as we note later.

38
In our discussion of the Raising principle we will take note of the fact that if the Raising principle is correct, there may well be no rule of extraposition that applies to sentential subjects. There are other rules of extraposition *from* subject which must be able to apply at S in any event. For example, Extraposition of PP and Extraposition of S Complement, both of which we will discuss. The first extraposes PP in an NP like *a picture* $_{pp}[of\ Fred]$, and the second, $\bar{S}$'s in NP's like *John's belief* $_s[that\ the\ world\ is\ round]$.

39

It does not seem that sentences like (115b) can be blocked by manipulating the structural description of the transformation that extraposes PP. In the derivation of (i), the effect of the rule is to move a PP from within an NP in a nonsubject context.

(i)
a. John gave a book *about amoebas* to Mary.
b. John gave a book ∅ to Mary *about amoebas*.

It appears that the structural description of the rule must be something like X - $_{NP}[Y$ - PP] - Z. Without a constraint like the Binary principle, this will derive (115b). We see no non-ad-hoc formal difference between the grammatical (i.b) and the ungrammatical (115b) except that in the latter case an $\overline{S}$ is between the subject NP and the PP that extraposes.

40

It is not likely that the rule of Complex NP Shift can be constrained in this way in the structural description, because a complex NP need not be a clause-mate of the V that it is moved away from. In examples like the following the complex NP is the subject of the complement.

(i)
a. We believe ∅ to be a fool the man who just left the room.
b. The governor showed ∅ to be unfounded the reports on the evening news that he was running a bookmaking operation in the mansion.
c. Bill considers ∅ to be obvious the reasons why the economy is going down the drain.

We presume that there is no rule of Raising into object position. As far as we can tell, there is no compelling evidence that there is such a rule. (See Chomsky 1973 and Lightfoot 1976 for discussion.) In fact, for reasons of learnability we have assumed in chapter 4 that no transformation changes only the structure and not the terminal string. (Cf. sec. 4.3.4.4 for details.)

Our statement of Complex NP Shift differs from that of Ross (1967), Postal (1974), and Bresnan (1975), all of whom adopt essentially the following statement:

X - NP - Y
1 - 2 - 3 $\Rightarrow$ 1 - ∅ - 3+2
Condition: 2 is complex.

This statement creates problems of overgeneration, since not just any complex NP can be shifted to the right:

(ii) *I climbed into ∅ on a ladder *the room that had been pointed out to me by the sergeant.*

Ross (1967, 226) blocks rightward movement out of PP by a specific constraint; Bresnan (1975) argues that this can be accomplished by the Relativized A-over-A principle if the second term is allowed to range over PP and NP. In case the complex NP is immediately dominated by PP, the latter will be maximal with respect to the proper factorization of the tree according to the structural description of the rule, and thus will be the constituent to undergo the rule. Postal (1974) notes that the rule as stated will apply incorrectly to subjects of *that*-complements. He proposes that a constraint prevents Complex NP Shift from applying to subjects.

(iii) *I believe ∅ is a millionaire the man that Mary married.

The problem noted by Ross and Bresnan can be avoided by restating the rule as we have done in the text. This means, of course, that Complex NP Shift will not be applicable to PP's internal to the VP which do not immediately follow the verb. However, it does not appear that the movement of PP's is due to the same rule, in view of the fact that a PP need not be complex in order to move to VP-final position:

(iv) We spoke yesterday to Fred.

As we pointed out in Culicover and Wexler 1977, the Binary principle will block application of Complex NP Shift to the subject of a *that*-complement.

41
It is also possible that the ungrammatical examples in (118) might be ruled out by the Internal S constraint. See Kuno 1973 for discussion.

42
We are assuming here the strongest position, which is that the theory does not allow for true exceptions to the Binary principle. Our assumption may be wrong, of course, and the theory may have to allow for certain classes of exceptions. It is conceivable that certain classes of exceptions may not have significant consequences for the learnability proof, but we have not investigated this possibility in detail.

Moreover, the learnability proof motivates the Binary principle to exclude grammars that can be excluded in other ways. If a complication of the class of grammars should yield a new motivation for the Binary principle, this new case might tolerate exceptions that might not be tolerated in the simpler model.

43
Still another possibility, suggested by J. Emonds (personal communication) is that Comp is substituted for by the fronted constituent. However, if we are to maintain successive cyclicity, Comp substitution must not cause freezing. As can be seen from the structures in (123) and (124), substitution for Comp will allow access to the fronted constituent only in the case of DV.

44
Bresnan (1976a,b,c; 1978) and Chomsky (1976; 1977) discuss the differences, both empirical and theoretical, between a theory that permits unbounded movement over a variable and one that does not.

45
See Bresnan 1972, Lasnik and Fiengo 1974, and Brame 1976.

46
VP_0 in (126) could be replaced by $_s$[Pro VP] without affecting the analysis.

47
An interesting fact is that the examples in (130) are far worse than those in (131). We have no explanation for why this should be so.

48
If the Binary principle is correct, the PP must be an immediate constituent of NP. Both versions require this, since PP can extrapose from subject position.

49
For many of the NP's in (138)–(139) it is impossible to front the PP when the NP is in object position, also:

(i)
a. ?Of what sort of potatoes does a pound cost $1.90?
b. *About what kinds of roses did you find a book?
c. *For what sort of success did the President announce his hopes?

In our discussion of the Raising principle we will argue that this is due to completely different factors: In order for the PP to be accessible to Wh Fronting at the $\bar{S}$ level, it must be either restructured into the VP, or extraposed from the object NP. In either case, there is a constraint against reordering of constituents that were originally generated in a particular configuration. Cf. sec. 5.5.2.2.

Bach and Horn (1976) propose the NP Constraint to block examples such as these. See Chomsky 1977 for discussion.

50
Under neither version should it be possible to move the object of the prepositional phrase out of the subject; in general, this prediction appears to be correct.

(i)
a. ?What does a pound of ∅ cost $1.90?
b. $\begin{Bmatrix} \text{*What kind of roses do you think a book about} \\ \text{*Which famous physicist do you think a book by} \end{Bmatrix}$ ∅ would sell enough to break even?
c. *What sort of success would our hopes for ∅ be well rewarded?
d. *What kind of wood did a house of ∅ on the next block burn down?
e. *Who did a friend of ∅ introduce you to Bill?
f. *What fruit is a bowl of ∅ sitting on the table?
g. *Which city was a man from ∅ standing on the podium and waving his hands around?

51
Notice that the statement of rules with labeled brackets in the structural description is not allowed by the formalism of chapter 4. Mention of such brackets may not be necessary here, but we have retained them in the interest of clarity.

52
We are comparing only the two versions of the Binary principle here. It is logically possible that a completely different constraint provides the best explanation for the data we are considering.

53
It would be helpful, of course, to provide independent syntactic arguments for Det. The kind of evidence needed would be a transformation that applied only to the set of categories that can appear in Det position: NP's, *the,* demonstratives, and so on. No such rule exists in English, so far as we can tell.

54

Unless otherwise specified, output structures such as that in (161) do not constitute any specific claims about the details of the transformations involved.

55

Assuming that grammars may contain last cyclic rules would constitute an undesirable enrichment of the theory of grammar, other things being equal. Such rules would apply to the entire phrase-marker (violating the Binary principle) when the topmost cyclic node was reached. It appears in this particular case that there would be no independent motivation for this ordering besides the problem at hand.

56

This assumption permits a generalization of Wh Fronting, and is found in much of the standard literature. See Chomsky 1977 and Culicover 1976b, among many others, for discussion.

57

A good reason for making this assumption is that when an interrogative pronoun has moved into a [+wh] Comp, it cannot be moved into a higher [+wh] Comp, even when it is within the domain of transformations applying at the higher cycle. For instance, consider the structure (i), where Q represents $\begin{bmatrix} \text{Comp} \\ +\text{wh} \end{bmatrix}$. This can give only (ii), not (iii).

(i) Q you wonder $_{\bar{S}}$[Q Bill saw what]
(ii) Do you wonder what Bill saw?
(iii) *What do you wonder (whether) Bill saw?

If we have a structure with two *wh* phrases, they must stay within their own clauses. For example, (iv) can give (v.a) and (v.b).

(iv)
Q you told whom $_{\bar{S}}$[Q you saw what]

(v)
a. Who did you tell what you saw?
b. *What did you tell whom (whether) you saw?

See Chomsky 1973, 1975b, 1976, 1977 for proposals along somewhat different but related lines.

58
Bresnan (1977 and elsewhere) has proposed that *that* relatives are not derived by fronting and deletion of relative pronouns but by deletion of nonrelative proforms in their original underlying position. Such a transformation, as Bresnan envisions it, would not function correctly in our framework because it would violate the Binary principle. We leave open the possibility of devising an analysis that does not violate BP, but does not treat *that* relatives as *wh* relatives at some stage.

59
The Binary principle blocks extraction from these *that* clauses when they have not been extraposed. The strict cycle blocks extraction first, and then extraposition.

In addition, there are certain examples suggesting that some extraposed *that* clauses (by Extraposition of S Complement) are analyzable, as in (i). For cases such as these we postulate a restructuring of the sort postulated for PP complements to be discussed in 5.5. The resulting structure will have the complement $\bar{S}$ as a sister to the verb, as in (ii).

(i) Who did John make the claim that he had met $\emptyset$?

(ii) . . . $_{VP}[V \ _{NP}[N \ \bar{S}]] \Rightarrow_R \cdot \cdot \cdot _{VP}[V \ _{NP}[N] \ \bar{S}]$

60
Examples (a) through (h) are taken from Culicover and Wexler 1977.

61
See the discussion in sec. 5.4.1.1 for motivation of this transformation.

62
Actually, the constraint is somewhat more general. For a formal statement, see sec. 5.5.

63
We are assuming here that adjunction of the extraposed constituent is Chomsky-adjunction. Freezing would also occur if PP_0 were daughter-adjoined to PP_1.

64
If, contrary to our assumptions, NP is not cycled on, the problems discussed here may be handled by the A-over-A principle. Suppose that PP can be extraposed only at S; then, by A-over-A, only PP_1 in (i) may be moved, avoiding the problem concerning us.

(i)

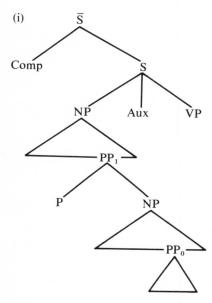

65

Chomsky (1973) proposes that restructuring rules are responsible for certain exceptions to his Subjacency condition. (These are the exceptions to the Binary principle.) So far as we can tell, Chomsky had in mind rules whose function was considerably different from those that we discuss in the following section. For example, he suggests that the analyzability of the *that* clause in *Who did John make the claim that Mary likes?* is due to a restructuring from $_V[make]$ $_{NP}[_{NP}[the\ claim]$ $_{\bar{S}}[that\ S]]]$ into $_V[make\ the\ claim]$ $_{\bar{S}}[that\ S]$.

Akmajian, Steele, and Wasow (1979) employ a notion of restructuring rules that is related in spirit to ours, though somewhat more restrictive. In particular, they wish to restrict restructuring to lexical items only. We are unable to find any clear motivation for this position, however, although it does appear that certain restructurings may be governed by lexical items. As should be clear from the preceding discussion, the sort of restructuring that we will employ must apply to categories, such as PP and $\bar{S}$, when they appear in certain configurations. An interesting possibility is that restructuring rules that apply to lexical items are lowering rules of the sort described by Chomsky, whereas those that apply to categories are raising rules. The lowering restructuring rules may very well have important applications in languages in which clitics—which are syntactically external to the $\bar{S}$—are incorporated with the verb, as in (i). Such a possibility was suggested to us by discussion with Ken Hale.

An analysis of the sort we are proposing in this section is proposed independently by Chomsky (1977, 144ff).

(i)

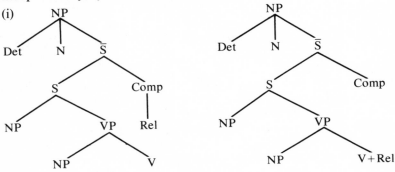

66
For discussion of the *make the claim* case, see Chomsky 1973.

67
Perhaps this is due to a generalized version of Repulsion (cf. sec. 4.3.3.1). The learnability motivation for such a generalization is unclear, however. See note 71 for discussion.

68
For discussion of how they get to be [+wh], see 5.5.4.

69
We can construct the same argument involving extraposing PP from object NP's: The Binary principle blocks direct access to a PP that is dominated by NP; restructuring cannot apply if the NP is not clause-final, and extraposition of the PP to the end of the VP raises the same problem.

(i)
a. John gave a pound of flour to Bill.
b. We expressed our hopes for future success to Mary.
c. I saw a man from Philadelphia last week.

(ii)
a. ?John gave a pound to Bill of flour (milled in Connecticut).
b. We expressed our hopes to Mary for future success.
c. I saw a man last week from Philadelphia.

(iii)
a. *Of what did John give a pound to Bill?
b. *For what sort of success did you express your hopes to Mary?
c. *From which city did you see a man?

70
Not all examples of this sort are fully grammatical, for reasons that we do not understand.

(i)
a. ?A pound costs $1.90 these days of white rose potatoes.
b. *?I think that a book would sell enough copies to break even
⌈about roses that do not bear flowers.⌉
⌊by that great physicist.   ⌋
c. ?A house on the next block burned down of expensive redwood.
d. *A friend introduced me to Bill of Susan.

But since some extrapositions are possible, the problem of blocking Wh Fronting after Extraposition of PP remains.

71
The class of structures to which this restriction applies is, strikingly, the class to which the principle of Repulsion applies, namely boundary constituents. This raises the possibility that some generalization of Repulsion may be able to subsume this case. Repulsion says, in essence, that when a constituent is moved from the boundary of another constituent by a raising transformation, it cannot move back to that boundary later by another transformation. A generalization of this principle which would yield the reordering constraint as a special case would be that a boundary constituent cannot be moved *up to* or *over* the boundary from which it was moved. Conceivably such a generalization would be required by another version of the learnability proof based on a different set of assumptions about the formal properties of transformational grammars from those in chapter 4.

Notice, incidentally, that a rule of Quantifier Shift deriving (i.b) from (i.a), would provide further motivation for a reordering constraint.

(i)
a. NP[The men all] will leave.
b. The men will all leave.

A reordering constraint would predict that VP Top should be unable to move the VP *all leave* over the subject NP *the men,* and this appears to be an accurate prediction.

(ii) *They said that the men would all leave, and all leave they will.

This ungrammaticality is not due to the presence of an adverbial in VP-initial position, as (iii) shows.

(iii) They said that the men would suddenly leave, and suddenly leave they will.

We suggest a similar explanation for the fact that Complex NP Shift cannot apply to an NP from which *all* has been moved. The following data illustrate:

(iv)
a. We believe the man in the funny suit to be a clown.
b. We believe to be a clown the man in the funny suit.
(v)
a. We believe the men in funny suits to have all been clowns.
b. *We believe to have all been clowns the men in funny suits.

Notice that *the men in funny suits all* cannot be moved, but this may be due to an independent constraint against sentence final lexical NP-*all* in surface structure.

(vi) *I saw the men all.

For discussion of Quantifier Shift in English cf. Postal 1974, Fiengo and Lasnik 1976. Kayne 1975 deals with similar phenomena in French.

72
The interpretation of the cycle suggested by Williams (1974a,b) allows an alternative account of the reordering facts. Williams proposes, in essence, that a transformation may apply only at the highest node that it applies at in any derivation. Ignoring the problems that this interpretation of the cycle raises for learnability theory, we see that such an account based on rule ordering will block the examples that lead us to a reordering constraint. It is important to recognize that in this book we assume simply that transformations apply at the lowest node in any given derivation at which their structural description is met (subject to the strict cycle), in contrast to Williams.

Suppose that Complex NP Shift applies at VP, but Extraposition of PP applies at S. Then (i) is ruled out: to derive (i), Extraposition of PP would have to apply before Complex NP Shift, and this is impossible because S dominates VP.

(i) *Sam gave ∅ to Susan by Fred *a picture of Mary*.

Extraposition of PP would have to apply at S, on Williams's theory, because it must apply at S when subject NP's are involved, as shown in (ii).

(ii) Two photographs are on the wall by Fred.

It is straightforward to extend this explanation to the restructuring case, but only if restructuring applies at S, that is, at a node higher than the node at which Complex NP Shift applies. (Strictly speaking, restructuring cannot apply at S if it meets the conditions assumed in 5.5.2, but we will ignore this.) Now, if restructuring applies at S, Complex NP Shift will never follow restructuring.

If this account is right, we would have two reasons to suspect that restructuring of PP is in fact a special case of Extraposition of PP. First, by definition restructuring cannot apply at S to a constituent of the direct object NP. Second, we would be missing a generalization if, in a theory that allowed statements of rule ordering, two distinct rules with the same effect were ordered at the same point.

But even if we do not adopt an explanation along the lines that Williams's theory suggests, we still find certain motivation for suspecting that restructuring is a special case of Extraposition of PP. For one thing, we have reason to question the validity of the Raising principle. (Cf. sec. 7.1.5.) Without the Raising principle, there is no difference between restructuring and Extraposition of PP in terms of their obedience to the constraints. We cannot propose that the Raising principle be dropped, however, because to do so we would first have to develop an alternative account of the data given in sec. 5.4, which it explains, as discussed in chap. 7. Notice, also, that if this restructuring is a special case of Extraposition of PP, we might be led to adopt the more restrictive notion of restructuring proposed by Akmajian, Steele, and Wasow (1979). See note 63 for some discussion.

73
The following examples, and the discussion, are taken from Culicover and Wexler 1977, with a few amendments.

74
We would have to require two *of*'s, one of which (*of interest*) prohibits restructuring. Even two *of*'s, however, would not explain the correlation with relative paraphrases.

75

If the subject were $\overline{\overline{N}}$, $\overline{\overline{N}}$ would have to be B-cyclic, so as to block extraction of or out of the PP to the left:

(i) *Of whom was a picture hanging on the wall?
(ii) *Who was a picture of hanging on the wall?

76

Greg Carlson has pointed out to us that some aspect of our restructuring analysis would follow if we adopted an approach in which a non-branching $\overline{N}$ node is pruned, as in (i). Assuming $\overline{\overline{N}}$ to be B-cyclic and $\overline{N}$

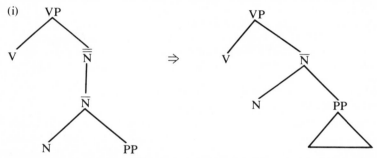

not B-cyclic, pruning $\overline{N}$ would move PP into the domain of transformations that were formally blocked by N. Significantly, $\overline{\overline{N}}$ PP would remain a constituent, avoiding some of the problems dealt with by the Reordering constraint. We have not pursued this alternative, but it appears promising. A potential problem is that the Reordering constraint applies not only to restructures but to the output of Extraposition of PP as well.

It should be pointed out that under this (or any other) approach to restructuring, there must be some device for blocking access to the Comp of a constituent that originated as a relative clause. A B-cyclic NP blocks access to the Comp by the Binary principle, but if the restructuring occurs (by definition, not causing freezing) the Comp Accessibility convention then would incorrectly allow the constituents of the Comp of this relative clause to be moved out of it. See sec. 5.4.1.2 for discussion of how this might be prevented.

77

In this discussion we are reporting only our own judgments. There may in fact be considerable disagreement among native speakers about particular sentences. A conclusive discussion of pied piping would have to take into account sufficiently many examples that the basic patterns could be convincingly distinguished from the minor individual variations due to uncertainty, complexity, and other external factors. Our intention here is simply to suggest an analysis of pied piping in the context of the learnability theory, and not to present a comprehensive account of the phenomenon.

78
The Reordering constraint predicts that it should be impossible to move PP_2 over PP_1 or vice versa after restructuring has derived (254). This accounts for the ungrammaticality of (252a). The following should also be ungrammatical, but again, it is difficult to form a sharp judgment.

(i)
These are the books which the government prescribes the height of the lettering of $\emptyset$ $_{PP_2}$[on the covers].

Here, PP_2 has been reordered to the right of PP_1, from which the *wh* word has been extracted.

79
Wh Copying is not a typical transformation. For one thing, it copies a feature and does not create a new constituent. This is just the sort of copying transformation that is not explicitly ruled out by the assumption of No Copying of chap. 4, which rules out constituent copying for reasons having to do with the proof.

   Second, Wh Copying cannot be formulated in terms of the usual structural description, since the constituent that receives the feature dominates the constituent that originally has it. Possibly this is a property of copying rules that would also follow from the requirements of the learnability proof if we extended the class of grammars to which the proof applies to those containing feature-copying transformations. We have not investigated this question, however.

80
We will not pursue the further consequences of this analysis here. As noted in note 77, any attempt at a comprehensive account of pied piping would take us well beyond the limits of this work.

81
This sentence seems to us to be clear evidence that it is impossible to

apply Extraposition of PP after Wh Fronting has moved an NP into Comp. This resolves the dilemma concerning the proper derived structure of *How many pictures did you lose of Mary?* and supports Chomsky's (1973) assumption, which we have adopted, that nothing can be moved out of Comp except into a higher Comp. Notice, though, that if our account of pied piping is correct, we don't have to make this assumption; it will follow from the Freezing principle. This is because, any constituent marked [+wh] which has internal structure is frozen by Wh Copying; hence it can be moved into Comp but cannot be analyzed after it has been moved there.

82
See Culicover 1976b for a sketch of one approach to the basic syntax of interrogative and relative proforms. The details of the mechanism by which such NP's are blocked in the base component depends on the particulars of the syntax that one adopts.

Notes to Chapter 6

1

For a discussion of the relation between theories of language acquisition and developmental data, see Wexler (in press).

2

It is sometimes claimed that transformational grammar is not based on empirical data. This judgment is simply wrong. The empirical data on which transformational theory is based consist of informant judgments of grammaticality, synonymy, etc. A theory is tested against such judgments. The situation is similar in many respects to the field of psychophysics (or perception). See Batchelder and Wexler 1979 for discussion.

3

Reaction time is a function of so many interacting processes that enter into production and comprehension of language that we may never be able to predict reaction time even by an extremely delineated theory of these factors. To our knowledge there is no reasonably articulated theory of production or comprehension based on reaction time data. See Wexler 1978b for discussion.

4

Consider, for example, *What did John drink ∅ yesterday and eat ∅ today?*

5

This was written before we saw Schlesinger 1977, and we will not take that newer work into account. Some of the central notions in that work were first proposed by Schlesinger in 1971 (Schlesinger 1977, 5).

6

This is also pointed out by Brown (1973, 123).

7

Finite-state grammars (Chomsky 1957) may be an exception, but the inadequacies of these are well known and no linguistic work is carried out according to finite-state theory.

8

In the sense of "strategy" or "heuristic" that we have been discussing, a strategy is simply a rule, but a rule in a performance rather than a competence system. Another sense of "strategy" sometimes employed in the literature is something like "hypothesis constructing procedure." If this is all that is meant, then of course any theory of language acquisition must contain strategies, as the theory presented in this book does.

9
Fodor, Bever, and Garrett have to argue that the syntax of children may be very simple, closely related to the character of the surface strings that they utter, "e.g., that the child represents all sentences by simple $((N) (V) (N))_S$ structures which are reduced to two-word surface forms by a mechanical computational constraint" (p. 490). If this were so, the problem of the ultimate construction of a transformational grammar would be an even greater mystery. Of course, FBG argue that such a grammar is never constructed, but they never give an explicit theory of what is constructed (aside from the claims about heuristics). If $((N) (V) (N))_S$ represents the child's abilities, what is the corresponding representation for the adult, and how does this representation relate to the empirical data of linguistics? No answer is given. More generally, there is no sense of a unified theory of language and of language acquisition (Wexler, in press).

10
Until recently, the theory of performance has been in a relatively rudimentary state. Unlike the situation in linguistic theory, there has been relatively little active testing of alternative hypotheses, with the theory growing as hypotheses and data interact. Given this lack of a performance theory, it is difficult to see how a serious theory of the acquisition of performance could be created. Trying to develop a theory of how performance strategies are acquired under these conditions would be something like trying to create a theory of the learning of syntactic competence before the development of transformational grammar. Essentially, it was not done, nor could it have been done. If a sufficiently precise theory of what is achieved does not exist, we cannot evaluate (or even do a reasonable job of creating) a theory of the learning of the achievement. More recently, some promising work has taken place in the theory of syntactic performance (Marcus 1977).

11
Another example is the claim (e.g., Putnam 1967) that multipurpose learning strategies can account for language acquisition, with no need for special structural linguistic principles. No such theory exists, however, and our formal results imply that procedures without specific

constraints cannot learn transformational grammar. It is clear that any fairly complex structured theory cannot be learned by these generalized, nonspecific procedures. Such a theory can be made coherent only if (adult) language is taken to be exceedingly simple. This last assumption will turn out to be clearly false empirically.

Notes to Chapter 7

1
Several assumptions made in chapter 4 will not be discussed here: No copying, no conjunction, no string preservation, Freezing-Principle Strict Determinism, strong NBC. The other assumptions were made for reasons either of convenience (in the proof) or because we could not see how to make the proof go through without them. This does not mean, therefore, that we believe, or have shown, that they are necessary for the proof. Nor do we wish to attribute any necessary empirical basis to them.

We will touch on other assumptions rather unsystematically. Several assumptions concerning heads are brought up in sec. 7.1.2, and the principle of Designated Representatives is referred to in sec. 7.1.5.2.

2
A further complication may be due to empirical factors, although it is only partially allowed for in the framework developed in chapter 4. Suppose that there were grammatical formatives that were unique in the sense that they could not be shown to be members of any particular lexical category. Such formatives might have to be mentioned in transformational rules, nevertheless. We have in mind such elements (in English) as *do* (in a *do*-Support analysis), *not, so, -ing, even,* and so on. If such formatives exist, and may be mentioned in transformations, we must adopt further assumptions governing their distribution and behavior in order to rule out the construction of counterexamples to theorem 2. Given appropriate additional assumptions, it will be seen, for example, that either of the following might rule out the application of transformations that cause errors that are not detectable in the absence of order-equivalence:

(i)
No transformation may move a grammatical formative.

(ii)
At most one instance of any given grammatical formative may appear in any binary-cyclic domain in the base.

The force of the first assumption is obvious. The second is more interesting. Suppose that there is a particular grammatical formative *G*. An example of the sort that we are trying to rule out can be created by moving one instance of *G* around another. Thus both instances of *G* must be accessible to the transformation that causes the movement. If only one *G* is allowed in any binary-cyclic domain, such a transformation will be ruled out by the Binary principle. Furthermore, if G is raised from one domain to another, the resulting structure will be frozen. In view of the fact that the empirical basis for this theoretical possibility is lacking, we will not speculate further on how the situation could be handled within linguistic theory. It is worth pointing out, however, that if there were grammatical formatives of the sort that we have been considering, independently motivated conditions on their distribution might render additional constraints unnecessary. It is also unclear how grammatical formatives would be accommodated in a theory having the assumptions about heads that we have adopted.

An additional minor point is that there is a special set of circumstances under which NULI can be eliminated in favor of other assumptions that have different empirical content. Suppose there were a category X^i that was expanded by the following rules:

(iii)
$$X^i \to X^{i-1}$$
$$X^{i-1} \to X^{i-2}$$
$$\cdots$$
$$X^1 \to X$$

The crucial property of this set of rules is that each X^j exhaustively dominates the next phrase down (and, in fact, each of the phrases that it dominates). Suppose that X were a lexical category containing just one lexical item. Movement of X^i would then be tantamount to movement of X. Thus we could construct a counterexample to theorem 2 without movement of lexical categories.

NULI would not be independently necessary, in such a case, if X is the only lexical category containing one member, and if, furthermore, a situation such as the one illustrated in (iii) is ruled out in the theory. There appears to be no reason to assume, however, that exactly one unique lexical category may occur in any language, nor is there any strong reason to rule out situations such as (iii). Jackendoff (1977a,b) argues for just such a set of rules for the category Modal in English, in order to maintain certain generalizations about the base component.

3
It is not difficult to find examples in which the order of PP's in the NP is fixed. What is difficult is to get clear judgments about the result of extraposing the PP's. For example,

(i)
a. Irritation with Bill over the fiasco will be useless.

b. Irritation over the fiasco with Bill will be useless.
c. Irritation will be useless with Bill over the fiasco.
d. Irritation will be useless over the fiasco with Bill.

It seems to us that (b) is bad. However, so is (c), although it is not as bad as (d). In the best case for the theory, (a) and (c) both would be good, and (b) and (d), both bad. Part of the complication here is that the individual PP's do not easily extrapose:

(ii)

a. Irritation will be useless with $\begin{Bmatrix} \text{Bill} \\ \text{any of the children who are here} \end{Bmatrix}$.

b. Irritation will be useless over the fiasco.
c. Irritation with Bill will be useless over the fiasco.
d. Irritation over the fiasco will be useless with Bill.

It seems to us that none of these examples is particularly felicitous. To test the principle of Adjacency, we would have to have examples in which extrapositions such as these were perfectly acceptable. At present we have been unable to discover such examples.

4
In contrast to the original example in chapter 4, we have used Chomsky-adjunction in this example. Without this it might well be impossible to construct the error at all with the structures that we are considering, but we have not investigated this possibility in detail.

Suppose that we restricted ourselves to sister-adjunction in this example. The only attachment error that we could then construct would be along the following lines:

(i) PP_0

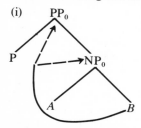

The example requires, however, that B not be raised explicitly from PP_0, but implicitly, through the raising of a constituent that dominates it. In this example, the only constituents that can be raised are P and NP_0. Though the latter dominates B, the former does not. So the raising of P and NP_0, given just this sister-attachment, will cause a detectable error immediately on the next cycle.

5
In fact, a constituent in Comp cannot influence the application of a transformation in a higher S. This follows from NBC. It is an open question whether a constituent in Comp can affect the application of a transformation in its own $\bar{S}$. Inversion in English might appear to be such a case, but quite possibly the feature [+wh] on the Comp into which a *wh* constituent is moved might be sufficient to trigger Inversion. Thus Inversion would not have to make reference to the presence of a *wh* constituent in Comp. Not allowing constituents of Comp to function as contexts in transformations would appear to be desirable purely on theoretical grounds, in the absence of any strong empirical evidence to the contrary.

6
Notice that the S.D. for NP Preposing contains the variable X between the dummy Δ and the context term **V**. The presence of this variable is crucial to example (i), which could not be constructed if constant terms were designated in its place. However, to replace this variable with constants would complicate the transformation considerably: as (i) shows, the passive construction is not particularly sensitive to the precise nature of the material between subject and verb.

(i)
a. John (*certainly*) *would* (*not*) $\begin{Bmatrix} \textit{have (obviously) been} \\ \textit{(obviously) be} \end{Bmatrix}$ arrested by the cops.
b. I believe John *to have* been arrested by the cops.

No doubt all possible intervening sequences could be mentioned in the S.D. of NP Preposing, but this would miss a significant generalization.

7
Wilkins's (1977) constraint on the interpretation of variables will rule out these cases as well. The NP *Susan* cannot undergo the rule on S_2, because the variable X would contain an NP *John* in the grossest analysis.

8
It is not clear that everything but *it* and NP can be eliminated from the S.D., as Wilkins suggests. In examples like the following, the italicized

NP cannot undergo TM, yet it may not be possible to group it with the *for*-phrase:

(i)
a. It takes *forty men* to lift this refrigerator.
b. *Forty men take to lift this refrigerator.
c. This refrigerator takes forty men to lift.

Similar examples can be constructed using the first *for*-phrase in sentences like (24a), which yields (24c). It appears, therefore, that a general constraint against moving subjects of infinitives will not block all misapplications of TM, since in (24c), for example, *the rich* is not a subject NP.

9
A configuration that we have not discussed in detail is (i). Nothing can

(i)

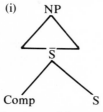

be moved from the S into the NP because of the Binary principle, and nothing can be moved from the Comp into the NP because of the convention against moving constituents from Comp anywhere except into a higher Comp.

10
Actually, in chapter 4 we allow only sister-adjunction. We could do so here, but the examples would be more complicated, and perhaps even more farfetched.

11
Recall once again that the proof in chapter 4 is given for sister-adjunction only. In the case of (34), and elsewhere in this chapter, we have used Chomsky-adjunction in order to be able to construct appropriate examples given assumptions about the English base. It would be interesting to consider the consequences for the learnability proof of allowing Chomsky-adjunction in the theory, both as an optional alternative to sister-adjunction and as a substitute for it.

12

In a formal theory of parsing we might relate unacceptability to the presence of unfilled *'s after the sentence has been parsed. Notice that in order for this to work, the parser would have to be instructed to seek a * in order for it to be in a state to perceive it. Otherwise all *'s would be noticed when encountered, and the parsing would take a considerably different course from the one we will suggest.

13

One other similarity between the PP subjects and the sentential subjects, though not strictly relevant to the present discussion, is worth mentioning. Sentences like (i)–(ii) contain sentential subjects and are unacceptable; Kuno (1973) suggests they contain an "internal S" and are therefore ruled out by a version of the "internal S constraint."

(i)   *How obvious is that Bill is a fink?
(ii) ?How interesting does that John is here seem to be?

We find that the same phenomena occur when the subjects are PP's.

(iii) *How far is from here to Boston?
(iv) ?How far does from here to Boston seem to be?

We suggest, but without analysis, that these sentences are unacceptable because of the problem they raise for a parser that is trying to find the subject NP—in neither case is the subject obviously an NP when it is first encountered. The second member of the pair ((iv)) appears to be somewhat more acceptable, perhaps because the inverted Aux *do* aids the parser slightly, as does the inverted modal in (v). Note the relatively lower acceptability of (vi)–(vii), where *do* is replaced by *is* in the comparable position in the sequence.

(v)   ?How far might from here to Boston seem to be?
(vi) *How loudly is that John is here being shouted?
(vii) *How far is from here to Boston said to be?

A similar pattern may hold for some speakers when the subject is sentential. Here (viii) would be worse than (ii).

(viii) How interesting is that John is here said to be?

Our own judgments are uncertain.

14

Assuming, of course, the standard theory of transformational grammar (as we have done in this book). Other theories are conceivable. It is quite possible that if transformations left behind traces, as Chomsky has proposed (1973, and elsewhere), the enriched surface structure might be sufficient for learning. The problem for the learner would then be to determine where in the surface structure the traces were located. We discuss this problem briefly in sec. 7.3.3.

No doubt there are other alternatives in which the conclusion that deep structure information is necessary would not follow. In a purely surface structure grammar, such as that proposed by Brame (1978), it would not even make sense to formulate the problem for the learner in terms of transformations. Nevertheless, it seems to us that the task for the learner is comparable, regardless of whether the theory is a transformational one or not, given that the language embodies a complex set of mappings between levels of representation.

15

It is important to stress the preliminary and speculative nature of this sort of investigation, since it appears not to have been noted by at least one person writing on linguistic universals, Pullum (1977). In commenting on our earlier unpublished work, he appears to take our attempts to evaluate potential universals as attempts to support these universals. It seems to us that Pullum has simply failed to understand why we were considering universals in the first place. Surely there is nothing particularly significant about a superficial linguistic universal unless is can be shown to follow from some interesting and deeper universal principle. We will return to this matter in somewhat more detail after the particular issues are made clearer.

16

In the strict sense of UBH, not only are the grammatical relations and the phrase structure rules universal, but the order of constituents also is universal. One could, of course, weaken UBH by relaxing the restriction that the order of constituents is universal. What is important to note is that even with the strongest hypothesis it is impossible to prove learnability without either a presentation scheme of (b, s) pairs or certain learnability constraints on the applicability of transformations, or both.

17

Such a language would be Japanese, in which the verb comes last. One could propose that there is a strict universal base but that languages differ in the rules that order constituents. This is essentially equivalent to the hypothesis that we will entertain initially, in which the constituents are unordered in the semantic representation and the task of the language learner is to discover the underlying constituent order, given the linguistic data. The only difference in the two approaches is that there is no particular reason to assume that the notion of constituent order has any relevance whatsoever in the semantic representation, whereas it is quite sensible to speak of constituent order as an aspect of syntactic description definable on syntactic deep structures.

18
Gold (1967). See also chap. 2.

19
The procedure is to simply list as a rule $A \rightarrow A_1 \ldots A_n$ whenever A is a nonterminal node appearing in a base phrase-marker and A directly and inclusively dominates $A_1 \ldots A_n$. In most cases, the base grammar doesn't have to be known in order for the transformations to be learned, because the procedure that hypothesizes transformations makes reference only to the base phrase-marker, not to the generating grammar. However, in order to apply the Freezing principle the base rules must be known.

20
We are assuming that there exists such a universal characterization of the human perception of events, objects, relations, properties, etc., in the world. This is reasonable to assume, given that any child will learn any language correctly in the environment in which the language is spoken. It is logically possible that more than one descriptively adequate semantic theory could exist, such that different schemes of semantic representation could appear in different languages; but the possibility cannot be seriously entertained in the absence of any empirical evidence. The difficulty of finding such evidence, of course, is greatly increased by our lack of understanding of what constitutes a descriptively adequate semantics and the fact that none has even been proposed. Some suggestions are given by Katz and Fodor (1964) and Katz (1972). For an alternative approach see Montague (1973).

21
We have in mind model-theoretic semantics, developed initially by Frege, Tarski, and Carnap and pursued by a variety of others.

22

We are assuming for the purposes of this discussion that the semantic representation is related to, perhaps contains, what has often been called *logical form*. It would be necessary to be quite precise about what semantic representation looked like if we proposed to make empirically testable claims about the mappings M and I. Although a lot rides on the choice, we must leave the question open here, because so little in fact is known about the proper form of representation at the semantic level. (For discussion of potential criteria for evaluating choices of logical form, see Harman 1972.)

23

Such a situation would be equivalent to that argued for by generative semantics, in which the mapping between deep structure and semantic interpretation is the identity mapping.

24

See, for example, Staal 1967 and Hudson 1972. Their assumptions differ from ours in that they propose that constituents in deep structure are unordered, whereas we are suggesting that there is ordering of constituents in deep structure but no ordering of functions and arguments in the semantic structure.

25

Chomsky (1965, 124–126) discusses other proposals for *set-systems* and points out that such systems will have to be supplemented by two types of rules: ordering rules, which convert set-systems into *concatenation-systems;* and grammatical transformations. This, of course, is exactly our proposal; thus his criticisms about set-systems without these rules do not apply. Why not have, then, what appears to be a simpler representation, namely, a concatenation-system to start with? The reason is that we want to represent an additional assumption in the notation, that the grammatical relations in deep structure are universal. This assumption is not implied by the usual notation of a context-free grammar for a specific language. Of course, if one supplements the concatenation-system for a particular language with the assumption that the concatenation-system incorporates a specific universal system of grammatical relations (i.e., the hierarchical relations are specified over all concatenation-systems), then the concatenation-system and set-system (with ordering rules) theories become notational variants. It is important to note in this regard that just because the order of constituents in a given sentence can be derived from a set-system without transformations applying (e.g., the passive in English) it does not follow that the sentence is necessarily derived without transformation. The analysis in a particular situation is an empirical question, for which various kinds of evidence can be offered.

Staal (1967) proposes that set-systems represent a universal base for natural language, with ordered strings derivable by transformation. Our proposal differs from his in that the ordering rules are not transformational in character; instead, they are limited (i.e., by the Invariance principle) and must operate before transformations. Which system is right is an empirical question.

26
Actually, all that needs to be learned is the order of constituents; the grammatical relations are implicit in the semantic grammar.

27
The tree corresponding to the semantic representation is, of course, an unordered tree.

28
The situation is actually more complicated than suggested here, because the learner has no a priori way of knowing whether the surface string has been derived via transformations or not. For some discussion of child data, see Wexler, Culicover, and Hamburger 1975.

29
See sec. 3.2.

30
In this example, we have hardly begun to exploit the full power of ordering rules if no constraint besides effectivity is put on them. It is quite clear that if no constraint is involved, the ordering of constituents could never be learned.

31
See Montague (1973) for a formal semantics based on an essentially subject-predicate analysis of English syntax.

32
We could try to make the subjicate analysis have the appropriate properties by changing the rules so that (i) would replace (53). The semantic rules to accomplish this would be those of (ii). Note that (ii) gives the internal structure of the semantic categories corresponding to syntactic S and subjicate.

(i)

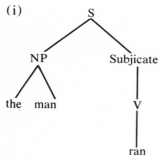

(ii)

a. S → {NP, Subjicate}

b. Subjicate → {V, (NP)}

By linearizing the structures generated by (ii) we would have, in essence, the syntactic structures that underlie English. However, the semantics corresponding to these structures would not be those of English. For the case in which subjicate expands as V NP, the NP would be (semantically) the subject, although it appears in predicate position in the syntactic structure. When subjicate expands as V, the NP that S immediately dominates would function as the semantic subject, that is, as the term that denotes the individual(s) of which the property designated by V is predicated.

It is interesting to observe that whereas (1) it seems to be possible to provide a semantics for a language of this sort, (2) the Invariance principle will rule it out. To consider point (1), note that we will have two rules of interpretation defined on the subjicate, depending on whether there is an NP or not. If the verb is intransitive, the interpretation of the subjicate will be an "active" one—the set of things that run. If the verb is transitive, however, the subjicate must be assigned a "passive" interpretation. For example, if we have the subjicate *open John,* the interpretation will be the set of things that were opened by John. The interpretation of S in either case can be expressed in terms of set inclusion: the sentence is true just in case the set denoted by the NP immediately dominated by S is a subset of the set denoted by the subjicate. For the intransitive case, *John runs* is true just in case the set containing only John is a subset of the set of things that run. For the transitive case, *the door open John* is true just in case the set containing only the door in question is a subset of the set of things that were opened by John (or that John opened).

Point (2) is that given the Invariance principle, a language like English cannot have the structure required by (ii), because the Invariance principle will linearize subjicate and NP of (ii.a) regardless of what subjicate dominates. Therefore it will be impossible to have both *John runs* and *John opened the door.* The only possibilities will be the examples given in the previous paragraph or their mirror images. If a set of rules like (ii) is possible, and if there is no principle that serves the function of the Invariance principle, then in order to describe a language like English, it will be necessary in any event to allow the linearization rules to be context sensitive.

33

Vennemann (1973) suggests that this order is "appositional." We are not certain exactly what he means, but we surmise from his discussion that the order N Det Quan Adj is derived from N_i Det Quan Adj N_i by (at least) deletion of the latter N_i.

34

Not the least problem is that subject and object are both of the category NP. It is therefore difficult to distinguish them by noncircular criteria. For an attempt to find universal independent characterizations of "subject," see Keenan 1976. Johnson (1977) argues that Keenan's criteria are generally inadequate because they are formulated in terms of a large number of poorly understood primitives. This raises the possibility that upon further examination it will be necessary to introduce the notion "subject" to explain what in fact these terms mean.

35

One example is Breton, discussed at some length by Anderson and Chung (1977).

It is important to point out that a language with very free word order is not a counterexample to the Invariance principle. Such a language simply does not bear on the correctness of the principle at all, unless there is an additional principle that somehow correlates particular deep structure constituent orders with surface structure possibilities. Nor do nonoccurring orders necessarily invalidate the Invariance principle. Independent principles may be required to explain why not all logically possible orders occur. Of course, we would want these principles to have strong theoretical motivation.

36

A language such as Dyribal is of the sort that Anderson (1976, 18) characterizes as "ergative in a fundamentally syntactic sense." In such a language, the patient in fact appears to function syntactically as a subject, at least to the extent that it is possible to settle independently on general properties of subjects (cf. Keenan 1976).

Pullum (1977, 261ff) observes that those languages that have been claimed in the literature to be OSV are also of the ergative type. Pullum tries to argue that there does not exist a strong case for any of these languages being OSV. But he bases his arguments (which appear to be suggestive at best) on superficial evidence only. Not only does he not attempt to introduce considerations about the grammars of these languages, but he explicitly rejects such considerations, as in the following remark about Rischel's (1970) analysis of West Greenlandic: "But the arguments given by Rischel (1970) for assuming patient-agent-predicate order in deep structures are extremely weak, and are in any case irrelevant from a relational point of view. All Rischel wants is to be able to predict morphological marking from standard, linearly ordered phrase-markers in a maximally simple way" (264). In view of Pullum's unwillingness to consider such arguments for deep structure constituent order in the first place, it would be a mistake to take his objections too seriously.

37
In addition to Breton (cf. note 35) there are numerous others. We agree with Pullum (1977) that the case for an underlying predicate would be needed for each such language if we intended to pursue seriously the Invariance principle.

It is important to sound a note of caution here. The available evidence may suggest that strong principles such as the Invariance principle are empirically inadequate in that they do not allow, in themselves, for the full range of observable variation. To conclude, as Pullum (1977, 271) does, that in testing the adequacy of such a principle we have accomplished "a conclusive reductio ad absurdum" of the subject-predicate hypothesis not only appears to us to be premature but goes against the usual principles of scientific methodology. Upon deeper investigation it may be found that a more abstract version or modification of an apparently too strong principle is precisely what is called for. A most striking and suggestive finding, in this regard, is the observation by Anderson and Chung (1977) that there is syntactic evidence for a VP in Breton, even though there are good arguments for Breton's being analyzed as underlying VSO. Continued careful analysis is necessary in order to determine the ways in which our hypotheses must be weakened; such analysis is necessary to theoretical questions having to do with the fundamental principles that underlie linguistic theory.

38
For some very comprehensive studies of syntactic universals, cf. Greenberg 1963 and Steele 1976; 1978a; 1978b.

39

Some linguists might even be prepared to dispute this. In view of this fact, intuitions about semantic markedness cannot be diagnostic for basic constituent orders, as we will argue.

40

In comparison, it is relatively easy to gather data about surface structure universals. It is interesting to note that Pullum (1977, 271), in discounting the approach to syntactic universals of Culicover and Wexler (1974), does find some value in the "massive tabulation of word order data" that appeared there. It is not surprising that Pullum discovers "occasional inaccuracies" in this tabulation, since it demanded no more than thirty hours of library research into over two hundred languages.

More seriously, it is important to emphasize that to a considerable extent the collocation of data on universals makes sense only in the context of a theory from which explanations can be developed and precise predictions derived. In our view, principles such as the Invariance principle will play a crucial role in such a theory. In contrast, Pullum's discussion of syntactic universals leads him to posit a "fundamental principle for linearization in natural language" no deeper than the following: "The NP constituents of a clause are linearized in their GR hierarchy order, from left to right" (p. 272). Here, the "GR hierarchy" is subject > direct object > indirect object > others. (Cf. in this regard our discussion of constraints as generalizations from data in sec. 5.1.)

41

Steele also suggests that native speaker intuitions may serve to give some indications as to basic and derived orders. We do not dispute this. However, it is difficult to see how such intuitions can reliably be directly translated into theoretical constructions on the basis of which deep universals may be inferred or hypotheses tested, though this methodology may be perfectly accurate in investigating superficial universals.

One fact that points up the difference between the two views that we discuss here is Steele's decision to ignore constituent order in subordinate clauses in her study of universals. It can be argued quite plausibly that German is underlying SOV, even though SOV may be judged to be the principle or basic word order only in subordinate clauses by Steele's criteria. If the syntactic arguments lead to the conclusion that German is SOV, what is the value of a universal for which German is counted as SVO, or the criteria by which this universal is arrived at?

42
See Siegel 1970 for convincing arguments that "unpassives" like *unemployed* are not derived by the passive transformation.

43
We are thinking of semantic representation as the level that expresses the aspects of interpretation of a sentence having to do with its truth value, like logical form (cf. Harman 1972). Other, so-called pragmatic aspects of interpretation (focus and presupposition, given-new, illocutionary inferences and intentions, conversational postulates, etc.) are not assumed to be represented at this level. We will ignore well-known problems having to do with surface structure interpretation of quantifiers and other scope-bearing elements.

44
This result follows from the requirement that the semantic interpretation of a constituent is a function of the semantic interpretations of its immediate constituents and the syntactic rule that combines them. There is still a problem here, in the case of VSO languages. If we suppose that a VSO language maps into a subject-predicate semantics, the syntactic analysis of a simple sentence will have to be something like the following: First, V and O are combined to form a constituent, the interpretation of which is the predicate. Then S and VO are combined, by putting S between the V and the O, and the interpretation of this is that of the sentence (the proposition). In order to carry out a derivation of this type, it will be necessary to allow the syntactic formation rules to analyze the structure of already interpreted phrases. If this is in fact the way to proceed, then something like the Binary principle will be required to set constraints on the depths to which such an analysis may go.

45
A possible solution is that every infinitive is dominated, both in semantic structure and in the corresponding deep structure, by S̄. For those infinitives that lack overt complementizers, we might assume that there is no underlying Comp node. Then, by convention, we may prune the nonbranching S̄'s. Alternatively, and more simply, primitive relations are defined only over finite clauses and VP's, for independent reasons.

46
Ken Hale (personal communication) cites Walbiri as an example. It is also possible in Walbiri to break up noun phrases, which violates the

to deep structure. Our assumptions commit us to the position that the breaking up of noun phrases is therefore transformational, since the Binary principle allows access into NP from S. We have no empirical reasons to adopt either analysis; however, it is interesting to note that the parts of the NP's that are broken up agree in case-marking, as they would if they were left intact. If case-marking is an early transformational rule, then the rule that breaks up NP's would have to be transformational and could not be part of the mapping into deep structure.

47

Note that the definition of *transformation* adopted for the formal proof does not employ a mechanism for specifying a set of constituents to which a transformation applies. This may be a simplification that will eventually have to be given up.

48

Assumptions that will work, but may not turn out to be plausible, involve the postulation of a universal finite set of filters which the learner supposes apply to all languages, in the absence of data to the contrary. For example, given a finite base component, there is a finite number of simple sequences of constituents (that is, sequences that involve no recursion). Assume that there is a node Comp, and that there can be at most one movement into Comp on any cycle. Then there is a finite number of simple sequences derivable from a simple base S. Suppose, finally, that a filter is a statement of the form $*_\alpha[\beta_1, \beta_2, \ldots, \beta_i]$ where α is a category and β_j are all constant terms (either lexical items or category labels).

We allow the learner to begin language acquisition with a full complement of filters, where each filter corresponds to a simple sequence derivable from a simple base S. Since there is a finite number of these sequences, there is a finite number of filters. Every time the learner encounters an adult sentence that violates a filter, that filter is eliminated. Thus we have learning of the filters from only positive evidence.

This characterization of the set of possible filters is a maximally general one; the account of learning just sketched would apply as well, and perhaps more plausibly, to more restricted sets. Conceivably there may be a perceptual basis for the choice of such a restricted set of possible filters. One must then explain why they are not all present in all languages. Surface word order may play a role, but how is not clear.

49

See Wexler (1978a) for discussion.

BIBLIOGRAPHY

Akmajian, A. 1970. On deriving cleft sentences from pseudo-cleft sentences. *Linguistic Inquiry* 1, 149–168.

Akmajian, A. 1975. More evidence for the NP cycle. *Linguistic Inquiry* 6, 115–129.

Akmajian, A., and F. Heny. 1975. *An Introduction to the Principles of Transformational Syntax*. Cambridge, Mass.: The MIT Press.

Akmajian, A., and A. Lehrer. 1977. NP-like quantifiers and the problem of determining the head of an NP. *Linguistic Analysis* 2, 395–413.

Akmajian, A., S. Steele, and T. Wasow. 1979. The constituent AUX in Universal Grammar. *Linguistic Inquiry* 10, 1–64.

Andersen, E. S. 1977. Annotated Bibliography. In C. E. Snow and C. A. Ferguson, eds., *Talking to Children*.

Anderson, S. 1976. On the notion of subject in ergative languages. In C. N. Li, ed., *Subject and Topic*. New York: Academic Press.

Anderson, S. 1977. Comments on the paper by Wasow. In P. W. Culicover, T. Wasow, and A. Akmajian, eds., *Formal Syntax*. New York: Academic Press.

Anderson, S., and S. Chung. 1977. On grammatical relations and clause structure in verb initial languages. In P. Cole and J. M. Sadock, eds., *Syntax and Semantics* vol. 8. New York: Academic Press.

Anderson, S., and P. Kiparsky, eds. 1973. *Festschrift for Morris Halle*. New York: Holt, Rinehart & Winston.

Arbib, M. A. 1969. Memory limitations of stimulus response models. *Psychological Review* 76, 507–510.

Bach, E., and G. M. Horn. 1976. Remarks on "Conditions on transformations." *Linguistic Inquiry* 7, 252–299.

Baker, C. L. 1977. Comments on the paper by Culicover and Wexler. In P. W. Culicover, T. Wasow, and A. Akmajian, eds., *Formal Syntax*. New York: Academic Press.

Baker, C. L. (in press). Syntactic theory and the projection problem. *Linguistic Inquiry*.

Bar-Hillel, Y. M., M. Perles, and E. Shamir. 1961. On formal properties of simple phrase structure grammars. *Z. Phonetik, Sprachwiss., Kommunikationforsch.* 14, 143–172.

Bartsch, R. 1973. The semantics and syntax of number and numbers. In J. Kimball, ed., *Syntax and Semantics* vol. 2. New York: Seminar Press.

Batchelder, W., and K. Wexler. 1979. Suppes' work in the foundations of psychology. In R. J. Bogdan, ed., *Patrick Suppes.* Dordrecht, Holland: D. Reidel.

Bellugi, U. 1967. *The acquisition of negation.* Doctoral dissertation, Harvard University.

Bellugi-Klima, U. 1968. Linguistic mechanisms underlying child speech. In E. M. Zale, ed., *Proceedings of the Conference on Language Behavior.* New York: Appleton.

Berman, A. 1974. On the VSO hypothesis. *Linguistic Inquiry* 5, 1–37.

Bever, T. 1970. The cognitive basis for linguistic structures. In J. R. Hayes, ed., *Cognition and the Development of Language.* New York: Wiley.

Blakemore, C. 1974. Developmental factors in the formation of feature extracting neurons. In F. O. Schmitt and F. G. Worden, eds., *The Neurosciences: Third Study Program.* Cambridge, Mass.: The MIT Press.

Bowers, J. S. 1977. On surface structure grammatical relations and the structure-preserving hypothesis. *Linguistic Analysis* 2, 225–242.

Braine, M. 1971. On two types of models of the internalization of grammar. In D. Slobin, ed., *The Ontogenesis of Grammar.* New York: Academic Press.

Brame, M. K. 1976. *Conjectures and Refutations in Syntax and Semantics.* New York: Elsevier.

Brame, M. K. 1978. *Base Generated Syntax.* Seattle: Noit Amrofer.

Bresnan, J. W. 1971. Contraction and the transformational cycle in English. Unpublished manuscript, Massachusetts Institute of Technology.

Bresnan, J. W. 1972. *Theory of complementation in English syntax.* Doctoral dissertation, Massachusetts Institute of Technology.

Bresnan, J. W. 1973. Syntax of the comparative clause construction in English. *Linguistic Inquiry* 4, 275–343.

Bresnan, J. W. 1975. Comparative deletion and constraints on transformations. *Linguistic Analysis* 1, 25–74.

Bresnan, J. W. 1976a. On the form and functioning of transformations. *Linguistic Inquiry* 7, 3–40.

Bresnan, J. W. 1976b. Toward a realistic model of transformational grammar. Paper presented at MIT and AT&T Convocation on Communications at MIT.

Bresnan, J. W. 1976c. Non-arguments for raising. *Linguistic Inquiry* 7, 485–501.

Bresnan, J. W. 1976d. Evidence for a theory of unbounded transformations. *Linguistic Analysis* 2, 353–393.

Bresnan, J. W. 1977. Variables in the theory of transformations. In P. W. Culicover, T. Wasow, and A. Akmajian, eds., *Formal Syntax.* New York: Academic Press.

Bresnan, J. W. 1978. A realistic transformational grammar. In M. Halle, J. W. Bresnan, and G. Miller, eds., *Linguistic Theory and Psychological Reality.* Cambridge, Mass.: The MIT Press.

Brown, R. 1973. *A First Language.* Cambridge Mass.: Harvard University Press.

Brown, R. 1977. Introduction. In C. E. Snow and C. A. Ferguson, eds., *Talking to Children.*

Brown, R., C. Cazden, and U. Bellugi. 1968. The child's grammar from I to III. In J. P. Hill, ed., *Minnesota Symposia on Child Psychology* vol. II, 1969.

Brown, R., and C. Hanlon. 1970. Derivational complexity and the order of acquisition of child speech. In J. R. Hayes, ed., *Cognition and the Development of Language.* New York: Wiley.

Campbell, R. N., and P. T. Smith. 1978. *Recent Advances in the Psychology of Language*. New York: Plenum.

Chomsky, N. 1957. *Syntactic Structures*. The Hague: Mouton.

Chomsky, N. 1960. On the notion "Rule of grammar." In *Structure of Language and Its Mathematical Aspects*, Proceedings of the Symposia in Applied Mathematics vol. 12. Providence, R.I.: American Mathematical Society.

Chomsky, N. 1963. Formal properties of grammars. In R. D. Luce, R. R. Bush, and E. Galanter, eds., *Handbook of Mathematical Psychology* vol. 2. New York: Wiley.

Chomsky, N. 1964. *Current Issues in Linguistic Theory*. The Hague: Mouton.

Chomsky, N. 1965. *Aspects of the Theory of Syntax*. Cambridge, Mass.: The MIT Press.

Chomsky, N. 1968. *Language and Mind*. New York: Harcourt, Brace Jovanovich.

Chomsky, N. 1970. Remarks on nominalizations. In R. Jacobs and P. Rosenbaum, eds., *Readings in Transformational Grammar*. Waltham, Mass.: Blaisdell.

Chomsky, N. 1973. Conditions on transformations. In S. Anderson and P. Kiparsky, eds., *Festschrift for Morris Halle*. New York: Holt, Rinehart & Winston.

Chomsky, N. 1975a. *Reflections on Language*. New York: Pantheon Books, a division of Random House, Inc.

Chomsky, N. 1975b. Questions of form and interpretation. *Linguistic Analysis* 1, 75–109.

Chomsky, N. 1975c. *Logical Structure of Linguistic Theory*. New York: Plenum.

Chomsky, N. 1976. Conditions on rules of grammar. *Linguistic Analysis* 2, 303–351.

Chomsky, N. 1977. On wh-movement. In P. W. Culicover, T. Wasow, and A. Akmajian, eds., *Formal Syntax*. New York: Academic Press.

Chomsky, N., and H. Lasnik. 1977. Filters and control. *Linguistic Inquiry* 8, 425–504.

Chomsky, N., and M. P. Schutzenberger. 1963. The algebraic theory of context free grammars. In P. Braffort and D. Hirschberg, eds., *Computer Programming and Formal Systems*. Dordrecht, Holland: North-Holland.

Clark, E. 1973. How children describe time and order. In C. A. Ferguson and D. Slobin, eds., *Studies in Child Language Development*. New York: Holt, Rinehart & Winston.

Clark, H. H., and S. Haviland. 1974. Psychological processes as linguistic explanation. In D. Cohen, ed., *Explaining Linguistic Phenomena*. Washington, D.C.: Hemisphere Corp.

Cross, T. G. 1977. Mother's speech adjustments: the contribution of selected child listener variables. In C. E. Snow and C. A. Ferguson, eds., *Talking to Children*.

Culicover, P. W. 1967. The treatment of idioms within a transformational framework. Technical report. Cambridge, Mass.: IBM—Boston Programming Center.

Culicover, P. W. 1971. *Syntactic and Semantic Investigations*. Doctoral dissertation. Massachusetts Institute of Technology.

Culicover, P. W. 1976a. A constraint on coreferentiality. *Foundations of Language* 12, 53–62.

Culicover, P. W. 1976b. *Syntax,* New York: Academic Press.

Culicover, P. W. 1977a. Some observations concerning pseudo-clefts. *Linguistic Analysis* 3, 347–375.

Culicover, P. W. 1977b. An invalid evaluation metric. *Linguistic Analysis* 3, 65–100.

Culicover, P. W., and K. Wexler. 1973a. An application of the freezing principle to the dative in English. Social sciences working paper No. 39. University of California, Irvine.

Culicover, P. W., and K. Wexler. 1973b. Three further applications of the freezing principle in English. Social sciences working paper No. 48. University of California, Irvine.

Culicover, P. W., and K. Wexler. 1974. The invariance principle of universals of grammar. Social sciences working paper No. 55. University of California, Irvine.

Culicover, P. W., and K. Wexler. 1977. Some syntactic implications of a theory of language learnability. In P. W. Culicover, T. Wasow, and A. Akmajian, eds., *Formal Syntax*. New York: Academic Press.

Davis, M. 1958. *Computability and Unsolvability*. New York: McGraw-Hill.

Dean, J. 1967. Noun phrase complementation in English and German. Unpublished manuscript, Massachusetts Institute of Technology.

Emonds, J. E. 1970. *Root and Structure-Preserving Transformations*. Doctoral dissertation, Massachusetts Institute of Technology. Indiana University Linguistics Club.

Emonds, J. E. 1974. Parenthetical clauses. In C. Rohrer and N. Ruwet, eds., *Actes du Colloque Franco-Allemand de Grammaire Transformationelle*. Tübingen: Max Niemeyer Verlag.

Emonds, J. E. 1976. *A Transformational Approach to English Syntax: Root. Structure-Preserving and Local Transformations*. New York: Academic Press.

Feldman, J. A. 1969. Some decidability results on grammaticality and inference. Artificial Intelligence Memorandum, Dept. of Computer Science, Stanford University.

Feldman, J. A., J. Gips, J. J. Horning, and S. Reder. 1969. *Grammatical Complexity and Inference*. Technical Report No. CS125, Dept. of Computer Science, Stanford University.

Ferguson, C. A. 1977. Baby talk as a simplified register. In C. E. Snow and C. A. Ferguson, eds., *Talking to Children*.

Fiengo, R. 1976. On trace theory. *Linguistic Inquiry* 8, 35–61.

Fiengo, R., and H. Lasnik, 1976. Some issues in the theory of transformations. *Linguistic Inquiry* 7, 182–191.

Fodor, J. A., T. G. Bever, and M. F. Garrett. 1974. *The Psychology of Language*. New York: McGraw-Hill.

Friedin, R. 1975. The analysis of passives. *Language* 51, 384–405.

Ginsburg, S. 1966. *The Mathematical Theory of Context-Free Languages*. New York: McGraw-Hill.

Ginsburg, S., and B. Partee. 1969. A mathematical model of transformational grammars. *Information and Control* 15, 297.

Gleason, J. B. 1977. Talking to children: Some notes on feedback. In C. E. Snow and C. A. Ferguson, eds., *Talking to Children*.

Gold, E. M. 1967. Language identification in the limit. *Information and Control* 10, 447–474.

Greenberg, J. 1963. Some universals of grammar with particular reference to the order of meaningful elements. In J. Greenberg, ed., *Universals of Language*. Cambridge, Mass.: The MIT Press.

Halle, M., J. W. Bresnan, and G. Miller, eds. 1977. *Linguistic Theory and Psychological Reality*. Cambridge, Mass.: The MIT Press.

Hamburger, H. 1971. On the learning of three classes of transformational components. Doctoral dissertation, University of Michigan.

Hamburger, H., and K. Wexler. 1973. Identifiability of a class of transformational grammars. In K. J. J. Hintikka, J. M. E. Moravcsik, and P. Suppes, eds., *Approaches to Natural Language*. Dordrecht, Holland: D. Reidel.

Hamburger, H., and K. Wexler. 1975. A mathematical theory of learning transformational grammar. *Journal of Mathematical Psychology*, 12, 137–177.

Hankamer, J. 1973. Unacceptable ambiguity. *Linguistic Inquiry* 4, 17–68.

Harman, G. 1972. On logical form. *Foundations of Language* 9, 38–65. Reprinted in D. Davidson and G. Harman, eds., *The Logic of Grammar*. Encino, Calif.: Dickenson, 1975.

Higgins, R. 1973a. *The pseudo-cleft construction in English*. Doctoral dissertation, Massachusetts Institute of Technology.

Higgins, R. 1973b. On J. Emonds' analysis of extraposition. In J. Kimball, ed., *Syntax and Semantics* vol. 2. New York: Seminar Press.

Hopcroft, J. E., and J. D. Ulmann. 1969. *Formal Languages and Their Relation to Automata*. Reading, Mass.: Addison-Wesley.

Horning, J. J. 1969. A study of grammatical inference. Doctoral dissertation, Stanford University. Stanford A. I. Project Tech. Report No. CS 139.

Hubel, D. H., and T. N. Wiesel. 1959. Receptive fields of single neurons in the cat's striate cortex. *Journal of Physiology* (London) 148, 574–591.

Hudson, G. 1972. Is deep structure necessary? In G. Bedell, ed., *Explorations in Linguistic Theory*, UCLA Papers in Syntax, University of California, Los Angeles.

Hudson, R. A. 1976. Conjunction reduction, gapping and right node raising. *Language* 52, 535–562.

Hull, C. L. 1943. *Principles of Behavior*. New York: Appleton.

Jackendoff, R. S. 1971. Gapping and related rules. *Linguistic Inquiry* 2, 21–35.

Jackendoff, R. S. 1972. *Semantic Interpretation in Generative Grammar*. Cambridge, Mass.: The MIT Press.

Jackendoff, R. S. 1976. Towards an explanatory semantic representation. *Linguistic Inquiry* 7, 89–150.

Jackendoff, R. S. 1977a. Constraints on phrase structure rules. In P. W. Culicover, T. Wasow, and A. Akmajian, eds., *Formal Syntax*. New York: Academic Press.

Jackendoff, R. S. 1977b. $\bar{X}$ *syntax: A study of phrase structure*. Linguistic Inquiry Monograph 2. Cambridge, Mass.: The MIT Press.

Jenkins, J. J. 1965. Mediation theory and grammatical behavior. In S. Rosenberg, ed., *Directions in Psycholinguistics*. New York: Macmillan.

Jenkins, J. J., and D. S. Palermo. 1964. Mediation processes and the acquisition of linguistic structure. In U. Bellugi and R. Brown, eds.,

The Acquisition of Language. Monographs of the Society for Research in Child Development, 29 (1).

Johnson, D. 1977. On Keenan's definition of "Subject of," *Linguistic Inquiry* 8, 673–692.

Katz, J. J. 1972. *Semantic Theory.* New York: Harper & Row.

Katz, J. J., and J. A. Fodor. 1964. The structure of a semantic theory. In J. A. Fodor and J. J. Katz, eds., *The Structure of Language.* Englewood Cliffs, N.J.: Prentice-Hall.

Katz, J. J., and P. M. Postal. 1964. *An Integrated Theory of Linguistic Descriptions.* Cambridge, Mass.: The MIT Press.

Kayne, R. 1976. *French Syntax: The Transformational Cycle.* Cambridge, Mass.: The MIT Press.

Kean, M-L. 1975. The theory of markedness in generative grammar. Doctoral dissertation, Massachusetts Institute of Technology.

Keenan, E. L. 1976. Toward a universal definition of "Subject." In C. N. Li, ed., *Subject and Topic.* New York: Academic Press.

Keenan, E. L., and B. Comrie. 1977. Noun phrase accessibility and universal grammar. *Linguistic Inquiry* 8, 63–99.

Kieras, D. E. 1976. Finite automata and S-R models. *Journal of Mathematical Psychology* 13, 127–147.

Klima, E., and U. Bellugi. 1966. Syntactic regularities in the speech of children. In J. Lyons and R. Wales, eds., *Psycholinguistic Papers.* Edinburgh: Edinburgh University Press.

Koster, J. 1978. Why subject sentences don't exist. In S. J. Keyser, ed., *Recent Transformational Studies in European Languages.* Linguistic Inquiry Monograph 3. Cambridge, Mass.: The MIT Press.

Kuno, S. 1973. Constraints on internal clauses and sentential subjects. *Linguistic Inquiry* 4, 363–386.

Kuno, S., and J. Robinson. 1972. Multiple wh-questions. *Linguistic Inquiry* 3, 463–488.

Labov, W. 1970. The study of language in its social context. *Studium Generale* 23, 30–87.

Lasnik, H., and R. Fiengo. 1974. Complement object deletion. *Linguistic Inquiry* 5, 535–571.

Levelt, W. J. M. 1975a. *Formal Grammars in Linguistics and Psycholinguistics*. The Hague: Mouton.

Levelt, W. J. M. 1975b. What became of LAD? *Peter de Ridder Publications in Cognition* I. Lisse, Holland: Peter de Ridder Press.

Lightfoot, D. 1976. The theoretical importance of subject raising. *Foundations of Language* 14, 257–285.

Lightfoot, D. 1977. Traces and conditions on rules. In P. W. Culicover, T. Wasow, and A. Akmajian, eds., *Formal Syntax*. New York: Academic Press.

McCawley, J. 1970. English as a VSO language. *Language* 46, 286–299. Reprinted in D. Davidson and G. Harman, eds., *The Logic of Grammar*. Encino, Calif.: Dickenson, 1975.

McNeill, D. 1966. Developmental psycholinguistics. In F. Smith and G. A. Miller, eds., *The Genesis of Language*. Cambridge, Mass.: The MIT Press.

McNeill, D. 1970. *The Acquisition of Language*. New York: Harper & Row.

McTear, M. F. 1978. Review of C. E. Snow and C. A. Ferguson, eds., *Talking to Children*. *Journal of Child Language* 5, 521–530.

Maling, J. A. 1972. On "Gapping and the order of constituents." *Linguistic Inquiry* 3, 101–108.

Marcus, M. P. 1977. A theory of syntactic recognition for natural language. Doctoral dissertation, Massachusetts Institute of Technology.

Mayer, J. M., A. Erreich, and V. Valian. 1978. Transformations, basic operations and language acquisition. *Cognition* 6, 1–14.

Miller, G. A., and N. Chomsky. 1963. Finitary models of language users. In R. D. Luce, R. R. Bush, and E. Galanter, eds., *Handbook of Mathematical Psychology* vol. 2. New York: Wiley.

Milner, J.-C. 1978. *De la Syntaxe à l'Interpretation*. Paris: Seuil.

Milsark, G. 1972. Re:doubl-ing. *Linguistic Inquiry* 3, 542–549.

Montague, R. 1973. The proper treatment of quantification in ordinary English. In K. J. J. Hintikka, J. M. E. Moravscik, and P. Suppes, eds., *Approaches to Natural Languages*. Dordrecht, Holland: D. Reidel.

Nelson, R. J. 1975. Behaviorism, finite automata and stimulus response theory. *Theory and Decision* 6, 249–268.

Newport, E. 1976. Motherese: The speech of mothers to young children. In N. Castellan, D. Pisoni, and G. Potts, eds., *Cognitive Theory* vol. 2. Hillsdale, N.J.: Lawrence Erlbaum Associates.

Newport, E., H. Gleitman, and L. R. Gleitman. 1977. Mother, I'd rather do it myself: some effects and non-effects of maternal speech style. In C. E. Snow and C. A. Ferguson, eds., *Talking to Children*.

Oehrle, R. T. 1976. The grammatical status of the English dative alternation. Doctoral dissertation, Massachusetts Institute of Technology.

Partee, B. 1975. Montague grammar and transformational grammar. *Linguistic Inquiry* 6, 203–300.

Perlmutter, D. 1971. *Deep and Surface Structure Constraints in Syntax*. New York: Holt, Rinehart & Winston.

Peters, P. S. 1972. The projection problem: How is a grammar to be selected? In P. S. Peters, ed., *Goals of Linguistic Theory*. Englewood Cliffs, N.J.: Prentice-Hall.

Peters, P. S., and R. W. Ritchie. 1973a. On the generative power of transformational grammar. *Information Sciences* 6, 49–83.

Peters, P. S., and R. W. Ritchie. 1973b. Non-filtering and local filtering transformational grammars. In K. J. J. Hintikka, J. M. E. Moravcsik, and P. Suppes, eds., *Approaches to Natural Language*. Dordrecht, Holland: D. Reidel.

Pfuderer, C. 1969. Some suggestions for a syntactic characterization of baby-talk style. Working paper No. 4, Language Behavior Laboratory, University of California, Berkeley.

Postal, P. M. 1971. *Cross-Over Phenomena*. New York: Holt, Rinehart & Winston.

Postal, P. M. 1972a. A global constraint on pronominalization. *Linguistic Inquiry* 3, 35–59.

Postal, P. M. 1972b. On some rules that are not successive cyclic. *Linguistic Inquiry* 3, 211–222.

Postal, P. M. 1974. *On Raising: One Rule of English and its Theoretical Implications*. Cambridge, Mass.: The MIT Press.

Pullum, G. 1976. The Duke of York's gambit. *Journal of Linguistics* 12, 83–102.

Pullum, G. 1977. Word order universals and grammatical relations. In P. Cole and J. M. Sadock, eds., *Syntax and Semantics* vol. 8. New York: Academic Press.

Putnam, H. 1967. The "Innateness Hypothesis" and explanatory models in linguistics. *Synthese* 17, 12–22. Reprinted in S. P. Stich, ed., *Innate Ideas*. Los Angeles: University of California Press, 1975.

Rischel, J. 1970. Some characteristics of noun phrases in West Greenlandic. *Acta Linguistica Hafniensia* 13, 213–245.

Roeper, T. 1978. Linguistic universals and the acquisition of gerunds. In H. Goodluck and L. Solan, eds., *Papers in the Structure and Development of Child Language*, Occasional Papers in Linguistics vol. 4. University of Massachusetts, Amherst.

Roeper, T., and M. Siegel. 1978. A lexical transformation for verbal compounds. *Linguistic Inquiry* 9, 199–260.

Ross, J. R. 1967. *Constraints on variables in syntax*. Doctoral dissertation, Massachusetts Institute of Technology.

Ross, J. R. 1969. Auxiliaries as main verbs. In W. Todd, ed., *Studies in Philosophical Linguistics*, Series One. Carbondale, Ill.: Great Expectations Press.

Ross, J. R. 1970. Gapping and the order of constituents. In M. Bierwisch and K. E. Heidolph, eds., *Progress in Linguistics*. The Hague: Mouton.

Ross, J. R. 1972. Doubl-ing. *Linguistic Inquiry* 3, 61–86.

Schlesinger, I. 1971. Production of utterances and language acquisition. In D. Slobin, ed., *The Ontogenesis of Grammar*. New York: Academic Press.

Schlesinger, I. 1977. *Production and Comprehension of Sentences*. Hillsdale, N.J.: Lawrence Erlbaum Associates.

Schwartz, A. 1977. Constraints on movement transformations. *Journal of Linguistics* 8, 35–85.

Shatz, M., and R. Gelman. 1977. Beyond syntax: The influences of conversational constraints on speech modifications. In C. E. Snow and C. A. Ferguson, eds., *Talking to Children*.

Siegel, D. 1970. On nonsources for unpassives. In J. Kimball, ed., *Syntax and Semantics* vol. 1. New York: Seminar Press.

Slobin, D. 1972. Children and language: they learn the same way all around the world. *Psychology Today* 6, 71–82.

Slobin, D. 1975a. Language change in childhood and history. Working paper No. 41, Language Behavior Research Laboratory. University of California, Berkeley.

Slobin, D. 1975b. On the nature of talk to children. In E. H. Lenneberg and E. Lenneberg, eds., *Foundations of Language Development*. New York: Academic Press.

Snow, C. E. 1972. Mothers' speech to children learning language. *Child Development* 43, 549–565.

Snow, C. E. 1977. Mother's speech research: From input to interaction. In C. E. Snow and C. A. Ferguson, eds., *Talking to Children*.

Snow, C. E., and C. A. Ferguson, eds. 1977. *Talking to Children: Language Input and Acquisition*. Cambridge, England: Cambridge University Press.

Solomonoff, R. T. A. 1964. A formal theory of inductive inference. *Information and Control* 7, 1–22, 224–254.

Staal, J. F. 1967. *Word Order in Sanskrit and Universal Grammar*. Dordrecht, Holland: D. Reidel.

Steele, S. 1975. On some factors that affect and effect word order change. In C. N. Li, ed., *Word Order and Word Order Change*. Austin: University of Texas Press.

Steele, S. 1978a. The category AUX as a language universal. In J. Greenberg, ed., *Universals of Human Language* vol. 3. Stanford: Calif.: Stanford University Press.

Steele, S. 1978b. Word order variations: a typological study. In J. Greenberg, ed., *Universals of Human Language* vol. 4. Stanford: Stanford University Press.

Stillings, J. 1975. The formulation of gapping in English as evidence for variable types in syntactic transformations. *Linguistic Analysis* 1, 247–274.

Suppes, P. 1969. Stimulus-response theory of finite automata. *Journal of Mathematical Psychology* 6, 327–355.

Vennemann, T. 1973. Explanation in Syntax. In J. P. Kimball, ed., *Syntax and Semantics* vol. 2. New York: Seminar Press.

Wasow, T. 1972. Anaphoric relations in English. Doctoral dissertation, Massachusetts Institute of Technology.

Wasow, T. 1976. McCawley on generative semantics: Review of *Grammar and Meaning* by James D. McCawley. *Linguistic Analysis* 2, 279–301.

Wasow, T. 1977. Transformations and the lexicon. In P. W. Culicover, T. Wasow, and A. Akmajian, eds., *Formal Syntax*. New York: Academic Press.

Wexler, K. 1977. Transformational grammars are learnable from data of degree less than or equal to 2. Social sciences working paper No. 129, University of California, Irvine.

Wexler, K. 1978a. Empirical questions about developmental psycholinguistics raised by a theory of language acquisition. In R. N. Campbell and P. T. Smith, eds., *Recent Advances in the Psychology of Language*. New York: Plenum.

Wexler, K. 1978b. A review of J. R. Anderson's *Language Memory and Thought. Cognition,* 6, 327–351.

Wexler, K. (in press). A principle theory for language acquisition. Paper presented at the *Workshop in Language Acquisition: The State of the Art,* sponsored by the Sloan Foundation at the University of Pennsylvania, May (1978). To be published in the proceedings of the workshop, edited by L. Gleitman and E. Wanner.

Wexler, K., and P. W. Culicover. 1973. Two applications of the freezing principle in English. Social sciences working paper No. 37, University of California, Irvine.

Wexler, K., and P. W. Culicover. 1974. The semantic basis for language acquisition: the Invariance Principle as a replacement for the Universal Base Hypotheses. Social sciences working paper No. 50, University of California, Irvine.

Wexler, K., P. W. Culicover, and H. Hamburger. 1975. Learning-theoretic foundations of linguistic universals. *Theoretical Linguistics* 2, 213–253.

Wexler, K., and H. Hamburger. 1973. On the insufficiency of surface data for the learning of transformational languages. In K. J. J. Hintikka, J. M. E. Moravcsik, and P. Suppes, eds., *Approaches to Natural Language.* Dordrecht, Holland: D. Reidel.

Wilkins, W. 1977. *The variable interpretation condition.* Doctoral dissertation, University of California, Los Angeles.

Williams, E. S. 1974a. Rule ordering in syntax. Doctoral dissertation, Massachusetts Institute of Technology.

Williams, E. S. 1974b. Small clauses in English. In J. Kimball, ed., *Syntax and Semantics* vol. 4. New York: Academic Press.

Williams, E. S. 1977. Discourse and logical form. *Linguistic Inquiry* 8, 101–139.

Williams, E. S. 1978. Across-the-board application. *Linguistic Inquiry* 9, 31–43.

NAME INDEX

SUBJECT INDEX